DATE DUE			

ANGLICIZING THE GOVERNMENT OF IRELAND

Map of Hibernia, 1567, by John Gough.

The map was done from reports of Ireland since Gough
never visited the country. Ireland is seen from an English
perspective, as if one were viewing the shores of Leinster
from the coast of Wales.

Anglicizing the Government of Ireland

THE IRISH PRIVY COUNCIL AND THE
EXPANSION OF TUDOR RULE, 1556–1578

JON G. CRAWFORD

IRISH ACADEMIC PRESS
in association with
THE IRISH LEGAL HISTORY SOCIETY

Typeset by Seton Music Graphics Ltd, Bantry, Co. Cork for
IRISH ACADEMIC PRESS LTD
Kill Lane, Blackrock, Co. Dublin.

A catalogue record for this book
is available from the British Library.

ISBN 0–7165–2498–8

Printed in Ireland by
Colour Books Ltd, Dublin

Preface

ONE OF THE FASCINATIONS of studying the sixteenth century is the underlying tension between tradition and reform. In the Elizabethan period every innovation was cloaked in the language of convention and the dynamism of the age was often concealed by a theoretical bondage to ancient wisdom and subservience to the natural hierarchy in all relationships. It is often the case that statesmen who know when changes must be made face massive indifference and occasional hostility to their ideas. Tudor officials in England and Ireland knew that the divided loyalties of the population could not be sustained indefinitely. They were tolerant of constitutional anomalies, and yet they understood the need for political and judicial coherence. What they achieved in Ireland was an incomplete and unsatisfying compromise. They offered detailed plans of reform and they launched campaigns to rebuild the superstructure of Tudor government, but they faced either apathy or opposition at critical times and they were periodically left penniless by the queen. It is important to realize that the government of Tudor Ireland was reformed in certain basic ways, but the effect was neither revolutionary nor confrontational. The Elizabethan chief governors and the council in Ireland made practical progress in the reform of the administration, but their efforts were often frustrated by lack of support, local resistance and political conniving. If politics is the art of the possible, then constitutional change must be the low-budget documentary of the manageable. Only over the span of several decades is it possible to assess the results of this undramatic accretion of institution-building. But the durability of structural changes in government makes them intrinsically worth studying.

This book grew out of an interest in the extra-parliamentary government of Tudor England. While engaged on a study of the privy council, I was led to a comparison with the provincial and regional councils such as the council in the North and the council in the marches of Wales. Turning to the Tudor government of Ireland, I was surprised to find that a fully-developed privy council in miniature, the council in Ireland, had never been investigated despite its importance to royal dominion. The lord deputy and council governed Ireland on behalf of the crown, following instructions carefully laid down by the queen and her advisers in Westminster. This executive forum possessed substantial initiative since the sovereign had to rule at a distance (no Tudor monarch ever visited Ireland). The council managed affairs from

Dublin, but it had an appellate jurisdiction over the law courts of the realm and it attempted to expand that jurisdiction through the creation of several new institutions. The foundation of council policy was the anglicization of Irish political architecture. The effort to impose its command throughout the country took several forms, including novel financial expedients. But the major thrust of conciliar planning was to govern by terms of the common law, bringing access to English justice and, ultimately, providing new sources of revenue to the crown. Military action was subordinate to the legal and constitutional aims of English rule in Ireland, despite the egregious perversions of provincial authority by notoriously cruel adventurers such as Humphrey Gilbert. In summary, it is to be hoped that a study of the council in Ireland during two decades of its existence will illuminate much about Irish government generally. But the chief objective of the book is to rescue the council from its undeserved obscurity and to place it securely in the firmament of the emerging institutions refined and reconstructed by Tudor statesmen.

From the long list of people to whom I owe thanks for their support of this project, the following cannot escape mention. Historians rely heavily on the accomplished work of archivists and librarians, so I must thank, collectively, the staffs of the British Library, the Public Record Offices in London and Ireland, the Royal Irish Academy, the Folger Shakespeare Library, the Huntington Library, and the college and university libraries of the University of London, Oxford University, Trinity College Dublin, the University of North Carolina, and my own institution, Mars Hill College. I am particularly grateful for the support of a sabbatical leave and institutional grants from Mars Hill College, a stipend from the National Endowment for the Humanities and a research grant for graduate study from the University of North Carolina. This book would have been impossible without their assistance. I am in addition most grateful to the Alfred Beit Foundation for a grant to enable John Gough's map of Ireland to be reproduced as a frontispiece. I would like to acknowledge the inspiration and the assistance of the Institute for Historical Research in London; and the permission of the editors of the *American Journal of Legal History* to allow me to republish here my article on the court of castle chamber. To my professors in graduate study I owe a large debt of gratitude, including the late Joel Hurstfield, and Professors Gillian Cell, Richard Soloway, Richard Pfaff and James Godfrey of UNC. To my mentor, Dr Stephen Baxter, I am profoundly obliged for many years of unfailing support. I should add that my contemporaries who toil in the field of Tudor Irish history have also been unstinting in their encouragement of my work. I am pleased to recognize here the letters and conversations with Steven Ellis, Ciaran Brady and Nicholas Canny over the past fifteen years. I owe my greatest intellectual debt to Professor David B. Quinn, who provided materials and ideas and showed the way through his own pioneering researches in the field of Irish administration. While I may disagree with them in certain ways, I have the greatest respect for their contributions to the history of Ireland. I should also like to acknowledge the assistance of Professor Nial Osborough, secretary of the Irish Legal History Society and former editor of the *Irish Jurist*: without his interest and indefatigable enterprise, this book would never have reached the light of day. And finally, for their forbearance with my singleness of purpose, I would like to thank my parents; my children, Gregory and Elisabeth; and my wife, Robin.

The spelling of words in quotations has been left in the original, although I have extended contractions and added punctuation where necessary. In the spelling of English surnames I have followed, wherever possible, the usage of the individual. This has resulted in some arbitrary nominative transformations of well-known officials (Sir Henry Sydney, rather than Sidney; Sir Thomas Cusake, rather than Cusack; Sir Edward Fyton, rather than Fitton), but the procedure has allowed me to be consistent with the names of all the councillors, including the most obscure (Henry Cowley, or Colley, and others). The English rather than the Gaelic spelling of all place names and personal names has, in general, also been used. The dates have been left in the original except that I used the Gregorian calendar to calculate the beginning of the year.

Contents

List of illustrations

Abbreviations

Add. MS	Additional manuscript
Am Hist Rev	*American Historical Review*
Am Jn Legal Hist	*American Journal of Legal History*
Anal Hib	*Analecta Hibernica*
Ball, *Judges*	F.E. Ball, *The judges in Ireland, 1221–1921*
BL	British Library
Bodl	Bodleian Library, Oxford
Brady, *Ir. ch. Eliz.*	*State papers concerning the Irish church in the time of Queen Elizabeth*, ed. W.M. Brady
Brit Acad Proc	*Proceedings of the British Academy*
Cal. Carew MSS	*Calendar of the Carew manuscripts*
Cal. pat. rolls	*Calendar of patent rolls*
Cal. S.P. Ire.	*Calendar of the state papers relating to Ireland*
Cork Hist Soc Jn	*Journal of the Cork Historical and Archaeological Society*
Cott. MS	Cottonian manuscript
d.	died
DNB	*Dictionary of national biography*
Dublin Hist Rec	*Dublin Historical Record*
EHR	*English Historical Review*
Facs. nat. MSS Ire.	*Facsimiles of the national manuscripts of Ireland*, ed. J.T. Gilbert
G.E.C., *Peerage*	G.E.C. [okayne], *The complete peerage*
Harl. MS	Harleian manuscript
Hist	*History*
Hist Jn	*Historical Journal*
H.M.C.	Historical manuscripts commission
Hughes, *Patentee officers*	*Patentee officers in Ireland, 1173–1876*, ed. J.L.J. Hughes
Huntington Lib	Huntington Library, San Marino, California
IHR Bull	*Bulletin of the Institute of Historical Research*
IHS	*Irish Historical Studies*
Ir Econ Soc Hist	*Irish Economic and Social History*

Ir Jur	*Irish Jurist*
Jn British Stud	*Journal of British Studies*
Jn Eccles Hist	*Journal of Ecclesiastical History*
JP	justice of the peace
Kildare Arch Soc Jn	*Journal of the County Kildare Archaeological Society*
knt	knight
Lib. mun. pub. Hib.	Rowley Lascelles, *Liber munerum publicorum Hiberniae*
Louth Arch Soc Jn	*Journal of the County Louth Archaeological Society*
LPL	Lambeth Palace Library, London
LQR	*Law Quarterly Review*
m.	married
MP	member of parliament
MS	manuscript
N.H.I.	*New history of Ireland*
OED	*Oxford English dictionary*
P.R.I. rep. D.K.	*Report of the deputy keeper of the public records in Ireland*
PRO	Public Record Office, London
PROI	Public Record Office of Ireland (= National Archives)
R Hist Soc Trans	*Transactions of the Royal Historical Society*
RIA	Royal Irish Academy
RIA Proc	*Proceedings of the Royal Irish Academy*
RSAI Jn	*Journal of the Royal Society of Antiquaries of Ireland*
Sidney S.P.	*Sidney state papers, 1565–70*, ed. T. Ó Laidhin
SP	State papers
S.P. Hen VIII	*State papers, Henry VIII*
s.v.	sub voce (under the heading)
TCD	Trinity College Dublin
UJA	*Ulster Journal of Archaeology*
Walsingham letter-bk	*The Walsingham letter-book, or register of Ireland*, ed. J. Hogan and N. Mc N. O'Farrell

CHAPTER ONE

The council and the government of mid-Tudor Ireland

INTERPRETING THE EVIDENCE

WHEN THOMAS RADCLIFFE, Lord Fitzwalter, arrived in 1556 as the new lord deputy of Ireland, he began a process by which new English political institutions were gradually added to the architecture of Irish government. The privy council in Ireland was given the responsibility for implementing these changes by instructions sent to 'the lord deputy and council' from England. The council was the engine of the administration; the apex of the judiciary; the centre of Irish politics; and the master builder of the policy of anglicization. This study of the council in Ireland analyzes its constitutional role, its membership, and its responsibility for the three interlocking policies of anglicization: (1) the expansion of common law rule; (2) the maintenance of order and stability through military garrisons and provincial presidencies; and (3) the increase of Irish revenue through the reform of fiscal administration. The full range of the Irish administration will be treated in some depth because of the virtual omnicompetence of the council. The medieval basis for expansive conciliar jurisdiction has been explained by Professor Otway-Ruthven in this way: 'The council thus constituted exercised all the powers of government in conjunction with the chief governor. No detail was too small for it; nothing not expressly reserved to the king was too great.'[1]

The purpose here is to examine the council itself, so it should be apparent that the study of other judicial, military and financial institutions is, of necessity, incomplete. Nevertheless, we may hazard some general observations linked to the state of Tudor historiography. In the first place, the slender resources of the government and the political vulnerability of the viceroys made it impossible to establish a tyrannical or 'absolutist' regime in Ireland in this period. Despite the occasions of political violence, this was not a systematic 'conquest' of Ireland nor a persecuting administration backed by military rule.[2] In the

1. A.J. Otway-Ruthven, *A history of medieval Ireland* (London, 1968), p. 151.
2. See S.G. Ellis, *Tudor Ireland: crown, community and the conflict of cultures* (London, 1985), pp. 234–46 for an account which strongly emphasizes the military exploits of Sussex to the exclusion of other endeavours.

second place, there is substantial evidence that the government was joined in its efforts to expand common law jurisdiction by cooperative local officials who thus participated in the institutionalization of English governance. There was sufficient complexity and variety in the reception accorded to anglicization to arouse our scepticism about the 'nationalist' opposition to Tudor rule.[3] And in the third place, the evidence for an active colonial policy is marginal to the central thrust of the Dublin administration. Efforts to establish small settlements in Ulster and elsewhere received only fragments of attention, and occasionally outright hostility, from the established interests in Irish government, including the chief governor and the local élites.[4]

The sources for a study of the privy council in Ireland are many, yet there are important gaps in the record as well. The policies and principles of Irish governance were established in instructions given regularly to the lord deputy and council. These objectives were further refined and amplified in the voluminous correspondence between officials in Ireland, the queen, and her leading advisers. The council was more than a conduit for policy-makers in Westminster, however, since the governing board in Dublin was given wide scope for the interpretation of general mandates, and the queen often deferred to the expertise of her Irish administrators. The executive activities of Irish government were manifested in the council books, proclamations and other records which revealed their daily routine. Both the actions and the intentions of the administration during the period 1556 to 1578 suggest that crown government was chiefly concerned with expanding its real effectiveness. The anglicization of Irish institutions flowed uncertainly from this general purpose, and it is from these reformed instruments of government that the sources for this study are mainly taken. The Irish state papers in both London and Dublin are a treasure trove of fascinating lore, much of it relevant to the activities of the government, and nearly all of it recorded unsystematically.

3. See, for example, the recent article by Nerys Patterson, in which she argues that the English government used certain Gaelic lawyers regularly as advisers, and that Gaelic land tenures were at times assimilated to common law principles. N. Patterson, 'Gaelic law and the Tudor conquest of Ireland: the social background of the sixteenth-century recensions of the pseudo-historical Prologue to the *Senchas már*', *IHS*, xxvii (1991), 193, 214–15.

4. Dr Canny has recently reasserted his view that colonization was the primary thrust of Elizabethan government, though he has also offered a more sensitive account of the contemporary understanding of colonial ideology. N. Canny, *From reformation to restoration: Ireland, 1534–1660* (Dublin, 1987), pp. 80, 84–86; *Kingdom and colony: Ireland in the Atlantic world, 1560–1800* (Baltimore, 1988), pp. 11–17, 29. But see M. MacCarthy-Morrogh, *The Munster plantation: English migration to southern Ireland, 1583–1641* (Oxford, 1986), for the view that settlement was conducted within constitutional limits using appropriate legal safeguards for the rights of the native Irish.

Private papers do much to illuminate the record of conciliar management of affairs, particularly the Carte MSS in the Bodleian Library, Oxford; the Carew MSS in the Lambeth Palace Library, London; and the scattered remnants of the correspondence of Sir Henry Sydney, the earl of Ormonde, Sir William Fitzwilliam, the earl of Sussex and others. The widespread legal authority of the council assured that all matters of consequence, and many of little moment, came within its purview. And because the council was the nucleus of government, it received reams of correspondence from the English and the native Irish alike. Thus it served to filter the aims and ambitions of English statesmen into the disparate milieu of a very complex Irish culture, and to a lesser extent, the reverse.

An objective critique of the sources would begin with two important survivals of the conciliar record: the council book of 1556 to 1571; and the entry book of the court of castle chamber, the star chamber jurisdiction of the council itself.[5] These are reasonably complete accounts of conciliar governance, yet they leave out as much as they reveal. There are very few entries for certain years; the recording of judgments does not include details of concilar proceedings; the practical enforcement of conciliar decrees and proclamations is rarely addressed; there is no record of deliberations, so the apparent management of consensus may mask vigorous debate on certain issues; and record-keeping was so undisciplined that it is nearly impossible to trace consistent patterns in the handling of the council's business. What is more, the state papers contain an implicit bias toward English concerns and policy alternatives, leaving the very existence of autonomous Irish politics very much in the shadows. The ordinary give-and-take in political discourse may be excessively muted in the case of Ireland because of the eccentric survival of the evidence. There are only tables of the now-missing Irish council books for other periods, in contrast to the virtually complete Acts of the Privy Council for the English parent body. There are no substantive record books from the regional councils established in this period for Munster and Connacht. What is more, the irregular accounts taken for the musters of the army and for the exchequer often create more problems than they solve. The accounts were subject to fraudulent practices by captains, escheators, sheriffs and clerks; they were not taken rigorously and so each record differs slightly (or more) from the others; many of them are condensed versions of longer documents with which they are difficult to reconcile; and the serendipitous survival of public records from Tudor Ireland

5. For an astute analysis of the surviving conciliar records, see D.B. Quinn, 'Calendar of the Irish council book, 1 March 1581 to 1 July 1586', *Anal Hib*, no. 24 (1967), 93–105. For the council book see RIA, MS 24 F 17; for the entry book see BL, Add. MS 47,172.

makes any generalization difficult. It is possible to glimpse into the administrative machinery of the Tudor governing apparatus, but the record is insufficient to reconstruct a reliable account of the whole.

Due to the apparent lack of rigour in conciliar record-keeping, it is not difficult to imagine why there has been no previous attempt to study the privy council in Ireland. And yet most writers have explicitly acknowledged its importance as a governing institution. When the Irish council is compared with other governing boards, the lack of a constitutional study is more remarkable. There are full accounts of the provincial councils in Wales and the North of England, and of the parent body in Westminster and its origins (see below).[6] Yet, despite the fact that the Irish forum was the only one to be modelled on the senior privy council, it is also the only one which has not been investigated by historians. This is the more difficult to understand because it was a more developed institution than the others. It was jointly responsible with the lord deputy for the standing army, a garrison far larger than any which was commonly known to Wales or the northern borders. It supervised the exchequer and the four courts of justice, an obligation which was not shared by the other councils. In addition, the judicial authority of the council in Ireland was greatly augmented by the creation of a star chamber jurisdiction, the court of castle chamber in Dublin. And, finally, the title of the chief governor in Ireland conferred a greater executive authority than the more limited power of the 'lord president of the council' in Wales and the North.[7] In sum, the council in Ireland was directly responsible for the entire government of the country, while the other bodies were restricted to a clearly defined judicial and policing authority.[8] In Dr Williams' account of the Tudor government, the role of the English privy council bulks large, though he elected not to bring Ireland within the scope of his investigation.[9] As a consequence of travelling this lonely road in constitutional

6. See, for example, R.R. Reid, *The king's council of the North* (London, 1921); P. Williams, *The council in the marches of Wales under Elizabeth I* (Cardiff, 1958); M.B. Pulman, *The Elizabethan privy council in the fifteen-seventies* (Berkeley, 1971).
7. In 1575 the instructions were addressed by Cecil to '. . . Sir Henry Sydney, Lord President of the Council in Wales, Lord Deputie of Irelande and one of her majesties privy counsell . . .': BL, Cott. MS Titus B XII, f. 155. When the subordinate lords president and councils for Munster and for Connacht were created under Sussex and Sydney, the model was explicitly the regional council in the marches of Wales. This would indicate that the privy council in Ireland was constitutionally a more developed and powerful body than the other regional councils under Elizabeth.
8. Williams, *Council in Wales*, pp. 50–51, 53–55, 58–59.
9. P. Williams, *The Tudor regime* (Oxford, 1979). We may be permitted to disagree in part with Williams' dictum that 'The complex field of Irish history would have needed a book to itself, so different were Irish society and Irish government from English' (p. vii).

history, the present study must be seen as a preliminary introduction. The conclusions offered here are necessarily tentative ones since we lack a comprehensive account of the Elizabethan government in Ireland, and new work on the institutions of that government (the exchequer, the courts, the military establishment) has only just begun. What is more, the precise relationship of the privy council in England to the council in Ireland remains to be investigated, and the policies of the leading English statesmen have not been analyzed systematically.

The tremendous variety and complexity of the work of the Irish council makes it difficult to offer a general statement about its effectiveness. Indeed, the distinction we wish to draw between achievement and aspiration is often blurred in the surviving records. Letters, proclamations, drafts and memoranda can be unreliable guides to action, though they are clearly suggestive of intention. In what follows, every effort will be made to explain both the practical limitations of Tudor government in Ireland and the struggle undertaken to reform itself. Along the way, it may be useful to point out how Irish political institutions may be compared with other European structures to propose alternative models for understanding the work of Irish government. If what emerges from this discussion is an uneven record of qualified success and intermittent failure, of high-minded intentions and crudely realized outcomes, the incompleteness of the record and the absence of a generous and expansive historiography of late Tudor Irish administration may be put forth by way of explanation. In addition, it is well to remember the limited effectiveness of sixteenth-century governments. Regarding the settlement of Munster, D.B. Quinn has said, 'The Munster plantation is an excellent example of the ideas of a sixteenth century government out-running its capacity for performance'.[10] The parallel difficulties of enforcing government policy in England have been described by G.R. Elton: 'This was the rough, superstitious, excitable and volatile society which the king's government had to rule . . .'.[11] As an example of the relatively high levels of violence in sixteenth-century societies, we might point to the use of provost marshals and commissions of martial law in both England and Ireland at the beginning of Elizabeth's reign.[12]

The selection of the mid-Tudor period for a study of the privy council in Ireland can be explained in several ways. The extant sources are fuller and more comprehensive than for the earlier history of the

10. D.B. Quinn, 'The Munster plantation: problems and opportunities', *Cork Hist Soc Jn*, lxxi (1966), 24. See also Williams, *Council in Wales*, p. ix on the limited resources of Tudor government.
11. G.R. Elton, *Policy and police: the enforcement of the reformation in the age of Thomas Cromwell* (Cambridge, 1972), p. 5.
12. See, for example, R.B. Manning, 'The origins of the doctrine of sedition', *Albion*, xii (1980), 107.

council. Furthermore, the new administration of Lord Fitzwalter in 1556 was an important bridgehead for Irish reform. As the young earl of Sussex in 1557, he chose a more active style of government, pursued his enemies relentlessly in the field, and promoted a series of important administrative changes which were shepherded by his successors and made permanent after his departure from Ireland. Sussex has been charged with ruthlessness, inflexibility, belligerence and propagandistic self-concern. Contrasts with the previous administration of St Leger have placed the work of Sussex in an invidious comparison since he increased the size of the military, demanded higher taxes on the Pale and caused an opposition movement to develop among the Anglo-Irish élite.[13] After St Leger's conciliatory government, Sussex was required to govern more frugally and to engineer fundamental reforms. He brought into the administration new personnel to assist him and to provide a loyal base of support. This nucleus of reforming privy councillors dominated Irish politics for the next twenty-two years. The unity of the period is thus based on continuities in policy, leadership, conciliar membership and ambition. Ironically, the accession of the new sovereign in 1558 made little difference in Irish government. Elizabeth was preoccupied with events in England and the continent, she had no wish to compel her Irish subjects to accept religious change abruptly, and she relied on her experienced viceroy to maintain her dominion in Ireland.

During the period from 1556 to 1578 Irish government was led by a reasonably stable nucleus of councillors and three lords deputy who all arrived in Ireland at the same time. The coherent policies of law reform and anglicization of the institutions of government were pursued with indifferent success by each administration; the implementation of religious change was deferred, due in part to moderating influences on the council itself; and overt resistance by Gaelic chiefs to instances of rash expropriation was confronted by each successive regime. Dr Canny has insisted that the first administration of Sydney was a key turning-point, but this rests on the dubious proposition that the entire government, led by Sydney, was now largely focused on the establishment of colonies and settlements beyond the Pale.[14] At

---

13. The works of Bradshaw, Canny and Ellis argue that Sussex's regime constituted a rupture with the past moderation of St Leger's government, although Brady views Sussex as less confrontational than opportunistic. See B. Bradshaw, *The Irish constitutional revolution of the sixteenth century* (Cambridge, 1979), pp. 260–63; Canny, *Reformation to restoration*, pp. 53–63; Ellis, *Tudor Ireland*, pp. 234–35; C. Brady, 'The Government of Ireland, *c.* 1540–1580' (unpublished Ph.D. dissertation, Trinity College, Dublin), pp. 110–27.

14. Canny, *Reformation to restoration*, pp. 75–80. For his original statement of the thesis see *The Elizabethan conquest of Ireland: a pattern established, 1565–1576* (New York, 1976).

the end of the period, in 1578, Sydney left Ireland in disgrace and the core of the privy council was quickly broken up. The lord chancellor and the interim viceroy both died soon after 1578 and the two aged chief justices expired within two years. Further, the large-scale rebellions which began in 1579 changed the assumptions of the government that piecemeal reforms and gradual acculturation would eventually bind the Irish to crown policy and common law rule. At the departure of Sydney a political crisis in the Pale became crystallized, instead of vanishing along with the *bête noire* of the Anglo-Irish, and a period of drift ensued. War and rebellion; opposition politics and confrontations on the council itself; weak leadership and foreign intervention; high prices and the militarization of Irish policy; all of these issues culminated in the new policy of confiscation and plantation following the Munster rebellion and the death of the earl of Desmond.[15]

However, we must not make too much of these apparently unifying themes. If history is indeed a seamless web, it is important to realize that the seeds of opposition must have developed earlier in the period, and that the reluctant embrace of colonization in the 1580s was the consequence of the limited effect of other policy alternatives. Nevertheless, by 1578 the anglicization of Irish political institutions was a genuine practical achievement. Since it was largely a matter of internal reform and a question of obtaining crown support for the creation of new mechanisms of government, the policy was not dependent on Anglo-Irish *bienfaisance* nor on the accumulation of public revenues. So its success was muted and its effect diminished by the very process through which it was accomplished. Nevertheless, as we shall see, Irish government was closely modelled on English institutions in 1578 and the ensuing decades of unrest and rebellion would do nothing to reverse the process.

The structural changes which gradually led to the anglicization of Irish government took place in an unspectacular and irregular fashion throughout the period. Consequently, we must seek evidence of these changes in the folds and crevices of the Dublin administration and in the obscure work of provincial officials. A topical arrangement of subjects will be used to allow deeper investigation into particular agencies of government, from the formal and dignified grand council to the national grocer, or victualler, who was responsible for providing

---

15. Most writers agree that the threshold moment in Elizabethan rule fell between the years 1578 and 1583. Dr Ellis concludes his study of the mid-Tudor period in 1579; Dr Canny in 1583, stressing the messy outcomes of Sydney's last administration; and Dr Brady also in 1583, though his treatment of the Munster rebellion serves largely as an epilogue to his analysis of Tudor governance. See Ellis, *Tudor Ireland*, p. 274; Canny, *Reformation to restoration*, pp. 106–07; Brady, 'Government of Ireland', pp. 420–25.

supplies for the garrison. In chapters two and three, the infrastructure of the council itself is discussed at length. Beginning with the viceroys, the entire membership is analyzed on the basis of age, education, experience, aptitude, connection and policy preferences. In addition, the council itself is examined for evidence of its places of meeting, clerical staff, record-keeping, level of activity, conduct of business and other practical matters. The constitutional role of the executive forum was essentially that of a fulcrum, balancing the interests of the queen and her Irish subjects, while at the same time serving the crown in a dependent role. The council was thus the nucleus of Irish politics and it will be necessary to examine the function of patronage, family networks, enrichment, dissension and other questions in order to assess the corporate personality of the board in this period. These inquiries will provide opportunities to test a number of assumptions about Irish government generally, such as the extent of opposition on the council, the level of corruption among leading officials, and the displacement of Anglo-Irish office-holders in favour of new English clients and partisans. Chapter three concludes with case studies of representative councillors who typify the distinct roles of the chief governor, the leading peers, the bishops, the judges and the military advisers.

While the council was a durable and coherent body which sustained a commitment to law reform and anglicization throughout the period, it was also quite diverse and its complexity makes generalization difficult. The remaining chapters, it is hoped, will reveal the extent of this complexity through a study of the three interlocking features of Elizabethan Irish policy: law reform, military defence and fiscal expediency. A full investigation of the council as a tribunal demonstrates that the forum possessed an original and an appellate jurisdiction; comprehensive supervision of the judicial structure; powers of enforcement for both its proclamations and its judicial decrees; and the right to use brehon law in appropriate cases. The council advocated reform of the judiciary and the courts, extension of the assizes and judicial commissions, and the expansion of its own role as a court through the creation of the court of castle chamber. In military affairs, the council enjoyed similarly wide powers of superintendence. The Dublin executive administered the garrisons, organized the musters of troops, called out the general hosting (militia), appointed the means for victualling and purveyance (the cess), and provided a small military contingent for the lords president and councils in Munster and Connacht. The accelerating costs for the military and other enterprises created a fiscal deficit which the Irish council also had to confront. The councillors, acting collectively, were given the responsibility for financial reform. This in turn took the form of commissions of account for the exchequer, studies of fiscal retrenchment, handling of abuses and complaints, and diplomatic manoeuvring in the constitutional crisis over the increase of the cess.

Although these matters took up the burden of the council's time and trouble, they did not exhaust the versatility of the governing board. Nevertheless, it has been necessary to exclude from this study questions such as the implementation of religious reform, the management of colonies and settlements (Leix and Offaly, for example), the handling of the economy and the administration of purely local matters. While the council took an important role in the parliaments of this period, no effort has been made here to examine the political manipulation of legislative hearings and enactments.[16] Further, the sensitive relations of the government with the Gaelic Irish chiefs and lords is not treated here despite the acknowledgment that the queen wished to govern all of her Irish subjects with equal force and justice. The conflict with the Scots and the Irish of Ulster varied considerably from the more tractable relations with the Irish chiefs nearer the Pale, and the subject deserves fuller investigation.[17] In matters of administrative practice, it has been necessary to omit consideration of such details as the problems of communicating with the queen and privy council in England; the difficulty of enforcing conciliar proclamations in the towns and regions distant from Dublin; the precise relationship of the council to the new regional councils in Munster and Connacht; and problems of a similar nature.

THE CROWN'S IRISH POLICY

Certainly the most important relationship for the Dublin administration was that between the council and the crown. Elizabeth could never settle on a single approach to the Irish problem, so every government was beset by contradictory instructions and ill-timed rebukes from the ever-parsimonious queen. Her objective was to develop a self-sufficient government in Dublin, but the need to preserve order

16. In a recent article, H.A. Jeffries has asserted that the reformation parliament of 1560 passed the statutes creating an Elizabethan religious settlement in Ireland in the remarkably short space of three weeks. Nine members of the council (eight of them English-born) were elected to the lower house and Sussex worked behind the scenes to manage a compliant delegation, excluding the potentially defiant Catholic bishops. He rejects Bradshaw's earlier view of a hostile confrontation during the session of 1560. See Jeffries, 'The Irish parliament of 1560: the anglican reforms authorised', *IHS*, xxvi (1988), 128–41. See also V. Treadwell, 'The Irish parliament of 1569–71', *RIA Proc*, lxv (1966), sect. c, no. 4, 55–89; 'Sir John Perrot and the Irish parliament of 1585–6', *RIA Proc*, lxxxv (1985), sect. c, no. 3, 259–308.

17. See the important work of Kenneth W. Nicholls, Katharine Simms, Bernadette Cunningham, Nerys Patterson, Anthony Sheehan, Hiram Morgan and Raymond Gillespie, among others, for the impact of conciliar governance on the provinces furthest from Dublin (see Bibliography for citations).

was always in conflict with fiscal constraints. The good shepherd of the queen's wayward Irish policy was Sir William Cecil. It was he who prevailed upon the queen to establish the court of castle chamber and the provincial councils, as well as other administrative changes and refinements. It was due primarily to Cecil, and later to Sir Francis Walsingham, that greater attention was increasingly paid to Irish affairs. At the beginning of the period, few English leaders understood the unique conditions of governing Ireland. But by 1578 the entire English privy council appreciated the complexities involved and saw Ireland, menaced by Spanish intervention, as one of the queen's gravest problems. Elizabeth was too prudent to move ahead with the implementation of religious change in Ireland, but she recognized that she would never govern all of the country unless she were able to expand the reach of the common law. Thus she gave fleeting commitments to expanded jurisdiction until local resistance led to financial burdens which her chief governors had not contemplated. The diversity of loyalties and allegiances in Ireland bewildered her and she was unable to settle on a policy that would both keep order and prevent the alienation of some of her subjects. Consequently, the council in Ireland pursued a cautious and conservative line in the knowledge that the queen might peremptorily withdraw her support for their initiatives. But the origin of reforming ideas came from the queen's administrators, both English and Irish, and she was beset with competing policy alternatives at the privy council and elsewhere.

Fifteen years after the accession of Elizabeth, one of her experienced statesmen returned to Ireland to gather evidence on the reform of the government. Edmund Tremayne had been personal secretary to the lord deputy in Ireland in 1569, and when he accepted preferment in England he did not forget the 'Irish problem' of Tudor government. Tremayne had become clerk of the privy council by 1573 when he wrote an extended essay for the use of Sir Walter Mildmay which rehearsed the estrangement of Irish people from English governance. In general, he blamed the arbitrary power of Irish chiefs and lords who used Irish laws and customs '. . . nothinge agreeinge with the lawes of England'.[18] He concluded that these Irish leaders had become local tyrants because the queen's writ did not run in their territories, even in parts of the English Pale (the loyal counties nearest to Dublin). The dangers of this reckless disregard of English rule were obvious to Tremayne. The queen stood to lose her revenue; the people received no impartial justice; the tenants were ruthlessly exploited; and the Anglican religion was not respected. A cultural divide separated the Anglo-Irish communities of Ireland from the larger Gaelic territories.

18. Huntington Lib, Ellesmere MS 1701, f. 1.

Tremayne argued that the queen's dominion should not tolerate the constitutional dualism which had thus emerged, saying, 'But as her majestie is the naturall lieg soveryne of bothe the Realmes, so shold there be made no difference of Subjecte so farre forthe as both shall showe like obedience to her majesties lawes'.[19] He argued forcefully for a programme of reform which would reach into every province, uniting all Ireland under the rule of the crown. He advocated the use of lords president and councils to furnish the administration of justice for distant regions and to bring all Irish subjects alike to pay as they could for the maintenance of the queen's government there. He summarized his argument thus: 'I thinke it will be yelded that ye gretest [not thonelie] disease whereon all others do depend is the Injustice or rather Tyrany as is there practised. And that being so it followeth consequentlie that the planting of justice must be the medicine.'[20]

The reform of Irish government by establishing common law principles and institutions throughout the country was accepted as a legitimate and practical goal by every chief governor from 1556 to 1578. Tremayne was certainly not alone in proposing it. In 1554 Edward Walshe composed a 'Treatise for the reformation of Ireland' which called for reform on constitutional grounds. Here, he relied upon a civil law tradition of political thought, with the aim of uniting the entire kingdom through the institutionalization of English governance. He proposed the establishment of new courts and provincial presidencies; shiring of new counties; creation of parliamentary boroughs; employment of English-style local officials and juries; and the maintenance of a small garrison of 600 English troops to stabilize the unruly elements until justice could take hold. Dr Bradshaw has argued that this proposal was a self-interested and partisan attack by a lawyer from the Pale against the weak government of St Leger, in the hope that reform would ultimately lead to increased litigation and enrichment of the governing élite.[21] However that may be, Walshe was certainly in agreement with the core elements of most reform pro-

19. ibid., f. 5. In his analysis of Tremayne, Dr Brady has stressed the means of compulsion ('a grand expeditionary force') and the composition arrangements for increased revenue instead of the ends of common law rule. See C. Brady, 'Government of Ireland', pp. 215–18. This excellent revisionist work is soon to be published.

20. ibid. Tremayne added that a new lord deputy must be above partiality; that he should have sufficient men in garrison to enforce the law while curbing their arbitrary exactions on the local tenantry; and that leading officials in the Dublin administration were to be experienced officials born in England (ff. 5–8).

21. E. Walshe, 'A treatise for the reformation of Ireland, 1554–5', ed. B. Bradshaw, *Ir Jur*, xvi (1981), 301–02, 305–13. See also 'Edward Walsh's conjectures regarding the state of Ireland [1552]', ed. D.B. Quinn, *IHS*, v (1947). Quinn noted that, 'The dominant theme, pervading the whole document, is the familiar one that only the erection of an effective system of law-enforcement throughout Ireland can bring peace and stability' (p. 311).

grammes which stressed the primacy of the common law. Rowland White's treatise, composed for Sir William Cecil in 1569, echoes the familiar theme: 'For when the lawe shall threaten punyshmente and deathe to thoffendours assuring the laborsome and weldoers quietlie to enjoye their owne (as is mente) then the let of the saulvage lyfe shall enforce men to cyvilitie, . . . the rote of unrule can then growe no longer, and so shall prosperitie springe.'[22] White added that the imposition of the queen's 'common justice' should be accompanied by a systematic reform of Ireland's political culture, including the calling of parliament, establishment of provincial councils, shiring of counties and concomitant abolition of Gaelic practices. White embraced the humanist nostrum that education would improve men's behaviour and he promoted the establishment of a university, twelve free schools, ten preachers and twelve hospitals for the poor.[23] A similar argument was written later in the period by Sir William Herbert. His essay, 'Croftus sive de Hibernia liber', argued that the 'nub of reform lay in law and civil government' using the model of the council in the marches of Wales. Herbert's cautious approach was based on the inculcation of public virtue from civic justice and he too stressed the need to replicate English governing institutions in Ireland.[24]

Each of the foregoing authors asserted the conventional expectation of increased revenue for the crown following upon law reform, and each of them included a clear preference for conciliation over coercion. Nevertheless, they also addressed the need for a military force, varying in size, to maintain order and to enforce the terms of the law. It may be, as Dr Brady has asserted, that the principal aim of this force was to overawe and to intimidate local lords.[25] But the writers and reformers of the mid-Tudor period offered balanced, integrated policies of law reform, fiscal management and military constraints. This harmony of interdependent features was designed to create a microcosm of the English commonwealth in Ireland, and the underlying tenor of most critics remained largely optimistic about the eventual outcome. In practice, however, the queen refused to maintain a large standing army in Ireland, primarily due to its enormous cost, and her reluctance to move forward with key aspects of the reform programme under-

---

22. R. White, 'Acts and orders for the government of Ireland and the reformation thereof', ed. N. Canny, *IHS*, xx (1976–77), 448.

23. ibid., 449–63.

24. Sir William Herbert, *Croftus sive de Hibernia liber*, ed. and trans. A. Keaveney and J.A. Madden (Dublin, 1992). And see B. Bradshaw, 'Robe and sword in the conquest of Ireland' in C. Cross, D. Loades and J. Scarisbrick, ed., *Law and government under the Tudors: essays presented to Sir Geoffrey Elton on his retirement* (Cambridge, 1988), pp. 143–44, 148–52.

25. Brady, 'Government of Ireland', pp. 215–16.

mined its credibility in the provinces. Expedient resistance to systematic anglicization emerged in English counsels and in Irish politics generally for a variety of reasons. Yet the possibility of peaceful reform by expansion of the common law gave the initiatives of the mid-Tudor period a distinctive tone. The cultural and political transformation of Ireland by gradual stages was accepted as a logical and practical end by most writers prior to the Desmond rebellion of 1579.

In contrast, recent writers have found an altogether different sentiment in the celebrated histrionics of Edmund Spenser's 'A view of the present state of Ireland', written under the circumstances of war and rebellion during the 1590s. This well-known diatribe from the pen of a gifted Elizabethan poet has been taken as evidence of the rapacious brutality of English adventurers in this period. Professor Myers included selections from 'A view' in his collection of strident invectives which he took to represent official thinking about Ireland.[26] Dr Bradshaw, on the other hand, saw Spenser's hot-blooded account as rather exceptional in its belligerent assertions that wholesale conquest, intensified by mass starvation and resettlement, must precede the establishment of civil government.[27] In a contextual interpretation of Spenser's ideas, Dr Canny has argued that most English officials at the end of the sixteenth century viewed Ireland as a colony and thus they justified extreme measures as a solution to disorder and heresy.[28] Certainly the context in which Spenser wrote must be considered here, and Dr Brady concluded that he was inspired by the fear of general rebellion in 1596, by the urgency of the immediate crisis, and by personal disappointment and tragedy. The apocalyptic thinking of the 1590s was thus the product of embittered disillusionment during a war with Spain and a rebellion in Ireland that lasted into the next century.[29] Nevertheless, we must still account for the unexplained reference of Spenser's protagonist, Irenius, to the possibility of cultural assimilation. He said,

But by the sworde I mean the Royall power of the Prince which ought to stretch yt self forth, in her cheif strength, to the redressinge and cuttinge off of those evills which I before blamed, and not of the people which are

26. J.P. Myers, ed., *Elizabethan Ireland: a selection of writings by Elizabethan writers on Ireland* (Hamden, Conn., 1983), pp. 68–74, 92–109. Myers treats this 'polemical literature' as part of a 'propaganda war' in the late Tudor 'ferocious war of conquest and attrition'. This one-dimensional approach to the period lacks sophistication and simply excludes those views which do not focus on Irish 'barbarity'.
27. Bradshaw, 'Robe and sword', pp. 139–40, 155–62.
28. Canny, *Kingdom and colony*, pp. 31–38.
29. C. Brady, 'Spenser's Irish crisis: humanism and experience in the 1590s', *Past & Present*, no. 111 (1986), 22–30, 41–49.

evill, for evill people, by good ordynance and gouernment, may bee made good, but the evill that is of yt self evill will never beecome goode.[30]

RECENT HISTORIOGRAPHY

The historiography of Tudor Ireland has traditionally been preoccupied with conflict and insurrection. From Elizabethan writers and chroniclers down to the present generation, there has been a persistent tendency to emphasize the record of violence and disorder. In addition, there has been a marked undertone of approval for the resistance of Irish leaders to English governance, on the assumption that the high level of disruption must have been somehow justified by the cruel tyranny of the queen's viceroy and his minions.[31] In a recent article, Dr Bradshaw has attacked the 'revisionist school' of modern Irish historiography by claiming that they practised 'tacit evasion' of the 'catastrophic dimension of Irish history'. His critique of the 'value-free' practitioners of historical writing is a shrill and unsympathetic reaction to the 'iconoclastic' authors who have chosen to 'evade the chronicle of violence' which suffused the work of early twentieth-century authors. Bradshaw decries the attention to 'complexity, ambiguity and discontinuity' which obscures the identity of the national pageant, the river of time running through the generations which connects the Celtic peoples of ancient times with the Irish of today.[32] The present-oriented nationalism of Bradshaw's appeal concludes with a reaffirmation of the work of earlier nationalist writers and a call to 'empathy' and 'imagination' in Irish historical writing.[33] Perhaps the best response to such a scathing rebuke would be to emphasize the primacy of the documents; to offer an approach to the subject

30. E. Spenser, *A view of the present state of Ireland*, ed. W.L. Renwick (London, 1934), pp. 123–24.
31. English writers such as Richard Bagwell perpetuated the notion that Irish political life was a turbulent, see-saw affair, coloured by violence and perfidy, lacking positive achievements. Bagwell said, 'The history of Ireland is at best a sad one . . .'. R. Bagwell, *Ireland under the Tudors*, 3 vols. (London, 1885–90), i, v. More recently the Irish historian R. Dudley Edwards caricatured the English government as an occupying force. See *Ireland in the age of the Tudors: the destruction of hiberno-norman civilization* (London, 1977).
32. B. Bradshaw, 'Nationalism and historical scholarship in modern Ireland', *IHS*, xxvi (1989), 339, 341–47, 350.
33. For an alternative model, see D.G. Boyce, 'Brahmins and carnivores: the Irish historian in Great Britain', *IHS*, xxv (1987), 234. Boyce stresses the importance of appreciating the 'cultural pluralism' of Irish history which has clearly resulted in a modern political form that denies 'unity in diversity'. Further, Dr Cosgrove rejects the simple dualism of English v. Irish, arguing the case for a distinct Anglo-Irish milieu in the later middle ages that was neither Gaelic nor English. See A. Cosgrove, 'The writing of Irish medieval history', *IHS*, xxvii (1990), 99–102, 109–10.

which combines ancillary disciplines and alternative modes of analysis; to recognize the plausibility of other hypotheses; and to analyze the evidence with a synoptic and integrative generosity.[34] Ironically, Dr Bradshaw's call for empathy is at odds with the tenor of his own essay. The suggestion of Dr Elton that modern historians avoid 'excessive schematizing' is not irrelevant here, though it will be taken up elsewhere in this essay.[35]

In spite of the raging tempests which periodically occlude the historiography of Tudor Ireland, the past twenty years have witnessed a significant expansion of our knowledge of the period. Building on the careful work of D.B. Quinn, whose researches paved the way to a more refined understanding of the interstices of Tudor government in Ireland, a new generation of Irish historians erected an imposing monument of scholarship. Writing in 1974 in his important work *The dissolution of the religious orders in Ireland under Henry VIII*, Dr Bradshaw offered this key insight: 'We are used to having sixteenth-century Ireland presented to us in very sombre colours indeed. I believe that its history is not nearly so gloomy as its historiography.'[36] The work of Dr Canny has done much to reveal the nature of late Tudor Ireland, commencing with his monograph *The Elizabethan conquest of Ireland: a pattern established, 1565–1576*. While the assertion that Ireland was treated thenceforth as a colony has come under some criticism, Canny illuminated the connections between English government and Irish society in important ways.[37] The publication of Bradshaw's seminal work, *The Irish constitutional revolution of the sixteenth century*, was an important milestone in Tudor historiography.[38] His argument that the Cromwellian reforms in Irish government were unprecedented

34. For related insights see S.G. Ellis, 'Nationalist historiography and the English and Gaelic worlds in the late middle ages', *IHS*, xxv (1986), 1–18; and 'Historiographical debate: representations of the past in Ireland: whose past and whose present?', *IHS*, xxvii (1991), 289–308. Ellis offers a comparative dimension to Irish studies which places events in a British and European perspective, and he argues that the constitutional position of Ireland in the fifteenth century was indivisibly linked to the crown in one body politic. He posits the anglicization of Gaelic culture as a useful balancing of the mono-cultural outlook reflected in models of gaelicization, and he sees the emphasis on proto-nationalist outcomes as unhistorical and acutely divisive.

35. G.R. Elton, *Reform and renewal: Thomas Cromwell and the common weal* (Cambridge, 1973), p. 4.

36. B. Bradshaw, *The dissolution of the religious orders in Ireland under Henry VIII* (Cambridge, 1974), p. vii.

37. Canny, *Elizabethan conquest*. See also his *Reformation to restoration*; and *Kingdom and colony*, cited above, where he reasserts the need to see the Irish experience as part of a larger process, using colonial and European comparative perspectives (pp. 140–41).

38. Bradshaw, *Irish constitutional revolution*, cited above.

has been challenged by Dr Steven Ellis in a series of analytical essays which has contributed much to our knowledge of late medieval government. Ellis' study of these changes, *Reform and revival: English government in Ireland, 1470–1534*, is a comprehensive analysis of the foundations of Tudor government. In this work, and in his complementary text, *Tudor Ireland: crown, community and the conflict of cultures, 1470–1603*, he shows that the sixteenth century was an age of reform that gradually changed the superstructure as well as the ethos and spirit of the Irish polity.[39] In addition, the publication of other works by these leading historians has done much to illuminate our understanding of the period. Any reassessment of their premises, including this one, should begin with an acknowledgment of the tremendous impact of their ideas.

Revisionist accounts of the Tudor experience have flourished in recent years, led by the work of Dr Ciaran Brady. In the volume of essays, entitled *Natives and newcomers: essays on the making of Irish colonial society, 1534–1661*, edited by him in conjunction with Dr Raymond Gillespie, the editors review the historiography of the period sympathetically while calling for a new paradigm:

> The simple and dismal account of inevitable military confrontation followed by subjugation and expropriation and accompanied by irreconcilable religious and cultural conflict between English and Scottish planters and dispossessed native Irish is slowly being replaced by a greater awareness of the subtlety and complexity of events between 1534 and 1641.[40]

The emphasis here on the 'essential complexity of early modern Ireland' is a call for further research as well as a claim for the appreciation of 'discontinuities and uncertainties' which have been under-appreciated by earlier historians searching for a 'schematic' understanding of Tudor Ireland. The model of gradualist reform under the mantle of conciliation was not suddenly replaced by a policy of conquest and coercion. Rather, the two alternatives co-existed in efforts to find a practical way to govern Ireland prior to 1603 which Brady and Gillespie have characterized by 'variety and contingency'.[41] Other historians have taken up the call to investigate these multiple factors in the evolution of Irish government and society. For example, Colm Lennon has studied the mercantile patriciate in Dublin; Anthony Sheehan has analyzed the growth and development of Irish towns; Katharine

39. S.G. Ellis, *Reform and revival: English government in Ireland, 1470–1534* (London, 1986); *Tudor Ireland*, cited above.

40. C. Brady and R. Gillespie, 'Introduction', in Brady and Gillespie, ed., *Natives and newcomers: essays on the making of Irish colonial society, 1534–1641* (Dublin, 1986), p. 11.

41. ibid., pp. 11–21.

Simms has examined the evolution of Irish chiefs from sovereigns to local warlords; and Bernadette Cunningham has written on the reaction of native Irish élites to the reforms initiated by the Dublin administration.[42] In his reflection on the research needs for an expanded view of Tudor Ireland, Dr Ellis has said,

Until we have for the lordship detailed studies of those problems which bulk large in histories of other European countries—such questions as the rule of law and the rise of absolutism, taxation and representation, warfare and the growth of state bureaucracy, and crown-community relations—we are not in a position to do justice to such themes as the Gaelic revival and 'Anglo-Irish separatism'.[43]

In summary, then, this is the first full-scale investigation of the privy council in Ireland. It attempts to make a contribution to the history of conciliar government in the early modern period. It addresses the general problem of Elizabeth's Irish policy and clarifies the process of policy formulation in the period under review. The study challenges the overworked argument that Sussex and Sydney were bent on wholesale conquest and colonization in Ireland. It argues instead that the administration was more concerned with extending the parameters of effective government by using the institutions of the common law. The earl of Sussex inaugurated a policy of territorial expansion and institutional growth which established the character of this period until 1578. The balance of native Irish and new English interests on the council also gives the period a distinctive coherence. Further, it rebuts the argument that the Dublin administration was culturally alienated from its milieu. Finally, the council is given a central role in the body politic. From the ligaments and sinews of administrative routine to the muscular boldness of military campaigns, the council exercised government by omnicompetence as the obedient heart of the queen's dominion in Ireland.

42. C. Lennon, *The lords of Dublin in the age of the reformation* (Dublin, 1989); A. Sheehan, 'Irish towns in a period of change, 1558–1625', in Brady & Gillespie, ed., *Natives and newcomers*, pp. 93–119; K. Simms, *From kings to warlords: the changing political structure of Gaelic Ireland in the later middle ages* (Dublin, 1987); and B. Cunningham and R. Gillespie, 'Englishmen in sixteenth century Irish annals', *Ir Econ Soc Hist*, xvii (1990), 5–21. Much other useful work is being conducted by other scholars, too numerous to mention here.
43. Ellis, 'Nationalist historiography', 6.

CHAPTER TWO

The council in an era of reform: durable hierarchies and altered structures

THE GOVERNMENT OF IRELAND in 1556 was passively inert. A prolonged period of gradualist reform had come to an inglorious end amid the corruption and compromise that characterized the administration of the veteran lord deputy, Sir Anthony St Leger. An era of genuine cooperation had met an early demise when the crown sanctioned belligerent initiatives under Lords Deputy Bellingham and Croft. St Leger then returned to Ireland in 1553 at the head of a caretaker government, a hollow vessel which had no particular programme.[1] Following his recall in 1556, a succession of three chief governors attempted to reform Ireland and each of them was replaced amid retrenchment and recrimination. Their ambitious programmes achieved less than they promised and they each retired in disgrace. However, the Ireland of 1578 was institutionally stronger. Despite the political disasters which befell the viceroys, the government itself was metamorphosing into a miniature version of the bureaucracy in Westminster. And the important network of local officials and commissions which did the work of this newly designed administration was being similarly anglicized. At the core of this portentous evolution was the privy council in Ireland.

The aim of this work is to introduce the council in Ireland as the chief organ of the central government. The executive board may be defined as a privy council, modelled in fundamental respects on its English parent. Like the superior forum in Westminister, the privy council in Ireland was omnicompetent. It was charged with general oversight as the engine of administration, giving instructions to the exchequer, the courts, the military, the towns, the church and nearly everything else. It had original jurisdiction as a court of law in certain cases and it managed both private suits and public matters, from an assault on a shipowner to treasonable offences arising from rebellion. The council was given added responsibility as a check on the independent power of the lord deputy after 1534, and the instructions

---

1. See Brady, 'Government of Ireland', pp. 71–111; and Bradshaw, *Irish constitutional revolution*, pp. 189–263 for full discussions of the mid-Tudor governments of St Leger.

from England were carefully preserved in council documents as a guide to sanctioned royal policy. The council was the most important political institution in Ireland, serving along with the lord deputy as the queen's representative and agent of her will in its multiple roles.

The infrastructure of the council in Ireland will tell us much about its mode of operation. There is sufficient evidence to estimate when and where the council met; who belonged to the board and which of its members were most active; what the council did at its meetings and how it was organized. Matters of policy occasionally collided with partisan interests, so it is important to study profiles of the councillors to see how well they worked together in the crown's favour. The council was required to implement policy set in Westminster by the queen and her advisers, but there was also room to manoeuvre. Consequently, we must examine the constitutional relationship of the council in Ireland with its senior institution in England. Within the council itself, there was a differentiation of function which became more formalized in this period. The council could split into two smaller groups; it could meet as a judicial body independently; and it could incorporate a larger institution, the grand council, to authorize fiscal exactions and military preparations. Finally, the council organized itself more efficiently, using a clerk and several deputies to create systematic record-keeping.

Irish history must be studied for its nuances. Increasingly, the paradigms of conquest and colonization, or proto-nationalist uprisings, appear to be the result of sophisticated models rather than painstaking reconstructions of the Elizabethan era. While we may argue that research design is important to all historical writing, we pursue in the last analysis a more exacting portrait of an age. And in this case, it is simply not a neat, or systematic, or patterned set of policies and behaviours that emerges from a study of the first two decades of Elizabethan rule in Ireland. The queen's orders were often contradictory; her advisers were positioned to take political advantage of any blunder by their rivals for power; and the complexity of Irish society itself made it difficult to rule by uniform regulations. No chief governor launched a policy which was pursued in a rigorous and disciplined way for more than three years. The politicians and officials in both Dublin and Westminster were practical men, capable of manipulating situations for their own profit. And the queen's Irish subjects were often unwilling to accommodate themselves to a programme which promised them further disruption in an already turbulent century.

Not surprisingly, in view of its characteristic incongruence, the first generation of Elizabethan rule produced both reform and retrenchment. The government was strengthened institutionally by a number of important structural changes even though the politicians who inaugurated these changes were often victimized by the impatient and parsimonious sovereign and her advisers. At the end of every succeeding administration there was a hastily cobbled interim government which was instructed to do nothing which would either produce change or cost money. Yet beneath the surface of this tempestuous era there were indeed important reforms being implemented. The council itself, after a long period of badgering the crown, ultimately received approval to create a star chamber jurisdiction, called the court of castle chamber. A principal secretary of state was created for Ireland, though with a different mandate from that of the powerful Tudor officials who held this office in England. New counties were shired and sheriffs appointed (see Map 2). The lords president and councils were finally named to administer the common law and govern according to English practices in Munster and Connacht. The council devised agreements to victual the troops and in the end stationed the military garrison outside the Pale, while trying to devise a composition for their maintenance. Reforms of the central courts and the exchequer were attempted with little success, but the recoinage was managed efficiently by the council so that a common standard was restored to Ireland for the first time in the century. In all of this, achievement was delayed, frustrated and avoided by the crown. Thus, there was no dramatically successful product of a well-considered and internally consistent programme. Instead, there was piecemeal reform, obtained by dint of tenacious management and thoughtful inquiries which eventually overcame royal obduracy. The process of change has been called anglicization. And, despite many fits and starts, the period ended with the achievement of a predominantly English administrative structure which the ensuing war and rebellion did nothing to reverse. This was the success of Elizabethan government, acquired virtually in spite of itself. The principle of rule in accordance with the common law was established, even though resistance prevented the comprehensive realization of this goal. And the institutions of government, modelled exactly on those of the Tudor state in England, were ultimately put in place in Ireland. The privy council was the instrument of those changes. We must begin now to examine how this English agency of reform, with its hybrid personnel, went about the business of governing.

HISTORICAL BACKGROUND

Any discussion of Tudor institutions of government must begin with a salute to the monumental corpus of research and writing achieved by Geoffrey Elton and his students over the past forty years. In a field which he has both revitalized and dominated, it is possible to cavil and to express important reservations about the conclusions he has reached. Yet the Eltonian model of skilful documentation and carefully crafted argument has been a boon to the historical profession and particularly to those who try to re-imagine the Tudor century. In regard to the central institution of government, the privy council, Elton has said, 'In England, as in most parts of sixteenth-century Europe, the King's Council was the centre of administration, the instrument of policy making, the arena of political conflict, and the ultimate means for dispensing the king's justice'.[2] In his view, the transition from a medieval king's council, made up principally of peers of the realm, to a working council led by a team of ministers of state was achieved rather suddenly, between 1534 and 1536. Elton initially argued that the administrative genius of Thomas Cromwell conceived the new privy council and gave it direction by his superintendence as principal secretary. Yet he subsequently offered a more complex argument. Since the privy council acted in such a variety of ways and reformulated itself to achieve such different purposes (commissions of inquiry, judicial hearings, councils of war), it would be exceedingly difficult to be precise about its origins or its definition.[3]

There is no dominant orthodoxy in regard to the 'administrative revolution' which Elton purported to discover in his seminal work of 1953, and the ferment in Tudor studies has never ceased since that time. One of his leading critics, Penry Williams, has claimed that the privy council which emerged by 1540 was clearly adumbrated by changes at the court of Henry VII and that the privy council continued to evolve well after 1540 when it obtained its formal record-keeping mechanism.[4] More recently, J.A. Guy has identified the stages of conciliar evolution toward the fully developed privy council. Under Henry VII the council was a large, undifferentiated body with multiple roles, yet the councillors attendant upon the king constituted an important 'inner ring' which continued to govern on behalf of the youthful Henry VIII after his accession in 1509. The architect of change, for Professor Guy, was Thomas Wolsey. Wolsey energized the king's council, emphasizing its judicial work in star chamber, and using committees to differentiate the public business of the governing board. He created the early model of the court of requests and anticipated the development of a privy council in the Eltham ordinance of

2. G.R. Elton, 'Why the history of the early-Tudor council remains unwritten', in his *Studies in Tudor and Stuart politics and government* (Cambridge, 1974), p. 308.

3. G.R. Elton, *The Tudor revolution in government: administrative changes in the reign of Henry VIII* (Cambridge, 1953), pp. 317ff; Elton, 'Early-Tudor council', p. 314.

4. P. Williams, *The Tudor regime* (Oxford, 1979), pp. 29–30.

1526. Guy has asserted that the changes initiated by Cromwell were 'progressive and pragmatic' rather than 'fundamental', or principled constitutional reform. The key event in the evolution of the privy council occurred as a result of the immediate need to respond to the Pilgrimage of Grace in the autumn of 1536. Here, a privy council was constructed to meet the exigencies of a political crisis and it became a permanent organ of central administration from that point forward. However, it had been anticipated by Wolsey and its development proceeded by episodes of practical refinement. Cromwell contributed meaningfully, according to this explanation, to one of the stages in the gradual evolution of the privy council.[5]

The privy council was certainly organized by 1540 to do the bidding of the crown. Unfortunately, the direction of royal policy went through a series of profound and sudden changes during the next generation which obscured the development of the institution. Writers have focused primarily on the council as the nexus of political rivalry and scheming intrigue. Nevertheless, recent treatments of the council have emphasized that the operations of government in the period between 1540 and 1558 were more efficient, more decisive and more coherent than tradition would have it. Dale Hoak, for example, has written that the coup d'état engineered by the duke of Northumberland which toppled the government of the duke of Somerset in 1549 was an effort to restore conciliar control. In his own interest, perhaps, Northumberland saw the need to 'create administrative stability and efficiency' by reorganizing the methods of administration. What he achieved was the structural equilibrium which could survive patches of rough political seas to emerge as the Elizabethan compromise, a government by conciliar superintendence which was devoted to good order and smooth sailing.[6] More recently, Hoak has argued that the unwieldy and ponderous privy council of Mary was the product of two distinct requirements which confronted the queen early in the reign. The first was her need for an ad hoc council of war to advise her in the dangerous moments of the transition to her new government. The second requirement, equally necessary but less dramatic, was for competent professionals to govern the kingdom. It was in this emergency that the shrewd Sir William Paget manipulated events at court to assure the return to power of the experienced governing

5. J.A. Guy, 'The privy council: revolution or evolution?', in C. Coleman and D.R. Starkey, ed., *Revolution reassessed: revisions in the history of Tudor government and administration* (Oxford, 1986), pp. 62–85.

6. D. Hoak, 'Rehabilitating the duke of Northumberland: politics and political control, 1549–53', in R. Tittler and J. Loach, ed., *The mid-Tudor polity, c. 1540–1560* (Totowa, N.J., 1980), pp. 29–51. See also his definitive study, *The king's council in the reign of Edward VI* (Cambridge, 1976).

élite.[7] Ann Weikel has argued that Paget's concern for order and stability in government led him to manage conciliar debate in order to minimize conflict and enhance cooperation. The gradual evolution of the Marian council from an unworkable body of forty-three men to a smaller core of active councillors by 1555 is indicative of the ability of the council to reform itself to meet the practical needs of government.[8] Based on these essential adjustments, crafted according to the needs of a situation, David Starkey has called into question the Cromwellian model of energetic, sharply focused reform. He maintains that, since institutions tended to change as circumstances demanded, there is a diminished role for the 'presiding genius' of amelioration who imposed a theoretical model of efficiency on Tudor government.[9]

Recent studies of the council in Ireland have, similarly, stressed its evolution toward a more independent role in government with a more formal structure. Steven Ellis has even argued that the Irish board was organized in a manner which anticipated the more celebrated establishment of the English privy council.[10] The foundation of the council, of course, lay in the council attendant upon the king's representative in Ireland, known throughout much of the medieval period as the justiciar. After a long period of general decline, the late medieval lordship entered upon a period of stronger government in 1470, led by reliance on powerful local magnates who governed as semi-autonomous viceroys. However, when this period ended with the Kildare rebellion of 1534, important structural changes were already in place. In his stimulating essay on Irish government, Ellis has traced the evolution toward new power realities in the lordship. Initially, the authority of the lord deputy was virtually unchallenged over military, judicial and financial matters and he commanded full control of an extensive patronage system in the Pale. However, beginning in 1478, the chief governors were at first limited to shorter terms of office and from 1534 they served only during royal pleasure. This deprived them of security of tenure and made them vulnerable to both open and covert criticism. Then, in 1479 the deputy's control of patronage was explicitly limited by reversion to the crown of the appointment to six leading civil offices. Further, by act of parliament in 1494–95 all judges and other principal officials were to serve during the king's pleasure,

7. D. Hoak, 'Two revolutions in Tudor government: the formation and organization of Mary I's privy council', in Coleman & Starkey, ed., *Revolution reassessed*, pp. 89–91, 113.

8. A. Weikel, 'The Marian council revisited', in Tittler & Loach, ed., *Mid-Tudor polity*, pp. 56–62, 66, 72–73.

9. D. Starkey, 'After the revolution', in Coleman & Starkey, ed., *Revolution reassessed*, pp. 200, 207.

10. Ellis, *Tudor Ireland*, p. 156.

placing them beyond the control of the deputy. And, of course, Poynings' law was passed in the same parliament, requiring the viceroy to obtain licence from the king to call a parliament and submitting bills to England for prior approval.[11]

Despite these efforts to limit the independence of the lord deputy, the earls of Kildare effectively dominated the period 1470 to 1534. They did so by a combination of clever politics, management of their power base in the Pale and inexpensive, 'undemanding' government. In practice, the reservation to the crown of appointments to the Dublin administration was no check on Kildare's partisan support, neither in the council nor in the bureaucracy more generally. While he was required to act only with the advice of the council and he employed an 'inner circle' from 1479 expressly for this purpose, his minions generally accepted the lord deputy's leadership. Yet the council itself retained a certain functional independence. Vacancies in the chief governorship were filled by order of the council and justiciars were chosen whenever the sovereign died. The emergence of a privy council was anticipated by several changes in the fifteenth century, but Ellis has maintained that this new model of a working council was formally erected during the viceroyalty of the earl of Surrey in 1520. The purpose in this case was to create an institution of government which could act independently of the chief governor under the leadership of the lord chancellor, if necessary, and which would serve as a restraint on the power of the incumbent viceroy. Gradually, this new privy council became a more sedentary part of the Dublin administration with broad powers to assist the lord deputy in governing. Ellis concluded that, 'While Kildare survived, his influence concealed the full extent of the changes, but in reality executive power in Ireland had come to lie more nearly with the deputy and council jointly, "and in thabsens of the deputy, the counsaill here"'.[12]

The significance of the 1530s in the administrative history of Ireland is not less than it was in England, and for similar reasons. While historians continue to debate the effectiveness and authorship of the 'constitutional revolution' described so ably by Brendan Bradshaw, it is clear that the government of Ireland had been transformed by 1540. According to Dr Bradshaw, a former student of G. R. Elton at Cambridge, the movement for fundamental reform in the lordship of Ireland came from a 'reforming milieu' of experienced observers among the leading officials and the patrician class of the towns in Ireland. Using a convention of humanist scholarship, these reformers convinced

11. Ellis, *Reform and revival*, pp. 14–23.
12. ibid., pp. 48, 32–36, 41–44. Interestingly, the acumen of Wolsey anticipated in Ireland the establishment of similar arrangements for the council in England. Cf. Guy, 'Revolution or evolution', and see above.

Cromwell that Ireland must be reformed on a commonwealth model, based upon assimilation of the native Irish and a systematic policy of general reform. Cromwell devised this constitutional realignment of the Irish polity beginning in the summer of 1533, according to Bradshaw, and the ensuing Kildare rebellion merely interrupted his plans for 'unitary sovereignty', the concept of all Ireland ruled directly through royal agents in Dublin. The formative instrument of this constitutional restructuring was the lord deputy and council. From 1534 until well into the next century, Ireland was governed by an English viceroy assisted by a council which employed a mixture of English and Anglo-Irish officials and peers of the realm. The alternative model of military conquest was explicitly disavowed. Bradshaw concluded that 'Cromwell's programme was designed to undermine the administrative and jurisdictional integrity of the government of the Irish lordship, to shift its centre from Dublin to London, and to transform the Dublin administration from a central government into a regional council'.[13]

In several respects, this model of institutional reform requires modification. It is beyond question that the lordship of Ireland was thenceforth governed by an English viceroy, assisted by a reformed privy council and supported by a regular, if small, military establishment. But the outcome of Cromwellian reform was much less coherent and less commanding than its intent. In part, this was due to the chronic failure to provide adequate financial resources for such an ambitious project. Cromwell's policy began with the staffing of the council in Ireland. He employed both Anglo-Irish and new English officials, a policy intended to foster conciliation. However, the immediate effect of this change was to polarize the council and to generate new factional disputes within the governing board. By insisting that the lord deputy govern only with the advice of the council, Cromwell hoped to restrain impetuous viceroys. But, in practice, he managed to create a composite structure which often produced stalemate. The intrusion of the commission of 1536–37 further debilitated the central government by introducing arbitrary oversight from Westminster. In sum, we can see that the constitutional revolution fell well short of its aims.[14] Yet, in some ways, the archetype of unitary sovereignty was a useful one. It introduced the possibility of governing systematically from Dublin under the aegis of royal supervision and control. The problem of Cromwell's model was not in its design but in its execution. Repeated examples throughout the century of financial retrenchment

13. Bradshaw, *Irish constitutional revolution*, p. 161. See also pp. 35–55, 89–99, 108–16, 140–42.
14. S.G. Ellis, 'Thomas Cromwell and Ireland, 1532–1540', *Hist Jn*, xxiii (1980), 497–515.

and arbitrary interventions undermined even the most talented and respected chief governors.

In 1541 the newly installed lord deputy, St Leger, called a parliament to complete the constitutional revolution. By the act 'for the kingly title', the lordship of Ireland with its implicit acceptance of subordinate status, exchanged this awkward dual sovereignty for legal parity with England under one sovereign. Henry VIII was now king of Ireland and his viceroy, acting with the privy council, would proceed to rule all of Ireland in accordance with the common law. For the crown, this meant the resumption of its legal rights to forfeited estates and the expansion of its taxing authority to pay for its new responsibilities. For the reformers in the Pale, the promise of administrative reform meant the restoration of stability and prosperity after a decade of civil unrest. Ciaran Brady has appraised the act thus: '. . . the new constitution of 1541 signified the Tudor resolution that civil society was to be established in Ireland through the instruments of government already available and by the conventional means of institutional development and reform.'[15] Nevertheless, he views the outcome of this optimistic legislation with considerable scepticism. He argues that Poynings' law continued to emasculate the work of the intermittent parliament; that the council in Ireland was wholly subordinate to the chief governors and to the privy council in Westminster; and that the politics of faction and patronage conspired to undermine even the most well-intentioned government. In his view, the reform of Ireland by the gradual extension of the common law throughout the realm was continually frustrated by the very officials who were invested with the authority to implement it.[16]

Were Tudor statesmen blind to the realities of their situation? Had they no idea that implementation of the constitutional change would be met with obstacles and impediments? Were Irish councillors merely opportunistic cynics who would seize upon every advantage, however slight, to make their fortunes in the anarchic wreckage of impending political upheaval? In contrast to these assumptions, we have Bradshaw's argument for the 'liberal formula', based on commonwealth humanism, which would lay the constitutional foundation for the new government. The conciliatory policy of St Leger was grounded on the pragmatism of surrender and re-grant, by which the Irish chiefs would release their estates to the crown and receive them back under title of the common law with the honour of a peerage. The objective of government was to change the infrastructure of Irish

15. C. Brady, 'Court, castle and country: the framework of government in Tudor Ireland', in Brady & Gillespie, ed., *Natives and newcomers*, p. 28. See also, Bradshaw, *Irish constitutional revolution*, pp. 195–205, 233–44, 263–66.

16. Brady, 'Court, castle and country', pp. 29, 40–41.

politics and society without changing its superstructure, that is, its landholding élite. Thus the council was expanded to include the newly ennobled lords and the role of the governing board now embraced the management of these delicate arrangements. The enhanced council continued to supervise the daily administration of the realm, including the central courts, while it attempted to expand its authority beyond the Pale. Proposals which were offered at this time anticipated the later establishment of itinerant justices, new shires and provincial councils. Bradshaw has argued that the earlier manifestations of cross-cultural conflict began to vanish in an 'erosion of hostility' which was evident at a great council meeting in Dublin in 1546.[17] However, in the view of Bradshaw, the promise of this new dawn was crushed by the militant 'radicalism' of the more aggressive deputies, beginning with Bellingham, and reaching a crescendo of cultural violence under Sussex and Sydney. The abrupt reversal of the policy of moderation has been characterized by Bradshaw as a programme of military conquest, a discontinuity with earlier reforms that formed a 'chasm' between compromise and confrontation which was ultimately tragic for Ireland.[18]

In this charged atmosphere of political change, the role of the privy council in Ireland has been concealed. It is difficult to imagine that the experienced councillors who had just survived the rousing decade of the 1530s would have simply acquiesced in the machinations of every chief governor, or that they meekly accepted the belligerent new policy so passionately described by Bradshaw. Indeed, it may be that their cynicism was not so great, nor their inaction so pervasive, as we have been led to believe. Were they really a den of thieves, as Brady seems to imply? Were they victimized by the 'tragic' aggression of the Tudor conquest? Neither model really takes us very far towards an understanding of the work of the council, its constitutionally altered role in the government, or its dynamic relationship with a series of new lords deputy. We do know, of course, that the council began its systematic record-keeping in the Red Council Book in 1543, but there is little else from this period that would suggest institutional reform of the kind which was implied in the 'constitutional revolution' of 1541 and after. Nevertheless, the council had clearly begun to take on the characteristics of the busy privy council in Westminster. It

17. Bradshaw, *Irish constitutional revolution*, pp. 242–55.

18. ibid., pp. 189, 244. Bradshaw's use of anachronistic terms such as 'radical' and 'conservative' is arbitrary and partisan. His characterization of St Leger's regime as one of 'truth and gentleness' lacks judicious balance and his discovery of 'Irish political nationalism' in this period is premature. ibid., pp. 82–83, 258–60. See also S.G. Ellis, 'Nationalist historiography', 1–17 for a more moderate statement of the case.

was the driving force of the central government and its widespread influence was acknowledged in the great variety of suits and cases brought before it in the period leading up to 1556. While we lack sufficient evidence for a detailed analysis of the privy council in this period, it would be useful to examine more fully the parliamentary intent of the act for the kingly title; the connection between institutional development of the privy councils in Westminster and Dublin; and the impact on the Irish board of factional strife within the English privy council from 1547 to 1553. Given the new evidence for comparable institutional changes under Wolsey and Cromwell in both England and Ireland, a new study of the 'mid-Tudor polity' in Ireland may be warranted.

THE LORD DEPUTY AND COUNCIL

Ordinarily, the council in Ireland incorporated the lord deputy as its presiding officer. To this extent, he was like the lord president of the council in the marches of Wales, the leading official on a provincial council. But his authority was traditionally greater. Lords deputy possessed broad powers to negotiate with Irish chiefs, to command the garrison in Ireland and to supervise the financial establishment, so they could not easily be mistaken for provincial presidents. In the instructions of 1575 Sir Henry Sydney's titles were described thus: 'Lord President of the Council in Wales, Lord Deputy of Ireland and one of her majeties privy counsell.'[19] It is significant that in Wales he was president of the council, whereas in Ireland he had greater scope as deputy under the queen for the entire realm. In this sense he was clearly above the council, although he was also part of it. And, whereas in Wales he frequently acted by deputy during long absences, his governorship in Ireland was more direct and continuous.[20] He was in fact a viceroy, not unlike those employed by Spain in the Netherlands, and his executive power was considerable. Hence, when he presided over the council it, too, was constitutionally superior to any provincial body, and when he was gone the council was restricted in what it could or would do, lacking the authority of his office.

The lord deputy could do a great many things without the council, but he was specifically enjoined to discuss with it all matters of importance. Thus the government could not be run arbitrarily by the strong hand of a dictatorial viceroy. In 1558 Queen Mary required Sussex

19. BL, Cott. MS Titus B XII, f. 155.
20. Williams, *Council in Wales*, pp. 137, 252. Williams makes clear that the Welsh council was primarily seen as a court of law and when it took up other administrative duties it lacked initiative of its own. See pp. 47–50, 106, 111.

to consult with the councillors she had just appointed. After naming each of them, she added,

In whose advice, wisedome, good counsell and service, their majesties repose great trust, and therefore require their said Deputie to use, cherisshe and esteme the same, as apperteyneth. And in all treaties, consultacons, devises and conclusions concerning the said affaires, to take their advise and good counsaill, as for his wisedome they doubt not he well do accordingly.[21]

It is significant that the choice of whom to consult would seem to lie with the lord deputy, although he was certainly under constraint to take the advice of at least some of his councillors. The queen implicitly understood this to mean the greater part of those who would usefully contribute, but in practice the chief governor may have asked only those most certain to agree with him. Instead of turning to those with breadth of experience and wise alternatives, he may have merely obtained sufficient assent to suit his own purposes. Dr Brady has argued that Sussex attempted to govern without the support of the entire council, relying instead on a 'tightly organized executive group' to manage affairs while he pursued a methodical plan designed to achieve immediate practical success. According to this view, the lord deputy could staff the council with a core of his clients and supporters and then proceed to call upon only those whose willing consent was guaranteed.[22] However, Sussex's management of the council was not so adept as this explanation would have it. And the queen certainly intended to circumscribe his executive authority. In 1561 Sussex was advised to announce openly to the council and to '. . . suche others of our nobilitie as you shall thinke fitt, declaring unto them the hole proceeding [with] . . . Shane Oneyle . . .'.[23] In this case we may infer that Sussex had the option to invite discreet supporters of the government in addition to the council itself.

An analogy can be drawn with the evolution of the privy council in England in the mid-Tudor period. Upon the death of Henry VIII the privy council was granted exceptional powers to govern, and this authority was usurped by the duke of Somerset, acting as lord presi-

---

21. PRO, SP 62/2/51. Instructions such as these form an important source of information on the council. They were usually given at the beginning or the renewal of a governor's term of office and covered the entire range of his activity. In most cases the orders required the lord deputy to take action in conjunction with the council.

22. Brady, 'Government of Ireland', pp. 124–28. See also Ellis, *Reform and revival*, pp. 32–34 for his view of 'conciliar eclipse' during the 'Kildare ascendancy' after 1470.

23. PRO, SP 63/3/194.

dent of the council. In the view of Dr Hoak, Somerset arrogated to himself the proper authority of the council and ruled arbitrarily until he in turn was removed and conciliar independence was restored. When the duke of Northumberland was made lord president in February 1550 he was less arbitrary and sought to build consensus for his policies, seeking 'collective authorship' of the privy council. And when he returned to a more autocratic style based on his new political supremacy, the duke managed affairs behind the scenes by using the young king's boyhood friend, Henry Sydney, as the conduit for policy.[24] Thus, the management of the privy council had created a national crisis and it is significant that Elizabeth did not make use of a lord president of the council after her accession. Government by an 'inherently conservative council, presided over by a determinedly unprogressive queen' and led in practice by the cautious Sir William Cecil would naturally resist the assertion of independence by a robust viceroy of Ireland. Indeed, the Elizabethan privy council implicitly rejected the precedent of its Edwardian ancestor in that it became more dependent on the queen to take action and it relied very heavily on a network of local officials to give effect to its decrees.[25] In that respect, the council in Ireland accepted this balanced constitutional position as its model.

The instructions given periodically to the lord deputy and council were the basis for governmental policy during each administration. They were ordered to be read before the council once in every quarter of the year by the clerk or the secretary. The articles of the queen to the council in 1556 made it plain that she wanted the council to be acquainted with all directions, instructions, establishments and warrants sent from England. However, a significant proviso was made in matters of great secrecy. Here, the queen said, '. . . in especiall matters which for secrecie sake are not to be openly read to all the Councell at Large, the lord Deputie maie in Discretion Direct the secretary to refer them to be Communicated only to such of thenglish counsell as for the most parte are ordinarily [attendant upon the lord deputie]'.[26] This may have been a tacit understanding reached with subsequent chief governors as well, but this secretive instruction does not recur in the period under discussion. In 1575 Sydney was sent a second time as lord deputy to Ireland with orders to peruse all the instructions of previous chief governors, to consider with the council

24. Hoak, *King's council in reign of Edward VI*, pp. 101–05, 153–54.

25. Pulman, *Elizabethan privy council*, pp. 150–53, 237–42.

26. BL, Add. MS 4,786, f. 24. The MS is torn at the bottom of the folio but we may surmise that the sentence ended with the formula 'attendant upon the lord deputie'. In April 1566 the new lord deputy and council reported that they had read their instructions as directed. PRO, SP 63/17/14.

how they had been executed, and to reprimand negligent officials.[27] The instructions, then, were viewed as cumulative, and each succeeding lord deputy must be aware of the full extent of his responsibilities. At times, this system could make for embarrassing contradictions, but on the whole it served the Dublin government well. In 1578 the reasoning behind these orders was partly revealed to the new lord justice, Sir William Drury. He was admonished to publish quarterly before the council all orders and instructions he had received so that no councillor could plead ignorance of his instructions.[28]

The relationship between the lord deputy and the council in Ireland was a practical one, of course, and they responded to different matters as the circumstances required. In judicial business the chief governor and council acted in concert, applying the principles of the common law publicly and conscientiously, since this was fundamental to the aim of eventual anglicization of social and political institutions. Financial policy was handled by the lord deputy and council acting under instructions from the privy council in Westminster. The council's independence of action was increasingly restricted as fiscal reform and retrenchment became the watchword. In this case, the council itself was employed to monitor and restrain the actions of the lord deputy. In military affairs, on the other hand, the viceroy often acted alone, though he was always accompanied by several councillors in the field and took their advice as needed. In matters of strategy he consulted the council, and often lamented the lack of 'martial councillors'.[29] In the impending crisis of 1578, anticipating an invasion by Thomas Stukeley, Sir Henry Sydney reported that he discussed with members of the council '. . . neere here unto me . . .' the contents of a letter from the privy council in England, although it was addressed to the lord deputy alone.[30]

Correspondence with the queen and her advisers helps to clarify the interdependence of the lord deputy and the council in Ireland. While Sydney and other chief governors corresponded privately with the principal statesmen in Westminster as well as with the queen, letters addressed to the lord deputy and council were generally more formal and ceremonious and dealt with matters of the gravest importance. In addition, formal statements of governmental policy, as opposed to more informal suits and technical matters of lesser importance, were

27. BL, Cott. MS Titus B XII, f. 155. See Ellis, *Reform and revival*, pp. 34–35 for earlier examples of instruction to seek the advice of the council.

28. ibid., f. 625–25v. In this case, the constitutional crisis over the cess was in full force and government policy was in a state of flux.

29. Fitzwilliam had no one to go on a military mission from the council in 1573 and complained to Cecil. PRO, SP 63/42/184–86.

30. PRO, SP 63/61/3.

commonly sent as the result of council meetings. For example, the council in 1561 offered the queen advice on how to negotiate with Shane O'Neill and in the following year provided an extended account of the state of Ireland.[31] Reliance upon the council's advice was intensified when a lord justice replaced the lord deputy temporarily, for his authority was of necessity more limited. The instructions to Sir William Drury in 1578 called upon him and the lord chancellor, Sir William Gerrard, to meet with the council immediately in order to discuss the state of the four provinces confronted by the rebellion of James Fitzmaurice.[32]

Although the lord deputy could not make a councillor, the council could, under certain conditions, make a lord justice. The lord deputy received his warrant from the queen, but a lord justice was chosen by the council to replace temporarily the chief governor when he was recalled to England or in case he was unexpectedly incapacitated. The warrant of the lord deputy lapsed on the death of the sovereign, so when the council received the news of Queen Mary's demise in December 1558, the lord chancellor issued writs for a meeting of the grand council. This formal caucus met at Christ Church cathedral in Dublin and chose Sir Henry Sydney to be lord justice while Lord Deputy Sussex travelled to England to seek the favour of the new queen.[33] There were, however, certain ambiguities in the procedure of selecting someone to replace the chief governor. In February 1560 the council attempted to clarify the matter by proclamation, reciting the conditions of election when the realm '. . . hath chaunced to be destitute of a lieutenant, deputie justice or outher hede gouvernour by death, surrender or departure out of the Realme of Irland . . .'.[34] It was agreed that the council had customarily assembled to elect a new chief governor, but that the laws on the subject left the matter in some doubt. Consequently, an established procedure was created in the 'act for the election of the lord justice', so that

. . . immediatelie upon the avoidaunce of enye the kinges lieutenant, deputie or justice of this realme by death, surrendre . . . or any other cause, the Kinges Chauncellor of this realme or keper of his grate seal . . . shal by the kinges writt or writtes call and assemble togither . . . the kinges counsaillors . . . to electe and choise one souch person as shalbe an Englishman and born within the realme of England to be justice and gouvernor of this realme of Irlande . . . . And yf therebe noo souch

31. PRO, SP 63/41/132–34; 63/5/223.
32. BL, Cott. MS Titus B XII, f. 378.
33. *Liber mun. pub. Hib.*, i, pt. 2, p. 3.
34. PRO, SP 63/2/12.

person then within this realme, then theye to electe and choise twoo persons of the said counsaill of Englisshe bloud and surname . . . .[35]

Traditionally, the council had the responsibility for electing a lord justice under the temporary leadership of the lord chancellor. But there was some confusion about the correct mode of naming a deputy when the chief governor departed the realm. The laws established under Henry VII required the election of the vice treasurer as lord justice, but this had been annulled by an act of Henry VIII.[36] The effect of the edict of council in 1560 was to reinstate an older practice with the proviso that the elected man be English-born. The proclamation was made in the wake of the election of Fitzwilliam as lord justice on 2 February 1560.[37] Clearly, the explicit preference for an English-born executive was a reflection of the well-remembered Kildare rebellion of 1534. Nevertheless, it is significant that two Anglo-Irishmen ('of English blood and surname') could hold the office jointly, and the possibility of having no English-born official available is eloquent of the pragmatism of Elizabethan government. Indeed, Dr Brady has warned against interpreting the replacement of office-holders in the top levels of the Irish administration as a purging of Anglo-Irish in favour of English officials. Despite the efforts of modern historians to discover racial politics at the heart of Tudor policy in Ireland, it seems that faction, patronage and 'interest' played the dominant role in the selection of leading officials of the Dublin government.[38] It is also significant that the conciliar decree of 1560 could thus abridge two previous acts of parliament and that the council could so amend its own latent powers. Of course, this was done only with the prior assent of the queen. The effect of the decree was to eliminate any single Anglo-Irish leader from eligibility for the chief governorship, but this had been the case in practice since 1534. It is possible to see here the emergence of the role of the council as intermediary, an arena for the reconciliation of interests in a period of transition.

The right of the council to replace the chief governor was limited and did not represent in itself a check on the incumbent lord deputy. Furthermore, the temporary nature of the lord justice's position undermined his authority to act. As a consequence of his political vulnerability, he commonly faced more widespread incidents of open criminality

---

35. ibid., ff. 12–13.

36. Ellis, *Reform and revival*, pp. 20–24; E. Curtis and R.B. McDowell, *Irish historical documents, 1172–1922* (London, 1943; 1968), pp. 81–83.

37. 'Colectanea de rebus Hibernicis', ed. C. McNeill, *Anal Hib*, no. 6 (1934), 365–66.

38. Brady, 'Government of Ireland', pp. 127–30.

and disobedience. In April 1562 the lord justice and council acknowledged that the '. . . vulgar sorte (of simplicitie) . . . [had] become slacke to obaye soche mandates as from tyme to tyme are sett furthe by us for executinge of thorders hitherto taken . . .'.[39] The council attributed this to rumours of a change in the government, and even lords deputy were the victims of attenuated authority when rumours of their imminent recall were circulated.

In most cases the council was not free to elect whom it pleased as lord justice because the queen sent instructions nominating certain men to replace the lord deputy. In March 1570, for example, when Sydney left for England, writs were directed to the sheriffs of every county to assemble the nobility and council to elect a new governor. On 31 March at Kilmainham this grand council '. . . according to the Queens majesties pleasure signified by her letters to her Majesties said Lord Deputy, elected and chosen Sir William Fitzwilliams, knight'.[40] In 1578 Walsingham wrote to Sydney urging him to expedite the transition of the chief governorship by finishing all his business and bringing the Pale to good order. He commanded the lord deputy to give Sir William Drury '. . . the best advice and direction that you can for his better abilitie to meet withe the attempts of the sayd [Thomas] Stukeley . . .'.[41] But Drury remained in office for only a year before he became fatally ill. On the death of a governor the council was left to its own devices to decide upon a successor, so when Drury died on 3 October 1579 the council wrote hastily to England and then promptly prepared for a grand council meeting in Dublin '. . . to make choice of a newe justice according to the lawes of the realme . . .'.[42] The mood of the council was one of gravity and determination mixed with great anxiety as they quickly prepared to choose a new viceroy in the middle of a rebellion. Sir William Pelham was elected as the new lord justice in a ceremony on Sunday 11 October, after which a council meeting was held.[43] It was only under the unusual circumstances of the death of the viceroy or of the sovereign that the council was able

39. PRO, SP 63/5/223.

40. 'Colectanea', ed. McNeill, 365–66. Letters were sent to 13 counties and the order was signed by 25 councillors, including bishops and peers. See also *Cal. pat. rolls Ire., Henry VIII—Eliz*, p. 545. On 22 April 1564 the queen recalled Sussex to England and in the same letter required the council to elect Sir Nicholas Arnold as lord justice. RIA, MS 24 F 17, f. 188v.

41. University of North Carolina, Chapel Hill, Southern Historical Collection, Preston Davie Papers, 3406, item no. 4. See also *Cal. pat. rolls Ire., Eliz*, p. 15 for the ceremony of Drury's election as lord justice in 1578.

42. *Walsingham letter book*, ed. J. Hogan and N. McN. O'Farrell (Dublin, 1959), p. 199.

43. LPL, Carew MS 597, f. 20–20v.

to exercise its right to elect freely a new chief governor without instructions from England.

The council was employed as a check on the power of the lord deputy and this was clearly articulated in a variety of ways. For example, in 1552 the conciliar authority to approve grants, leases and warrants was entered into the council book with this instruction: '. . . noe letters, writings or orders of importance be signed before they bee read before the counsell.'[44] Due to the enrichment of sycophants like Walter Peppard, and many of the councillors themselves, a procedure was devised to protect the estates of the queen from arbitrary alienation. In 1578 the instructions ordered Lord Justice Drury and the lord chancellor to grant no extraordinary charges over the value of £10 wihout calling '. . . all those of our Counsell beinge within viij milles of the place where you or eyther of you shalbe . . .'.[45] The queen wanted to curb the excessive charges from warrants, leases and gifts, so she required the lord deputy to confer with at least four other councillors on the merits of the proposed allowance and only then to subscribe to it. As the queen and privy council extended their control over Irish financial administration, they demanded more of the council in Ireland as a check on the powers of the chief governor.

The council could hardly be used to balance the power of the lord deputy if it were largely subordinate to him. On the other hand, little business could be conducted if the council were an adversary and refractory body, refusing to be led by the viceroy. There is evidence to support both these hypotheses and it would therefore be misleading to suggest that the council was habituated to either extreme. The personality and character of the lord deputy was perhaps the principal basis for accommodation with the council, but a lot depended on the current membership, the political situation in Ireland, and the support of the English Pale. The assiduous and principled lord chancellor, Sir William Gerrard, found that Sydney exercised considerable control over his councillors in 1577. Gerrard told Walsingham,

I find heare one ill and daungerouse custome which I learne by ymitacion is soe taken holde of as growen comen and that is when sutes are maide to the deputie for thinges to be letten for allowances or giftes by Concordatum, yf the Lord deputie putt his hand to the fiant . . . then all the Councill like Sheepe to the Water subscribe the same when theye are nothinge acquainted with the matter.[46]

44. H.M.C, *Haliday MSS* (*H.M.C. rep 15*, app. iii (1897)), p. 281 (f. 295v).

45. BL, Cott. MS Titus B XII, f. 382. The enrichment of councillors and others is amply demonstrated by the grants in *Cal. pat. rolls Ire.*, *Hen VIII—Eliz* and *Cal. pat. rolls Ire.*, *Eliz.*

46. PRO, SP 63/57/97.

Gerrard had remonstrated with the lord deputy and obtained limited success, but he sought from Walsingham a directive that '. . . mye Lord to have speciall regarde that before he passe anie thinge by waie of graunte . . . that first he have the cause . . . debated by the Counsell and then agreed upon by the most parte to passe and to be subscribed by those who gave their assentes'.[47] It is likely that the council commonly agreed upon ordinary grants in a perfunctory way, but this does not establish a functional subordination of the council to the lord deputy on more vital matters.

In fact, many of the viceroys had confrontations with the council, although this was not typical of their relationship. In 1562 Sussex alleged that the master of the rolls, John Parker, had attempted to circulate a petition against him. On this occasion the council closed ranks behind the lord deputy and Parker was forced to defend himself alone.[48] In March 1563, however, Sussex wrote that '. . . ther mette with me not on of the nobylyte and very fewe of the Counsell . . .'.[49] The issue of the cess was disputed at that time and some of the council took the side of the Pale against the chief governor. Sussex pronounced himself bitterly disappointed and claimed that Lord Slane and others had disavowed their previous consent to the cess on the Pale. It was often the nobility, as in this case, who proved the most refractory in conciliar disputes, since they did not depend on the favour of the lord deputy to hold office. But when Sir Nicholas Arnold was lord justice he faced the resistance of the entire council. Arnold wrote to Cecil in April 1565, saying the queen needed

. . . a governour and counsaill here, as will rather bende themselfes to her best shrvice and welthe of the countrey then as sume of them nowe daily doe, to the Impungnyng [sic] or crossing of anything I can doo or speake, howe reasonable or necessarie so ever it maye seme to the rest of the counsaill here, if it agree not with the former governementes and advertisementes into Englande . . . so that no faulte can be amended as long as we that rest here of her Majesties counsaill do stande at suche division as we do nowe except that such as have devided this counsaill, maye . . . be tried out and . . . her highness maye remove the offender and fill the place with sume suche as will further and not hindre shrvice . . . .[50]

The insecurity of tenure of the lord justice may have contributed to this bitterness, as well as the acerbic temperament of the dictatorial

---

47. ibid. It seems clear from this account that the lord deputy could not simply overrule the council, but must have its consent by whatever means he could obtain it.
48. BL, Add. MS 40,061, ff. 43, 45–46v.
49. PRO, SP 63/8/22–24.
50. PRO, SP 63/13/77.

.Arnold. In any case, the removal of unruly councillors was an extreme measure and nothing came of his suggestion.

In general, the council was an active force without being fractious or intractable. It was usually supportive of the chief governor, even lamely subordinate at times. Although in most cases it deferred to the lord deputy, the council could also act against him. From 1575 to 1578 the council was badly split by the controversy over the cess, the customary taxation in kind for the lord deputy and the garrison. This eventually developed into a constitutional crisis involving the queen, the council and the gentlemen of the Pale (see chapter six). But even then a distinction was evident between the more passive civil servants, who were often clients of the lords deputy, and the active dissidents among the nobility. It must be remembered that the officials of the government were also men of distinguished Anglo-Irish families, so perhaps the most the lord deputy could expect from them in such a crisis was a restrained neutrality. For the most part, however, the council as a whole was an active partner with the lord deputy in the government of the realm.

CHARACTERISTICS OF THE PRIVY COUNCILLORS

Although there was no typical councillor, no mould from which an ideal casting could always be obtained, there were certain features common to all or most of them. The councillors were generally able and experienced men when they were administered the oath of office. In age they ranged from the superannuated veterans of previous administrations to the young scions of great families. The great variety of character, temperament and training among the councillors makes categorization difficult (see chapter three, 'Personalities and Politics'), so a caveat must be issued forthwith: the following analysis and summary should not obscure the genuine differences between the councillors nor the heterogeneous nature of the council. The majority were representatives of the great Anglo-Irish families, but there were also a few English adventurers like Sir Peter Carew. Formerly sheriff of Devon, Carew decided, at the age of fifty-four, to press his dubious claims to the barony of Idrone in Co. Carlow. He obtained the queen's blessing for his project and was made a councillor, yet he represented no interest but his own and continually requested personal favours of the government. Carew was not a typical councillor, and it is certainly misleading to suggest that the primary thrust of government policy was to promote his opportunistic schemes for colonization.[51] But his

51. Note, for example, Canny's discussion of Carew's role in colonization. Despite the attention given to this subject, only two active councillors (Carew and Warham St Leger) fit the model of classic adventurers. Canny, *Elizabethan conquest*, pp. 68,

case illustrates the difficulty of neatly summarizing the backgrounds of this diverse body.

There were forty-four privy councillors during the period from 1556 to 1578. Actually, a larger number signed documents of the council, but they signed very rarely and there is no supporting evidence to indicate that they were councillors. I have used five criteria to identify privy councillors. They are: (1) signing the council book, or other document from the council; (2) designation by official instructions; (3) holding an office presumed to confer membership; (4) attendance at meetings; (5) independent description as a councillor. Signing the council book would presumably be an act which only members could do, but this approach has some problems. A small number of non-councillors did sign the council book, albeit quite rarely. Also, the grand council assembled a large number of notables who were not privy councillors, yet all of them signed the council book. Hence, it is necessary to discount the grand council meetings (ceremonious formal occasions) when trying to determine who belonged to the privy council. Oswald Massingberd, the prior of Kilmainham until 1559, signed the council book eight times. However, only twice did he attend meetings of the privy council and these sessions were probably held at Kilmainham where he might be expected to join in the deliberations.[52] Signing a letter from the lord deputy and council is also persuasive evidence of membership, although perhaps not so clear as signing the council book.

Most members were named as councillors in instructions or patents from the queen. This would seem to be conclusive evidence of formal participation on the council, but in fact it is indicative only of the intention to place someone there. For a number of reasons, that intention might never be realized. In the case of three Anglo-Irish earls who were formally named to the council, a sub-category has been used. The two earls of Desmond and the earl of Clanricarde in this period were seldom seen in Dublin except as prisoners, and their inclusion on the council was probably honorific. In fact, it was never intended that they should meet regularly with the privy council because they were needed as the symbols of authority in their own dominions. They were thus inactive councillors, named but not in attendance. For

---

72–76, 78–82; Ellis, *Tudor Ireland*, pp. 256–57, 264. See also John Hooker's 'Life of Sir Peter Carew' from Carew MS 605 in the Lambeth Palace Library. *Cal. Carew MSS, 1515–74*, pp. lxvii–cxviii.

52. RIA, MS 24 F 17, ff. 69v, 72v. Massingberd signed the council book for the first time on 2 May 1558 and for the last time on 31 July 1559. If he had been a councillor, his membership would probably have lasted longer than a year. It is possible that he was named to the council and dropped by Elizabeth for religious reasons.

.different reasons, the membership of Valentine Browne, who was made a councillor in the instructions of 16 July 1559, was virtually still-born.[53] Browne came to Ireland briefly as a commissioner to inquire into administrative irregularities, but he only signed the council book on two occasions, and he left shortly thereafter.[54] He was not, therefore, a councillor in any meaningful sense. The purpose here is to identify the active councillors whose membership contributed to the unique character and quality of the institution. Browne clearly was not one of these.

Three further criteria for membership may be used. First, if a man were described as a councillor this could support other evidence of his membership. Secondly, certain men held offices which were deemed to carry with them membership on the council. One of these was William Walsh, bishop of Meath under Mary. It is clear that the bishops of Meath before and after him were councillors, and he signed the council book with some regularity. He was not mentioned in the instructions and his tenure of office (1554–63) was interrupted by the Elizabethan settlement in 1560. Perhaps the turmoil and uncertainty in his diocese may explain his lack of stature in the council, and he was certainly not called to the board after he refused the oath of supremacy.[55] Finally, we must consider regular and continuous attendance at council meetings as evidence of membership on the board. An example of this is the case of Roland, Viscount Baltinglas. His successor was not on the privy council and he was never named to the body by patent or instruction, yet he was the most assiduous peer in attendance next to the earl of Kildare. He came to forty-five meetings, thirteen of which were sessions of the privy council, but he was never described as a councillor. A last difficulty is the role of David Hay. He held no office and was never mentioned in the instructions. Yet he signed the council book and was apparently a mainstay of the council during 1556 and 1557.[56] He was probably the same David Hay of Slade, Co. Wexford, who was tried for treason by the council in 1564, but no mention was made at his trial that he was a former councillor.[57] Nevertheless, both Hay and Baltinglas were used as

53. *Cal. Carew MSS, 1515–74*, p. 279.
54. RIA, MS 24 F 17, ff. 101v, 102v. Browne sat at the council on 22 and 31 August 1559 and one of those meetings was a grand council.
55. See H.C. Walshe, 'Enforcing the Elizabethan settlement: the vicissitudes of Hugh Brady, bishop of Meath, 1563–1584', *IHS*, xxvi (1989), 356–63.
56. Hay first signed an order of the council on 17 June 1556, and last signed on 30 November 1557. ibid., ff. 5, 60v. In all he signed some eleven council orders and documents.
57. Hay was accused with his son, James, on 13 January 1564 and they were imprisoned for 25 weeks. They were released when no evidence of treason was found. ibid., f. 194–94v.

councillors and may be described as de facto members despite the lack of formal authorization.

The size of the council varied somewhat from year to year, but the average number of active councillors in Ireland was about twenty-two. In comparison, the privy council in England from 1568 to 1582 included twenty-five men who formed a relatively stable governing board. There were twenty-one selected by Elizabeth to be councillors in England in 1558 and by 1578 the number declined to eighteen.[58] In Ireland, by contrast, the instructions reveal a significant increase in the size of the council from 1553 to 1558. At the beginning of Mary's reign only twelve men were named to the board and in 1556 Lord Deputy Fitzwalter was attended by only eleven men.[59] However, in Elizabeth's first instruction to Sussex she named twenty-four councillors, a two-fold increase. Many of these were civil officials, but the new council was designed to represent diverse groups and interests. In fact, there was no serious purge of the Marian council on the accession of Elizabeth. Only William Walsh, bishop of Meath, was removed from office after refusing the oath of supremacy, but he was treated mildly by the authorities. The queen explained the large increase on the council board thus:

. . . hir majestie willeth the sayd deputy to consider, that the usuation [sic] of so many and so diverse is because, as the varietie of the cases may arise for hym to have advise, so may he therein to make choise, and yet as the circumstance of thinges maye beare it to communicate with as many of them as he shall think mete, that thereby the governance maye have the most partes both to ayd him and to allowe and mayneteine determinacions passed . . . but to conclude [she] requireth hym to cherish and mayneteine suche of them chiefly as he shall fynd carefull, willing and paynefull.[60]

In doubling the size of the council, the queen provided more expertise and more diversity of opinion for conciliar deliberations. Further, this measure prevented the sycophancy likely to grow from a small

58. Pulman, *Elizabethan privy council*, p. 17.

59. Mary's last instruction in 1558 left Sussex with thirteen councillors. PRO, SP 62/1/3; PRO, SP 62/2/51; *Cal. Carew MSS, 1515–74*, p. 252. Dr Hoak has argued that the Marian council in England incorporated two distinct memberships in 1553 for political reasons, making the board appear larger than it really was. The outcome was to 'assure the triumph of . . . the principle of government-by-Council . . .'. See Hoak, 'Formation of Mary I's privy council', pp. 111–13.

60. PRO, SP 63/1/104. See also *Cal. Carew MSS, 1515–74*, pp. 284–85. George Dowdall, archbishop of Armagh, had died in August 1558 and was not yet replaced. In general, there was a conscious gradualism in implementing the religious changes, and nearly all the councillors either conformed or kept their religious opinions closely guarded.

body subordinate to the chief governor. The effect of this reform was specifically to include the leading members of the administration by office, rather than to invite selected individuals to serve as members. This larger body was not less efficient than the Marian councils, for its efficiency depended on how many members came to the meetings. The working council still averaged about seven men at its sessions, but the clear intent of the crown was to provide opportunity for a broader spectrum of opinion in governance. This was typically careful and prudent, and it suggests that Elizabethan rule was not committed to a policy of conquest in Ireland from the outset.[61]

In spite of the general continuity of personnel throughout the period, each viceroy governed with a slightly different council. The sovereign might name twelve or more members by instruction, and individual councillors were commonly added on the death of a principal office-holder. In the administration of Sussex under Mary the total number of active councillors was about eighteen. During the remainder of Sussex's administration and the first government of Sir Henry Sydney some twenty-six men were active members of the council. Elizabeth's instructions plainly called for a remodelling of the institution to reflect more diverse interests, and to serve as a check on the chief governor's exercise of power. The shorter terms of office of Fitzwilliam and Sydney from 1571 to 1578 witnessed a gradual decline in the number of councillors. Under Fitzwilliam some twenty-three men were active, while under Sydney's second administration only seventeen were commonly used. This decline may be explained by the death of a number of councillors whose presence was justified by their long years of experience or by their unique perspective on Irish affairs. For example, the deaths of Sir Thomas Cusake, Sir Francis Herbert and Sir Peter Carew, all of whom served on the council without office, created vacancies which were not filled. The result was that, at the end of the period, the council was more of an 'official' body, tied closely to the leading officers of the administration.

Most councillors served by virtue of the office they held, and this was true even in 1556. Yet all the leading officials were not included systematically in the instructions of Queen Mary, and some who were named came only rarely to the council. By 1578, however, the notion of being a councillor ex officio was well-established in fact as well as in theory. There were five basic categories of council members: peers, clerics, civil officials, military officials and councillors without office. Three Anglo-Irish peers served by virtue of their titles, but only two of them were active councillors. Gerald, earl of Kildare, was

---

61. There is no evidence here of a 'conquistador' mentality or of 'colonialist theory' as suggested in recent treatments of the period. See Ellis, *Tudor Ireland*, pp. 238, 245–48.

among those most frequently in attendance, while Thomas, earl of Ormonde, was less active, although he was the most prominent Irish peer. These two men served on the council from 1556 when they were first named by Queen Mary.[62] Kildare was only thirty-one years old and Ormonde was but twenty-four. The earls of Desmond were named to the council in 1556 and thereafter, but they rarely came to Dublin willingly and were thus not active councillors. Three bishops commonly served on the council. Foremost was the archbishop of Dublin, who, during much of the century, was also the lord chancellor. The successive bishops of Meath and the archbishops of Armagh were also ex officio members of the council. The Elizabethan holders of these bishoprics were tireless in their attendance on the council. Adam Loftus, archbishop of Dublin, Hugh Brady, bishop of Meath, and Thomas Lancaster, archbishop of Armagh were all industrious councillors who spent most of their time in Dublin.[63] The deans of Christ Church, Thomas Lokwood and John Garvey, served regularly on the council, though we may doubt whether they were members ex officio.

The council was mainly a civil body, despite the large number of lords spiritual and temporal who were named to it. The principal state officials had the highest authority in government, and the majority of active councillors were civilian crown officers. The lord deputy and lord chancellor took precedence over all other councillors including peers and bishops. Hardly less important was the beleaguered vice treasurer, on whom the fiscal burdens of the government rested heavily. The four senior judges were required to be present at council meetings and formed the judicial element of the council board when it sat as a tribunal. The two chief justices, the master of the rolls and the chief baron of the exchequer were ordinarily diligent in their attendance on the board, and they were often employed on judicial commissions from the council. Lastly, the secretary of state, more a clerk than a statesman, was an ex officio member who sat at council sessions regularly. In England, where Cecil as principal secretary of state acted as an unofficial lord president of the council and set the agenda for its meetings, the officer was a powerful influence in government.[64] But the distinctive role of the viceroy in Ireland made the duties of the secretary of state less important, since no chief governor would wish

---

62. *Cal. Carew MSS, 1515–74*, pp. 252–57.

63. It should be noted that the primate of all Ireland, the archbishop of Armagh, found his see often troubled and restive, so remained for the most part in Dublin. A recent treatment of Hugh Brady as bishop of Meath demonstrates the importance of faction on the council and the schism, even among Protestants, in the episcopacy. See Walshe, 'Enforcing the Elizabethan settlement, 370–73.

64. Pulman, *Elizabethan privy council*, pp. 30–33.

to brook a rival for power and patronage comparable to the Cromwellian secretaryship which had emerged under Henry VIII.

While the administrative and juridical functions of the council constituted the locus classicus of its mandate to govern, the board was also at times a council of war. The two leading military officers, the marshal and the master of the ordnance, were ex officio members of the council. They were the principal military advisers of the chief governor, but they were not particularly reliable in their attendance. Sir George Stanley, the marshal under Sussex, came to the council often, as did John Travers, Sussex's master of the ordnance. But their replacements, Sir Nicholas Bagenall and Jacques Wingfield, seldom attended council meetings despite their long years of service.[65] After 1569, the presidents of Munster and Connacht held ex officio seats on the council, but they were not very active because of their commitments in the provinces. Consequently, the chief governor obtained his most consistent military advice from the older veterans of Irish campaigns, especially the redoubtable Francis Agarde. He was not a member ex officio, but he was the single most diligent councillor over the entire period. Other captains like Humphrey Warren and Henry Cowley were effective military advisers without principal office. And civil officials like Sir Edward Fyton and Sir William Fitzwilliam had obtained considerable military experience during their years in the Irish administration. In sum, then, the council was given significant responsibility for the conduct and maintenance of the military establishment in Ireland with only nominal participation from senior military councillors. If the governing board had been designed to pursue military conquest, its leadership would have been a different one.

Membership on the council was, in general, limited to a closed circle of bureaucratic intimates joined by some of the leading peers of the realm. However, Tudor institutions were always defined pragmatically and the council in Ireland was opened to select former officials and others on occasion. This ad hoc participation was sometimes quite extensive. For example, two former lords chancellor, Sir Thomas Cusake and Sir John Alen, were shrewd, experienced former councillors who were both past sixty years of age in 1561. They had served in the Irish administration since 1534 and Cusake was an active coun-

---

65. Wingfield became master of the ordnance in 1558 and was replaced in 1587 after nearly thirty years in office. Hughes, *Patentee officers*, p. 140. Bagenall had been marshal in 1547 but was replaced in a Marian purge in 1553. When he regained his post in 1565 he clung to it tenaciously until 1590 when he resigned in favour of his son. ibid., p. 6. Bagenall's role in Ulster as both patron and governor in Newry shows that military men were pragmatists who '. . . did not provoke universal hostility among the native lords . . .'. See Brady, 'Sixteenth century Ulster and the failure of Tudor reform' in C. Brady, M. O'Dowd and B. Walker, ed., *Ulster: an illustrated history* (London, 1989), p. 94.

cillor until his death in 1571.[66] On the other hand, two councillors had never held office. The cases of Francis Herbert and David Hay are quite enigmatic, yet it can be shown that Herbert was a trusted informer of Cromwell and obtained certain preferment from him. He was named to the council as early as September 1546.[67] Hay's place on the council, as we have seen, cannot be explained by a record of office or experience. On rare occasions, Englishmen without offices of state were admitted to the board. Sir Nicholas Arnold and Sir Peter Carew came to the council from England on specific missions, both public and private. Their presence on the council was notable as the extension of an active English interest in Irish affairs. Arnold led a commission to inquire into financial irregularities and later served briefly as lord justice, while Carew had licence to pursue his personal fortune in Ireland.

On such a relatively stable council there were few disagreements over the placing of members and issues of precedence were generally solved by custom. Nevertheless, occasional contentions did arise. Soon after Sydney assumed the office of lord deputy in 1566, he was faced with such a dispute. Writing to Cecil in March, he explained that,

I have sent you a scedule herein closid [with] the names of the Counsellors here, of whose plasing their [is] grown some construction because some who might claime higher place either by office or Custome were in the instruction signed by the Queene named after their inferiors. And therein I send in the same scedule both their names as they be and as they claime to be . . . .[68]

Whether this flawed alignment proceeded from clerical error or a mistaken impression of the status of the councillors, the queen promptly agreed to the new statement of precedence. On 4 April she wrote to Sydney to '. . . authorise you to place the said persons in our Counsell there, in such Ordre as their names ar heere Under written, which is according to the note which you sent us for that purpose'.[69] There were only three major changes. Ormonde insisted that he should be placed before Kildare because he was the lord treasurer. Plunket averred that as chief justice of the queen's bench he was the superior

66. Hughes, *Patentee officers*, pp. 2, 137. Cusake was a reformer and client of St Leger while Alen had been his adversary and St Leger's opponent on the council. See Brady, 'Government of Ireland', p. 82.

67. Herbert was apparently a military figure in the 1530s with command of a garrison. *Cal. S. P. Ire., 1509–73*, pp. 19, 29, 36, 38, 75, 77.

68. PRO, SP 63/16/109.

69. D.B. Quinn, ed., 'Additional Sidney state papers, 1566–70', *Anal Hib*, no. 26 (1970), 94.

of both the marshal and the master of the rolls, with whom he exchanged places. And Warham St Leger wished to be placed ahead of the chief justice of common pleas because he had been appointed the new president of Munster. The rest remained in their customary order,[70] as follows:

1. lord chancellor, archbishop of Dublin	10. vice treasurer
	*11. chief justice of queen's bench
2. archbishop of Armagh	*12. marshal
*3. earl of Ormonde	*13. master of the rolls
*4. earl of Kildare	*14. Sir Warham St Leger
5. earl of Desmond	15. chief justice of common pleas
6. earl of Thomond	16. chief baron of the exchequer
7. earl of Clanricarde	17. Sir Thomas Cusake
8. earl of Clancare	18. Francis Agarde
9. bishop of Meath	19. secretary of state

The typical councillor would have been about 50 years of age, experienced in administration and reasonably well-educated. The stable element which presided at the core of the council entered Irish administration at a fairly young age and grew old in office, so the same men represented different generations at the beginning and end of the period. The composite data in this case, however, conceal a 'generation gap' which gradually narrowed. The council in 1559 was basically composed of older, more experienced administrators, combined with the younger scions of great families, to make a council with an average age of 48. For example, Sir Henry Sydney, the earl of Kildare, and Sir William Fitzwilliam were all between the ages of 30 and 34 in 1559. On the other hand, Sir Thomas Cusake was already 70 and Sir Robert Dillon was 59. In 1570 the same core or nucleus of the council, now eleven years older, was still active. The younger members at this time were the archbishop of Dublin and the bishop of Meath at about 37, while Cusake was then 81 and Plunket was at least 63-years-old. This was a well-seasoned council, both in terms of the average age, which was 51, and the declining vigour of its senior members. By

70. Asterisks denote those whose places were changed. St Leger, whose membership was based on his provisional appointment as president in Munster, was originally placed between Cusake and Agarde. See PRO, SP 63/16/109; Quinn, ed., 'Sidney papers', 94.

1579 the average age was 54 and the youngest councillor was at least 46. Clearly, then, this very stable council was ageing in office, yet the average age was generally about 50 for the entire period. In 1579 the number of councillors whose own ages were close to the average was far greater than in 1559. There were both fewer young and fewer elderly men.

Most councillors had received some formal education, but few were university graduates. Seven of the Anglo-Irish lawyers and judges were formally trained at the inns of court in London, and nine others, including five bishops, had extensive schooling at Oxford and Cambridge. The councillors and their affiliations were:

Oxford
Thomas Lancaster, archbishop of Armagh
William Walsh, bishop of Meath (D.D.)
Hugh Brady, bishop of Meath
Sir Richard Weston (All Souls, D.C.L.)
John Garvey, dean of Christ Church (D.D.)

Gray's Inn
Sir John Alen (1522)
Sir William Gerrard (1543)

Lincoln's Inn
Sir Nicholas White (1552)

Cambridge
Hugh Curwen, archbishop of Dublin (B.C.L.)
Thomas, earl of Sussex
Adam Loftus, archbishop of Dublin (Trinity, D.D.)
Sir William Drury (Gonville)

Middle Temple
Sir James Bathe (1522)
Sir Lucas Dillon (1551)

Inner Temple
Sir Thomas Cusake (1522)
Sir John Plunket (1518)

In addition, the presumption may be made that some seven councillors, men such as George Dowdall, archbishop of Armagh, and Sir Robert Dillon, chief justice of common pleas, studied theology and law at the university level, in spite of the absence of any record to this effect. This assumption is based on the offices they held, for which university training was ordinarily a prerequisite. Two other members of the board had been instructed at the prestigious cathedral schools of St Paul's (London) and St David's.[71] And two of the most prominent councillors were educated at the court of Edward, prince of Wales. Sydney and Ormonde joined the precocious boy prince, who was known for his exceptionally rigorous academic work, and they were favoured by him at his accession. They were united at court in 1547 with Gerald, earl of Kildare, who had been in the service of the Medici

71. These were Sir Peter Carew and Sir John Perrot. See *DNB*, s.v.

in Italy during his years of exile from Ireland. He was then 23. Soon thereafter, William Fitzwilliam, aged 21, was presented at Edward's court by Sir John Russell and was made a gentleman of the king's privy chamber.[72] The remaining councillors were largely veteran military men who, we may assume, lacked a university education.[73]

Perhaps the most common characteristic of the councillors was their lengthy experience in service to the crown. Thirty-nine of the councillors had occupied various offices of significance before they were named to the council. Among the more remarkable was Henry Draycott, who obtained his first office as comptroller of the pipe rolls in May 1541. He spent most of his career in the Irish exchequer as chief remembrancer, chancellor and third baron of that institution. On his promotion to the office of master of the rolls in December 1565, Draycott was made a councillor. After twenty-five years of administrative experience he was at last elevated to the governing board and served there for six years until his death in 1572.[74] Draycott was an Englishman, but most councillors who served in a judicial capacity were Anglo-Irish. Sir Robert Dillon the elder was the grandson and namesake of a previous chief justice of the common pleas, but it took him twenty-five years to obtain the rank of his forebear. He became attorney general in 1535; was second justice to the queen's bench in 1554; and was at last preferred to the chief justiceship of common pleas in 1559. He was then 59 years old and he served on the council for another twenty-one years.[75] It would be easy to dismiss the venerable Dillon as a judicial antique in his declining years, but it is important nonetheless to recognize that, in general, the council was a significant repository of administrative experience on which the crown could draw for sage advice.

Certain councillors were promoted on the basis of their previous experience in high office. One such veteran of Irish administration was Sir John Alen. He had been master of the rolls in 1533 and a

---

72. These four men became principal figures in the Irish government for over two decades from the time they were all named simultaneously to the council in Ireland in 1556. Their early relationships at the court of Edward VI would bear some investigation. The state papers are silent on this except for the evident dislike of Sydney for Ormonde. See *DNB*, s.v. 'Sidney, Sir Henry', 'Fitzwilliam, Sir William', 'Fitzgerald, Gerald', and 'Butler, Thomas'; *Cal. Carew MSS, 1515–74*, p. 252.

73. Of the sixteen remaining councillors, twelve were military men with long experience. For the rest, we may surmise that the English leaders Sir William Fitzwilliam and Sir Edward Fyton had considerable formal training. Both were prolific writers and literate men whose advice was sought in the highest circles. John Chaloner was trained as a clerk. We know nothing about the education of David Hay.

74. Hughes, *Patentee officers*, p. 44.

75. ibid., p. 41; *DNB, supplement*, s.v. 'Dillon, Sir Robert'.

clerk of the council. He was later lord keeper and lord chancellor from 1538 until he was removed for his hostility to St Leger's programme in 1547. His reinstatement on the council in 1554 was symptomatic of St Leger's declining influence. At his death, in 1561, Alen had served on the council board, intermittently, for twenty-eight years.[76] On the other hand, veteran military officers were occasionally elevated to the council because of their accumulated experience in the management of conflict. Henry Cowley, the former seneschal of King's County, was summoned to the council when he was too old to continue as a captain.[77] And Sir Wiliam Drury, the marshal of Berwick since 1564, was brought into the executive board in 1576 as the new president of Munster. The lords chancellor were perhaps the most experienced administrators among the official element on the council. Hugh Curwen, the archbishop of Dublin and lord chancellor, had taken his bachelor of civil laws at Cambridge in 1510 and thereafter went to Oxford. He became a chaplain to Henry VIII and was created a doctor of civil laws at Oxford in 1532. He was a pragmatic churchman who became a client of Cromwell, and he served on several commissions to inquire into the use of scripture in Hereford and Calais. In 1541 he was made dean of Hereford and, after being passed over for an English bishopric several times, he was made archbishop of Dublin by Queen Mary in 1555, apparently in spite of his erstwhile Protestant connections. He was undoubtedly a 'trimmer', like so many others in this era.[78] Like Curwen, the queen's councillors in Dublin had commonly gained two decades of experience in civil, military or ecclesiastical office before joining the council.

Only five of the councillors were named as members without ample previous experience. Of these, two were rapidly elevated to the bench. Adam Loftus had been chaplain to Lord Deputy Sussex before he became the new archbishop of Armagh and Hugh Brady had been preferred as bishop of Meath after he became a professor of divinity at Oxford.[79] Two others were the young earls of Kildare and Ormonde, who were senior in rank and owed their membership on the council solely to their degrees of nobility. The last was Henry Radcliffe, brother of the lord deputy, who was only about 26 when brought to Ireland and made lieutenant of the forts in Leix and Offaly. Two of these young men provided the greatest continuity in service of all the councillors

76. Hughes, *Patentee officers*, p. 2; Ball, *Judges*, i, 198–99; Brady, 'Government of Ireland', pp. 99–101, 107.

77. PRO, SP 63/45/184.

78. *DNB*, s.v. 'Curwen, Hugh'. See also, Walshe, 'Enforcing the Elizabethan settlement', 354.

79. *DNB*, s.v. 'Loftus, Adam' and 'Brady, Hugh'. See also Walshe, 'Enforcing the Elizabethan settlement', 352 ff.

of the Tudor period. Although placed on the council when they were only about 30, Ormonde and Loftus outlived Elizabeth and each served in Ireland for over forty-three years.[80]

A nucleus of leadership emerged in 1556 which gave the council a unique identity, an almost self-contained character during the period to 1578. When Lord Fitzwalter came to Ireland for the first time, he brought with him two remarkable men, Sir Henry Sydney and Sir William Fitzwilliam, who were to become successive lords deputy. As the earl of Sussex, Fitzwalter governed during the first decade of the period from 1556 to 1565. Sydney followed him in office, and was succeeded by Fitzwilliam. So the chief governorship was dominated for twenty-two years by Sussex and his former followers. Indeed, Dr Brady has claimed that the successive governments of Sydney after 1565 fostered a continuation of Sussex's initial programme, arguing that it was perhaps more systematically applied.[81] Three members who were placed on the council between 1553 and 1556 also served to the end of the period. Sir John Plunket, Francis Agarde and Gerald, earl of Kildare, each representing distinct interests, were among the most active councillors.[82] Each man was on the council for over twenty-five years. They gave the government unusual stability of leadership and the opportunity for a balancing of views during an era of reform. All the holdovers from the St Leger era had been named to the council within the previous three years.[83] In addition, the ambition and enterprise of Sussex's remodelled council were leavened initially by the wisdom of experienced administrators like Sir Thomas Cusake, Sir John Alen and James Bathe. Bathe, who had become chief baron of the exchequer in 1535, finally died in office in 1570 and Cusake was laid to his final rest one year later.[84]

Others on the council knit the body into a loosely woven fabric of seasoned leaders who accumulated years of training in attendance on the executive board. Adam Loftus, the ambitious cleric from Oxford, was brought to Ireland as Sussex's chaplain in 1560 and by 1562 he was a councillor and the new archbishop of Armagh. He became lord

---

80. For a recent assessment of Ormonde see C. Brady, 'Thomas Butler, earl of Ormonde, and reform in Tudor Ireland' in C. Brady, ed., *Worsted in the game: losers in Irish history* (Dublin, 1989), pp. 49–59.

81. Brady's argument contains an implicit repudiation of the theme of discontinuity so prominent in Canny's claim that a 'new chapter' was unfolding in Irish history that ushered in the conquest of Ireland. Brady, 'Government of Ireland', pp. 164, 172, 176–78; Canny, *Elizabethan conquest*, p. 65. See also *Cal. Carew MSS, 1515–74*, p. 252.

82. *Cal. Carew MSS, 1515–74*, p. 252; PRO, SP 62/1/3; 62/2/51.

83. Stanley became marshal of Ireland in 1553; Curwen was named archbishop of Dublin in 1555. Hughes, *Patentee officers*, pp. 36, 122.

84. ibid., pp. 2, 8, 37.

keeper and later lord chancellor and died in Ireland in 1605.[85] Another newcomer in 1560 was the freshly appointed secretary of state, John Chaloner, who served as a councillor for twenty-one years until his death in 1581. Robert Dillon (the elder) became chief justice of the common pleas in 1559 and was a diligent councillor for at least fifteen years, until blindness and ill-health forced him into inactivity. Still, he died in office in 1580 and remained formally a councillor until then. His son, Lucas Dillon, became chief baron of the exchequer in 1570 and served on the council until his death in 1593. Another stalwart was Hugh Brady, bishop of Meath, who was a faithful and industrious councillor from 1564 until his death twenty years later.[86] While some Irish office-holders may have obtained their posts as sinecures, it is also true that all these men frequently met at council sessions and those councillors who were longest in service to the crown proved to be the most dedicated and responsible members. It was this nucleus of veteran leadership that gave the body its distinctive qualities of stability and practical wisdom during twenty-two years of expansion and change. Doubtless, there was ample evidence of internal dissension on the council, based on the pull of faction and of divergent interests. But it is important to view the Irish privy council as more than an arena of conflict. Despite assertions that the council was rent by political purges when a new viceroy took office in Dublin Castle, there is evidence for continuity in both membership and policy formation throughout this period. Although Canny has argued that Sydney brought on the council six new men as a clique, only two could be identified as his clients and the vast majority were holdovers from Sussex's government.[87]

The privy council in Ireland closely resembled its English parent in several respects, yet its membership was quite distinctive. In the first place, there were no counterparts in Ireland of the important English officials of the royal household. In the Edwardian and Elizabethan privy councils the lord chamberlain; the treasurer, comptroller, and vice chamberlain of the household; keeper of the wardrobe; and master of the horse all possessed membership on the council, and some were notably intimate with the queen herself (Knollys, Leicester among them). Also, the admiralty of Ireland was a titular

---

85. *DNB*, s.v. 'Loftus, Adam'.

86. Hughes, *Patentee officers*, pp. 25, 41; *DNB, supplement*, s.v. 'Brady, Hugh'; Walshe, 'Enforcing the Elizabethan settlement', 352 ff.

87. St Leger and Bagenall were part of a Sydney faction, but Loftus, Brady, Lucas Dillon and the earl of Desmond were not really dominated by the viceroy. Canny, *Elizabethan conquest*, pp. 52–54. See Brady, 'Government of Ireland', pp. 174–75 and Ellis, *Tudor Ireland*, p. 252 for an argument that stresses continuity on the council.

honour which conferred only a subordinate and minimal role on the incumbent, while the judges of the admiralty court lacked influence in this period.[88] Consequently, there was perhaps a greater concentration of judicial and ministerial officials on the Irish council than in England. On the other hand, there were also a number of Irish peers without office and senior clergy who were regularly members of the council in Ireland. Nine of the nineteen councillors in 1566 were members of the traditional aristocracy and only one held high office at the time (Ormonde's role as lord treasurer was honorific). By comparison, the privy council in England in 1568 included only five peers out of fifteen members. The English peers and gentlemen named to the privy council were typically men of substantial experience and education who also held high offices of state, although two of them were regarded as token appointments (Norfolk and Arundel) who served by virtue of their senior rank in the aristocracy.[89] Therefore, the council in Ireland was both more traditional (containing more non-office-holding aristocrats) and more bureaucratically modern (comprising more purely civil officials) than the English council. Yet it was also far more than a provincial body which was largely limited to a judicial role such as the council in the marches of Wales.[90] By its membership and its mandate, the council in Ireland was thus a distinctive governing body, operating with substantial continuity of personnel in the period 1556–78.

There is another reason to see these years as a unit, for the old guard passed on rather quickly after 1578. To be sure, a number of those like Adam Loftus, the earl of Ormonde and Sir Lucas Dillon lived on for decades. But the leadership changed dramatically from 1579 to 1582. In the first place, Sydney left the chief governorship under a cloud of disapproval. This was the first time it had passed out of the hands of the triumvirate of lords deputy that had held office since 1556, and it took the queen nearly three years to find a suitable replacement. A measure of the change that took place was the total ineffectiveness of the inexperienced Lord Grey from 1580 to 1582. The honest, energetic lord chancellor, Sir William Gerrard, gave way to the less honest, more ambitious Archbishop Loftus in 1581. Of the eight leading civil officials in 1578, only two remained by 1582 after the deaths of Chief Justices Plunket and Dillon, Secretary Chaloner and Vice Treasurer Fyton. Agarde had died in 1577. With the demise of these men, the core of the old council passed out of existence. Their

---

88. Pulman, *Elizabethan privy council*, p. 38; Hoak, *King's council in reign of Edward VI*, pp. 80–81; J.C. Appleby and M. O'Dowd, 'The Irish admiralty: its organisation and development, *c.* 1570–1640', *IHS*, xxiv (1985), 300–05.

89. Pulman, *Elizabethan privy council*, pp. 20–30.

90. Williams, *Council in Wales*, pp. 142–45.

replacements gave the new council a very different appearance, more contentious and more aggressive than before. New men like Vice Treasurer Sir Henry Wallop and Secretary Geoffrey Fenton were soon at odds with the lord deputy. The 1580s witnessed many contentions and disputes among themselves. After 1578 the council quickly developed a new temperament, a different countenance from the one which had prevailed since 1556, as it met new crises and faced greater internal divisiveness than ever before.

COUNCIL MEETINGS

The council in Ireland was a vigorous, active institution meeting about once a week to conduct the affairs of government. However, the evidence of its activity is so spotty that we must go beyond the surviving records of council meetings to recapture the essence of the governing board at the heart of the Dublin administration. The extant council books and letters have left a very uneven log of conciliar activity, ranging from the full record of intense and prolonged business to lacunae which omit any documentation for over a year. From the registers alone we might conclude that the council was a loosely constructed organ, meeting only occasionally or in times of crisis, which often went months without convening at all. On the other hand, the tenor of other surviving documents indicates that the council was composed instead of a tightly-knit nucleus of officials which met regularly. In 1572, for example, Lord Deputy Fitzwilliam was advised to retain the councillors who remained from Sydney's tenure as chief governor, and '. . . to use diligence in frequent assemblies of Counsell with hir Depute wherby he may be the better assisted with advise to governe . . .'.[91] It is clear that some meetings were not recorded in the council book, and that for others the records were merely filed instead of entered, and have since been lost. The cumulative record from all archival sources indicates that the council sat continuously and that it convened with some regularity. It is clear, in addition, that a preponderance of meetings occurred during the summer, when there were 116 sessions (winter meetings numbered only 72 during this period). And the formidable judicial obligations of the council explains the greater frequency of meetings during the legal terms.

A comparative analysis of the business of the English privy council may clarify the level of activity we could expect for the Irish board. According to Dr Hoak, the privy councillors signed two documents for every action they took, that is, (1) a letter or decree authorizing official action, and (2) a copy of the original entered into the council

91. PRO, SP 63/36/22.

book and retained by the clerks there. This established the 'corporate responsibility' of the council for acts of government which then took on enhanced validity and authority. Council meetings were organized around a set agenda for business and certain items were prepared in advance for approval, while some matters were referred to special committees for further deliberation. Perfunctory acts of the council were certainly frequent, but there is also evidence of heated exchanges between councillors and animated debate. Clerical staff handled routine business, but the necessity of obtaining signatures to letters and decrees often caused delay or redrafting of the correspondence.[92] What is more, Dr Pulman has found that the Elizabethan privy council often met privately to discuss matters of state, expelling the clerks and thus leaving no permanent record of very important deliberations. He points out that independent evidence must be used to verify the business of the privy council. For example, the Walsingham Day Book, an account of conciliar business for 1583, is a very full record of council agendas for that year.[93]

The work of particular sessions for which the evidence is plentiful provides a more credible picture of conciliar activity than does the simple record of total meetings based on the extant documents. In many cases, the entries for one day may be more numerous than for an entire month.[94] If we were to accept the aggregate figure from the surviving evidence as representative of council business, we would find that the council convened an average of one session every twenty-one days from 1556 to 1578. Yet for some years in this period the records show only seven meetings or less, while for other years there is evidence for as many as twenty-nine gatherings of the council. Using the years of consistently greatest recorded activity, from 1561 to 1564, the average interval between meetings was about fifteen days.[95] The gaps in the records are in some cases enormous and cannot be

92. Hoak, *King's council in reign of Edward VI*, pp. 124–32, 145–49, 156–60.

93. Pulman, *Elizabethan privy council*, pp. 52, 60, 154.

94. On 1 August 1560, for example, the council rendered four orders which took seven folios of the council book to describe. RIA, MS 24 F 17, ff. 134–43.

95. The total figures are 403 meetings in 24 years. In the period from 1570 to 1573 the average was also about one meeting every 15 days. The totals were:

1556	24	1564	29	1572	28
1557	23	1565	1	1573	21
1558	21	1566	28	1574	13
1559	12	1567	10	1575	7
1560	15	1568	7	1576	2
1561	28	1569	15	1577	4
1562	20	1570	22	1578	17
1563	17	1571	21	1579	18

seen as typical or as part of a conscious reform. The case of 1565 is clearly aberrant, because, while only one meeting was recorded, the years 1564 and 1566 had twenty-nine and twenty-eight sessions, respectively. The patterns of distribution in the archival remains fall unpredictably in any part of a given year, so that from 12 June 1568 to 1 June 1569 only one meeting was recorded in the surviving documents.[96] It may be possible to explain the absence of council records from 1565 as partly due to the irascible temperament of Lord Justice Arnold who early declared that he could not work with the council.[97] On the other hand, we know from independent sources that the council was very busy during the dispute which raged over the cess between 1575 and 1578. Despite the general opposition to Sydney's proposal for change in the annual levies, the conciliar record shows long intervals between council meetings during this period, a fact which may be attributed to the divisiveness of the issue among the council's membership. Over the span of two decades, however, the vagaries of record-keeping are perhaps a more convincing explanation of the lacunae in the annals of the council. By comparison, Pulman's analysis of the English privy council shows 412 meetings from 1570 to 1575 with three large gaps in the records. The beleaguered council recorded no meetings at all during the political crises of 1568 to 1570 and again of 1575 to 1578. Pulman argues that verbal instructions concealed much important work and that the council registers are at best an incomplete sketch of the actual conduct of conciliar business.[98]

The activity of the council is more completely revealed in those occasional spurts of energy when business required almost daily meetings. At times, the board convened once every three or four days during a month or longer. From 27 May to 27 June 1556, for example, the council met ten times, an average of about one meeting every three days. In 1561 it met daily to consider the implementation of the Elizabethan recoinage, making eight proclamations in four days.[99] Also, it is clear that the council often met more than once a day, for there are many examples of four or more entries on the same date. In June 1573, for example, the council convened at nine in the morning and again at four in the afternoon, and the tenor of the document

96. The largest gaps are in 1565, 1568–69 and 1576. There are also gaps of about six months in 1560 and 1563.

97. PRO, SP 63/14/77. Also, there might be missing documents among Arnold's papers if he, like other chief governors, left office with state correspondence in his possession. However, only the Carte Papers amassed by Fitzwilliam add much to the evidence for the council in this period.

98. Pulman, *Elizabethan privy council*, pp. 164, 168.

99. RIA, MS 24 F 17, ff. 1–7v, 164–70. From 3 to 26 May 1563, six meetings were held at intervals of about four days. And in 1570 from 8 January to 4 March ten meetings were held with about five days between each one. ibid., ff. 327–34v.

suggests that this was common practice.[100] If this activity were typical it would mean an average of about two or three meetings a week. But even if this were not usual, it is difficult to reconcile with a view of the governing board as a casual or occasional forum, little-used by the deputy. If we may extrapolate from the period after 1578 when council meetings were held every six days, we may get closer to the actual figure for our period, perhaps once a week or a little more.[101] The English privy council in this period met about 1.5 times each week, and again the records are quite incomplete.[102] Dr Hoak found the Edwardian council met on average 4.3 times weekly after February 1550. This figure is perhaps closer to the actual level of business, both in England and in Ireland.[103]

To expand the paucity of surviving records for much of the council's enterprise, we must turn to other evidence. Most of the extant documents are found in two primary sources, the council book for 1556–71 and the State Papers Ireland in the Public Record Office, London. In general, we cannot rely on the council book to demonstrate the extent of conciliar activity, for the council did far more and met more often than the document reveals. It is basic for certain kinds of business but it is not definitive. The council book is the primary source for the work of that forum during the early years from 1556 to 1560, but during 1562–63 the state papers are of far more importance. For 1565 there is very little information in either source, and from 1567 to 1571 both records are needed to fill out the picture of conciliar activity. The uneven and sketchy records for certain years after 1571 may be partly explained by the loss of the third council book, for which the extant table is an inadequate and often misleading substitute. Council records from other sources, particularly the Carte and Carew manuscripts, amplify the range of council business, but the signed documents of the council itself are found infrequently outside these collections. Family records, which might contain the council's letters to sheriffs, commissioners, mayors, peers and other local officials, have seldom come to light.

The omission to record certain acts of the council was common, and this characteristic may have been more typical in conditions of

---

100. PRO, SP 63/41/54–54v. The council was already sitting when the obstreperous vice treasurer, Edward Fyton, was brought before it at 9 a.m. and the lord deputy urged the vice treasurer to be seated when he appeared again at 4 p.m. citing the burden of business that awaited the council's attention.

101. See 'Council book', ed. Quinn, for the number of meetings after 1581, recognizing that the record is fragmentary and needs to be supported with the other council book, now lost.

102. Pulman, *Elizabethan privy council*, p. 167.

103. Hoak, *King's council in reign of Edward VI*, p. 106.

stress or when no formal action was taken due to a stalemate at a council meeting. Also, minor administrative decisions were not usually
recorded. Quinn has said,

It is clear that although the more formal administrative decisions of the
privy council found their way into the council books before 1581, a substantial part of the business of the privy concil is not recorded—minor
administrative arrangements, provisions for arbitration, judicial decisions,
some of them between party and party, and the record of recognizances
taken before the council.[104]

In the council book for 1581–86, recognizances and other minor acts
of the council form a great part of the business recorded there. In
1581 alone there were at least seventy-five recorded meetings, an average of one every five days. The average number of meetings annually
during those five years was about fifty-one. Although these were war
years and the council was then in effect a council of war, the business
recorded in the 1581–86 council book was generally not of a military
nature. This reflects the change in the records of the council which
allowed for the entry of simple administrative acts which were generally
not recorded before 1581. Quinn pointed out that, 'As there is no reference to a journal or minute book before 1581, it may be assumed
that documents concerned with these matters were filed rather than
entered . . .'.[105] Hence, the omission to record certain kinds of evidence, together with oscillations in the scale of Irish politics and the
accidents of documentary preservation, may go a long way to explain
the incomplete sources for council meetings.

Sessions of the council were ordinarily convened in Dublin where
the lord deputy could take the advice of his colleagues at the seat of
government. Most of the meetings were held in the council chamber
of Dublin castle, the medieval fortress sited on the rise overlooking
the Liffey. It was here that a new residence was erected for the lord
deputy at the beginning of Elizabeth's reign, so that thereafter the
council most frequently resorted to the state apartments of the chief
governor. Sydney built a 'stately drawing room' over the medieval

104. 'Council book', ed. Quinn, 97. Ellis agrees that the registers from the early Tudor
period omitted sessions and recorded only the most important affairs of state.
Ellis, *Reform and revival*, p. 39.

105. 'Council book', ed. Quinn, 97–98. Quinn has further suggested that many pages
are missing for 1584 and 1586, making the actual activity of the council even
greater. The calendar may represent only two-thirds of the original. ibid., 93,
99–100. It is, of course, still possible to see the council as less active before 1581
than it was thereafter. However, it is difficult to explain why it would suddenly
issue commissions, recognizances and grants in that year if it had not done so
before as a matter of course. The council was, after all, a creature of habit and
its authority as well as its functions were based on long-standing custom.

chapel in 1567 and this was where the council sat most often.[106] The council was responsible for its usual place of meeting, and care was taken to see that it was enlarged, cleaned and maintained. In November 1570 the council provided for a permanent housekeeper to preserve the council room and the lord deputy's lodgings in a fit state to receive suitors. The act of the council declared,

Whereas there hath been erected of late within her Majesty's Castle of Dublin certain lodgings and other fair and necessary rooms both for a . . . fit seat for the placing and receiving of any governor hereafter, and for the better and more commodious resort and assembly of the council, and for the greater ease of all suitors, both rich and poor, which heretofore were accustomed to travel to and from places both farther distant and less commodious . . . .

We have therefore thought fit that, as well for the keeping of the said house and rooms newly erected as for the . . . keeping of the clock within the said castle which requireth daily attendance to be tempered and kept in frame, to appoint some honest, careful and diligent person . . . [namely] George Arglass of Dublin, gent . . . .[107]

Dublin castle was also the site of the four courts throughout this period, as well as the storehouse of munitions and powder, the state prison and the usual residence of the lord deputy. It was unquestionably the centre of government. The council also met frequently at other places in Dublin that possessed predominantly ecclesiastical functions. The suppressed priory of Kilmainham served both as an official residence of the chief governor and a frequent meeting-place of the council. It was located just west of the city walls near the Liffey.[108] The council also met often at the palace of St Sepulchre which was the official residence of the archbishop of Dublin. It was found south of the city and outside the walls. For certain ceremonial occasions which usually required a grand council, meetings were held in Christ Church cathedral and, less frequently, in St Patrick's.

When the board met outside Dublin, the full privy council did not usually travel with the lord deputy, though some of its formal meetings were held in the Pale at Navan, Drogheda, Dundalk and Trim. In

106. J.L.J. Hughes, 'Dublin castle in the seventeenth century', *Dublin Hist Rec*, ii (1940), 81–97.
107. 'Colectanea', ed. McNeill, 364–65. This concordat was also registered in *Cal. pat. rolls Ire., Hen VIII—Eliz*, p. 541, and renewed in April 1578. See *P.R.I. rep. D.K. 13*, pp. 71, 116.
108. F.E. Ball, *History of the county of Dublin*, 6 vols. (Dublin, 1902–20), iv, 156–58. In 1578 Sydney had a stone bridge built across the river at Kilmainham with his insignia on it, and he had other bridges erected, notably at Athlone. See P. O'Keeffe and T. Simington, *Irish stone bridges: history and heritage* (Dublin, 1991), pp. 30, 176, 190, 268–69.

general, we may distinguish three types of meetings outside Dublin. First, council sessions were held at the important towns in the Pale and in the areas which were effectively governed from Dublin. Part of the council travelled with the lord deputy to confer with local magnates and officials, to hear causes and to settle disputes. The typical places for such meetings were Leighlin, Waterford, Kilkenny and Wexford, but the council also appeared occasionally at Newry, Limerick, Athlone, Philipstown (the modern Daingean) and even Carrickfergus. We may take these conciliar perambulations as evidence of the intent to expand effective rule by the terms of the common law since most sessions involved some judicial hearings. Secondly, meetings were held less frequently at towns en route to a campaign or when the lord deputy went on progress. These were generally impromptu, unscheduled assemblies conducted at places where the chief governor and his entourage chose to rest. Towns such as Armagh, New Ross, Athboy, Arklow and Youghal received such visits during the period. Thirdly, the council convened in the field wherever the lord deputy was sited when he chose to take the advice of those councillors who accompanied him. These meetings were held at military camps or castles with no traceable link to towns of any significance. In fact, these were more like councils of war which were used to represent the views of the lord deputy and council to the queen and her advisers.

In most cases when the lord deputy left Dublin the council was split and each part continued to function as an executive board with contingent, and reciprocal, responsibilities. This had the effect of limiting the authority of each part of the council, especially the one remaining in Dublin. The lord chancellor was the presiding officer in the absence of the lord deputy. The active Sir William Gerrard made full use of this opportunity, but his predecessors, Curwen and Weston, ventured nothing before the return of the viceroy. In matters of state the chief governor sometimes travelled with the entire council, as when he visited Waterford on 1 August 1560 to resolve outstanding differences between the earls of Ormonde and Desmond. This exceptional proceeding required an increment of provincial magnates whose presence added dignity to the occasion.[109] The flexibility of the split council was revealed by an expedient adopted in 1561 by the lord deputy and council in the field. This body was able to control the work of the council remaining in Dublin, sending a direction on 14 July 'from the lord Lieutenant and council at camp to the body of the council remaining at Dublin'. The attenuated council was ordered to proclaim the recoinage and to print forty proclamations for distribution

109. RIA, MS 24 F 17, ff. 134–41v. The order drawn up to reconcile the differences between Desmond and Ormonde had eighteen signatories, including seven lay peers and two archbishops.

in every county, an act which ordinarily would have required the attention of the full council.[110] On the other hand, the division of responsibilities occasionally resulted in a predictable failure of communication. In one such instance, Sussex and the council in the field called for more supplies and kerne to be sent to the north. After several entreaties and two months of waiting, the viceroy gave up and called instead for a general hosting.[111]

Splitting the council was particularly necessary in times of rebellion when the lord deputy was needed in the field indefinitely. In July 1573 Fitzwilliam left Dublin to reside at Maryborough (the modern Portlaoise) where the O'Connors were engaged in desultory warfare. He took with him only two civil officials (the chief baron and the master of the rolls), leaving open the question of the relative authority vested in the truncated board resident in Dublin.[112] By contrast, in January 1580, the new lord justice, Sir William Pelham, joined with the rest of the council to address the constitutional basis for conciliar decrees which were issued when the body was divided. Noting that the lord justice was soon to depart with other councillors to Munster, the order declared that this bifurcated council could act with full authority from two different venues. The decree explained that

Wher as . . . others of her Majesties Counsell likewise are to remaine here in the English pale, so as the Counsell, for theis respects beinge devided into the severall partes of this realme asonder, are to pass severall actions and consultations, for advancement of her highnes service . . . . It is agreed by us therfore, that what so ever action or consultation be concluded on or executed by us the lord Justice and the Counsell repaired in the entended Jornie . . . . And likewise such actions as shalbe determined by those of us of the Counsell in the Englishe pale remaininge shalbe in every respecte as well of the one side as of the other, as available, perfaict and permanent as yf all we the bodie of the whole Counsell were or had bine altogether present . . . .[113]

This resolution glossed over the potential for conflicting or contradictory decrees issued by the two distinct branches of the executive board, although they were in frequent communication with each other. While in theory the council remaining at Dublin retained full authority to act in the absence of the viceroy, the council in the field took up the most vital matters and left administrative routine in the fraternal partner in the Pale. On 8 July 1580, for example, the lord justice and council heard several cases of Munster peers at a meeting in Limerick.

110. PRO, SP 63/4/6–7, 35.
111. PRO, SP 63/8/63–64, 69, 95, 99–101.
112. Bodl, Carte MS 57, f. 609.
113. LPL, Carew MS 597, f. 176v.

From 1 to 3 July 1580, 'The Counsell satt dailie to determine controversies and had many complaints brought in againste the lord
Barrie'.[114] Clearly, even in a time of open rebellion such as this, the
council offered to extend its judicial role.

When the council met regularly in Dublin, a nucleus of civil officials
regularly formed its core. The lord deputy and the lord chancellor
were nearly always present, but meetings could be held without one
of them. If neither of the two highest officials could attend, no meeting
of the council was possible. There were about seven men present at
every council meeting during the period, and the council rarely met
with less than five. In comparison, Elizabeth's privy council in England
averaged between 7.4 and 8.9 members in attendance, depending on
where the meeting was convened.[115] Besides the lord deputy and lord
chancellor, six civil officials were also commonly found at council
meetings: the vice treasurer, the two chief justices, the master of the
rolls, the chief baron of the exchequer and the secretary of state. The
privy council at Westminster, by contrast, was dominated by eight
officials, including four from the royal household. Elizabeth's advisers
were chosen for their personal qualities and their respective offices
mattered less than their connection with the queen.[116] In Ireland,
conciliar participation, if not political effectiveness, was more closely
tied to office-holding. The attendance of these officials depended on
the personal qualities of the incumbent. For example, the involvement
of the chief justices declined as age overtook them, while more active
men like Nicholas White, on their entry to office, became vigorous
advocates of reform, and members of key political factions. The archbishop of Dublin was nearly always at council meetings, and the bishop
of Meath and the dean of Christ Church were diligent councillors.
Among the peers, the earl of Kildare was the most assiduous member.

We may assume that a quorum of four was needed to do the business of the council. There were only thirty-four council meetings
with under five present, and twenty-four of these assemblies convened
with four councillors in attendance.[117] These meetings commonly

114. ibid., ff. 63v–64. See Ellis, *Reform and revival*, pp. 42–43 for earlier examples
     (from 1520) of the council acting independently of the viceroy under the
     leadership of the lord chancellor.

115. Pulman, *Elizabethan privy council*, p. 164. For the Edwardian council the average
     was 10.8 members at each meeting. Hoak, *King's council in reign of Edward VI*,
     pp. 106–07.

116. Pulman, *Elizabethan privy council*, p. 168. Sir Francis Knollys and Sir James
     Croft were treasurer and comptroller of the household, respectively, and the
     earl of Leicester was master of the queen's horse, yet they occupied roles at the
     pinnacle of power in the Elizabethan state.

117. RIA, MS 24 F 17, ff. 7, 9v–10, 28v–29, et seq. On one occasion the lord deputy
     and Francis Agarde signed an order regarding some galloglasses in Wexford,

registered indentures, submissions or licences. By comparison, the Edwardian privy council in England had established a rule in 1553 whereby a quorum of four officials could do business, though six men were needed to make a 'perfect conclusion'.[118] It has been argued that Dudley's employment in practice of a closed membership, an 'inner ring' of key advisers loyal to him, was replicated in Ireland. The existence of a 'council attendant' upon the viceroy in Ireland was, however, more a function of the need for flexibility than part of a conscious desire to exclude refractory councillors from participation in key decisions.[119] Brady's assertion that Sussex sought to govern exclusively through a 'tightly organized executive group' reflects the 'programmatic' approach of his administration, not its practice. In fact, Sussex and others had to contend with the council in Ireland if they wished to lead the Irish polity successfully. And the dominance of faction in Irish political life did not, in the last analysis, make it wholly derivative or utterly dependent on the viceroy or the English privy council.[120]

THE GRAND COUNCIL

For the most important actions of the Irish government, a grand council was summoned to attend on the lord deputy. This was a body composed of the privy council together with the lords spiritual and temporal who were summoned to give their assent to some weighty matter. At the height of the dispute over the cess, the role of the grand council became something of a *cause célèbre*. The gentlemen of the Pale argued that only a parliament or grand council could give its assent to the cess, while the government contended that '. . . her Majesties Prerogative was suche as myghte Impone a charge, for defence of the Contrie withoute Parliamente or graunde Counsell'.[121] The issue of legislative consent to taxation in kind was to be of great political and constitutional significance, and the right of the grand council to act as a modified legislature was implicit in the arguments

but that is the only record of a meeting of only two men. ibid., ff. 336v–37. In one case the lord deputy signed alone, but this was a letter to the local men of Waterford which had been copied into the council book and hence did not represent all those present at the meeting itself, which in fact was quite large. ibid., f. 144.

118. Hoak, *King's council in reign of Edward VI*, pp. 107, 124–25.
119. See Hoak, *King's council in reign of Edward VI*, pp. 108–10; Elton, ed., *Tudor constitution*, p. 90, for the development in England of a distinct body of loyal followers of the lord president within the privy council itself.
120. Brady, 'Government of Ireland', pp. 56–57, 124–25.
121. PRO, SP 63/58/47v.

fo. 312

H Sydney

Dublin the first day of June An° 1569

Eliz.

It is condiscended concluded and agreed by us the Lorde Deputie the Lordes spirituall and temporall of this Realme and the rest of the Comons ma[?] k comber of the same whose names be [here] unto subscribed assembled at Dublin the daie and yeare above written the rest beinge absent upon necessarie causes or imployed elsewheare; that for sondrie benefitts respected for the furtherance of her ma[jesties] service and more securitie of this realme the termes and redinnge of relieffe unto their subvecion and obedience, that ther shalbe a generall cesse[inge?] proclamed by month after the anncient custome for fower weekes after the ende of their ploweland to a cartes the same to assemble att Castle Knagge the 24th day of Julie next to come or at such day proroged after that day as by writtgen proclamacon set forthe by us the said L Deputie and Compaire shalbe assigned, the same generall cessinge to be [there] divided furni[shed] [appointed] and sortid as by precincts in that behalfe directed to the precincts of the severall Comities and Cessors of the severall Baronies within [...] there shalbe prescribed:

Robert Ibetson rarr.   C. Armacan   G Kildare

Roland Buttingham   H Midens   R. Dim[...]ton

J Trevitt[...]

B [...]   H [...]

H Dracott

Thomas [...]   James [...]

[...]   Henry Edwards   John Chaloner   [...]

Dublin the first day of June
Ano 1569

H Sydney

11 Eliz. It is condiscended concluded and agreed by us the Lorde
Deputie the Lordes spirituall and temporall of this
Realme and the rest of the Queenes maties Counsell
of the same whose names be here unto subscribed
assembled at Dublin the daie and yeare above written
the rest beinge absent upon necessarie causes or
emploied otherwaies: that for sonderie ernest respectes
for the furtherance of her maties service and more
securitie of this realme, the terror and reducinge of
rebells unto dew subiection and obedience, that ther
shalbe a generall hostinge pclaimed by writt after
the auncient custome for six weekes after the rate of
thre plowland to a carte: the same to assemble att
Ratheskeaghe the xvth day of Julie next to come or
at suche day p[ro]roged after that day as by further
pclamacon set forthe by us the said L. deputie and
Counsaill shalbe assigned, the same generall hosting
to be levied divided furnished appointed and sorted as
by scedules in that behalf directed to the Sheriffes
of the severall Counties and Cessors of the severall
Baronies wthin everie shire shalbe prescribed:

Robert Weston canc.	T. Armachan [Armagh]	G Kyldare
Roland Baltinglas	H. Miden [Meath]	R. Trimletiston
T Lowthe	————	W Fitzwilliams
		H Draycott
	Thomas Cusake	James Bathe
? J Alen	Frances Agarde	John Chaloner
		N. White

1 Extract from the Irish privy council book, 1556–71. The lord deputy and
council in a large session with 17 councillors present declared a general hosting
on 1 June 1569 for the '. . . reducinge of rebells unto dew subiection and
obedience. . .'. The hosting was to commence on 25 July according to a
schedule which would be forwarded to the sheriffs of every county and cessors of
several baronies. The councillors present were: Lord Deputy Sydney, Lord
Chancellor Weston, Archbishop Lancaster, the earl of Kildare, Roland Viscount
Baltinglas, Bishop Brady, Lord Trimleston, Lord Louth, Edward Fyton, William
Fitzwilliam, Henry Draycott, Thomas Cusake, James Bathe, Francis Agarde,
John Chaloner, Nicholas White and (barely visible in left bottom margin) Peter
Carew.

on both sides. However, the debate focused principally on the liability of the Pale to this unique exaction and the precise role of the grand council was made no clearer.[122] Lucas Dillon, master of the rolls, departed from his customary indulgence of the English-born officials to remind his colleagues that '. . . this manner of layinge of the Cesse as it was, was by a graunde Counsell, and vouched the opinyon of his father, yet livinge, learned in the lawes and of great yeares'.[123] A marginal note in the letter to England explained the character of the institution thus: 'The governor, nobilitie and counsell dothe make the graunde counsell.'[124] Of course, the concept of a grand council was not new to Ireland, for parliament had grown out of it during the fourteenth century. There were numerous references to grand council meetings in extracts from the earlier council books. For example, a grand council held before St Leger in 1551 comprised eight peers in addition to the privy council, invited gentry and select captains of the military establishment.[125]

Professor Quinn has suggested that recognizing a threefold division of the council in Ireland more accurately reflects the distinction of the grand council from the privy council in the Tudor era. Apart from the working, or privy, council he has defined two other distinct manifestations thus: 'The afforced council consisted of the privy council together with a small number of ecclesiastical and lay magnates. The great council, in theory, consisted of the lords, lay and ecclesiastical, and such other persons as might be formally summoned from time to time . . . .'[126] Quinn has distinguished the manifestations of the council by membership, by function and by the use of different formulae stated at the beginnning of every order issued by them. The afforced council, Quinn believes, was smaller and concerned itself only with the ordering of a general cess. The great council was (rather inexactly) larger and concerned itself only with the ordering of a general hosting. The formulae differed slightly in wording: '. . .

122. Ellis has asserted that the grand council could be equated to a 'great council' and that they were in practice 'scarcely distinguishable from a parliament'. S.G. Ellis, 'Taxation and defence in late medieval Ireland: the survival of scutage', *RSAI Jn*, cvii (1977), 19.

123. PRO, SP 63/58/47v.

124. ibid.

125. In 1551 Caher McArte Cavanagh was compelled to renounce the name of MacMurrough '. . . at ye Grand Council and general assembly holden at Dublin ye 4th of November anno 4 Edw. VI before Sir Anthony St Leger knight of the order, Lord Deputy of ye Realme afforesaid and ye Council . . .'. PROI, MS 2,532, f. 5. The document appears to be misdated as 6 July 1549. The definitive study of the medieval parliament is H.G. Richardson and G.O. Sayles, *The Irish parliament in the middle ages*, 2nd ed. (Philadelphia, 1952).

126. 'Council book', ed. Quinn, 97.

by the lord deputy, the lords and nobility of the realm, with the rest
of the queen's majesty's council . . .' (afforced council) [and] 'That
upon summons given to the lords spiritual and temporal and other
her majesty's council, it is concluded by us, the lord justice [or lord
deputy], the lords spiritual and temporal and the rest of her majesty's
council of this realm . . .' (great council).[127] The lord deputy and
privy council were common to both formulae, so we may ask how
the 'lords and nobility of the realm' differs from the 'lords spiritual
and temporal'. The meaning appears to be quite the same, although
the lords spiritual were expressly named in the second model. In any
case, this difference does not suggest a substantive distinction in the
character or the formation of the council.

Professor Quinn's hypothesis should be amended in a number of
ways. In the first place, while the grand council was clearly a working,
functional aspect of the council in Ireland, to which many documents
refer, there is no mention in the records of a 'great' or an 'afforced'
council. If these distinctions were essential then it is difficult to explain
why they were not at some point articulated or at least contrasted with
the predominant functions of the privy council and grand council.
Secondly, it is possible that Quinn's paradigm was too narrowly
conceived, based as it was solely on the evidence from the council book
for 1556 to 1571. Here, certain superficial distinctions, primarily
those based on the formulae of the council, appear to have greater
substance than they in fact possess. The formulae were used to
distinguish the kind of business conducted by a grand council rather
than to characterize the precisely delimited work of two putatively
separate bodies. Furthermore, not all grand councils used formulae
to indicate the nature of the affairs being considered. In January 1557
consecutive meetings of the grand council were held, one to levy a
tax on the Pale and the other to make seven decrees for the better
maintenance of public order. In each case the meeting noted the
presence of the 'nobilitie of this realme nowe assembled', in addition
to the lord deputy and privy council. The meetings were attended by
eighteen men, thirteen of them peers or bishops. However, in neither
case did they employ the specific formula which Quinn thought necessary to demonstrate the sitting of a 'great' or 'afforced' council.[128]
On 2 May 1558 another meeting was held to provide against a foreign
invasion. This forum was composed of only eight men, seven of them
peers, but because the formula was repeated, however inexactly, Quinn
averred that this was indeed an 'afforced' council.[129] The inflexible

127. ibid.
128. RIA, MS 24 F 17, ff. 32–34v.
129. ibid., f. 69–69v.

application of this dubious standard is arguably too rigid, for it leaves uncertain the identity of a very large and unquestionably important meeting (that of 1557), while confirming the significance of a relatively small one. It is clear that two distinct formulae were regularly used to authorize the general cess and general hosting, but this does not, in itself, prove the existence of two separate councils, nor does it confute the use of a grand council without an established formula.

Quinn also suggested that there was a formal distinction in the membership of the 'afforced' and 'great' councils. However, we can see that 'a small number of ecclesiastical and lay magnates' differs little from 'the lords, lay and ecclesiastical, and such other persons as might be formally summoned from time to time'.[130] In any event, the 'afforced' councils identified by Quinn were not uniformly smaller than his 'great' councils. In 1563, for example, a general hosting was called in January, using Quinn's formula for a 'great' council. At this meeting sat sixteen councillors, of whom only five were peers. On the other hand, a general cess was called in August of the same year, using the formula for an 'afforced' council. Twenty councillors sat at this meeting, including nine peers.[131] A further comparison reveals that in May 1563 a general hosting was called at which only nine signers were present, and only four of these were peers.[132]

The malleable and practical nature of Tudor institutions compels us to seek a simpler and more flexible distinction for the work of the governing board. To distinguish the existence of a grand council which incorporated the privy council when it met, we should use a number of criteria, of which the formula is only one. The number and the profile of members, the gravity of the business conducted and the manner in which it was presented should all be taken into account. We could argue that even the smallest grand council must have at least four peers sitting. However, the vagaries of the evidence compel us to balance these criteria, especially when we see that sixteen men convened in 1569 to declare war and only three of them were peers. In this case there was also the indisputable use of a formula appropriate to a grand council.[133] In September 1563 a letter to the queen describing the state of the realm was signed by fourteen men including eight peers.[134] The letter was almost certainly the product

130. 'Council book', ed. Quinn, 97.
131. RIA, MS 24 F 17, ff. 98, 102–02v. Examples of this kind of contradiction are found many times in the council book. In 1568 and 1569 the members attending the council to authorize the cess and the hosting were about the same, between nine and eleven councillors. ibid., ff. 308v–09, 323v–24.
132. RIA, MS 24 F 17, f. 183.
133. RIA, MS 24 F 17, f. 313.
134. PRO, SP 63/9/34.

of a grand council meeting to discuss the affairs of the realm, even though no formula was used to declare its existence. In general, the number and the social standing of councillors attending a given meeting often reveal the nature of the council more readily than a rigid formula. No forced distinction in membership, formula or function can sustain a further articulation of the privy council beyond the unquestionable existence of the grand council.

The constitutional role of the grand council in the period was more than merely perfunctory, although it was plainly subordinate to the lord deputy and council. Ellis has confirmed the continuous existence of two distinct working councils before and after the creation of the privy council in 1520. His explanation for the use of a larger council, '. . . to associate leading magnates and gentry with government . . .', offers a clear practical argument for the political usefulness of a grand council, although he follows Quinn's distinction for the post-1534 period.[135] Here again, the constitutional position of the Irish executive diverged from English practice, since the use of a larger king's council resembling the grand council in Ireland, was ended after 1536.[136] By the Elizabethan period the privy council acted alone as the governing board in England, whereas the viceroy in Ireland could augment the working council, as we have seen. It should be noted that on certain occasions the grand council was essentially a substitute for the parliament in Ireland. Dr Treadwell has recently suggested that the grand, or great, council was used in the crisis of the 1570s to obtain consent to taxation and that it later became '. . . more representative of the cess-paying section of the community and less amenable to official management, perhaps, than parliament itself'.[137] The elected legislature was called into session during only six of the years in the period 1556 to 1578.[138]

The grand council was thus a regularly functioning body which met about three times a year for a variety of purposes. It was not tied to a set of rigid procedures and ceremonies but was flexible enough to deal with a multitude of difficult situations. It incorporated, on average, seven peers in its normal membership of fifteen councillors. After 1565 there was a trend away from very large meetings of the grand council. The largest grand council assembled twenty-five men, but the last meeting with over sixteen in attendance was in 1564. Prior to 1565 the average attendance at grand councils had been seventeen

135. Ellis, *Tudor Ireland*, p. 156; *Reform and revival*, pp. 36–39, 46.

136. Elton, ed., *Tudor constitution*, pp. 90–91.

137. V. Treadwell, 'Sir John Perrot and the Irish parliament of 1585–6', *Proc RIA*, xxxv (1985), sect. c, 260–66.

138. Ellis, *Tudor Ireland*, p. 335. The years: 1557, 1558, 1560, 1569, 1570, 1571.

men. Thereafter the average declined to about thirteen, and the smallest grand council had about eight men.[139] Apart from the declaration of the general hosting and the cess, the grand council was habitually summoned to elect a new chief governor; to declare war; to participate in the swearing in of a new viceroy; and to observe the delivery of new seals at the accession of a sovereign. The largest assembly of the period, twenty-five councillors, met on 13 December 1558 after hearing of the death of Queen Mary. This was clearly a grand council, summoned to hear the news of the sovereign's death and to elect a lord justice.[140] In February 1560 the council established a clear procedure for the selection of a new lord deputy. The lord chancellor was to send writs of summons to the sheriffs of the counties of the Pale and Kilkenny, Tipperary, Wexford, Waterford, Cork, Kerry and Limerick.[141] Even a moderate response by the local peers who were thus invited to attend would have ensured a very large meeting of the grand council in this case.

The grand council was frequently used to obtain the symbolic assent of the country to an act of the government, and this was nowhere more evident than in the levy of the general cess. In 1580 the lord deputy '. . . assembled a graund Counsell of the Nobility and gentlemen, and their consent had for the levieing of 600 men . . . to be victuallid, furnished and paid . . .'.[142] The queen's instruction suggested that their consent was expected as loyal subjects. She said, 'And therefore our pleasure is that the lord deputie Cause to be Assembled the Nobilitie and Graund Counsell according to former usadg in lik Cases and to move them to renewe and accepte the said composicion . . .'.[143] A summons to 'sundry councillors' on 15 December 1579 beckoned them to an important meeting which must have been, in essence, a grand council. The letter declared, '. . . thiese are to require yow for consultation to be held in matters weightelie emportinge her highnes present service, that yow will repaire hether to the Counsell, on fridaie the firste of January without farder delaie . . .'.[144] The

139. This is partly due to changes in the evidence in the 1570s for which the council book is missing. Also, the drop in the number of peers was partly due to the non-noble lords deputy and lords chancellor after 1567.

140. *Liber mun. pub. Hib.*, i, pt. 2, p. 3.

141. PRO, SP 63/2/12–13. On 11 October 1579 Sir William Pelham received the sword of state in Christ Church as the new lord justice before a grand council of fifteen men including nine peers and a large assembly of knights and gentlemen as well. LPL, Carew MS 597, f. 20–20v.

142. PRO, SP 63/78/7v.

143. BL, Add. MS 4,786, f. 24. See also Treadwell, 'Irish parliament of 1585–6', 264–66.

144. LPL, Carew MS 597, f. 160.

likely explanation for this meeting in the early stages of the Desmond rebellion is that the government was seeking political consensus for its anticipated response.

The versatility of the grand council extended to less formal occasions, although it is often difficult to distinguish when a grand council was meeting from when a privy council of unusual size was convened on an important matter. The distinction was blurred when the council considered the delicate matter of the Elizabethan recoinage in January 1561. Several sessions were attended by about fourteen men, but no more than five peers came to any single meeting.[145] A clearer case of a grand council occurred in January 1557 where the characteristic formula was used and eighteen men were sitting. Several orders for the taxation of the Pale were given on two successive days, with the enforcement of decrees and other technicalities occupying much of the time of the grand council.[146] The grand council here acted on a number of minor administrative matters, indicating its flexibility as an institution of government. It is apparent that no simple recitation of formulae could encompass the multiple roles of the grand council, for it was not so easily circumscribed. In several instances grand councils were convened to hear the chronic grievances of the rival peers in Munster, Ormonde and Desmond.[147] Increasingly, the grand council was employed to consider the state of the realm and to report on it periodically to the queen and privy council.[148] In sum, we may view the institution as complementary to the privy council, capable of working on a variety of problems. The grand council had a considerable responsibility to act in certain prescribed affairs of state, but it also had an inherent capacity to meet the problems of the government on an ad hoc basis, much as the privy council did.

INFRASTRUCTURE OF THE COUNCIL

The infrastructure of the council in Ireland experienced a metamorphosis early in Elizabeth's reign which reflected the more ambitious programme of the new administration. With the addition of a new privy seal for Ireland and the creation of a new secretary of state, the silhouette of the administration was theoretically streamlined and governance was to be made more efficient. While these initiatives did

145. RIA, MS 24 F 17, ff. 165–70.
146. ibid., f. 32–32v. In May 1558 a small council met to plan for a system of watches and couriers in the event of foreign invasion. Despite its size, this was manifestly an occasion for a grand council meeting. Although only eight men sat at the council board, seven of them were peers. ibid., f 69–69v.
147. ibid., ff. 140–41.
148. PRO, SP 63/4/64.

not, in practice, revolutionize conciliar record-keeping, they were a part of the comprehensive plan to anglicize the Irish polity. And in this respect, as in many others, the eventual development of an Irish administration modelled completely on that of England rested on Elizabethan foundations.

Council business in the early Tudor period was not formally registered in a council book, although Ellis has argued that systematic record-keeping must have pre-dated the earliest known register of 1542–43. The clerk of the council had also served as the viceroy's personal secretary under the earl of Kildare in 1513, but the office of clerk became independent after 1520.[149] By the early Elizabethan period, the clerks of the council were responsible for the writing and keeping of all conciliar records, particularly the council book itself. They usually attended council meetings and their reports generally summarized the action that was taken by the councillors, who in turn signed the council book. More often, they copied into the council book submissions witnessed by the council, proclamations ordered by it and other conciliar business. They also entered important documents which were functionally related to the council, such as instructions from the queen or petitions from the provincial towns. Their work was not confined to the council book, for they also wrote letters for the council and penned orders and proclamations. Their counterparts in the English privy council numbered twenty-eight men, including secretaries of Latin and French and four clerks of the signet seal. This large and rather specialized staff met in small rooms adjoining the council chambers to write letters, register decrees and file petitions. They produced fair copies from the rough drafts earlier drawn by senior clerks and they used prototypes of letters and other communications to which signatures could be affixed days later. One copy was sealed and sent to the recipient and another was entered in the council book.[150] We may assume that an abbreviated form of this procedure was adopted by clerical staff of the council in Ireland.

Although they were rarely made councillors, most of the clerks were important enough in their own right to be named to commissions of the council. They often took conciliar messages to London with the admonition to declare the state of the realm to the queen and privy council, and some of them became trusted informants of Cecil and Walsingham. These well-informed intermediaries, acting as conduits

149. Ellis, *Reform and revival*, pp. 37–39. References to a council book have been traced back to 1486 and John Alen, when he was clerk of the council, copied proceedings before the council into the archbishop's register in the 1520s from a similar document which he kept for the governing board.

150. Pulman, *Elizabethan privy council*, pp. 155–64; Hoak, *King's council in reign of Edward VI*, pp. 145, 156–60.

.for the communication of state business, occupied an enhanced role in the government of Ireland based on their position at the axis of executive power. By analogy, we may consider the position of Edmund Tremayne, clerk of the English privy council. He was well-educated, a client of Sir James Croft and later of Cecil, a member of parliament for Plymouth, and frequently active on commissions from the privy council.[151] He was sent into Ireland by Cecil in 1569 and he served as Sydney's secretary until 1571. On the basis of his experience he drafted an astute critique of Elizabethan policy and devised the comprehensive agreement for cess which Sydney adopted on his return to Ireland in 1575. Tremayne's work illustrates how a senior clerk with intimate knowledge of the workings of government could exercise influence out of all proportion to the intrinsic authority of his office.[152]

Personal qualities of the individual clerks determined how important they were in the government. Some, like Robert Cowley, rose to become higher officials, though few reached the stature of master of the rolls as he did. Cowley, who took office under Surrey, was later a minion of Cromwell and held the position of clerk until 1529. He corresponded with the secretary of state on matters of great importance and later fell out with the lord deputy over his proposals for reform.[153] His successor was John Alen who also became master of the rolls and a reforming lord chancellor.[154] John Goldsmyth was named to the position of clerk of the council in 1542 and in 1551 was sent to London to declare more fully the proceedings of the council regarding the north of Ireland.[155] On the other hand, the work of Ralph Coccrell, who succeeded Goldsmyth, has vanished almost completely from the records.

From 1569 until 1582 the clerkship of the council was in the hands of uniformly able men who tended to amplify the duties of the position because of their personal energy. Edmund Molyneux became clerk of the council sometime in 1569. On 15 November he entered his name in the council book to record the fact that he had personally delivered to three agents certain writs for the cities of Cork, Waterford, Limerick and Galway.[156] This evidence gives us an insight into the

151. Pulman, *Elizabethan privy council*, pp. 159–60.
152. Brady, 'Government of Ireland', pp. 213–18. See Huntington Lib, Ellesmere MS 1,701 for his critique done 'at the request of Sir Wa. Mildmay' in 1573.
153. *Cal. S.P. Ire., 1509–73*, pp. 40, 63, 78.
154. Ellis, *Reform and revival*, p. 37.
155. ibid., pp. 65, 86, 111. Goldsmyth entered his name in the council book during 1557 and 1558 as the copier of several memoranda of council actions, signing 'Concordat cum originali. Ex per me Johannem Goldsmyth'. RIA, MS 24 F 17, ff. 59, 71v, 72v.
156. The writs were for the attainder of those convicted of treason in the recent rebellion of James Fitzmaurice. RIA, MS 24 F 17, f. 314v. The earliest mention of Molyneux as clerk was on 26 October 1569. *Cal. S.P. Ire., 1509–73*, p. 422.

multiple functions of the senior clerks as representatives of conciliar authority, helping the board to expand its constitutional dominion. Molyneux was thus often sent on commissions by the council, an example of the high confidence that was had in his abilities. For example, in 1570 Molyneux was engaged in two commissions during the winter. On 9 January he went to examine the Cavanaghs after they had submitted to the council, and on 21 February he journeyed with two others to advise Lord Mountgarret to stay in Dublin pending the action of the council in his case.[157] Because the clerks were used to bear messages and to take depositions, they employed deputies to do the regular work of writing and recording in Dublin.[158] Rowland Cowyck succeeded Molyneux, who had gone to England with Sydney, in 1574 and Lodowyck Bryskett took office in 1577 after unsuccessfully seeking the office of secretary of state. The latter was a valuable reporter of conditions in Ireland to Cecil and Walsingham during the Munster rebellion and he was perhaps the most active of the long line of clerks of the council. In 1581, for example, he was sent to Turlogh Luineach O'Neill to arrange a conference with the lord deputy.[159]

The work of the clerks of the council was supplemented and in some ways overshadowed by the personal secretary of the chief governor. This unique official was useful to the council as well as the lord deputy, and certain holders of the office also became significant advisers of the principal secretary in London. Sir Henry Sydney revived the practice of employing a personal secretary in the affairs of state, perhaps as a result of the difficulties experienced by his predecessor, Sussex. Sydney's choice was excellent, for his secretary, Edward Waterhouse, swiftly became a mainstay of the Dublin administration and remained so for over twenty years. Waterhouse had unusual ability. He was educated at Oxford and spent several years at court under the patronage of Sydney. In 1566 he accompanied Sydney to

---

157. RIA, MS 24 F 17, ff. 327–27v, 333.
158. The deputies used by the clerk of the council were sometimes called 'registers' to denote their peculiar function with respect to the council book. Robert Kendall and Thomas Chaloner were both registers of the council in 1576. *Cal. pat. rolls Ire., Hen VIII—Eliz*, p. 558.
159. *Cal. S.P. Ire., 1509–73*, p. 443. *Cal. S.P. Ire., 1574–85*, pp. 102, 135, 169, 290, 297, 299, 301, 304, 330, 315. It should be noted that the dates of succession to the office have been muddled by Hughes in *Patentee officers*, pp. 16–17, 34. Cowyck succeeded Molyneux at least as early as 10 September 1574 (not simply 'long before 1580') when he signed an order of the council to rebuild Athenry. PRO, SP 63/47/137v. And Cowyck was in turn succeeded by Bryskett in 1577 (not in 1582) when he received the patent of office as clerk. *Cal. S.P. Ire., 1574–85*, p. 102. When his suit to replace the secretary failed, Bryskett was relieved of office by Nathaniel Dillon in 1582. ibid., pp. 301, 330; Hughes, *Patentee officers*, p. 41.

Ireland and was there made clerk of the newly designated court of castle chamber. He was used by Sydney and the council on missions to London and he frequently sent dispatches reporting the activity of the government.[160] He left Ireland with Sydney in 1570 but returned to serve there as secretary under Essex in 1573. He became secretary to Sydney again in the latter's second administration between 1575 and 1578, and in 1579 was made a councillor in his own right, serving under Lords Deputy Grey and Perrot.[161] Waterhouse was exceptional in that he attained such high office. But others had similarly long careers. Philip Williams, secretary to Fitzwilliam in 1572, returned to Ireland to serve under Lords Deputy Perrot and Lord Burgh until 1597. In 1573 Williams copied a document of the council in his correspondence to England, an act which demonstrated the interdependence of the clerks of the council and the secretaries of the chief governor.[162]

A portent of significant change in the hierarchy of Irish government took place in 1560. When the office of secretary of state was created for Ireland, modelled on the office of principal secretary in England, the incumbent was given a place on the privy council. However, the actual exercise of executive authority was never realized by this lowly councillor for a number of reasons. In the first place, the viceroy was unquestionably vested with formidable powers as chief governor and by his instructions he had control of significant patronage. Secondly, the administrative echelons were fixed by long tradition, and matters of priority and place were guarded jealously. Thirdly, the clerical work of the new principal secretary was already divided among senior staff, notably the viceroy's personal secretary and the clerk of the council. The highly intricate matrix of Irish politics and government, therefore, made the foundation of a new and independent writing office impossibly difficult, so the novelty of the secretaryship quickly evaporated. The lord deputy remained unchallenged and the hierarchy of Irish government stayed intact.

160. *Cal. S.P. Ire., 1509–73*, pp. 406–08. See Ellis, *Reform and revival*, p. 37 for the earlier history of the office of personal secretary.
161. *DNB*, s.v. 'Waterhouse, Edward'. Waterhouse certainly became far more than a clerk. Besides his two initial offices, he at times served as vice treasurer and chancellor of the exchequer and as a commissioner for the recovery of concealed lands. He was the confidant of Burghley and in 1584 mediated the dispute between Lord Deputy Perrot and Lord Chancellor Loftus. He died in England in 1591.
162. PRO, SP 63/40/129; J.L.J. Hughes, 'The chief secretaries of Ireland, 1566–1921', *IHS*, viii (1952), 59–60. Hughes confuses the personal secretaries to the viceroys with the higher office of secretary of state for Ireland. While admitting there is a good deal of confusion both in their titles and responsibilities, it seems needlessly obfuscatory to call the personal aides of the chief governors either 'chief secretaries' or 'principal secretaries' as he does. One of the most notable of these personal secretaries was Edmund Spenser, who served under Lord Deputy Grey from 1580 to 1582.

Although the first holder of the office never developed its full potential, it was initially recognizable as the analogue of the position held by Cromwell, Cecil and Walsingham. The instructions to Lord Lieutenant Sussex in May 1560 included this order:

> Item becaus at this present ther ar none appointed to bie Clerk of our Counsaill there, and consydering how more meet it wer that in that our realm there wer for our honour one to be our Secretary there, we have condescended that one shalbe alwayes hereafter placed as our Secretary there for thaffaires of our Realm. And [he]shall hold and kepe the same place there as our Secretary doth here. . .[163]

It appears that Ralph Coccrell was named clerk of council in 1559, but there is no record of his actions in office and the appointment of a secretary may be partly explained as a result of his absence. However, the description of the office is more clearly aligned with the powerful principal secretary of state and the queen may have sought more than a scribe in creating the position. Once again, we are left with the impression that the aim of English government was to establish in Ireland a model of Tudor rule on a smaller scale. The secondary impression, which the first one always invites, is that the queen's advisers were groping toward a policy which was insufficiently grounded upon a working knowledge of Irish affairs. If the queen wished to increase her 'honour', why would she nominate a simple clerk to this new office? The contradictions must have been obvious to members of the Irish administration.

Initially, at least, the function of the secretary of state for Ireland was largely clerical. The instructions required that '. . . for his fee [he] shall have the like as hath ben alwayes assigned to the clerk of our counsaill there with such fees and other commodities as the same clerk use to enioye . . .'.[164] A postscript was added in Cecil's hand which noted: 'Where in ye 7 [article] which we have ordeyned a secretary and to have ye fee of ye Clerkshipp of the counsell; we be content to augment ye same with xx Marks by yere . . .'.[165] Evidently, then, the standing of the secretary was intended to be greater than the clerk of the council since he was also to be awarded custody of the new seal, the signet of Ireland, which formed the basis for the office. The viceroy was instructed to offer the secretary

. . . the custody of our Signet, and ther with [he] shall seall all such writting as shalbe warranted by your hand and subscription in like manner

163. PRO, SP 63/2/38. See also *Cal. Carew MSS, 1515–74*, p. 293.
164. PRO, SP 63/2/38.
165. ibid., f. 42.

as our Secretary doth here by warraunt of our hand. And for sum further augmentation of his enterteynement our pleasur is that ye shall there by advise of our Counsaill or the more part thereof, make a rate of certeyn fees to be receyved by him uppon warrauntes, leasses, grauntes, lettres, missives and such like, as our four clerkes of the signet have here, using nevertheless such moderatenes therein as to your discretion shall seem mete.[166]

The secretary thus stood in relation to the deputy much as the principal secretary did to the queen, although Dr Ellis has argued that the new seal was akin to a 'royal privy seal' and its use was strictly conditioned to limit the independent power of the viceroy.[167] His role in the council was limited to reading the instructions for the board four times each year and he did not set the agenda for council meetings as did his English counterpart. Many years later, in 1586, the queen found it necessary to guarantee full control of the signet to the secretary as a protection against the encroachments of the lord chancellor, '. . . with all fees and Duetyes appertaininge as our principall Secretary in England doeth'.[168] The constitutional subordination of the secretary of state to the chief governor was unique to Ireland and Dr Brady's claim that the Irish viceroy's position was an exceptionally powerful one is certainly valid. However, his related thesis—that constitutional reform in Ireland was a superficial gossamer which only paid 'lip service' to the commitments made in the act of 1541 for the kingly title—too easily dismisses the incremental innovations of the period.[169] Gradually, but productively, the government of Ireland was changing. The superstructure was indeed the political plum of ambitious rivals for power. But the substructure would provide the basis for a more complete anglicization of Irish institutions over time.

Sussex had apparently recommended John Chaloner, a gentleman and former auditor of Calais then living in Ireland, as the new secretary. He was ordered to administer the oath of office to Chaloner and to deliver the new signet to him after receiving assurances of his '. . . diligence, secretie and discretion . . .'.[170] Chaloner was a curious choice from the beginning, for he never sought the office and spent a long time trying to be relieved of it. In May 1563 he wrote to Cecil that he was unworthy of his new position, yet feared to refuse it because the queen would think him unwilling to serve. He complained that he

166. ibid., f. 38. See Appendix 1 for a description of the signet.
167. S.G. Ellis, 'Privy seals of chief governors in Ireland, 1392–1560', *IHR Bull*, ii (1978), 193.
168. BL, Add. MS 4,786, ff. 24–25.
169. Brady, 'Government of Ireland', pp. 27–31, 40–44.
170. PRO, SP 63/2/38.

was wholly unfit for the office, saying, 'As for the trade of a Secretarie, and namelye for ye state of a Realme, I was never treyned therein, and so in ye practise thereof ye more to seeke'.[171] Furthermore, he alleged that the costs of running the office were more than the fees brought in, so that he could only employ one clerk as an assistant. He humbly asked to be relieved of the post and sought some more fit employment in the queen's service, but in the event he died in office some eighteen years later.[172]

In light of Chaloner's attitude about his new position, it is not difficult to explain his performance in it. In his first fourteen years of service he wrote only seven letters to England and these were mainly requests for land or money.[173] He never became the informant of Cecil or Walsingham as both Waterhouse and Molyneux had been, and on the one occasion when he offered his advice on matters of state, the lord chancellor subsequently warned Burghley against taking it.[174] Chaloner never attempted to amplify his position into one of greater authority and hence was of little significance in the council. He was more of a scribe than a secretary, although he was occasionally used on commissions from the council.[175] As a token of his inferior standing he was made to sign the council book last after all others had signed it. He did not come to council meetings as regularly as the three leading officials but his attendance was quite frequent from 1560 to 1564, and again during 1569–70. However, from 1571 until his death he came infrequently to the council, a fact which was attested by Fitzwilliam. In April 1572 the lord deputy complained to Cecil that Chaloner, who earnestly sought to be replaced, '. . . wrote me not two lettres this xiiij monethes nor foure tymes with me in Counsell . . .'.[176]

171. PRO, SP 63/8/109. Chaloner told Cecil that, 'Indeed the Facultie I have been treyned in was but for an Auditor and therein I coulde serve and did serve for Caleis while it was Englishe . . .'.

172. ibid., ff. 109–10. Chaloner complained that he was 'infirm of the stomack' and that his condition was aggravated by the daily writing occasioned by his position.

173. In 1564 Chaloner wrote twice to Cecil to appeal for a new position and to press his suits for land. *Cal. S.P. Ire., 1509–73*, pp. 225, 242.

174. In 1578 Chaloner advised Cecil not to accept the offer of the gentlemen of the Pale in lieu of cess. Gerrard subsequently warned Cecil not to take the secretary's advice. *Cal. S.P. Ire., 1574–85*, pp. 141, 162.

175. Chaloner was named a commissioner of martial law for Co. Dublin in 1564 and in 1569 he was sent to Ormonde to ensure the safe keeping of the earl's two indicted brothers. RIA, MS 24 F 17, ff. 192–92v, 323. See Lennon, *Lords of Dublin*, p. 237 on his role in Dublin's municipal affairs.

176. PRO, SP 63/36/10v. Fitzwilliam noted that Chaloner would rather be a clerk of the council and wanted to give up his fee and be relieved. In a wide-ranging article on the secretary of state, H. Wood argued that the office was an important one from the beginning. He credited Chaloner and his successors with corresponding regularly with the crown and with supervising the clerks of the council.

This default was apparently balanced by the work of other clerks like Waterhouse, Molyneux and Bryskett, but the office of secretary was effectively dormant for long periods after 1570 until the replacement of Chaloner in 1581. Despite the implication in the original instructions that the new office-holder would wield powers similar to those of the principal secretary in England, it is evident that the government initially intended the secretary of state in Ireland to be no more than a senior clerk, responsible for the efficient functioning of the signet seal. Chaloner's successor, Geoffrey Fenton, was considerably more vigorous and ambitious and he figured prominently in the politics of the 1580s, but the later development of the office is beyond the scope of this study.

Clerical staff attached to the council were primarily engaged in record-keeping and the focus of their attention was the council book. This register was kept by the clerks in Dublin Castle and new entries were usually made whenever the council met. However, it appears that many meetings may have gone unrecorded, so the council book was probably viewed as a record of important documents rather than a chronicle of all conciliar acts. This interpretation is borne out in part by the character of the entries themselves. The council book contained the essential records generated by the council, including orders, proclamations, submissions, memoranda, and commissions. But the inclusion of a large number of other documents suggests that the council book was also used to record significant acts, letters, instructions and petitions originating elsewhere, of which the council should remain cognizant. For example, the petition of the corporation of Galway to have a free school was memorialized in the council book.[177] And the instructions from the queen and privy council to the council in Ireland were systematically incorporated as a matter of record.[178] If we surmise that the council book was intended to serve as a repository of significant documents and not as a journal of all conciliar business, then the gaps in the surviving records may be partly explained by the omission to register the technical and the trivial actions of the council. This was also suggested by the 1579 memorandum of the Pelham administration which concluded that 'Many other things were determined

It is almost certain that he read back into the early period what was true for the subsequent history of the office, for there is nothing in the state papers to show that Chaloner was nearly this active. Wood noted that the secretary had a considerable fee of over £50 and travelling expenses of 10s. per diem. In 1579 Waterhouse apparently acted as Chaloner's deputy in an effort to get things done, but this arrangement received no official sanction. See Wood, 'The offices of secretary of state and keeper of the signet or privy seal', *RIA Proc.*, xxxviii (1928), sect. c, no. 4, 51–68.

177. RIA, MS 24 F 17, ff. 309v–10v.
178. ibid., ff. 186, 254–55v, 261.

duringe my lord beinge in Dubline, wherof tyme would not permitt Coppies to be taken; Some wherof are inserted in the Counsell booke, And some nothing materiall to be observed'.[179]

Only one council book has survived from the sixteenth century. It was begun by Sussex in 1556 and concluded in 1571. The register was copied out mainly in one hand, most entries beginning with the signature of the lord deputy and ending with the signatures of the councillors in attendance. Subsequent rebinding of the document has resulted in a disorder of the foliation, but the council book remains intact.[180] The first council book, often called the 'Red Council Book', was begun about 1543 and ended in 1556. The table of this document is extant. There is also a table for the Sussex council book, called the 'Black Council Book', which covered the period to 1619.[181] Professor Quinn has explained that a differentiation of function in 1581 caused the development of a second council book as an entry book for ordinary affairs of the council. This slim volume was a more truncated version of the original council books, and its creation supports the view that, until 1581, there was no record of the diurnal, common business of the council.[182] This book probably ended in 1589 and Fitzwilliam then began another which was concluded in 1599. A third council book for ordinary affairs was then begun by Essex, but its origins are less clear than the others.[183] The council books, had they all survived intact, would have given us a great deal more detailed information on the council under Elizabeth. But the outlines of the council and its business are nevertheless quite clear, and the supporting documents from the state papers and other collections present us with a comprehensive picture of conciliar practice.

CONCLUSION

The privy council in Ireland was matched with the lord deputy in a symbiotic relationship, one in which it served as an active partner

---

179. LPL, Carew MS 597, f. 21v. As in the English privy council, we can assume that verbal agreements, matters referred to committee, heated discussions, and technical matters went unrecorded. Hoak, *King's council in reign of Edward VI*, pp. 145–60.

180. RIA, MS 24 F 17. This is the core document of this study. It is in the library of the Royal Irish Academy, Dublin, and is in fine condition.

181. The tables to the three basic council books may be found in BL, Add. MS 4,792, ff. 117–24, 127–33, 135 and 136–44. See Ellis, *Reform and revival*, p. 38 for evidence of earlier registers dating from the late fifteenth century.

182. 'Council book', ed. Quinn, 98–100, 102. Ordinary matters like the recognizances, for example, proliferate after 1581 but are not found in earlier council books at all.

183. Brief tabular extracts from the three later council books, or journals, may be found in BL, Add. MS 4,792, ff. 125–26v, 134. Longer extracts from all the missing council books are found in BL, Add. MS 4,763, ff. 229–50; LPL, Carew MS 628, ff. 3–352; TCD, MS 843, ff. 1–189; and PROI, MS 2,532.

with the chief executive. It is clear from the instructions received by the lord deputy and council that the board was used as a check on the independent authority of the chief governor. While it acted constitutionally as a counterweight to the ambitious designs of Elizabethan viceroys, it also worked to balance the equities of competing interests in Irish politics more generally. Furthermore, statements of policy and decrees of the government were harnessed to the corporate responsibility of the lord deputy and council in order to enhance their legitimacy for the queen's Irish subjects. The council was functionally interdependent with the viceroy on matters of law and finance since the leading law officers and exchequer officials served regularly on the board. And while the lord deputy was more independent in his management of military policy, this certainly did not give him 'absolute' power except in extreme emergencies. The chief governor was required to seek the advice of the council on all vital matters of state, but there was no requirement that he must obtain a majority vote, or any particular showing of general support. Yet, while we may view the executive largely in terms of the stature and dominance of a vigorous lord deputy, it is also clear that he must maintain conciliar backing both for the reconciliation of interests and the presentation of policy to the crown.[184]

Missing records of conciliar activity present us with a barrier to a full understanding of the work of the privy council in Ireland. Nevertheless, it is evident from available documents that the council met regularly and often; that it resembled the English privy council in its omnicompetent management of crown affairs; that it was the centre of Irish politics and policy-making, both as a working board and as a formal grand council; that it was the apex of the judiciary, serving both as an appellate court and as the fulcrum of judicial administration; and that it was the driving force of administration, from financial and military policy to relations with the towns and with Gaelic chiefs and lords. The council acted through its agents and messengers (often the clerks of the council itself), through commissions on which the councillors themselves commonly served, and through local officials on whom it depended. In this respect, some have argued that the council's effectiveness was not great, since it lacked the full complement of English-style local administrators.[185] But a comparison with the English privy council itself makes clear the practical limits of government in the Tudor century. Dr Pulman has suggested that Cecil and his colleagues in Westminster were forced to rely on an extensive but fragile network of self-serving local aristocrats, boroughs and counties chafing at royal management, and other local officials whose

184. Brady, 'Government of Ireland', pp. 61–62.
185. Ellis, *Tudor Ireland*, p. 179.

connection with the centre was tenuous in the extreme. What is more, the government was seriously hampered by limited resources and often mystified by the antics of the queen. In sum, he argues, the Elizabethan privy council was a 'paradoxical political animal' which was 'grand, respected and even feared' but which was also dependent on the crown for its institutional authority and used as a scapegoat for policies that went wrong.[186]

The privy council in Ireland suffered from similar problems, but the council was indeed distinctive in a number of important ways. In the first place, it was a characteristic Tudor hybrid, an executive board modelled on the governing privy council at Westminster yet subordinate to the policy-makers there. Since it had been only recently created and it lacked the intimacy with the crown of its English progenitor, the Irish council had to improvise its blended functions by a kind of inventive pragmatism, responding as necessary to circumstances which erupted with a vicious suddenness onto the comparatively tranquil world of Dublin Castle. The council retained its earlier function as a legislative body when acting through the enhanced grand council and it added a new star chamber jurisdiction when it acted as the court of castle chamber. The governing board managed its way to a more fully realized anglicization of the other institutions of government in Ireland, trying to inculcate a rare harmony of Irish custom and English law while conforming to orthodox, traditional methods. Yet the board was also innovative, compelled to find the reconciliation of interests between its suitors and the crown, balancing the views of its Irish and English members, seeking the imagined equipoise of order and stability in a reformed Irish polity. By virtue of its membership, its leadership, its subordination to English institutions and its own executive role, the privy council in Ireland was a unique Tudor institution. And the early Elizabethan council developed a corporate personality which made it still more distinctive.

In this second sense, the council in Ireland from 1556 to 1578 had a collective identity which distinguished it from the earlier governments of St Leger and from those which followed during and after the Desmond rebellion. As we have seen, the chief governors in this period all arrived in Ireland at the same time under the leadership of Lord Fitzwalter. They each pursued policies which had been originated in concept by the first of these viceroys and pursued with determination and tenacity by his successors. The stable core of Irish administrators in this period gave the council a seasoned, veteran appearance by 1578 and the remarkable continuity of personnel and policy helped to shape the transformation of the government below the surface of

186. Pulman, *Elizabethan privy council*, pp. 237–50.

patronage and politics. This is not to say that there was not abundant friction on the council itself, nor is it meant to suggest that policy differences were muted in a general comity of purpose. The intent here is merely to suggest another way to view Irish government in a period of reform and retrenchment. If stability and order in Ireland were the primary desiderata of the queen's advisers, then the place where they were most likely to be found was on her own governing board. The councillors in the period lent their distinctive conservatism to the work of the crown, making its innovations realistic and flexible in practice. This essential forming of an Irish equilibrium has often been misunderstood as the failure of policy, but in effect the council helped to refine English policy toward Ireland by restraining the ambitious and over-extended goals of the government in ways that gave them a chance to succeed.

Metamorphoses occur in every living organism. The council in Ireland exhibited its own form of dynamism as it presided over a period of substantial change from 1556 to 1578 which was perhaps unusual for the Irish body politic. Yet this did not constitute a 'constitutional revolution'. There was a good deal of continuity throughout the period, but for every change in government there were tactical retreats which punctuated the era of reform. A discernible pattern of anglicization emerges from a study of the institutions of government, but we must resist the temptation to label these changes 'progressive' or, even less sensibly, 'radical', since they were merely attempts to bring the government of Ireland more fully into conformity with the apparatus of the Tudor administrative structure. These were certainly not measures which the cautious statesmen in Westminster regarded as trail-blazing. What is more, the policy of anglicization was not pursued with single-minded rigour. Instead, the changes which occurred were put in place over a long period of time and in some cases allowed to lapse before being resurrected. We can observe this in the many delays leading to the establishment of the court of castle chamber and the refusal of the queen to concede the necessity of establishing lords president and councils in Munster and Connacht. On the other hand, the installation of the new secretary of state for Ireland and the introduction of the signet seal were both accompanied at the outset of Elizabeth's reign with comparative speed. The overall effect was to systematize Irish government on the English model, but the approach adopted was piecemeal and hesitant. Changes in the bureaucratic interstices of the Dublin administration were largely concealed by more dramatic events in the realms of politics and religion. Yet the government was finally anglicized at the end of the period, following the logic of the 1541 act for the kingly title and pursuing the goals first articulated by St Leger. The abandonment of his minimalist strategy, however, should not be mistaken for a commitment to wholesale conquest and confiscation.

The use of paradigms to construct a clearer picture of past events is part of the historian's work. But these models of behaviour and mentality must be employed carefully to avoid distortions. In particular, the employment of a sharply-focused research design can lead to a narrowing of the perspective which leaves out the complex, contradictory, ragged and inconvenient narrative of events which must be interpreted organically. In a generally unprogressive atmosphere, convinced of the static hierarchy of an unchanging world, the government of Ireland groped toward changes which would ultimately bear fruit in a microcosm of English institutions. Any framework which would dismiss the practical and tentative nature of these transformations runs the risk of dangerous over-simplification. The 'thesis of discontinuity', for example, sees sudden shifts in policy, accompanied by dramatic changes which then characterize an era as 'liberal', or otherwise.[187] However, an alternative approach might be employed to appreciate the delicate balance which was precariously maintained by untidy compromises and threatened by entrenched interests. There was indeed a discordant tone throughout the period under discussion, but the historiography of the epoch has been unduly concerned with riot and rebellion. Another paradigm, the 'thesis of calculated violence', seeks to brand the government as an imperialist aggressor which systematically planned and promoted the expropriation of land and culture from a largely defenceless people. The rupture with the past is explained in terms of anthropologically-derived models and the language of the interpretation is suffused with provocation and outrage.[188] There is, further, an attitude of inevitability to this argument which sees, for example, that the opportunity for reform was lost by 1570 and that anglicization would have to proceed by force.[189] However, based on a new understanding of the closely limited resources and conceptually harnessed aims of the Elizabethan government, it is surely an exaggeration to label it 'absolutist'. On the other hand, a deeper understanding of the operations of government may lead to a more complex and less hostile exegesis of the period. The 'colonialist' characterization of Elizabethan government, in particular, is too simplistic to be a convincing explanation of the rich diversity which competing plans and campaigns of reform have exhibited.

187. Bradshaw, *Irish constitutional revolution*, pp. 252–53.

188. Canny, *Elizabethan conquest*, chs. 4, 6; *Kingdom and colony*, chs. 1, 2. Bradshaw wishes to re-focus our attention on the 'catastrophic dimension' of early modern Irish history. See Bradshaw, 'Nationalism and historical scholarship in modern Ireland', *IHS*, xxvi (1989), 341.

189. Ellis, *Tudor Ireland*, p. 180.

Finally, we may turn to another prototype, one which demonstrates a sensitivity to the nuances of Irish government and its relations with the crown. Dr Brady's analysis of government in this period has emphasized what we may call the 'thesis of faction', that is, he suggests the preponderant influence of English politics on Irish government as refracted through the work of the lord deputy. He diminishes the political significance of the council in Ireland, choosing to focus instead on the intricate network of patronage and clientage which, alternately, sustained and threatened the legacy of Anglo-Irish interest and culture. The argument, while ingenious, uses still another paradigmatic narrowing of focus so that the chief governor is made solely responsible for Irish policy. Political troubles in both England and Ireland conspired to unseat every viceroy in the Tudor period, creating an unsettled and unimproved administrative milieu in which reform could not take root. In an unusually perceptive essay, Brady concluded that government policy in the localities was highly erratic, moving from neglect to intrusion, and in sum largely ineffective. He argues that the aim of making Ireland a miniature version of English society and institutions was inherently flawed and feebly supported. Brady explains that the viceroys operated in a political vacuum of sorts, their power unrivalled, as they pursued their 'master-styles' of proposed reform in an effort to realize personal ambition at Elizabeth's court. His thesis concludes that,

It became, in other words, all too easy for the officers of the crown to regard the national reform policy which they were under orders to implement as an unrealistic ideal, and to substitute for that unsatisfactory fiction the far more practical aim of making the best of their service in Ireland in whatever way lay open to them. Thus it was that while the reform of Ireland through the gradual extension of English law throughout the whole island remained the officially declared objective of each succeeding Tudor regime, the policy itself was continually undermined by the fact that no one involved in the process was prepared to make a firm and determined commitment to it.[190]

While, on the one hand, Brady offers the confident assertion that a 'national reform policy' was being pursued by semi-autonomous viceroys who had carefully crafted their 'programmes' for Ireland in advance, he concludes that they betrayed the promise of their grand strategies. He finds the Irish administrators, as a group, to be cynical, grasping opportunists who lacked the requisite firmness of purpose to complete needed reforms. Hence the dissonance in Irish government between policy and practice, according to Brady, was a function of

190. Brady, 'Court, castle and country', p. 41.

lapsed idealism. On the other hand, we may see that both Sussex and Sydney returned to Ireland despite their earlier disappointments, and that the government never ceased to formulate plans for change. What is more, the council in Ireland was the principal forum of high politics there and chief governors could not afford to ignore manifestations of resistance or discontent within the executive board. It is important to remember that the fitful and episodic movement toward anglicization of Irish institutions was the only path open to them. There was no turning back, despite the evident obstacles to improvement. And, not surprisingly, the finding that reform proceeded slowly is consistent with what we know about Tudor government generally. In the next chapter, we will examine the political setting of Irish governance and test the argument that influence, patronage and power were the sole determinants of its course of action.

CHAPTER THREE

Personalities and politics: family, faction and favour

INTRODUCTION

THE ANGLICIZATION OF IRISH government did not foretell the wholesale removal of Anglo-Irish officials on the privy council in Ireland.
Instead, the gradual institutionalization of English bureaucratic
government worked in parallel with the slow increase of English-
born officials at the senior levels of the administration. This was not
a political purge, as some have implied, but an extension of the patronage system from England to Ireland.[1] Every English administrator
sought to make private profit from public office and the employment
of clients in the government of Ireland was simply an obvious Tudor
mechanism for rewarding servitors and loyal followers. Dr Brady's
astute analysis of the matrix of Irish politics offers a complex and
subtle appreciation of influence and connection. He views the role of
faction as the key to understanding Irish governance, from the
making of policy to the undermining of successive viceroys. At the
outset, rival groups at the English court allied themselves with key
Irish reformers and adopted their programmes in whole or in part.
Leading Irish councillors offered their advice to English statesmen in
the hope of securing advancement or defeating their rivals, thus mating
English patronage with Irish politics in a symbiotic relationship. These
volatile connections had tremendous potential for conflict at many
levels, and in many cases personality counted for more than principle.
While Brady has identified several key groups such as the Kildare and
Ormonde interests in Ireland, and the Leicester and Sussex factions
in England, he is careful to mention the highly volatile and unstable
character of these combinations. Therefore, in appraising the unrivalled

---

1. Ellis, for example, has argued that the government 'militarized' Irish policy and
   excluded the 'Old English' from positions of influence which went to a new governing élite of English-born administrators. This, he said, forced the Anglo-Irish
   into 'oppositionist politics and [they] eventually ceased to act like Englishmen'.
   See S.G. Ellis, 'Crown, community and government in the English territories,
   1450–1575', *History*, lxxi (1987), 196, 201–02. Brady, however, rejects the concept of a political purge of the Anglo-Irish prior to the 1580s. See Brady,
   'Government of Ireland', pp. 129–30.

power and influence of the viceroys over Irish politics, he has perhaps lost sight of his own cogent argument that they were at the same time vulnerable to criticism from Irish rivals and English opponents. Unlike St Leger, who succeeded for a time in uniting all the disparate Irish factions under his genial leadership, his successors lost their jobs when they forfeited the support of key advisers to the crown at the same time that they expended all their political capital in fruitless military commitments in Ireland.[2]

It is the purpose of this chapter to assess the personal characteristics of the Irish councillors in relation to the themes of patronage, corruption, training, enterprise and dissension within their own ranks. Of course, it is important to acknowledge that there is insufficient evidence for a full treatment of the councillors themselves, and there is really no satisfactory discussion of political life in Ireland below the level of the council. As a consequence, most studies of Elizabethan Ireland offer an inherently unbalanced picture which exaggerates the real impact of English policy-makers on Irish political life.[3] The sources for Irish political patronage and family connections which might correct the resulting distortion are few and largely unexplored. Therefore, we must recognize that at this point we rely very heavily on English sources which emphasize the influence of courtiers and rivalries centred on Westminster. Nevertheless, we may gather from the extant letters and papers of selected councillors that they participated actively in the competition for place, preferment and profit from the crown. In that regard, they were no different from English officials. They depended on their roles in government to provide access to further advancement and favour, including grants, leases, licences, commissions and other evidence of royal largesse. And while this supplication did not necessarily make them blindly obedient to crown policy, the effect of their constant petitioning was to bring them within the embrace of royal influence. It is, therefore, difficult to sustain the view of recent writers that this period also witnessed the emergence of a nascent Irish patriotism among the Anglo-Irish families of the Pale.[4]

The places of origin of members of the council in Ireland were, of course, both English and Irish, but this does not necessarily posit a

2. Brady, 'Government of Ireland', pp. 55–70, 81–84, 97–107, 124–30, 156–59, 182–87.
3. Brady, for example, argues that office-holders were only important as placemen in the patronage networks and that Irish politics was largely derivative, based on factions in England and directed by the overwhelming power of the viceroy. See Brady, 'Government of Ireland', pp. 56–57, 61–62. Canny views Irish politics as only an 'extension of the power struggle at court'. *Elizabethan conquest*, p. 42.
4. See, for example, Bradshaw, *Irish constitutional revolution*, p. 287; Ellis, *Tudor Ireland*, pp. 246–49.

simple dichotomy of political views. The English councillors differed from each other and from the viceroy, just as did the Anglo-Irish members, and the leading peers, Kildare, Desmond and Ormonde, were persistent adversaries. Therefore, we must be careful in trying to appraise the 'corporate personality' of the forum. In view of the collision of interests which, at times, attended the policy of anglicization, we may be justified in seeing the period as one of unremitting distress and alienation. However, there is plenty of evidence to suggest that the councillors themselves and their many allies in the Pale offered cooperation and counsel to each English viceroy throughout the period. One of the most important explanations for this level of agreement is the role of patronage itself. The Anglo-Irish community had relied on royal favour to sustain its vital interests for many years and the tradition of loyal service did not come to a sudden end in this period. Dr Lennon has suggested in his recent study of the patriciate in Dublin that municipal leaders continually petitioned the crown for redress of grievances at the same time that they sought place and preferment.[5] And when the Palesmen confronted both Sussex and Sydney on the constitutional legitimacy of the cess, they did so by seeking the benign intervention of the crown. These were not, then, the acts of a badly alienated proto-nationalist group, isolated from its own government. The discovery of an inchoate patriotism among various Irish populations prior to the 1580s is simply an artifice of modern historiography, largely unsupported by the vast body of the evidence.[6] Studies of dissension on the council in Ireland itself generally reveal hostilities between members of the same interest and background, such as the rivalry between Lord Deputy Fitzwilliam and Vice Treasurer Fyton, both of English birth.

The background to a study of Elizabethan patronage politics in Ireland is highly intricate. When the decision was made after the Kildare rebellion in 1534 to employ only Englishmen as viceroys in Ireland, the stage was set for the development of a new model in Irish politics. Yet even after the rebellion, the lords deputy selected the loyal Anglo-Irish reformer Thomas Cusake to be lord chancellor and he served as the principal adviser to the admired chief governor, Sir Anthony St Leger. Cusake was a client of Thomas Cromwell, but he parted company with the secretary and found favour with the Howard faction and later with the Dudley group under Edward VI and

---

5. C. Lennon, *Lords of Dublin*, p. 64.

6. Ellis, for example, has argued that the 'Old English' developed an 'embryonic concept of nationalism' from the 1550s due to the erosion of their influence and their estrangement from government policies. Yet he acknowledges that the exile Richard Stanihurst was not typical and that, in general, nationalist ideas were not widespread prior to 1600. See *Tudor Ireland*, pp. 246–48.

Elizabeth. His arch-rival was John Alen, also a protégé of Cromwell, who became lord chancellor in his own right for a time and aligned himself with Cecil in Elizabeth's reign. Both of these veterans of Irish politics were named to the council in 1558 in recognition of their experience and in spite of their personal animosities. If it were the intention of the government to secure pliant conformity to the views of each chief governor, the selection of these two ancient enemies would be difficult to explain. Whereas Alen was allied with the Butler interest of the earls of Ormonde, Cusake favoured the cause of the earl of Kildare. Yet it was often the case that rivals such as these could reach agreement on matters of policy. The study of Irish politics may reveal greater complexity than the chronic opposition of leading courtiers and their retainers would suggest.

In the view of Dr Brady, Lord Deputy St Leger provided a unique alternative to the sterility of hostile camps locked in uncivil combat. The veteran administrator found the field of Irish politics crowded with conflicting interests and yet he managed to combine all the factions without actually uniting them. He did this by promising reward and favour to all and sundry, regardless of their particular patron or indeed their own clients. He combined the two domains of English and Irish politics by serving the petitioners of all parties. The outcome of this clever manipulation of competing factions was to create a stable and interdependent network of cliques which all relied on his personal management of their affairs. St Leger hoped to develop an Irish interest with greater influence, if not common purpose, but he relied entirely on benefactions to secure his ends. He dominated Irish politics from 1540 to 1556 and established an enormous personal following, yet he became in the end merely a broker of patronage and not an advocate of principle. Many of his clients secured great personal wealth, but they were also guilty of corruption and fraud, while some earned the unsavoury reputation of profiteers. By 1556 St Leger fell from power amidst an avalanche of criticism. His personal gain from office implicated him in the 'colossal fraud' of his leading supporters and a series of investigations placed four of his principal clients in gaol.[7] The new administration inherited a web of intrigue which St Leger had carefully managed among the competing interests of Gaelic, Anglo-Irish and English politics.

By comparison with other Tudor institutions, the council in Ireland was relatively free of internal friction. Wallace MacCaffrey has described the relationship of Cecil and Leicester at the court of the queen as 'coldly hostile' in the early years of the reign, yet he also caricatured them as 'surrogate husbands' who had become reconciled

7. Brady, 'Government of Ireland', pp. 68–69, 81–107.

to the balancing of their interests at court by 1572. He described the operation of the patronage system as a form of theatre in which the players knew and appreciated the limits of their roles, acknowledging the absolute primacy of the queen, and he concluded that 'the unity of English leaders provided a strong nucleus for the whole political order of England'.[8] More recently, studies of Elizabeth's English privy council have stressed the coherence of their policy positions, noting that real conflict emerged primarily in the private battles for preferment of their respective clients. Simon Adams has suggested that the contest between Leicester and Sussex has been exaggerated, and he has emphasized the family connections which served to unite most of the privy councillors of the 'inner ring'. While the politics of the court were exceedingly complex below the level of her closest advisers, only the queen controlled patronage and she restrained the rivalries of her intimates while making it necessary to combine their counsel if they wished to influence her in matters of state.[9]

The link between office and politics was an intrinsic one in the early modern period, and it should not be surprising that all Elizabethan officials sought to make the most of their respective positions. Service to the crown also meant advancement of the servitor's private ends. By the very nature of this explanation, it is easily seen that a simple dualism between opposed elements in the government does not offer a convincing model of patronage politics. G.E. Aylmer has reminded us that government is about the direction of human affairs by human agents, and the various ways in which officials were beholden to each other constituted a highly complicated pattern of alliances and relationships. In his view, it is important to stress the heterogeneous interests of the servants of the crown, and to recognize that some were practically independent of court factions altogether.[10] In his analysis of provincial government, Penry Williams has discovered a system of interlocking parts which reflected both national and local politics in Elizabethan Wales. Williams identified six distinct regions which were each dominated by a prominent family. Leicester himself was most influential since he had extensive lands in north Wales and he was allied with practically all the other patrons except Sir James Croft. It would be worth analyzing more fully the connections between

8. W.T. MacCaffrey, *The shaping of the Elizabethan regime, 1558–1572* (Princeton, 1968), pp. 18–20, 466–76; *Queen Elizabeth and the making of policy, 1572–1588* (Princeton, 1981), pp. 431–44, 503.

9. S. Adams, 'Eliza enthroned? The court and its politics', in C. Haigh, ed., *The reign of Elizabeth I* (Athens, Ga., 1985), pp. 57–76. See also D. Loades, *The Tudor court* (Totawa, N.J., 1987), pp. 134–35, 144–47, 163–65.

10. G.E. Aylmer, *The king's servants: the civil service of Charles I, 1625–1642* (London, 1961), pp. 337–40, 454–58.

Ireland and Wales in this period since it appears that at least four of the six leading patrons in Wales were intimately connected with mid-Tudor Ireland (Croft, Leicester, Sir John Perrot and Walter, earl of Essex).[11]

Personalities and politics were thus clearly intertwined with office-holding in Elizabethan Ireland, and we must attempt in what follows to analyze the varied networks of family, faction and favour on the council at that time. The Anglo-Irish members were leaders of their respective kinsmen who had risen to the pinnacle of power and influence. It is often forgotten that these clerks and lawyers were men of great consequence in Ireland, although they were clearly subordinated to the policy-makers in Westminster. Englishmen who took up residence in Ireland competed with the Anglo-Irish for patronage, yet they also became neighbours and landlords whose support of anglicization and resistance to new taxes closely mirrored that of their native-born colleagues. A careful assessment of the placing of English officials in Irish government will show that the council provided a balance between English and Irish interests, while the tenure of Anglo-Irish officials below the conciliar level remained largely undisturbed. Finally, case studies of the actions and attitudes of several leading councillors will demonstrate the diversity of type and the level of interaction on the queen's governing board.

ANGLO-IRISH AND NEW ENGLISH: TRADITION AND INFLUENCE

The character of the council in Ireland can best be studied through its members, although too little personal information is available for a biographical treatment of each man.[12] An overview of the aggregate personality of the council must be preceded by analyses of the independent networks of patronage politics. Interpretations of the conciliar temperament in that microcosm of English government must contend with the divisive forces contained within it, but the occasional clash of interests may have concealed the more durable congruence of policy and purpose which was commonly exhibited at the council board. In fact, the family connections of both Anglo-Irish and new English councillors may explain how the council, and the entire administration, were interlaced with men of like backgrounds and attitudes. Yet the official correspondence of all the councillors is not impressive

11. Williams, *Council in Wales*, pp. 230–38.

12. Of the forty-four active councillors, some twenty-seven have merited articles in the *DNB*. Of the rest, some were lesser men in Irish politics while others like Francis Agarde and George Stanley were officials of real influence whose careers deserve investigation. See Appendix 5 for a list of the active councillors with biographical sketches.

in size, and in any case it seldom reveals much about them as individuals. A few, like Sir Nicholas White and Sir Edward Waterhouse, were the informants of Cecil and many of their letters are extant. Others, such as the contentious Sir Edward Fyton, were in frequent correspondence with the queen's advisers, but his self-serving pleas and exculpatory petitions should not be taken as characteristic of the council's work. Hence, the councillors must be studied first as a group to gain a satisfactory impression of their collective behaviour. There is ample evidence from the work of certain leading officials to construct a profile of the personal and professional qualities of men of their rank and office.

The Anglo-Irish were the key personnel in Irish government below the level of the council and the leading members of this governing élite participated as councillors in roughly equal numbers with their English counterparts until late in the Tudor period. By definition, they were men of English ancestry who were born in Ireland and who largely respected English customs, language, laws and values. Their families had become well-established in Irish society and they were connected with each other in a reciprocating symmetry of allegiance and interest. The Anglo-Irish were prominent throughout the Pale and the loyal towns, but there were shadings and gradations of English influence which makes any clear-cut distinction difficult. In the first place, the leading Irish peers were themselves Anglo-Irish, yet most of them had become significantly gaelicized over the centuries and they preserved both English and Irish customs and language in their centres of influence. Ormonde became an Elizabethan courtier and built, in the late Tudor style, a manor house at Carrick-on-Suir, while Desmond remained at the periphery of English control and was culturally distanced from the terms of English governance. Sir Thomas Cusake was often used on embassies because he was bilingual in English and Irish, and many Anglo-Irishmen were similarly bi-cultural, at home in both societies. Bernadette Cunningham has recently stressed the complexity of Irish society and noted in particular the absence of a generalized racial animosity among the inhabitants of Ireland. This fact she attributed to the local and dynastic character of Irish politics, and she sees no sharp division between native and newcomer until the early seventeenth century.[13]

Dr Canny has recently argued that the Englishmen who came to govern or to reside in Ireland after the 1580s should be distinguished from the traditional governing élite by referring to the latter as the 'Old English'. These native inhabitants who were English in manner

---

13. B. Cunningham and R. Gillespie, 'Englishmen in sixteenth century Irish annals', *Ir Econ Soc Hist*, xvii (1990), 18–20.

believed themselves to be inherently superior to the Gaelic Irish. They were the loyal representatives of English civility, yet they also advocated the programmes of persuasion and assimilation by which Irish government would gradually anglicize the Gaelic population. Canny believes that the Old English suffered a loss of influence and became alienated from English government after 1579 when they entered into a kind of permanent opposition to the ascendancy of new English settlers.[14] Dr Ellis has also argued for a more coherent characterization of the 'English' elements in Tudor Ireland, noting that the 'Old English' actually called themselves 'English' during this period. He makes the connection with other Tudor borderlands in Wales and the North to show how each population shared a common link with England south of the Trent.[15] And Aidan Clarke has traced the 'political disinheritance' of the Old English back to the 1580s when the gradual transfer of power began to move from the traditional élite to the new English settlers. Nevertheless, Clarke was sensitive to the gradations of meaning closeted within these rather arbitrary categories. Among the Old English families of the seventeenth century, he discerned a wide variety from gaelicized lineages at the periphery to Protestant loyalists at the core of the administration. Therefore, it may be less useful than some have argued to superimpose on the untidy reality of Irish society too precise definitions of 'English' elements within it.[16]

In the current study, I have used the term 'Anglo-Irish' to describe the inheritors of ancient English descent who were born in Ireland and lived there in the Elizabethan period. While recognizing that this may appear to be somewhat confusing, I can only defend the choice by suggesting that it readily identifies persons who combined both of these backgrounds, as opposed to the newly arrived mono-cultural English. And, in any event, the cachet is employed to describe a group which is defined with an unanimity quite uncommon among scholars of this period. As Clarke has explained, this community later became estranged from the government and ultimately went into rebellion in 1642 over issues of politics and religion, yet they retained their special identity as loyal English subjects who refused either to adopt the new religion or to claim a right of disobedience as late as 1625.[17] This lengthy political transformation must be respected, and recent attempts to discover a sweeping mid-Tudor embrace of Irish nationality

14. N. Canny, 'Identity formation in Ireland: the emergence of the Anglo-Irish', in N. Canny and A. Pagden, ed., *Colonial identity in the Atlantic world, 1500–1800* (Princeton, 1987), pp. 160–64.

15. Ellis, 'Nationalist historiography', 3, 14.

16. A Clarke, *The Old English in Ireland, 1625–42* (Ithaca, N.Y., 1966), pp. 15–19.

17. ibid., p. 9.

cannot be harmonized with the gradually evolving political beliefs of the 'Old English'. Dr Bradshaw's argument, for example, that the juncture of interest and principle which was shared between Anglo-Irish and English reformers was so badly ruptured after 1556 that the Anglo-Irish sought refuge in a new concept of 'patria' is an unfortunate conclusion to an otherwise sensitive analysis.[18]

Did the Anglo-Irish move from cooperation to confrontation during the mid-sixteenth century? There is general agreement that they gave the creative impetus to the constitutional changes of the 1530s, leading to the act for the kingly title in 1541. In Brady's view, the Anglo-Irish joined with St Leger's government to wield power and influence on behalf of the crown, and men like Cusake and John Travers made their personal fortunes in this period of general rapprochement.[19] In addition, later Anglo-Irish reformers called for persuasive and conciliatory approaches in the implementation of reformation policies, restraining the advocates of militancy such as Archbishop Loftus.[20] On the other hand, some writers have claimed that the mid-Tudor period witnessed a dramatic change in the relations of Anglo-Irish and English. It has been alleged that native-born officials opposed the new policies of conquest and colonization and that, in turn, the new English adopted a hostile attitude to the Anglo-Irish, referring to them as 'degenerate English', holding them in suspicion, and joining them with the Gaelic Irish in a common denunciation.[21] According to this view, the Anglo-Irish were removed from their roles as informed participants in a policy of moderation and forced into political oblivion. They emerged from their eclipse as a transformed opposition fundamentally estranged from the new 'colonialist' government.[22] This argument for discontinuity can only succeed, however, if we accept the 'evil' characterization of English viceroys from 1556 as 'conquistadores' pursuing a reckless policy of military conquest.

A more balanced view of the role of the Anglo-Irish must take into account both their forceful resistance to change and their general acceptance of reform measures after 1556. In the first place, we should

18. Bradshaw, *Irish constitutional revolution*, pp. 287 ff.

19. Brady, 'Government of Ireland', pp. 81–85; Bradshaw, *Irish constitutional revolution*, pp. 193–94, 243.

20. B. Bradshaw, 'Sword, word and strategy in the reformation in Ireland', *Hist Jn*, xxi (1978), 480–85.

21. N. Canny, *Kingdom and colony: Ireland in the Atlantic world, 1560–1800* (Baltimore, 1988), pp. 2–4, 32–38.

22. K. Bottigheimer, 'Kingdom and colony: Ireland in the westward enterprise, 1536–1660' in N. Canny, K.R. Andrews and P. Hair, ed., *The westward enterprise: English activities in Ireland, the Atlantic and America, 1480–1650* (Liverpool, 1978), pp. 49–51.

recognize the great diversity of opinion which existed within the Pale élite, especially on matters of religion, for the Anglo-Irish did not speak with one voice.[23] Secondly, the conciliatory role of men such as Cusake at the higher levels of government was paralleled among junior officials who practised a kind of self-interested pragmatism in their service to the crown. Thirdly, the Anglo-Irish were the heirs of a venerable indigenous legacy of tradition and influence, in contrast to the newcomers from England. Dr Lennon has shown that several generations of the Dublin Stanihurst family served the crown dutifully throughout the Tudor period. But he has also written that James Stanihurst, the lawyer-merchant who served as recorder of Dublin, could act in concert with his rival to hide the Catholic reformer Edmund Campion from the authorities.[24] This merely indicates the inconvenient fact that Stanihurst, like many others, strove to reconcile his loyalty to the crown with his private acts of conscience. When James became speaker of the Irish house of commons in 1570 he spoke as a critic of immoderate policies, although he had voted for the reformation settlement previously. His son, Richard, was educated at Oxford and London before returning to Ireland as tutor to Kildare's son and heir, and he enjoyed the favour of Lord Deputy Sydney in the 1560s. Despite his subsequent departure for exile and recusancy, Stanihurst exemplified the typical Anglo-Irish balancing of English attitudes and Irish values.[25]

Even after 1580 there was a significant Anglo-Irish 'lobby' on the Irish council promoting moderate reform and aligned with the lord deputy in pursuing anglicization by extension of common law rule. Cunningham has claimed that the composition of Connacht actually strengthened local lords by compensating them directly for their loss of traditional rights such as coyne and livery.[26] And Brady's argument for the emergence of a 'permanent country opposition' within the Pale élite claims that the estrangement of the Anglo-Irish only occurred after 1578 with the Desmond rebellion. Their disillusionment led them to overt resistance and 'subversion', but they followed constitutional procedures in carrying out their conspiracy to resist unfair taxation.[27] In sum, the Anglo-Irish were neither summarily excluded from government

23. N. Canny, 'Why the reformation failed in Ireland: une question mal posée', *Jn Eccles Hist*, xxx (1979), 429–32.

24. C. Lennon, *Richard Stanihurst, the Dubliner 1547–1618* (Dublin, 1981), pp. 13–22.

25. ibid., pp. 24–31.

26. B. Cunningham, 'The composition of Connacht in the lordships of Clanricarde and Thomond, 1577–1641', *IHS*, xxiv (1984), 8–9.

27. Brady, 'Conservative subversives: the community of the Pale and the Dublin administration, 1556–1586', in *Radicals, rebels and establishments* (Historical Studies: XV), ed. P.J. Corish (Belfast, 1985), pp. 28–29.

nor entirely alienated from its policies in the period under discussion. Yet the gradual evolution of the political matrix which culminated in the dominance of new English officials was clearly under way by the third decade of Elizabeth's reign.

As we have seen, the entire administration was staffed with Anglo-Irishmen from the Pale and the loyal counties and towns. The extended families of Cusakes, Dillons and Bathes were found in every corner of the government, although only a relative few were on the council. Sir John Plunket and Sir Gerald Aylmer represented other great families of the Pale on the council in this period, and native-born councillors like Sir Nicholas White, who was proxy for the Butler interests, were key members of the Anglo-Irish establishment. The remarkable interrelationship of the leading families of the Pale was what ensured the survival of an Anglo-Irish sentiment throughout the Tudor century. In part, the influence of these men was based on their dominance of key judicial positions. For example, the venerable lawyers Sir Thomas Cusake and Sir John Plunket were linked to the prominent Sarsfield clan as the fourth and fifth husbands of the long-lived Jenet Sarsfield. Plunket's son-in-law, Nicholas Nugent, briefly succeeded Sir Robert Dillon as chief justice of common pleas in 1580. Sir Thomas Luttrell, chief justice of common pleas until 1554, had married a sister of his colleague, Sir Gerald Aylmer. His daughter in turn maried Luke Netterville, second justice of queen's bench in 1559.[28] During the course of the sixteenth century these same Anglo-Irish surnames recur frequently in the legal establishment and elsewhere in Irish government.

The network of family ties extended both horizontally, that is across a particular level or rank of Irish office-holding, as well as vertically, from the most senior officials to the most subordinate roles in the administration. Some leading Anglo-Irish families were not represented in the council in this period, but they were nevertheless a force in the administration. The Barnewalls, Nugents, Sarsfields, Talbots and Dowdalls, for example, were traditionally involved in the patronage system of the Dublin administration at both the municipal and the national levels. The vertical integration of a family network may be illustrated by the success of the Walshes in obtaining places in the government. Just for the period of 1556 to 1578, we may count George Walsh as the first chief justice of the council in Munster in 1569; James Walsh as constable of Dungarvan castle in 1550; Sir Nicholas Walsh as second justice of the council in Munster in 1570 and later chief justice; Richard Walsh as searcher at Cork and Kinsale in 1560; Thomas Walsh as first clerk of the court of castle chamber in

28. Ball, *Judges*, i, 199–202, 208–09, 213.

1563; and William Walsh as an escheator in the exchequer as early as 1535.[29]

Since the leading Anglo-Irish officials were frequently related to each other and they gained employment for their relatives and clients, they were often charged with corruption and nepotism. This favouring of relatives so exercised Sir William Gerrard that he compiled a complete list of all the chief officials in 1576, with '. . . a gesse at theyr dispositions'. He described Sir John Plunket as '. . . aged, restrained but of small learning, greatlye allyed, wilfully affected in his frendes cawses withowte regard to troth or equitye, yet without corruption'.[30] He invariably mentioned that the individual was 'alyed in the Pale', although he described the education and honesty of each official according to his merits. As an example of horizontal integration of office-holding, we might instance the Bathe family. John Bathe, the queen's attorney general in 1575, was unusually well-connected through his marriage to Viscount Gormanston's sister and through his own relations with the Bathes and the Dillons. James Bathe, chief baron of the exchequer until 1570, was the son of an earlier chief justice, Sir Thomas Bathe. His own son, John, became chancellor of the exchequer in 1577. A kinsman, another John Bathe, became chief justice of common pleas briefly under Mary and died in 1559. William Bathe, his son, was appointed second justice of common pleas in 1581. The impact of certain key Anglo-Irish families on the administration of justice in this period must have been considerable and certainly would repay fuller investigation. The herculean stature of Sir Thomas Cusake during a career of nearly forty years was not matched by any of his progeny, but they were certainly not excluded from the patronage system. He was a kinsman of a former judge and his eldest son Robert became an accomplished lawyer and served as second baron of the exchequer for nine years until his death in 1570. Bartholomew was an examiner in the chancery in 1553 and another kinsman, possibly a son, served as third baron of the exchequer from 1581 until 1590.[31]

Perhaps the greatest Anglo-Irish family associated with the administration was that of the Dillons. This important household among the ruling élite provided over a century of reliable support for crown policies in return for a long succession of offices and preferments.

29. Hughes, *Patentee officers*, pp. 7, 97, 126, 135.
30. LPL, Carew MS 628, f. 311v. See below, chapter four, for further discussion of Gerrard's accusations against the judiciary.
31. A more comprehensive investigation might show that these offices were passed along as estates in tail to kinsmen, a fact which would account for the preponderance of officials of one family name in one branch of the administration. The consistent presence of Cusakes in the exchequer might be a case in point. See Ball, *Judges* i, 200–06, 209, 220; Hughes, *Patentee officers*, p. 37; LPL, Carew MS 628, f. 312v.

The progenitor of the family was James Dillon, of Riverston, Co. Meath. A relatively obscure clerk who rose to become first baron of the exchequer, he was the first of a line of able men which produced four judges and eventually an earl. His eldest son, Sir Bartholomew Dillon, was the product of a union with Elizabeth Bathe. This was not the last conjugal link of Bathes and Dillons which produced a claimant for office. Sir Bartholomew became chief baron of the exchequer in 1514 and subsequently chief justice of king's bench. He married, successively, two daughters of the houses of Plunket and Barnewall. The third son of James Dillon was Sir Robert, who became chief justice of common pleas in 1559. The brother of Sir Bartholomew, he was born in 1500 and became attorney general in 1534. Only after twenty-five years of service did he obtain the chief justiceship, and his later years of service on the council were frustrated by blindness and ill-health. Gerrard and others sought his removal, but he remained in office until his death in 1580.[32]

Certainly the staunchest supporter of the government among the Anglo-Irish was the eldest son of Sir Robert Dillon. In the legal tradition of his family, Sir Lucas Dillon was trained at the Middle Temple and became solicitor general in 1565. A year later he was named attorney general and in 1570 he was appointed chief baron of the exchequer. He died in that office in 1593 after a law career spanning nearly three decades. Sir Lucas had obtained further credit among the Anglo-Irish families by marrying the daughter of Sir James Bathe, whom he succeeded as chief baron. Sir Lucas was generally regarded as the ablest of the native-born judges in Ireland. Gerrard said that he was '. . . greatlye allyed, [and] the honestest of his profession there . . .'.[33] He was a most industrious councillor and he often accompanied the lord deputy on military progresses in the field. Furthermore, he was a reliable informant for both Cecil and Walsingham, as well as a supporter of the chief governor against his adversaries on the council. In 1580 Waterhouse commended him to Walsingham for his service to the lord justice, noting his willingness to afford 'a good table in town and campe'.[34] Clearly, Sir Lucas was a member of the inner circle of advisers on the council and he was one of the key reformers in the 'unofficial intelligence system' of the English privy council, according to Brady.[35] His eldest son was made the first earl of Roscommon in 1622.[36]

32. Ball, *Judges*, i, 190–91, 206; *DNB*, *supplement*, s.v. 'Dillon, Sir Robert'; LPL, Carew MS 628, f. 311v.

33. LPL, Carew MS 628, f. 312.

34. PRO, SP 63/72/147.

35. Brady, 'Government of Ireland', pp. 56–57.

36. G.E.C., *Peerage*, s.v. 'Roscommon, first earl of'. James Dillon secured large grants from James I and was created a baron in 1620, later obtaining the earldom.

Three other notable office-holders were direct descendants of this great judicial family. The most celebrated was the younger Sir Robert Dillon, son of Thomas Dillon of Riverston and grandson of Sir Bartholomew. Thomas Dillon had made a well-considered union with Anne, the daughter of the former chief justice Sir Thomas Luttrell, so the younger Robert was bred to the law. He attended Lincoln's Inn and later received his first appointment as second justice of Connacht in 1569. He became chancellor of the exchequer, second justice of common pleas and, finally, chief justice of that bench in 1581. In 1580 Sir Edward Waterhouse recommended him to Walsingham with these words: '. . . he is reported one of the most sufficient in knowledge and Judgement and he is of very good hability to beare out the Countenance of a Counsaillor, being born to fair living as the chief of that surname . . .'.[37] His career, unlike that of his great uncle, was strewn with the shattered fortunes of his adversaries. He was a partisan, aggressive, even combative office-seeker and he nearly ruined the good name of his family. A confrontation with Nicholas Nugent in 1580–81 allowed him to replace that unfortunate man as chief justice. But in 1592 he was himself removed and then imprisoned in a vindictive countermeasure by William Nugent and others. Though restored in 1594, he died soon thereafter.[38] The prestige of Sir Lucas Dillon also plummetted during this reversal, as did that of Sir Robert's brother, Gerald Dillon. Gerald was third justice of queen's bench when he was implicated in the political disgrace of his sibling in 1592–93 and lost his office, but he was finally restored to favour and became a clerk of the crown in 1605. Another son of Sir Robert Dillon the elder suffered for his cousin's excesses. Thomas Dillon had been chief justice of Connacht in 1577 and was made third justice of common pleas in 1593. He was restored after being imprisoned briefly and died in 1606. On the other hand, a kinsman, Sir Theobald Dillon, was sergeant at arms for the council in Connacht and became in 1622 the first Viscount Dillon of Costello-Gallen.[39]

---

37. Waterhouse noted that he had the support of most men learned in the law. PRO, SP 63/72/147. At his first appointment as second justice of Connacht, Sir Robert obtained the assistance of the council for an increase in the level of his financial support. The council requested that he receive lands worth £20 to help defray the charges of his new office. PRO, SP 63/32/105.

38. *DNB, supplement*, s.v. 'Dillon, Sir Robert Dillon, the younger'; Ball, *Judges*, i, 218–19.

39. Ball, *Judges*, i, 224; Hughes, *Patentee officers*, p. 41; G.E.C., *Peerage*, s.v. 'Dillon, first viscount'. Two other kinsmen held important posts in the Dublin administration during the period. The first was Richard Dillon, second justice of queen's bench in 1560; the second was Nathaniel Dillon, who was named clerk of the council in Ireland in 1582. Ball, *Judges*, i, 209; Hughes, *Patentee officers*, p. 41.

Judging from the elevation of two of their number to the peerage under James I, the stature and reputation of the family cannot have suffered permanently from the contentiousness of the younger Sir Robert.

In view of the durable successes of the Dillon clan throughout this period, it is difficult to accept the view that the Anglo-Irish faltered in their allegiance and collapsed in political extinction. Of course, the traditional terms of entry of Anglo-Irish families into the government were amended after 1534 to incorporate the addition of senior English administrators. But the active participation of the Anglo-Irish in the administration was practically undiminished and native-born officials continued to receive advancement and rewards. Yet we find R. Dudley Edwards has claimed that 'The old English . . . began to experience the loss of offices which they had come to regard as their exclusive perquisites . . .'.[40] He argued that the Anglo-Irish were alienated by their systematic exclusion from office, though he also acknowledged that the government was careful to associate some of them with the administration in order to afford the crown a cloak of legitimacy. Hugh F. Kearney agreed that it was difficult for an Anglo-Irish Catholic to enter the administration after the mid-sixteenth century, though he also saw that '. . . the links of the towns and the Pale with the Crown proved stronger than were the religious differences'.[41] More recently, Dr Ellis has described a polarization within the administration between the incumbent Old English civil administrators and the military leaders who were mainly new English, blaming Sussex for his efforts to 'pack' the administration against the Palesmen.[42]

The prevailing view of an estrangement between Anglo-Irish office-seekers and the government rests on a narrowly focused analysis of the rhetoric of Elizabethan policy-makers. The English did, indeed, wish to replace certain Anglo-Irish officials. They were concerned that the old family connections would subvert justice, that the judges would be too partisan, too corrupt and too self-interested. English observers blamed the Anglo-Irish officials for slow process in the courts, for faulty accounts in the exchequer and for a myriad of other ills. They were often regarded as inept, maladroit and under-trained for their positions. In fact, there is no evidence to show that the entire burden

40. R. Dudley Edwards, 'Ireland, Elizabeth I and the counter-reformation' in S.T. Bindoff, J. Hurstfield and C.H. Williams, ed., *Elizabethan government and society* (London, 1961), p. 316.

41. H.F. Kearney, *Strafford in Ireland, 1633–41: a study in absolutism* (Manchester, 1959), p. 3. Kearney also pointed out the cooperation of Protestant English and Catholic Anglo-Irish during the rebellions of Elizabeth's reign, a condominium of interests which lasted until the mid-seventeenth century. ibid., p. 1.

42. Ellis, *Tudor Ireland*, pp. 169, 246–48.

of misgovernment should be borne by these men and their junior functionaries, but it is significant that the English blamed them. The result was a preference for replacing leading and middle-ranking Anglo-Irish officials with English ones. For example, Lord Chancellor Weston wrote to Cecil in October 1567 complaining of the bias in judicial rulings and requesting new English lawyers:

Such partiallitie and slackness both in counsell and Judgment is for the most parte used as is a pittie to behold. If therefore it might please the Quenes highes, to send two or three learned men in the lawes to be moderators in courtes, it shuld do very well and a neadfull and charitable [thing] were it.[43]

The policy of anglicization of the Irish government essentially required competent and learned justices, yet the English training and 'civility' of Anglo-Irish families such as the Dillons assured the crown of an indigenous judicial élite which proved to be reliable and loyal over several centuries.

From the correspondence of the queen and her advisers, however, it is easy to come away with the impression that the Anglo-Irish were being removed. In 1565, for example, the queen found that the administration of justice suffered because some principal judges had rendered decisions favouring their kin and allies. While this fault was equally a feature of judicial practice in English counties, she instructed Sydney that if she heard of any further lapses in the course of justice she would replace the judges with men sent from England.[44] The leading English officials often complained to the queen that the councillors were too old and incompetent to serve effectively. In 1567 Sydney fretted to the queen that the entire burden of the administration fell on his shoulders because of the lack of able administrators. In fact, however, a number of those he complained of were new English placemen, and in any event Elizabeth repeatedly omitted to excuse older councillors from their tenures in office.[45] By 1575 the aged chief justice of common pleas, Sir Robert Dillon, was no longer fit to hold office, and the queen announced that she would send over an Englishman to replace him. In the same letter, however, she recommended three noted Anglo-Irish lawyers to be the principal law officers of the crown. When Dillon the elder finally died in 1580, the English secretary Edward Waterhouse recommended Sir Robert Dillon the younger to the office. In writing to Walsingham, he noted that the younger Dillon would surely succeed his great-uncle unless the

43. PRO, SP 63/22/37.

44. PRO, SP 63/14/3.

45. PRO, SP 63/20/142. In 1572 Fitzwilliam recommended that a number of councillors be pensioned off and replaced.

queen named '. . . some speciall English person'.[46] The tone of his letter indicated that he hardly expected the queen to do this. An indication of what might happen if the queen did nominate an English successor to office in Ireland was provided by the new attorney general, Thomas Snagge, in 1577. Snagge, one of Elizabeth's few English appointees, charged the reliable Sir Nicholas White with maladministration before the council in Ireland and sequestered his office.[47] Even the normally astute Lord Chancellor Gerrard offered the quixotic proposal that English judges who would replace the Anglo-Irish justices should thereafter be assisted by them in a subordinate capacity.[48]

In the event, however, the equilibrium of the Dublin administration remained finely balanced between English and Anglo-Irish office-holders. The major offices of lord deputy, lord chancellor and vice treasurer had been exclusively in English hands since the trauma of the Kildare rebellion. On the other hand, the judiciary was solidly Anglo-Irish and the entire infrastructure of clerks and deputies and secretaries who ran the government was dominated by the Palesmen. While the last Anglo-Irish lord chancellor was Sir Thomas Cusake, who left office in 1553, the two chief justiceships and the office of chief baron remained in the possession of well-connected Anglo-Irishmen. Among the leading civil officials, only the position of master of the rolls was displaced from one connection to the other, and in this case two successive English incumbents were replaced by the Anglo-Irish lawyer Sir Nicholas White in 1572.[49] When the aged chief baron Sir James Bathe died, he was replaced by another Anglo-Irishman, the talented and astute Sir Lucas Dillon, who had earlier assured his route to success, as we have seen, by marrying Bathe's daughter.[50] And after all she had said about the removal of Sir Robert Dillon, the queen replaced him with two Anglo-Irishmen in succession. When Sir John Plunket expired in 1582, his successor was another Anglo-Irishman of considerable experience. Sir James Dowdall, the new chief justice, had been solicitor general in 1554 and became second justice of queen's bench in 1565.[51] Evidently, then, patronage

---

46. PRO, SP 63/72/147. The younger Dillon had been executing the office since 1575. SP 63/72/142.

47. PRO, SP 63/59/159. As an English official, Snagge received an extra stipend on taking office. *Cal. pat. rolls Ire., Eliz*, pp. 11–12.

48. 'Gerrard's report', ed. McNeill, p. 184.

49. Sir John Parker and Sir Henry Draycott were succeeded by White. Hughes, *Patentee officers*, pp. 44, 101–02, 138.

50. ibid., pp. 8, 41.

51. Dillon was replaced first by Nicholas Nugent and then by Sir Robert Dillon the younger. Plunket's successor, Dowdall, was a member of another great Pale family of the judicial élite. Hughes, *Patentee officers*, pp. 41, 43, 97; Ball, *Judges*, i, 210, 213, 218–19.

and faction among the Anglo-Irish governed judicial replacements and influenced royal favour. A useful analogy might be made to the judicial bench in the reign of Mary when lawyers and judges practised 'political dexterity of the highest order' and made a 'virtue of conformity' to avoid the political wreckage of the previous reign.[52]

The policy of anglicization did not lead to a 'colonization' of the Irish bureaucracy, as Brady has explained. The 'major displacement of personnel' which Sussex introduced into Ireland after 1556 was intended to empower his own faction rather than to weaken the Anglo-Irish links to office-holding. Real influence on the council under Sussex was therefore limited to a few men including his close relations, his brothers-in-law Sydney and Fitzwilliam, and his brother Henry Radcliffe. Personal allegiance to Sussex was the key to a successful career, and it is misleading to claim that the chief governor conducted a purge of the Anglo-Irish at this time. His decision to replace the two chief justices and the attorney general was motivated by patronage politics, and the new men were all members of the Anglo-Irish élite (Plunket, Dillon, Barnewall). His employment of new captains in the garrisons assured him of their loyalty, but it did little to alter the balance of Anglo-Irish administrators in government.[53] Sydney followed his example, bringing a large number of new military leaders to Ireland as captains of the garrisons, but this exercise in patronage politics must be seen as a characteristic of the Elizabethan political scene rather than as evidence of a 'colonial' mentality.[54]

The composition of the council in Ireland in 1556 differed little from that of 1578 in the relative proportion of its Anglo-Irish and English members. Of twenty-one councillors identified in 1556 at the outset of Sussex's administration, ten were English and eleven were native-born Irishmen of English descent. Twenty-two years later, the number of Englishmen was the same, ten on a smaller council of eighteen members. By this time the Anglo-Irish membership had declined to eight, but this fact conceals a number of basic changes. Lords president had replaced military captains, but they were largely absentees; the secretary of state was added as a new office, but the master of the ordnance was removed from the council in this period;

52. The Marian judges retreated from political brinksmanship to the safety of the patronage system and their conservatism won them favour in the reign of Elizabeth, who removed only one judge from the bench at her accession. See L. Abbott, 'Public office and private profit: the legal establishment in the reign of Mary Tudor', in Tittler & Loach, ed., *Mid-Tudor polity*, pp. 139, 143, 155.

53. Below the level of the council, the replacement of the auditor and the clerks of the council and the hanaper were similarly dictated by the requirements of faction. See Brady, 'Government of Ireland', pp. 124–30.

54. Brady, 'Government of Ireland', pp. 134–40, 172–75.

members without office such as David Hay, John Alen, William Fitzwilliam and Viscount Baltinglas were not replaced; and the archbishop of Dublin ceased to combine the office of lord chancellor with his ecclesiastical duties after the departure of Hugh Curwen. While it is indeed clear that efforts were being made to create a model of English bureaucracy in Ireland, there is no evidence that this policy was implemented in a way which excluded the Anglo-Irish from office or from membership on the executive board. Over the entire period, a total of forty-four councillors served the two queens regnant and twenty-six of them can be described as English (60%) versus eighteen Anglo-Irish (40%) members. For the most part, institutional growth and factional politics accounted for the changes within this period, and the relative decline of Anglo-Irish officials on the council by 1578 was not the result of any systematic expulsion of the membership.

Among the non-judicial councillors, the archbishopric of Dublin remained in English hands with the appointment of Adam Loftus. But when vacancies occurred for the bishopric of Meath and the deanery of Christ Church, the queen elevated two promising Anglo-Irishmen. Hugh Brady, as bishop of Meath, became an active councillor and a force for moderate reform in the church. He was friendly with both Sussex and Sydney and a close ally of the temperate new English lord chancellor, Sir Robert Weston, whose daughter he married in 1568.[55] The council actively supported John Garvey, the dean of Christ Church, for the bishopric of Ardagh in 1572. Writing on 1 October to both the queen and Cecil, the council praised his 'Englysshe mynde' and said,

May it please your Majestie this Garvie is so Englisshe harted that we thincke if it stand with your Majesties pleasur, he might do good service if it please you to assigne him for one of your counsell here, by the credit and countenance whereof he should be hable to do muche the moer good in the Bisshopricke.[56]

Within the episcopate, only Thomas Lancaster, who had a long connection with Ireland, could be named as a gain for the English interest on the council when he became archbishop of Armagh in succession to George Dowdall.[57] The English-born Jacques Wingfield, who replaced an Anglo-Irishman as master of the ordnance, was excluded

55. Walshe, 'Elizabethan settlement', 354, 365–71.
56. The council commended his wisdom and his learning and noted he was uniquely suited to bring the gospel to such a distant area. PRO, SP 63/38/1, 3–3v.
57. Walshe, 'Elizabethan settlement', 367–69. Lancaster is viewed by Walshe as a force for moderate reform through education and preaching, and thus an opponent of Loftus on the ecclesiastical commission. See also Bradshaw, 'Sword, word and strategy', 484–89.

from the council board after 1562 as a result of his defeat in a skir-mish at the hands of Shane O'Neill. And the addition of the new lords president to the English interest on the council was neutralized by their long absence in the provinces and the intervals in naming their successors.[58] Only the new secretary of state, John Chaloner, proved to be an active councillor among the new English officials created in this period. Thus, the imposition of English councillors was altered in small ways although the number of them remained exactly the same as in 1556.

One writer has supported the idea of a turning-point in 1580 when some members of the leading Anglo-Irish families were refused judge-ships and other posts, but this view does not account for the placement of three new Anglo-Irish chief justices between 1580 and 1583.[59] It was not until 1586 that a hint of change was seen in the appointment of Sir Robert Gardiner as chief justice of queen's bench. The feisty Gardiner served in Ireland for seventeen years and participated actively in the dispute that fractured the council during Perrot's adminis-tration.[60] The turning-point for the new English complexion of the council really came in 1593. In that year alone, three new Englishmen were named to traditionally Anglo-Irish posts. Sir Robert Napier became chief baron; Sir William Weston became chief justice of common pleas; and Sir Anthony St Leger became master of the rolls.[61] The latter two were kinsmen of previous chief governors, but among them only Weston died in Ireland. The others returned to England, breaking the connection established by earlier office-holders. Nevertheless, there remained a core of Anglo-Irishmen on the council. Sir Nicholas Walshe succeeded Weston on the bench as chief justice of common pleas. And below the level of the council, the staff of law officers and other mid-level posts continued to be filled by the Anglo-Irish until at least 1603.[62]

Between 1556 and 1578 the nucleus of the council was roughly split between the first rank of English officials and the second rank of Anglo-Irish judges and bureaucrats. However, there was no simple

58. Lords president were not appointed until 1569 and they represented no long-term addition to the working nucleus of the council. Sir Edward Fyton was replaced in Connacht by Nicholas Malbie after a hiatus of five years, and Sir William Drury came to Munster three years after the departure of Sir John Perrot, in 1576.

59. See D.F. Cregan 'Irish Catholic admissions to the English inns of court, 1558–1625', *Ir Jur*, v (1970), 100. The new chief justices were Nicholas Nugent (1580); Sir Robert Dillon the younger (1582); and Sir James Dowdall (1583).

60. Ball, *Judges*, i, 222–23.

61. ibid., i, 151–52.

62. C. Kenny, 'The exclusion of Catholics from the legal profession in Ireland, 1537–1829', *IHS*, xxv (1987), 339.

dichotomy between them, as we have seen. Some of the new English councillors who settled in Ireland established links with the Anglo-Irish and adopted certain of their attitudes. Henry Cowley, for example, married the daughter of Sir Thomas Cusake and obtained the property of the Berminghams at Castle Carbery.[63] Edmund Tremayne remarked that English settlers generally balked at their taxes, particularly the burden of the cess, and they became 'degenerate' (that is, like the Irish) in one generation.[64] Although Elizabeth failed to remake the council in Ireland, she altered the balance slightly in favour of the new English. She could have reformed the entire government by sending over able men to replace the old and decrepit judges who clung to their places. She could have filled the presidencies quickly with competent replacements. But she was by nature a cautious sovereign who understood the impact that a policy of exclusion and replacement would have had on the fragile Irish polity. Her government could not continue without the full support of the loyal families of the Anglo-Irish, and widespread resentment and ill-will would have undermined her modest reforms. What is more, she could not afford it. The men she would have chosen would only go to Ireland with very large stipends and assurances of adequate support.[65] It was precisely this new commitment of men and money that the queen was most anxious to avoid.

The success of the Dillons in gaining access to the highest judicial offices was unparalleled by any other Anglo-Irish family. But the new English who became connected with Ireland through the Dublin administration attained equally great stature and prominence. Some English councillors were simply adventurers, men who were frustrated in their ambitions for office in England and who sought the favour of the queen by first obtaining some years of service in Ireland. Most of these men never returned to England. A full study of the fortunes of these men as a group would probably show that they entered into the matrix of Anglo-Irish and Gaelic culture, competed for patronage and favour and made dynastic alliances with their neighbours and clients. While no such analysis will be attempted here, it is important to try to gain a sense of the character of the new English. Just as we may regard with suspicion the inflated rhetoric of Elizabethan statesmen regarding the displacement of Anglo-Irish officials, we would be equally justified in our scepticism of the persistently negative attitudes of the new English toward Ireland which have been the subject of much discussion. Dr Ellis, for example, argues that the English view

---

63. *DNB*, s.v. 'Cusake, Sir Thomas'; Lewis, *Topographical dictionary of Ireland*, i, 242.
64. PRO, SP 63/32/182.
65. *Sidney S.P.*, p. 64.

of Ireland changed from that of a borderland to a 'degenerate' colony.[66] And Dr Canny claims to have discovered a view of the Irish, held by such varied Elizabethans as Humphrey Gilbert, William Gerrard and Thomas Smith, that branded them as 'anthropologically inferior'. What is more, he finds that the distinguished lawyer, Sir John Davies, justified the expropriation of Irish lands by reference to the unredeemable barbarity of Irish culture.[67] He explains that the substantial risk of cultural 'debasement' through gaelicization of the new English population was used to justify extreme measures against the natives.[68] Yet in more recent studies Canny has found that new English settlers from William Piers to Richard Boyle adopted aspects of Irish manners and culture. He noted that there were only sixty career officials of English birth working in Ireland in 1560 and still only 200 such men by 1603.[69] Who were these men, after all?

In the first place, Ireland was seen by many leading English politicians as the graveyard of reputations and the drain of personal fortunes. Lord Leonard Grey was an exceptional soldier and an energetic chief governor but he was recalled in disgrace in 1540 and then executed for his brutal transgressions in Ireland. Sir William Brabazon and Sir John Alen were both deprived of office during their years of service, and later Sir John Perrot suffered a similar fate. The Elizabethan chief governors, who initially sought the position energetically, came to regard Irish service as the origin of political discredit and they all endeavoured to leave office well before they were finally dismissed. All except Sussex carried a huge burden of debt into their retirement from Ireland and some claimed to have contracted lifelong illnesses in their service. Perrot died in the Tower of London awaiting trial for his alleged offences as lord deputy. In view of this pattern, it is difficult to imagine why an ambitious man would choose to pursue his career in Ireland, yet Brady has found that the viceroys sought the office because they believed they had developed a promising programme for the reform of the country.[70] Others, less ambitious for political power, aimed simply for private gain. Among these was the hapless secretary of state, John Chaloner, who remained in office for twenty-two years and died in Ireland. Within months of his nomination, he sought to be revoked because the work of the office and the costs of maintaining his staff were too great. He tried for many

66. Ellis, *Tudor Ireland*, p. 249.
67. Canny, *Elizabethan conquest*, pp. 118–19, 131.
68. Canny, *Kingdom and colony*, pp. 37–38.
69. Canny, 'Dominant minorities', pp. 53–55; *The upstart earl: a study of the social and mental world of Richard Boyle, first earl of Cork, 1566–1643* (Cambridge, 1982), pp. 126–33.
70. Brady, 'Government of Ireland', pp. 62–64.

years to obtain another, less demanding, position in Ireland but without success.[71]

Despite this evidence of profound disillusionment, however, most of the Englishmen who were named to positions in Ireland remained there to establish their personal fortunes. Of the twenty-six councillors who were English by birth, only six men returned to England to pursue their careers. Four of them were chief governors (Sussex, Sydney, Fitzwilliam and the interim viceroy Sir Nicholas Arnold); a fifth was Archbishop Curwen, who died shortly after his translation to the see of Oxford; and the last was Henry Radcliffe, brother of Sussex, who followed him on his return to England. The rest of the councillors ended their careers in the Irish service.[72] It was, in effect, a permanent post rather than a way-station to greater preferment. Yet most Englishmen managed to profit from their careers in Ireland, using the system of patronage and preferment to good effect despite the lack of strong family connections there. For example, Henry Draycott, a native of Derbyshire, came to Ireland in 1544. He was named treasurer of the lordship of Wexford and received crown lands in Co. Wexford. He became chief remembrancer and then chancellor of the exchequer and obtained leases of forfeited lands in Counties Meath and Louth. He was MP for Naas in the parliament of 1559 and in 1566 he became master of the rolls. Draycott clearly profited from his advancement and acquired many estates during his long service in Ireland.[73]

Another example of the successful English office-holder in Ireland was the military veteran. These men were employed as sheriffs, seneschals, constables and captains in isolated garrisons, yet the majority of them became known for their versatility and competence rather than the belligerence which has been so noted by historians. An interesting case in point is the career of Sir Nicholas Malbie. Born to a Yorkshire family in 1530, Malbie had a chequered career in England before he was sent to Ireland in 1566. Sydney named him sergeant major of the army and he served for a time with William Piers in the lonely outpost of Carrickfergus He was the only councillor involved personally in the plantation schemes before 1584 and he had tried to obtain a barony in Co. Down in 1571 with the promise to settle it before 1579. His project was undermined by the ill-fated efforts of Smith and Essex in the north, but in 1576 he was knighted by Sydney and made colonel of the province of Connacht. His effectiveness

71. PRO, SP 63/8/109–10.

72. Sir William Gerrard managed to return to his native Chester in early 1581 during his final illness. He died there in May. And Sir John Perrot returned to England frequently before his last government ended with his imprisonment in the Tower.

73. Ball, *Judges*, i, 209–10.

there earned him the renewed title of president of Connacht in 1579, and he also obtained the manor and lordship of Roscommon plus other lands in Co. Longford. He won important concessions from the landholders in anticipation of the composition of Connacht, and although he was reportedly in debt at his death, he possessed a large estate and a formidable reputation as governor of the province.[74]

English office-holders who served on the council in Ireland came from diverse backgrounds, but most of them were the scions of the political élite, or the ambitious sons of the gentry class, or simply adventurers in their own right. First, there were the sons of prominent families whose endeavours in Ireland were explicitly to advance their political reputations and thus enhance their careers in the service of the queen. These were men such as Sussex, Sydney, Sir Warham St Leger and more marginal figures like the earl of Essex. Secondly, there were the gentlemen of substance, or the sons of armigerous gentry, who sought professional advancement in the Irish service. Sir William Gerrard and Sir William Drury, for example, came to Ireland in the twilight of their careers in the borderlands of Wales and Scotland. Gerrard had been elected vice president of the council in the marches of Wales under Sydney in 1562 and he was well over fifty years old when he was summoned to Ireland in 1576. Drury had been the marshal of Berwick since 1564 when he was called to Ireland as president of Munster. Both of these able and experienced men were called to Irish service by Sydney, not as landless adventurers who would despoil the countryside, but as veteran officials who would rule according to the principles of the common law. Both died in the Irish service, little thinking they would spend the remainder of their days there.[75] Sir Edward Fyton and Sir Nicholas Bagenall, on the other hand, seized the opportunity to settle in Ireland from the time they first held office in the Dublin government.[76] Thirdly, there were men of limited means yet full of ambition who came to Ireland to make their personal fortunes. Dr Canny has offered an excellent account of the later exploits of Richard Boyle[77], and the foremost of these men in the Elizabethan

74. *DNB*, s.v. 'Malby, Sir Nicholas'. Malbie was probably the most effective English soldier during the Desmond rebellion, for he managed to keep Connacht quiet while at the same time leading successful expeditions against the rebels in Munster. He died at Athlone in 1584. See also Canny, *Elizabethan conquest*, pp. 70, 76, 114, 158.

75. *DNB*, s.v. 'Gerard, Sir William', 'Drury, Sir William'. Drury became lord justice in 1578, but illness overtook him and he died, aged 52, at Dublin in the following year.

76. Fyton, in particular, showed a willingness to remain in Ireland despite his inheritance of Gawsworth in Cheshire. He guarded jealously his rights to Athlone and his other estates, even after he was removed as president of Connacht. He died in Ireland in 1579. *DNB*, s.v. 'Fitton, Sir Edward'.

77. See Canny, *Upstart earl*.

period was probably the grasping archbishop of Dublin, Adam Loftus. He fathered twenty children and three of his sons were knighted in the seventeenth century, including the eldest, Sir Dudley Loftus. The latter made the most of his family connections by marrying the daughter of the well-established marshal of Ireland, Sir Nicholas Bagenall.[78]

English families often became connected with Ireland through the initial involvement of one particularly successful individual. Other members of the family subsequently viewed the Dublin administration as a place where one could seek profit and preferment. One such family was the St Legers of Kent. Sir Anthony St Leger was perhaps the most effective English lord deputy of the early Tudor period, a shrewd negotiator and a competent soldier. He was lord deputy three times between 1540 and 1556 and was succeeded, at the age of sixty-two years, by Sussex, as Lord Fitzwalter.[79] His second son, Sir Warham St Leger, was sponsored by his Kentish neighbour, Sir Henry Sydney, as the first lord president of Munster. Although he finally obtained the office and was made a councillor, he was suspected of being a partisan of the Desmond interest and was recalled in 1568.[80] Sir Warham attempted to fashion an English colony at Kerricurrihy, near Cork, in February 1569 but the infant settlement was overrun by Fitzmaurice in June and the project failed due to a lack of financing.[81] In 1579 he was given the new post of provost-marshal of Munster and he remained in the provincial government until his death in 1597. A younger Sir Warham St Leger began to serve in Ireland in 1574. This was the son of William St Leger, who was the disinherited eldest son of Sir Anthony. This nephew of the elder Sir Warham became the seneschal of Queen's Co. in 1584 and in 1589 was made a member of the council in Ireland. He was knighted in 1597 and became provisional governor of Munster in 1599, a year before his death.[82] His son, yet another military figure, was Sir William St Leger. He became lord president

78. *DNB*, s.v. 'Loftus, Adam'.
79. *DNB*, s.v. 'St Leger, Sir Anthony'. See Brady, 'Government of Ireland' and Bradshaw, *Irish constitutional revolution*, for two outstanding interpretations of the career of St Leger.
80. Sydney sought his inclusion as a councillor in the instructions of 1565, but the queen expressed concern because his father had quarrelled with Ormonde and she withheld her support for several years. PRO, SP 63/13/14; 63/14/18, 22v; 63/16/204.
81. Canny, *Elizabethan conquest*, pp. 77–84, 144. The St Leger colony was an ambitious failure, despite the relentless efforts made to attract crown support, mercantile trade and subscriptions from the gentry for the purchase of land. Canny argues that St Leger viewed himself as a 'conquistador' although he had a close friendship with the earl of Desmond for nearly two decades. ibid., p. 133.
82. *DNB*, s.v. 'St Leger, Sir Warham'. The younger Sir Warham consolidated his position in Munster by marrying Elizabeth Rothe, of the great Anglo-Irish merchant family of Kilkenny.

of Munster in 1627 and served there until his death in 1642. Sir Anthony St. Leger the younger, son of the former lord deputy's brother, was a prominent lawyer in Ireland. He spent over twenty-five years at Gray's Inn and eventually became master of the rolls in Ireland in 1593. His ties to Ireland were not so strong as those of his cousins and he retired in England in 1610 where he died in 1613.[83] But the original office-holder had set in motion a remarkable association for this Kentish family which led to several generations of officials in Ireland. While they became influential landholders, not all of them were principally known as planters or military leaders. It is important to remember that the English interest in Ireland was as diverse as the men who came to settle there.

Certain English families with less favoured status than the St Legers eventually obtained substantial estates and consistently held high office as well. The Bagenall family was uniquely successful in obtaining its hold on the office of marshal, and the consolidation and improvement of the estates at Newry had a great deal to do with this. Sir Nicholas Bagenall, the second son of the mayor of Newcastle-under-Lyme, was first sent to Ireland in 1539. He later campaigned in France in 1545, and in 1547 was made marshal of Ireland by Edward VI. He lost office in 1553 because of his Protestant views, but Sydney sponsored his restoration to the marshalship in 1565.[84] He executed the office jointly with his son from 1584 until he resigned in 1590. Bagenall was originally favoured by Edward VI with a grant of the Cistercian abbey of Newry and its surrounding territory. During his tenure of office he rebuilt the town, brought in Protestant settlers, erected the church of St Patrick's and restored the castle. Sir Nicholas spent a great deal of his time at Newry, which was then regarded as the northernmost edge of the Pale and a substantial buffer against Ulster.[85] His son, Sir Henry Bagenall, succeeded him as marshal of Ireland and proprietor of Newry. This unfortunate man is known to history as the soldier who allowed Tyrone his greatest victory over the English at the battle of the Yellow Ford. Sir Henry was killed in this key conflict of the Tyrone rebellion in 1598, but another son, Sir Samuel Bagenall, was made marshal of Ireland in 1602.[86] While the Bagenalls clearly developed colonial interests and proved to be able proprietors of the settlement at Newry, the foundation of their interest in Ireland predated the putative 'conquest' of Ireland by nearly twenty years.

83. *DNB*, s.v. 'St Leger, Sir Anthony' and 'St Leger, Sir William'.
84. PRO, SP 63/15/34–36.
85. Lewis, *Topographical dictionary of Ireland*, ii, 393–95.
86. *DNB*, s.v. 'Bagnal, Sir Nicholas' and 'Bagnal, Sir Henry'.

The objective of office-seekers like the Bagenalls was primarily to obtain wealth and status and the function of patronage was to provide opportunity for enrichment in return for personal allegiance. The reciprocal obligations of patron and client served the interests of each, and yet it would be misleading to suggest that these connections were akin to modern party discipline. Private gain was the social cement in the edifice of the patronage system, but the work could become unbonded in the high winds of political and financial risk-taking. While the aim of all courtiers' influence was to increase power and develop a reliable faction, the ends of their many petitioners were less grand. The latter sought grants, reversions, leases, freeholds, pensions and sinecures for themselves and their families. And they would look for advancement from any source, promising loyalty in return for access to favour. The competition for office and income was fierce, so the petitioning from suitors resembled, on the surface, an élitist anarchy, a graceless free-for-all in which all the contenders were rival sycophants. Yet, over time, a discernible pattern of relationships evolved from the attachments of various suitors to their particular benefactors. The various connections which developed were of great importance and provided a stabilizing influence in Irish politics, but it is possible to make too much of these essentially impermanent unions which were no more than political marriages of convenience. The long-term interests of the Anglo-Irish families such as the Stanihursts could be served by reliable accommodation to the governments of Edward VI, Mary and Elizabeth in succession.[87]

VENALITY IN OFFICE

The widespread practice of venality in office makes it difficult to distinguish between outright corruption and the legitimate use of patronage. Regular attendance at the court of Elizabeth was regarded as critical to the success of a powerful broker of interests, but the queen made strenuous efforts to appear impartial and fair in her distribution of royal favour. The number of offices and grants available for patronage remained static while the crowd of petitioners increased.[88] Dr Guy has estimated that there was a 'patronage log-jam' under Elizabeth because the 1,200 offices available represented no increase since the the time of Henry VIII. Despite the act against buying and selling of offices passed in 1552, there was evident trafficking in preferment. Substantial gifts made to courtiers in return for their influence might lead to later increments in the fees charged by officials who

87. Lennon, *Richard Stanihurst*, pp. 13–14.
88. Loades, *Tudor court*, pp. 133–35.

obtained office. Embezzlement within the exchequer resulted from the practice of storing the royal treasure in the private homes of the tellers, and Lord Treasurer Winchester owed the crown £46,000 at his death. Cecil managed to curtail some corruption after he became treasurer, but he accepted £3,301 in arrangement fees for wardships during the last two and a half years of his life. While the common law courts in England were less corrupt, we must be aware that charges of maladministration which were commonly levelled against the Irish government must be weighed against the low standard of official rectitude which was set by crown officials in England.[89]

A general study of private gain through public office in Ireland would have to begin with an assessment of the indigenous network of patronage among the Anglo-Irish families. Dr Brady has suggested that they treated office-holding as their own particular domain, but he rejects the argument that the heated contests for preferment which characterized the Elizabethan period were mainly fought between new English claimants and Anglo-Irish pretenders to favour. Brady's description of 'inter-factional politics' suggests that the chief governors arranged advancement for both their new English and Anglo-Irish clients, building a foundation for political support among highly volatile elements. It was this extensive network of reciprocal dependencies which St Leger used to form and maintain his genial coalition in office from 1541 to 1556. However, the well-liked St Leger apparently encouraged his followers in their 'widespread conspiracy to defraud the crown', allowing them to create a highly profitable market for crown estates by sensationally undervaluing the properties under their control. Sir William Brabazon as vice treasurer amassed a huge personal fortune through his purchases of manors and estates, aided by the Anglo-Irish Chief Baron Bathe and others, including Councillors John Parker, Thomas Cusake and Henry Draycott. The contagion of bribery and embezzlement spread to all ranks of the administration and led directly to the downfall of St Leger, whose generous policy of conciliation was grounded on duplicity and fraud.[90] Later in the century, the covetous Englishman Richard Boyle built a private estate from public trust by using his office of deputy escheator to discover flaws in land titles, particularly in Munster. He obtained titles to crown lands at low rents and married into several wealthy local families en route to founding an earldom.[91] These examples of corruption, however, were probably the exception to the general rule for the Elizabethan period.

89. J.A. Guy, *Tudor England* (Oxford, 1988), pp. 391–97.

90. Brady, 'Government of Ireland', pp. 65–68, 82–93, 97.

91. Canny, *Upstart earl*, pp. 5–6.

Any view of the enrichment of councillors in Ireland through the patronage system must take into account the desperate pleas of some of them for relief from financial distress. The new English members, in particular, often found to their dismay that the expenses of their offices were greater than their incomes. What is more, they argued with some conviction that they were stuck in the morass of Irish politics and disabled from further advancement because they were tainted with the financial shortcomings of the government there. The Elizabethan administrators were sent to Ireland with the strong admonition to govern economically and to reform the bureaucracy. In some cases, they arrived with no wish to remain and settle in Ireland, so they accumulated no estates in land that would compensate them for their losses in office. They did not seek other lucrative positions for their family nor sinecures for themselves since they wanted to leave as soon as a good opportunity arose. These features applied in particular to the senior members of the government whose positions required greater expenses to maintain the standard of comfort proper to the dignity of their office or rank. Thus, Lord Chancellor Weston wrote to Cecil in 1567 to request an increase of 100 marks in his living allowance.[92] And Lord Deputy Sydney complained in 1570 that he had to borrow for his dinner.[93] The most strenuous objections were raised by Fitzwilliam in 1571 when he was made lord justice. The vice treasurer then claimed that his thirteen years of service had brought him to the brink of financial ruin and pleaded that some worthy who possessed greater resources than himself be named as chief governor.[94] The importunate John Chaloner, having successfully won the office of secretary of state, sought an increase in his fee and the lease of an estate to rescue him from a mountain of debt. He had evidently miscalculated the real costs of his office, including the hire of a clerk and the keeping of horses for his journeys with the lord deputy.[95]

Unlike these senior English officials, most councillors clearly benefited from their tenures in office. Sir Robert Dillon the younger, for example, was reputedly the wealthiest commoner in Ireland, and Archbishop Loftus was said to have amassed a large fortune. Sir Nicholas Bagenall could afford to build a church in Newry in 1578 and Sir John Plunket added a chapel to his house at Dunsoghly in 1573.[96] The Anglo-Irish, of course, had an established network of

92. PRO, SP 63/22/37.

93. H.M.C., *De L'Isle and Dudley MSS*, ii, 12.

94. PRO, SP 63/33/72–72v.

95. PRO, SP 63/8/109–10. The council supported his suit in 1566, claiming he was reduced to poverty from the charges of his office. SP 63/17/20.

96. Ball, *Judges*, i, 205; H.G. Leask, *Irish castles and castellated houses* (Dundalk, 1964), pp. 118–21.

family and kinsfolk, for whom they obtained lucrative positions and sinecures, while accepting for themselves the bribes and gifts that were often regarded as the perquisites of office. More remarkably, the majority of the new English administrators also settled in Ireland at this time, becoming landholders in different counties and establishing themselves in quite the same manner as their Anglo-Irish colleagues on the council. The new lord chancellor in 1576 charged nearly every incumbent official with corruption, largely because of their personal enrichment in office. As we have seen, of course, this was a some-what dubious standard for an English statesman to impose in Ireland. Nevertheless, the sober Gerrard accused even the reliable Sir Lucas Dillon, saying that he '. . . dealeth and conveyeth conninglye, nothing furtheringe the Just causes in the Court where any profit may grow to him self, which is a great impediment to the due answering of the Quenes revenewes'.[97] Sir Nicholas White was similarly characterized as '. . . a depe dissembler, greatly corrupt and wilfully affected . . .'.[98] White had long benefited from his relationship with Ormonde, for the queen had granted his petitions for lands in the Pale and the loyal counties, and at the same time elevated him to the council in 1569. He obtained leases and reversions of the monastic houses of Dunbrody (Co. Wexford), Baltinglas (modern Co. Wicklow), and the manor of Leixlip (Co. Kildare). However, in 1580 the privy council called for an investigation into the very large sum of 1,000 marks received by White when acting as interim lord chancellor.[99] The charge of corrup-tion against these and other officials should perhaps be interpreted as placing self- interest above service to the crown, an accusation which could have been made against most officials in the early modern period of the 'venality of offices'.

Personal enrichment was keenly pursued by the councillors, yet this did not always mean either derogation of their responsibilities in office or loss of revenue to the crown. The greatest sources of profit to the councillors were the grants which they obtained from the queen. These took the form of outright gifts, leases, pensions, rewards, licences and other royal largesse. In 1558, for example, Sir John Plunket received an award of lands in the barony of Balrothery, Co. Dublin, valued at £12 per annum.[100] John Parker, master of the rolls, demon-strated his entrepreneurial virtuosity by establishing a 'tapyssery' and a millinery in Ireland. He obtained a licence to export wool in 1559

97. LPL, Carew MS 628, f. 312.

98. ibid., f. 311v.

99. White had disputed the right to retain the great seal with Loftus, who had actually received a patent as lord keeper. BL, Stowe MS 160, ff. 123v–24. See also *Sidney S.P.*, pp. 100–02, 129.

100. PROI, Lodge MSS, Records of the rolls, 6 August 1558.

in order to obtain in Flanders those items needed for his industry.[101] Three councillors received substantial leases in January 1561. Viscount Baltinglas obtained New Abbey and other lands in Co. Kildare; Sir Thomas Cusake received at least five rectories in Counties Meath and West Meath; and Sir George Stanley acquired substantial property which was taken from the O'Connors.[102] The queen received so many importunities from suitors in Ireland that she often dealt with their petitions in a group, instructing the lord deputy how to make the grants. On 20 April 1568, for example, over twenty individuals received grants from the crown. Over half of these were crown officials and they included Sir Robert Dillon, who received land in Connacht worth £30 per annum, and Sir John Plunket, who obtained a lease in reversion worth £10 a year for thirty years.[103] This evidence of preferment shows the extent of officials' reliance on the crown for personal success and the normal working of the extensive patronage system. It is important to remember how pervasive this system was in Elizabethan Ireland when discussing the extent of the 'estrangement' of the Palesmen from the government. For politics and patronage went hand-in-hand. While the councillors and other officials might be free to criticize royal policy, they remained bound by the nexus of faction and favour which ultimately formed and conditioned the milieu in which the Anglo-Irish thrived.

Elizabeth was celebrated for her stinginess. Therefore, when she recognized one of her servants with royal favour she often lauded his extraordinary commitment to Tudor rule. Most petitioners, of course, cited their particular merits as crown officials, but the sovereign reserved exceptional praise for her most dedicated servants. For example, in a letter dated 13 January 1559, she granted the manor of Grange Gorman to Francis Agarde because '. . . she much tended the convenient Preferment of her well beloved Servant Fraunces Agard, one of her Councillors of Ireland, to the intent he might be the more encouraged, and the better enabled to continue his effectual service towards her . . .'.[104] Another councillor, James Bathe, was similarly rewarded.

---

101. Parker complained of the '. . . extreme los in ye exchange of ye money . . .', and got around this by arranging to trade directly for the coloured wool and 'cruell' [crewel] that he needed. *P.R.I. rep. D.K. 11*, p. 40, no. 92.

102. ibid., pp. 65 (nos. 309, 314), 67 (no. 326).

103. Others receiving grants were Captains Robert Harpole, Anthony Colclough and Henry Cowley. PRO, SP 63/24/32–38; PROI, Lodge MSS, Extracts from the patent rolls, pp. 114–19. In a similar letter of 1558 the queen granted the petitions of the earl of Ormonde, Sir John Plunket and Henry Draycott. PROI, Lodge MSS, Extracts from the patent rolls, pp. 84–85.

104. PROI, Lodge MSS, Records of the rolls, i, 140. The manor was attached to the cathedral of Christ Church, so the letter was addressed to the dean, requiring him to lease to Agarde an estate in fee farm.

A grant of 1565 explained that, because he had been continuously involved in the judicial and conciliar business of the crown, he was compensated with a grant of land near his estate in Drumcondra.[105]

Certain military officers were often awarded more substantial estates because their service took place in regions far distant from the seat of government and hence were less attractive to suitors. Also, the queen, in granting these estates, ensured a more effective military presence in these areas. In 1579 she made an unusual grant, consolidating several previous bequests to Sir Nicholas Malbie. For a total rent of £32 she leased him the manor, lordship and friary of Roscommon, plus the friary of Longford. In addition, Malbie was to receive a yearly rent of £200 from the people of the Annaly (Co. Longford). It was up to him, of course, to collect it and it is doubtful whether such a sum was ever produced by the residents of the newly shired county. Malbie had earlier received the castle of Roscommon in 1577, described as having a great hall, two chambers and seven turrets along the walls. The town immured only seven cottages and the fields contained some 190 acres of arable and 60 acres of pasture. In effect, the bargain was not the munificent act it seemed to be, since Malbie would be hardpressed to defend his lands in order to make them profitable.[106] In 1568 the queen had given a similar endowment to Jacques Wingfield, the master of the ordnance, of a lease in Limerick, Cork or Kerry. The clear object of this was to establish a military interest there which Wingfield would willingly defend.[107] It should be remembered that patronage was exploited for political advantage by the crown as well as the suitors. The policy of anglicization was promoted by selective compensation as well as judicious appointments to royal service.

DISSENSION ON THE COUNCIL

Tudor Irish politics has traditionally been studied as if it were largely an extension of politics in England. While the sources oblige the historian to follow where they lead, it would be of interest to conduct a thorough examination of the political life of Elizabethan Ireland which focused primarily on the Dublin government and its relations with the rest of Ireland. The intent of this work is simply to explore some aspects of the internecine politics of the council in Ireland, however, and to a limited extent the external world of Elizabethan politics more generally. As we have seen, the patronage system in

105. ibid., pp. 157–58.
106. ibid., pp. 180–81.
107. *Sidney S.P.*, p. 92.

Ireland offered an intricate setting for the interaction of varied interests, competing policies and complex alliances. The Anglo-Irish competed for office and favour with the new English, but political life was not based on the simple dualism of native versus newcomer. Rather, as Dr Brady has shown, the chief governors so arranged and manipulated office-holding that competition itself was subordinated to the interlocking features of crown policy. Personal loyalty to the viceroy was so important in the political environment that dissension within the Dublin government was the exception rather than the rule in Irish politics prior to the Desmond rebellion.[108] Furthermore, the stable core of office-holding clients on the executive board during this period militated against the outbreak of politically motivated hostility, and the generally conservative tone of the government in Westminster wholly disapproved of fraternal discord in the council. After all, the primary aim of faction was to enrich one's family and to obtain increments of favour, so the goal of influencing policy was of secondary importance to the councillors themselves.

It would be difficult, if not impossible, to study dissension on the Irish council without reference to the persistent realities of political life in England and in the wider arena of Ireland beyond the Pale. In the mid-Tudor period, the intensity of partisan scheming on the privy council which was unique to the reign of Edward VI led to a more moderate balancing of interests under Mary.[109] Recent studies of the Elizabethan court, too, have found more concord and cooperation than the earlier interpretation associated with Sir John Neale allowed. For example, Christopher Haigh has argued that Elizabeth sought to balance the interests represented on her privy council, and Simon Adams suggested that even Leicester and Sussex became reconciled to each other during the 1570s.[110] All the leading courtiers were related to each other by marriage and alliance and few outsiders made it into the inner circle of trusted royal advisers. The 'political homogeneity' of the court and council was the product of Elizabeth's management of royal patronage and of Cecil's careful crafting of policy alternatives. Adams concluded that explanations of factional conflict at court have been exaggerated and too narrowly focused on periodic crises.[111] And Wallace MacCaffrey has argued that the critical years of the regime (1559–63) which culminated in a 'testing time' between 1569 and 1572 ultimately witnessed a convergence of interests which

108. Brady, 'Government of Ireland', pp. 6, 54, 65–68, 174.

109. D. Hoak, 'Rehabilitating the duke of Northumberland', pp. 29–36; A. Weikel, 'Marian council', pp. 68–73.

110. C. Haigh, *Elizabeth I* (London, 1988), p. 82; Adams, 'Eliza enthroned?', pp. 56–70.

111. Adams, 'Eliza enthroned?', pp. 69–70.

was largely 'free of the tensions of rivalry' that characterized the courts of Paris and Madrid. He offered the view that the privy council collectively controlled patronage and adjudicated disputes, and that Leicester was the only leader of a faction who consistently sought partisan ends. MacCaffrey saw the role of Cecil as increasingly passive in the period after 1569, leaving the field to the ambitious rivals Leicester and Sussex. But he also said that the role of faction itself was limited to placing clients in office, since the queen had final authority and would not permit the destruction of a competitor in the race for official favour.[112]

Irish politics were altered substantially after 1534 when viceregal government was no longer delegated to the Geraldine earls of Kildare and direct control of the administration was assumed in London. Cromwell's multiple initiatives were implemented by able commissioners and the aggressive new lord deputy, Lord Leonard Grey, attempted to expand political power arbitrarily by making a series of military expeditions which led to a widespread rebellion against his rule.[113] After Grey was recalled in disgrace, St Leger as the new viceroy gathered a large and varied coterie of supporters and pursued a more conciliatory programme. As we have seen, he managed to wield great influence by tolerating the fraudulent schemes for personal enrichment conceived by his vice treasurer and others. Nevertheless, the apparently rock-solid coherence of his government suffered from the fissures of ancient enmities among veteran councillors. For example, Cusake and Alen were both lords chancellor in this period and they became arch-rivals within the Dublin administration. As we have already noted, Cusake tended to favour the interests of the earl of Kildare and Alen was aligned with the Butler faction, but the permutations of their various allegiances defy easy description. Cusake had conceived the policy of conciliation and St Leger used it on the council as well to bridge the alien cliques and ally himself with both Anglo-Irish and English councillors. Thus, he developed a 'reform party' from Cusake, Sir Thomas Luttrell (chief justice of common pleas), John Travers (master of the ordnance), Gerald Aylmer (chief justice of king's bench) among the Anglo-Irish; and Thomas Agarde (treasurer of the mint), John Parker (personal secretary) and William Brabazon (vice treasurer) of the new English.[114]

---

112. MacCaffrey, *Elizabethan regime*, pp. 67, 454, 460–66, 486; *Queen Elizabeth and the making of policy, 1572–1588* (Princeton, 1981), pp. 432–37, 441–46. See Williams, *Council in Wales*, pp. 231–48 for an account of Leicester's powerful influence on that provincial body.

113. Ellis, *Tudor Ireland*, pp. 130–36.

114. Brady, 'Government of Ireland', pp. 54–68, 81–86, 99–108.

St Leger's clever policy of accommodation of rival interests worked well until his last viceroyalty in 1553. He had survived earlier accusations by the Butler faction which resulted in the removal of Alen as lord chancellor in 1556. But he entered his familiar role as lord deputy in 1553 with a new mandate. St Leger was required to initiate fiscal reform, and a commission led by two English auditors resulted in the dismissal of the Anglo-Irish vice treasurer, Andrew Wise, a former deputy of Brabazon. In 1554 a new commission led by a powerful young courtier, William Fitzwilliam, quickly undermined the position of St Leger. Fitzwilliam was made a councillor by instructions from England and St Leger was compelled to reinstate the fallen John Alen on the council as well. George Stanley was sent to Ireland to replace Nicholas Bagenall as marshal and the new earl of Ormonde came to Ireland in 1554 to secure his interests and his title. Even the loyal Thomas Cusake was replaced as lord keeper of the seal and called to London to answer inquiries about misgovernment.[115] The administration of St Leger had been undermined, its malfeasance exposed and the lord deputy personally disgraced by the work of the commissions sent to investigate his regime. This demonstrates the frailty of the Dublin government, vulnerable to charges from the Pale and the hinterlands as well as to policing from England.

The constitutional position of the viceroy was distinctive to Ireland and while it is clear that the lords deputy were maligned by their enemies at the Tudor court, they were exceptionally powerful executives. To an extent, the chief governors in this period were indeed capable of managing the Dublin administration without serious hindrance. The chief governor's right to recommend councillors at the beginning of his term allowed him to construct a powerful base within the council on which he could rely. Both Sussex and Sydney obtained consistent succour from their own appointees. The fact that Lord Deputy Fitzwilliam was urged to retain most of Sydney's councillors may explain to a degree his failure to control the council at various times in his administration. Also, Fitzwilliam did not receive his initial appointment in England but was elevated from lord justice to lord deputy. This meant that he continued to be viewed as a temporary, or at best an interim, chief governor. It was commonly understood that the lords justice had far less support both in the country and on the council than did the lords deputy. Brady has argued that the council in Ireland was 'impervious' to the influence of Irish politics since it was wholly dependent on the court at Westminster and the viceroy had neither patronage nor a proper court of his own.[116] Yet

115. ibid., pp. 102–08.
116. ibid., pp. 6–8.

other writers have insisted that these men were indeed powerful and ambitious courtiers who sought in Ireland the opportunity for gain and glory.[117] This inconsistency in the assessment of the political position of the governor may be explained by the delicate equilibrium which he was forced to maintain. He was empowered to govern and yet provided only with the barest essentials in men and money. He was allowed to nominate his own men to office, yet he faced a large rank of incumbents left over from previous administrations who might prove hostile to his new initiatives. He was generally placed in Irish service by the influence of a great patron at court, and thus he was seen as the standard-bearer of a particular faction, open to criticism by those who wished to discredit the queen's adviser by attacking his minions. In sum, we may view the viceroys in Ireland as exceptionally vulnerable to political defeat, an Achilles heel which was largely the result of their unwieldy power and high ambition. But it would be misleading to assume that Irish political life revolved exclusively around the viceroy alone. We must turn to an investigation of the council in Ireland as the isolated, but not sterile, 'court' of the ruler in her distant dominion.

Most analyses of this period in Irish history have emphasized a record of resistance, hostility and rebellion, but it is important to view the entire spectrum of Irish politics in order to provide some balance to this rueful picture of discontent. In succeeding chapters we will consider the problem of law and disorder more generally, examine the judicial and military initiatives to expand the jurisdiction of the Dublin administration, and assess the reactions to the vigorous policies which we have described as anglicization. Within the administration, and particularly inside the council itself, the occasions of disagreement were relatively few. The sources are inadequate to provide us with a clear picture of debate within the council. There are no diaries and few private letters in comparison with the abundance of conciliar correspondence which represents only their corporate judgment. But we may make certain negative inferences with some confidence. For example, there is no convincing evidence that dissension within the government was motivated by hostility between the new English and the Anglo-Irish officials, despite the chronic protests launched by the Pale community against the cess. Further, the rivalries which emerged were not uniformly based on the factions at the court of Elizabeth, except in so far as they paralleled the realities of Irish political life. And the role of ideology and principle which may have formed the judgment of some observers of Irish politics did not apparently dominate the interaction among Irish politicians.

117. Canny, *Elizabethan conquest*, pp. 42–47, 53–56.

Rather, the slim documentation available for angry exchanges on the council is reflective of indigenous problems in the courts, in the Pale, in Connacht and elsewhere. Hostilities which developed were not generally part of a consistent pattern, but they often concerned questions of preferment and precedence and protocol. The emphasis on matters of high drama during periods of crisis may obscure the political reality of a durable, if frayed, convergence of interests on the council and within the government.

Sussex first entered Ireland as chief governor in 1556 and he transformed the council immediately, placing his own followers in key positions and elevating new men to the leading roles among the traditionally Anglo-Irish judiciary. He managed the patronage opportunities in Ireland with a rigorous attention to detail, yet he never succeeded in creating a humbled or dependent infrastructure and he faced resistance to his initiatives on several fronts. When he began to use the cess to augment his fiscal base, contrary to tradition, Sussex incited the animosity of the Pale. By 1558 he was faced with the opposition of the archbishop of Armagh, George Dowdall, and the earl of Desmond. Both senior Irish politicians travelled to England to accuse Sussex of arbitrary expansion of the tax base, but the viceroy survived this challenge when both men died in the same year as the sovereign. The protest did not expire with the demise of the principal dissidents, however, and Sussex faced renewed opposition to the cess in Elizabeth's reign. For the most part, however, this movement took place outside the confines of the council and we see only occasional evidence there of the incipient rivalries that would soon colour his administration.

Sussex blamed the earl of Kildare for his alleged leadership of the opposition, although the earl denied complicity in any political resistance to the lord lieutenant. The chief governor had opposed Kildare's suit for the recovery of certain estates as part of his patrimony, and he certainly feared that the Fitzgerald interest would become an obstacle to his leadership.[118] However, Dr Lennon has argued that Kildare was a cautious and traditional aristocrat who appreciated his vulnerability to charges of undermining the government and sought only to re-establish his own power base in the Pale and the loyal counties.[119] The argument that Kildare might have been used at this point to re-establish a sympathetic government managed by the Irish peerage takes no account of the political distance travelled since 1534 and ignores the capacity of the man himself.[120] It has been asserted

118. Brady, 'Government of Ireland', pp. 141–42, 157.
119. Lennon, *Richard Stanihurst*, pp. 35–36.
120. Ellis, *Tudor Ireland*, p. 229.

that Kildare was used by Dudley to establish a rival faction on the council which would eventually unseat Sussex, but there is little to show that Kildare himself was an active participant in such a manoeuvre.[121] In 1561, when Kildare had openly stated that he had obtained permission to have £2,000 from the queen, the council objected. The earl was prepared to go to England and Sussex was concerned that he would challenge the viceroy's leadership there. Furthermore, the council contradicted Kildare's claim that only he was privy to the queen's instructions. However, it is clear that Kildare was a useful symbol as a leading Irish peer associated with the administration and the council did not wish to risk the queen's reproof.[122] For the most part, Kildare's role on the council was an active, but not a divisive one. He was employed to negotiate with O'Neill and with Desmond; he was given a role as defender of the Pale and he governed the plantation of Leix and Offaly; and despite a brief flirtation with the rebels, he helped to defend the government during the Munster rebellion. Kildare was rewarded for his loyalty and service when the parliament of 1569 reversed the attainder against his lands.[123]

It is tempting to divide Irish politics into neat categories which can be analyzed separately, but in many cases the confluence of English patronage and Anglo-Irish politics blurs the apparent distinctions. In the controversy over the cess, for example, the Dudley faction at court seized upon the opportunity to discredit Sussex, and Dudley himself gave assistance to the law students who petitioned the crown for redress in 1562. He supported the Anglo-Irish lawyer William Bermingham who came from Ireland as a representative of the interests of the Pale, and he engineered the commission of inquiry into the cess by his own protégé, Sir Nicholas Arnold. Dr Brady has shown that resistance to the cess in 1561–62 was widespread throughout the Pale, and it should not be surprising that the council in Ireland reflected this disturbance in Irish politics.[124] The English-born master of the rolls, John Parker, had become fully assimilated within the life and culture of the Pale community after years of service in Ireland, and he allegedly petitioned the queen against Sussex. He was brought before the council where he denied that he had instigated the slander of the chief governor. Sussex complained to the privy council in England that 'I know ther is one that went from place to place to gett mens handes unto a booke agaynst me'.[125] After several months,

121. Brady, 'Government of Ireland', p. 157.
122. PRO, SP 63/4/132–34.
123. Ellis, *Tudor Ireland*, pp. 242–44, 252, 263, 270–82.
124. Brady, 'Government of Ireland', pp. 157–65; 'Conservative subversives', pp. 22–24.
125. BL, Add. MS 40,061, ff. 43, 45–46v.

during which he divested Parker of his farms and livings, Sussex obtained the authority of the queen to censure him for his fault. Parker was soon lamenting the loss of his property due to the vindictive Sussex, and he was interrogated by the council in November and December 1562. He retained his office, however, until his death in 1564 and he was restored to the council by Arnold.[126]

After Sussex was removed from office, he in turn became a resident critic of the chief governors in Ireland, and he worked to ruin his successors, Arnold and Sydney. Sussex intrigued against Sydney's nominees for office and found a ready ally in the earl of Ormonde, whose influence in Munster politics would be challenged by the placement of Sir Warham St Leger there as lord president. The queen's refusal to accept a St Leger presidency was a political success for the Sussex faction.[127] Yet the most difficult problem facing Sydney and Fitzwilliam in the years after 1565 was the Palesmen's refusal to co-operate in the administration of the cess. The impact on the council was felt on several occasions. In 1574, for example, Lords Gormanston and Delvin refused to sign a conciliar proclamation of rebellion against the earl of Desmond, explaining that '. . . the said proclamation of Rebellion ment [meant] was grounded uppon a lettere sent from her highness to the Lord deputie and counsell whereof they wear none, and therfore they thought it a presumptious part for them to take uppon them the office of Counsellors or to deale in so weightie a matter without warrant'.[128] They claimed that they were not privy to the dealings of the council with the earl, and, alluding caustically to the dispute over the cess, said, 'It was also Straunge to them to be called to this [meeting] and before this tyme never requested to any consultacion other than to chardge the poore subiectes of the pale and many tymes not to the same'.[129] The council, however, retorted that the two peers had indeed known of the council's actions but withdrew when negotiations with the earl broke down.[130] Further evidence of the fractious nature of the conflict was provided by Nicholas Malbie who wrote to Walsingham in September 1577 to describe the breach in the council which had developed over the cess. He said,

here ys . . . Dyvision among us councell, for what we of thinglyshe do agree upon in her Majesties behaulfe, those of this cuntrie byrthe will eyther Dyssent from yt or absent them selves coulorably, only Sir Lucas

126. *Cal. S.P. Ire., 1509–73*, pp. 194–95, 198, 203, 206.
127. Brady, 'Government of Ireland', pp. 174–94, 206–09.
128. PRO, SP 63/48/42.
129. ibid.
130. PRO, SP 63/48/49–50.

Dillon the cheffe baron of thexchequer who in causes of the state ys nothing behind any of us in affection and Duetie.[131]

Malbie and other observers foresaw an erosion of English authority if the government forfeited the willing support of the Pale. In the following year the reliable Nicholas White was removed from office by the council, though he petitioned to have his case heard before the queen and was afterward reinstated. During the cess dispute, White was an informant of Cecil and his temperate advice was sought as well during the Munster rebellion.[132]

Despite Malbie's assertion that the council was divided against itself along the lines of new English and Anglo-Irish partisan interests, many of the disputes on the council did not involve adversaries of different backgrounds. While the presumed estrangement of the Pale from the Dublin government was certainly at the core of Irish politics throughout this period, the most celebrated case of a heated dispute among councillors was the enmity which developed between Sir William Fitzwilliam and Sir Edward Fyton. The latter became the first lord president of the council in Connacht in 1570 and soon thereafter fell out with the leading nobleman of the province, the earl of Clanricarde. In May 1571 he filed charges against the earl before the council, blaming Clanricarde, a rather pathetic figure, for the rebellion of his two sons.[133] Nearly a year later, in March 1572, the council again heard Fyton's charges against the earl and committed the peer to Dublin castle. But when Fyton brought a book of charges against Clanricarde in April, the council found them lacking in 'solydytie and force' and decided to release him.[134] In July, Fyton made new charges amounting to treason and once again the earl was imprisoned. But the lord president, appearing before the council on 22 July, refused to reveal the gravity of the specific offences charged to the earl. The council was properly incredulous at this and Sir John Plunket wrote that he might as well be dead for all the information he provided.[135] Cecil attempted to resolve the impasse by pointing out the usefulness of Clanricarde against the rebels, since the queen was set against the use of English troops there. He required both a full revelation of the basis for Fyton's accusations and 'pollitique proceedings with the said Earle'.[136] Cecil ended his letter with this reproof:

131. PRO, SP 63/59/59.
132. PRO, SP 63/62/43; Ellis, *Tudor Ireland*, p. 291.
133. PRO, SP 63/32/116–17, 124–25.
134. Bodl, Carte MS 56, f. 69; Carte MS 57, ff. 192, 513–14.
135. PRO, SP 63/37/26; Bodl, Carte MS 57, ff. 196, 443. Fyton excused his reticence by saying he would await the queen's decision on jurisdiction in the case against Clanricarde.
136. BL, Add. MS 32,323, ff. 27v–29v.

And by cause we finde by some of your lettres sente unto us that you Sir Edward Fitton have in a generallitye pronounced that you have matter whear with to charge the said Earle as an offender in treason, which being required in specialtye you have forborne, we cannot but merveyle of suche a manner of proceedinge to give suche Cause to Charge a noble man of soche good Credyte as he hath byne, and neyther to utter it to you the Lord Deputye nor to any other of that Counsell, nor yett to advertise her majestie thereof nor any of us of her Counsell . . .[137]

The upshot of the proceedings against the earl was the recall of Fyton as lord president in Connacht. Although Fyton brought specific charges against the earl on 5 August 1572, the council refused to judge Clanricarde without further examination. To test his loyalty, the council accepted his submission and his promise to bring in his rebel sons.[138] On 24 September 1572 the council responded to the renewed admonition to restore amicable relations between Fyton and Fitzwilliam with these reassuring words: 'for suspicion of unkindenesse emongest oure selves generallie, we dare and will avow it to your Lords that we knowe of no manner of unkindenesse or iarre [jar] emongest us that we maie eche for other saie and (we beleeve) swere for eche to others good will . . . .'[139] This was rather unconvincingly signed by Fitzwilliam and only three others, with the notable exception of Fyton. The council excused its actions because of the urgent need for Clanricarde's presence in Connacht, while acknowledging that the reputation of Fyton had suffered. By early 1573 the queen had altered the government of Connacht, but Fyton had meanwhile been busily shoring up his support in England, and he was named to return to Ireland as vice treasurer. In May 1573 the episode between the earl and Fyton ended in an unsatisfactory stalemate when each charged the other with responsibility for the misgovernment of Connacht.[140] In general, it seems that Fyton was a prickly colleague, yet he must have been valued as an insider by the privy council in England despite his reputation as an acknowledged renegade among Dublin officials.

A second, and even more explosive, confrontation began a month later when the obstinate Fyton was briefly imprisoned by the council. During the spring of 1573, James Meade, a yeoman of Dublin, killed a gentleman in the service of Fyton, one Rowden. Both the principals in the dispute were in fact adherents of Fyton and Fitzwilliam, for Rowden had first killed one Burnell, a friend of Captain Harrington who was in turn the nephew of the lord deputy. Meade, who was also

137. ibid., f. 28v.
138. Bodl, Carte MS 57, f. 569v; PRO, SP 63/37/64–66v.
139. PRO, SP 63/37/121.
140. PRO, SP 63/40/95–95v, 130–33.

a servant of Harrington, was thus avenging the death of his fellow retainer. The jury had acquitted Meade of manslaughter, accepting his plea of self-defence, but this decision was to be reversed in the queen's bench, whereupon the lord deputy then gave Meade a general pardon. The lord deputy delivered the pardon to the clerk of the rolls to be sealed, but Fyton asked to see the fiant and then refused to return it, so the clerk appealed to the council. The lord deputy first sent his secretary to Fyton to recover the fiant, and then dispatched Chief Justice Plunket to demand that he give it up in the council chamber. On 4 June the council, noting Fyton's written refusal to give up the fiant, found the act to be '. . . a dangerous contumacie, disobedience and contempte against the dignitie, credit and authoritie of this her majesties state . . .'.[141] The council concluded that 'sharp correction' was needed and ordered Fyton placed in the gaol at Dublin castle. Only Nicholas White dissented from this form of penalty.

On the following day, 5 June, the council released Fyton at nine in the morning and brought him before the council board. It should have been expected that the vice treasurer would not be so easily dealt with, for he promptly announced his refusal to sit at the council since he had been declared guilty of contempt of the state. Although Fyton then returned to his work at the treasury, when he was called to the council meeting three hours later he again refused to sit. The lord deputy said that he had been sufficiently corrected for his fault, but Fyton retorted that he thought himself disabled and unworthy to sit, while he still disagreed with the humiliating punishment he had received.[142] On 12 June the council reported that, as Fyton still refused to sit at council meetings, he was ordered to '. . . attende his chardge in Connaughe . . .'.[143] On the following day the lord deputy poured forth to Cecil his venomous dislike of Fyton in describing his 'disdainful speeches' and haughty manner with the council. Fyton meanwhile used his son to ply the secretary of state for copies of all official correspondence concerning himself, justifying this dubious practice by virtue of his isolation from the governing body.[144] It is unlikely that the council was often so embroiled in internecine contentions, especially since in this case the personal rancour and resentment of the two principal adversaries had made reconciliation nearly impossible.

At this point the queen intervened decisively. Hearing that the lord deputy had granted a general pardon to an alleged murderer, she mounted a vigorous defence of Fyton's actions. In doing so, she enun-

141. PRO, SP 63/41/52–52v; Bodl, Carte MS 56, f. 44–44v.
142. PRO, SP 63/41/54–54v; Bodl, Carte MS 56, f. 46–46v.
143. PRO, SP 63/41/56–56v.
144. PRO, SP 63/41/66–67v, 133–33v.

ciated the principles of a councillor's responsibility more clearly than in any other document of the period. On 28 June the queen wrote to Fyton, assuring him of her support because he regarded murder so gravely. She declared, 'And in that respecte we do Judge and esteme that our Counsell there did you wrong to put you to any Imprisonment for doeng that which every good counsellor ought to do'.[145] The queen then required Fyton to return to the council board and restore his concord with the lord deputy while continuing to '. . . stay temerite and rashnes'.[146]

When the queen turned to the council's role, she was by turns outraged, disillusioned and concerned. She berated the councillors for pardoning the murderer of a gentleman, saying they should have judged the acquittal as done by a 'corrupt' jury. Further, general pardons should never be used to excuse a single offence. Then she turned to the basic responsibility of the councillors, explaining that they had all served her badly by failing to check the excesses of the lord deputy. Her rebuke constitutes the clearest statement made on the duty of the council to nurture good government by their sage advice, given in conscience and independent of the influence of the lord deputy. She said,

Yet as aperith you the rest of our Counsell there have done as little your duties to god and us that you wold put your hands to it [i.e. the pardon]. As whatsoever our Deputie for the tyme should allow or do, you wold streight ronne into the same rashnes, and affirme whatsoever he wold will yow with the subscripcion of your hands, what nede there then eny cownsellers, if the Counsellers be but the handes and applauders of our Deputie. Yow are put there to be grave and sage advisers, to temper such sodeyn affections either thone way or thother, of love or hatred, as may chaunce to our Deputie, being a man made of flesh and blood, who lightly can not be without them. And to have regarde to god first, and then to our honor, and the saufetie and good government of our Realme . . . You showld all have done as he [Fyton] did in such rashe doings, and required the Deputie to stay, to take better advisement . . . Yow arr adioyned to him from us, as cownsellers and in one commission, not to follow on [one] head, whatsoever the Deputie willeth, but to consider what is iust and reason to be done, and so agrea with him, and set to your hands, and none otherwise. And therefor be yow more then one, that one may temper the other.[147]

The queen specifically berated the council for incarcerating Fyton, saying he was 'the onely good and true cownseller' because he alone

145. PRO, SP 63/41/152.
146. ibid.
147. ibid., f. 154v.

perceived that the pardon was unreasonable and acted on his independent judgment. She further urged the councillors not to take the matter
lightly, reminding them that '. . . if this had bene in our fathers
tyme, who removed a deputy there for calling one of the Cownsell
dissenting from his opinion churle, you may understand how it wold
have been taken. Our moderate reigne and government can be content
to bere this, so that you will take this for a warning . . .'.[148]

For reasons of her own, the queen put the best light on Fyton's
motives for withholding the pardon. She chose to ignore his record of
cantankerous obstinacy before the council and the evidence of partiality in this case to his own servant. But the queen made the most of
the occasion of this deep rift in the council to articulate in the clearest
terms the interdependence of the lord deputy and council. The
council was a check on the viceroy to correct his errors of judgment
and to prevent misfeasance and maladministration. Out of dissension
came a more exacting definition of the responsibility of the council.
The sequel to her intervention unfortunately followed the pattern
already established. The reaction was one of great dismay, the council
pleading both for the clemency of the queen and the restoration of
their credit in London. Fyton, however, told Cecil that matters had
not been patched up, alleging that the lord deputy had publicly rebuked
him in the presence chamber before one hundred persons and had
even refused to recall him to the council. Fyton claimed that he had
humbly offered to rejoin the council, '. . . but having no annswer from
the keeper, and being very bitterly annswered by the Lord Deputy, it
was playnely sayed to me, I should not be called . . .'.[149] He was
admitted, however, the following day and on 4 November Nicholas
White reported hopefully to Cecil that the adversaries had been reconciled by him out of respect for the queen.[150] But the bitter personal
rivalry between Fyton and Fitzwilliam was not healed by the queen's
discourse on the duty of councillors. On 22 November Fyton refused
to accompany others on a mission from the council to Munster. He
claimed he was a poor choice since he had been thrown out of a
presidency himself and argued that his house and fortune depended
on his continuous supervision of the treasury. Fitzwilliam bitterly
remarked that when he had served as vice treasurer he had '. . . no
such tender foresights of his house'.[151]

Elizabeth and her advisers had made it clear that they sought an
end to the unproductive disharmony on the Irish council without pro-

148. ibid., f. 155.
149. PRO, SP 63/42/52.
150. ibid., ff. 148–49.
151. ibid., ff. 184–86, 188–88v. See chapter six for Fyton's refusal to accept Sydney's
     admonition to sign a council letter affirming the increase of revenue.

ducing a sycophantic dependency on the chief governor. The aim of policy-makers in Westminster was to form a governing board in Dublin which was stable, obedient, observant and orderly. How shall we assess whether this ambition was realized in the period 1556 to 1578? Because of the limited evidence for dissension on the council board, we may hazard only negative inferences pending a fuller study of the character of Irish politics. First, there was no simple dualism of native versus newcomer which explains friction on the council and within the government generally. As we have seen, the most intense rivalry was between two leading English councillors. Secondly, Irish politics was not entirely controlled from England by Elizabethan courtiers who ruled through elaborate factions. There were indigenous preoccupations, such as the cess dispute, which dominated the political dialogue throughout the period, and the independent role of the Palesmen demonstrates that political contests in Ireland were not always derived from preponderant English interests. Thirdly, the influence of ideology and principle was rather small. Few of the rival councillors appealed to some exalted ideal when they disputed the succession to office or the trial of a loyal retainer. When the council acted as an arbiter in the case of the accusation of treason against the earl of Clanricarde, the argument from utility seemed to predominate. Rather than undertaking an exhaustive trial of the communications which the earl had made with his sons, the council anxiously returned the aged peer to his dominions where he might extract political concessions from his rebel progeny. In summary, then, it appears that Irish political life was rather conservative, perhaps somewhat parochial, and significantly more complex than the colonialist model would argue. In what follows, we shall examine case studies of individual Irish councillors to deepen our understanding of the influence of personalities and politics in the government of Ireland.

SELECTED CASE STUDIES

The councillors in Ireland were a varied lot. In the succeeding pages, we shall attempt to rescue from undeserved obscurity leading politicians and administrators who served as councillors. The chief governors, for example, should be seen as exceptional because of their unusual power. And yet they were required to seek conciliar sanction for policy decisions according to official doctrine. In fact, the vast distance between the policies of the viceroys and the achievements of their administrations illustrates the real limits of their personal authority. The roles of other councillors may be investigated by using representatives of each type, that is: the earl of Kildare for the Irish peerage; Archbishop Adam Loftus for the ecclesiastical leadership; Sir Lucas

Dillon for the civilian officials; and Francis Agarde for the military administrators on the council. The aim of this section is not to offer a biographical treatment of each man, but rather to analyze certain qualities of their respective roles as councillors. In particular, the age, experience, family and connections of each man will be discussed in order to place him within the political and cultural matrix of Irish government and society. And finally, the professional competence and policy preferences of each councillor will be analyzed in relation to the expectations and the performance of crown officials.

Sussex

The chief governors were extraordinary men and each made his distinctive mark on the government during his tenure in office. Thomas Radcliffe, third earl of Sussex, was originally sent to Ireland as lord deputy in 1556. At the time, he was Baron Fitzwalter but he succeeded to the earldom in the following year. Sussex was the model of a soldier-statesman. He was educated at Cambridge and he served in campaigns in France (1544) and Scotland (1547). He was commander of a band of demi-lances at the battle of Pinkie at the age of only twenty-one. In 1551 he was sent on an embassy to France and in 1553 he sat as a member of parliament for Norfolk. He was named warden and captain of Portsmouth in 1549 and in 1553 was appointed captain of the gentlemen pensioners for life. He undertook three embassies for Mary during the first three years of her reign, including a brief sojourn at Brussels in early 1556. In April of that year, at the age of thirty, he was nominated to succeed St Leger as lord deputy of Ireland. Clearly, his star was on the rise. Although he was chosen to fill a difficult position at a time of political and fiscal crisis in Irish government, few thought that he would remain in office for long. Yet Sussex remained in Ireland during nearly eight years and, toward the end of his service, was hounded by critics in both Westminster and Dublin.[152]

At the outset of his administration, Sussex was endowed with ample authority and resources. He was allowed £1,000 sterling for his entertainment as well as the farms and manors of Kilmainham, Carlow, Wicklow, Carlingford and Monasterevan. He had fifty horse and fifty foot in his personal service, and he also had the gift and disposition of most temporal offices below senior rank.[153] His nominations to high office were normally accepted and he staffed the council with his adherents including his own brother, Henry, and two brothers-in-law, William Fitzwilliam and Henry Sydney. The queen further provided eight castles to be used by the lord deputy during his expeditions.

152. *DNB*, s.v. 'Radcliffe, Sir Thomas, third earl of Sussex'.
153. *Cal. Carew MSS, 1515–74*, pp. 252–57; PRO, SP 62/2/51–52; 63/1/105.

2 Portrait of Thomas Radcliffe, third earl of Sussex (1525–83). Artist unknown.
Sussex was lord deputy and lord lieutenant of Ireland from 1556 until his recall
in 1564; subsequently named lord president of the council of the North from
1568 until 1572. A moderate pragmatist, Sussex became a prominent spokesman
within the English privy council and lord chamberlain of the queen's household.

They were: Roscommon, Athlone, Monasterevan, Carlow, Ferns, Enniscorthy and the forts in Leix and Offaly.[154] Sussex brought to Ireland a number of veteran military figures who manned the garrisons during his regime and he succeeded in placing his own personal stamp on the Dublin administration. His administration has been accused of making a radical break with the past, militarizing Irish government and using coercion where St Leger had employed persuasion.[155] Dr Ellis has shown that Sussex's government began by expropriating lands from the midland clans in Leix and Offaly to provide estates for English settlers. The governor raided the septs in Leinster and Ulster, increased the size of the army and generated resistance to his rule by increasing the burden of cess on the Pale.[156] Yet Brady has emphasized his basic acceptance of the terms of the previous government while noting that Sussex was far more commanding and systematic in pursuing those ends.[157] It should be recalled that the instructions of 1556 were rather brief and called on the viceroy mainly to increase the revenue and to reform judicial practice.[158] How can these different characterizations of the Sussex regime be reconciled?

In the first place, Sussex's military policy was gradually moderated during his tenure in office. He began his administration in 1556 with a journey of forty days into Ulster, during which he spent at least thirty days in camp beyond the frontiers of the Pale. The army marched through wooded passes, routed the MacDonnell Scots in Antrim and took thousands of their cattle.[159] This expedition was typical of many undertaken by Sussex during his government, and it is clear that he chose coercion as his first method of bringing order to Ulster. Nevertheless, he also showed himself a thoughtful observer and administrator. His defence of this aggressive policy was predicated on the need to bring lasting peace to the provinces, after which he would proceed with the more refined 'civilizing' mission of anglicization. For Ulster he sought the establishment of a provincial council assisted with 400 troops to keep order and to bring even-handed justice to the region. It is worth noting that he believed the brehon law could be made to work within the framework of English law. His proposals for Ulster were based first of all on the presence of warring factions there, so he called for a strong lord president and a large budget

154. PRO, SP 62/2/51–55.
155. Canny, *Elizabethan conquest*, pp. 58–63; Bradshaw, *Irish constitutional revolution*, pp. 260–62.
156. Ellis, *Tudor Ireland*, pp. 234–39.
157. Brady, 'Government of Ireland', pp. 105–11.
158. PRO, SP 62/2/51–52.
159. *Cal. Carew MSS, 1515–74*, pp. 257–62.

of £5,623. But his long-term policy was a moderate one, for instead of large-scale expeditions he advocated regular meetings with the Irish captains and at least provisional toleration of the Scots in Antrim. He wanted to rebuild the towns as English strongholds and to expel Shane O'Neill from Tyrone, but he saw the need for compromise on other issues.[160] For Munster and Connacht he also sought the establishment of provincial councils, but there he believed the association of leading peers on the council would have a more salutary effect than a contingent of troops. He advocated a small complement of forty soldiers in each province, hardly enough to be called military rule.[161]

It should also be remembered that Sussex worked under an extremely cautious sovereign. The political conservatism of the queen was evident in her first instructions to the viceroy. She called on Sussex to reach an accord with both Shane O'Neill and the Scots in Ulster, blaming them for regional turbulence, yet worried at the same time that she would lose her authority there. She was prepared to consider an English settlement in Ulster, but she cautioned Sussex that any overt movement in that direction would be premature.[162] She asked the earl to remain in Irish service at her accession and she increased his compensation by £500 'for his estate in nobilitie' and made him lord lieutenant in 1560.[163] Many things were left to his discretion, for the queen was initially reluctant to pursue an active policy or to dictate terms to her experienced viceroy. For example, when Sussex was called upon to inaugurate important religious changes in Ireland, Elizabeth's rather sanguine but hesitant approach took this form:

And that specially the sayd depute and such others of that Counsaill which be natif borne subjectes of this our Realme of Ingland . . . Do as much as conveniently maye with good order lye in them, use the cures and ceremonies of the service of god [in the church] at ye lest in there howses which is by lawe here approved and appoynted . . .[164]

These instructions reveal that a carefully balanced moderation was expected of Sussex, despite the rampant tergiversation of the queen. He was advised to use force and persuasion alternately to get the obedience of the cunning Shane O'Neill. He was ordered to reform the infrastructure of the Dublin administration. And at the same time he was required to control costs and to avoid incitement to disorder or disobedience.

160. *Cal. Carew MSS, 1515–74*, pp. 330–34.
161. ibid., pp. 334–36, 342–43.
162. PRO, SP 63/1/105; 63/2/37.
163. PRO, SP 63/2/36.
164. PRO, SP 63/1/123. The phrase 'in the church' is crossed out in the manuscript.

The earl of Sussex 'matured in office' during his tenure in Ireland, and his final proposal for Irish governance indicated a pragmatic grasp of the difficulties with which he was faced. In 1562 he called for the establishment of three provincial presidencies to govern the outlying areas of Ireland; for English captains to encourage the Gaelic septs in the Pale to seek remedies at the common law; and for a new star chamber jurisdiction for the council, to be named the court of castle chamber.[165] Sussex had found that resistance to the forceful government of his earlier years only led to widespread opposition and this had ultimately made his 'programmatic' style of administration too unwieldy. Yet he persisted with an energetic application of his policies because he was charged with the full actualization of the new constitutional role of the sovereign, based on the 1541 act for the kingly title. Elizabeth's caution and Sussex's bitter experience in Ireland did nothing to deter either of them from working toward the final purpose of Elizabethan rule: the complete authority of the sovereign over the whole of Ireland under terms of the common law. While Sussex and others have been charged with a kind of quixotic persistence in this ambition for governmental control, it should be remembered that this was the consistent aim of each of the queen's viceroys. Brady has criticized Sussex for his apparent attachment to the 'quick victory' in Ireland and for his 'fixity of purpose', but the tenacity with which he pursued his ends for nearly eight years would seem to belie this interpretation. And if the chief governor sought to endow his regime with the gold leaf of personal glory in the process, this ambition was certainly not exceptional at the court of Elizabeth, particularly for one who was 'desperate' in the political wilderness of Ireland.[166]

In the end, Sussex was brought down by a combination of his opponents at court, led by Leicester, and his adversaries in Ireland, particularly the Palesmen who opposed his use of the cess. His administration had been marked by bitter personal disputes and recriminations, for Sussex had a singular capacity for making enemies that was only exceeded by his disposition to take offence. In 1562 he was charged with misgovernment by the Irish law students and the Pale representative, William Bermingham; by the earls of Leicester and Kildare; and allegedly by the Irish councillor John Parker. With all these critics he could ill afford to err in his handling of Shane O'Neill. In fact, however, Sussex's ravaging of Ulster had little lasting effect and Shane obtained an interview with the queen which was the ultimate humiliation for the chief governor. The viceroy had been consumed with affairs in Ulster and so gave little attention to the rest of Ireland,

165. Ellis, *Tudor Ireland*, pp. 243–45; Brady, 'Government of Ireland', pp. 112–16.
166. Brady, 'Government of Ireland', pp. 121–25.

preferring at the time to leave the government of the other provinces in the hands of the feudal magnates. He left Ireland nearly every spring so that he was there in total less than six of the eight years he served as viceroy. The queen denied him full support and undermined his efforts by alternately invoking measures for peace and calling for the removal of Shane and the Scots. Sussex retired to England at last in 1564 to face his arch rival, Leicester, leaving behind a debilitated government and frustrated by the lingering difficulties in Ulster.

An assessment of the Irish career of the earl of Sussex, however, must take into account his subsequent successes. He became a notable rival of the dominant Elizabethan patron, Leicester, and the two nearly fought a duel in the heated atmosphere of 1565. When he was made the lord president of the council in the North as a 'reliable outsider', it became clear that Sussex had retrieved his credibility as a provincial administrator. He proved his loyalty during the Northern rebellions and was made a privy councillor late in 1569 at the age of forty-three. Thereafter, Sussex became a voice for moderate Protestantism and the queen sought his advice independently on the great questions of the realm.[167] By 1575 he was admitted to the 'inner ring' of elder statesmen along with Leicester, Burghley, Walsingham and Hatton.[168] The essential conservatism of his subsequent career makes it difficult to envision Sussex as a 'radical' exponent of colonialist expansionism in Ireland. Brady has asserted that Sussex gradually developed a lighter touch during the course of his career, ultimately arriving at policies for Ireland that were flexible, moderate and realistic.[169] While we must acknowledge that his initiatives were often regarded as failures, such as the sterile experiment with the plantation of Leix and Offaly, Sussex's statesmanship better accords with the judgment of Dr Pulman who regards him as the 'great proconsul of Elizabeth's reign'.[170] In his ruthless expeditions to Ulster, in his disciplined understanding of the myriad problems of the Irish polity, and in his advancement of new proposals for provincial government, Sussex offered his consistent and unrelenting support for the primary purpose of crown government in Ireland: the expansion of royal authority and the fashioning of a 'civil' commonwealth ruled by the terms of the common law.

---

167. Haigh, *Elizabeth I*, pp. 52–54; MacCaffrey, *Elizabethan regime*, p. 256; Pulman, *Elizabethan privy council*, pp. 48–50.

168. Loades, *Tudor court*, p. 145. See Pulman, *Elizabethan privy council*, pp. 48–50 for evidence of the cooperation of Sussex and Leicester after 1568, noting their daily contact and mutual interests on certain questions of national importance.

169. Brady, 'Government of Ireland', pp. 112–16; Bradshaw, *Irish constitutional revolution*, p. 260.

170. Pulman, *Elizabethan privy council*, p. 25.

Sydney

After the brief tenure of Sir Nicholas Arnold as lord justice, the way was cleared for Sir Henry Sydney to return to Ireland as lord deputy. Sydney was one of the ablest chief governors of the sixteenth century. He was an effective military leader, a statesman, a reformer and a judge. Like Sussex, his fortunes were in the ascendant when he was named lord deputy for the first time. Sydney had been raised in the company of Prince Edward at the court of Henry VIII, for his father was chamberlain and steward of the prince's household from 1538. Once the prince became Edward VI, Sydney was named one of the four gentlemen of the privy chamber and in 1550 was knighted along with Cecil and others. At the age of only twenty-one he was sent on an embassy to France and on his return he obtained other marks of royal favour. In 1551 he made a fateful link with the Dudley family that influenced the course of his career and the fortunes of his progeny. He married Mary Dudley, daughter of John, duke of Northumberland, and in the next two years he continued to gain offices and stature. On the death of Edward VI, however, his fortunes plummetted and he was only able to recover some standing at court by repudiating the arrangement of his father-in-law to alter the succession. He was sent in 1554 to arrange for the Spanish marriage of the new queen, and Philip II, who liked him, stood as godfather (and namesake) to his eldest son. But Sydney chafed at the unwonted subordination of his interests in the new reign. In 1556 he obtained permission to go to Ireland as vice treasurer with his brother-in-law, Sussex. The incipient connection with Radcliffe held some promise, since Lord Fitzwalter had married Sydney's sister, Frances. In fact, Sydney's successor, Fitzwilliam, had married Anne, another sibling. So, in effect, the Dudley interest was little more attractive at this juncture in his career than was the Sussex faction for the ambitious young courtier from Penshurst.[171]

Sydney demonstrated his aptitude for leadership in his first stint in the Irish administration. In three years as vice treasurer there, he served as lord justice for nearly thirteen months. As interim chief governor in 1557, Sydney put down the uprising of the O'Connors and defeated the O'Mulloys. He levied a cess on the Pale to provision the forts in Leix and Offaly and he forbade the export of corn. A second lord justiceship in 1558–59, occasioned by the death of Queen Mary, led to his nomination as the successor to Sussex. However, the new queen would not consent to this, so Sydney returned to England late in 1559. In 1560 he was named to succeed Lord Williams as president of the

---

171. *DNB*, s.v. 'Sidney, Sir Henry'; *Letters and memorials of state*, ed. A. Collins (London, 1746), pp. 82–85. Sydney's son Philip later married Frances, the daughter of Walsingham, and Sydney was also the brother-in-law of the earl of Warwick.

3 Portrait of Sir Henry Sydney (1529–86). By, or after, Arnold van Brounckhorst, *c.* 1573. Sydney was vice treasurer in Ireland under Sussex from 1556 until he became lord president of the council in the marches of Wales in 1560. His long tenure there was interrupted twice by his appointments as lord deputy in Ireland. He served as lord deputy from 1565 until his recall in 1571; he then sought a second term which lasted from 1575 until 1578. His energetic and creative administration was frustrated by local resistance and by the fiscal austerity of the queen. A client of Leicester, he gradually regained the favour of the crown and served on the English privy council until his death.

council in the marches of Wales, an office he held without interruption until his death in 1586. Sydney found the Welsh council badly in need of reform and his moderate proposals were designed to expedite judicial process. Two major themes of Sydney's Irish administrations emerged in these early years. First, he became an active, energetic leader, convinced that a prompt response to domestic turbulence would prevent it from accelerating into rebellion. Secondly, he showed himself to be a practical reformer with a decidedly judicial temper. He was determined that the effective extension of the common law would curb the 'incivility' of Celtic peoples.[172] Sydney was a tough, seasoned veteran of provincial administration, a soldier-statesman like Sussex, who accepted the lord deputyship in Ireland with some confidence and left it with a great deal of remorse. Reflecting on his Irish experience in 1583, he wrote: 'How pleasant a life it is that time of year [December], with hunger and after sore travail, to harbour long and cold nights in cabbanes made of boughs and covered with grass, I leave to your indifferent judgment.'[173]

When the terminal weakness of the Arnold government in Ireland made it clear that a new viceroy would be selected, Sydney campaigned for the role with the help of Leicester. He formulated a comprehensive plan for the reform of Irish government and society, borrowing heavily from the experience of Sussex and his own considerable awareness of Irish conditions. While it was not the 'radical departure' which some writers have claimed for Sydney's proposal, there were novel elements in it and Sydney made the plan most attractive to the queen by promising to cut expenditures drastically. But in most respects he was consciously building upon the foundation established by the government of Sussex and addressing the problems which his brother-in-law, and new rival, had posed. Anglicization had become the order of the day.[174] In a thoughtful memorandum of 20 May 1565, Sydney laid out the key issues which the queen must decide and later wrote privately to ask that he might be allowed to keep his office of lord president in Wales. He advised her to consider revising the government of Thomond, who was too weak to rule his people; to tolerate the Scots until a more propitious time to expel them from Ulster; and either to remove Shane O'Neill or create a buffer of fortified towns between the Pale and Ulster.[175]

172. Williams, *Council in Wales*, pp. 251–55, 259.

173. *Cal. Carew MSS, 1575–88*, p. 336.

174. Brady, 'Government of Ireland', pp. 172–81. See Canny, *Elizabethan conquest*, pp. 48–50, 64–65, for the view of Sydney's government as 'radical' in its ends and means.

175. PRO, SP 63/13/108–11.

Dr Canny has asserted that these rather pitiful efforts to establish tiny citadels of English influence on the perimeter of the Pale led to a 'new chapter in Irish history', pointing the way to 'more forceful' methods of plantation and settlement. But he also acknowledged that the Ulster project was a complete failure from the beginning and his assertions that Sydney masterminded these efforts at colonization are purely speculative. It is not at all clear, for example, that Sydney imbibed an enthusiasm for colonial projects during his embassy to Madrid under Mary.[176] A more reasonable assessment of Sydney's policies by Dr Brady stressed the fundamentally 'eclectic' nature of his government, emphasizing the need for flexibility and moderation.[177] The argument that Sydney was a champion of plantation who was 'determined to establish colonies of Englishmen throughout the country' has been too uncritically accepted. It is important to remember that his proposals for Irish government mention colonies only indirectly and they are in no way central to his plan. As Canny himself has often stressed, the chief aim of these and other policies was to bring the Irish to 'civility' through a systematic extension of the common law.[178] Nevertheless, we must be aware of the connection between the isolated, quasi-legal expropriations of adventurers like Carew and St Leger and the advent of rebellions against English encroachments of this sort in 1569. Sydney was forced to confront rebels who claimed that their property rights in Munster had been violated and his success against them was largely a Pyrrhic victory. The disorders of 1569–71 humbled the veteran chief governor, leading directly to his removal from office, and thereafter he was certainly no supporter of colonial experiments.[179]

Sydney's formal instructions of July 1565 were the most comprehensive and detailed of the period. It is probable that the queen expected more of Sydney, both because she was by then more aware of the problems in Ireland and because of the confidence she had in his ability. He was called upon to reform judicial practice, to curtail expenses and increase the revenue, and to reduce the garrison. Beyond these conventional guidelines, however, Sydney was expected to initiate new programmes and reinvigorate others. He was directed to look into the foundation of a college at St Patrick's cathedral in Dublin, to provide for commissions of oyer and terminer beyond the Pale, to publish the statutes of the realm and, most importantly, to

176. Canny, *Elizabethan conquest*, pp. 66–77.
177. Brady, 'Government of Ireland', p. 202.
178. Canny, *Elizabethan conquest*, pp. 49–52, 69. See also Ellis, *Tudor Ireland*, pp. 249, 255–56 for a recent restatement of the colonialist thesis.
179. Ellis, *Tudor Ireland*, pp. 259–61.

establish the new provincial councils in Munster and Connacht. He was also required to find a place for Irish judges to reside when they came to Dublin, and in general to expand recourse to the courts of law. In religious matters, Sydney was ordered to prevent the alienation of church property and to organize an ecclesiastical commission to correct abuses in the Irish church.[180] As an earnest of her new commitment to Irish government, the queen agreed to Sydney's proposal '. . . that it may please your Majestie to name and appoint iii or iiij Counselors to whom I may speatially address my Letters and from whom I may accordingly expect answer and Reasolucion'.[181] This wise counsel was not taken up for several years, but a sub-committee of the privy council for Irish affairs was ultimately created, made up of Leicester, Cecil, Croft, Sussex and Walsingham.

As lord deputy, Sydney became the principal advocate of anglicization of the central government and expansion of common law jurisdiction. His military expeditions were generally combined with a kind of ad hoc jurisprudence and his basic approach was dominated by his judicial temper. In his first year as lord deputy he personally presided over extended assizes, travelling with the judges in Leinster and conducting sittings in Munster, the object being to provide a forum for those unable to sue their overlords at common law.[182] He vigorously challenged the use of private baronial courts and Gaelic judicial practices, and he imposed royal justice on more areas of Ireland than any previous chief governor. What is more, he always brought with him a few councillors to assist with the judicial work. On 27 January 1567, for example, Sydney left Dublin for an expedition that would take him through all of Munster and Connacht in eleven weeks. He held sessions in Leix, Kilkenny, Limerick, Waterford, Youghal, Cork and Galway, as well as in other towns of lesser significance. He intervened in many local disputes, and he met the leading nobles and gentlemen of every county. His conclusion was that in neither province was there a man of quality sufficient to govern it.[183] In contrast to Sussex, who was eternally preoccupied with conditions in Ulster, Sydney made more practical the ambition to extend English authority throughout all of Ireland.[184] An acknowledgment of Sydney's '. . . good zeale to direct causes accordinge to the comon Lawes of this Realme . . .'

180. PRO, SP 63/14/2–15, 18–23.

181. PRO, SP 63/13/111. It is an error to suppose that the sub-committee of the governing body was solely created to promote the establishment of colonies in Ireland. See Canny, *Elizabethan conquest*, p. 84.

182. Canny, *Elizabethan conquest*, pp. 53–54.

183. PRO, SP 63/20/135–43.

184. Sussex certainly sought more in his government than merely to defend the Pale, however. See Ellis, *Tudor Ireland*, pp. 252–53.

came from a number of English judges to whom Sydney had referred the question of the validity of a Dublin episcopal lease. With some reluctance, the judges put forward an authoritative opinion based on common law practice which would serve to instruct the Irish judiciary and assist the viceroy.[185]

The key to Sydney's programme of expansion was the establishment of provincial councils. When he found that no one among the leading men of Munster and Connacht could govern the provinces effectively, he concluded that an English-born president was sorely needed. In theory, the presidents and councils would bring order to each province and at the same time would begin to dispense even-handed common law justice to distant regions. The lords president were not primarily military men, as some have indicated, and they were each assisted by an experienced judge as well as a small troop of retainers for defensive purposes. Confrontations, however, were unavoidable since it quickly became clear that Sydney's provincial government would directly threaten the private jurisdiction of feudal magnates like Ormonde and Desmond.[186] Sydney based his confidence in this dissemination of conciliar government on the usefulness of the council in Wales where he had been lord president since 1560. As chief governor there, Sydney earned a reputation for tolerance, moderation and leniency. He preferred to use common law remedies against disorder and he worked through competent provincial administrators who shared his views, men such as William Gerrard and John Throckmorton.[187] In 1567 he and the council in Ireland wrote to the queen in this vein:

For it is not your Majesties lawes exercised within ye englishe pale that ever did or can rule this your whole realme, for yf the counsell in wales or in the northe of England be necessarie one m [thousand] tymes more nedefull and expedyent soundry counsells and regyments by your highnes appoyntment to be within this realme for dutie and consciences sake . . .[188]

Unfortunately, the queen was more concerned with what it would cost than with the extension of the common law. Sydney was, if anything, an impatient and a forthright man. His letters from 1565 to 1571 are full of recriminations for the delay in approving the presidents and councils. Cecil wrote hopefully in November 1568 that

185. *Dignitas Decani*, ed. N. White with intro. by A. Gwynn (Dublin, 1957), pp. 147–48.

186. Canny, *Elizabethan conquest*, pp. 49–50, 93, 99–108, 114–15. There is no solid evidence that the presidents 'were stalking horses for colonization', despite the fact that some planters had been employed in leadership roles in Munster and Connacht.

187. Williams, *Council in Wales*, pp. 252–254, 265, 274–275.

188. PRO, SP 63/21/80.

'. . . I laboured so much with her Majestie, as she was well content to accord to establish ij Counsels, one for Mounster and an other for Conacht . . .'.[189] But the queen still balked at the expenses and nothing would be done until Sydney reconsidered the anticipated cost and the size of the garrison. A week later Sydney complained peevishly to Cecil that if the queen had accepted his proposal of two years before there would be no need to request additional money and men now.[190] In May 1570 he blamed the insurrections in Munster on the failure to send a lord president to that province several years before.[191] Dr Brady has argued that the principal explanation for the sovereign's failure to act was the intense opposition of the earl of Ormonde. His dominions were threatened by a new layer of regional administration headed by a potentially hostile president, Sir Warham St Leger, who had given succour to Ormonde's sworn enemy, the earl of Desmond, when the latter was in England. The fusion of patronage politics and fiscal restraint was thus deadly to Sydney's plans for the government of Munster.[192]

At the commencement of his deputyship, Sydney recognized that his programme of anglicization must be built on a reformed central administration. He was thus a leading proponent of improvements in the government. He was credited with such mundane but important achievements as the start of dependable record-keeping, the rebuilding of Athenry and the erection of a gaol at Mullingar. He attempted to reform the exchequer, the judiciary and the military and he called for the replacement of aged councillors. Sydney brought into the administration many talented and well-educated officials who were equally committed to reform. The conscientious lord chancellor, Sir William Gerrard, who joined Sydney from Wales during his second term of office, was the most incisive critic of the judiciary in this period. It was Sydney who selected as his personal secretaries two dynamic and clever junior administrators, Edmund Tremayne and Edward Waterhouse. And he chose two of the most active clerks of the council during this period as his able assistants, Edmund Molyneux and Lodowick Bryskett. However, Sydney did not always succeed in completing his administrative restructuring, as we have seen. For example, his relentless appeals to English statesmen to forward the rules of procedure

189. PRO, SP 63/26/60.

190. ibid., f. 71. See also his letter of 30 June 1569 to Cecil in the same vein. PRO, SP 63/28/131.

191. PRO, SP 63/30/97; Brady, 'Government of Ireland', pp. 180–86, 194–208.

192. Brady, 'Government of Ireland', pp. 182–86. Canny has argued that Sydney wished to discipline the unruly Munster lords and undermine the 'overmighty subjects' by ending their palatinate jurisdictions. See *Elizabethan conquest*, pp. 49–50.

for the newly established court of castle chamber were barren until he left office in 1571.[193] Sydney's reforming energy was often frustrated by the bureaucratic inertia of the Tudor court and by the lack of congruence between English and Irish systems of government. Although he created the new office of victualler in 1568 as a response to the turmoil over the administration of the cess, this innovation failed to produce a logistical solution. In sum, Sydney was forced to govern under the severest fiscal constraints, so his work as a reformer was handicapped by delay, deception and debt. Nevertheless, he was appreciated as a man of boldness and energy who applied himself systematically to the task of governing Ireland.

Sydney's return to Ireland as chief governor in 1575 is, at first blush, something of an enigma. He was disillusioned with Irish service and he already had a senior role in the government as lord president of the council in the marches of Wales, yet he campaigned vigorously to be reappointed as lord deputy in Ireland. He had been vice treasurer and knew the vulnerability of Irish viceroys to charges of excessive spending, yet he offered to govern with only £20,000 per annum from England. He apparently accepted the risk that his opportunity to save the queen's government in Ireland would be unacceptable to the Pale and improvident beyond it. Sydney conceived a two-fold policy which, he believed, would soon restore the good faith and credit of Elizabethan rule. First, he launched an ambitious expedition throughout Ireland during which he prepared the way for the new lord president in Munster, Sir William Drury; held court at Cork for six weeks and received all the Anglo-Irish lords and Gaelic chiefs of the region; managed a truce with Turlogh Luineach in Ulster and recognized the rights of the Scots in Antrim; erected the two new shires of Mayo and Sligo and marked out the borders of four counties in Connacht; and took submissions of the rebellious Burkes and O'Connors. By 1576 he had placed Sir Nicholas Malbie in office as the second lord president of the council in Connacht, and his long-sought programme for provincial government was finally in place. What is more, by this time the court of castle chamber had become well-established as the judicial arm of the council in Ireland and a new court of high commission heard cases in ecclesiastical law as well.[194] The reform of the central administration, so long delayed, was now practically complete and Sydney's government was poised to reap the benefits of anglicization and moderate rule.

However, the second feature of the new government's policy met with less success and quickly developed into a constitutional crisis

---

193. PRO, SP 63/16/110; *Cal. S.P. Ire., 1509–73*, pp. 303, 307, 309–10.

194. Ellis, *Tudor Ireland*, pp. 215–16, 269–74.

which overwhelmed the energetic work of Sydney in a wave of unrest and opposition. Despite the bitter legacy of resistance which Sussex had left behind, Sydney now bargained with the Pale to substitute a regular tax on property in lieu of the cess. As lord deputy in 1565, he had tried to relieve the Pale of the onerous burden of victualling by placing soldiers on the frontier, and he had agreed to the victualling contract of Thomas Might in 1568. But in 1575 Sydney recognized the urgency of meeting his financial obligation to the queen and he was determined to produce more revenue in Ireland to prevent the need for subventions from Westminster. His undertaking coincided with bad harvests, an incipient opposition movement within the Pale community, and a growing need for military reinforcement in the face of a threatened invasion. In the end, Sydney found his policy under attack by agents of the Pale who travelled to England. He failed to reach a compromise with the Pale representatives and his government was £9,000 in debt by 1578. While his administration confidently established the infrastructure of English governance, it was soon undone by political crises both in Dublin and at court.[195] Ironically, it was the legal and constitutional questions raised by the agents of the Pale which finally brought Sydney down. While they may have been alienated from government policy, the experienced lawyers, gentry and merchants of the Pale well knew that they could manipulate the levers of the common law and thus provide for their interests a protection which the uncertainties of Irish politics did not afford.

It is remarkable, in some ways, that Sydney should have fallen from power so precipitately. He numbered among his friends and supporters both Leicester and Cecil, now Lord Burghley, as well as the powerful Walsingham. But the groundwork had been prepared for years by his enemies at court, and he was in a real sense the victim of palace intrigue. When he came to Ireland in 1566 he bluntly noted the deterioration of the country under the administration of Sussex and Arnold, a misstep which cost him a great deal. Sussex, Leicester's rival, would not brook such criticism, and in July 1566 Sydney wrote that Sussex was already working against him.[196] Sydney knew also that Ormonde had sought his removal since 1566 and he accused him thus: 'The Earl of Ormond (my professed foe) sometime with clamour, but oftener with whispering, did bitterly backbite me, saying that [his] brethren were driven by my cruelty to rebel. . .'.[197] He

195. For a fuller discussion of the controversy over the cess, see chapter six, below, and Brady, 'Government of Ireland', pp. 319ff.

196. PRO, SP 63/18/133. Perhaps too much has been made of Sydney's challenge of Sussex to a duel in 1566. Neither man had a 'feudal' mentality. Ellis, *Tudor Ireland*, p. 253.

197. *Cal. Carew MSS, 1575–88*, pp. 350–51.

wrote to Leicester that '. . . masters be so factius and servantes so corruptyble in thys cuntry as I assure your lordship I hardly dare confer with any concelor in this matter till I know what the queene will do nor trust my secretary to wryte yt'.[198] By 1570 he had acquired the undesirable reputation at court of a prodigal spender. He had been a popular lord deputy, but during his second administration he forfeited his support in the Pale, and his bargain with the queen to limit spending led to the miscarriage of his entire programme. In 1578 Walsingham wrote to warn him of his imminent recall thus: 'Her Majesty, on knowledge how far you had exceeded the proportion agreed on, was greatly moved. Somwhat she is appeased; notwithstanding I find her disposed to revoke you.'[199] Sydney fretted to Leicester that he had been badly served. He wished for an end to the rumours of his downfall so the government would not be hamstrung by his evident loss of favour.[200] His friends could not save him, for the queen had decided that his administration was too expensive and, perhaps, too provocative as well. The lack of support from the crown brought him down more surely than any combination of his enemies could have done. Perhaps Sydney remembered his earlier complaint to Cecil, penned in 1570:

No servant in Christendom endures greater toil of mind and body than I; as in the proceeding I find little comfort, so in the end I find less thanks. I am forced to borrow, yea almost to beg for my dinner . . . I am hated of all here; of the nobility, for deposing their tyranny; of the merchant, who not receiving his money is become bankrupt; of the gentleman, who cannot get his rents through keeping soldiers; the husbandmen cry out on me and will do no work, for they are never paid for bearing the soldiers; the soldiers have twice refused to go to the field, when I punish one the rest are ready for mutiny.[201]

The reputation of Sir Henry Sydney did not suffer irreparably, however. He was extremely well-connected and the principal advisers of the queen, Cecil and Walsingham, had been his trusted confidants during his long years of service in Ireland and Wales. He had been named to the privy council itself in 1573 and he retained that role in high politics until his death in 1586. His son, Philip, and his many

198. PRO, SP 63/16/90.

199. H.M.C., *De L'Isle and Dudley MSS*, ii, p. 75. Philip Williams counselled Sydney that '. . . because integritie is seldom a sufficient buckler against Irisshe malice, I will undre correction presume to wysshe you to provyde for all objections, but specifically for matters of chardge and expence . . . .' ibid., p. 78. See also pp. 59, 69, 76, 78–79.

200. ibid., p. 62. See also pp. 61, 66.

201. ibid., p. 12.

relations at court were important allies and Sydney emerged from the shadows of royal displeasure to resume his work as lord president in Wales. In that role he was comfortably away from court life but not insulated from criticism. The unfortunate Sydney soon discovered that the stable and well-ordered society he had described in the Welsh marches was now the scene of turbulence and political feuding. There were disorders in Monmouth, riots in Glamorgan, and allegations of corruption by sheriffs. In his absence, Sydney had been charged with responsibility for the discord in Wales and blamed for excessive leniency towards ruffians and recusants. Gerrard had earlier defended his work, but the arrival of the stern bishop of Worcester, John Whitgift, in April 1577 led to new complaints just at the moment when the crisis in Ireland had reached epic proportions. His former ally, Gerrard, now abandoned him on the matter of the cess dispute and his reliable lieutenant, Throckmorton, was tainted by corruption, so Whitgift's charges against Sydney went largely unopposed. Sydney was on the defensive until Whitgift became archbishop of Canterbury in 1583, but the new bishop of Hereford, John Scory, proved equally nettlesome.[202] It is clear, then, that Sydney's government in Ireland closely paralleled the fortunes of his simultaneous administration in Wales. Until 1575, his efforts were well regarded, his lieutenants exceptionally able, and his policies of temperance and forbearance were accepted as practical and realistic. Thereafter, Sydney's deft management of politics and government failed to contend with the increasingly vigorous forces for intolerance and dissension.

Fitzwilliam

The interlude (1571–75) between Sydney's two administrations was filled by the seasoned bureaucrat, Sir William Fitzwilliam. He had extensive experience as lord justice in Ireland, having served on four occasions prior to his appointment to replace Sydney. In fact, he had governed in Sydney's absence for almost a year in 1567–68, but he was not highly regarded as a military leader and Sydney was returned to face the rebellion of Fitzmaurice in 1568. Fitzwilliam was employed again in the spring of 1571 as a temporary replacement while the queen sought a new chief governor. Consequently, his imminent recall was rumoured from the beginning. Unlike his predecessors, he had no opportunity to devise a programme of reform or to bargain with the queen for the terms of his entry into office. It is thus quite understandable that he had no clear mandate which he covenanted to implement. He was advised to retain Sydney's council, so he had no chance to

202. Williams, *Council in Wales*, pp. 252–67, 270–75; Pulman, *Elizabethan privy council*, pp. 38–49.

develop a coterie or following of his own. And he was never allowed to return to England during the four years of his office, so he was unable to negotiate for more men and money based on the new conditions he faced in Ireland. When he was finally made lord deputy in his own right in December 1571, his authority was already diminished and his limited influence was derived largely from the Sussex faction at court.[203]

The youthful Fitzwilliam was a well-placed junior courtier whose grandfather had been sheriff of London and served Wolsey for a time as treasurer and chamberlain. The family estates in Northamptonshire served as a power base and the young William was introduced at the court of Edward VI by Sir John Russell. He must have known there the younger aristocrats Henry Sydney and the future earl of Ormonde, with whom he would serve later on the Irish privy council.[204] In 1554 at the age of twenty-eight Fitzwilliam was chosen to conduct the delicate matter of a special commission to investigate charges of misgovernment against St Leger. He was appointed to the council in Ireland and given the unusual title of deputy chancellor. Within a year he had replaced the respected lord chancellor, Sir Thomas Cusake, who was called to account in London for his alleged misconduct in office. The main function of Fitzwilliam's commission was to inquire into the accounts of the treasury and make accurate reports of his findings to the privy council in Westminster. By the middle of 1556 he had uncovered evidence against the entire administration, including the lord deputy, and accused the government of profligate spending which consumed £66,600 of royal revenue. Fitzwilliam was joined in Ireland by the young earl of Ormonde and he made use of St Leger's critics like Sir George Stanley and Sir John Alen to form an influential opposition to the lord deputy. When St Leger was finally replaced by Sussex, then Lord Fitzwalter, Fitzwilliam remained on the council in Ireland. Though he had earlier relinquished his duties in the chancery to the newly appointed archbishop of Dublin, the erstwhile constable of Athlone continued his notable career in Irish service which culminated in his last lord deputyship in 1594 after twenty-six years in office.[205]

203. Ellis, *Tudor Ireland*, pp. 264–265.
204. *DNB*, s.v. 'Fitzwilliam, Sir William'.
205. Brady, 'Government of Ireland', pp. 104–09. He replaced the earlier commissioners, Valentine Browne and Edmund Rouse, when the latter joined St Leger in his fraud and became the new vice treasurer in Ireland. Fitzwilliam served in Ireland continuously from 1554 to 1575 and again as lord deputy from 1588 to 1594. He has been largely ignored by writers on Tudor Ireland despite his many years of service and his regular correspondence. A biographical essay would be merited.

It is clear that Fitzwilliam formed no independent faction and he quickly sought the favour of the new lord deputy, to whom he was related by marriage. He had married Sydney's sister, Anne, while Sussex had earlier married another sibling, Frances, so the three chief governors of the period had close family connections. Fitzwilliam, however, remained loyal to the Sussex interest and the two men corresponded for many years after the latter had left Ireland in 1564. He relied as well on Ormonde for support in Ireland and at court, so Fitzwilliam's interests were woven into the pattern of Elizabethan politics, though he was not a leading courtier. When Sydney returned to service in England and Wales in 1559, Fitzwilliam became vice treasurer and treasurer at wars along with his other military duties and he retained those responsibilities during his lord deputyship from 1571 to 1573. It was at this time that he began to suffer from the crushing burden of financial debt that he amassed during his years of work at the Irish exchequer. Despite his earlier experience in the unreformed treasury and with full knowledge that the crown wished to govern frugally, Fitzwilliam failed to gain control of receipts and expenses. He allowed unsupervised deputies to do the work of nearly every department and amassed a debt to the crown of £7,000 by 1569. When the Arnold commission arrived in Ireland in 1562 to launch an investigation into Sussex's management of finances, Fitzwilliam declined to cooperate. He sabotaged the interim Arnold government of 1564–65, leading the captains in their refusal to yield up their accounts. Nevertheless, Sydney retained him in office (perhaps as a brother-in-law) during his administration and Fitzwilliam served frequently on commissions and as lord justice in Sydney's absence. His accounts had been audited only once by 1569, but in fairness to Fitzwilliam it should be added that both Sydney and Fyton as vice treasurers also slid helplessly into debt.[206]

In some respects, Fitzwilliam was the ideal choice to replace Sydney in 1571. The queen sought an economical regime and she chose to allow her principal financial officer to combine his roles with that of chief governor. Fitzwilliam was known to be opposed to the bold new schemes of Sydney for lords president and councils in the provinces, and when both Perrot and Fyton left their posts in 1573, they were not replaced. He generally favoured a decentralized form of government which would rely heavily on local lords and Anglo-Irish officials to manage affairs cheaply and efficiently. Elizabeth cut the army down to 1,300 men and relied upon ambitious private schemes in Ulster to sustain the momentum for anglicization of Irish institutions. But Fitzwilliam distrusted the intrepid earl of Essex and

206. Canny, *Elizabethan conquest*, pp. 35, 53; Brady, 'Government of Ireland', pp. 47–50, 160, 165, 170, 180.

feared that his efforts would produce a rebellion for which insufficient troops and resources were available to contain it. Fitzwilliam was without a plan to reform the government and his incessant carping won him no praise at Westminster.[207] The departed Sydney, along with Leicester, criticized his government, and his weakness was illustrated by his failure to address the needs of the Pale. In 1573 Fitzwilliam had reached an accord with the Palesmen to alleviate their burden from cess. He contracted to provide the victualling himself and to withdraw the troops to the frontiers of the Pale if the agents would agree to forgive the large debt already due to them. However, the deputy found that supplies broke down, prices rose, and the delays in receiving English money forced him to borrow heavily. A new crisis arose in 1574 when the victualler defaulted and only a subvention from England saved Fitzwilliam from further embarrassment.[208]

Fitzwilliam was kept at arm's length, in part because he was the target of persistent censure at court, and in part because he had two formidable rivals for power in Ireland. The Ulster plantation schemes of Sir Thomas Smith, which failed disastrously, were succeeded by the enterprise of the earl of Essex. The latter had obtained far greater support from the queen, and her approval of the government in Dublin had diminished proportionately. This diversion of men and resources meant not only a contraction of the available supplies, but also a split authority in Ireland. For Essex's plantation was controlled directly from London, circumventing the Dublin administration and thus weakening it. This was a significant example of the increasing involvement of the English government in Irish affairs. Fitzwilliam therefore lacked a clear warrant at the start of his period in office, and his attenuated authority was diminished still further by the Essex plantation. He responded with a cascade of criticism and protest against the colonization schemes and he was proven tragically correct in his belief that they were intrusive, brutal, expensive and ruthless. The earl of Essex massacred innocent civilians, murdered his rivals and arrested the earl of Kildare for supposed complicity with Gaelic chiefs. The disgraceful conduct of the planters in Ulster discredited their future projects for confiscation and settlement as folly, and worse. It is significant that Sydney did nothing to further these plans when he returned as lord deputy in 1575.[209]

207. Canny, *Elizabethan conquest*, pp. 87, 115; Brady, 'Government of Ireland', pp. 219–22.

208. Brady, 'Government of Ireland', pp. 340–41. The agents of the Pale threatened to go to England with their protest in 1574.

209. Brady, 'Government of Ireland', pp. 64, 170, 219; Ellis, *Tudor Ireland*, pp. 266–69. Canny argues that Fitzwilliam advocated the colonialist theme of military conquest prior to acculturation of the Irish, but his virulent opposition to Essex's

Although Fitzwilliam was theoretically freed by the arrangement with Essex to attend to other problems, he badly neglected the provincial government. He was not a military man and he showed no inclination to pursue the active policies of his predecessors in taking the field every year. As a result, the English presence in the provinces declined, and Sydney's programme of extending judicial reform beyond the Pale was allowed to lapse. The lords president in Munster and Connacht departed in 1573, so there were no strong figures there to support the government and to control disorder. In November 1573 the lord deputy complained to Cecil that he lacked 'Marciall Counsellors'. The escape of Desmond from his detention in Dublin was a great humiliation for Fitzwilliam, because he was unable to convince any of his colleagues on the council to go to Munster and apprehend him.[210] He was gravely concerned when Ormonde was recalled to the court in 1571 and only when the earl returned in 1574 could Fitzwilliam move into Munster successfully and demand the submission of Desmond. When Rory Oge O'More rebelled in 1573, Fitzwilliam was again without adequate resources and lamely tried to negotiate with him.[211]

His efforts to reform the central government were similarly ineffective. He held the posts of vice treasurer and chief governor simultaneously until 1573, despite entreaties to be relieved of his fiscal duties. He could not convince Agarde to take the vice treasurership and ultimately the place was given to his enemy, Sir Edward Fyton, surely a mark of Fitzwilliam's lack of influence at court. The council had been badly split in 1572 and 1573 by the disputes between Fyton and Fitzwilliam when the former was lord president of the council in Connacht, as we have seen. When these scars on the body politic were nearly healed, the death of Lord Chancellor Weston threw open the office of lord keeper and both White and Loftus fought bitterly over it. No serious judicial reform could be achieved without a committed lord chancellor to guide it, so little was accomplished in the courts despite the fact that the new court of castle chamber finally received the long-awaited instructions and rules of procedure in 1571. The abysmal state of conciliar record-keeping during this period is also testimony to the ineffectiveness of Fitzwilliam, since the council book ended with the departure of Sydney. Fitzwilliam sought his recall from the moment he was named to office, noting that he was wholly unfit to serve as chief governor.[212] As the years went by, this became

scheme calls this hypothesis into question. See *Elizabethan conquest*, pp. 87, 115, 128.

210. PRO, SP 63/42/184–86.
211. Ellis, *Tudor Ireland*, pp. 264–66.
212. PRO, SP 63/36/10–11. As early as August 1571 he appealed to the queen that he was unfit for the office. SP 63/33/72–72v. In 1572 he told Cecil that he

abundantly clear. Both Essex and Fitzwilliam fell from power at the same time, helped along by the acrimonious exchanges between themselves.

In 1574 four leading English councillors wrote privately to Fitzwilliam that his government was 'misliked' by the queen. They cited the refusal of Desmond to submit; the rebellion of the O'Mores and O'Connors; the deterioration of the English presence in Munster; the failure of the Essex enterprise in Ulster; and the expenditure of prodigious sums from England.[213] It was impossible to believe that Fitzwilliam could last as chief governor, but he was not replaced until the following year. He was an able bureaucrat, but not a leader. He had no policy because he earnestly sought his removal from office and expected his superiors to understand that this was no empty request. He has been pitied because the queen denied him adequate support, but it is doubtful whether more ample spending would have produced an effective administration under his leadership. In contrast to his predecessors, Fitzwilliam was reluctant to move forward with the general restructuring of Irish government which we have termed 'anglicization'. His government, then, represents a hiatus in the implementation of Elizabethan rule throughout Ireland, and it is significant that it was no more peaceable, or less turbulent, than other regimes in this period.[214] When Fitzwilliam was returned at the head of another caretaker government in 1588, he was sixty-two years of age. Once again, he proved to be inactive and unimaginative in the face of an impending crisis and much that was undertaken in the period was done in spite of him. By the time he was replaced in 1594, the Tyrone rebellion was already under way.[215]

Kildare

While the lords deputy gave each administration a certain individual countenance, it is also important to recognize the factors tending to continuity and stability. Many of the leading councillors served in their respective roles throughout the first two decades of Elizabeth's reign, having entered the government along with Sussex in 1556, or

feared a foreign invasion and lamented the state of Ireland. This was a constant refrain during his entire administration.

213. PRO, SP 63/45/112. The councillors were the Irish experts, Cecil, Sussex, Leicester and Walsingham.

214. Fitzwilliam was neither 'amply supplied with money' nor did he advocate military conquest, so he must be seen as an exception to the supposed Elizabethan policy of paying for 'quick results' led by 'powerful vested interests'. This model of a systematic and disciplined approach to governing Ireland must be viewed with suspicion in any case. See Ellis, *Tudor Ireland*, pp. 245–46.

215. ibid., pp. 294–97.

even before. They contributed much to the corporate identity of the council in Ireland and they provided a reliable core of experienced opinion. They occasionally offered passive resistance to some of the bolder initiatives of the new viceroys, yet their longevity in office bespeaks a willingness to compromise, to seek personal advantage by conforming to the will of the crown, and to accept the basic outlines of the policy of anglicization. In this respect, the political career of the eleventh earl of Kildare has great interest. Among the Anglo-Irish peers, he was the most constant in attendance at the council board and he was used by the council on embassies and military expeditions. His unquestioned pre-eminence as the greatest landholder and the most important personage in the Pale gave him tremendous potential power. Yet, because of the political legacy which he inherited and the real, or imagined, frustration caused by his exclusion from high office, the earl was mistrusted. His service to the crown was expected, and accepted with good will, but his usefulness was always tainted by the suspicion that he sought more than the queen could give.

This result was not wholly unanticipated, considering the remarkable events of his youth. At the age of nine his father was declared a traitor and his half-brother led the Kildare rebellion against Tudor rule in Ireland. When his five uncles were captured along with the tenth earl and sent to England in 1535, the young Gerald was removed from the Pale to Thomond, and finally to distant Donegal, from which he escaped to France in 1540. He was regarded by Francis I as a pawn to use against Henry VIII in Ireland, but he was soon sent to Brussels. From there he was summoned by his relative, Cardinal Pole, to Italy. For several years he was educated at the courts of Verona, Mantua and Florence, and he became master of the horse to Cosimo di Medici.[216] After eight years abroad, at the age of twenty-three, Gerald returned to England. His mother was Elizabeth, daughter of Thomas Grey, marquis of Dorset, and he was thus related to Lord Leonard Grey, the lord deputy who had been charged with apprehending him. At the court of Edward VI he met and married Mabel, the daughter of Sir Anthony Browne.[217] He was thus half-English and, with his English wife and his continental education, he was not an entirely typical Irish peer. Through his father-in-law he obtained

216. B. Fitzgerald, *The Geraldines: an experiment in Irish government, 1169–1601* (London, 1951), pp. 241–45. See also Rev. A. Valkenburg, 'Gerald, eleventh earl of Kildare (1525–1585): a study in diplomacy', *Kildare Arch Soc Jn*, xiv (1966), 293–315. These two pieces are among the small number of works on Kildare and both are largely impressionistic. Fitzgerald, in particular, was plainly disappointed that Kildare was not more openly rebellious and 'patriotic'. See also Lennon, *Richard Stanihurst*, pp. 35–36.

217. *DNB*, s.v. 'Fitzgerald, Gerald, eleventh earl of Kildare'; G.E.C., *Peerage*, s.v. 'Kildare, eleventh earl, Gerald (Fitzgerald)'; Ellis, *Tudor Ireland*, pp. 5–6, 130.

preferment and became a knight of the garter. After his important service to Mary during Wyatt's rebellion he was restored to the earldom and he finally returned to Ireland in November 1554.

The Pale had presumably evolved in new directions during the absence, for nearly two decades, of its leading nobleman. Yet the earl of Kildare was ambitious to retrieve his influence in the region and he was soon accepted in his traditional role as defender of the Pale's interests. As a stabilizing influence, he was uniquely positioned to bridge the cultural divisions in Ireland. He was part-English and was well-connected at court; he was knowledgeable about European affairs, including the new renaisssance diplomacy; and he spoke Irish and used Irish customs such as coyne and livery. It is no wonder that questions have been raised about his allegiance, but the earl may well represent a type of Anglo-Irish peer whose position was both threatened by crown policies and dependent on royal support. As the acknowledged leader of the Geraldine clan, he was powerful in the Pale and beyond it. He was thus relied upon by successive governments to control the Gaelic septs living in the midland counties and to defend the Pale against rebellious or marauding Gaelic chiefs who preyed upon vulnerable settlements. Nevertheless, he accepted a subordinate role in Irish policy-making. He did little if anything to seek the deputyship, but even his largely dormant influence was treated with suspicion by the merchants and gentry who had no wish to return to the social tyranny of the old Geraldine patriarchy.[218]

In 1556 the earl of Kildare was made a member of the council in Ireland during Sussex's first administration. He was born in the same year as the lord deputy and the two men soon became rivals. Yet Kildare was an industrious councillor who came frequently to meetings and he was sent on many commissions in the Pale. For example, he was employed to hear cases in the five counties beyond the immediate jurisdiction of the royal courts in 1558.[219] His role as emissary for the government to the Irish chiefs was perhaps his most important service to the crown. He undertook several embassies to Shane O'Neill from 1560 to 1562 and he conducted the crafty rebel to England in the latter year, a ploy which led to the humiliation of Sussex.[220] He served as a mediator to the O'Mores and other insurgents, and he was also used to guard the Pale in the absence of the lord deputy. In 1574, for example, the council made a proclamation for the defence of the Pale, naming Archbishop Loftus and Kildare as governors there, and leaving the general hosting in the command of the earl. He was

218. N. Canny, *Formation of the Old English élite in Ireland* (Dublin, 1975), pp. 6–10.
219. *P.R.I. rep. D.K. 9*, p. 81, no. 214.
220. *Cal. S.P. Ire., 1509–73*, pp. 169, 179, 183.

given free rein to decide the deployment of troops and allowed to levy more support if he needed it.[221] His significance on the council lay primarily in his representation of the interests of the Pale. In that regard, he may be seen as a characteristic Anglo-Irish peer, a feudal magnate with great estates and personal power yet willing to work with the new English, to conform to the policies of a new age. Canny has noted that the lesser peers whose estates were to be found nearer the coast were even more inclined to follow the lead of the government.[222]

Kildare has been called a 'trimmer', and undoubtedly he harboured some misgivings about the course he took. But it was the only one open to him. Unlike Desmond or O'Neill, he could not withdraw to the wilds of Munster or Ulster when he fell foul of the government. And his vulnerability was often proved. In this respect, he served as an example to the other noblemen of the Pale, those who attended the grand council meetings and observed, perhaps uncomfortably, the gradual expansion of English control. On the council, Kildare's loyalty was questioned by his colleagues and to some extent he earned their mistrust. As early as 1561 he was working against Sussex in England, bargaining for a more conciliatory policy towards O'Neill. He encouraged the law students of the inns of court to write their critical book against Sussex, and earlier, in 1560, he was upbraided for his 'disloyal' speeches in the parliament.[223] Sussex regarded Kildare as the primary threat to English rule as early as 1560, but the Geraldine leader was on better terms with Sydney, who managed the final restoration of his estates in 1569.[224] He was suspected of dealing with James Fitzmaurice in 1569, and in 1575 he was incarcerated and sent to England on charges of treasonable relations with the rebel Rory Oge O'More. At this time, Kildare was accused of plotting to kidnap the lord deputy so that he could force the queen to let him govern. Many of the charges were similarly specious. Kildare was arrested in May, and in June was examined closely by Knollys, Walsingham and

221. Bodl, Carte MS 56, ff. 50–51v. In 1579 he served on a commission to govern the Pale and Ulster in the absence of the lord deputy. *P.R.I. rep. D.K. 13*, pp. 124–25, no. 3601.

222. Canny, *Old English élite*, pp. 9–10. Ormonde, too, constituted a special case, and his loyalty to his own interests was just as strong as his fidelity to the crown. See C. Brady, 'Thomas Butler, earl of Ormond (1531–1614) and reform in Tudor Ireland', in C. Brady, ed., *Worsted in the game: losers in Irish history* (Dublin, 1989), 52–57.

223. PRO, SP 63/2/15; G.E.C., *Peerage*, s.v. 'Kildare, eleventh earl'. Kildare complained that he was excluded from influence in Leix and Offaly, arguing that his own government of the midlands would be cheaper for the queen and less belligerent toward the Gaelic Irish. However, the Geraldine interest did not always conform to that of the Pale generally and Kildare served his own needs before those of the Palesmen. See Canny, *Elizabethan conquest*, pp. 38–39.

224. Brady, 'Government of Ireland', pp. 113–21, 141–43.

Bromley in London.[225] After three years' detention, he returned to Ireland in April 1578 and led the forces of the Pale during the early stages of the Munster rebellion. But once again he was tainted with suspicion of treason, and in 1580 he was detained a second time.[226] In the last ten years of his life he spent nearly eight years in custody. He was nevertheless an effective councillor and he proved useful to the government on many occasions, though no one ever forgot his origins and he was not careful enough to avoid provocative dealings with the Irish chiefs. While he served on the council he was probably the most influential spokesman for the concerns of the Pale and for a conciliatory policy toward the Irish.

Loftus

Along with lay peers of the realm, the leading Elizabethan bishops in Ireland were senior members of the council. However, unlike the nobles who were uniformly Anglo-Irish and Catholic, the episcopal councillors of the period varied widely in religion, policy, background and temperament. In general, there were twice as many ecclesiastical councillors as there were noblemen, and the former were among the most consistent in their attendance at council meetings. This may be explained, in part, by the fact that they were resident in Dublin and their churches were often used as the venues for the executive board. Substantial differences of opinion divided the Marian bishops, and the act of supremacy in 1560 which restored the Anglican settlement in Ireland did nothing to repair the rent fabric of eccesiastical policy. Nor was there a single approach to reform that characterized the Elizabethan episcopate in Ireland. As we have seen, the Anglo-Irish bishop of Meath, Hugh Brady, was a consistent voice for moderation. He was joined by Thomas Lancaster, archbishop of Armagh, and Dr Robert Weston, the seasoned English churchman who was sent in 1567 to be the new lord chancellor.[227] On the other hand, the most notable ecclesiastical figure of Elizabeth's reign was certainly the ambitious archbishop of Dublin, Adam Loftus, who represented the aggressive policy of strict enforcement of the new religion. He was a consistent advocate of the legal imposition of Anglican religious practices throughout Ireland, and he held high office in the Dublin administration from 1562 until his death in 1605. Yet he was profoundly

---

225. *Cal. S.P. Ire., 1574–85*, pp. 53–54, 64, 69. At this time his son, Lord Garret, was brought to London by Stanihurst to complete his education. Lennon, *Richard Stanihurst*, p. 38.

226. *Cal. S.P. Ire., 1574–85*, pp. 265, 276, 284, 290, 295, 297.

227. Walshe, 'Elizabethan settlement', pp. 352–76; B. Bradshaw, 'Sword, word and strategy in the reformation in Ireland', *Hist Jn*, xxi (1978), 480–81.

unsuccessful in his efforts to impose new doctrine and by the 1590s a significant indigenous opposition to Anglicanism had emerged.

Adam Loftus was educated at Trinity College, Cambridge and in 1556 he obtained a rectory in Norfolk. He went to Ireland as chaplain to Sussex in 1560, and in the following year he was nominated to the vacant see of Armagh. Both the town and the bishopric were in the hands of Shane O'Neill, so it was impossible to proceed to the election in the normal way. Loftus went to England in 1562 and obtained the rights to the temporalities of the office. In March 1563, when he was apparently just thirty years old, Loftus was consecrated archbishop of Armagh and primate of all Ireland. However, this title left him with little real power and a revenue of only £20 a year. He resided in Dublin, rarely visited his diocese, and pressed for a more profitable living in England.[228] One year later the establishment of a new court of high commission in Ireland gave Loftus the unusual opportunity to advance the tenets of the reformation in Ireland. He directed this organ of the central government for forty years and gradually came to dominate it.

In 1568 the new ecclesiastical court, with Loftus at its head, sought a renewal of its patent. Several of the councillors were members, but a large number of non-councillors were also included. Twenty-eight men were named and the nucleus of the commission was ten notables, of whom one was always to sit on the commission. The fixed core of the court included: Loftus, archbishop of Dublin since 1566; Weston, the lord chancellor; Lancaster, archbishop of Armagh; Brady, bishop of Meath; the bishop of Kildare; Fitzwilliam; Draycott, master of the rolls; Francis Agarde; James Weston; and Sydney. Eight of these ten were on the council, and at least four of them consistently preferred moderation in religious policy.[229] The mandate of the court was broad, including the prosecution of masterless men and even simple assaults. But the effectiveness of the new tribunal has been widely questioned and it was certainly not a powerful force for the reform of the church. The corruption of the Irish clergy was compounded by the poverty of their livings, so the effect of rampant simony, pluralism, absenteeism, lay patronage and other abuses was to permit a substantial erosion of corporate authority over the parishes.[230] A change

228. *DNB*, s.v. 'Loftus, Adam'. When he campaigned to become archbishop of Dublin in 1566 he also spent nearly a year at Cambridge and earned his D.D. degree prior to returning to Ireland. In 1567 he nominated a fellow Puritan, the scholarly firebrand Thomas Cartwright, to be the new archbishop of Armagh. *Cal. S.P. Ire., 1509–73*, p. 351.

229. PRO, SP 63/25/115–16. The moderates: Weston (the lord chancellor), Lancaster, Brady, Sydney.

230. A. Ford, *The Protestant reformation in Ireland, 1590–1642* (Frankfurt, 1985), pp. 19–21; A. Ford, 'The Protestant reformation in Ireland' in Brady & Gillespie, ed., *Natives and newcomers*, pp. 52–55.

in religious dogma was perhaps not the most relevant or timely measure for the Irish church of the mid-sixteenth century.

Loftus' policy of strenuous enforcement of church doctrine and law was covertly resisted by most of the nobles and gentry in the Pale, and in associated contexts he would complain to the queen and to Sydney that he could get no assistance from local juries, who were all connected with the leading families. What is more, his own colleagues on the high commission court were alienated by his uncompromising position and he soon came into direct conflict with Bishop Brady of Meath, essentially a moderate in dealings with the laity, over the fining and imprisonment of recusants.[231] Brady's pastoral care in Meath had been complicated by the interventions of the former Marian bishop, William Walsh, until the latter was proceeded against by the court of high commission in 1565 and incarcerated for seven years. Bishop Brady also advanced the cause of a new Irish university to be based in Dublin at the deanery of St Patrick's. Loftus had agreed to support this plan but in 1565 he betrayed the trust of Brady by obtaining the deanery for himself. While this peremptory decision has been seen as evidence of his hostility to policies of lenity and restraint, it is equally clear that Loftus was seeking to advance his own cause in the church. Since he subsequently provided his son-in-law with the deanery of St Patrick's, it can be argued that Loftus was simply using the instrument of patronage politics here rather than contending against the education of the Irish clergy. Brady's proposal for advanced theological training in Ireland would, if implemented, have been at the expense of his rival, after all. When the two men campaigned earnestly for the vacant see of Dublin in 1566, Loftus engaged in a vicious calumny againt his fellow bishop and used his new alliance with the Leicester faction to advance his cause.[232] Though Loftus was to be successful it should be noted that a moderate course was chosen by the government in the following year when Weston was made lord chancellor to balance the partisan views of Loftus. Thus the policy of the court of high commission was not consistently arbitrary or autocratic. While Loftus led the investigation and incrimination of the papal appointees Richard Creagh and David Wolfe in 1567, most of the fines and sentences imposed by the court were never carried out.[233]

---

231. *Cal. S.P. Ire., 1509–73*, p. 261; Walshe, 'Elizabethan settlement', 367; Bradshaw, 'Sword, word and strategy', 480–83, 499–501.

232. Walshe, 'Elizabethan settlement', 364–69. Loftus reluctantly gave up the deanery of St Patrick's to Weston in 1567.

233. Ellis, *Tudor Ireland*, pp. 216–21. It was notorious that many nobles and gentry of the Pale often kept Catholic priests as chaplains, but when Loftus imposed a huge fine on the leading Palesmen in 1591 to require their attendance at his sermons, Elizabeth restrained his proselytizing zeal.

The work of Adam Loftus has been characterized as emblematic of the coercive strategy of conquest and colonization. He was unquestionably a difficult colleague.[234] Apparently not content with his standing as the leading churchman in Ireland, he actively sought further preferment as lord chancellor. In 1570 he mentioned an interest in the post, noting that Weston was very sick and commenting obliquely that, 'The new Chancellor should neither be a dissembling Papist, nor a cold or carnal Protestant'.[235] He became lord keeper in 1573 on the death of Weston and immediately engaged in a struggle with Nicholas White, the master of the rolls, for the rights to the office.[236] In the same year his house in Co. Dublin was attacked and his nephew was killed. He wrote to Sydney that only force would compel obedience and he urged prompt action before conditions in Ireland deteriorated beyond recall.[237] In the less familiar role of arbitrator, Loftus mediated the dispute between Essex and Fitzwilliam in 1575, obtaining the lord deputy's consent to pay Essex's soldiers without a special warrant from the queen.[238] Two years later, Loftus challenged the jurisdiction of the newly created commission of faculties, designed to confer licences, dispensations and grants in the Irish church.[239] He also quarrelled with Sydney over the imposition of religious conformity, and he led conciliar opposition to Perrot in the 1580s. He finally obtained the coveted lord chancellorship in 1581 and he served as lord justice three times thereafter. In 1590 he accused Sir Lucas Dillon, the stalwart defender of English interests in the Pale, of harbouring Catholic enthusiasms. When Loftus became the first provost of Trinity College, Dublin in 1592, his leadership of the institution created an English enclave rather than an educational opportunity for the training of Irish clergy. At the end of his life he encouraged James I to expel Catholic priests and to enforce strictly the Anglican settlement in Ireland, but the privy council refused to follow such a disruptive course and Loftus died in 1605 with little of his programme in effect.[240] He was estranged from many of his fellow councillors and

234. Bradshaw, 'Sword, word and strategy', 480–83, 499–501.

235. *Cal. S.P. Ire., 1509–73*, p. 432.

236. *P.R.I. rep. D.K. 12*, p. 102, no. 2281. The praise for Loftus' judicial leadership throughout the Elizabethan period has, in effect, telescoped the reign since he possessed much more influence in the law after he became lord chancellor in 1581. See Ball, *Judges*, i, 131.

237. *Cal. S.P. Ire., 1509–73*, p. 503.

238. PRO, SP 63/50/164; *Cal. S.P. Ire., 1574–85*, p. 60.

239. BL, Harl. MS 35, ff. 253–58; BL, Cott. MS Titus B XIII, ff. 263–70v; *Cal. pat. rolls Ire., Eliz*, pp. 24–25; PRO, SP 63/65/150–50v.

240. Ford, 'Protestant reformation', pp. 58–59; Ellis, *Tudor Ireland*, p. 287; Walshe, 'Elizabethan settlement', 374–75. Despite his political isolation in various

spent his career in chronic bitterness, like a weakly belching volcano in the archipelago of competing interests in Irish government.

His influence was limited for many reasons. The Anglo-Irish Protestant councillors such as Thomas Cusake, Nicholas White, Lucas Dillon and Robert Dillon were anchored in the local community and pleaded for tolerance and persuasion. As for the bishops, they were heavily engaged in local administration, with little time to spare for the enforcement of religious conformity: they were placed on commissions of the peace and involved in provincial councils and courts of law. What is more, local officials on whom the policies of the government primarily depended were disinclined to offer their unqualified support to arbitrary breaches of public trust (for so it must have seemed to them). When Loftus himself became lord keeper and later lord chancellor, his career was divided between matters spiritual and temporal after 1573. And the Irish church was highly idiosyncratic. The Gaelic areas were so anomalous that neither Anglican nor Catholic doctrine was particularly effective, most of the local clergy were poorly educated, and the incidence of reform varied in each town and province.[241] For this reason, it is difficult to accept the 'extensive polarization' of the Elizabethan church as a simple contest between two different strategies for reform.[242] Not only was there genuine reluctance to support militant Protestantism on the council in Ireland, but the queen's advisers in Westminster were unwilling to commit adequate resources to the extensive reform of the Irish church. The anglicization of Irish social and political institutions was an inherently moderate policy, and the gradual restructuring of Irish government and society would have to precede the imposition of Protestant doctrine. In sum, the enforcement of the reformation in Ireland had made very little headway prior to 1580, and the resistance to Anglican reforms was still at the time largely inchoate.[243]

> governments, Loftus managed to enrich himself with substantial landholdings near Dublin. He built an imposing castle in 1590, perhaps to house his prodigious family of twenty children, and he provided for their respective futures through manipulation of the patronage system.

241. Ellis, *Tudor Ireland*, p. 216; Ford, 'Protestant reformation', 50–55; N. Canny, 'Why the reformation failed in Ireland: une question mal posée', *Jn Eccles Hist*, xxx (1979), 429–32.

242. Bradshaw, 'Sword, word and strategy', 480. The persistently Manichean tone of this article and the inflammatory language (an 'apartheid constitution in law and practice') are singularly unfortunate lapses in an otherwise sensible argument. The debate over persuasion versus coercion is thoughtfully stated.

243. For the fusion of secular and religious policies in a comprehensive programme for anglicization in Ireland, see Ford, *Protestant reformation*, p. 13; C. Lennon, 'The counter-reformation' in Brady & Gillespie, ed., *Natives and newcomers*, p. 80; K. Bottigheimer, 'The failure of the reformation in Ireland: une question bien posée', *Jn Eccles Hist*, xxxvi (1985), 207. Walshe has argued that the departure

Dillon

The bishops and the peers occupied the chief places in the council, but the largest number of councillors were civil officials. Beneath the superstructure of the forum lay this second rank of members who atttended regularly, acted on commissions, heard cases and formed the most active stratum of the council. These judges and bureaucrats were characterized by longevity in office, a legal education, and consistent loyalty to the crown. Perhaps the best representative of this type of councillor was Sir Lucas Dillon, chief baron of the exchequer from 1570 to 1593. A member of the distinguished legal family of Dillons (see above), Sir Lucas entered the Middle Temple in 1551 and by 1565 he had become the queen's solicitor general. In the following year he was named attorney general. Even before he came on the council, Dillon was used on conciliar commissions and was thus involved in the transaction of the business of that body. In 1570, for example, he was sent to explain to the queen the means to be used to erect a university in Dublin.[244] In 1566 he was employed on a commission to hear civil causes in Kilkenny, and four years later he was sent on a deputation to Viscount Mountgarret by the council.[245] Sydney nominated him to be chief baron in 1570, and the queen sent him back from England with her letters and an instruction that he be preferred to the office.[246]

Dillon was a remarkable example of the active privy councillor. Talented, experienced, loyal and energetic, he combined all the best attributes of the council member and he was free of the infirmities of old age. He was the ablest of the Anglo-Irish judges, and he was frequently employed as an itinerant councillor.[247] He was reliable and diligent, yet he was also capable of independence in thought and action. His letters to Cecil indicated a practical turn of mind and he certainly personified the judges and lawyers to whom Colum Kenny refers as the 'willing instruments of administrative policy in Ireland'.[248] Writing to Cecil in June 1570, for example, he agreed with the

of Sydney and the retreat from a policy-making role by Cecil after 1577 allowed more militant advisers to dominate. 'Elizabethan settlement', 373.

244. RIA, MS 24 F 17, f. 334v. In 1567 he carried letters to the queen and was charged with explaining council actions to her. *Sidney S.P.*, p. 83.

245. RIA, MS 24 F 17, ff. 216v, 333.

246. *Sidney S.P.*, pp. 124–25; PRO, SP 63/30/115v. The chief baron earned a salary of £67 10s. and in this respect he was the equal of the chief justice of common pleas. BL, Add. MS 4,767, ff. 112–14.

247. Dillon received the commendation of Sydney and the English privy council for his service in the field with the lord deputy in 1576. *Cal. Carew MSS, 1575–88*, pp. 37, 43.

248. Kenny, 'Exclusion of Catholics', 338.

4 Photograph of the tomb of Sir Lucas Dillon (d. 1593) at Newtown Trim, Co. Meath. Dillon was the scion of a great political family who married well and became chief baron of the exchequer. He was a loyal follower of crown policy and a competent judge. The tomb is decorated with elaborate bas-reliefs containing the armorial bearings of the Dillon family and of the Bathe and Barnewall families to which Sir Lucas was linked by marriage. The two recumbent figures atop the tomb are of Sir Lucas and his first wife, Jane Bathe, daughter of his predecessor as chief baron of the exchequer.

principal secretary '. . .that it stode better with good polecy to procede by degrees (as wherein stode safetie) then to take in hande so moche as we should not be hable to welde . . .'.[249] Dillon was promoted by Sydney in 1565 and he may be regarded as part of the Leicester faction along with the recently reappointed Sir Thomas Cusake. His support for the policy of moderation in both religion and politics would suggest that he was part of a 'reforming milieu' which did not, in fact, simply disappear in this period. It is possible to see him as performing a role similar to that which Cusake filled for St Leger prior to 1556, and he was a useful counterpoint to the aggressive ambitions of Archbishop Loftus. While some have argued that Dillon was merely a sycophant, others have claimed that his moderate policy threatened to isolate him from both the Palesmen and the new English in the government.[250] However, it is unlikely that loyalty to the crown meant social and political ostracism in this period, since most of the Anglo-Irish nobles and gentry practised a kind of covert Catholicism while maintaining their support for the anglicization of the realm.[251] Kenny has argued that religious changes were largely accepted by the Irish legal profession since they benefited directly from the dispersal of monastic properties and they would profit from the expanded jurisdiction of the common law.[252]

The most significant contribution made by Sir Lucas Dillon was by his display of competence on the judicial bench where he served as chief baron of the exchequer from 1570 to 1593. In 1572 Fitzwilliam recommended him to replace his father, then chief justice of common pleas, observing that he would be an industrious and useful chief magistrate.[253] In 1576 Sydney censured both chief justices and sought English replacements for them, noting that 'There is none here so meet for those places as is to be wished, Sir Lucas Dillon excepted, who is Chief Baron'.[254] And Lord Chancellor Gerrard accorded him a singular compliment, saying that he was the most honest and most enterprising judge among the generally incompetent Irish judiciary![255] Dillon was crucially involved in Sydney's policy of extending the jurisdiction of the common law. He went with

249. PRO, SP 63/30/130. He informed Cecil that 'I have made me a patent of thoffice of chiefe baron and placed me in Councell here as my predecessor was'.

250. Brady, 'Government of Ireland', pp. 37, 174.

251. Lennon, 'Counter-reformation', p. 80; Ellis, *Tudor Ireland*, p. 218.

252. Kenny, 'Exclusion of Catholics', 337.

253. PRO, SP 63/53/53.

254. *Cal. Carew MSS, 1575–88*, p. 52. Sydney knighted Dillon for his service to the crown in 1575. *DNB, supplement*, s.v. 'Dillon, Sir Lucas'.

255. LPL, Carew MS 628, f. 312.

the lord deputy on numerous expeditions and served on the small caucus of councillors who tried cases in town and camp while outside
the Pale. In 1578, for example, when Sydney was concerned to apprehend and punish those who had maintained Rory Oge O'More, he
noted that 'On Christmas eve I came to Kilkenny, Sir Lucas Dillon
only accompanying me thither'.[256] The chief baron manifested his
remarkable loyalty even during the bitter disputes over the cess. In
1577 Dillon acted with Lord Chancellor Gerrard to investigate, abridge
and interpret the statutes regarding purveyance for the government,
despite his many connections in the Pale.[257] During the 1580s he
opposed Loftus and supported the beleaguered Lord Deputy Perrot,
a risky endeavour which earned him the enmity of the archbishop. It
was Loftus who, in 1590, revealed the covert Catholicism of the steadfast chief baron to Burghley.[258] In the event, this did nothing to alter
his place in the Dublin administration or his reputation for constancy
as a stalwart supporter of anglicization. Sir Lucas served as lord justice in 1584. He finally died in office in 1593 and was buried at the
family estate in Newtown, outside Trim. Sir Lucas' fine renaissance
tomb may still be seen.[259]

Agarde

While the civil officials composed the bulk of the active membership,
military councillors were nearly equal in number. The council needed
competent military opinion and nearly one fourth (nine of forty-four)
of the councillors were professional soldiers. However, most of these
men were not particularly active due to their obligations in the garrisons, so the council was heavily dependent on a few veteran captains,
whose advice became correspondingly weighty. After the dismissal of
Sir George Stanley, the marshal under Sussex, and the disgrace of
Jacques Wingfield as master of the ordnance, only Francis Agarde
was consistently involved in conciliar deliberations. Yet he was also the

256. *Cal. Carew MSS, 1575–88*, p. 126. In 1580 Waterhouse commended him in a
   letter to Walsingham, noting that he had served with the lord justice during the
   entire expedition into Munster. PRO, SP 63/72/146v.

257. *Cal. Carew MSS, 1575–88*, p. 66.

258. Walshe, 'Elizabethan settlement', 374–75. Loftus had earlier condemned Dillon
   as corrupt when he was a candidate to be named chief justice in 1582, and in
   1583 a letter from an Irish exile made the claim that Dillon kept a Catholic
   priest named Charles and that he was 'catholick at hart' despite his pretensions
   to Anglicanism. It was during the 1580s when Irish Catholics at the inns of
   court were subjected, for the first time, to religious examinations and occasional harassment. C. Kenny, *King's Inns and the kingdom of Ireland* (Dublin,
   1992), pp. 51–53.

259. *DNB, supplement*, s.v. 'Dillon, Sir Lucas'; Ball, *Judges*, i, 211–13; J. Jocelyn, 'The
   renaissance tombs at Lusk and Newtown Trim', *RSAI Jn*, ciii (1973), 153–66.

5 Photograph of the monument to Francis Agarde (d. 1577) in the south
transept of Christ Church cathedral, Dublin. Agarde was a veteran of the Irish
military establishment, one who became a trusted commissioner for the lord deputy
and council. He was admitted to membership of the council in Ireland in 1553,
his service culminating as chief commissioner in Munster, an office which he
held 1574–75. The monument was erected in the renaissance style by Captain
Henry Harrington, Agarde's son-in-law. The two panels show a kneeling Agarde
with his wife and their six children.

There are inscriptions under both panels of the Agarde monument. That under the left-hand panel is in Latin, and reads:

Hic situs est Franciscus Agarde armiger, quondam
cohortis equitum in Scotia sub domino Seimor de Sudley
Angliae Admirallio praefectus, postea comitatui Wexfordiae
praepositus. In bello contra O Nealum centu equitum
ductor, provinciae Momoniae commissarius primarius,
regionum O Birne & O Tolo seneschalius, regni Hiber-
nici per annos xxvi (regnantibus Maria & Elizabetha)
consiliarius prudentissimus. obiit xi Octobris 1577
cum Henricus Sidneius amicus eius longe,
honoratissimus iam secundo esset Hiberniae
priorex; unaq sepelitur uxor eius charis
sima Iacoba de la Brett cum Thoma filiolo.

A rendering into English is this:

Here lies Francis Agard, gentleman, formerly
cavalry officer in Scotland under Lord Seymour de Sudley,
admiral of England, afterwards appointed prefect (seneschal) of Co.
    Wexford.
In the war against O'Neill a leader of one hundred cavalry,
chief commissioner for the province of Munster,
seneschal of the lands of the O'Byrnes and O'Tooles.
A very sagacious councillor of the kingdom of Ireland for twenty-six
    years
in the reigns of Mary and Elizabeth. He died 11th October 1577
when his long-time friend, the honorable Henry Sidney, was
viceroy of Ireland for the second time. Together with him is interred
his very dear wife, Jacoba de la Brett, with their infant son, Thomas.

The inscription under the right-hand panel is in English:

Here lyeth entombed Ladye Cecilie Harrington, daughter and coheyre
    of
Francis Agard, Esq. Most deare and lovinge wife of Sir Henry
    Harrington,
Knight, with whom she had lyved seven years most virtuously and had
brought forth two sonnes James and John. She ended this lyfe the
8th of September in the year 1584. For whose memorial and her father's
Syr Henry Harrington, Knight, her loving husband and his successor in
office erected this monument at his owne charge.

most reliable councillor of the entire period, attending more meetings than anyone else.[260] Agarde was another of the uniquely able admin- istrators of the mid-Tudor period, an English captain whose father had been notorious for his malfeasance as the deputy to Vice Treasurer William Brabazon in St Leger's government. Thomas Agarde had come to Ireland as part of a commission of inquiry sent by Cromwell in 1535. He quickly attached himself to Brabazon and the lord deputy, and reaped large profits from undervaluing crown estates. St Leger used him often on embassies to England and he was ultimately made treasurer of the mint in Dublin. Although he died before 1556, Thomas Agarde surely did what he could to pave the way for his soldier son's subsequent career in Ireland.[261] Francis Agarde was first mentioned as captain of a troop of cavalry in Scotland under Lord Seymour de Sudeley in 1548 and he probably returned to Ireland in 1551. In 1553 he was named constable of Ferns castle and appointed to the council in Ireland, probably at the urging of his father.[262]

Although Francis Agarde was practically the sole military adviser to no less than four chief governors, he was not known to favour a coer- cive strategy for the government of Ireland. Rather, he was known primarily for his versatility and his pragmatism. Agarde was initially constable of the two garrisons in Ferns and Wexford and he was retained as a captain when Sussex became lord deputy in 1556. He was responsible for a contingent of 100 soldiers at musters and general hostings, and in 1559 he went with Lord Deputy Sussex and the mar- shal on an expedition to Leix and Offaly where the siege of Meelick castle was successfully conducted.[263] In 1560 he was required to supervise the delivery of money by the victuallers to the cessors in the Pale after it had been revealed at the council board that these accounts were delinquent.[264] After Sussex had left Ireland, the conflict between Ormonde and Desmond broke out into open hostilities in 1565 and Agarde served on a commission to govern Munster in the absence of the two earls.[265] The engagement of Captain Agarde in such a wide

---

260. Of the 500 plus documented meetings of the council, many of which are unsigned, Agarde sat at 166 of them.

261. Brady, 'Government of Ireland', pp. 83–84, 92.

262. PRO, SP 62/1/3–7; Hughes, *Patentee officers*, p. 1. In 1584, on the death of his wife Cecilie, Sir Henry Harrington erected a mural monument in Christ Church cathedral, Dublin, to her and to her father, Francis Agarde. Harrington was also an English captain who served in Ireland and he was the successor to Agarde as senseschal in Wicklow. The monument is in the wall of the south transept of Christ Church cathedral (hereafter cited as Agarde monument, Christ Church).

263. *Cal. Carew MSS, 1515–74*, pp. 265–67, 349.

264. RIA, MS 24 F 17, f. 145–45v.

265. *Cal. S.P. Ire., 1509–73*, p. 254; Agarde monument, Christ Church.

variety of purposes and policies may serve as a corrective to the view that military officials in Ireland were committed exclusively to a policy of conquest and coercion.

In 1565 the arrival of Sir Henry Sydney as lord deputy caused a turnover in the civil and military administration, but Agarde and others kept their jobs. Sydney employed the policy of his predecessor in innovative ways and he chose Agarde to be the new seneschal of east Wicklow. This turbulent mountainous region had been transformed by Bellingham into three military zones, each to be ruled by an English captain from a convenient fort. Both of Sussex's appointees, Jacques Wingfield and Nicholas Heron, had been accused of criminality and negligence, allowing Gaelic chiefs to use brehon law. Sydney now drew up a plan for the gradual imposition of common law rule by seneschals empowered to keep order and obedience without recourse to Gaelic practices. He placed Agarde in the most important zone, nearest to Dublin, with command of the O'Byrnes and O'Tooles, and thereafter Captain Agarde brought with him to musters and hostings a small group of Irish kerne.[266] It is significant that the veteran councillor was selected to govern this region in accordance with common law principles; he was presumably quite experienced in adjudication at the council board. He governed the area bounded by Arklow and Bray from his principal military base of Newcastle and from there he was also within easy reach of Dublin for council meetings.[267] Agarde had acquired the manor of Grange Gorman just outside Dublin in 1560 and he wrote often from here in his later years.[268] In the Sussex administration he had gone on long campaigns against Shane O'Neill, but after 1566 he was generally occupied in his office of seneschal.[269] As the sole military adviser to Fitzwilliam in 1573, Agarde was the obvious choice to capture the earl of Desmond after the lord deputy failed to convince the more senior councillors Fyton or White to undertake the task. Agarde offered to go to Munster but he could not be spared from his '. . . continuall overlooking of the Byrnes and Tooles'.[270]

266. Canny, *Elizabethan conquest*, pp. 34–36, 54.

267. *Cal. S.P. Ire., 1509–73*, p. 295. While Agarde checked the O'Byrnes and O'Tooles on the east, Robert Pipho was seneschal of the foothill area in the west bordering on Co. Kildare. Heron kept his role as seneschal of the Kavanaughs and captain of the forts of Leighlin and Ferns. The ruins of Agarde's reputed house (close to the Church of Ireland parish church at Newcastle) are still pointed out. R. Jennings, *Glimpses of an ancient parish: Newcastle, Co. Wicklow 1189–1989* (n.d. [1989]), pp. 8–9.

268. PROI, Lodge MSS, Records of the rolls, i, p. 140.

269. Hughes, *Patentee officers*, 1; RIA, MS 24 F 17, f 226; *Cal. Carew MSS, 1575–88*, pp. 44–45; Agarde monument, Christ Church.

270. PRO, SP 63/42/184–86.

It is clear that Francis Agarde was valued by many for his well-seasoned competence. He was doubtless counted a member of Sydney's faction in Ireland, but he was widely admired and enjoyed the support of such adversaries as Fitzwilliam and Essex. In 1566 Sydney wrote to the privy council that he was '. . . the most sufficient servaunt of the Queene . . .' in all Ireland.[271] Cecil considered him in 1567 for the presidency of a council to be erected in Ulster, but the tribunal was never established.[272] Agarde was frequently occupied on commissions from the council. He was employed in 1567 to take to the queen the news of the defeat and death of Shane O'Neill. He explained the conciliar proposal for a plantation in Ulster and suggested how the garrison should be dispersed. On his return the queen entrusted him with £2,000 for the immediate support of the government.[273] In 1572 Fitzwilliam wrote to Cecil that Agarde had refused the offer to become vice treasurer, probably on account of his age.[274] Perhaps his most important commission came in the twilight of his career as the struggling Fitzwilliam wrestled with his difficulties in Munster. Agarde was named to be the chief commissioner there in 1574, assisted by James Dowdall, in lieu of a lord president. But he apparently fell ill, and he was recalled to the council in Dublin in 1575.[275] The privy council in England was well aware of his merits. During the crisis which began in 1576 the council ordered the lord deputy to take the advice of the council in Ireland and send the opinion over in the custody of his most trusted advisers, Sir Lucas Dillon and Francis Agarde '. . . being of each nation one'.[276]

In matters of policy-making, Francis Agarde was rarely among the leaders on the Irish council. He served with distinction on many commissions, conducted embassies to the Gaelic chiefs and Anglo-Irish peers, campaigned in the field against the enemies of the crown, and undertook council business in England in great matters of state. Though Agarde was infrequently sought out for his advice on the direction of government strategy until near the end of his career, he was certainly not without opinions. He wrote to Walsingham in 1576

---

271. *Cal. S.P. Ire., 1509–73*, p. 296. He is described in his epitaph as 'consiliarius prudentissimus'. His death, on 11 October 1577, occurred in the company of '. . . Henricus Sidneius amicus eius longe honoratissimus . . .'. Agarde monument, Christ Church. In 1575 Essex had written to Walsingham that Agarde was a 'perfect honest gentleman, the most sufficient for wisdom in this state'. *Cal. S.P. Ire., 1574–85*, p. 55.

272. *Cal. S.P. Ire., 1509–73*, p. 343.

272. *Sidney S.P.*, pp. 70–72.

274. *Cal. S.P. Ire., 1509–73*, p. 470.

275. *Cal. Carew MSS, 1515–74*, p. 484; *Cal. S.P. Ire., 1574–85*, pp. 14, 38–40, 51.

276. *Cal. Carew MSS, 1575–88*, p. 53.

that Ireland had never known such peace, and that in order to preserve it the laws must be enforced and the provinces must be governed by 'uprighte ministers'.[277] It is important to realize that the emphasis on political crises during this period sometimes obscures the intervals of genuine stability in different regions of the country. In 1577, six months before his death, Agarde advised Walsingham to send over experienced English officials for the exchequer, and he defended the reasonableness of the new composition for the cess. To lay it aside, he argued, would not '. . . win the hearts of the disloyal and little persuade the disobedient'.[278] It is little wonder that Sydney was vexed at the absence of his veteran supporter when he was posted to Munster during 1575. The viceroy pestered the privy council in England for his return, saying 'I cannot but lament the lack of Mr. Agard so long from hence; surely the loss of £1,000 should not so much have grieved me as the wanting of him hath troubled me'.[279] The work of Agarde reveals that his role as a civil administrator was an important complement to his career as a military captain. And the ideas of Agarde, expressed late in his career, articulate a genuine hope for peace in Ireland and strong support for the policy of anglicization through the extension of the common law.

In summary, we can observe that the leading members of the council in Ireland were surprisingly diverse. They represented competing factions, rival policies, opposed religious doctrines and different family networks. But the councillors were also joined by certain common elements. Their versatility was conspicuous, although few were as active as Lucas Dillon and Francis Agarde. Their senescence in office gave the council a composite durability. The presence of experienced councillors in each new administration gave the appearance of gradualism and continuity in the midst of change. In a period of many crises which threatened to divert the progress of anglicization, the forces for stability on the council worked to maintain an orderly transition. For these were generally conservative men, accustomed to working within the system of Irish government despite the strategic and fiscal reforms which occasionally caused tremors in the body politic. The chief governors devoted themselves energetically to a wide range of problems and, while they were unable to make Irish government work well, they were clearly not obsessed by a single one-dimensional policy. Most of the councillors shared this eclectic, flexible and utilitarian

---

277. PRO, SP 63/55/169.

278. *Cal. S.P. Ire., 1574–85*, p. 116.

279. *Cal. Carew MSS, 1575–88*, p. 32. In the following year Sydney protested again that 'The cause of my deferring [to write] was, that I expected the arrival of Mr. Agard, whose miss hath been no small maim to me in this my travail . . .'. idid., p. 46.

approach to administration. And, while Loftus may have been largely isolated in this period and Kildare was surely alienated from crown policy at times, the council members generally worked well together. The rogueish caricature of conquistador newcomer versus truculent native obscures and distorts the clear evidence of subtle and multi-form interests on the council.

CONCLUSION

The modern distinction between bureaucrats and politicians did not exist in the sixteenth century. The councillors in Ireland were there-fore not merely functionaries, but statesmen and ministers whose duty it was to inform and to serve the interest of the crown. They were also leading members of the great families of the Pale and experienced crown administrators who were sent from England. They represented the dominant factions of the court and the more extensive network of Irish cliques and associations. As a group, the councillors were a stable, durable, conservative and experienced executive board which devel-oped over the period in question a distinct corporate personality. They proved to be pragmatic, adaptable and generally moderate in their collective decisions. Their function was explicitly declared by the queen herself to be independence of judgment, a responsibility which required them to offer sage advice to the viceroy even when it meant opposing him. The role of the councillors was thus to balance the ambitions and preferences of the chief governor and to restrain him from unwise actions. While this constitutional injunction to restrain sycophancy might have led to greater conflict at the council board, it was the habit of each chief governor to consult an 'inner circle' of advisers on whom he could effectively rely for advice and support. As the membership changed, so did this privileged core of collegial advis-ers. We might identify Francis Agarde, William Fitzwilliam, Hugh Curwen, Robert Weston, Lucas Dillon and William Gerrard as the most active members of this fraternal confederacy.

Policy and principle were subordinated in the work of the coun-cillors to common expediency. This is not to say that they were drones who were unable to conceptualize the problems of the country. Many of them were frequently in correspondence with Cecil and Walsingham in England, and some members such as Gerrard provided exceptionally thoughtful analyses of Irish government. But the dominant traits of most of the councillors were their adroitness and their versatility. Of course, the character and personality of the council depended a great deal on the leadership of the queen's representative in Ireland. Two of the chief governors in the period demonstrated remarkable energy and ambition, while the other (Fitzwilliam) was exhausted and dispirited by his humbling experience as viceroy. Consequently, the period of Fitzwilliam's weak deputyship opened the door to a dangerous power vacuum which, in turn, permitted a sterile interval in the anglicization of Irish government. Nevertheless, as we have seen, the lords deputy were not tyrants who ran roughshod over the legitimate concerns of the council. Rather, they employed the ablest of their colleagues in a variety of missions which offered proof of their all-round expertise. The council was thus a 'working committee', in modern parlance, which expected its members to participate actively in the multifarious roles of the executive board. Agarde and Dillon went on embassies to Gaelic chiefs as well as to the privy council in England; Loftus and Curwen served as both archbishop and lord chancellor; and Fyton combined the offices of lord president of Connacht and vice treasurer. The broad spectrum of dynastic and political allegiance on the council was paralleled by the universal resourcefulness of its most active members.

Irish politics in the Tudor period has been the subject of much discussion in recent years, as we have seen. The reckless patriotism of some writers has deliberately obscured the modest ambition of the mid-sixteenth century Dublin administration to maintain the rule of law. The general policy of anglicization which was pursued with limited success by each of the chief governors was viewed by the Anglo-Irish élite with qualified approval. The incumbent office-holders were not removed, despite evidence that some were Catholic recusants and others were well past their prime as judges. The entire administrative edifice was staffed with Anglo-Irish clerks and other functionaries, so a policy of exclusion or confrontation would simply have been a dead letter in practice. But the creation of a microcosm of English government and its gradual extension throughout the country was accepted as a benefit to sympathetic Anglo-Irishmen who anticipated that they would thereby extend their patriarchal family interests. On the council itself, a small number of English officials were added as members and some Anglo-Irish veterans such as Cusake were not replaced when they died. But there was no comprehensive policy to displace the governing élite and they continued to support the government even when they conspired against the governor. The perennial loyalty of the Anglo-Irish to the crown was also a matter of practical politics, since they depended almost entirely on royal favour for grants, leases, preferment and other attractions to the magnet of Tudor benevolence and reward.

What are we to make of assertions that the new English administrators came to Ireland with a single-minded determination to re-conquer the queen's dominion and to exploit vast tracts of land for their own ends? In the first place, it is well to remember that the constitutional forms of crown government were uniform in their essentials in both England and Ireland. Experienced English administrators who joined the council in Ireland were generally veteran officials, accustomed to the rule of law, valued for their sage wisdom, men like William Drury, William Gerrard and Robert Weston. The enlistment of hapless adventurers like Peter Carew was rare. In the second place, the relationship of English and Anglo-Irish councillors was not an adversarial one, as we have seen. Some of the newly arrived English officials became successful landowners and espoused the views of the Palesmen on the issue of the cess. Men like Nicholas Bagenall and Nicholas Malbie were culturally assimilated to a large degree and defended their interests in Ireland quite like native proprietors. And while Bagenall and Warham St Leger became involved in small-scale colonial settlements in Ulster and Munster, they were hardly the prototype of ruthless 'conquistadores'. It is obvious that the campaign against the cess pitted the Anglo-Irish community of the Pale against the chief governors in a relentless political battle which stained the careers of both Sussex and Sydney (see below). But this is evidence of the indigenous character of Irish politics, not the basis for racial animosity. The recent efforts to demonstrate an incipient Irish nationalism prior to the 1580s seem to argue that this ordinary dissension concluded in the polarization of two hostile and separate communities. This is too tragically modern and it does not fit the evidence.

Perhaps an improved model for understanding the mid-Tudor Irish polity lies in a deeper study of patronage politics. While it is true indeed that the dominant Elizabethan courtiers shaped and formed the development of Irish politics in this period, it is important to realize that the court of the viceroy must have had a separate, if not altogether independent, structure. We need a study of Irish politics which takes into consideration both native and newcomer, mercantile and gentry interests, noble connections and ecclesiastical perspectives. A new paradigm might get beyond the mono-causal approach to the 'Tudor conquest' and the simple dichotomy of coercion versus persuasion. The interstices of Irish government were surely no less complex than other early modern states, and possibly more so. English patrons worked to keep their retainers faithful by plying them with favour and benefaction. The conservative queen would not risk a policy which would alienate her tax-paying subjects even if the long-term interests of the crown might suffer. The aim of patronage politics was different for the courtier and the client. For the former, it was power and influence. For the latter, it was simply an opportunity to enrich himself, provide for his family, expand his estates and retain his office. The character of patronage politics is inherently to conserve one's position and to compete, without great risk, for further advantage.

This political and cultural milieu does not encourage rebelliousness, although it certainly permits dissension and a high level of corruption in government. In that regard, Irish political life was no more divisive than politics at the English court, although it was no mere reflection of the now de-mystified conventions of Elizabeth's closed society.

CHAPTER FOUR

The council and reform of the legal system: judiciary, litigation and the court of castle chamber

INTRODUCTION

SOVEREIGNS OF THE mid-sixteenth century sought to associate their rule with the timeless and universal themes of order, security and stability. The ideal of a fixed social hierarchy rested upon the amplitude of divine authority, supported by human conventions. Laws were assumed to be consonant with divine justice, and the aim of Tudor government was to maintain social order by preserving stasis. Not surprisingly, then, the mutability of political fortunes in this period generated anguished concern.[1] Recent treatments of the reigns of Mary and Elizabeth I have stressed the conservative nature of their regimes. Beset by intrigues, plots, factions and rebellions, their respective governments showed a distinct unwillingness to hazard innovation. Instead, needed reforms were cloaked in the language of tradition, and obedience to the crown from the true and loyal subject was constantly promoted.[2] Social order and the rule of law were inextricably connected in the state religion of Tudor rule, from pulpit to proclamation. Indeed, the prevailing concept of an organic hierarchy of being, with its interdependent parts linked in a cosmic chain of 'degree, priority and place', was well-known and understood.[3] Unruly and heedless behaviour was intolerable in a country with such limited means of enforcement, but this fact led to an interesting dichotomy. In England as well as in Ireland, the privy council remonstrated continuously against all manner of rogues, renegades, rebels and other dangerous elements, leaving the impression that government was

1. S.L. Collins, *From divine cosmos to sovereign reality: an intellectual history of consciousness and the idea of order in renaissance England* (Oxford, 1989), pp. 3–7. Collins finds the idea of cosmic order in the later Tudor period 'precarious' as it continued to ignore the realities of political and social change (pp. 15–28).
2. See C. Haigh, *Elizabeth I* (London, 1988), pp. 7–9, 66–74, 144–46; Ann Weikel, 'The Marian council revisited', in Loach & Tittler, ed., *Mid-Tudor polity*, pp. 52–73; D. Loades, *The reign of Mary Tudor: politics, government and religion in England, 1553–58* (London, 1979).
3. See E.M.W. Tillyard, *The Elizabethan world picture: a study of the idea of order in the age of Shakespeare, Donne and Milton* (London, 1943).

effectively restraining the ebullient disorderliness of a wilful people.[4] However, the evidence from court records at all levels reveals an unusually restive populace which was only marginally controlled through a combination of force, judicial remedies and carefully orchestrated civic images such as the Elizabethan symbol of majesty.[5]

Few historians have ventured into the obscure, but fascinating realm of comparative social conditions and related judicial practices.[6] However, it would be useful to know more about the relative levels of disorder in England and Ireland during the late sixteenth century. The evidence of increasing crime in Elizabethan England should be compared with the incidence of crime in Irish court records.[7] While it is important to measure the extent of social unrest and incivility in late Tudor Ireland, it would also be instructive to compare how the English government there dealt with disobedience, crime and disorder, and to contrast this again with the turbulent conditions of France or Germany or the Netherlands in this period. What may emerge from such a study is that Ireland was no more disordered than other countries or regions disturbed by the age of religious wars.

Prior to 1556, the effectiveness of judges and law officers in Ireland was limited by the political weakness of the government and circumscribed by the lack of a mature constitutional framework. The common law was accepted as the dominant medium for adjudication only in parts of Ireland, and often in combination with brehon, or native Irish law. And the essential infrastructure for the extension of common law jurisdiction in the countryside, a system of shires and sheriffs which was so familiar in England, was at best erratic in Ireland beyond the Pale. Assizes were infrequent, intermediate jurisdictions were unformed, justices of the peace and sheriffs were only moderately active on judicial business, and lords lieutenant were yet unknown.[8] These

4. Williams, *Tudor regime*, pp. 222, 236–39, 350–54, 389, 402–05; *The proclamations of the Tudor queens*, ed. F. Youngs (Cambridge, 1976), pp.52, 67–71.

5. See K. Wrightson, *English society, 1580–1680* (London, 1982), pp. 150–55, 175–82; J.S. Cockburn, 'The nature and incidence of crime in England 1559–1625: a preliminary survey' in J.S. Cockburn, ed., *Crime in England 1550–1800* (Princeton, 1977), pp. 49–71; Joel Samaha, *Law and order in historical perspective: the case of Elizabethan Essex* (New York, 1974), pp. 16–17, 43–45.

6. See S.G. Ellis, *The Pale and the far North: government and society in two early Tudor borderlands* (Galway, 1988). Also see Williams, *Tudor regime*, pp. vii, 11, 345, wherein he overstates the extent and the intensity of Irish rebellions in comparison to English ones. See Ellis, *Tudor Ireland*, pp. 13–16, 316, 319–20.

7. Ellis has explained that before 1534 the availability of common law justice in the Pale was similar to that in the more settled shires in England, while in outlying counties the level of violence was hardly worse than in the borderlands of Tudor England. *Reform and revival*, p. 164, and see ch. 7, 'Local government'. See also Cockburn, 'Crime in England', p. 49.

8. Ellis, *Reform and revival*, pp. 188–95, 205.

and other defects led to several basic reforms initiated by the council in the legal hierarchy. The most fundamental change was the creation of a complementary and parallel legal jurisdiction within the council itself. This new tribunal was modelled on the star chamber and called the court of castle chamber.

The aim of the council was to extend its effective jurisdiction by using the instrument of the English common law. Conciliar government as practised in England and Wales rested upon the assumption that all subjects should have customary recourse to courts of law. English privy councillors and chief governors in Ireland continuously restated the argument that Ireland should ultimately be governed in accordance with the principles of common law.[9] It was believed that the availability of legal remedies would gradually incline all the queen's Irish subjects to set aside their feuding and rebelliousness in favour of settled means of arbitration. Indeed, the resemblance between the government in Ireland and in the north of England shows a consistent purpose which was to effect the pacification of a turbulent region by extending the effectiveness of judicial remedies.[10]

This policy has recently been labelled 'anglicization' in its Irish context, and some writers have concluded that the aims were 'programmatic' departures from traditional forms of Tudor administration.[11] But the councillors who proposed the policy in England and those who implemented it in Ireland shared a rather conservative outlook on government. They saw themselves not as intrepid reformers but as the representatives of royal government which aimed at the closer alignment of policy and practice in Elizabethan Ireland. They were not the conscious purveyors of a superior cultural mode, but administrators charged with specific mandates to improve the quality of the queen's dominion. And, for the most part, they discharged these duties in the belief that common law practices would both improve Irish government and bring it into conformity with English rule.

In 1556 the council had a very irregular and tenuous jurisdiction over the areas outside the Pale and the loyal towns (see Map 1).[12] But by 1578 the legal system had been extended through commissions,

9. PRO, SP 63/15/19v–20. Ciaran Brady, for example, has said, '. . . the gradual extension of English law and social structures remained the explicit objective of English policy in Ireland'. Brady, 'Government of Ireland', p. 9. See also, pp. 7–8, 114–15, 209, 214–15, 358.

10. Ellis, 'Nationalist historiography', 5, 9–10, 17; Ellis, *Pale and the far North*, p. 25 ff. Ellis, however, also sees the two cultures as distinct and argues they were often better governed by local magnates than by crown representatives sent from London.

11. Brady, 'Government of Ireland', pp. 38–39, 42–43, 240–46; and, more forcefully, Ellis, *Tudor Ireland*, pp. 243–51.

12. Ellis, *Reform and revival*, pp. 112–13, 135–38.

provincial councils, itinerant justices and other means, to include a far greater territory under the common law. What is more, the council itself expanded its own caseload, handling more litigation when sitting as the court of castle chamber, and thus exercising a more systematic jurisdiction over the Pale and traditionally loyal counties. It will be necessary to describe the outlines of the judicial hierarchy and to give some account of the immediate background of the council's adjudicative function before an analysis of this expansion can be made. Fundamental changes as well as refinements were resisted by entrenched Anglo-Irish interests and the net effect was small in terms of the sanguine objectives of the council. But the real impact of the proposals was to change the judicial temper of the legal establishment and to commit the government of Ireland to a wholesale restructuring and improvement of Irish justice which lasted well into the next century.[13]

The legal jurisdiction of the Irish council was closely connected with the unquestioned judicial competence of the lord deputy from the early thirteenth century. Otway-Ruthven has said, 'It would seem that in the early days of the colony the justiciar's *curia* was the sole source of centralized justice . . .'.[14] Long after it had been modified and differentiated into other courts, the justiciar's court remained the greatest court in Ireland. From about the middle of the thirteenth century, the burden of his judicial responsibilities led the chief governor to associate with himself one of the itinerant justices who became known as the justice of the justiciar's pleas.[15] In 1286 a judge was specifically named to assist the justiciar, and in 1324 he became the chief justice of a court which was the forerunner of the king's bench.[16]

The justiciar's court thus very slowly developed into a distinct tribunal. However, the separation was not made complete for over a century and a residual authority remained in the king's council which also derived from the judicial powers of the governor. Because of the incomplete separation in the records of the council, it is not surprising that conjectures about the division of judicial responsibility between court and council have differed. H.G. Richardson and G.O. Sayles have pointed out that '. . . there was brought before the justiciar's court much business that we should not regard as strictly matters of law, and it is sometimes difficult to differentiate the work of the court

13. See H. Pawlisch, *Sir John Davies and the conquest of Ireland: a study in legal imperialism* (Cambridge, 1985). But see Brady, 'Government of Ireland', pp. 420–22, for the assertion of deteriorating government effectiveness prior to 1579, based on political and social discontent among the Anglo-Irish and Gaelic populations.

14. Otway-Ruthven, *Medieval Ireland*, p. 158.

15. G.J. Hand, *English law in Ireland, 1290–1324* (Cambridge, 1967), pp. 40–41.

16. ibid., p. 45; Otway-Ruthven, *Medieval Ireland*, p. 160.

from that of the king's council in Ireland'.[17] It is generally agreed, however, that the council had a continuous judicial function from the early thirteenth century, regardless of how that function was shared with its subordinate courts.

During the era of Gaelic resurgence, the jurisdiction of the common law in Ireland was substantially reduced. From the period 1290–1324 (which G.J. Hand saw as the 'climax of medieval Ireland')[18], the area wherein the king's writ was effective became gradually limited to the Pale and the loyal towns and counties, mainly in the south-east. Although the 1331 ordinance *una et eadem lex* extended the benefits of English common law to all free Irishmen, the initiative appears to have been still-born, for succeeding years witnessed an upsurge in resort to Gaelic legal practices. By the mid-fifteenth century the amount of business done in the king's courts had declined substantially, while the brehon law and amalgams of both systems came into more common use.[19]

Recent writers have described the hybridization of two legal systems in Ireland, suggesting that the traditional explanation of rival and mutually exclusive approaches to justice has understated the complexity of the situation. Kenneth Nicholls has shown that the common law was often refined to accommodate certain brehon law principles ('march law'), and he argues that significant assimilation had occurred from at least the early fifteenth century.[20] While it is clear that Gaelic law and custom was 'local and particularist' and thus inherently at odds with the more systematic common law tradition, it is no longer acceptable to discuss the two approaches in terms of a 'radical estrangement'.[21] In his revisionist study of late medieval government, Steven Ellis asserts that the royal courts began to recover substantial legal business after 1470. While the effective jurisdiction of the courts narrowed

17. H.G. Richardson and G.O. Sayles, *The administration of Ireland 1172–1377* (Dublin, 1963), p. 37. Hand has taken rather a different tack, arguing that the amount of judicial business done by the council was apparently small. Hand, *Eng. law in Ireland*, p. 50.

18. Hand, *Eng. law in Ireland*, p. vii.

19. B. Murphy, 'The status of the native Irish after 1331', *Ir Jur*, ii (1967), 116; R. Frame, 'The immediate effect and interpretation of the 1331 ordinance *una et eadem lex*: some new evidence', *Ir Jur*, vii (1972), 109. Also see Ellis, *Reform and revival*, p. 139; Ellis, 'The common bench plea roll, 19 Edw IV (1479–80)', *Anal Hib*, no. 31 (1984), 19. For the brehon law, see Katharine Simms, 'The brehons of later medieval Ireland', in D. Hogan and W.N. Osborough, ed., *Brehons, serjeants and attorneys* (Dublin, 1990), p. 51.

20. K.W. Nicholls, *Land, law and society in sixteenth century Ireland* (Dublin, 1976), p. 6; Nicholls, *Gaelic and gaelicized Ireland in the middle ages* (Dublin, 1972), pp. 44, 47–50, 54; Ellis, *Reform and revival*, p. 210.

21. See Bradshaw, *Irish constitutional revolution*, p. 14.

from *c.*1330 to 1460, the period from 1470 to 1534 saw increased litigation and a general recovery of the legal system based on the new judicial activity of the chancery and the council. Judicial commissions also expanded the perimeters of English common law after 1500 to include annual visits to Counties Kilkenny, Tipperary, Wexford, Waterford, Cork and Carlow.[22]

The impact of the Kildare rebellion on judicial practice in Ireland was slight, but the accompanying and subsequent reforms have been the subject of considerable controversy. Brendan Bradshaw has argued that Thomas Cromwell's reforms of the central administration in Dublin were carefully considered by an Irish 'reforming milieu' and actually preceded Kildare's uprising in 1534–35. The aim of these reforms was a comprehensive constitutional realignment of Irish government based on assimilation of English practices, which Bradshaw has called 'unitary sovereignty'. On the basis of humanist principles associated with a commonwealth strategy of governance, reformers in the Pale who were associated with Cromwell helped to conceive a broad strategy of conciliation and compromise leading to full integration of Ireland into the dominions of the crown.[23] Steven Ellis, on the other hand, has challenged the importance of 1534 as a turning-point in Tudor Ireland. In the view of Ellis, there was a continuous presence of English law and administration under the leadership of Kildare prior to 1534, even beyond the Pale. He sees the reforms of the 1530s as piecemeal efforts which were poorly funded and inadequately supported by political will in London.[24] Nevertheless, both writers seem to agree that the post-1534 era constituted a new departure in Irish government, based on the cumulative results of changes in administration, personnel and intention.

The assertion of a more direct connection between the governments in Dublin and London led to a continuous review of the Irish judicial system, beginning with the 'Ordinances for the government of Ireland' in 1534. As the recipient of most of the correspondence from Ireland, Cromwell may have authored this extensive document. Article 11 of the ordinances called for a regular meeting of the judges together with the lords of the council to hear complaints brought by the king's subjects in the council chamber. The presence of lords of

22. Ellis, *Reform and revival*, pp. 8, 138–39, 162–64, 207–09. See also K.W. Nicholls, 'Some documents on Irish law and custom in the sixteenth century', *Anal Hib*, no. 26 (1970), 103–09.

23. Bradshaw, *Irish constitutional revolution*, pp. 33, 49–54, 118–19. Also see B. Bradshaw, 'Cromwellian reform and the origins of the Kildare rebellion, 1533–34', *R Hist Soc Trans*, 5th ser, xxvii (1977), 73ff.

24. Ellis, *Reform and revival*, pp. 208–12; *Tudor Ireland*, p. 129; 'Thomas Cromwell and Ireland, 1532–1540', *Hist Jn*, xxiii (1980), 504–11, 517–18.

the council, and the choice of the site of the council chamber would suggest that this was intended to be a meeting of the Irish council.[25] In fact, it seems to adumbrate the development of the court of castle chamber over thirty years later. Significantly, there seemed to be no clarification of the particular jurisdiction of this tribunal, a feature which was unique to the council itself. No records of this court were kept and nothing is known of its sessions. We may surmise that it was an abortive judicial experiment and that the novel authority created in 1534 was subsumed in the ordinary judicial power of the council some time after it was created.

The ordinances also anticipated later developments in legal administration. They called upon the lord deputy and council to establish gaols in Counties Dublin, Meath, Kildare, Louth, Waterford and other areas where practicable. Article 15 required mayors, bailiffs and portreeves of towns to assist the judges coming to hear causes within their jurisdiction. Quarter sessions were ordered to be held in each of the shires and their marches every term. The lord deputy was directed to extend the king's writ to Carlow, Kilkenny, Waterford and other counties, and the judges who were now to be so busy were in consequence commanded not to go on hostings but to send a substitute, armed and accoutred according to their wealth and status.[26] These orders demonstrated the ample judicial powers of the council, and the considerable extent to which it relied upon local officials to implement its instructions. The ordinances offer convincing evidence of the determination of the English government to reform the Irish judicial system from top to bottom, using the council as the instrument of its policy. It was clear from succeeding instructions, however routinely they may have been offered, that the English government of Ireland was to proceed with dispatch to refine and expand its judicial competence. Law reform was at the core of successive administrations after 1534, and it remained so through the deputyship of Sydney, ending in 1578.[27]

25. PRO, SP 60/2/66; *S.P. Hen. VIII*, ii, 207–16. Ellis dismisses the importance of the ordinances as a 'ragbag of instructions' routinely given to new chief governors. See Ellis, *Tudor Ireland*, p. 123. However, the ordinances were exceptional both in their timing and in the fact that they were printed as a pamphlet, a strategem usually reserved to statute law. If, indeed, aspects of the reforms were anticipated by earlier instructions (1493, 1499, 1524), this is indicative of the careful and comprehensive approach to institutional change initiated by Cromwell and his advisers. See Ellis, 'Thomas Cromwell and Ireland', *Hist Jn*, xxiii (1980), 502–05.

26. PRO, SP 60/2/67, 70. Articles 14, 16 18, 29.

27. See C. Brady, 'Court, castle and country: the framework of government in Tudor Ireland' in Brady & Gillespie, ed., *Natives and newcomers*, pp. 27–28, 41.

While aspects of the intervening period, 1534–56, have been studied in some depth, the judicial activity of the council and the superior courts has not received detailed attention. Ciaran Brady has noted that the Dublin administration and the royal courts were unusually susceptible to partisanship in local causes of action. The judges and other officials resisted the demands from Westminster for strong central government which would be the instrument of royal policy. Brady argues further,

However loyal they were to the English crown and anxious to fulfil its objectives, the Palesmen continued to regard their administration in Dublin less as the royal instrument for the rule of the whole island, than as the seat of their own local government. And, like contemporary English countrymen, they looked to its courts as means of processing their own affairs, settling their internal differences, and defending their own interests rather than as channels for the implementation of reform policy.[28]

While it is generally agreed that '. . . the gradual extension of English law throughout the whole island remained the officially declared objective of each succeeding Tudor regime . . .',[29] the period down to 1556 witnessed a collective resistance by Dublin administrators to commit themselves wholly to the aims of anglicization in this manner.[30]

In constitutional terms, the period from 1534 to 1547 is central to an understanding of Tudor rule in Ireland. Cromwell committed the government to an extension of conciliar administration on the basis of recommendations from a group of lawyers in Ireland, including the Anglo-Irish judge, Thomas Cusake, and the English judge, John Alen. These reformers called for more judicial commissions and they crafted the new policy of surrender and re-grant. The role of parliament in 1536–37 was expanded to give legislative authority to the reformers' aim of extending effective administration within the Pale. The parliamentary session of 1541 was held in Dublin in the presence of many Gaelic lords to announce the bill which declared Henry VIII king of Ireland. This act created the foundation for what Bradshaw has called 'unitary sovereignty', in that it ended the implicit dualism of Irish government and stimulated the reformation of both central and local admininistration in conformity to the English model. While these aims were not achieved in practice at this time, they later served as the principles underlying systematic extension of the common law beyond the Pale.[31]

28. ibid., pp. 36–37.
29. ibid., p. 41.
30. ibid., p. 41. See also Ellis, *Tudor Ireland*, pp. 144–45, 147–48.
31. Bradshaw, *Irish constitutional revolution*, pp. 233–41; Ellis, *Tudor Ireland*, pp. 139–42.

The chief governor who was most closely associated with the reform movement in Ireland throughout this period was Sir Anthony St Leger. In the view of leading historians, St Leger wielded the most effective leadership of the Dublin administration and he was joined by sympathetic advocates of change within the Pale community, including the clever and judicious Thomas Cusake. From his first appearance in Ireland as commissioner in 1537 until his last lord deputyship ended in 1556, St Leger practised a moderate reform policy. This was designed to assimilate the local lords into a generous constitutional framework which would allow them to retain their lands and local influence while exchanging their titles for English ones. The policy of surrender and re-grant involved a legal transformation from the Gaelic practice of partible inheritance among surviving sons and other male relatives to English land tenure based on primogeniture. In a related process called indenture, Irish chiefs promised to renounce Gaelic titles and to accept English ones held directly of the king. The clear aim of this conciliatory policy was to achieve stability in land law and to commence the anglicization of Irish society. The emergence of the difficulties over the feudal rights of the king and over obtaining full fiscal dues owing from the land were initially delayed by the moderation of St Leger and his council.[32]

Despite the promise of this new dawn in Irish constitutional relationships with the sovereign, efforts to build upon the emergent feudal structure in the Irish lordships soon foundered. There were many reasons for this. Claimants to an Irish inheritance were unlikely to accept the primacy of a very young heir. The policy led to occasional military expeditions which were meant to enforce adherence to the new English land law, but which occasionally became simply menacing and retributive. And the rising costs of maintaining the Dublin administration caused politicians in Westminster to withdraw support from the moderate policies of St Leger and his reformers. Before the death of Henry VIII in 1547, the initial success of the moderate reformers had been only partial, and thereafter a succession of chief governors with more radical mandates interrupted the progress made under surrender and re-grant.[33]

32. Bradshaw, *Irish constitutional revolution*, pp. 193–212. The usefulness of labelling this policy as 'liberal' seems to me rather dubious and perhaps too arbitrary. See also Ellis, *Tudor Ireland*, pp. 137–43; Brady, 'Court, castle and country', pp. 44–45.

33. Bradshaw, *Irish constitutional revolution*, pp. 242–44, 252–55. The partisanship evidenced by the use of charged language (St Leger's regime ended 'tragically' along with 'truth and gentleness', p. 258) does not necessarily mitigate the basic argument in praise of St Leger's statesmanlike leadership. See also Ellis, *Tudor Ireland*, pp. 143–48.

During a period which has been called the 'mid-Tudor crisis' in English history, from 1547 to 1556, it is hardly surprising that the government of Ireland experienced a series of critical discontinuities. Changes in the leadership occurred with greater frequency and the official policy of the Edwardian and Marian governments in Westminster alternated between leniency bordering on aloofness and stridency which was wedded to religious zeal. Although St Leger returned to the helm as lord deputy in this period no less than three separate times, his mandate was very limited and his replacements were generally military men who were chosen to put down rebellions in Leix and Offaly and to defend the kingdom against the Scots. Early in Mary's reign, the government made the fateful decision to send three young Irish peers who were educated in England back to Ireland. The return of the earls of Kildare and Ormonde and the lord of Upper Ossory soon caused a schism in the ranks of the political élite. As the scions of rival noble families, these youthful aristocrats became the leading magnates in Ireland for the next generation, and they exacerbated the problem of consensus government under St Leger. Furthermore, the corruption and financial maladministration which occurred under St Leger's later deputyships tainted his regime. And the debasement of the coinage did nothing to create stability and order in the Pale.[34]

If the records of the council from 1534 to 1556 had survived it might have been possible to trace the development of its judicial function during that crucial period more clearly. The extant table from the council book begun in 1542 is too brief and too cryptic to be an accurate guide.[35] For example, it is difficult to tell from the summaries whether an order given by the council was pursuant to a case adjudicated before them or merely the result of arbitration conducted on its behalf by an ad hoc commission. Nevertheless, it is possible to learn something of the judicial character of the council prior to 1556. Most cases involved peers of the realm in disputes over land, such as the 1549 decree exempting the barony of Ferney and Maguire's lands from the authority of the earl of Tyrone.[36] The council also heard cases involving the Gaelic Irish, although less frequently than those in which the Anglo-Irish peers were disputants. In an unusual departure from the administration of English justice the council once ordered that the 'Controversie [be] referred to brehownes',[37] a reminder that

34. W.R.D. Jones, *The mid-Tudor crisis, 1539–1563* (London, 1973); but see also Loach & Tittler, ed., *Mid-Tudor polity*, pp. 1–8. For causes of instability see Ellis, *Tudor Ireland*, pp. 228–34; Brady 'Government of Ireland', pp. 86–108.

35. BL, Add. MS 4792, ff, 117–24. Another table was found in TCD, MS 843, ff. 1–18.

36. BL, Add. MS 4792, f. 122.

37. ibid., f. 118–18v. See Nicholls, 'Documents on Irish law', 109.

there were still two rival (but not wholly unrelated) legal systems in the early sixteenth century.

Other cases apparently decided by the council included disputes involving the loyal towns, particularly in commercial litigation such as the rights to prise wines between Waterford and New Ross.[38] In October 1543 the lord deputy and council heard a case which illustrated the nature of conciliar jurisdiction. Both litigants, Richard Blake and Andrew Kyrwan, were merchants of Galway and both alleged superior and legitimate claims to certain fishing rights '. . . in the river of Galway . . .', relying upon crown documents. The council determined that Blake had the superior claim based upon the weight of the evidence from as early as 1373 and transcripts of rentals from the reign of Richard III. However, since Kyrwan had letters patent on a lease of a mill with attendant fishing rights, he was excused from paying court costs or other burdens.[39] The same Richard Blake had sued successfully before arbitrators meeting at Galway in January 1543 to reclaim lands which had been leased for 80 years to the sept of Walter fitz Thomas de Burgh. The arbitrators decided the case in favour of the Blakes, who had superior documentation and were represented by an assiduous lawyer, against the de Burghs who were repeatedly cited for failing to appear.[40] We can surmise that recourse to the common law was the preferred remedy for leading townsmen and that possession of sufficient documentation weighed heavily with the council as well as with arbitrators.

In general, the period after the Kildare rebellion witnessed an increase in litigation. The English-born exchequer official Thomas Alen, for example, said in a letter to Cromwell in October 1538, 'Peace has made men resort to the law'.[41] Although the records are scanty, it seems reasonable to conclude that the council did not hear many cases of riot and other disturbances, nor did it hear litigation connected with the administration of the law in the ordinary courts. The penalties assessed were various and it is difficult to determine on the basis of the table for 1542–56 how the council punished malefactors. After 1556 the answers to these and other questions became somewhat clearer.

38. ibid., f. 121. These towns share a common estuary formed by the meeting of two rivers, the Barrow and the Suir.
39. *Blake family records, 1300–1600*, ed M.J. Blake (London, 1902), no. 104, pp. 83–85.
40. ibid., no. 103, pp. 81–83.
41. *Cal. S.P. Ire., 1509–73*, p. 46.

The council in Ireland was both a part of the legal system and above it, for the council did far more than adjudicate lawsuits and render decisions. The council was responsible for the smooth operation of the entire judicial system, which, by the middle of the sixteenth century, was modelled in its essentials on that of England.[42] The courts of king's bench, common pleas and exchequer originated in the thirteenth century, although the differentiation between them was not clearly worked out until the fourteenth century; the development of chancery as a court of law was to come later, probably in the mid-fifteenth century.[43] It is not intended here to address the judicial role of parliament in this period. After 1494 only twelve parliaments met during the Tudor regime and their judicial functions were absorbed by the more active council and the chancery.

The judicial hierarchy was headed by the lord chancellor, who was primarily responsible for the effective operation of the entire judicial apparatus. When the Irish council received instructions relevant to the administration of justice, the lord chancellor was expected to carry them out.[44] He was second in importance only to the lord deputy and was from 1555 always an Englishman. Of course, the virtual omnicompetence of the lord deputy allowed the latter to hear causes of action outside of term and to deliver quasi-judicial judgments by decree, but his was an extraordinary jurisdiction which was employed in a very casual and occasional manner. The chief governor usually gave decisions of this kind in concert with a small number of the Irish councillors and so his authority was, in practice, ordinarily combined with that of the council.

42. The subordination of the Irish council to its parent body in England was, in practice, a kind of acknowledged appellate jurisdiction. Nevertheless, despite recent claims of friction between the two councils, the board in Westminister heard few Irish cases apart from those involving Irish peers. See Ellis, *Tudor Ireland*, p. 162.

43. Otway-Ruthven, *Medieval Ireland*, pp. 153–59. Although the courts were held for a brief time (1548–55) at St Patrick's cathedral, they were normally convened in Dublin Castle. But this was apparently not an ideal site. In 1586 the lord deputy and council were required to consider a suitable place to which the courts could be moved as they were dangerously near both the prison (called 'the Grate') and the powder magazine. See also C. Kenny, 'The Four Courts in Dublin before 1796', *Ir Jur*, xxi (1980), 107; letter of Lord Deputy Perrot to Walsingham, 21 August 1584, in W.M. Brady, ed., *State papers concerning the Irish church in the time of Queen Elizabeth* (London, 1868), p. 90.

44. PRO, SP 63/56/105. See Ellis, *Reform and revival*, pp. 159–64 on the growth of chancery as a court and its role in strengthening the recourse to common law jurisdictions by 1534. Also see Nicholls, 'Documents on Irish law', *Anal Hib*, no. 26 (1970), 105–09, for evidence regarding the mediation in chancery between brehon law and common law; Nicholls, 'A calendar of salved chancery proceedings concerning Co. Louth', *Louth Arch Soc Jn*, xviii (1972), 112.

The chief justice of queen's bench was the next most prestigious of the senior occupants of the bench, and his court was referred to as the 'chief place' to distinguish it from the inferior 'common place' or court of common pleas. The chief justice of common pleas was next in order of dignity. Subordinate in rank were the chief baron of the exchequer and the master of the rolls. The lord deputy usually initiated both the appointment and advancement of judges to the highest offices, and it was imperative for aspirants to secure his goodwill. During the sixteenth century these four judges appeared invariably as members of the council, and their notorious subservience to certain lords deputy may be explained by the need to curry favour with them. On the other hand, elderly justices like Sir John Plunket and Sir Robert Dillon, having reached the pinnacle of their profession at an advanced age, owed nothing to the chief governors after Sussex, and they were correspondingly slack in attendance on their respective offices.[45]

The second justices of queen's bench and common pleas, the barons of the exchequer and the masters in chancery had similarly subordinate roles within their courts, and formed the next rank in the judicial hierarchy. They were joined in that level of dignity by the principal law officers who pleaded the cause of the queen: the serjeant at law, the attorney general and the solicitor general.[46] After 1569, there were presidency courts in Munster and Connacht, each of which employed a chief justice, second justice and attorney general.[47] Although none of these officials was a member of the Irish council, a few of them became councillors once they were elevated to higher rank. Sir Robert Dillon (the younger), who was appointed second justice at the commencement of the Connacht presidency, ultimately became chief justice of the common pleas in 1581. The relationship of the judges and law officers with the council was always a close one because they were frequently employed on investigative commissions and named to commissions of the peace.

45. Brady, 'Court, castle, country', pp. 35–36.
46. A recent study which claims for the king's serjeant at law a membership on the council demonstrates the importance of the council's judicial role. However, the serjeant was a pleader only and as such had no right to participate in conciliar judgments, though he often went on commissions appointed by the council. He was not named as councillor in any official instructions in this period. See A.R. Hart, 'The king's serjeant at law in Tudor Ireland, 1485–1603', in Hogan & Osborough, ed., *Brehons, serjeants and attorneys*, pp. 81, 91, 97. Also see the law officers' joint advice with the judges to the council on how to proceed against Archbishop Hurley (1 June 1584) in Brady, *Ir. ch. Eliz.*, p. 83.
47. See Liam Irwin, 'The Irish presidency courts, 1569–1672', *Ir Jur*, xii (1977), 106. For Connacht, see the decrees of the court in litigation in regard to Co. Galway (nos. 144A, 150) in *Blake family records*, ed. Blake, pp. 115–17, 120–22.

Two surviving statements on judicial procedure in the common law courts, written around 1565, list the kinds of cases these tribunals heard.[48] These findings will in turn amplify the role of the Irish council in supplementing the ordinary course of justice. The court of queen's bench had jurisdiction in three general categories of proceedings: (1) indictments for treason or other felonies for which the punishment was death unless excused by the queen's pardon or a claim of benefit of clergy; (2) indictments for forcible entry, riot, trespass or other offences for which the punishment was a fine at the discretion of the court; and (3) suits between party and party using a jury and the ordinary common law writs and pleadings to reach a decision.[49] Cases heard in the court of common pleas were markedly different, at least in theory, from the other courts. The court's principal function was to hear all real, personal or mixed actions by chancery writ and proceed according to the common law. Recognizances were frequently taken to preserve the peace and to guarantee payment for debt or appearance in court. In either court the defendant would be proclaimed an outlaw if he could not be found, and his goods sequestered for the queen. The jurisdiction of the exchequer court reflected its role in revenue collection since it was mainly a court of audit. However, competition between all the central courts for litigation governing crown rights, real property actions, customs and trade continued during this period.[50]

The litigation taken up before the council was similar to that which was heard in the court of queen's bench, but conciliar procedure was more typical of the court of chancery. However, the council was not just another court. It acted as a judicial referee, deciding where cases should be heard and arbitrating the results of disputed cases in the other courts. Beyond its superintendence of the legal administration, the council also took the responsibility for enforcement of judicial decrees. In spite of its unquestioned pre-eminence in the judicial hierarchy, the council was not arbitrary, nor was it inquisitorial. In a reference to the English chancery which is also valid for the Irish court, W.J. Jones has suggested that

48. This date is based on letters patent for officials of the court. Hughes, *Patentee officers*, pp. 43, 106, 114.
49. BL, Cott. MS Titus B XII, ff. 568v–69. The chief justice received a salary of £100 plus the profits of the seal of queen's bench as a perquisite. The second justice received £49. See PRO, SP 63/64/6–10 for a complete list of salaries of all leading officials and Ellis, *Reform and revival*, pp. 110–32 for a full account of the respective roles of king's bench, common pleas and exchequer to 1534.
50. BL, Cott. MS Titus B XII, ff. 569–70, 667–67v. The chief justice of common pleas received £67 10s. and the second justice £30 per annum. The clerk of common pleas had a fee of £7 and many perquisites from bonds, recognizances, etc. while the clerk of queen's bench had £10 and similar perquisites. All the legal officers were poorly paid by standards in England. Ellis, *Reform and revival*, pp. 106, 123–32, 142.

Distinctions which have so often been made between 'common law' and 'prerogative' courts can be both misleading and dangerous. Most courts found their origin in the royal prerogative to do justice, the royal responsibility of maintaining law and order, and most courts upheld the royal prerogative. The classification of courts into groups according to their equitable or conciliar nature, in presumed distinction to those of common law, is almost equally inappropriate.[51]

In assessing the character of the council as a tribunal, it is necessary to strike a balance between its several powers and responsibilities. For while the council used common law procedures at its formal sessions, even observing the authority of legal precedent, it also exercised extensive discretionary powers in areas of legal administration where no precedent was considered binding and the use of the prerogative was restrained only by the judicial temperament of the members of the council themselves. We must therefore be prepared to look beyond the council sitting formally as a court of law to appreciate the full extent of the council's actual role in the legal system.

THE COUNCIL AS A TRIBUNAL, 1556–71

During the period from 1556 to 1588 the judicial business of the council grew significantly. As the number of cases increased and the legal system assumed a larger work load, the council turned its attention to the expansion and reform of the system itself. The establishment of admiralty jurisdiction and, as regards ecclesiastical law, the linking of a prerogative jurisdiction with that of faculties to create the court (or commission) of prerogative and faculties will not be discussed here.[52] By 1588 the entire judicial apparatus had been extended to embrace a far larger area than the Pale and the loyal towns. Although some reforms were less effective, the structure of the judicial hierarchy was amplified; caseloads were augmented; record-keeping was systematized; and the quality of the individual judges was finally improved after two decades of proposals, instructions and replacements aimed at the entrenched Anglo-Irish bench.

After 1556, litigation was more extensively reported in the council book. Besides hearing a greater number of lawsuits during the law

51. W.J. Jones, *The Elizabethan court of chancery* (Oxford, 1967), p. 18.
52. In 1573 the English privy council reprimanded the council in Ireland for exceeding its jurisdiction in an admiralty case arising in Munster over the seizure of a ship with a rich cargo. See J.C. Appleby and M. O'Dowd, 'The Irish admiralty: its organization and development *c.* 1570–1640', *IHS*, xxiv (1985), 302. See also H. Wood, *Guide to the public records of Ireland* (Dublin, 1919), p. 222 and W.N. Osborough, 'Ecclesiastical law and the reformation in Ireland', in R.H. Helmholz, ed., *Canon law in Protestant lands*, Comparative Studies in Continental and Anglo-American Legal History, Bd. 11 (Berlin, 1992), pp. 223–52.

terms, the council took action generally in a greater variety of legal questions. More recognizances were used in cases where the council was unable to intervene directly, and more commissions were employed to gather evidence and to hear cases.[53] Despite this new activity, the records are not full enough to describe completely the details of conciliar organization and procedure. Most documents recorded only the allegation of the plaintiff and the decision of the council, omitting the specific details of venue, pleadings and arguments. It is difficult to form a sense of the procedural rights enjoyed by the respondent save where some peremptory defence (such as the pleading of the queen's pardon) is advanced.[54] The *ratio decidendi* of a case was almost never recorded and the council seemed to regard itself more as a trier of fact than an interpreter of law.

The Irish council was a prerogative court which operated very much like the council in the marches of Wales. Actions were usually begun by the plaintiff's bill in equity, the defendant's response, a replication and an answer preceding the hearing of evidence.[55] It is quite likely, indeed, that the council followed star chamber procedure as early as 1556, or even before. After the initiatives of Sussex in 1562 led to the development of the court of castle chamber, the chief governors made frequent requests to England for the precise instructions of star chamber procedure.[56] In any event, from the clear erection of the court of castle chamber in 1571 this was the procedure that was applied.[57]

If the hearings and deliberations of the council were too often omitted from the records, the interlocutory orders and decrees were not. Recognizances appeared in increasing numbers during this period. They were generally used to guarantee the performance of obligations associated with the progress of the suit. Many of the recognizances, or bonds, were simply to ensure the appearance of the defendant at the next session of the council, or the court of castle chamber, or one of the common law courts; others guaranteed that the defendant would

53. Canny, however, has characterized the Dublin administration as 'ineffectual', 'inept' and 'perplexed' in its role as the centre of legal administration. His claim that the Gaelic and Anglo-Irish lords did not recognize the courts in Dublin rests on only one example, the notorious dispute between Ormonde and Desmond, and he exaggerates the distinction between an orderly England and an instinctively rebellious Ireland. Canny, *Elizabethan conquest*, pp. 29–30.

54. BL, Add. MS 47,172, f. 21. There are many other examples of this plea in the entry book of the court of castle chamber.

55. Williams, *Council in Wales*, pp. 47–59, 65–66. Also note the bill in equity brought by Giles Nugent in 1581 in 'Council book', ed. Quinn, 153.

56. PRO, SP 63/16/203.

57. Sydney wrote to Cecil complaining of the delay in establishing the court because it lacked a form of procedure. PRO, SP 63/19/109.

not leave Dublin without licence of the lord deputy and council.[58] The council commonly enforced the decrees issued by the other courts or by arbitrators.[59] The recognizance thus became an important instrument in the administration of justice, especially where the threat of a subpoena was not always effective. It was used in quasi-judicial cases of debt involving former officials, and in the guarantee of an indenture between two former litigants.[60] As the number of lawsuits and other legal proceedings continued to grow, the council increasingly resorted to the assurances of a written guarantee such as a recognizance to enforce obligations which the council itself lacked the time to pursue. Indeed, by the end of the period, the recognizances had become ubiquitous in the records of the council, numbering over one half of the entries for 1581–86.[61]

The council increasingly resorted to ad hoc commissions to relieve the pressure of legal business. Although commissions were employed before 1556 for a number of reasons, their proliferation after Sussex became lord deputy occurred because the council had come to rely on them to hear cases that could not be taken up at the council board. In addition, commissions were part of conciliar procedure because at any point in the litigation the case might be interrupted to allow a commission to collect evidence or obtain a deposition. On 4 October 1566, for example, the council commissioned three gentlemen to take depositions regarding the ownership of Cotlandstown, Co. Kildare. The council took up the matter again when it sat next term.[62]

The number of cases heard by the council depended in part on the energy and judicial inclinations of the lord deputy. Lucas Dillon, then attorney general, commended Lord Deputy Sydney to Cecil on 6 November 1568 for holding sessions at Dublin for the important gentlemen of the provinces. He described as 'marvelous' the resort of the chief Anglo-Irish and Irish men to the council to defend and prosecute their rights. He was also among the many observers who saw the need to extend a continuous judicial presence to the remoter parts of Ireland to ensure peace among the Irish.[63] Few were as energetic as Sydney, but every chief governor presided at a large number of judicial sessions. Sydney and the council heard three cases on 20 February

---

58. 'Council book', ed. Quinn, pp. 111 (20), 114 (41, 42), 116 (54), 117 (64) and others. Numbers in parentheses indicate the entries on the pages. See also pp. 117 (59, 60), 128 (150, 151), and others. See also Ellis, *Reform and revival*, p. 158.

59. ibid., pp 129 (162), 136 (183, 184) and others.

60. RIA, MS 24 F 17, ff. 5v, 79.

61. 'Council book', ed. Quinn. Totals: 180 recognizances out of 359 entries.

62. RIA, MS 24 F 17, ff. 256–58v. For the use of commissions in the early Tudor period, see Ellis, *Reform and revival*, pp. 134–42.

63. PRO, SP 63/26/68.

1566, naming arbitrators in each instance to investigate the allegations and to render an appropriate decree. The council itself first heard the full complaint and answer in each suit, then commissioned others to ensure a complete hearing of witnesses and to guarantee the peace between the two parties. Another plea was heard and determined on 21 February and, on the 25th, the council had to defer new litigation, after taking recognizances of both parties, until the succeeding term.[64]

Of course, this spate of proceedings cannot be taken as evidence of daily recourse to the conciliar court. The judicial activity of the council characteristically ran in spurts, due to the press of other business. Indirect evidence for the legal activity of the council comes from a grant of 5 November 1565 to James Bathe, then chief baron of the exchequer, which awarded him a considerable amount of land because he had been '. . . daily employed in deciding Causes relating to the State, Government and writ of the kingdom in the Privy Council, as well in as out of Term time, to his great costs and charges, without any Allowance for the same'.[65]

As the council came to hear more litigation, the tendency for cases to be delayed and forestalled also increased. On 1 August 1560 the council rebuked those on local commissions who '. . . negligently or willfully deferre or delaye the juste ordering of the matter . . .',[66] that is, the cases referred to them by the council itself. One of the longer cases taken up at the council board involved the fraudulent sale of Spanish merchandise by a Flemish captain at Waterford. The council first heard the case on 26 December 1556 and held for the plaintiffs, ordering the goods to be restored or the fair market value paid to their agent. When it appeared that the original order was not performed, Lord Justice Sydney heard the plaintiff again on 2 February 1558, ordered a commission to investigate, and directed the mayor and aldermen of Waterford to make a final order. The plaintiff appeared once again before the council on 25 November 1559 to complain that the defendant had escaped. Finally, the council decreed that the men of Waterford who stood surety for the appearance of the defendant should forthwith pay the agent 200 marks, and allowed that the agent could recover his damages from the now-departed respondent wherever he could find him.[67] After all the delays and nearly three years of litigation in several courts, the Spanish merchants were without a practical remedy at law.

64. RIA, MS 24 F 17, ff.210–12v.
65. PROI, Lodge MSS, Records of the rolls, pp. 157–58.
66. RIA, MS 24 F 17, 134v.
67. ibid., ff. 61v–63, 109v–12. See below, pp. 201 ff., for discussion of related issues in this case.

Other frustrations attended the unwary litigant who approached the conciliar tribunal. The council took up the dispute of Sir Edmund Butler against Oliver Fitzgerald on 25 February 1566, but then, '. . . beeng for the present occupied with other matters of weightie importance and entending shortly to travaill on our apoynted journey to the parties of Leynster . . .',[68] put off the hearing until the next term. The council was often too busy with other non-judicial matters to take on another case, or to follow up on an award which was in practice unenforceable. For reasons of this kind the entire legal establishment was expanded and the focus of general reform was evidently on the common law.

a) litigants

The judicial competence of the council in Ireland was so wide that a summary of its actions must employ appropriate classifications. However, we must remember that the systematization of cases before the council tends to understate the variety and complexity of those cases. As W.J. Jones has said, 'The historian must be wary of inventing classifications which are convenient, but which may have little connexion with the realities of Tudor legal existence'.[69] The identity of a conflict of interests as inherently a legal question poses some additional problems. Penry Williams has noted that 'It is never easy to separate the judicial and the administative aspects of medieval and Tudor institutions; nor is it desirable that we should make a rigid distinction where many contemporaries saw none'.[70] The dispute between the earl of Clanricarde and the irascible lord president of Connacht, Sir Edward Fyton, had many ramifications. The case was complicated at the outset by military overtones arising from the rebellion of Clanricarde's sons, and when the lord president levelled charges of treason against the earl, the council was faced with a number of difficult options. The case was ultimately heard at the council board, but the issue was at least equally a matter of provincial administration stemming from the council of Connacht as well as a military question.[71]

As the judicial business of the council increased, a greater variety of cases was heard. Indeed, the council's jurisdiction tended to overlap that of the common law courts, rather haphazardly in some instances, and this led to the attempted rationalization of conciliar jurisprudence by the creation of the court of castle chamber. Proceedings

68. ibid., f. 212v.
69. Jones, *Elizabethan chancery*, p. 5.
70. Williams, *Council in Wales*, p. 106.
71. PRO, SP 63/32/116–17, 124–25.

involving a threat to public order were widely interpreted as lying within the purview of the council. These might include murder, treason, forgery, slander, and robbery, but until the advent of the court of castle chamber they rarely included riot. The council also heard proceedings involving certain special litigants, that is: the legal interests of the queen, peers of the realm, Gaelic Irish, and foreigners (especially merchants). Finally, the council might also hear miscellaneous actions, such as those between husband and wife, and those involving the loyal towns.

An indictment for treason was normally considered by the council itself, rather than a lower court, since it was the highest tribunal in Ireland and the queen was vitally interested in these proceedings. It is noteworthy that what, at bottom, were political trials were not usually transferred to the English courts for closer scrutiny there. This is significant evidence of the degree of independence of the Irish council in exercising its judicial function.[72] On 7 June 1569, Thomas Masterson, constable of Ferns, charged Thomas Stukeley before the council board with consorting with the rebels and conspiring to make war on the queen's subjects. Stukeley was immediately placed in gaol, with '. . . the Counsell depely debating bothe for the maner of Triall, and carefull ordering of this cause that so highly touch the Quenes highnes her Crowne and dignitie'.[73] After Stukeley had been imprisoned for eighteen weeks and no evidence of treason had been produced, the council released him on a bond of £500 and told him to remain available for further questioning. Stukeley set sail for Spain in the following spring, leaving Waterford on 17 April 1570, which raises a question about the perspicacity of the council on that occasion.[74]

The case of David Hay is interesting because it involved a former privy councillor. On 12 January 1564, seven years after he last signed the council book, he was charged with a felony as well as '. . . high treason towching the queenes majesties most royall person . . .',[75] along with his son, James. Since no one produced any evidence of their treason, they were released after twenty-five weeks in prison on a bond of £5,000. This proceeding seems inquisitorial and arbitrary,

---

72. See S.G. Ellis, 'Henry VIII, rebellion and the rule of law', *Hist Jn*, xxiv (1981), 513, for an excellent discussion of the law of treason which was applied somewhat moderately in the aftermath of the Kildare rebellion. Ellis follows Elton in viewing the Henrician government as too constrained by fiscal, political and constitutional limitations to proceed by wholesale revenge (pp. 529–31). But he exaggerates the extent of military rule under Elizabeth, claiming that moderate policies were quickly superseded by colonial conquest (p. 514). See Elton, *Policy and police*, pp. 374–75; Williams, *Tudor regime*, pp. 389, 463.

73. PRO, SP 63/28/64.

74. RIA, MS 24 F 17, f. 319–19v; Bagwell, *Ireland under the Tudors*, ii, 199.

75. RIA, MS 24 F 17, f. 194–94v.

since in both Stukeley's and Hay's cases the defendants were detained
for over four months without bail and no trial was ever held. However,
this example of malign justice was rarely repeated by the council and
may be explained by its genuine concern over rebellion and foreign
invasion.

In the class of special litigants seeking redress of grievances before
the council, the peers were the most frequent suitors and among these
the earl of Ormonde was foremost, despite his frequent absences in
England. Because he was a favourite of Elizabeth and was recognized
as the most important Irish peer during her reign, he probably thought
his chances of succeeding in an action before the queen's court were
very good. He had lands in four Irish counties and interests all over
Ireland, especially through his unique privilege of the collection of
the prise wines (a form of customs duty owed to the crown on imported
wine).[76] He had a corps of able lawyers and representatives, such as
the loyal Kilkenny merchant, Richard Shee, who were described as
Ormonde's 'officers' in legal matters.[77] Since he was the most anglicized
of the leading Irish nobles, he more easily accepted the jurisdiction of
the royal courts. In addition, his lands were more nearly within the ambit
of conciliar control than those of Desmond, Thomond or Clanricarde.

Although Ormonde and others resisted all encroachments on their
dominions, the council in Ireland was determined to extend its
judicial authority over the Anglo-Irish peers in order to prevent the
desultory fighting so common among them.[78] As a result, the council
heard a greater number of actions involving the peers, and this contributed to its growing caseload. Ormonde's most dangerous adversary
was his neighbour, the earl of Desmond. In July 1558 the council
undertook to resolve their disputes over the prise wines and the liberty
of Tipperary, binding each of them to the final award by a recognizance
of £2,000.[79] In 1565, when the two earls met in private combat in

76. *Calendar of Ormond deeds*, ed. E. Curtis, 6 vols. (Dublin, 1932–43), v, 211.
    Hereafter cited as *Ormond deeds*. The queen granted Ormonde the office of lord
    treasurer by letters patent dated 26 August 1559. He had the prise wines by
    earlier grants (pp. 110–11) and he continued to obtain more land in Ireland
    throughout the period.

77. PRO, SP 63/40/140. Ormonde's suits were increasingly plentiful in this period,
    as were those of the aristocratic Butler family generally. However, Brady has
    argued that Ormonde was an overmighty subject in Ireland who used his
    unique influence to avoid common law jurisdiction and to undermine the lord
    deputy's authority. C. Brady, 'Butler and reform', pp. 54–57.

78. Sydney said, '. . . I am credibly enformed that the whole country is made to
    beleeve by soche as come out of England, that all under the rule of my lord of
    Ormound are exempted from my authority, and that this is the principal cause
    why they seek for no redresse here'. H.M.C., *De L'Isle and Dudley MSS*, ii, 9.

79. RIA, MS 24 F 17, ff. 77v–79. In July 1559 both earls petitioned the queen over
    the rights to prise wines in Youghal and Kinsale. The privy council advised

Co. Waterford, the queen was outraged. She ordered the peers to be fined, called for pledges to be given, and required full submissions and a complete investigation. In the first article of her order she directed the chancery in Ireland to hear the disputes over property and to pursue charges of riot, unlawful assemblies and other public disorders.[80] Despite the direct intervention of the queen in this dispute, she was forced back upon the machinery of justice in Ireland to give effect to her judgments. Hence, even when a case was initially removed from the jurisdiction of the Irish council, its continued advice and cooperation were often needed to reach a final decision.

Another rival of Ormonde was the neighbouring baron of Upper Ossory, head of an Anglo-Irish family which became actively sympathetic to the English government. Sir Barnaby Fitzpatrick was educated at the court of Prince Edward, heir apparent to Henry VIII, along with Ormonde himself. The first baron, his father, was frequently at odds with the earl and demonstrated a characteristic disdain for those orders of the council which adversely affected his interests. By 1576 this feud had become a chronic affair with charges and counter-charges taking up the time of the council. In February 1575 the council decreed that the baron must surrender possession of the castle at Durrow to Ormonde, since the earl had produced a deed leasing the manor to him from the bishop of Ossory.[81] Ormonde wrote to Sydney in August 1576 that the baron was still in possession of the castle, and prayed relief from the council since he '. . . forbore to use force'.[82] However, the baron alleged he had been in possession of it for forty years and his father had built it originally. Besides, the castle and its appurtenances were located on the opposite side of the river Elkin from the old town of Durrow, and Upper Ossory claimed that it formed part of the town of Mayne. The lord chancellor, having heard all the evidence, returned to Dublin and recommended a finding in favour of Ormonde based on his lease from the bishop. The council once again ordered the baron to give up the lands and castle to his adversary,

referral of the case to the two English chief justices who subsequently held for Ormonde by virtue of his letters patent of 12 March 1557. *Ormond deeds*, v, 111. This does not necessarily derogate from the authority of the council in Ireland, as Canny insists. See Canny, *Elizabethan conquest*, pp. 29–30.

80. *Letters and memorials of state*, ed. Arthur Collins (London, 1746), ii, 44–47. Desmond fell foul of the law once again in March 1567 when he was committed by the council to prison in Dublin castle for failing to observe the orders made two years before. The council, then at Limerick, heard complaints from all over Munster against the earl and noted '. . . for lack of administration of justice the shires of Cork, Limerick and Kerry are in manner waste in his default . . .'. H.M.C., *De L'Isle and Dudley MSS*, ii, 5.

81. *Ormond deeds*, v, 259–60.

82. H.M.C., *De L'Isle and Dudley MSS*, ii, 42.

rejecting the plea that his failure to obtain a deed was merely Irish custom.[83] The fact that the council was willing to send the chancellor to Munster and to hear the pleadings twice in two years indicates that the tribunal had some difficulty in reaching an equitable decision. However, when a signed instrument of conveyance was produced, the council had little choice but to follow the common law and order the castle to be surrendered to Ormonde.

As the litigation before the Irish council increased, suitors soon learned the usefulness of appearing to defend the queen's interests. It is difficult to know whether the council stretched this definition to include occasional suits they wanted to hear for other reasons. On the other hand, it is almost certain that the suitors strove to formulate their cases in such a fashion that the council would hear them. If a plaintiff could allege he was defending the interests of the queen he was almost sure to gain a favourable decree. John and Walter Bermingham, for example, alleged before the council in 1557 that the castle of Kannafad '. . . pertayned to the quenes majestie by reason that a certayne somme of money was defrayed for the buylding thereof out of the kinges Majesties treasure and a common cesse was levied of the countrey by ordre directed from the lorde deputie and counsaill . . .'.[84] The Berminghams claimed the rights to the castle as it was erected on their property, and they obtained an interim settlement of a small rent for three years until the title could be finally decided.

Questions of the queen's grants and interpretations of their provisions were frequently brought before the council. In June 1583 the lords justices decreed that a lease made in the name of Emery Lee of Co. Kildare should include the name of his brother, who had defrayed part of the costs of his journey to England. The council found that the queen's letter of 9 August 1582 was obtained in trust for both men and ordered that they share the property equally.[85] Here the council was exercising an equity jurisdiction to award the moiety to the brother who may have had difficulty in demonstrating the intent of the original contract at common law. Similarly, the council had to decide the rights to two manors in Co. Wexford when the tenant was dispossessed before the end of his lease. The incumbent found that the seneschal of Co. Wexford had obtained the rights to his property by a new lease, and the council referred the matter to the judges and law officers. On the basis of their interpretation of the law, the council

83. 'Report on the state of Ireland, 1577–78', ed. C. McNeill, *Anal Hib*, no. 2 (1931), 162, 164–67. The council had ordered Upper Ossory to deliver up the possession of Durrow to Ormonde on 6 August without any result. PRO, SP 63/56/36.

84. RIA, MS 24 F 17, f. 48v.

85. 'Council book' ed. Quinn, 143 (244).

reinstated the original tenant.[86] At times, the queen's appointees initiated proceedings to recover their places. On 5 March 1583, the council imposed a fine of £20 on Anthony Fitton for usurping the office of collector of the imposts in Galway. The council was indignant that twenty-six townsmen should have petitioned the queen to rescind the actual appointment that had been made, and fined them all £10 each.[87] Cases such as these greatly expanded the business of the council, since men were more likely to pursue their property interests at law if they could allege the queen's interests were affected. And this, in turn, assured the council that the overarching policy of anglicization through expansion of the common law would gradually have its desired effect.

The most notorious case was that of Sir Peter Carew, the grasping Devon adventurer, who appealed to the queen to support his claims to lands in Ireland. With the aid of the antiquarian, John Hooker, Carew convinced the queen and privy council that certain records proved his title to lands in Ireland by an inheritance long since lapsed.[88] Hooker claimed that the barony of Idrone, Co. Carlow and certain estates in Co. Meath were legally the lands of Carew.[89] These estates were currently in the possession of the sept of the Cavanaghs and of Sir Christopher Chyvers, respectively . When Carew brought suit before the Irish council in 1568, Chyvers appeared with eight lawyers to challenge the jurisdiction of the court. They claimed that '. . . that court was no ordinary court for trial of lands, and therefore the Lord Deputy and Council were no competent judges; secondarily, that no person should be impleaded for any lands but by the order and course of the common law, and not otherwise . . .'.[90] But William Peryam, Carew's English lawyer, argued that the queen could call before her any matter depending in any court by virtue of her prerogative. On somewhat less provocative grounds he retorted that,

. . . every man being driven to an extremity or wanting just trial, may bring his cause before her Majesty, either in the Chancery or before the Council; lastly, that there were sundry precedents to be shewed how, in the like cases before this, the like matters had been decided there in that land before the Lord Deputy and Council.[91]

86. RIA, MS 24 F 17, ff. 70v–71v.
87. 'Council book', ed. Quinn, 137 (192). Many of these fines were remitted in part by an order of 26 March 1583.
88. *Cal. Carew MSS, 1515–74*, pp. xcvi–xcvii. See the 'Life of Sir Peter Carew' by John Hooker in LPL, Carew MS 605.
89. *Cal. Carew MSS, 1515–74*, p. 383.
90. ibid., p. c.
91. ibid.

The two chief justices and the queen's solicitor concluded that, because Carew could not expect a fair trial at common law, the case could be argued before the council. Chyvers then saw how matters stood and, before a trial of title could be had, pleaded for a settlement with Carew. Perhaps the latter perceived the implications of the hostility he generated among the Anglo-Irish and retreated prudently from his near-triumph. In any case, he settled the estate on Chyvers for a small sum without a hearing on the merits.

In the second action, Carew prosecuted his claim through to a successful conclusion. In a bill of complaint before the council he claimed that he was likely to be defrauded of his due inheritance by the Cavanaghs. The three defendants alleged a kind of prescriptive right, based on their family's possession of the barony since before the conquest and their claim of descent from the king of Leinster. The council rejected this claim and accepted instead Carew's demonstration of his descent from the original barons of Idrone.[92] In general, the council found for the disputant who could demonstrate his title by a showing of ancient deeds, wills or other records, which gave its decrees a distinctly English bias. The example of the Carew case demonstrates how the queen's interests could be manipulated to the advantage of an opportunist, although it is clear there was an element of mutuality in Carew's claim and the queen's support. Nevertheless, the Carew case is not enough, by itself, to taint the administration of justice with the stain of a now archaic Tudor 'despotism'. Neither is it sufficent evidence for the putative irreconcilability of interest between the new English and the Palesmen. Prior to 1578 there was general consensus on the evident worth of the policy of extending the common law despite its intrinsic bias in favour of the apparatus of constitutional (basically English) forms.[93]

The treatment of the Gaelic Irish as suitors before the council is a controversial issue. The evidence, however, would suggest that in practice they were dealt with equitably enough according to the terms of English law and custom. The Cavanaghs' rights were obviously abridged in the Carew case, but other Irish suitors received generally even-handed justice as long as they were prepared to accept it on English terms. In most cases involving Irish litigation, the council named commissioners or arbitrators to investigate the dispute after a

92. *Cal. pat. rolls Ire., Hen. VIII–Eliz*, pp. 520–21.

93. Brady, 'Court, castle and country', pp. 22–23, 36–38, 39. Brady overstates the 'implicit tension' between the Dublin administration and the local community. See also Canny, *Elizabethan conquest*, p. 68. Canny sees the Carew episode as evidence of Sydney's determination to promote colonies, even through spurious lawsuits, but Carew was rarely prominent in Irish government and he was the sole example of an English adventurer on the council.

preliminary hearing at the council board. The cases themselves were quite various, ranging from murder and assault to the abuse of rights to tax and to cess. The council occasionally heard cases which dealt with Irish custom exclusively. For example, after they had established William O'Carroll as chief and captain of the O'Carrolls of Ely, Co. Tipperary, he was accused of 'traytorous' behaviour and deprived. The council then obtained the consent of the O'Carrolls and other freeholders of Ely to call Tege O'Carroll to be 'capitayn of his nacyon' and to exercise his jurisdiction according to letters patent which combined both English law and Irish custom. Tege was ordered by the council in August 1558 to restore the goods of Mulroney O'Carroll and '. . . for all other controversies betwene party and party in the contrey every man to stonde to suche order as shalbe by the breghouns taken betwene them in the presence of Tege or by his assigmente . . .'.[94] In a similar instance, the council issued a decree on 26 July 1583 awarding the tanistship of the O'Kellys to Connor Oge O'Kelly as the eldest in line of succession.[95] As the council expanded its jurisdiction territorially, more suitors came before it seeking the arbitration of local disputes. The Gaelic Irish thus often found themselves embroiled in a lawsuit which they did not initiate, as the Anglo-Irish and other rival chiefs would sue to obtain at law what they could not achieve by force. For example, the O'Tooles sued to establish their right to the 'spending' of the estate of Glancapp, that is, the authority to impose a levy of taxes on land in case an offending party should not abide by the decision of the brehons in Irish litigation.[96] The council, however, rejected the Irish claim in this case and established an exemption which became enforceable at common law.[97]

Occasionally, however, the interests of the Gaelic Irish prevailed even over the influence of an important figure such as Nicholas White, master of the rolls, and a councillor himself. White sued out a writ of appeal seeking to reverse the pardon given to Brian McCahir Cavanagh and Feagh McHugh O'Byrne for the murder of his son-in-law, one Browne. The council took up the case in a preliminary proceeding to decide whether to allow the writ of appeal to be sealed. After long deliberation, the council declared that,

94. RIA, MS 24 F 17, f. 86–86v.
95. 'Council Book', ed. Quinn, 145 (231). In this case the council took depositions of '. . . the ancient men of Imany . . .', and thus based their decision on Irish custom and law. The tanist was the appointed successor to the chief of an Irish sept. He was often a relative but usually not the son of the chief, and rivalry for the position could be intense.
96. *Cal. pat. rolls Ire., Eliz*, p. 328.
97. RIA, MS 24 F 17, f. 51. See also *Cal. pat. rolls Ire., Eliz*, pp. 328–29.

. . . it apperithe that it is no great derogacion to the due corse of Justice and lawe (the state of this government considerid) to deny unto the sayd Browne the Benefit of the lawe in this behalf. And Forasmuche also as it is apparaunt that the graunting of that writ wold renue a blooddie rebellion which withe great travell we have appaysed, whereof were lyke to insue the shedding of muche innocent blood and the spoile of many a good subiecte[98]; And so by indiscreet graunting the corse of Justice to one, we should do great iniustice to manie.[99]

The council continued in that vein, arguing that the object of having the Irish honour the queen's word, especially her pardon, would be frustrated by allowing the writ of appeal. This case was complicated by the anticipation of sudden outbreaks of violence, and most Irish suits were not handled in this timorous fashion. But the council was reluctant to prosecute to the fullest extent of the law when incipient rebellion loomed on the horizon.[100]

There is increasing evidence that the practical hybridization of Gaelic Irish and English social institutions (which one would expect after several hundred years) had advanced to a stage of refinement which permitted some tacit acceptance of real diversity. Katharine Simms, for example, has recently discussed the use of both brehon and common lawyers by Irish chiefs, and the incorporation into brehon law of common law concepts.[101] An article by Nerys Patterson demonstrates the existence of a mixed legal system from the fourteenth century, and shows that Sussex, as late as 1562, was willing to admit the brehons to plead before the governor and council and to have fees for their professional services. Patterson shows how the O'Dorans, a school of brehon lawyers, were employed in 1570 to assist in determining cases before the council, and how they continued to argue for the practical benefits of cooperation with crown policy until the end of the century.[102] Kenneth Nicholls has convincingly argued for study of the fusion of two rival sytems into a hybrid which was a practical juxtaposition

98. The following is crossed out in the MS. '. . . the avoyding whereof is to be preferred farre before the privat interes and comoditie of anie one subiecte . . .'. Bodl, Carte MS 56, f. 65v.

99. ibid. Brady has argued that attempts to establish English law among the Gaelic Irish ended in failure, but the claim is too broad and ignores the inherent complexity of the social and political landscape prior to 1579. See 'Government of Ireland', pp. 358–59.

100. For examples of the selective application of common law principles and the difficulty of requiring compliance with legal mandates and awards in the modern period, see W.N. Osborough, 'Executive failure to enforce judicial decrees: a neglected chapter in nineteenth century constitutional history' in J.F. McEldowney and P. O'Higgins, ed., *The common law tradition: essays in Irish legal history* (Dublin, 1990), p. 115.

101. Simms, 'Brehons of Ireland', pp. 71–75.

102. Patterson, 'Gaelic law and the Tudor conquest of Ireland', 200–01, 207–09, 214.

wherever conflicting claims to land existed.[103] And Steven Ellis has discussed the manner in which the Elizabethan chancery reconciled the conflicting claims of Irish and English justice.[104] Consequently, the older view of a dual system, irreconcilably hostile and mutually antagonistic, must give way to a more complex, nuanced and pragmatic understanding of the condition of law in Ireland. This may make it possible to revise the somewhat overstated claims of Tudor conquest and to envision rather the myriad possibilities which Elizabethan administrators addressed in their attempts to govern Ireland.[105]

When the council heard cases involving foreigners, its problems of jurisdiction and enforcement were intensified. In most of these actions the council was exercising an admiralty jurisdiction because in nearly every suit a ship was involved. However, the ordinary principles of equity would apply, just as they did in England when an admiralty suit was held in chancery alleging a breach of contract.[106] The cases usually involved foreign merchants seeking a remedy which was not available to them at common law. The council took up the suits because in every instance the custody of the ship was in the hands of someone in Ireland, and, in most cases, there were significant international implications.

In a proceeding heard at the council board on 26 December 1556, Francisco Dias, acting for certain Spanish merchants, sued Henry Corneilson of Middelburg for the embezzlement and fraudulent sale of merchandise laden on his ship. Dias charged that the goods were laden in Flanders and discharged at Waterford where they were illegally sold by the ship's master, Corneilson. The council took in evidence certificates of sale from the mayor of Waterford, and noted that the defendant also gave away some goods and sent others to La Rochelle in France to be sold. A decree was handed down requiring all goods then unsold to be delivered into the custody of the mayor of Waterford. The latter was also to receive all money taken in from the sale of goods and the market value of merchandise simply given away.[107] The defendant was ordered to give himself up at Waterford

103. Nicholls, 'Documents on Irish law', 109.

104. Ellis, *Tudor Ireland*, p. 164

105. See Canny, *Elizabethan conquest*, pp. 18, 28. Canny rather extravagantly claims that the 'aggressive' adventurers used advanced anthropological concepts to justify their contempt for the native Irish, while the Irish rebels were proto-nationalistic in their rejection of English rule. See chs. 8, 9. Also, see Bradshaw, *Irish constitutional revolution*, pp. 276–78, for his view of 'political patriotism', in opposition to crown government.

106. Jones, *Elizabethan chancery*, pp. 380–81.

107. RIA, MS 24 F 17, ff. 61v-63. The value of the commodities sold at La Rochelle was disputed because a certificate from La Rochelle showed 2,649 francs received while the factor of the defendant claimed he had only taken 1,910 francs.

and put up a £500 bond to ensure his performance of the order. Repeated council orders over a period of three years were to no avail. When the agent appeared a last time before the council in November 1559 to aver that the defendant had escaped and the decree had never been performed, the council was left without a remedy to provide. It ordered the bond of the defendant surrendered to Dias and limply proclaimed that he might recover from Corneilson the balance of the goods and receipts 'whersoever he shall finde his bodie . . .'.[108]

The order of the council in this case was comprehensive. After hearing all the evidence on both sides of the dispute, the decree ordered the restoration of the goods to the plaintiff and an equitable fee to the defendant. Yet the agent for the plaintiffs, after years of litigation to earn the recovery of their goods, was left without recourse. What went wrong? In the first place, the venue in this case was distant Waterford, where the council had difficulty getting the local men to enforce its decrees. Secondly, the merchandise in question had been spirited away in whole or in part, and the council had to leave the formidable questions of fixing the market value of the goods and of arranging reparations to buyers in the hands of the municipal government of Waterford. Thirdly, the case involved not one but two foreigners and there were no clear means to obtain the original contract in the dispute or, even more, to restore the goods sold at La Rochelle. Finally, the defendant proved unusually resourceful in obtaining several delays and a bond from Waterford merchants which ultimately facilitated his escape. Faced with all these difficulties, the resources of the council were simply not able to provide a remedy at law. In most cases, however, the suit was brought by a foreigner against someone in Ireland, so the council had less difficulty with the appearance of defendants. This case illustrates both the continuous effort to expand conciliar jurisdiction and the practical difficulties of doing so in a time of transition to a more fully developed English model of governance.[109]

Occasionally, the English privy council intervened in cases involving foreigners, perceiving the international complications that might arise. In a letter of March 1572 directed to the lord deputy, the privy council related a complaint made by a Spanish official that a ship of Spain had been taken at sea by an English vessel and her sailors incarcerated and abused in a Dublin gaol. The privy council reminded the lord deputy that the queen was not at war with Spain and advised the release of the Spanish sailors, even if they were guilty of offering the

108. ibid., ff. 110v, 112.
109. Even Canny acknowledges that plans for the presidency system in Munster were based on the ultimate expansion of common law jurisdiction, though he emphasizes the military nature of the endeavour. See Canny, *Elizabethan conquest*, pp. 48, 50.

first provocation.[110] In most cases the privy council allowed the council in Ireland to act independently, and apart from the cases involving foreigners and certain peers, the council was normally free of interference from London.

b) venues

Ordinarily, the council heard complaints while sitting in Dublin, but it was quite common for the lord deputy and a small number of councillors to hold sessions while on progress. The notion of the justiciar's court was still alive, at least in theory, and the lord deputy could hear causes at any venue in Ireland without waiting for the commencement of regular judicial sessions. Precedents for an itinerant council were many, and active governors such as Lord Leonard Grey held sessions of the council wherever he went on progress.[111] This was perhaps the clearest example of the way in which the council could extend its territorial jurisdiction and increase its caseload. The councillors, or certain among them, were ready to encounter the hazards and annoyances of a long, wet journey in order to bring the distant parts of the country under the common law.

In the early Elizabethan period, the expansion of conciliar justice was accelerated. On 12 March 1566 Sydney heard a suit at Youghal with only two ordinary councillors, Sir Thomas Cusake and John Chaloner, but he also joined the bishop of Waterford and Lismore and Warham St Leger to the tribunal.[112] This ability to travel with a few councillors and augment the forum with leading local officials when it was sitting made the council a much more mobile instrument of justice than even the provincial council in the marches of Wales. On 13 April 1566 the council in Dublin reported that Sydney had left at the beginning of Lent with four other councillors for a long progress. This itinerant council went south through the Irish septs of Wicklow, to Wexford, Kilkenny, then north through Leix, Offaly, West Meath and Meath, a journey which roughly circumscribed the periphery of the council's effective jurisdiction at that time.[113] This journey demonstrated the council's sway in the Pale and the surrounding counties

110. BL, Add. MS 32,323, f. 71–71v. See Ellis, *Reform and revival*, pp. 42, 48, 157–58, for the early Tudor origins of conciliar jurisdiction.

111. *Cal. S.P. Ire., 1509–73*, p. 47. In January 1539 Grey heard cases in Carlow, Kilkenny, New Ross, Waterford, Wexford and Clonmel. In October 1543 St Leger and eight councillors heard a case in Galway and issued a decree which was later exhibited in the court of exchequer and enrolled there. *Blake family records*, ed. Blake, pp. 83–85.

112. PROI, Lodge MSS, Records of the rolls, p. 163. See Canny, *Elizabethan conquest*, pp. 48–54, 61 and Ellis, *Tudor Ireland*, pp. 167–70.

113. PRO, SP 63/17/17.

while it extended the council's judicial authority beyond the traditionally loyal areas. In June 1579 Lord Justice Drury, who was holding sessions with Sir Lucas Dillon and Sir Edward Fyton at Kells in Co. Meath, articulated the widely accepted reasoning behind the promotion of itinerant justice. He ordered certain leading O'Reilly chiefs to appear once a year at every session held in Co. Meath and once a year in Dublin at the queen's bench, declaring that

This device ys thought good not onlie to kepe peace in that borders, but also to be a meane to make those wild headed people acquainted and more familiar, with their more Civile neighbeures and so to enure them with seinge and heringe of Civilitie, Lawe and iustice.[114]

THE LEGAL ESTABLISHMENT AND MOVEMENTS FOR REFORM

In addition to its adjudicative functions, the council had the responsibility for the broader legal administration of Ireland. This involved mainly administrative and quasi-judicial acts as opposed to the formal decrees and orders issued by the council acting as a court. The delegation of conciliar authority may be viewed as part of the widening scope of the council's legal responsibility from 1556 to 1578. Although the number of lawsuits heard by the council clearly increased after 1556, much more impressive, in one sense, was the progress made by the council in the carrying out of the important ancillary or supplementary tasks of issuing recognizances, deputing commissions, organizing the assizes, disseminating the statute laws and reforming the courts. The pattern of increased administrative and legal activity demonstrates once again the determination of the council to extend and consolidate its authority in Ireland.

The police functions of the council were broad, but were usually delegated to local men. However, in some cases the attention of the council itself was directed by the privy council in England to suspected felons who escaped to Ireland. The council was required to notify the port towns to search for a suspected offender in 1579, for example.[115] The correction of errant officials was a more characteristic function that it fell to the council to undertake. In June 1585 the council decreed that all justices of the peace who had not executed or performed mandates and commissions sent to them for the preservation of order would be punished according to their offences.[116] The malfeasance of non-judicial officers needed reproof as well, and here the council acted with dispatch, particularly when prompted by the

114. PRO, SP 63/67/24. See also PRO, SP 63/65/64v.
115. BL, Stowe MS 160, f. 19v.
116. 'Council book', ed. Quinn, 122 (99), 118 (73–74).

queen. In the case of Captain Harrington, who blundered into the house of the earl of Kildare in Dublin and executed one of the O'Tooles by martial law, the queen took offence at his action. Harrington had been expressly told not to execute O'Toole and the erring soldier was committed to Dublin castle at the queen's orders.[117]

Due to the increase of legal business in Dublin, and in the Pale generally, the council used ad hoc commissions in the investigation and determination of suits. The origin of these commissions has been traced to the early sixteenth century by Steven Ellis, and he has shown that English legal and administrative forms were relatively well-preserved in Munster.[118] Commissions named by the Irish council usually included at least one councillor as well as local men or other officials. Most of the commissioners sent from the council were law officers or judges, while non-judicial office-holders like the secretary and vice treasurer were rarely included. Men of great experience who spoke the Irish language were also frequently sent, hence the presence of Sir Thomas Cusake, Francis Agarde and Francis Cosby on many commissions. Commissions were always ad hoc, and were used in cases within the Pale as well as beyond it. The council employed characteristic formulae when rehearsing the need for a commission:

. . . forasmouche as for other more waightye affaires we can not convenyently ourselves attende to call the partyes before us, . . . we have thought good by theas our lettres to auctoryse you or any two of you as well to call the saide partyes before you . . . and to here and examyn at large their severall grieffes and varyaunces, as also to order and determyne the same betwixte them as to justice shall appertayne.[119]

In one case, anticipating the breach of the recent proclamation regarding the re-sale of stolen goods, the council declared it would '. . . remytt any mattier in controversye betwene partye and partye to the hearing and determynyng of . . . a commission . . .'.[120]

The delegation of conciliar authority to arbitrators appears at first blush to be little different from the use of commissions, and at times it is difficult to tell them apart. However, commissions were more formal in nature. They were engaged in the determination of a solemn

---

117. BL, Stowe MS 160, ff. 133v–34v. Two months later Harrington was released because the O'Tooles had entered into a dangerous confederation with the O'Briens.

118. Ellis, *Reform and revival*, pp. 136–40. He explicitly repudiates Canny's assertion that royal justice had practically ceased to exist in Munster. Ellis, p. 181. See Canny, *Elizabethan conquest*, p. 55.

119. RIA, MS 24 F 17, f. 23v. See Ellis, *Reform and revival*, pp. 135 ff. on the use of judicial commissions of oyer and terminer, gaol delivery and assize.

120. RIA, MS 24 F 17, f. 33v.

legal cause of action while arbitrators were named to decide an issue between two adversaries which, however heated, had not been joined in a court of law. Generally, arbitrators were to decide between the claims of disputants whose arguments were of relatively equal merit. They were to deliver an equitable, balanced judgment, fair to both sides. The commission, on the other hand, determined questions of liability based on fixed principles and took evidence impartially without attempting to balance the equities of the case. Arbitrators were generally local men selected by each side in a contest, with the approval of the council, while commissioners were always appointed directly by the council. The distinction was made on one occasion by the council with at least theoretical clarity, when it declared, '. . . the parties are to elect arbitrators, who are to compose differences, and such as they cannot compose to submit in proof to the lords justices or to commissioners appointed by them'.[121] In this case, the arbitrators were to attempt to settle outstanding issues before legal process was instituted, and this may have been their most characteristic function.

The commissions of martial law varied substantially from ad hoc commissions, but they illustrate the efforts of the council to supplement the common law with a military presence. In 1559–60 commissions to use martial law were issued for all the counties of the Pale. This might have been a device to enable local officials to expel idle men and vagabonds without the evidentiary obstacles of common law or the sympathies of local juries to deter them. The commission declared that all persons who had less than a forty shilling freehold or £10 in chattels and were found to be felons, rebels or 'notorious malefactors' were to be put to death.[122] Commissions of martial law were certainly a provocation to those Irishmen who were commonly loyal to the crown, and they were usually issued only when circumstances seemed to require a strong hand. Leading policy-makers such as Lord Chancellor William Gerrard opposed the use of coercive justice, and the commission of martial law was expressly discouraged by Elizabeth in 1586 except in cases of rebellion. She required that from that time forth martial law would be used only by the lord deputy with the advice of the council because it was dishonourable to use simple coercion when complete justice could be rendered at common law and, not least important, because the queen obtained no profits from forfeitures or escheats when the offender was executed by martial law.[123]

121. 'Council book', ed. Quinn, 151 (251).

122. *P.R.I. rep. D.K., 11*, pp. 33, 52–53.

123. BL, Add. MS 4,786, ff. 37–38. The queen ordered that sheriffs and justices of the peace replace captains and seneschals wherever possible, and she proscribed the use of martial law by sheriffs.

Most cases in which commissions were appointed were of a judicial nature. In 1567 the council named Lucas Dillon and two others to go to Wexford to hear the verdict of a jury on the forfeiture of rebels' lands. When the jury found that the lands of the O'Mores were annexed to the crown it was difficult to escape the conclusion that the mission of the three men from the council had been mildly coercive![124] The council might even name a commission to hear a suit in Dublin city, noting that '. . . our leisure then would not suffer us to heare the controversye . . .'.[125] In a complaint by the mayor and corporation against the Trinity Guild of Dublin it was alleged that the guild unlawfully detained certain privileges and franchises from the whole city. The council dispatched Francis Agarde, a councillor himself, and three others to hear the case, and after perusing the relevant charters they finally held for the complainant. It was more common for the council to name commissioners to hear causes far from Dublin. In August 1560, for example, the council, having been overwhelmed with local business, sent letters to the five leading men of Co. Waterford, requiring them to be commissioners for that county. The council explained that '. . . whereas at our last being at Waterforde the tyme served us not for to determyne the sutes and complaintes whiche were there exhibited unto us, we sende unto you herewith bounde together suche of the saide billes as were not by us there determyned . . .'.[126]

The largest number of suits which required the appointment of a commission were those involving peers of the realm. Here the council had to proceed with care. In 1556 Robert Dillon and John Plunket were sent to the countries of the earl of Ormonde and the baron of Upper Ossory with instructions to '. . . learne and understonde, by all the lawfull wayes and meanes they maye, eyther by deposition of wittnesses or otherwyse, what hurtes and damages have byn donne by the saide erle and baron one againste another or by any their tenantes, servauntes and followers . . .'.[127] In 1564 the council named four commissioners to travel to Munster and there determine the particulars of the disagreement between Ormonde and Desmond, a political feud of long standing. The chief justice of queen's bench, the master of the rolls, the attorney general and the adroit ex-chancellor Sir Thomas Cusake were given this task and directed to take recognizances

---

124. *Cal. pat. rolls Ire., Hen VIII—Eliz*, pp. 505–06.

125. ibid.

126. The five men were: the bishop of Waterford, Lord Power, Sir Maurice Fitzgerald, the mayor of Waterford and the sheriff. RIA, MS 24 F 17, f. 144. In January 1572 the council dispatched three of its own members, including the chief justice of queen's bench, to hear the causes in Kilkenny. When they returned after six months they had levied fines totalling £3,316 5s. PRO, SP 63/35/20.

127. RIA, MS 24 F 17, f. 28v.

from the earls for their future good behaviour.[128] The leading lawyers and judges were almost invariably employed on politically sensitive and potentially explosive missions such as this one.

The effectiveness of the commissions would vary, reflecting the influence of factors such as the subject-matter of individual suits, the identity of those who sat as members and the choice of venue. The pressure of legal and other business meant that the council had to rely increasingly on commissions, although it became necessary to intervene at times when a commission failed to do its work. In the case of John Horne, a mariner of Gloucester, a commission was named to discover the offenders who robbed his ship of £90 in the river of Wexford, murdered the ship's master and wounded Horne's agent. This heinous crime went unsolved by local authorities, and the council named a commission to hear the evidence and find the malefactors. In February 1571, after the commission had failed to discover the culprits, the council reprimanded them and required them, together with the leading men of Wexford, to devise a penalty of £90 to be levied equally on the entire county and paid in to the council before 20 May.[129] Such decisive action was uncommon, however. At the other end of the spectrum of judicial effectiveness, we find the cause of William Sarsfield of Cork. A commission of July 1564 ordered David Oge Mantagh Barry to pay Sarsfield the rent due for his property in Kilvellan. Twelve years later, in October 1576, the unfortunate Sarsfield was still trying to recover his long overdue rent.[130]

In spite of their occasional ineffectiveness, the commissions were viewed as useful and necessary by the council and were employed continually up to the end of the century. The court of castle chamber also used commissions to hear evidence and occasionally to render a decree in a suit begun at that court. The advent of the provincial councils in Munster and Connacht meant that certain functions of the commissions there would be taken up at Limerick or Galway or wherever those tribunals were sitting. Sydney anticipated these developments by several years when in 1566 he called upon Sir Warham St Leger to hear the case of the baron of Dunboyne against Piers Butler and Patrick Shurlocke.[131] St Leger's commission was the abortive beginning of the council in Munster. The commissions were really the vanguard of the council's policy of extending its territorial

128. *Cal. pat. rolls Ire., Hen VIII—Eliz*, pp. 485–87. In the event, the two earls were drawn into battle over a series of land disputes, but it is not clear that they simply ignored the Dublin administration in this case. See Brady, 'Butler and reform', p. 53; Canny, *Elizabethan conquest*, pp. 29–30; Ellis, *Reform and revival*, p. 140.

129. RIA, MS 24 F 17, ff. 341v–43.

130. TCD, Caulfield papers, ff. 74, 102.

131. RIA, MS 24 F 17, f. 216.

jurisdiction, using the instrument of the common law. Nevertheless, the level of enforcement of judicial decrees remains unknown so it would be difficult to define precisely the geographical areas in which conciliar jurisdiction was effective. It would not be too much to say, however, that the perimeter was expanding.

The establishment of new provincial councils or presidencies was designed to offer a more systematic judicial presence in regions distant from Dublin than the ad hoc commissions could provide (see Map 3). These regional governments in miniature combined both the legal machinery of conciliar jurisprudence with a small military retinue, and a fuller description of them will be found in chapter five. Nicholas Canny has suggested that the provincial presidencies constituted a key element in the Elizabethan policy of conquest and colonization, despite much evidence of the judicial role which had been planned for them.[132] Ciaran Brady has recently challenged the assertion that the aim of these regional councils was to reduce the power of local lords, but he also sees them as primarily military jurisdictions.[133] Yet all the recent writers acknowledge that instructions to the presidencies incorporated the objective of assimilation through the implementation of a widened common law jurisdiction. Anthony Sheehan, writing of the post-rebellion period in Munster when expropriations might have been more easily justified, explains that the government proceeded carefully and equitably to examine the lawful claims to land, and calls for a more sophisticated picture of English policy in Ireland.[134] Cross-currents in policy formulation and ambiguous assertions of crown dominion in the regions of Ireland require a re-conceptualization of the now familiar argument for a Tudor conquest. Anglicization, assimilation, acculturation and agreement need to be considered in a new investigation of the origins of the provincial presidencies.

The reform and improvement of the judicial system was another aspect of the council's strategy of extending its effective control. Basic

132. Canny, *Elizabethan conquest*, pp. 47–51, 90–92, 93–99. But see p. 64 for the importance of the judicial role in the presidencies. See also P. Piveronus, 'Sir Warham St Leger and the first Munster plantation, 1568–69', *Eire-Ireland*, xiv (1979), 32.

133. Brady, 'Desmond rebellion', 295; 'Court, castle and country', pp. 39–40; Canny, *Elizabethan conquest*, p. 106. But see Pawlisch, *Sir John Davies and conquest of Ireland*, pp. 38–39 for the view that provincial councils were essentially tribunals by design.

134. A. Sheehan, 'Official reaction to native land claims in the plantation of Munster', *IHS*, xxiii (1983), 298. See also, B. Cunningham, 'The composition of Connacht in the lordships of Clanricard and Thomond, 1577–1641', *IHS*, xxiv (1984), 7–9; M. MacCarthy-Morrogh, *The Munster plantation: English migration to southern Ireland, 1583–1641* (Oxford, 1986), pp. 2–3; R. Gillespie, *Colonial Ulster: the settlement of east Ulster, 1600–1641* (Cork, 1985), pp. 1–3.

changes in the traditional legal establishment, coupled with the extension of the common law through new tribunals and commissions, were
the two principal components of the conciliar strategy. And the reform
of the Irish judiciary was the first object of every observer of the legal
system in Ireland. Although the judges served during pleasure and
not for life, as did some clerks of the crown, it proved very difficult to
get rid of aged and incompetent justices. J.E. Neale and others have
noted how much English office-holders in the sixteenth century depended on their stipends, treating their offices like property, unwilling to
let them go without the security of an ample pension,[135] and the same
certainly held true for Irish officials.[136] This was one of the basic criti-
cisms by the lords deputy who, like Sydney, called for replacement of
decrepit judges. Writing to Leicester on 1 March 1566, Sydney said,
'In Concell the chancelor the ij cheefe Justyces & the cheif baron are
all decayed and almost spent men. What shold I discoors of the rest?
In troth my Lord if I have not help in this all will be to wreck and I to
shame'.[137] Sydney was able to pack off Lord Chancellor Curwen, who
desperately wanted to leave, in the following year, and Chief Baron
Bathe was replaced in 1570 by Lucas Dillon. But the two chief justices
were certainly octogenarians before they died in their respective
offices in 1580 and 1583.[138]

Many judges were accused of failure to attend regularly at their
respective courts, but the most damning allegation against the Irish
judiciary, and in the long run the most telling, was that of partiality in
their decisions. Because they were so closely allied to leading families
in the Pale, they were charged with dealing unfairly in cases affecting
the interests of friends and relatives. It was not simply advanced age,
because Englishmen such as Curwen and Weston grew old in Ireland,
but alliance that told against the Anglo-Irish judges. Gerrard put the
case quite clearly in a letter to Cecil on 15 November 1576:

After I had spent one fortenighte in the Chancerie Corte in Tearme
tyme, sene [seen] unto the kings benche, Comen pleaz and Exchequer (in

135. J.E. Neale, 'The Elizabethan political scene', *Brit Acad Proc*, xxxiv (1948), 97–
117; W. MacCaffrey, 'Place and patronage in Elizabethan politics', in J. Hurstfield,
S. T. Bindoff and C.H. Williams, ed., *Elizabethan government and society* (London,
1961), pp. 111–26.

136. Brady, 'Court, castle and country', pp. 33–38. See also Ellis, *Reform and revival*,
pp. 210–14.

137. PRO, SP 63/16/87.

138. Ball, *Judges*, i, 140. Ball puts the case perhaps too strongly, saying, 'the insufficiency of the judges . . . was a subject of complaint for three-fifths of Elizabeth's
reign. She was singularly unfortunate. Apart from want of legal knowledge, it
was the exception to find anyone on the judicial benches who was not suffering
from age or ill-health'. ibid., i, 139.

truthe my Lord onlie showes and shadowes of Cortes) and had considered of the justices and officers, who I see rather overlepte [overleaped] as Scarecrows than reverenced as magistrates, and howe hardlie before them, any cause maye receave Indifferente triall by Jurie, I toke the hearing of all causes, all thoughe more aptlie apperteiginge to the other Cortes.[139]

The English themselves were not above partiality, of course, while some Anglo-Irish judges earned a reputation for honest dealing.[140] Yet the most common charges were levelled by men like Sydney, who claimed that there was too great an affinity between judges and judged, that the Gaelic Irish never got a fair trial, and that the judges kept part of the fines and amercements due to the queen.[141]

This being the state of the judiciary, there were, understandably, many proposals for reform throughout the period. Certainly the most common suggestion was to install an English judiciary in Ireland, but such a scheme was considered too impractical at this time since no distinguished jurists would go to Ireland without a large stipend. In a letter of 1567 Elizabeth demonstrated her awareness of the problems of low stipends for English judges and potential recriminations by Irish justices relieved of their offices. She declared that,

We perceive by your letters and have thought it always to be true, that the insufficiency of our iustices both of our Bench and of our Commen Please, with others in our Exchequer there, is a great hindrance to our service, and a lack to the due adminstration of justice, wherfore we do lyke well to have them charged and some sent from hence to hold their

139. PRO, SP 63/56/105. Gerrard had deliberately engineered an extension in the sphere of competence of the Irish chancery in order to improve the quality of judicial treatment of litigants in the common law courts. See also K. Nicholls, 'Calendar of salved chancery pleadings', *Louth Arch Soc Jn*, xvii (1969–72), 250. He argues that the lack of local courts in unshired territories, the difficulty of finding impartial juries, and the unique ability of equity jurisdiction to hear cases involving Irish customs and brehon law drove suitors to the chancery court.

140. See the remarks by Gerrard on each of the queen's law officers in LPL, Carew MS 628, ff. 311v–14. Gerrard listed the men and their 'dispositions' in this thoughtful memorandum done in 1576. He found the two aged chief justices quite ill and said of Sir Robert Dillon that he was '. . . of late yeares unapt to travell and past service, he cometh not to the court . . .'. James Dowdall and Richard Talbot, second justices in the queen's bench and common pleas, respectively, were impugned as corrupt and well-connected in the Pale. In the chancery, Gerrard found Sir Nicholas White, master of the rolls, '. . . greatlye allyed in the pale by his marriages . . . a depe dissembler, greatly corrupt and wilfully affected with oute regard of troth or equitie . . .'.

141. PRO, SP 63/32/186. For the influence of faction on the Dublin administration, see Brady, 'Court, castle and country' pp. 29–30, 35–38. See also Hart, 'The king's serjeant at law', pp. 80, 94–95. For comparison see W. Prest, 'Judicial corruption in early modern England', *Past & Present*, no. 133 (1991), 67–95.

places. Wherein is to be considerid that the interteynment of theim which be there will not be thought sufficient for such as wer meete to be sent from hence for those places, the choice of whom must be the better because they which shal be removid there and their freends wil be ready to deprave theim which shal succeede.[142]

Undaunted by these difficulties, on 13 September 1577 she nominated Thomas Snagge to be attorney general and, because of his learning and experience, awarded him the unusual pension of £100 per annum in addition to the fees of his office.[143] In 1579 she noted the infirmity of the two chief justices and called for the chief governor, with the advice of the lord chancellor and the rest of the council, to choose two of the most qualified lawyers to 'occupy' the chief justiceships.[144] This was to be a temporary expedient until she could appoint an English judge, but the fact remains no English judge was named until 1585. Despite the recommendations and clear intentions of the government, the Anglo-Irish, even if Catholic, continued to enter the legal administration until at least 1593.[145] The systematic substitution of English judges for native-born incumbents began in earnest after 1603 with the adoption of a rigorous policy of 'legal imperialism' following the Tyrone rebellion.[146]

Since it appeared that the wholesale replacement of the Irish judiciary was impracticable, other proposals were made to bring them more into line with English standards. In 1580 the privy council thought that if judges and chief barons used the robes and attire that the justices used in England they '. . . would greatly countenance ther place . . .'[147] and inspire more respect for their positions. The council also wanted four men of the coif chosen to place exclusively in the court of common pleas, and sought to have only qualified serjeants at law appointed to the senior positions on the bench.[148] Sir

142. *Sidney S.P.*, p. 64.

143. *Cal. pat. rolls Ire., Eliz*, pp. 11–12.

144. BL, Cott. MS Titus B XIII, f. 274v. Dr Kenny has argued that Anglo-Irish lawyers were 'willing instruments of administrative policy . . . and of the extension of English rule to Gaelic areas'. Kenny, 'The exclusion of Catholics', 338.

145. Ball, *Judges*, i, 151–52. Gerrard understood the resentment which might be visited on an English interloper and, to soften the blow, propounded that each chief justice of the royal courts and provincial councils be assisted by an experienced Irish judge. 'Gerrard's report', ed. McNeill, p. 184.

146. Pawlisch, *Sir John Davies and conquest of Ireland*, pp. 39–42; Kenny, 'Exclusion of Catholics', 338–42.

147. BL, Stowe MS 160, f. 120. The initiative appears to have been stillborn. See Kenny, *The Kings's Inns and the kingdom of Ireland: the Irish 'inn of court', 1541–1800* (Dublin, 1992), p. 62.

148. BL, Stowe MS 160, f. 120–20v; Kenny, *King's Inns*, p. 62. For the strictly regulated English practice, see E.W. Ives, 'Promotion in the legal profession of

James Croft recognized early in the reign that England could not spare the number of judges needed to provide Ireland with the protection of the law. Therefore, he suggested in 1561 that 'Graund scoles' be erected to instruct the Irish in English laws and customs and meanwhile to use commissions to bring the common law to every part of the Pale.[149]

The legal administration of Ireland would have been far more effective if the majority of the people had been aware of the statute laws. The printed ordinances of 1534 represented a start in this direction, and the king declared his intention to publish all relevant Irish statutes in response to a petition of the parliament of 1541–43.[150] This project was soon dropped, and Sussex's attempt to get the statutes printed in 1556 also failed. By 1562 Cecil had perused notes of the earlier compilation and called for a survey of laws currently in force to be printed,[151] and Elizabeth incorporated these orders in her instructions of 4 July 1565.[152] The statutes were finally printed in 1573 but they were apparently not widely disseminated. Gerrard sought a further publication of certain laws in 1577,[153] and subsequently both Drury and Perrot called for the printing of statute laws as a means to achieve greater public order.[154]

Of all those who offered proposals for the reform of Irish justice, Sir William Gerrard was perhaps the most perceptive. Indeed, he was probably the most active, and the most competent, of the Irish lord chancellors of the sixteenth century.[155] From his landing in Ireland on 23 June 1576 he was given enlarged powers as lord chancellor.[156] Gerrard wasted little time in adjusting to Irish customs, for he took his oath and seal of office on 25 June and six days after he landed he called the judges and law officers before him. He wrote to Walsingham on 29 June, saying,

Yorkist and early Tudor England', *LQR*, lxxv (1959), 348–63; Ives, *The common lawyers of pre-reformation England* (Cambridge, 1983), ch. 4.

149. PRO, SP 63/3/42. For a complete study of the development of Irish legal education, see Kenny, *King's Inns*, passim.

150. PRO, SP 60/2/64–71. For a discussion of the problems of publishing the laws of the kingdom see D.B. Quinn, 'Government printing and the publication of the Irish statutes in the sixteenth century', *RIA Proc*, xlix (1943), sect. c, 45–109.

151. Quinn, 'Government printing', 50–55.

152. PRO, SP 63/14/2–15. Article no. 26.

153. BL, Add. MS 4,763, f. 413. See also PRO, SP 63/56/105.

154. Quinn, 'Government printing', 56–61.

155. But see Ball, *Judges*, i, 137, who claims he lacked dignity.

156. 'Gerrard's report', ed. McNeill, 93.

I have had before me the hole crew of Judges officers and Counsaylors and . . . I see not eny so sownde in religeon so hable in knowledge and honest conversacion . . . as I colde wishe, I see a show or a shaddow of Justice and the admynistracion of it, but farr from such dexteritie as is requisite.[157]

In a memorandum prepared for Walsingham on the competence of all the law officers, he briefly noted the spouse of each man, his family connections, the quality of his learning, the disposition of his rulings, and the extent of his corruption.[158] Writing to Cecil in November 1576, he described his frustration (see above, pages 210–11) with the condition of the four senior courts and explained that he had decided to hear all cases in chancery, holding sessions every day of the vacation.[159] It is difficult to imagine a more auspicious beginning for an energetic lord chancellor, or a less tractable one.

The most convincing proposal made by Gerrard was his insistence on holding assizes regularly throughout the Pale and the borders. He sought to bring itinerant justice wherever idle men and vagabonds terrorized people in the towns, forcing them to stay within their walls. He declared to Cecil that, 'Sitting tearmes in Dublin will never by lawe suppresse them [idle followers]'.[160] Gerrard conceived of a broadly based, systematic extension of the common law to areas which had seldom experienced it. He wanted seasoned judges to conduct regular sessions at the principal towns in Connacht and Munster and these judges, additionally, to hold assizes twice each year throughout the provinces. In recommending assizes he also lauded the success achieved in Wales, saying,

I tolde their Honnors that justice would be delivered to itinerant circuitinge the whole pale and everye other partie made counties twoe tymes in the yeare to deliver the same at the doores of such poore creatures as either for feare or wante of abilitie could not travell to Dublin. A better president . . . colde not be found then to imitate the course that reformed Walles . . . [for] . . . Walles contynued their Walshe disorders untill kinge H. the viijth established Justices Itinerant to travell throughout all partes of Walles . . . .[161]

---

157. PRO, SP 63/56/105.

158. LPL, Carew MS 628, ff. 311v–14 (see above, note 140, for details).

159. PRO, SP 63/56/105.

160. ibid., f. 105v.

161. 'Gerrard's report', ed. McNeill, 124. For the assize reforms of the early seventeenth century see now J. McCavitt, ' "Good planets in their several spheares"— the establishment of the assize circuits in early seventeenth century Ireland', *Ir Jur*, xxiv (1989), 248.

The lord chancellor was nothing if not ambitious, for he even called for an inroad into Ulster, recommending Richard Belyng, the queen's solicitor general, to hold sessions twice a year at Newry. He wanted all the laws then in force to be printed, explained and made available for the use of the judges. Gerrard not only named the counties that each judge should travel, but he even named specific officials and peers to guard the judges as they journeyed throughout each county.[162] If this scheme had been effectively carried out, all Ireland save Ulster might have been governed from Dublin. He tried to make the administration of justice less burdensome to the local inhabitants by suggesting that the judges should scrupulously pay for all their own victuals, and that the lord deputy should order provisions stored for their use in select places. He carefully laid out the costs of the scheme, totalling £1,306 13s. 4d., and suggested ways to defray the expenses.[163] Unfortunately, Gerrard's proposals were brought forward just on the eve of the Munster rebellion, and after 1585 the conditions on which Gerrard based them had changed significantly.

Gerrard's proposals were sound enough, of course, to outlast the insurrection, but they were only implemented in part and the subjugation of Ireland was ultimately undertaken by the sword in the 1590s. Gerrard was opposed to coercion, despite his desire for severity of justice, and his views deserve to be quoted at length:

Soche as affirme the swoord muste goe before to subdue theise 'Englishe degenerates' greatly err. For can the swoord teache theim to speake Englishe, to use Englishe apparell, to restrayne theim from Irishe exaccions and extorcions, and to shonne all the manners and orders of the Irishe. Noe it is the rodd of justice that must scower out those blottes. For the sword once went before and settled their auncestors and in theim yet resteth this instincte of Englishe nature, generally to feare justice . . . And untill this course and devise to purge those Englishe degenerates, the second sorte of English rebells, of and from all Irish staynes be taken in hande, the pollecye to wade further to gayne territories is as it were to suffer the parties nier home to burne, and to seek to quenche a fyer afarr of [off].[164]

162. 'Gerrard's report', ed. McNeill, 185–87. For the chief justice of queen's bench: Cos. Louth, Meath, West Meath, Dublin, Kildare, King's, the city of Dublin and town of Drogheda; the chief justice of common pleas: Cos. Queen's, Carlow, Wexford, Waterford, Kilkenny, and Tipperary; the chief justice in Munster: Cos. Cork, Limerick and Kerry; the chief justice in Connacht: Cos. Sligo, Roscommon, Mayo, Galway and Clare. For the handling of reform in Ulster and its prospects for success, see H. Morgan, 'The end of Gaelic Ulster: a thematic interpretation of events between 1534 and 1610', *IHS*, xxvi (1988), 8–32.

163. 'Gerrard's report', ed. McNeill, 185–87.

164. ibid., 96. Gerrard appears to agree that the basis for 'general reformation' should be the expansion of the common law. However, he demonstrates here a

While he was in Ireland Gerrard became seriously ill, but he remained indefatigable. In 1579 he assured Walsingham that he would go on circuit himself in the summer because the chief justices were no longer able to travel. He intended to go on assize to Drogheda, Louth, Meath, West Meath, Longford and Offaly unless sickness deterred him. In January 1581 he left Ireland to return to Chester and died there in May. Had his plans been carried through, the effective jurisdiction of the Irish council might have been substantially greater. In Gerrard's design, the two aspects of conciliar strategy, judicial reform and the extension of the legal system, were finally united, only to be supplanted by coercion and plantation after 1585.

THE COURT OF CASTLE CHAMBER

The wide-ranging judicial competence of the lord deputy and council was further refined and amplified by the creation of a distinct tribunal, the court of castle chamber, which acted in partnership with the residual judicial authority of the council itself.[165] Thus, the council became both author and actor in the expansion of the common law. The government in London wished to model the Irish council more precisely on its English parent. It was assumed that this structural assimilation would improve the effectiveness of the administration by imposing a systematic and continuous review on the judicial establishment. A council strengthened by this new star chamber jurisdiction would be able to hear more cases, to keep better records and to call the rich and powerful to the bar of justice. The process of anglicizing the administration was intended to filter down into the native culture itself by this buttressing of the judicial apparatus.

a) origins and evolution

This court was explicitly modelled on the English court of star chamber, but the difficult questions of its origins, its jurisdiction and the reasons for its creation are no more easily resolved than for its parent court. G.R. Elton has said, 'The history of the court of star chamber sets a number of problems all arising from the fact that it was in effect the king's council sitting as a tribunal'.[166] Assumptions about

profound distrust of the alien Gaelic culture which reform sought to displace. For a comparison of reforming schemes in this period, see E. Walshe, 'A treatise for the reformation of Ireland', ed. B. Bradshaw, *Ir Jur*, xvi (1981), 299–303; Brady, 'Government of Ireland', pp. 209–14, 235–37.

165. See my essay, 'The origins of the court of castle chamber: a star chamber jurisdiction in Ireland', *Am Jn Legal Hist*, xxiv (1980), 22–55.

166. G.R. Elton, ed., *The Tudor constitution: documents and commentary* (Cambridge, 1960; rev. ed., 1982), p. 158. The council had long heard suits and its original

the benefits of star chamber relieving the council for other work may have been too readily accepted, since the new court was simply a judicial gathering of the council itself. The development of a special arm of the council for the hearing of certain causes was difficult to trace, because it repeatedly merged in the ordinary council and was never intended to be physically separate. Elton has shown that the court of star chamber was created at least by the 1530s. In 1540 it obtained a distinct clerical organization and began its own entry book. Nevertheless, he said,

. . . the Court of Star Chamber rested upon no statute but derived from the immemorial authority of the old Council to receive petitions and redress grievances. The date at which the Council sitting as a court became a true court with a full public procedure still remains unsettled.[167]

The origins of the court of castle chamber are at least equally obscure. The Irish council had traditional judicial powers which were substantially augmented in the course of the sixteenth century after the Kildare rebellion of 1534–35. The 'Ordinances for the government of Ireland' were drawn up during the years of the emergence of the court of star chamber, and the substance of article 11 of the ordinances may have been an effort to extend that institution to Ireland. The lord chancellor was ordered to convene a special court,

. . . callyng to hym a juge of every of the kynges courtes, & such other of the lords and counsayle as shalbe present in terme tyme, shal syt twies every weke, duryng terme season in the counsayle chambre, there to receyve and here such compleyntes as the kynges subjectes shal exhibite; and take order therein accordingly.[168]

This article clearly required a meeting of at least some of the Irish council, although it is not clear whether the judges were in every case to be councillors. Herbert Wood suggested that it was '. . . the germ of the court which was afterwards to develop into the Court of Castle Chamber'.[169] A form of the court of star chamber may have been intended by this, but the records show no evidence of its continued existence as a regular tribunal apart from the council itself. It lacked

jurisdiction was acknowledged well before the fifteenth century. See C.L. Schofield, *A study of the court of star chamber* (Chicago, 1900), pp. 1–11. The most recent study is J.A. Guy, *The court of star chamber and its records to the reign of Elizabeth I* (London, 1985).

167. Elton, ed., *Tudor constitution*, pp. 160–61; Guy, *Star chamber*, pp. 2–4.

168. PRO, SP 60/2/66.

169. H. Wood, 'The court of castle chamber, or star chamber of Ireland', *RIA Proc*, xxxii (1914), sect c, 154.

the specific jurisdiction over certain classes of litigation which characterized the star chamber, and it had no distinct clerical organization. Furthermore, the ordinance made no reference to the reformed court of star chamber as a conscious model.[170]

No mention was made of the further amplification of the council as a court until 1562. In that year the lord lieutenant, Sussex, made a detailed report of the state of Ireland to Elizabeth, calling for the erection of a new forum. He said,

> Great numbers of disorders and riots and taking of possession by force be daily committed and left unpunished, for that there is no place to hear and determine those mattters but at the Council Board, which for the most part is occupied with other affairs of greater weight; and therefore it were necessary to have a like court of record established here by Parliament as the Star Chamber is in England, to order the like causes here.[171]

The records of the council book support the contention that cases of public disorder went largely unheard before 1562. Based on the claims of Sussex, the pressures of other business before the council now led to another expansion of the legal establishment, this time within the council itself. If it is correct to assume that Sussex's undated report was delivered to England before July 1562, then the queen must have directed him to consider the creation of a court modelled on star chamber.[172] The first article ordered that,

> . . . where we understand that dyvers grete ryottes piriuryes and such lyke publick offences be often tymes committed within that our realme, ye punishment wherof wold be also notable for example. We have thought mete that by conference with our counsell there a place might be apoynted for ye oppen hearinge [and] determyning therof lyke to our Counsell chamber called sterr chamber at Westminster and the lyke authoritie and Jurisdiction might be devised for you our lieutenant or for ye deputy, is for our great counsell of our realme sittye [sic] in our counsell in ye sayd place called ye sterr chamber. The devise whereof we referr to be furder consydered by you and our Counsell there.[173]

170. It may also have been an unfinished aspect of Cromwellian reform that fell on rocky soil in Ireland, but there is little direct evidence to sustain this. See Ellis, *Reform and revival*, pp. 39–48, 154–58; Bradshaw, *Irish constitutional revolution*, pp. 99–101.

171. *Cal. Carew MSS, 1515–74*, pp. 342–43.

172. The attribution of the original idea for this court is difficult, but the queen's letter appears to be a response to Sussex's description of public disorders committed in Ireland. If this is the case, the order of the documents in *Cal. Carew MSS, 1515–74*, pp. 330 and 342–43 ought to be reversed. See also Wood, 'Castle chamber', 154.

173. PRO, SP 63/6/101.

A dearth of information prevents us from tracing the development of the court step by step, and the surviving evidence often leads to contradictions. However, the appointment of Thomas Walshe as the first clerk of the court of castle chamber on 5 October 1563 indicates that the queen's command was carried out in the following year.[174] But the formal establishment of the court had to wait until the commission of 1571, and during the intervening nine years the court left few, if any, records of its adjudication. Although clerks of the castle chamber were continuously re-appointed, there was no entry book for decrees of the court and the extant council book contains no marked increase of conciliar proceedings during these years. Of course, the court of star chamber had developed as an institution before it obtained a distinct clerical organization in 1540. And the court of castle chamber may also have been created in effect prior to the commission of 1571 and before the establishment of an entry book for orders and decrees. However there is little internal evidence to show that the Irish court attained a separate institutional existence before 1571.[175]

The idea of the court was not allowed to lapse, however, for Sir Henry Sydney wrote to England frequently to obtain details of the rules of procedure of the star chamber. In a letter to Cecil dated 3 March 1566, Sydney, confident of the court's prospects for success, called for the full development of the court by the next term. He declared,

In the last government of my lord of Sussex here, A sterre chamber was by hym erected by the name of the Castell chamber, whereof by his lords short departur he sawe no greate effect followe. Nevertheless I finde yt a Court so necessary and of so great consequence here, as I must both allow and greatly commend the erection and allso desier you that yt may be farder established by sending us hither the orders of the starre chamber, especially that which is to be observid by the Clerke, and the order of the processes and the forme of the Seale therunto belonging togither with full auctority as the Clerke hath there for the accepting of recognizances, and cancelling of bandes, whereof yf advertisement might come before the next terme, the Court shuld be fully established which being yet but in his infancy was worth to the Queene this last terme in ————[176] abought one hundreth poundes.[177]

---

174. Hughes, *Patentee officers*, p. 135. He was followed by John Bathe (10 July 1565), Edward Waterhouse (1 February 1566) and John Harepenny (11 October 1569). ibid., pp. 8, 63, 136.

175. But see Wood, 'Castle chamber', 154–55, who implies that the court obtained a more clearly autonomous standing.

176. Word torn from MS.

177. PRO, SP 63/16/110.

It would appear from this document that the court was created by Sussex shortly before he left Ireland, probably in 1563, and that his departure may have arrested its development. Sydney's reference to the profit of £100 from the court in the last term was designed to stimulate the queen's interest, and it may be taken as evidence of the actual functioning of the court during his tenure. The clerk at that time, probably Edward Waterhouse, needed more precise instructions to execute his office, a fact which suggests that the court was struggling to establish an identity separate from the council. Nevertheless, Sydney anticipated the full operation of the court by the Michaelmas term of 1566. Toward this end, the queen wrote to Sydney on 28 March of that year,

Where you requyre to have some ordres sent you for the direction of yourself and our Counsell there in the heering and determining of the causes in that place which was erectid by our cosin of Sussex and named the Castell Chambre, to resemble our Sterre Chamber at Westminister; you shall have the same sent to you . . . before the next terme.[178]

Throughout the summer of 1566 Sydney repeatedly requested a statement of the formal rules of procedure for the star chamber, but there is no evidence to indicate that he finally received it.[179]

For the ensuing five years the status of the court of castle chamber is uncertain, although there can be little doubt that it was indeed created by Sussex about 1563 and that Sydney actively championed it before the privy council in 1566. The positive testimony of the queen and Sydney must be set against the lack of any concrete internal evidence of the court's continued existence from 1562 to 1571. It is possible, of course, that the first creation of the court proved abortive and that it was re-erected after a long hiatus. Deprived of guidance in the form of the rules of procedure of the star chamber, the court probably had a poorly articulated and largely subordinate relationship within the council for the first nine years of its life. After 1566 the court must have merged once again into the judicial function of the council, since there is no further mention of it for five years.

In any case, there was a clear determination to proceed with the development and organization of the court by 1571. On 4 June of that year Cecil's memorandum again mentioned a new Irish court, and on 14 June a commission to erect the court of castle chamber was drafted.[180] When the commission received the privy seal on 28 June

---

178. *Sidney S.P.*, pp. 19–20. This is clearly a response to Sydney's letter of 3 March, although Wood has the order reversed. See his 'Castle chamber', 154–55.

179. *Cal. S.P. Ire., 1509–73*, pp. 303, 307, 309–10.

180. ibid., p. 449.

the court at last secured formal organization.[181] With the enabling document which commissioned the court, however, we must confront a new problem: the absence of a continuous record of its formal decrees from its inception. The earliest memorandum in the entry book, that of 4 November 1573, was not based upon the first suit heard by the court since two undated judgments were recorded on the first two folios of the entry book.[182] In some instances, a subsequent order refers back to a case begun before November, such as the suit of John Garrahall, initiated on 7 October 1573, or the bill of riot on 25 January of that year.[183] Another suit was heard by the court on 30 January.[184] In addition, the fourteen pages now missing from the beginning of the entry book may have encompassed as many as eight more suits.[185] By extrapolating from these very inexact figures, we may link the arrival of the commission of 1571 with the approximate beginning of the entry book. Indeed, there is evidence to support this contention in the list of charges of riot dismissed on 7 November 1582. Cases of very long standing were then terminated and one entry referred to an original bill of 29 November 1571, while another bill was dated 30 November 1572.[186] These are the earliest records of the court found to date.

b) organization and procedure

The development of the court of castle chamber was a direct result of the commitment by the council to extend the entire judicial establishment. Besides the general objective of the improvement of the judicial hierarchy, the aim of the council was to provide a new tribunal for the litigation of specific cases previously unheard at the conciliar level. Sussex mentioned riot, disorders and forcible dispossession in 1562 as cases the council was unable to adjudicate because of the press

181. *Cal. pat. rolls, Eliz, 1569–72*, pt. 13, vii, pp. 276–77. Wood took note of the draft commission but was unable to find the formal commission of 28 June. See 'Castle chamber', 155. A subsequent commission was solicited by the lord deputy and council in 1581, '. . . the court not being competent under a lord keeper in the absence of the lord chancellor . . .'. See 'Council book', ed. Quinn, p. 112 (23), and Wood, 'Castle chamber', 155.

182. BL, Add. MS 47,172, ff. 1–3. The entry book is a bound vellum document, the cover of which is badly mutilated. The title is scratched out but the words 'Castel Chamb[er] [I]rela[nd]' can be made out along with the probable date, either 1570 or 1576.

183. ibid., ff. 7–8v.

184. TCD, MS 852, f. 95v. Trinity College has several manuscript copies of cases heard in the court of castle chamber, some of which are not in the entry book.

185. In the first six years of the entry book there were an average of four cases a year occupying approximately one and one half folios for each entry.

186. BL, MS 47,172, f. 67–67v.

of other business.[187] And in 1571 the draft of the commission to erect the court of castle chamber was most specific. The preamble recited the '. . . perversion of justice in Ireland . . .' and detailed a list of

. . . unlawfull mayntaynancyes, embracyries, confederacyes, alyancies, false bandinge and taking of mony by the common Jurors . . . and also by untrue demenying of sheriffs in making of pannels and other untrue retornes . . . .[188]

The new court was intended to deal with such breakdowns of public order and thus to expand conciliar authority by dealing with violence through litigation rather than through martial law or military action. After 1571 the most characteristic suit before the court of castle chamber was one involving some alleged violence. The commission declared that,

For the better remedye whereof & to the intent that suche execrable & pernicious evels & greffes shall not escape without just and dew correction & ponyshement we have thought mete to appoint that a particular court for the hering & determynacion of those detestable enormyties faultes & offences shalbe holden within our castell of our cyttie of Dublin . . . & that the same our court shalbe cauled & namyd the castell chamber of our said raelme of Irland.[189]

The organization of the new court was fundamentally the same as that of the council sitting as a tribunal, except that what had been merely customary was now reduced to a specific formula. Orders and decrees entered in the book begin with the statement, 'By the Lord deputie and counsell . . .'[190] just as do the entries in the council book for 1556–71. It has long been established that the court of star chamber, on which the Irish court was based, was also a judicial

187. *Cal. Carew MSS, 1515–74*, p. 343.
188. PRO, SP 63/32/162. The Elizabethan star chamber dramatically increased its business while at the same time limiting its jurisdiction to criminal cases of the sort noted above. See Guy, *Star chamber*, pp. 47, 52–58.
189. PRO, SP 63/32/162. It should be noted that nowhere in the enabling documents was there an intent '. . . to protect the Commons against the high-handed proceedings of the Anglo-Irish nobility . . .' which Wood intimated was the reason for creating the court. See Wood, 'Castle chamber', 158–59. See *Irish historical documents*, ed. Curtis & Mc Dowell, pp. 98–102 for the 1581 copy of the writ establishing the court and four representative cases.
190. BL, Add. MS 47,172, f. 22. In the case of *Browne* v. *Isham*, the suit was heard '. . . before your L[ordship] and her majestes Counsell in her highnes Court of Castell chamber'. ibid. Also see ff. 2v, 3, passim for orders taken by the lord deputy and council in the court of castle chamber.

meeting of the privy council.[191] The judges of the court were, therefore, always councillors but the commission of 1571 was even more specific. The lord deputy or chief governor, the lord chancellor or lord keeper, the lord treasurer, the two chief justices, the chief baron of the exchequer and the master of the rolls were appointed to be on the court, as well as any who succeeded them or temporarily held the office. The lord deputy was particularly enjoined to come to the court and when he did he was to be reckoned the 'chief head and principal judge' in all causes.[192] The commission gave the power to the lord deputy, lord chancellor or lord treasurer '. . . to call or assocyat unto him or them suche and so many of the lordes spyrituall, & temporall & suche of our previe counsell or Justices [of] any our benches in our said raelme of Ireland as they or everye of them . . . shall think mete . . .'.[193] This statement appears to differ slightly from star chamber procedure, since no one who was not on the privy council, as opposed to the more ceremonial grand council, could ordinarily sit as a judge at the court of star chamber.[194] The powers described in 1571 appear to have allowed a judge to sit on the Irish court even if he was not a councillor, although in practice all of the signers of the entry book before 1590 were councillors.[195]

Attendance at each session of the court of castle chamber averaged about five or six members for the seventeen years during which the entry book was signed.[196] Officials who came most frequently to the

191. Elton, ed., *Tudor constitution*, p. 158. See also Guy, *Star chamber*, pp. 7–8; Scofield, *Star chamber*, pp. 36–37. This explains away the difficulty of understanding why military men would sit on the court, as well as the secretary or the dean of Christ Church. They were there because they were councillors and as such they could be asked to serve on the court of castle chamber. See Wood, who poses this query, in 'Castle chamber', 159.

192. PRO, SP 63/32/163–65. The quorum for hearings was three councillors present, with the lord deputy, lord chancellor or lord treasurer to be one. The presence of only two councillors was required to decide whether to hear causes in a special session of the tribunal.

193. PRO, SP 63/32/163.

194. Elton, ed., *Tudor constitution*, p. 162; Scofield, *Star chamber*, p. 11. But see Guy, *Star chamber*, pp. 7–8, who argues that practical politics could occasionally overrule constitutional principle in admitting some who were not councillors to sit at star chamber.

195. I have doubts about only two, but all of them ultimately became councillors.

196. The last signed entry was on 6 November 1590. BL, Add. MS 47,172, f. 92. The quorum was clearly established at three judges, and at least three of the five cases where only one was sitting were aberrant. Lord Chancellor Gerrard signed one entry which was actually an interlocutory decree in a case of chancery, while Lord Deputy Perrot signed another which was no hearing at all but a warrant enforcing a previous decree. BL, Add. MS 47,172, ff. 17–19, 76. The average attendance rose slightly after 1580, and the number of different officials who sat on the bench increased as well. This would indicate that the more tightly

court were the lord deputy and lord chancellor, followed by the master of the rolls and chief baron of the exchequer. This was intended by the plan of the commission and was unremarkable. However, the chief justices rarely attended, with one exception, while the secretaries, who were not mentioned in the commission, were regular in their attendance. Basically, the presence of officials depended at least as much on their personal qualities and presumed judicial aptitude as it did on their respective offices. Hence, Hugh Brady, bishop of Meath, attended the court frequently (twelve times) while his successor came only twice. The vice treasurer was unmentioned in the commission, but Sir Henry Wallop sat on the court frequently, while his predecessor, Sir Edward Fyton, sat only occasionally. Perhaps most remarkable, as we have just observed, was the non-attendance of the two chief justices throughout the period. Only Sir Robert Dillon the younger sat at the court regularly, and his predecessor and namesake never sat at all. Of course, the chief justices were busy at their own courts during term, but presumably so were the lord chancellor, the master of the rolls, and the chief baron, all of whom methodically heard cases at the castle chamber.

The chief law officers of the crown conducted litigation frequently before the court of castle chamber. They argued both civil and criminal cases, as well as those involving the apparatus of judicial administration. In a case heard on 8 May 1578, the attorney general, Thomas Snagge, presented an information against three juries in Co. Kilkenny who had refused to bring an indictment against three confessed defendants.[197] Snagge argued the case for the queen against counsel for the three juries and proved that the testimony against them was true. The presentation of testimony and the denial of allegations by the defence were usually the province of the chief law officers when proceedings were tried at the court. When cases were begun outside Dublin, or when witnesses were unable to come to the court, ad hoc commissions were sent to take testimony and to send in depositions and arguments from the venue of the alleged offence.

The appointment of a special clerk for the work of the court of castle chamber may be taken as evidence of the expectation that the court would soon be very busy. The clerk of the council had previously assumed the clerical responsibility for conciliar adjudication. But after 1563 the continuous presence of two clerks suggests the intention of the council to separate its judicial and administrative functions.[198] It was not until 1577 that the clerks of the castle

grouped nucleus of judicial councillors under Lords Deputy Fitzwilliam and Sydney had broken up after 1580.

197. BL, Add. MS 47,172, ff. 33v, 39, 49v, 80v.

198. The two holders of the offices were ordinarily different men, but on two occasions the clerkships were held jointly by one man. Edmund Molineux and Robert

chamber became a force to be reckoned with, and they soon demon-strated a talent for administration. There is far greater evidence for the activity of the energetic clerks of the castle chamber than for that of the older clerks of the council, a fact which may also indicate the increase of judicial business done at the court. Although the salary of £13 6s. 8d. was not great, the office was probably quite lucrative, for the clerk handled a great deal of money in court costs, fines and other fees.[199]

As with any Tudor court, costs and charges could be extremely bur-densome to the litigant and he occasionally needed an official reminder to prompt his willing payment. Thus there were frequent orders in the entry book to pay fines and court costs that were overdue. On 14 November 1577, the court heard a complaint against Robert Kendall and other officers of the court for taking excessive fees for their clerical work. The court demonstrated an awareness of the plight of its contestants, declaring that '. . . wee weinge [weighing] the dis-abilitie of a nomber of the sewtors followinge theyre cawses and sewtes in the saied Courtes . . . to avoyde the dislyke of the complained excessyveness, the same mought in tyme growe to be over burden some to those sewtors and partyes sewed . . .'.[200] Kendall retorted that the rates charged were those used by previous clerks there and were also then used by the court of star chamber, so the court then prudently required that all fees due to the clerk should be paid in Irish money rather than in English currency.

Perhaps the most assiduous of the clerks of the court was the redoubtable Laurence Holinshed, who was also keeper of the records in Bermingham Tower during the four years of his clerkship.[201] Whereas Kendall was apparently grasping and willing to exploit his office, Holinshed was more concerned to streamline the proceedings and wil-ling to harass the litigants in order to expedite the adoption of his pro-posals. His concern for the slow process of the court was demonstrated most clearly in his letter of 1581 to Lord Deputy Grey. He declared,

Kendall held the two posts for about nine months during 1576 and 1577, respectively. The clerks were mostly obscure men below the second rank in the Dublin administration, but John Bathe rose to become solicitor general and attor-ney general, while Edward Waterhouse came to be a councillor himself in 1579. Hughes, *Patentee officers*, pp. 8, 136. See Wood, 'Castle chamber', 170 for a list of the clerks and other functionaries.

199. Anthony Wilcocks and Robert Kendall deemed it worthwhile to sue to hold their clerkships for life. PRO, SP 63/41/58; *Cal. pat. rolls Ire., Eliz.*, p. 14.

200. BL, Add. MS 47,172, f. 23. On the following day Kendall was again receiving court costs from an unsuccessful defendant. ibid., f. 24v. See also f. 33 and f. 84v. For a full discussion of the more sophisticated clerical organization, fees and pleadings of the English star chamber see Guy, *Star chamber*, pp. 10–14.

201. Hughes, *Patentee officers*, p. 67.

That whear the bookes of actes and orders of the same Court ar nowe very imperfecte and far out of order by reason the actes and orders hearetofore pronouncyd in Corte have not bene entered into the same, before the nexte courte theare holden, after the day that they were pronouncede; but set downe most commonly in Lewse papers, and by that meanes often cast aside and lost and so not at all entered into the saide bookes . . . .[202]

Holinshed contended that the entries themselves were often carelessly made in haste because of the dilatory habits of the councillors and requested Grey to direct that orders be speedily written and signed at court, so that the clerk should have sufficient time to enter them in the book before the next session was held. Grey signed the back of the letter, granting Holinshed's request, and from that time forward councillors' names were entered on the decree by the clerk rather than signed personally.[203] The sense of urgency in Holinshed's letter suggests that the court was very busy at this time, a fact which the entry book would not reveal if the records were lost, as he claims.

The conscientious Holinshed occasionally came to grief in his aggressive pursuit of lapsed orders and unenforced bonds and decrees. On 22 June 1582 the clerk brought two suits against Anthony Colclough of Wexford for misfeasance in office while he was sheriff. However, the court held for the defendant in both cases because the commission to Colclough of 1581 could not be found in the records.[204] Acting upon a complaint by Holinshed, the court ordered on 5 July 1582 that all plaintiffs must give bond for the 'effective prosecution of their suits' beginning at the next Michaelmas term.[205] As a result, the court initiated on 7 November a retrospective scrutiny of cases pending, and dismissed no less than fifteen charges of riot of very long standing, one of which dated from 1571.[206] Holinshed had accomplished two major objectives: the curtailment of future dilatory pleadings, and a clean sweep from the records of cases which had been allowed to lapse without a decision. At times, the chronic needling of Holinshed must have annoyed the court. On 4 August 1584, for example, the

202. BL, Add. MS 47,172, f. 52.

203. ibid. It was probably also Holinshed who discovered the blank in an order of 1579 and caused the council to repair the omission by an order of September 1581. ibid., f. 48.

204. BL, Add. MS 47,172, f. 52.

205. ibid., f. 63. The implicit claim here of dilatory pleadings and of using the court as an instrument of harassment has been discussed in T.G. Barnes, 'Due process and slow process in the late Elizabethan and early Stuart star chamber', *Am Jn Legal Hist*, vi (1962), 233, 236. There is too little evidence to allow us to investigate the '. . . deliberate inconvenience caused by plaintiffs to their adversaries . . .' examined by Williams in *Council in Wales*, pp. 70, 72 et seq.

206. BL, Add. MS 47,172, ff. 65v–74.

clerk was ordered to cease harassing the plaintiffs in a Limerick case because their suit had already been heard and determined by a commission from the court.[207] There is reason to believe that members of the court were relieved when Holinshed's tenure was ended in 1586, for thereafter his meddlesome contrivances vanish from the records.[208]

Among the most important functions of the clerk was, of course, the proper maintenance of the entry book of orders and decrees of the court.[209] This book contains many gaps and apparent lacunae. It omits all the pleadings, and frequently the details, of litigation, advising the indulgent reader to refer to the plaintiff's bill '. . . as more at large in the saied information dothe and maye appeare . . .'.[210] There are less than four entries for each year from 1573 to 1590, and five of these years have no entries at all.[211] However, certain other evidence explains this apparent lack of substance from the court records. For example, there are at least five leaves missing from the document at precisely the folios where large gaps in the record are indicated.[212] And we should recall that in 1582 Holinshed claimed that orders and decrees had been 'cast aside, and lost' because of the inefficient means of recording decisions.[213] It is clear from the proceedings in several cases that earlier decrees may have been made which were not placed in the entry book.[214] We must recall that the court was enjoined to convene twice weekly during term and that it was modelled on the very busy star chamber. Some orders are to be found in TCD MS 852 which were not placed in the entry book now

207. ibid., f. 76.

208. The marshal, another officer of the court, played a smaller role in proceedings, the usher even less. In November 1577 the marshal was ordered to arrest litigants who neglected to pay their fees. ibid., f. 23v. See Wood, 'Castle chamber', 160.

209. This was calendared by Sophie C. Lomas in H.M.C., *Egmont MSS* (*H.M.C. rep., Manuscripts of the earl of Egmont*, 2 vols. (London, 1905, 1909)), i, pt. 1, pp. 1–60. Mrs Lomas never intended a full transcription of the document although she was advised by J.J. Cartwright that 'Some of the more important entries might be treated more fully'. The calendar reverses the order of proceedings in the entry book and omits a great deal of technical detail, but on the whole it is reasonably accurate. BL, Add. MS 47,172, Lomas to Cartwright, 18 November 1898.

210. This is the reverse of the case with star chamber, where pleadings were preserved and the judgments lost. See Elton, ed., *Tudor constitution*, p. 158.

211. The years 1575–76, 1582–84 and 1584–86. For the years 1573–90 there was about one case recorded each year in Trinity and in Michaelmas terms and less than one in each of Easter and Hilary terms.

212. BL, Add. MS 47,172, ff. 12v–13, 74v–75, 75–76, 76–77. As we have seen, fourteen pages are missing from the front of the volume as well.

213. ibid., f. 52.

214. ibid., f. 64.

in the British Library. This suggests again that judgments of the court were not systematically recorded in the entry book. It is probable that no entries were recorded in cases which were begun in the court of castle chamber but were settled in other courts, or where proceedings were never completed, since only final judgments were recorded in the entry book of 'Orders and decrees'.[215] Pending the discovery of additional cases and fragments of information about the court, it is difficult to know more.

It is possible to provide some information on the litigants before the court of castle chamber, despite the gaps in the records. We cannot accept the inference of Wood that the court was '. . . instituted as a protection for the poor against the rich, and which was mainly so till the end of Elizabeth's reign . . .'.[216] When the poor were mentioned in the entry book, it was nearly always as defendants in a larger action alleging riot, usually as the servants of a gentleman or peer.[217] On the other hand, the majority of cases (36) involved the gentry, knights, peers and merchants, both as plaintiffs and defendants.[218] In fact, the court became the resort of many Anglo-Irishmen of gentle families, for family names such as Dillon, Eustace, Bermingham, Talbot, Nugent and Cusake recur frequently as suitors throughout the period. Another class of suits can be discerned in those contests (ten in all) involving local officials. Although no definitive list of causes can be attempted, it would appear from the extant records that the court dealt in the main with the suits of the rich, and also served the secondary purpose of supplying an instrument for the correction of local officials.

The new tribunal was part of a general scheme designed to bring the common law to areas beyond the Pale and to expand the territorial jurisdiction of the council. The majority of cases heard in the period 1573–90, however, involved only three counties: Dublin, Meath and Wexford.[219] Prior to 1580, nearly all the cases brought before the

215. The unpublished researches of Thomas Barnes on star chamber would suggest, by analogy, that up to 90% of bills initiated in the castle chamber would not have come to a hearing. Hence, they would not show up in a book of orders and decrees. Thomas G. Barnes to the author, 23 August 1974. But see 'Council book', ed Quinn, p. 98, who contends that the court was not in fact very busy.

216. Wood, 'Castle chamber', 129.

217. BL, Add. MS 47,172, ff. 2v, 5, 7, 8, passim. See also *Irish historical documents*, ed. Curtis & McDowell, p. 101.

218. Of a total sixty-eight cases, the gentry alone were involved in eighteen of them. The identity of many litigants cannot be known, but most of these were defendants in large actions. Only eight cases specifically identified servants, husbandmen, cottagers or artisans, and among them only Joyce Adryan, the litigious leatherdresser of Dublin, was involved in a suit as plaintiff (twice). ibid., ff. 55, 90. Most litigants before the bar of star chamber also came from the upper ranks of society. See Guy, *Star chamber*, pp. 61–62.

219. Eight of the sixteen cases involving Dublin were from Dublin city.

court of castle chamber were from counties where the government had traditionally maintained effective control.[220] Thereafter, the court heard suits from more distant or less well-governed areas such as Cork, Cavan, Galway, Limerick and Roscommon. This may have had a great deal to do with the results of the Munster rebellion, but there was no great upsurge in the number of cases heard after 1580 or even 1584. It may be surmised that most cases begun in Munster or Connacht were heard before the provincial councils there, but the court of castle chamber clearly retained a jurisdiction over provincial actions which were not routine.[221] In those cases touching questions of legal and judicial administration, where the court was in a position to support the authority of a local magistrate or provincial tribunal, the court exercised its broadly conceived jurisdiction most effectively.

One of the reasons that the court of castle chamber had such a tentative and measured beginning was the lack of a definitive statement on procedure. The commission of 1571 at last granted all the powers of star chamber to the new court and enclosed the rules of procedure of the parent tribunal. The judges were ordered to sit twice a week, on Wednesday and Friday, during all four legal terms of the year. They received the power to hear and determine all bills, complaints, supplications and informations submitted to the court, as well as to give orders and award process for bills and contempts of court.[222] In a case brought on behalf of the queen, the attorney or solicitor general would present an information against the defendant.[223] Otherwise, a plaintiff would seek redress from the court, which was authorized to issue a subpoena for the defendant to appear and give answer to the bill. The answer alleged as a matter of course that the court lacked jurisdiction, but then proceeded in fact to discuss the issues raised in the bill. The plaintiff then had four days in which to draw up interrogatories, or he could take until the next term to file a replication to the defendant's answer, and the latter might then make a rejoinder. The parties then produced their witnesses and the issue was thereafter joined, with counsel arguing for both sides before the tribunal.[224]

220. This was true for Cos. Dublin, Meath, Louth, West Meath, Wexford, Kilkenny, and some of Waterford and Tipperary, but not for Queen's Co.

221. But see the important case of certain Galway merchants who successfully sued to retain their ancient privileges of exemption from cess and other exactions, both English and Irish, before the lord president and council of Connacht in 1571. *Blake family records*, ed. Blake, pp. 115–17 (no. 144A). In this case, the provincial council was fully competent to offer an appropriate judicial remedy.

222. PRO, SP 63/32/163–65.

223. BL, Add. MS 47,172, ff. 74, 79–79v, 82–82v.

224. Elton, ed., *Tudor constitution*, p. 168. Answers and depositions were usually given before clerks and examiners, often out of term time. See also Guy, *Star chamber*, pp. 25–29; Scofield, *Star chamber*, pp. 73–75.

Even after the court had received a clear delineation of its powers and procedure, however, cases did not always run smoothly. The problem of 'slow process' apparently plagued the court of castle chamber just as it did other Tudor courts. For example, a trial in April 1580 took up several court days with the hearing of witnesses' depositions on both sides. When the plaintiff refused to appear in court after a writ had been issued to require his attendance at the proceedings, the defendant moved for acquittal.[225] The case was summarily dismissed, but the plaintiff had achieved his presumed objective of harassing his adversary and causing him to bear a needless expense. According to Thomas G. Barnes, the pleadings in star chamber were scrupulously observed and cases were very often protracted as a result.[226] The same may have been true of the castle chamber, for Holinshed claimed that there were thirty or forty cases pending in July 1582. He declared, however, that the reason was '. . . that divers, both plaintiffs and defendants, now in town, do not prosecute the same . . .'.[227] In other cases the court had trouble requiring litigants to appear. Henry Ealand, sheriff of Roscommon, defaulted on his summons after the answer and rejoinder were made and witnesses examined. In his absence, the court found all twenty-seven allegations against him proven. In many cases the court used recognizances of as much as £1,000 to secure the appearance of litigants at the next session.[228]

Once the judges had proceeded to a decision, giving their opinions one at a time in reverse order of seniority, they had to decide an appropriate penalty. In this they were limited by the injunctions of the commission of 1571 to fine or imprison offenders and to penalize those who failed to obey a summons or other order of the court.[229] Some defendants could obtain immunity from further prosecution merely by claiming the queen's pardon.[230] However, most offenders were fined, based on their ability to pay and according to the nature of the offence.[231] It is probable that the court of castle chamber reviewed the severity of fines at the end of every quarter, just as the star chamber did, for it commonly reduced these penalties.[232] Lord Howth

---

225. BL, Add. MS 47,172, ff. 43v–44.

226. T.G. Barnes, 'Star chamber mythology', *Am Jn Legal Hist*, v (1961), 5–6; Guy, *Star chamber*, pp. 26–27.

227. BL, Add. MS 47,172, f. 63. In one case a suit was taken up again eight years after it was settled (f. 64).

228. ibid., ff. 15v, 82–82v.

229. PRO, SP 63/32/165.

230. BL, Add. MS 47,172, ff. 8–12v, 21, 38v.

231. ibid., ff. 28, 29v, 41.

232. Barnes, 'Star chamber mythology', 7–8; Elton, ed., *Tudor constitution*, p. 169.

suffered the crippling amercement of £1,000 after he was convicted of the vicious beatings of his wife and daughter, but the amount was reduced to £500 nearly three years after it was levied.[233] Bonds were often required of the respondent to ensure his payment of a penalty.[234] The clerks of the court became so frustrated by the non-payment of fines in 1577 that they petitioned to have the marshal arrest and incarcerate those who were in default until they paid their penalties.[235] The court used its power to imprison less frequently because it was less profitable to the crown, but the occasional use of the pillory was viewed as an admonitory punishment, serving as it did to demonstrate the effectiveness of royal justice.

The establishment of the court of castle chamber, with its distinct organization and procedure, had a substantial impact on the management of the council's records. A manifest intent to distinguish the legal from the administrative work of the council may be discerned in the new pattern of record-keeping which emerged in 1571. The council book of 1556–71 was an erratic document, comparatively full in places, containing a miscellaneous record of formal actions taken by the council, including both judicial and administrative decrees.[236] In 1571 another council book was begun which seems to omit completely all judicial orders and decisions.[237] If we accept that the entry book of the court of castle chamber was initiated in 1571 and not in 1573, then the reason for establishing another council book could be that the procedure for making entries had changed. From 1571, then, the entry book would record the judicial acts of the council sitting in castle chamber, while the council book recorded administrative orders.[238]

Others have argued, however, that little was changed. David B. Quinn has said that '. . . the proportion of the judicial work of the

233. BL, Add. MS 47,172, ff. 43, 59, 62. See below for details of Lord Howth's case leading to this heavy fine. Perhaps more typical was the case of the jury in Co. Meath, whose fines were reduced from £50 apiece to a range of from £3 to £20 for each defendent only five days after they were first sentenced (f. 47–47v).

234. ibid., f. 41.

235. ibid., f. 23v. Occasionally a defendant might be held responsible for the appearance of his co-defendants, particularly if they were his tenants or servants. See ff. 3v–4, 7–7v.

236. RIA, MS 24 F 17, calendared by J.T. Gilbert in H.M.C., *Haliday MSS*, 'Acts of the privy council in Ireland, 1556–1571'.

237. This council book has been lost but the table of its contents survives in BL, Add. MS 4,792, ff. 136–44. The distinct clerical organization of the two institutions would seem to require two separate entry books although one may be permitted to wonder what Walshe and the other 'incumbents' were doing from 1563 to 1571.

238. The initiation of the new council book in 1571 also coincided with the beginning of the tenure of Lord Justice Fitzwilliam, but this certainly does not argue the need for a new record book, and it fails to explain why the judicial records were left out of it.

council transferred to the court of Castle Chamber was not large'.[239] Quinn based this interpretation on the fact that the entry book was evidently rather thin and dealt predominantly with only two classes of litigation. It is, of course, difficult to reconcile his view with the one offered here. There is only negative evidence and inference to support the contention that the lacunae in the entry book were characteristic of spotty record-keeping rather than typical of the court's caseload. We do, however, have the word of Laurence Holinshed on the backlog of thirty or forty cases in 1582, and we should recall that only decrees and judgments were entered, so that cases which were settled out of court or were allowed to lapse may not have been recorded. Furthermore, we should note that the enabling document, the commission of 1571, required the court to sit twice a week during each legal term and in general to follow the example of the unquestionably busy star chamber.[240] In any event, the intent to distinguish the judicial and administrative functions of the council seems clear from the very creation of the court of castle chamber, and the differentiation of the records emanated from this intention.

There were, then, two distinct records of the council for the decade 1571 to 1581. When a third record was created in 1581, a further differentiation of the conciliar documents was made. The number of folios in the council book of 1571, called the Black Council Book, dropped after the development of the third record book from about forty pages a year to about ten.[241] The new record was called a 'Giornal', reflecting the less formal nature of its contents, such as routine administrative and quasi-judicial acts of the council. Over half of its entries were recognizances, while only a few entries actually recorded specific cases heard before the council itself. As Quinn has said, '. . . administration and adjudication cannot be sharply differentiated . . .'[242] and several of these cases had important political implications which may explain their presence in the council book. Indeed, it may be that they were actually heard in the castle chamber, for the memberships of the council and the court were customarily the same. The commission of 1571 did not, in any case, prevent the

239. 'Council book', ed. Quinn, 98.

240. Suits under Wolsey's leadership of star chamber averaged 120 per annum and he systematically attracted more judicial business from rival courts. This number increased by mid-century to 150 per annum and in the last year of Elizabeth's rule the court heard 732 cases. See Guy, *Star chamber*, pp. 5–9.

241. 'Council book', ed. Quinn, 99. Quinn has suggested that the new entry book was created due to the need for more precise record-keeping in the aftermath of the constitutional struggle over the cess (see below, chapter six, for fuller discussion).

242. ibid., 104. The fragmentary condition of the calendar to the journal makes it difficult to say whether the cases were actually tried before the council or the court.

council from hearing suits at all. The journal recorded only twelve suits heard by the council (or court), as opposed to other judicial acts such as interlocutory decrees, orders to proceed in another forum and quasi-judicial decisions on administrative malfeasance.[243] During the same period, 1581–86, the entry book of the court of castle chamber recorded twenty-one cases, although five of these were new orders dealing with previous actions.[244]

What is the relationship, then, between the entry book of the court of castle chamber and the journal of 1581–86? It would appear that the entry book recorded more cases decided before the conciliar tribunal during that period, while the journal recorded all the recognizances and a number of the quasi-judicial orders and decrees of the council. There was nothing to prevent the council from hearing cases outside of term when urgency or expediency required it, but for the most part the council seems to have conducted judicial proceedings during legal terms in the castle chamber. Since this body was simply the council or a number of the councillors sitting as a court, it should not be difficult to understand how the proceedings in some cases would be entered in the journal of acts of the council, particularly when council meetings interrupted or overlapped hearings in progress. The two forums should be seen as functionally interdependent, since either could hear cases in practice and would commonly support the actions of the other. While they were not totally separate institutions, neither were they entirely merged in one body.

c) jurisdiction

The court of castle chamber apparently heard the majority of cases presented before the council after 1571, and the entry book of the

244. ibid. The twelve cases are nos. 111, 168, 174, 176–77, 224, 231, 240, 241, 255, 258, 289, and 335. Quinn has claimed that because the council entered a decree mitigating a fine ordered in castle chamber, '. . . the council regarded the court as subordinate to itself'. ibid., 104. However, the nature of this subordination should be understood as part of the fabric of the council. These were not rival institutions but fundamentally one body acting in two separable spheres of activity. It was quite proper for the council to reduce a fine levied by the castle chamber and not a derogation of the latter's authority. See Elton, ed., *Tudor constitution*, p. 158.

244. BL, Add. MS 47,172, ff. 44v–78. Whereas the council book has only a minor lapse in continuity in the spring and summer of 1584, the entry book of the court has two major gaps, from 28 November 1582 to 4 August 1584, and from 28 November 1584 to 23 June 1586. Hence, while the council book records the work of about five years, the entry book records the work of just over two years. In addition, the records are inconsistent. In 1582 the entry book shows the court taking action on no less than 32 separate issues, including 16 cases. Fifteen of these issues were administrative orders, but the fact remains that the court was on occasion very busy indeed. We may guess that activity in 1582 was not wholly aberrant, but without more evidence we can do little else.

court seems to have pointed the way toward a substantial differentiation of records of the Irish council based on the intended separation of its judicial and administrative responsibilities. However, the interdependence of the council and the court meant that certain basically administrative questions were also brought before the court and recorded in the entry book. The most celebrated example of this was the attempt of the council to obtain submissions from the reluctant gentlemen of the Pale during the dispute over the cess.[245] The court also heard cases of forgery and sedition as well as administrative or jurisdictional questions over such matters as the prise wines and the general hosting.[246] In two respects, however, the litigation before the court of castle chamber differed greatly from that of the Irish council acting as a court before 1571. First, after 1571, a majority of cases heard by the court alleged riot or other forms of public disorder, a class of actions seldom heard before 1571. Secondly, the court heard many more cases involving judicial administration, particularly the correction and punishment of erring jurors and the enforcement of decrees from other courts. The commission of 1571 declared that riots, forcible entries, and unlawful assemblies as well as the false swearing of jurors and '. . . misdemeanors of semblable nature . . .' were the reasons for creating the new tribunal.[247]

Apart from the hearing of cases for which it possessed original jurisdiction, the court of castle chamber also served as an appeals court at the apex of the judicial system and supervised all litigation in the lower courts. Indeed, the castle chamber offered institutional support to inferior jurisdictions from the sheriffs to the chancery. However, since the four greatest magistrates normally sat on the court it would appear that their own tribunals rarely came under the close scrutiny of the castle chamber. In fact, the relationships between the highest courts were governed largely by the incumbent office-holders' judicial fitness and aptitude. Hence, Lucas Dillon and William Gerrard brought to the court great energy and commitment, while Chief Justices Robert Dillon and John Plunket robbed it of needed talent and support. Criticism of the chief justices by William Gerrard was not advanced in the court of castle chamber but rather in his letters

---

245. ibid., ff.26v–28v. This important contest pitted the Pale gentry against the queen's government over the rights to impose the Irish equivalent of purveyance on the lands of the Pale. The administration in Dublin was driven to find new ways to increase its revenue and drove headlong into a constitutional confrontation with its most loyal citizens on the eve of the Munster rebellion (see chapter six for discussion).

246. ibid., ff.79–79v, 89, 96, 17–19, 29–31v (see chapter five for a discussion of general hosting; see above, page 238 note 252 for a description of prise wines).

247. *Cal. pat. rolls, Eliz, 1569–72*, pt. 13, vii, p. 276. See also the draft commission in PRO, SP 63/32/162, 164.

and memoranda. Thus, we may assume that the formal meetings of the tribunal managed to suppress the political rivalries and recriminations which surfaced elsewhere in the surviving correspondence.

While the court busied itself with cases of public disorder and admonitions to errant local officials, it only occasionally engaged in active supervision of the courts of chancery, king's bench, common pleas or exchequer. The bench was always certain, however, to hear a case that reflected on the dignity of the council itself, especially when that case had serious political implications. Hence, the court imprisoned and fined Christopher Barnewall, who had been foreman of a jury in the queen's bench in 1577, for disputing the validity of the cess and putting in doubt the legality of the council's actions.[248] A more provocative case in point is the sequel to the trial in queen's bench of Maurice Fitzgerald on 27 January 1582. Despite the ominous presence of leading privy councillors at the hearing, a jury acquitted Fitzgerald of high treason when he was accused of aiding in the rebellion of Viscount Baltinglas. On 7 February the jurors in question were brought before the court of castle chamber on the charge that they had committed perjury by acquitting Fitzgerald. It was then recorded that the evidence at the original trial '. . . was verified unto the Courte to be true both by the Judges that sate in Judgment and by some of the pryvie Counsell that sate there . . .'.[249] Citing the great harm such an example would do to the fabric of English justice if it were followed, the court levied a fine of £100 apiece on the jurors.[250] This is an example of the way the council, the court and the other tribunals operated interdependently, although it was somewhat unusual to learn of councillors being present in the queen's bench (as is recorded for the Fitzgerald trial). Most cases involving the verdicts of juries did not have such grave political implications. In non-political actions the court would first determine where the interest of the queen lay and then conduct the proceedings on that basis. For example, in 1581 the court fined and imprisoned jurors who had decided a case of wardship and escheat against the queen, contrary to the weight of evidence.[251]

The issue of the prise wines demonstrates the correlation of the English and Irish judicial systems at the highest level and exemplifies the tortuous route of complex litigation between two vested interests in Ireland. The grant of prise wines was hereditary in the Butler

248. BL, Add. MS 47,172, f. 20–20v. See also TCD, MS 852, f. 82.
249. BL, Add. MS 47,172, f. 51v.
250. They added that the jurors of greater means should help poor men pay their share because they were '. . . the chiefest doers in leading the simple sort . . .'. ibid., ff. 33v–35v. In July 1582 the fines were reduced by order of the council. 'Council book', ed. Quinn, 131 (172).
251. BL, Add. MS 47,172, ff. 44v–47v.

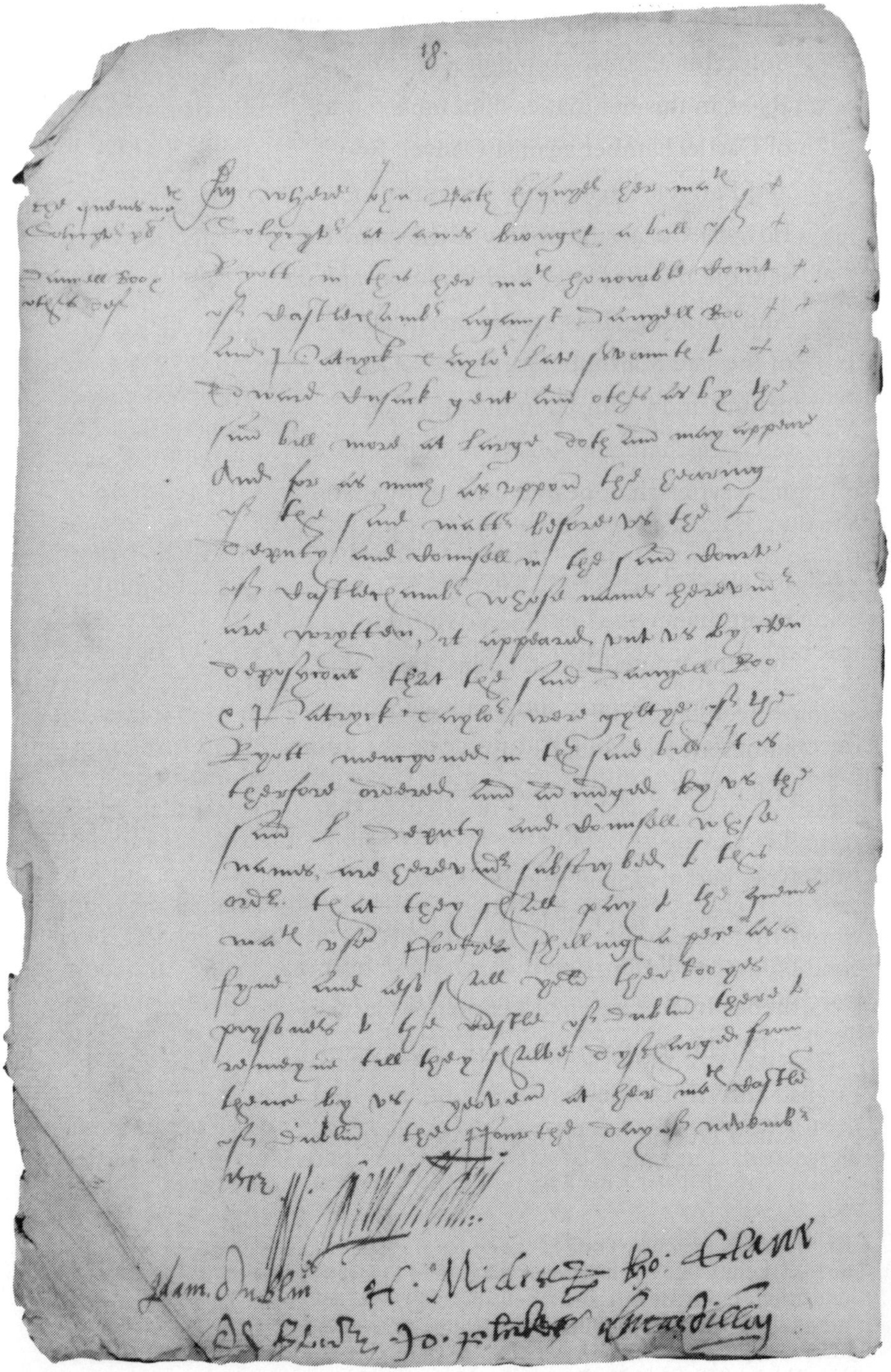

18

The quenes ma^tie
Colbright ag^t
Donnell Boo
& others

Sir whereas the [illegible] the ma^tie [illegible] Colbright at [illegible] brought a bill of Ryott in the the ma^ts honorable Court of Castlechamb' agaynst Donnyll Boo and Patryk Taylor [illegible] Edward [illegible] and others as by the said bill more at large doth and may appere And for as moche as uppon the heryng of the said matt[er] before us the L Deputy and Counsell in the said Court of Castlechamb' whose names hereunto are wrytten, it appeared unto us by ther deposicions that the said Donnyll Boo & Patryk Taylor were gyltye of the Ryott menconed in the said bill, It is therfore ordered and adiudged by us the said L Deputy and Counsell whose names are hereunto subscrybed that they shall pay to the quenes ma^tie [illegible] shillings a pece for a fyne and also shall [illegible] be prysoned in the Castle of Dublin there to remayne till they shalbe discharged from thence by us. Geven at the ma^ts Castle of Dublin the [illegible] day of Novembr [illegible]

H. Sidney

Adam. Dublin   H. Miden   Tho: Slane
[illegible]   Jo. Plunket   Lucas Dillon

I[de]m where John Bath Esqwyer her maties
Solycytor at Lawes brought a bill of
Ryott in this her maties honorable Court
of Castlechamber against Danyell Roo
and Patryck Taylor Late servannte to
Edward Cusack, gent and others as by the
said bill more at large doth and may appeare
And for as much as uppon this hearing
of the said matter before us the L[ord]
deputy and Counsell in the said Courte
of Castlechamber whose names hereunder
are wrytten, it appeared unto us by their
deposycons that the said Danyell Roo
& Patrick Taylor were gyltye of the
Ryott mencyoned in the said bill. It is
therfor ordered and adiudged by us the
said L[ord] Deputy and Counsell whose
names are hereunder subscrybed to this
order. that they shall pay to the quenes
maties use ffortye shillinges a pece as a
fyne. and also shall yeld their bodyes
prysoners to the Castle of Dublin there to
remayne till they shalbe dyscharged from
thence by us / geven at her maties Castle
of Dublin the ffourthe day of november
1573 W Fitzwilliam

Adam Dublin   H[ugh] Miden [Meath]   Tho. Slane
      Jo[hn] Plunkett   Lucas Dillon

---

6 Extract from the entry book of the court of castle chamber, November 1573.
The lord deputy and council heard the case of Danyell Roo and Patryck Taylor,
found them guilty of riot and fined them 40 shillings each. They were committed to the prison in Dublin Castle by this decree, signed in November 1573,
by Lord Deputy Fitzwilliam, Archbishop Loftus, Bishop Brady, Thomas Lord
Slane, Edward Fyton, John Plunket and Lucas Dillon.

earldom by letters patent from 46 Edward III, and it was renewed on 11 March 1557.[252] The Irish council heard a dispute between Ormonde and Desmond over the prise wines of Youghal in 1558, and a year later the arbitration of the two chief justices in England awarded them to Ormonde.[253] In 1576 the earl won a suit in England against the citizens of Drogheda and Dublin, who claimed that '. . . all Marchauntes Straungers, commenge withe any Wynes to thiere fortes, have used, Tyme out of Minde, to pay no Prise Wynes, and that alwaies theie have bene discharged of such Prise Wynes'.[254] In the following year Ormonde alleged before the court of castle chamber that alien merchants continued to unload wine at Dublin and Drogheda without paying prise wines. Lord Deputy Fitzwilliam and the Irish council were '. . . by vertue of letteres dyrected frome the Quens majestie to the saied Lord Deputie to Call the same Matter before hyme and to heare and order the same'.[255] On 4 February 1577, the court ordered the remainder of the unpaid prise wines delivered to Ormonde's agent. Ormonde was confirmed in his rights to the prise wines by the council in 1578 and again in 1581, but each time he gained a theoretically definitive award a new complaint would arise.[256] By the end of the period the chancery, the court of castle chamber, the Irish council, the English privy council, and the chief law officers of England had all heard ramifications of the case. The problem was unusually complicated because of Ormonde's stature and the vast territory covered by his grant. The litigation over the rights to prise wines illustrates how inefficient the overlapping jurisdictions of the crown courts could be and how difficult it was to enforce judgments of even the highest tribunal.

The second class of actions heard in greater number before the court of castle chamber involved cases of riot. From this it might seem that Irish society was in a state of chronic unrest, but such a facile interpretation must be examined carefully if we are to understand the conditions of Elizabethan Ireland. All sixteenth century societies experienced the frequent breakdown of public order, although disorder in

---

252. H.M.C., *De L'Isle and Dudley MSS*, ii, 46. The earl claimed one ton of wine from every ship of nine to twenty tons lading and two tons of wine from each vessel over twenty tons. PROI, Lodge MSS, Records of the rolls, 12 February 1584, *Ormonde v. mayor and bailiffs of Galway* (see above, page 194 and chapter three for prise wines and Ormonde).

253. RIA, MS 24 F 17, f. 77v; *Ormond deeds*, v, 110–11.

254. Collins, ed., *Letters and memorials*, ii, 130.

255. BL, Add. MS 47,172, f. 17. The court required the forfeiture of a sufficient pawn in case they defaulted on payment of the last ton within fifteen days.

256. 'Gerrard's report', ed. McNeill, 163; 'Council book', ed. Quinn, 122–23 (101–11).

Ireland verged nearer to insurrection or rebellion than perhaps it did elsewhere, at least in the eyes of English observers. The cases of riot brought before the court often alleged another cause of action as well, and when they did not they were often dismissed peremptorily. This may indicate that the charges of riot were occasionally spurious. Furthermore, a riot was defined rather loosely by the common law and could be used in the sense of a mere misdemeanour. Because there was always potential for an outbreak of violence, a 'riot' was regarded as a serious breach of the peace.

Cases of riot formed part of a larger class of litigation taken up by the court which was connected broadly with public order. The court heard charges of fraud, conspiracy, forgery, forcible entry and cognate offences.[257] In fact, the original purpose of the court, insofar as it mirrored the practice of star chamber, was to enforce the king's peace. Speaking of star chamber, Elton has said, 'Even if the violence alleged was often imaginary it does not alter the fact that the court was essentially occupied with crimes: it was, in a sense, the chancellor's court of criminal jurisdiction'.[258] The star chamber in England was intimately connected from its inception with the lord chancellor, and thus it tended to merge both equity and criminal jurisdictions. In Ireland, the court of castle chamber could be joined to the semi-autonomous jurisdiction of the chief governor as well as that of the lord chancellor, augmenting a potentially powerful juncture of two complementary sets of common law principles and remedies (equity and criminal law). It was widely supposed in 1571, therefore, that this expansion of conciliar adjudication would lead to a vastly increased caseload.

An allegation of riot might be contained in an indictment charging a series of other disorders or be brought forward in the context of a suit to recover property. When Thomas Masterson and Brian Cavanagh came before the court in August 1576, they charged each other with various murders, robberies and riots, but the suit basically claimed title to certain lands in Co. Wexford.[259] Some allegations of riot arose from apparent domestic conflicts and involved a very limited use of force. The earliest case was heard in January 1573 when Dame Jennet Sarsfield accused Margaret Howth of '. . . the ryotous taking awaye of the said Dame Jennett the fourth of October 1571'.[260] The court found the defendant guilty as charged, fined her £20, and committed

257. See Guy, *Star chamber*, pp. 52–58; E.P. Cheyney, 'The court of star chamber', *Am Hist Rev*, xviii (1912), 735.

258. Elton, ed., *Tudor constitution*, p. 171.

259. BL, Add. MS 47,172, f. 15.

260. TCD, MS 852, f. 95v.

her to the prison in Dublin castle. Other suits might be presented which contained no allegation of violence suffered by the complainants. In 1579 the court heard a case of an unlawful assembly of nearly 200 persons at the sea shore in Co. Wexford where the offenders dismantled and carried away parts of the plaintiffs' wrecked ship.[261]

In many cases of riot, however, substantive acts of violence were allegedly perpetrated on the person of the plaintiff or on those of his entourage. In an aggravated case heard in 1588, William Power of Co. Cork charged that the defendants had come to the town of Loghan and had beaten and terrified his tenants with guns, swords and spears, driving them away from their ploughs. Despite his claim that they came on three successive days and stole many horses, the court held that there was insufficient proof and dismissed the charges.[262] The court may have handled this case so inflexibly, without even naming a commission to hear the evidence, because its jurisdiction in Co. Cork was still ineffective or because the incident was simply too stale, since it had occurred three years before. In a case which involved the enforcement of justice, the council levied heavy fines and imposed prison sentences for preventing the apprehension of Manus O'Rourke, a suspected felon and traitor. Manus was apparently a guest in Ross O'Ferrall's house, and when the queen's officer tried to apprehend him a riot broke out during which he escaped.[263]

In addition to cases involving judicial administration and public disorder, the court continued after 1571 to hear other classes of suits that were entertained before then by the Irish council. The court also occasionally heard extraordinary cases where the remedy at common law was inadequate and the case itself was sufficiently unusual. A suit was brought against the baron of Howth in 1579 charging him with the assault and battery of his wife, his child and his butler. Probably because the case was so heinous, the court accepted testimony about the baron's dissolute life, his 'filthy conversacion' and his 'life with strange weomen', concluding that '. . . yt alsoe appeared that by this his usuall hauntinge & kepinge of hores, his wiffe became soe hatefull to him as he Could not without strikinge and beatinge of her suffy-cientlie satisfie the Crueltie of his mynde . . .'.[264] Lord Howth did in fact beat his wife so badly she had to stay in bed for many days, and when his butler gave her bread and drink he beat the man after tying

261. BL, Add. MS 47,172, ff. 40v–41. The court fined John Rochford £10 in 1578 for a riot committed in breaking down a device made by Roger Dillon to convey a water-course to his grist mill in Co. Meath. ibid., f. 36.

262. ibid., ff. 86–87v.

263. ibid., f. 84–84v.

264. ibid., f. 41v.

him to a post. He whipped his daughter for going to Dublin without his permission and she died within two days of the beating when he sent her away to a 'yeelding howse'. For this and other '. . . seacreat Causes known to the Lord Justice and Counsell and not fitt to be remembered in this order . . .',[265] the court fined Lord Howth £1,000, noting that he truly deserved the penalty of death. By the standards of the entry book this case was unusually bizarre in its features and extreme in the penalty awarded, but it may illustrate the wide competence of the court to entertain the most extraordinary cases, particularly if they involved a peer of the realm.

CONCLUSION

The Irish council possessed a judicial authority which was in theory as broad before the advent of the court of castle chamber as it was after it. We may ask, then, how the creation of the court changed the judicial function of the council. Perhaps the most fundamental change in 1571 was in the refinement and amplification of the court's judicial responsibilities. The judges were clearly named and the power to associate other judges with the court's work was expressly stated. The procedure of the court was firmly based on that of star chamber, and this had the effect of defining precisely the pleadings, the process and the penalties the court might employ. The addition of clerks of the castle chamber resulted in improved record-keeping and the speeding up of suits through the court. Substantive changes in litigation before the court took place, particularly in the increase of judicial decrees based upon actions taken in the lower courts. By expanding the judicial role of the council in this way, the entire legal framework in Ireland was brought directly under the supervision of the Irish government. The effectiveness of the council was enhanced because it heard more cases from a greater variety of litigants. Although most complainants were wealthy and powerful, the scope of conciliar authority now encompassed actions of riot. Bringing disorder more clearly within the purview of the council was intended to encourage greater stability and to stimulate recourse to English justice. There is evidence that more galled and vexed disputants sought the arbitration of the council, but the resultant adjudications did not substantially calm the unstable character of Irish society, and the latter continued to be disfigured by acts of violence. Finally, the court was a principal factor in the central policy of anglicization. The court of castle chamber made the Irish council more closely resemble the parent privy council in England. Cecil and other leading advisers of

265. ibid., f. 42v. One wonders whether the secret causes would go further to explain the baron's presence in the court than do the public charges.

the queen believed that Irish society would be made more tractable, even 'civil', if the queen's government in Ireland were made uniform with that of England.

After 1571 the court of castle chamber broadened the scope of conciliar authority and more clearly articulated its formal procedure. The work of the court both exemplifies the wide jurisdiction of the under-investigated council and helps to bring into sharper focus a Tudor court of star chamber. The establishment of the court itself signifies a willingness to extend the use of the royal prerogative in Ireland by employing the concept of star chamber jurisprudence in the expansion of the common law. It also indicates the direction of Elizabethan policy toward Ireland. The effort to reform Ireland in an English mould expressed itself continuously in projects for the gradual replacement of incompetent officials, expansion of the system of assize circuits, assignment of councillors to hear proceedings outside the Pale, and many other proposals. The thrust of government policy was law reform, not colonization.[266] Despite the establishment of several small colonies during the period, colonization schemes were not the principal focus of English policy. Instead, plans for the improvement and expansion of common law jurisdiction were the primary objectives of English statesmen.[267] The court of castle chamber was one of these initiatives. Its function was both supervisory and juridical, hence it was one of those characteristic Tudor hybrids, an institution with both legal and administrative functions. This may explain, in part, why it has laboured so long in comparative obscurity. A thorough investigation of the court in the context of Irish administration will help to complete the picture we have of Tudor justice.

The early Elizabethan regime in Ireland was a paradox. It was compelled to innovate and to reform while maintaining a vehement denunciation of all change and variety. It was confronted with the

266. Canny's claim that the government sought to bring order to Ireland through colonization and settlement is too exclusive. The documents indicate a persistent inclination to extend the common law through quarter sessions, circuit judges and the provincial presidencies and other means. Finally, government leaders were more directly involved in law reform since colonization was at least equally a private undertaking at this time. Canny, *Elizabethan conquest*, chs. 3–4, pp. 158–63. A more recent summary emphasizes the 'savagery' of the 'conquest' while acknowledging its incompleteness. See Ellis, *Tudor Ireland*, pp. 266–74. Brady, in contrast, views the policy of law reform as a key aspect in the 'eclectic' approaches taken by chief governors, though he emphasizes the setbacks and contradictions, concluding that the policy was a failure by 1579. See Brady, 'Government of Ireland', pp. 211–12, 358–59, 420–22.

267. The moderate and cautious policies of Cecil are wrongly characterized as 'aggressive' by Canny, who acknowledges his painstaking approach to Irish problems generally. A thorough analysis of Cecil's Irish policy would clarify much about the Elizabethan government of Ireland. See Canny, *Elizabethan conquest*, pp. 62–65.

necessity of making judicial and administrative transformations which would bring Ireland into conformity with the 'natural' order as it had evolved in an English setting. Yet the government was ill-equipped to impose the rule of the common law upon distant Irish countries. In much of Ireland, people observed the 'old religion', followed provincial leaders and spoke the Irish language. The eventual metamorphosis which would follow a thorough programme of education and evangelism must be preceded by garrisoning of troops and by erecting the preliminary scaffolding for the complete architecture of English government. Thus did a profoundly conservative sovereign embark upon a policy of reform in Ireland. The tentative character of these changes did nothing to make them more palatable in the Irish countryside, and yet there were areas of agreement and cooperation. The judges went on assize; the new provincial councils heard causes of action in Munster and Connacht; commissions were sent from the council into every shire on judicial and other business; bonds, recognizances and decrees were issued from the council to buttress the work of the judiciary; and the statutes were finally published for the edification of the queen's Irish subjects. In all of this new activity the clear aim was to govern all of Ireland under the rule of the common law. But in practice the work was complicated, the progress unsteady and the results ambiguous. The irony of changing the complex Irish infrastructure out of respect for venerable English tradition may not have escaped the cleverest Tudor administrators. But in any event, they pursued the policy of anglicization soberly, if not relentlessly, while acknowledging the difficulties of their task.

The rule of law was an essential Tudor commonplace. The aim of Elizabethan statesmen was to impose restraints on society which, in turn, would encourage the habit of litigation and repress the instinct to aggressive behaviour. Stephen Collins has recently argued that the reign of Elizabeth witnessed a profound intellectual revolution which worked itself out in the next century. He explained that the late Tudor period experienced dramatic changes which challenged the dominant assumptions of immutability and tradition as primary foundations of human society. Disorder was understood to be synonymous with change and it represented a dangerous threat to the natural harmony of the divine cosmos. It was thus the aim of every Elizabethan administrator to restrain the reckless and divisive habits of the queen's subjects, in England or in Ireland. Writers such as Thomas Smith and William Lambarde worked out elaborate arguments in support of the rule of secular law just as the practical basis of the Tudor commonwealth was becoming fractured.[268] Of course, we must necessarily be

---

268. Collins, *Divine cosmos to sovereign state*, pp. 71–78.

aware that reports of disorder, brutality, tyranny and corruption were constantly on the lips of all the queen's officials. Did this mean that royal agents and ministers responded to a rising tide of social violence with iron-fisted authoritarianism? Probably not. As Dr Elton has explained, the basis of English governance was the rule of law and constitutional norms. Despite occasional evidence of savagery, partisanship and malfeasance, the Tudor state relied primarily on statute law and representative institutions to govern.[269] Its utter dependence on private landholders in the localities to bring offenders to justice and to empanel reluctant juries is further evidence of the commitment to common law procedures. In summary, Dr Williams has challenged the lingering presumption of a Tudor despotism thus:

In practice the complete suppression of violence, the creation of an effective machinery for prosecution, and the removal of corruption and partiality from trials were impossible. The monarchy had to rely upon landowners for continuous service and could not afford to alienate them by excessive severity or constant nagging. The most it could do was to bring violence within tolerable limits and to make marginal improvements in the execution of the law.[270]

In the following reign, common law principles were employed to justify important changes in the policy of the government towards land law, again using the cloak of traditional conservatism. Dr Pawlisch has argued that Sir John Davies, the Englishman appointed Irish solicitor general in 1603 and attorney general in 1606, constructed a theoretical justification for the lawful expropriation of Irish land after 1603. Pawlisch termed the policy one of 'legal imperialism'. According to Davies' argument, the military conquest of Ireland would remain impermanent and reversible unless the imposition of common law rule were established comprehensively throughout Ireland. In this sense, the common law became the instrument of colonization. Davies used the opportunity presented by the Tyrone rebellion to justify a new doctrine of property based on 'conquest right' and he then proceeded '. . . to refashion all rights to real property in former Gaelic districts'.[271] The penultimate challenge to property rights of Gaelic landholders was thus legitimized and traditional concepts of gavelkind and tanistry were invalidated by the Irish judges acting collectively. Pawlisch has termed this approach 'judge-made' law and he argued that Irish tenures thereafter had no validity apart from that which the

269. G.R. Elton, 'The rule of law in sixteenth century England', in A.J. Slavin, ed., *Tudor men and institutions* (Baton Rouge, La., 1972), pp. 282–84.

270. Williams, *The Tudor regime*, p. 222.

271. Pawlisch, *Sir John Davies and conquest of Ireland*, p. 10.

common law provided. Gaelic inhabitants could retain their lands only by voluntary surrender and re-grant or by commissions which were created to investigate and repair defective titles. After 1603 the reformed Irish judiciary, acting in conclave at the instigation of Davies, created judicial precedents which functioned as *stare decisis* (binding precedents in case law) for all subsequent litigation. In taking this approach, Pawlisch argued that the Dublin government superseded statute law because of the inherent weakness of the Irish parliaments and the partisan spirit of the Irish judiciary when acting alone. By the time he retired from his position in Ireland, Davies had successfully challenged the financial independence of Munster towns, reformed Irish currency, extinguished Gaelic land law and expropriated lands in Ulster for the plantation of that province.[272]

In contrast to the authoritarian programme of Davies after 1603, the early Elizabethan officials pursued a conventional approach to the extension of the common law. The leading advocate for this policy was certainly Sir William Gerrard. His energetic propulsion of the campaign for law reform was not sustained, of course, because of his early death and the lasting interruption of civil peace after 1579. While significant attention has been paid to Spenser's later proposals for a 'drastic programme in social engineering', little work has been done by leading scholars on the pragmatic social and legal arrangements which allowed the inhabitants of Ireland to live together.[273] Dr Brady has recently argued that the views of both Anglo-Irish and English reformers of the sixteenth century 'stressed the value and political efficacy of existing English laws in Ireland', choosing to adopt legal means of governance among Irish people willing to accept it.[274] But further research is needed into the operation of the common law prior to 1593 in order to evaluate properly the lively debates and excessively taut characterizations surrounding the Dublin administration. Was the judiciary hopelessly compromised by favouritism, nepotism and corruption? Were the initiatives to increase the number of venues from which common law adjudication could be implemented throughout Ireland even marginally effective? How did the commissions operate in the provinces and what was the outcome of litigation which was begun in the central courts and then continued in the localities? To what extent did political considerations influence judgments in the central courts and what was the role of religious dissent prior to 1593? And, finally, how did the two rival legal systems co-exist in the

272. ibid., pp. 3–5, 9–14, 34–36, 42–51.
273. N.P. Canny, 'Debate: Spenser's Irish crisis: humanism and experience in the 1590s', *Past & Present*, no. 120 (1988), 203, 207.
274. C. Brady, 'Reply: Spenser's Irish crisis: humanism and experience in the 1590s', *Past & Present*, no. 120 (1988), 211, 213.

later decades of the reign? Since the policy of Davies apparently destroyed the residual claims of Gaelic land law, it would be useful to investigate how much influence that law retained before its terminal decline after 1603. In summary, this study of the judicial adminis-tration of the council is an incomplete one, resting on an analysis of the records of the central courts prior to 1578. A thorough assessment of the influence and the expansion of the common law will have to await new scholarship on the confluence of two legal traditions in areas beyond the Pale.

CHAPTER FIVE

The council as architect of order and stability: garrisons, general hostings, provincial councils

INTRODUCTION

CONTRARY TO A WIDELY HELD OPINION, the government of Ireland in the sixteenth century was not an occupying force, continually menaced by a hostile enemy and commonly engrossed in military planning. As we have seen, the lord deputy and council exercised virtually omni-competent authority on behalf of the crown. A principal element in the regular correspondence and memoranda of the council was, indeed, the maintenance of order and an aspect of this responsibility included the garrisoning of troops in strategically positioned sites throughout the country. And, when rebellion threatened the peace, the council met this imminent peril with unaccustomed energy and determination, much as did the privy council in England. However, the instructions and recommendations to the council in Ireland con-sistently linked the pursuit of military activity to a more fundamental objective: the extension of the common law throughout the realm. In areas beyond the Pale, this aim was often frustrated by resistance from the Gaelic Irish chiefs and Anglo-Irish magnates. But the council doggedly pursued the principle of anglicization through the common law using a complex system of constables, presidency courts, shiring of new counties and citadels of English influence.

Writers on Tudor Ireland have traditionally taken the view that Irish society was infused with violence and disorder, and some have recently argued that Irish resistance to Tudor rule was, at base, politically motivated.[1] This contention is often linked to another basic assumption which has been called the Tudor conquest. Since Ireland was irredeemably beyond the control of English courts and customs, it was necessary to embark upon a wholesale, often ruthless, campaign of conquest and colonization.[2] This explanation is generally

1. Canny, *Elizabethan conquest*, chs. 6, 7; Bradshaw, *Irish constitutional revolution*, pp. 267–87; Ellis, *Tudor Ireland*, pp. 245–49.
2. Canny, *Elizabethan conquest*, ch. 4. More recently, Canny has reformulated the argument in *From reformation to restoration: Ireland, 1534–1660* (Dublin, 1987), chs. 3, 4; and in *Kingdom and colony: Ireland in the Atlantic world, 1560–1800* (Baltimore, 1988), pp. 3–6, 11–16.

accompanied by assertions that the nature of Irish society was a simple dualism of irreconcilable opposites. The new English became increasingly hostile to the native Irish and their writings betrayed an anthropologically-based contempt for Gaelic (or gaelicized) incivility.[3] On the other hand, it is claimed, the native Irish viewed the new English with deep suspicion and eagerly sought religious and other justifications for protracted rebellion.[4] On this model, it would seem, government would be impossible and only military conquest could pave the way for a more enlightened administration based on the social compact of an English polity.

An alternative model for understanding the context of government in Ireland employs greater complexity and gradations of meaning. Ciaran Brady and others have recently pointed out that the government used a variety of approaches, from conciliation to coercion, in order to pursue the end of anglicization through extension of the common law. Brady sees the predominant attitude of a succession of governors as pragmatic and eclectic.[5] Steven Ellis has shown an appreciation for the diversity of Irish society, noting that some Gaelic chiefs accepted English forms while Anglo-Irish families had become gaelicized in varying degrees.[6] The loyalties of these divergent types cannot therefore be automatically assumed. Furthermore, most writers acknowledge the intensely local and particularist nature of Gaelic and border societies where the forces of dynastic competition were assuredly of greater influence for many localities than were the pretensions to sovereignty of a distant Dublin administration. Nevertheless, a recent article by Cunningham and Gillespie has indicated that the reception of new English forms of government such as the presidency courts in Munster and Connacht could be reconciled to Gaelic concepts of hierarchical society, despite evidence of resistance by local chiefs. They declared, 'The emergence of the presidency as an influential institution in Connacht society was not seen by the native Irish population as the product of conquest by an outside element but rather in the traditional terms of a new lord arising following the decline or failure of an old line'.[7]

3. Canny, *Kingdom and colony*, pp. 16–26. See also D.B. Quinn, *The Elizabethans and the Irish* (Washington, D.C., 1966).

4. B. Bradshaw, 'Native reaction to the westward enterprise: a case-study in Gaelic ideology' in K.R. Andrews, N. Canny and P. Hair, ed., *The westward enterprise: English activities in Ireland, the Atlantic and America, 1480–1650* (Liverpool, 1978), pp. 65–80.

5. Brady, 'Government of Ireland', pp. 116–17, 178–80, 202–09, 358–59.

6. Ellis, *Tudor Ireland*, pp. 46–50.

7. B. Cunningham and R. Gillespie, 'Englishmen in sixteenth-century Irish annals', *Ir Econ Soc Hist*, xvii (1990), 15.

The setting in which Tudor government attempted to extend its control was exceedingly diverse. Contemporary observers noted the difficulty of the terrain, which ranged from stony mountain passes and heavily forested districts to plains laced with bogs and rivers. Few roads and bridges existed to make transportation easier and military expeditions of over 1,000 men, horses and carts caused enormous logistical problems. If the English were heavily armed in contrast to their Gaelic Irish foes, the latter were experienced in tactical retreats and knew their territories well. As in any military campaign, the tactical advantage typically lies with speed and surprise. Gaelic Irish soldiers thus led a kind of desultory warfare and this made their forces more difficult to engage on terms favourable to the English. Recent treatments of the provinces beyond the Pale have stressed the complexity of local dynastic politics, and the rivalries which occasionally broke out into battle resembled feudal affrays rather than resistance to Tudor rule. The earl of Desmond, for example, struggled to maintain his control against the McCarthys as well as the Butlers on his borders.[8] Regarding the presidency of Connacht, Bernadette Cunningham has said,

Apart from its military role the institution of the presidency also provided legal and other services previously provided by the native Irish lords. The president acted as arbitrator in disputes. The holding of sessions and other features of the common law were noted in the annals, and it is evident that the native Irish were eager to use the machinery of the common law to resolve disputes among themselves.[9]

In Ulster, by contrast, two recent writers have explained the failure of Tudor reform by reference to the 'militarisation' of the province and the successful resistance of Gaelic leaders to the sporadic and ill-timed incursions of English chief governors and colonizing adventurers.[10] Despite this evidence of aggression and reaction, however, the English garrisons of Newry and Carrickfergus maintained themselves by a series of accommodations with the native chiefs and clans.[11] It is deceptively simple to claim that an abiding racial animosity lay behind every confrontation in Tudor Ireland, but the reality is far more complex. Further study of local and regional concordance, as well as conflict,

8. MacCarthy-Morrogh, *The Munster plantation*, pp. 1–2.
9. Cunningham & Gillespie, 'Englishmen in Irish annals', 14.
10. H. Morgan, 'The end of Gaelic Ulster: a thematic interpretation of events between 1534 and 1610', *IHS*, xxvi (1988), 8; C. Brady, 'Sixteenth century Ulster and the failure of Tudor reform', in C. Brady, M. O'Dowd and B. Walker, ed., *Ulster: an illustrated history* (London, 1989), p. 77.
11. Brady, 'Sixteenth-century Ulster', p. 94.

will doubtless make the variegated setting of Tudor government more convincing, and perhaps more clear.

The key to understanding the nature of Tudor government in Ireland and its use of coercion is a definition of order. Order was a common ideal in English society, from top to bottom, according to Anthony Fletcher. The body politic relied on familiar recognition of a few key principles: (1) the 'Great Chain of Being' as a divinely sanctioned hierarchy in which all things had their place and humans accepted reciprocal obligations to society and to each other; (2) the ideal of law as a common bond and a superior justice to which all persons might appeal; and (3) the ideal of stability which assured the survival of the system and committed individuals of each social class to undertake particular roles which would guarantee respect for the law.[12] Order was thus the business of everyone, from the family to the church to the government. When disorder occurred in this context, it was important to distinguish between the commonplace disturbances and the more serious insurgencies. Penry Williams has indicated two forms of disorder which have been used to identify rebellion and protest. In the more menacing example, the leaders attempt to seize, or to alter, political power, while in the more typical model they merely demonstrate in force against a policy or draw attention to some grievance.[13] Tudor policy on disorder was exceedingly harsh in either case. Whether it was the ordinary prosecution of masterless men or a reaction to the collective violence of genuine rebellion, the response of the government was often a ruthless and disproportionate retribution framed in the language of law and justice.[14]

We do not have similar studies of order and disorder for Tudor Ireland, so any comparison must necessarily be tentative. General histories have pronounced that the century was exhausted by 'constant war'.[15] Yet Ellis has suggested that Henry VIII's government responded to the Kildare rebellion of 1534 with practical moderation, born of limited means and the need to retain the political allegiance of the Pale élite.[16] While Ellis sees a sharp discontinuity beginning with the reign of Elizabeth, whose policies he regards as more aggressive, it is

12. A. Fletcher, 'Introduction', in A. Fletcher and J. Stevenson, ed., *Order and disorder in early modern England* (Cambridge, 1985), pp. 1–39.

13. Williams, *Tudor regime*, p. 314.

14. R.B. Manning, 'Violence and social conflict in mid-Tudor rebellions', *Jn British Stud*, xvi (1977), 21–22, 35–36; A.L. Beier, 'Vagrants and the social order in Elizabethan England', *Past & Present*, no. 64 (1974), 14–17.

15. Quinn, 'Ireland in 1534', p. 31; Williams, *Tudor regime*, p. 345. Williams said, 'By comparison with the pacific revolts of the English, Irish rebellions were brutal and violent', citing C. Falls, *Elizabeth's Irish wars* (London, 1950).

16. S.G. Ellis, 'Henry VIII, rebellion and the rule of law', *Hist Jn*, xxiv (1981), 517–30. But see at 514 and 531 for his view of aggressive Elizabethan policy.

important to recognize that the military establishment suffered frequent force reductions throughout the period leading to the Desmond rebellion. Canny argues that the policies of both Sussex and Sydney were at base military and belligerent, yet he acknowledges the very limited achievements of those policies, particularly in Ulster.[17] Brady, on the other hand, views the military establishment of mid-Tudor Ireland as weak, undisciplined and amateurish. In his view, these governments were restrained by fiscal limitations and legal objectives. They sought law reform as a basis for governance and hence rejected ruthless exploitation and military conquest.[18] The bloody exploits of notoriously reckless leaders such as Sir Humphrey Gilbert in Munster can thus be explained only by reference to the seriousness of the rebellion which he was chosen to put down. The picture which emerges from these observations is a muddled one indeed. Tudor military policy can be seen as a blend of approaches, from moderation to oppression, but in any event it is difficult to validate the assumption that a monolithic and draconian plan of campaign was taken up after 1558. Rather, Elizabethan government, like those before it, responded in practical ways to crises as they unfolded, revealing preferences that were indeed consistent with the primary aim of extension and reform of the common law. Speaking of Sydney's instructions for 1565, Canny has said, '. . . the scheme outlined by Sidney apppeared realistic and promised to open the way for the extension of English common law over a wider area, and eventually through the entire country'.[19]

The following analysis of the military responsibilites of the council in Ireland will focus primarily on administrative matters such as the size of the garrison, the taking of musters, the establishment of regional councils and the onerous burdens of victualling and the cess. When all is taken into account, including the traditional militia, or 'general hosting' of the Pale and its environs, the concept of an Elizabethan conquest of Ireland as a model for understanding the period prior to the Desmond rebellion must be rejected.

HISTORICAL BACKGROUND

The complex origins of the Anglo-Norman conquest of Ireland have some relevance to the history of Tudor military policy. In their very intricacy, these Anglo-Norman events illustrate the difficulty of sorting out a clear and consistent policy for the conquest of an entire country.

17. Canny, *Reformation to restoration*, pp. 59–62.
18. Brady, 'Government of Ireland', pp. 45–47, 145–46, 198–209.
19. Canny repeats this assertion often, despite his insistence that Sydney's aims were primarily military and led the way to conquest and colonization. Canny, *Elizabethan conquest*, pp. 48–50, 52, 54, 64, 99.

Indeed, when Henry II arrived at Waterford from Milford Haven with 4,000 troops he did not intend to do more than to control Leinster and the populous towns under the leadership of the capable Strongbow, who was named royal constable in Ireland. During the Tudor period, by contrast, no English army of 4,000 troops was used until the Munster rebellion made this necessary. Furthermore, all the Anglo-Norman lords and many leading Gaelic Irish chiefs offered their submission to Henry II at Waterford, acknowledging him as their feudal overlord. F.X. Martin has argued that the Gaelic Irish leaders were far more concerned with their internecine rivalries than with the protocols of swearing fealty to a powerful foreign king. Similarly, in the Tudor period, the act of 1541 which declared Henry VIII king in Ireland caused little political resistance and the process of surrender and re-grant which followed was accepted by many leaders among the Gaelic Irish. Finally, it is important to recognize that the aims of Henry II, like those of his Tudor successors, were based on a new kind of dominion. Martin has said, 'The rule of feudal law, under a centralised monarch, in its sophisticated Angevin form, was about to make its entry into Ireland'.[20]

In the fifteenth century, English rule was profoundly weakened due to a series of incompetent chief governors who were mainly absentees and to the disorders of the protracted Wars of the Roses. Anglo-Irish nobles built up private armies while Gaelic chiefs struggled to build up and maintain their primacy among related clans. Despite the debilitated condition of the Dublin administration, there is little support for the traditional view of a Gaelic revival in this period. Rather, the misfeasance of government and general neglect of Irish affairs made the practical independence and political power of Irish lords appear greater than they were. After 1470, the earls of Kildare exercised an ambiguous, but effective, hegemony over the lordship on behalf of the crown. There were spasmodic efforts at comprehensive reform led by English viceroys, but for most of the period 1470 to 1534 the Kildare magnates were provided with authority to govern and allowed to use a combination of English and Gaelic practices which proved unusually effective. The realm was relatively stable, peaceful and orderly during this period because the crown delegated power to a capable aristocratic leader who claimed a right to govern according to medieval concepts of dominion. Based on regional loyalties and control of the Pale, Kildare ruled Ireland in the tradition of the justiciar whose power was widely acknowledged and rarely challenged.[21]

20. F.X. Martin, 'Allies and an overlord, 1169–72' in A. Cosgrove, ed., *Medieval Ireland, 1169–1534: A new history of Ireland, ii* (Oxford, 1987), pp. 87–89.

21. Ellis, *Tudor Ireland*, pp. 27–31, 62–66, 85–105.

Prior to 1534 the 'Kildare ascendancy' was occasionally interrupted by brief intervals during which an English viceroy was sent to govern Ireland. There were three notable examples. In the first case, Sir Edward Poynings was appointed deputy lieutenant and sent to Ireland in the face of a threatened invasion by Perkin Warbeck in 1494. Poynings had a small garrison at his command, and he arrested Kildare on suspicion of treason, but his primary aims were civil, not military. He was assisted by three able lawyers who served as the principal judges in Ireland and he set about fiscal reform in the Dublin admin-istration. The famous parliament agreed to a practical withdrawal of its independence of action by statute and thereby accepted limitations on Irish government imposed from England. However, the return of Kildare in 1496 and the restoration of aristocratic governance proved to be of greater immediate significance. In 1520, Henry VIII sent the earl of Surrey to Ireland as lord lieutenant to attempt a comprehen-sive restructuring of the lordship. Surrey held a parliament, promoted financial retrenchment and tried to bring the Gaelic chiefs under the effective dominion of the chief governor. In the process, he alienated nearly every parochial interest in the country. His conclusion was that Ireland must be brought under military rule at great cost to the crown, but Henry preferred moderate means (as would both his daugh-ters) and Surrey was recalled in 1522. In the third example, Sir William Skeffington was named lord deputy in 1530 with a diminished set of expectations. He had only 300 troops, certainly not enough to begin an aggressive strategy. His role was to be an arbiter between the lead-ing Anglo-Irish magnates and to encourage others to submit to royal government. Within two years he was again replaced by Kildare.[22] It would apear, then, that the sending of experienced English military leaders to Ireland as viceroys did not necessarily herald the commence-ment of a campaign of conquest.

For many years it has been assumed that the Kildare rebellion and its consequences identified a key turning-point in Irish history. The current debate on the reforms initiated by Thomas Cromwell before and after that rebellion should not obscure the impact of the rebellion itself.[23] In the first place, the uprising quickly escalated into a full-scale challenge to royal authority, unlike earlier disturbances. Secondly, the rebels threatened the very stability of the Pale and laid siege to Dublin castle, the stronghold and symbol of English authority. Thirdly, the revolt was led not by the disendowed and disaffected border chiefs

22. Ellis, *Tudor Ireland*, pp. 75–81, 108–14, 119–21. Poynings arrived with a com-plement of 653 soldiers while Surrey struggled to obtain 550 troops who were suitable for service in Ireland.

23. See Bradshaw, *Irish constitutional revolution*, pp. 87–133, 164–67; Ellis, *Reform and revival*, pp. 211–15; Canny, *Reformation to restoration*, pp. 15–32.

and lords, but by Silken Thomas, son of the earl of Kildare, scion of Ireland's ruling family. Fourthly, the insurrection generated an important and lasting English response, that is, an English viceroy and a standing army which was thereafter garrisoned in strategic places throughout the country. When Skeffington brought up to 2,500 troops to Ireland in 1534 this was the largest contingent of English soldiers since Richard II arrived in 1399. While this is not evidence of a Tudor conquest, since it can be compared to the response to other rebellions in England (the Pilgrimage of Grace, for example), it is clear that the crown now became convinced of the need to maintain order and to change the nature of the Irish government.[24] And despite the relatively moderate response in the aftermath of the rebellion, Tudor policymakers were now inclined to argue the need for wholesale restructuring of the Dublin administration instead of the ambiguous compromise which had worked until this time under the earls of Kildare.[25]

In the somewhat artificial dichotomy currently in use, English policy towards Ireland veered unsteadily from coercion to conciliation throughout the sixteenth century. The Kildare rebellion was met with a military expedition led by Sir William Skeffington which effectively ended the fighting in 1535 after a campaign which was notable for the slaughter of the Geraldine garrison at Maynooth. Lord Leonard Grey had accompanied Skeffington to Ireland as marshal of the army and he succeeded as lord deputy on the death of the latter in 1536. Despite reductions in the military establishment after the surrender of Kildare from 2,500 troops down to only 700 men and a further reduction to 340 men by the commission sent to Ireland in 1537, Grey's tenure as lord deputy was known for its aggressive and belligerent posture. He tried to widen the authority of English governance by making extended progresses to such distant points as Athlone, Armagh and Dungannon. In the process, he agitated the Ulster chiefs who combined in a surprisingly united rebellion and sacked several towns in the Pale. Grey routed them easily, but in the process he acquired a reputation for gratuitous violence and he was recalled, charged with treason, and executed in 1541.[26]

The discrediting of Grey for using excessive force launched the celebrated career of Sir Anthony St Leger. St Leger was a member of the 1537 commission of inquiry sent into Ireland. He is closely associated with the policy of conciliation in Irish government and he viewed the disorder of the Kildare rebellion in a different light. Dr Bradshaw

24. For a comparison with the English response, see Elton, *Policy and police*, chs. 5, 8, 9.

25. Bradshaw, *Irish constitutional revolution*, pp. 114–23, 140–46; Ellis, *Reform and revival*, pp. 214–15; Canny, *Reformation to restoration*, p. 32.

26. Ellis, *Tudor Ireland*, pp. 126–31, 135–36.

has argued that both rebellions of the 1530s were essentially feudal reactions, protest demonstrations rather than insurrections. After 1534, resistance to the garrisons in the Pale was caused by the excesses of soldiers rather than by incipient opposition to English rule. When St Leger became lord deputy for the first time in 1540, he proceeded with characteristic caution. He began the policy of surrender and re-grant by which the Gaelic chiefs could exchange their corporate landholding and vulnerable social position for the greater security of English tenure and title. The constitutional and military significance of this policy was very great. Some of the leading Irish lords such as O'Neill, MacWilliam Burke and O'Brien took earldoms and swore fealty to the crown.[27] On the other hand, border chiefs generally refused to accept the olive branch and resisted encroachment on their territory by either English custom or coercion.[28] The aims, of course, were to provide general access to the common law and to prevent dynastic feuding which so often led to widespread disorder. St Leger's restrained military policy, thus, was designed to complement civil and social reform through persuasion and gradual amelioration. When he went on campaign he used force only to convince his adversaries of the superiority of the new legal arrangements, and he maintained his garrison at very low levels (500 troops in 1542 and again in 1553).[29]

We may judge the achievements of St Leger by other standards as well as by the policy of the 'commonwealth humanism' which is attributed to him. He was apparently successful in balancing the competing factions at court and council in Dublin, but he was vulnerable to factional struggles in England and he was recalled from office frequently. While he strove for a respectful rapprochement with many of the Irish chiefs, he failed to prevent them from raiding each other on occasion and his studied neutrality may also be regarded as singularly unambitious. Brady has shown that many leaders among the Gaelic Irish simply refused to accommodate themselves to the opportunity of surrender and re-grant.[30] Those who champion the work of Kildare and St Leger on the basis of their willingness to permit local dynasts to rule according to their own lights must, in some fashion, reconcile this approval with the evident and increasing intention of Henry VIII and his successors to rule the entire country and to extend the common law to all their subjects.[31] St Leger was content to probe

27. Bradshaw, *Irish constitutional revolution*, pp. 195–210.
28. Brady, 'Government of Ireland', pp. 72–78.
29. Ellis, *Tudor Ireland*, pp. 143, 233.
30. Brady, 'Government of Ireland', pp. 72–78.
31. See Ellis, *Reform and revival*, pp. 1–31; *Tudor Ireland*, chs. 3–5, for Kildare's tenure; Bradshaw, *Irish constitutional revolution*, pt. iii, 'The liberal revolution', for the work of St Leger.

for practical advantages. He accepted the status quo when he found it too difficult to change and he allied himself closely with reformers in the Pale. As the aims of Tudor policy-makers evolved after 1547 toward a more comprehensive restructuring of Irish government, his was increasingly regarded as a 'caretaker' administration, suitable in the intervals between reforming programmes. It is possible that the tolerant gradualism for which St Leger is duly famous was simply temporizing, although one could hardly blame such a prudent states-man for trimming his sails when the storms of mid-Tudor politics blew unpredictably on the shores of Erin.

A final comparison may be made between the viceregal tenures of two lords deputy who replaced St. Leger for brief intervals. In the first case, Sir Edward Bellingham went to Ireland as captain general in June 1547 and became lord deputy in 1548. He was a military leader who was sent initially out of concern for foreign invasion, but his expeditions were concentrated mainly in the midlands of Ireland. He built forts at Daingean and Ballyadams and erected smaller garrisons at Athlone, Nenagh and Leighlinbridge, and before he retired from Ireland he obtained the submissions of the rebel leaders of the O'Connors and O'Mores.[32] The garrison strategy for extending the authority of the government had been conceived by reformers work-ing under Thomas Cromwell, and the mid-Tudor period witnessed the erection of substantial fortifications which would become key elements in the military policy of Elizabethan governors.[33] The second example of the military-style governor in this period was Sir James Croft, who was sent to fortify Ulster and Munster in case of foreign invasion in 1551. He brought an enormous military force, including 2,134 English troops and added 484 Irish kerne. While he failed to engage either the Scots or the O'Neills, Croft managed to establish garrisons in the key northern outposts of Armagh and Carrickfergus. Later, he subdued disturbances in the midlands, a feat which encour-aged Lord Chancellor Cusake to call for shiring the entire area and bringing it within the purview of the common law.[34] Although Brady sees the more aggressive policies of both Bellingham and Croft as fully consonant with St Leger's moderation, their approaches were different and their results were more substantial, since they laid the foundation for garrisoning an expanded frontier.[35] In any case, it is important to emphasize the opportunity which the new garrisons presented to the efforts of the crown to extend its authority.

32. Ellis, *Tudor Ireland*, p. 229.
33. Bradshaw, *Irish constitutional revolution*, p. 167.
34. Ellis, *Tudor Ireland*, pp. 230–32.
35. Brady, 'Government of Ireland', p. 102.

a) the council and military policy

A substantial military establishment was maintained in Ireland under the control of an English viceroy, then, well before the arrival of Sussex as lord deputy in 1556. The chief governor shared with the council in Ireland the formal responsibility for its administration. The lord deputy and council recommended increases or reductions in the size of the army, hired galloglasses (Scots mercenary soldiers, generally native to Ireland) and Irish kerne (light infantry of the native Irish),[36] gave instructions to the captains and constables in the field, determined where the garrisons should be manned, heard grievances against the soldiers and planned the response to foreign invasion.[37] In addition, the council had to find money to pay the troops. This meant repeated entreaties to the English privy council or it might require the Irish council to contract a loan with local merchants or even to make assessments among the individual councillors. Responsibility for victualling led to several confrontations with the Palesmen, and the council would gladly have surrendered that obligation. The issues of military policy for a specific campaign, and the recruitment and training of troops were left to the English council acting in concert with the lord deputy.

In general, the privy council in England retained control of Irish military policy in every significant area, taking the advice of the council in Ireland as needed. Through the periodic instructions to the lord deputy and council, policies were initiated and strategies developed. The English privy council governed the payment of the troops and the sending of English bands as well as the declaration of war. However, there was a great deal of shared responsibility with the council in Ireland in such areas as the deployment of the army, the advancement of captains, and anticipated foreign invasions. During the period from 1556 to 1578 the structure of military authority gradually changed to reflect the crown's growing concern at the accelerating costs of governing Ireland. The effect was to increase the power of the London administration while tightening the pressure on the council in Ireland to control expenses. In May 1557, for example, the queen accepted the notion that the council in Ireland could act independently, augmenting the forces as they thought best, so long as the cost did not exceed £5,000 per annum. But by 1565 the instructions to Sydney mandated only limited increases and soon thereafter the queen compelled her Irish government to implement comprehensive retrenchment.[38]

36. See G.A. Hayes-McCoy, *Scots mercenary forces in Ireland, 1565-1603* (Dublin, 1937); K. Simms, 'Warfare in the medieval Gaelic lordships', *Ir Sword*, xii (1975-76), 1.

37. BL, Stowe MS 160, ff. 34-35v; PRO, SP 62/2/27-28; RIA, MS 24 F 17, f. 116.

38. PRO, SP 62/1/110-11; 63/15/18-25; 63/2/23.

The military authority of the council in Ireland was thus circum-scribed by the enhanced responsibility of the English privy council. Nevertheless, it played an important part in its advisory role, deliver-ing reports of campaigns on which new strategies could be based. In every year from 1556 to 1578 the council sent to London a detailed summary of the military expeditions and the state of the realm. During the stress of actual warfare the council's advice turned to more weighty strategic questions. In 1562, for example, Sussex and the council offered the opinion that Shane O'Neill must be forced to obedience since he had frustrated all their attempts at persuasion. The council advised what forces should be used, what provisions would be needed and even proceeded to build a garrison at Armagh to harbour and defend the troops. It was thought best to defer the invasion until the dry months, storing provisions during the winter season '. . . to be used utterly to subverte and expell him and not to reforme him . . .'.[39] The timing of military expeditions and the size of force increases were frequently the responsibility of the council in Ireland, as in 1572 when it decided to pursue Rory Oge O'More late in March.[40]

Not surprisingly, certain areas of military practice were uniquely the province of the Irish council because it alone was able to make prompt decisions. Hence the defence of the borders of the Pale was left to the council. In 1564 the council placed bands of horsemen on the borders next to O'Reilly's country and ordered a close watch kept in all the towns against possible raids while commissioners parleyed with the Irish chief. Two years later certain leading Anglo-Irish noblemen of the Pale were ordered to defend Kells and Navan with horsemen and archers and to supervise the watches.[41] The hiring of kerne and galloglasses was also peculiarly the council's responsibility. In 1563 Sussex led an expedition to the north and found he lacked sufficient men. He wrote back to the council at Dublin ordering 300 more kerne to be hired for twenty days beginning on 20 April. By 24 April neither Irish kerne nor the promised victuals and ordnance had arrived, so Sussex wrote a scathing rebuke to the council on 3 May,

39. PRO, SP 63/7/105–07. In 1561 the council's reports detailed the number of cattle taken by the lord lieutenant, the victuals he used, the allies he employed and the skirmishes he fought. Sussex proposed to pursue Shane at night during the 'bright mone' in Tyrone, '. . . and so contynuing everye bright mone in offending and the dark mone in defending, to waste and destroy corne, Cattle, and all other thinges for their sustenance in that country'. PRO, SP 63/4/57, 112, 115, 132–34.

40. Bodl, Carte MS 56, f. 73–73v. In 1579 the council had to increase the number of horsemen, juggling the force strength of several bands and adjusting the dis-tribution of others. *Walsingham letter-bk*, pp. 239–40.

41. RIA, MS 24 F 17, ff. 198v, 227. In 1573 the council hired 300 English troops to defend the northern borders. PRO, SP 63/40/125.

noting that the troops were restless from the enforced idleness and were hungry to boot! By 20 May Sussex was desperate. He wrote to the council, ordered a general hosting (see below), and then explained the situation to the privy council in London. Without bread and reinforcements, he complained, no fighting was done and the queen's victuals were consumed without anything to show for it.[42] This lapse of conciliar responsibility went unexplained, but it certainly casts doubt on the ability of the council, lacking the leadership of the chief governor, to provide troops and victuals at short notice. The council had more success in establishing new leaders in the field when circumstances required prompt action. In October 1569, for example, Humphrey Gilbert was made colonel of the forces in Munster against Fitzmaurice, the government of the entire province being placed in his hands.[43]

Fundamental strategic considerations were shared unequally between the governments in Dublin and London. Military policy was grounded on the fundamental question of whether to use force or persuasion against an adversary, and this issue was continually being debated among the queen's councillors. The deployment of troops was basically up to the lord deputy, assisted by the council in Ireland, while the English privy council would occasionally suggest places to be garrisoned or fortified. Tactical manoeuvres, on the other hand, were generally the province of the lord deputy, as commander of the garrisons. Although the council in Ireland, acting independently, might re-distribute the troops in the field to obtain a mixture of horsemen and footmen in the bands as a 'terror' to the rebels, the lord deputy often complained of the lack of experienced military men as councillors to assist him in planning and implementing strategy.[44] Sydney was particularly vexed by this omission, saying,

But alas, Madam, howe can your highnes thincke that I can attende that your martiall service when aswell for the providinge and furnisshing of it as also for governinge in all other civill causes, there is none in effect to commaund or execute but myself . . . so as I am no soner returned from any Jorney and can unwrappe myselfe any one hower oute of martiall actions and devises, but that causes of all thies Courtes by swarmes flye in unto me to the great confondinge of my memorie and hinderance of your service . . .'.[45]

42. PRO, SP 63/8/63–64, 69, 95, 99–101.

43. PRO, SP 63/29/133. Malbie was chosen as leader of the army in Munster in the rebellion of a decade later, replacing the dying lord deputy, Drury. At that time, Gilbert had returned with a combined naval and military command. *Walsingham letter-bk*, pp. 120–21, 194.

44. Bodl, Carte MS 56, ff. 61–62.

45. PRO, SP 63/20/142. See also Fitzwilliam to Cecil, SP 63/42/185.

This accusation exposes to view the clumsy stratification of civil and military jurisdictions which plagued all the chief governors, and it demonstrates emphatically the press of judicial business on the lords deputy and council.

Certainly the most serious threat to the peace in Ireland was the potential menace of foreign invasion. In questions of this sort, the privy council and the council in Ireland worked closely together and the latter body was not unwilling to remind the queen occasionally that '. . . we have both the Irishe and Scottes in our Bowelles allready . . .'.[46] A combined descent on Ireland by both French and Scots was anticipated in 1558 as a sequel to the loss of Calais, and the Irish council was caught with diminished forces and low supplies. Noting the projected invasion of Tyrone by the Scots, Sydney asked Sussex '. . . that we may have spedy succour or els to be revoked . . .'.[47] The council in Ireland was reasonably vigilant about regular watch-keeping to see that the Palesmen were not suddenly overrun by hostile Irish forces, ensuring that nightly watches were kept in all the towns. In times of extreme danger the watches were augmented with beacons erected along the sea coast, as in 1558.[48] A more serious threat emerged in 1571 when the council at Dublin feared Spanish intervention during the rebellion of James Fitzmaurice. At that time, the Irish council called for engineers to erect defences against the Spanish, as well as experienced commanders and 'engines of war'.[49] In 1577 when the council was expecting Thomas Stukeley's forces to land, it obtained the unusual power to send for 2,000 more men without first getting the queen's permission. News of Stukeley's preparations reached Ireland from the privy council in London, and more men and victuals were made ready in 1578 along with three of the queen's ships. Finally, in July 1578 the privy council sent word that Stukeley had been killed and no invasion was likely. At the same time, steps were immediately taken to withdraw the men and supplies so hastily mobilized for war.[50] This vacillation in official policy was largely unavoidable due to the difficulties of maintaining regular correspondence between London and Dublin, but the impact of hasty mobilization of forces

46. PRO, SP 62/2/15.

47. ibid., ff. 27–28, 32.

48. In 1556 the watches were continued, especially in the winter months against marauding bands. Constables, sheriffs and justices of the peace were to supervise the watch-keeping. RIA, MS 24 F 17, ff. 22v–23, 69–69v, 116–18. See also BL, Cott. MS Titus B XIII, ff. 114–15v.

49. PRO, SP 63/32/9–11v.

50. PRO, SP 63/59/11–11v; 63/61/82–83v; *Walsingham letter-bk*, pp. 4–6, 8–9; BL, Stowe MS 160, ff. 34–35v.

and the imperative of providing reinforcements from England made conciliar planning particularly troublesome in a crisis.

In 1575 the queen had determined to reform her Irish government, and in doing so she and the privy council in England assumed more control over Irish military affairs. When the bargain made with Sir Henry Sydney in 1575 subsequently failed to work, new orders were drawn up for the anticipated retrenchment in the army. In 1579 the privy council established in considerable detail how the reforms would be effected.[51] The intent of this renewed effort at reform was to establish control of the military expenses and activities in Ireland by reducing the troop levels during peace time. Ironically, the ensuing rebellion created even more favourable conditions for the assumption of military control by the queen and privy council, although it obviously cost a great deal more. Among the more important changes was a fundamental shift in policy-making which concentrated power in the hands of a committee of the privy council in London. It was proposed that,

. . . there be thre or foure selected persons to be assigned out of her majesties privie counsell, whear of the Lord High Threasurer to be one, and they to be as a speaciall or private counsell for thiese warres, and to take the care thereof and that some one or two men of experience to attend upon them, wiche may give direction and order, aswell to all officers, purveyors and mynisters that have alreadie any charge as that hereafter shalbe occupied in that service, as well in England as Irelande.[52]

Such a committee, had it been established prior to 1579, might have been able to give some harmony and coherence to an Irish military policy notorious for its shifts and starts before the Munster rebellion.

Although more control over the military was gradually transferred from Dublin to London, the desired retrenchment was never completely achieved. But the efforts of the queen and privy council to reform the military establishment resulted in a significant accretion of command over everything from the troop strength and musters to the victualling of the forces. By 1578 all that was left solely to the council in Ireland was the responsibility for calling out the general hosting. While the precise role and function of the military, indeed its legal and constitutional status, were still not clearly resolved, the problems created by the standing army promised to endure indefinitely.

Before treating the military responsibility of the Irish council in depth, we should discuss the opponents of the government who made the expedient of a standing army necessary. Very few of the Irish chiefs

51. BL, Cott. MS Titus B XII, ff. 265–68; *Walsingham letter-bk*, pp. 62–68.
52. BL, Add. MS 32,323, f. 187–87v.

merit the praise of later writers who, like Hayes-McCoy, championed their bitter and relentless opposition to English rule.[53] For, even the inveterate hostility of Shane O'Neill or of the earl of Clanricarde's sons was tempered by a willingness to come in to the government when the opportunity was right to sue for peace. After the death of Shane in 1567, the greatest menace to the Pale was ended and his successor, Turlogh Luineach O'Neill, was more tractable, and exclusively concerned with his dominion over Ulster. The MacDonald Scots represented a challenge to any ruler of Ulster, and the government tried to enlist O'Neill's support to oust them. But the Scots never threatened the Pale and were content to establish a limited, almost seasonal, kind of hegemony in north-east Ulster, the modern Co. Antrim.

Recent studies of Gaelic political and social practices have demonstrated that the structure of traditional lordships was changing in relation to the expansion of the central government. Although most accounts stress the restive and unruly elements in Gaelic society and argue that it was primarily organized for war, Katharine Simms has argued that the Gaelic lordships of the later middle ages gradually accepted a diminished role and began to cooperate with agents of the English crown. They submitted to the lords deputy, accepted conditions of surrender and re-grant, and employed mercenaries to do their fighting. This is not to say that the Irish lords became conventionally placable. The intent here is to demonstrate the intricacy of social and political relations in the Tudor period. Simms explains that some of the lords readily accepted Tudor jurisdiction and sought the protection of captains and constables such as Nicholas Malbie, while others who continued their warlike manner often pursued local and dynastic ends which did not aim at resistance to conciliar governance under the crown. The petty warfare of particular Irish chiefs should not be mistaken for rebellion against English rule, and no Gaelic lords of the sixteenth century asserted the traditional rights of kingship as they were understood prior to the rule of Henry VII.[54]

Some of the Anglo-Irish magnates such as Desmond, Thomond, and Clanricarde were hardly more trustworthy than the more sympathetic Irish chiefs, but they were far more dangerous in combination. Each of them rebelled at one time before 1578 and then meekly submitted. Desmond spent seven years in detention in the Tower of London and elsewhere. The Irish chiefs living near the Pale were also

53. G.A. Hayes-McCoy, 'The renaissance and the Irish wars', *Iris Hibernia*, iii, no. 5 (1967), 44; idem, 'The Protestant reformation, 1547–71', in T.W. Moody, F.X. Martin and F.J. Byrne, ed., *Early modern Ireland, 1534–1691: A new history of Ireland, iii* (Oxford, 1976), pp. 50, 80–86.

54. K. Simms, *From kings to warlords: the changing political structure of Gaelic Ireland in the later middle ages* (Wolfeboro, N.H., 1987), pp. 72–79, 121–28, 147–50.

a threat to peace, but their periodic uprisings were localized and largely confined to the vicinity of Leix and Offaly (the O'Mores and O'Connors) and the Wicklow mountains (the O'Byrnes and O'Tooles). These septs sporadically raided the borders of the Pale and occasionally attempted to overthrow the yoke of English domination. The council was forced to send troops to engage them many times, but the Irish were too mobile and no conventional battles were ever fought between them. The single most dangerous threat to the government was that of foreign invasion. When news was received of an impending attempt on Ireland, the council burst into furious activity, arranging for beacons to be lit and for the militia to be called up on a few days' notice. During this period no invasion occurred until the landing of James Fitzmaurice in 1578, but the alarms were often sounded and the council demanded constant vigilance from the towns, havens and garrisons under its supervision.

b) military infrastructure—personnel

Military forces in Ireland were variously identified as the 'army', or the 'garrison', or, rather enigmatically, the 'establishment'. The use of the term 'establishment' may have had reference to the semi-permanent nature of the army's mission in Ireland, in contrast to the lack of a standing army in England. Proposals for retrenchment in the number of troops quartered on the Pale usually mentioned the 'establishment' or the 'garrison' while the expeditionary forces used against Shane O'Neill were referred to as the 'army'.[55] However, in practice the terms were all used interchangeably to describe the permanent military force. The garrison included many bands of soldiers quartered on the Pale or attached to one of the leading military officials, so the simple impression of an immobile, defensive posture linked to a castle or fortress would be only partly correct.[56] The ambiguous

55. A military reform devised by Cecil in May 1578 was sent to the council as 'Orders . . . for putting in execution the said Establishment . . .'. BL, Cott. MS Titus B XII, f. 265. See also *Walsingham letter-bk*, p. 50. But the most common reference was in the computations made by clerks of the check of the 'state of the garrisons'. See, for example, the 1575 muster book of Owen Moore in PRO, SP 63/54/45–48v, and the book of rates and fees of the garrison in 1565 in PRO, SP 63/15/31–33. In the latter year, however, Matthew King drew up an 'abstract of the army'. PRO, SP 63/13/147–149.

56. The *OED* gives several definitions of 'garrison', including that of soldiers stationed in a fortress for purposes of defence. But one clearly sixteenth-century definition seems to fit, that of a 'body or troop of persons' as a military unit. *OED*, s.v. 'garrison'. The concept of an 'establishment' has many variations, including that of 'an organized body of men, maintained at the expense of the sovereign . . .'; orig. said of the military service . . . . The quota of officers and men in a regiment . . .'. *OED*, s.v. 'establishment'. These very general definitions will be employed in the text hereafter.

status of the military in Ireland stemmed from the fact that England had never employed a permanent occupying force there until 1535 and the government had no intention of keeping an army in Ireland any longer than a case could be made for its continuance.

Since the military establishment remained at a substantial level from 1535 throughout the rest of the century, it is surprising that so little note has been taken of the permanence of the army in Ireland. Quinn has said,

From 1534 onwards—and it is important to emphasize it as being one of the most important features of the Anglo-Irish connexion from that time forward—Ireland had a regular standing army, largely paid for and wholly supervised by the English Government.[57]

But others such as Cruickshank have cited Fortescue approvingly in discussing Elizabeth's '. . . failure to provide a permanent paid army'.[58] Cruickshank mentioned the permanent organization of pensioners in Ireland as a body of reservists, then proceeded to demonstrate the failure of English proposals for a standing army. But in Ireland all the attributes of a permanent armed force seemed to be present, including the requirement of a full complement of military administrators.

The 'garrison' was kept at a minimum of 1,200 men and its average size from 1556 to 1578 was 1,861. The permanent defences in outposts such as Monasterevan, Carrickfergus, Carlow and Dungarvan were constantly manned by a small ward of soldiers (generally about 15 troops, variously armed) and occasionally augmented by forces of up to 200 men.[59] The administrative hierarchy of the army was a permanent feature of the Dublin government. Of course, the lord deputy and treasurer at wars had other duties, but the marshal, the clerk of the check and the master of the ordnance were solely military officials. Each of these leading officers commanded a permanent retinue of soldiers, and these bands could be increased as occasion warranted.

57. Quinn, 'Tudor rule', p. 561.

58. C.G. Cruickshank, *Elizabeth's army* (Oxford, 1946), p. 285 and Cruickshank, *Army royal: Henry VIII's invasion of France, 1513* (Oxford, 1969), pp. 188 et seq. See also the famous quotation from Fortescue, charging that Elizabeth '. . . hated straight dealing for its simplicity; she hated conviction for its certainty; above all she hated war for its expense'. J.W. Fortescue, *A history of the British army*, 13 vols. (London, 1899–1930), i, 130. Even Hayes-McCoy agreed with the received opinion in his 'Strategy and tactics in Irish warfare, 1593–1601', *IHS*, ii (1941), 260.

59. The reliable William Piers was employed at Carrickfergus as captain with 20 footmen and up to 50 horsemen with three officers. On the other hand, Captain Thomas Cheston at Monasterevan commanded only eight footmen and Constable Robert Harpoole at Carlow led a ward of 8 archers, 4 arquebusiers and 6 horsemen in 1571. PRO, SP 63/35/7–9.

It is indisputable that an army was stationed in Ireland during most of the twenty-two years from 1556 to 1578. Despite the reluctance of the queen to maintain a large armed force in Ireland, her lords deputy perennially claimed that the Pale would not be safe and her government would fail if it were not supported militarily. Although the forces were reduced from 2,900 in 1567 to 1,483 in 1569, no further reduction of the armed force was then achieved. The constant pressure of military threats during the ensuing decade warranted a full complement of soldiers ready to defend the Pale and to confront a rebel chieftain in his own dominions. A core or nucleus of armed forces was stationed in Ireland during the intervals between the major campaigns against Shane O'Neill, James Fitzmaurice and the earl of Desmond. The retinues, the strongholds and the pensioners were always supported by a fixed number of bands led by such veteran captains as Francis Agarde and Nicholas Heron. These men and others served in Ireland for an average of nine years at a time and their continuous service demonstrates the permanence of the army. After 1569 the presidencies in Connacht and Munster harboured mobile forces of from 50 to 200 troops, and the failed plantations in Ulster employed many soldiers during 1571–75.

Although the army lacked a regimental organization, this would have been anachronistic in the sixteenth century, so the absence of a conventional chain of command may be explained away. The army was quartered on the Pale and in strongholds and retinues, so it was difficult to bring it all together in a short time, but, again, this disadvantage was characteristic of most Tudor armies. Even though it was permanently situated in Ireland, its status was never certain from year to year as Elizabeth looked for a solution to avoid the drain of men and money across St George's Channel. The queen would have preferred to maintain troops in readiness at a few strategic trouble spots as she did in England, and this conditional status was reflected in the persistent refusal to recognize the army as anything more than a 'garrison' except when it took the field. As late as 1576 Sydney felt compelled to remind the queen that she should reconcile herself to keeping a permanent force in Ireland.[60] While the queen never formally acquiesced in the maintenance of a military establishment in Ireland, her refusal to countenance such an open-ended commitment of resources was a kind of executive fiction. The core structure and staffing of the garrison remained largely the same throughout the early years of her reign.

60. *Cal. Carew MSS, 1575–88*, p. 52. Sydney looked for a permanent garrison in Ireland of 300 horsemen and 700 footmen, hoping that the burden could be spread evenly among the Irish and Anglo-Irish. In 1562 Cusake told Cecil that, despite the peace then current, the government should always keep 2,000 English troops in readiness in case the Irish should rebel. PRO, SP 63/5/88.

At the head of the military establishment stood the lord deputy. He was invariably the commander in the field, and, with the exception of Fitzwilliam, all the lords deputy in the later sixteenth century were experienced military men. The relationship between the council and the lord deputy was always a close, though ill-defined one, but in 1534 the 'Ordinances for the government of Ireland' clearly articulated the conciliar restraints on the chief governor. The first article required that,

. . . the Kinges deputie make no warre ne peace with any Irish man or other person . . . to the charges of the holle countrey, without the assent of the lordes and the kynges counsayle assembled, or the more part of them.[61]

In practice, then, the lord deputy and council planned in concert most of the details of military support, although the deputy acted alone in tactical and in some strategic matters. The treasurer at wars, who was paymaster of the army, was also the vice treasurer of Ireland, and like the deputy, had many other obligations. Both of these officials kept permanent retinues varying in size up to 200 men. After 1565 the lord deputy consistently led 106 men, including his officers, and the vice treasurer retained 41 men, a standardization we may attribute to Sydney's penchant for bureaucratic orderliness. By 1572, however, Burghley was considering the elimination of the band for the treasurer at wars.[62]

The marshal was the highest official with exclusively military obligations. He maintained a full band of 106 men and occasionally more, and he had a seat on the council. Military discipline was his responsibility and he held courts martial and generally enforced the military regulations. The masters of the ordnance, John Travers and later Jacques Wingfield, were responsible for the care and maintenance of the munitions and tools of the army. Masters of the ordnance had a more specialized band composed of gunners, smiths, bowyers and artificers as well as a complement of 30 horsemen. The clerk of the check had a small retinue of ten horsemen. His obligations for taking musters were so onerous that it is doubtful if he took part in field operations.[63]

The four leading military officials formed a nucleus of military expertise on the council. The holders of these offices, aided by certain captains elevated to the rank of councillor, shaped and adapted the crown's military policy in Ireland. Other council members demon-

61. PRO, SP 60/2/65.
62. PRO, SP 63/31/153; 63/35/2.
63. *Walsingham letter-bk*, pp. 51–53.

7 Woodcut of Sir Henry Sydney riding forth from Dublin Castle. From John Derricke, *The image of Irelande* (1581). Written during the Munster rebellion, Derricke's work offered a flattering account of Sydney's deputyship together with a critical appraisal of Gaelic society and its primitive unruliness. The text draws attention to the 'traytours heddes' hanging from the gate of Dublin Castle as Sydney rides out as chief governor with his military retinue.

strated a singular lack of aptitude for martial affairs. After 1569 the lords president of Munster and Connacht were theoretically resident in their provinces and they each had retinues of about 50 men. They were members of the council, but attended the formal meetings only occasionally. With the exception of Fyton, these were military men and their presence was designed, in part, to inspire awe of the English government on the frontiers of its nominal authority. Francis Agarde, the experienced captain and constable of several forts, was a long-time member of the council and sat regularly at its meetings, while Sir Henry Radcliffe, brother of Sussex, was in frequent attendance at the council board until 1565.[64]

Since no regimental organization existed, the next level of authority was that of captains of companies. These men were hired in England to lead their bands into Irish service, and some of them spent long careers in Ireland. A few, like Agarde, Nicholas Malbie and Henry Colley, eventually became councillors on account of their unique experience of Irish affairs.[65] But most captains served an average of three years in Ireland and then, presumably, returned to England, for their names were dropped from the musters. Some 54 captains served in Ireland during the twenty-two years of this period, but only about nine were in service in any given year. During 1567 eighteen captains led 2,933 troops, the largest contingent yet assembled in Elizabethan Ireland. A nucleus of five or six captains was permanently stationed there, even during the years of peace.[66]

Among the captains, only Francis Agarde was resident in Ireland throughout the period, but Sir Nicholas Bagenall returned in 1560 as a captain and successfully reclaimed his post as marshal in 1565 from George Stanley. Bagenall had been marshal of Ireland in 1547 but was removed by Mary in 1556. His return marked the commencement of a core of Sydney supporters in the new administration, but it also gives evidence of the survival in office of men of long experience in Ireland, whether natives or newcomers. After his reinstatement he remained in office till 1590 and he was succeeded by his son.[67] William

64. PRO, SP 63/31/153–53v; 63/62/3v–4v.
65. In 1574 the council recommended that Colley be replaced in the field because of his age. However, they showed their respect for his long experience, saying,
> But as his bodie is so decayed as he is lesse fit for that chardge . . . so is his Judgement and experience so increased as (if it seeme good to her Majestie and your Llordships) we thincke we should have good and sownde assistance of his Counseil . . .; we therefore humilie pray your llordships to be meanes to her majestie for warraunt to admit him one emongest us.

The council further asked for a reward and stipend for his long service and his new dignity. Colley was not long on the council before he died. PRO, SP 63/45/184.
66. PRO, SP 63/21/196.
67. Brady, 'Government of Ireland', pp. 128–29, 175; Hughes, *Patentee officers*, pp. 5–6.

Piers was both constable of Carrickfergus, the lonely outpost in Ulster, and captain of a band of footmen. He served in Ireland for nearly the entire period and became a trusted adviser of Cecil.[68] Nicholas Malbie made his career in Ireland, at first as a captain, then as an unsuccessful planter, then as colonel and lord president of Connacht. He was indefatigable in the field and kept the western province quiet after Fyton had stirred up virulent animosities.[69] Malbie was another whose opinion was sought by the English privy council. Henry Radcliffe held the unusual post of lieutenant of the forts in Leix and Offaly, and had the responsibility for blunting the resistance to the plantations from 1556 to 1565.[70]

Most captains did not rise to the rank of councillor, but they generally became important local men if they chose to settle in Ireland. The majority served in the field with their bands and were quartered with them in the Pale. Some captains were employed as constables in important garrisons in addition to fulfilling their responsibilities in the field. During most of the period Ireland was the only theatre of conflict for professional soldiers, so many of them pursued their careers in the Irish service. Several also stayed on in Ireland after they gave up their commands, living on a pension and settling in the Pale. Men like Nicholas Heron and William Portas were captains and constables and became independent farmers as well. Others like Humphrey Gilbert and Edward Moore continued to pursue their military careers. The captains were rotated into Ireland on an irregular basis, but changes usually accompanied the arrival of a new lord deputy. In 1565, for example, when the retinues were systematically reduced, the captains in service were also changed. It is unlikely that Sydney brought his own men with him from Wales, but some have charged that redundancies even at this level were politically motivated.[71]

Changes in the military leadership were made about every five years. In 1567 Sydney brought Humphrey Gilbert, Edward Moore and Thomas Cheston to Ireland. By 1571 these men had been replaced or supplemented by George Furres, William Collier and George Bourchier. Most captains arrived in Ireland with bands gathered from Berwick, Chester, Bristol or the West Country and were charged with the responsibility for disciplining, paying, quartering and arming

68. Brady, 'Sixteenth-century Ulster', p. 94.
69. Cunningham & Gillespie, 'Englishmen in Irish annals', 12–13.
70. Radcliffe became the fourth earl of Sussex in 1583. Malbie and Bagenall merited articles in the *DNB* by virtue of their unusual careers, but steady and reliable captains like Piers and Agarde did not, in spite of their long service and undeniable importance.
71. Canny, *Elizabethan conquest*, pp. 53–54; but see also, Brady, 'Government of Ireland', pp. 175–76.

their troops. For all this they were paid at the rate of 4s. per diem. It is notorious that they further enriched themselves at the expense of their companies and were guilty of mismanaging their accounts, but these machinations could do them little good if the pay were not forthcoming, as was usually the case in Ireland.

The companies were the functional units of the army in Ireland. They varied in size, but were usually composed of bands of 100 men, led by a captain, a peticaptain and four officers. The band of the lord deputy included a standard-bearer, a trumpeter, and a surgeon among its officers and the other bands might have some or all of these men in their complements of officers.[72] A distinction in pay was made between the lord deputy's standard-bearer (18d. per diem) and the guidon or ensign of the other companies (12d. per diem). But the other officers were paid equally according to rank. Peticaptains received 2s. in wages, trumpeters, guidons and other officers 12d. per diem. The most important distinction in pay was made among the soldiers, who were compensated according to the arms they bore. Hence, a horseman with lance and musket received 9d., a harquebusier 8d., an archer only 6d. and the lowly Irish kerne but 3d. per diem.[73] In Ireland, as elsewhere, the archer was fading into obsolescence. As early as 1562 there were 767 harquebusiers and only 393 archers, and parity between them was found only in the wards and a minority of companies of foot. In 1566 a proposal was made to the lord deputy and council to harmonize all units by finding muskets for every band. Citing the use of muskets by the Spanish, Dutch and French armies, the writer looked for an Irish source of muskets to reduce the charges of sending them from England.[74]

The native Irish employed a ragged light infantry called kerne and these men were also hired as mercenaries by the council. They served at low pay and were lightly regarded as fighting men unless supported by English companies. The proscription of Irish men from the English units meant that the bands of kerne were the only means of employing these roving Irish soldiers in the service of the government. When not in service, they were a menace to public order, but there is little doubt that they proved useful when emergencies arose. For example, in 1557 and 1558 the council swiftly called up several bands of kerne to protect the borders against the raids of the O'Mores,

72. PRO, SP 63/35/2.

73. PRO, SP 63/62/4.

74. PRO, SP 63/19/184. In 1562 there were 420 horsemen. Similarly, there were fewer pikemen to be found in the average company except as a kind of honour guard, for hand-to-hand fighting as a mobile unit was unsuited to Irish warfare. PRO, SP 63/7/193–94. See also PRO, SP 63/13/147–49. In 1565 there were 442 harquebusiers and only 180 archers. PRO, SP 63/15/33.

charging the Pale with £200 for their sustenance.[75] On the other hand, the council proclaimed in 1558 that all kerne retained in Leix and Offaly must be registered on pain of a £100 fine because they were habitually aiding the outlaws and rebels, even raiding with them at night.[76] The council annually employed about 300 kerne in several companies from 1558 until 1575, except for three years when the rebellion of Shane O'Neill caused sudden increases.[77] The regular employment of kerne received formal recognition with the appointment of Francis Cosbie as 'general of the queen's kerne' (a small but constant retinue of 32 troops) in 1558.[78] After 1560 Owen McHugh, a native Irishman, joined Sir Barnaby Fitzpatrick as perennial leaders of the Irish light infantry in conjunction with Cosbie. It was common for certain officials, such as the marshal and the master of the ordnance, to lead a company of kerne along with their other troops, while Anglo-Irish lords such as Kildare, Ormonde and Dungannon retained them as needed. In 1575 Sydney's financial retrenchment halved the number of kerne employed and for the next four years the number was fixed at 135 troops under four captains.[79] In general, the period witnessed a gradual decline in the employment of the kerne as the privy council in England assumed more and more responsibility for policy.

In addition to the Irish kerne, the council in Ireland hired Scots mercenary forces, galloglasses, to augment the forces of the government. These native professional soldiers were reputedly good fighters, having originally come from Scotland as mercenaries in the thirteenth

75. RIA, MS 24 F 17, ff. 27, 61, 75v–76. In 1558 the council agreed to raise temporarily the low wages of the kerne to 6*d.* per diem as an enticement, insisting that this should establish no precedent. See the full description of the kerne in Quinn, *Elizabethans and the Irish*, pp. 93–94, 97. In 1564 the kerne served as the bulwark of defence for the Pale against the rebel O'Mores. The council cessed the Pale for many bands of kerne to provide for their defence. The bands of Kildare, Wingfield, Radcliffe, Owen McHugh, Cosbie, Edward Butler and others were called into service. PRO, SP 63/11/93, 97–98, 100, 113; RIA, MS 24 F 17, ff. 197v, 203–05v, 206–06v.

76. RIA, MS 24 F 17, f. 56.

77. In 1561–62 the number of kerne hired was about 525, and in 1567 it jumped again from 300 to 412 kerne. After a slight increase to 352 in 1571 the number dropped to 270 in 1572. PRO, SP 63/21/196; 63/1/8–9; 63/4/130; 63/7/193–94; 63/13/147–49; 63/31/153–55v; 63/35/2–16v.

78. PRO, SP 62/2/135. He was named to the position on 13 July 1558, primarily because of his long service against the rebels of Leix and Offaly. In July 1548 he wrote six letters to Lord Deputy Bellingham describing his actions against the O'Mores and O'Connors. *Cal. S.P. Ire., 1509–73*, pp. 81–82. See also *DNB*, s.v. 'Cosby, Francis'.

79. Sydney cut the bands of Cosbie, Owen McHugh, Francis Agarde and Lord Upper Ossory, leaving the earl of Kildare with 100 men and smaller units attached to Baron Dungannon, Edward Moore and Sir Brian MacPhelim O'Neill. PRO, SP 63/35/10v.

century, and they hired themselves out to English and Irish alike.[80]
The clan MacDonald galloglasses were hired by the Irish council on
an ad hoc basis as the need arose. Whereas the kerne were employed
mainly in defence of the midland borders of the Pale, galloglasses
were used everywhere. The three captains of the queen's galloglasses
were hired for one-fourth of a year in 1560 with their 300 troops and
furnished with bonaught (a levy of provisions on the country by a
military force) from the Annaly.[81] In the following year the council at
Dublin was compelled to intervene among the galloglasses on the
death of their chief captain. An outbreak of fighting was prevented
when the council declared that the chief captain would not be replaced
and the bonaught would be shared out equally among the three septs.[82]
On the other hand, the galloglasses relied on the Irish council to
protect their interests at common law when, in 1564, they were sued
for debt in Dublin because they were unable to collect their bonaught.
The council arranged to have three of its own members stand surety
for the indebted chiefs until they could recover their due charges.[83]
The council in Ireland was not unwilling to apply native Irish law
and methods in the resolution of certain problems, for the cross-
cultural authority of the government was augmented in this way, just
as the application of the common law to the Gaelic Irish advanced the
effective control of the council. Galloglasses were hired occasionally by
the council in 1564 and 1566 for short terms, but thereafter they
played a much smaller role in the military force of the government,
and a correspondingly larger one in the forces of rebels like
Fitzmaurice and Desmond.[84]

The military establishment also included the non-combatant men
and the supplies under the supervision of the master of the ordnance.
The master employed about twenty-seven men who were skilled crafts-
men, from the master gunner and master smith to the simple artificers.

80. For a full description of them see Hayes-McCoy, *Scots mercenary forces*; and
Quinn, *Elizabethans and the Irish*, p. 40 ff.
81. RIA, MS 24 F 17, f. 127. The council outlawed the practice among the Anglo-
Irish.
82. ibid., f. 176v. The council provided that no injustice should be done, arranging
for a throw of the dice to decide which chief should pick first his own area of
bonaught. The captains were leaders of three septs of the MacDonald Scots.
83. ibid., 187v–88.
84. Unlike the regular troops and some kerne, galloglasses were hired for short
terms and paid partly in kind. In 1566, for example, 300 men were hired for six
weeks, to be paid half in victual and half money at the discretion of the countries
where they were quartered. RIA, MS 24 F 17, ff. 209v, 240–40v. In all the
muster accounts there is no list of galloglasses retained and no account of the
rate of pay for them, although they were undoubtedly paid in money for at least
half of their service.

The bowyer and fletcher were the most highly paid at 16*d*. per diem. The artificers and other gunners were paid 8*d*. or 6*d*. according to their skills.[85] The munitions were stored in Dublin castle for the most part and the mere storage of weapons and tools must have created great difficulties for Wingfield. In one year the master had been provided with 1,000 bows; 2,000 sheafs of arrows; 300 harquebuses; 1,000 morris pikes and black bills; 400 pikeaxes and felling axes; 1,200 spades and shovels; 3,000 shot for four different sizes of cannon; and assorted other wares, including matches, powder, lead, rope, harnesses and planks.[86] The tremendous costs of such an enterprise and the frustrating losses from spoilage, stealth and sheer incompetence led the government into efforts at retrenchment. In September 1558, Mary required the lord deputy to return all the brass cannon sent to Ireland since 1547.[87] Twenty years later the privy council wrote to the council in Ireland in disbelief that the stores had been so rapidly depleted in one year and required a firm accounting before any more would be sent. The privy council admonished the council in Ireland to ensure that the munitions were better stored and kept if a full re-supply were to be expected.[88] The attention to detail in this case illustrates the broad powers of supervision delegated to and by the council in Ireland and it also reflects the structural limitations on its use of military coercion.

The pensioners were mainly superannuated former soldiers who drew daily wages depending on their rank. Certain former captains won substantial pensions, the size of which depended in the main on how well-connected they were. Thus, Brian Fitzwilliams earned a pension of 5*s*. per diem, George Thornton had 4*s*. and William Portas but 3*s*., although the latter had served in Ireland the longest of the three. Others earned stipends for military-related service, such as the victualler, Thomas Sackford. The ordinary soldiers, however, rarely received substantial pensions. The queen had little sympathy for these men and recommended that they be employed in supportive roles in the wards of Irish castles. The privy council wrote to the council in Ireland in 1566 that an amputee sent over from Ireland could not be pensioned in England, 'consydering that the same cannot well be doon without some extraordinary chardges to the quenes majestie,

---

85. *Walsingham letter-bk*, pp. 58–59.

86. PRO, SP 62/1/96. See also PRO, SP 63/1/47, 129–30.

87. PRO, SP 62/21/156–57.

88. *Walsingham letter-bk*, pp. 10–11. In 1573 the council received instructions to employ the auditor in a full survey of the ordnance, making three account books for the exchequer, the privy council and the master of the ordnance. Citing recent 'disorders' in the ordnance office, the government required the lord deputy to restrict payments made for ordnance. PRO, SP 63/41/190v.

no beadmens roomes being presently voyde to be bestowed uppon them . . .'. The privy council, '. . . seing this man hath the use of his lefte arme, and can . . . weld the same as well as he was woont to doo his right arme . . .', ordered the man and his colleagues '. . . to be placed in the roome of sume porter, warder, or other like officer within sume of her majesties holdes or castles there that stand farthest from danger and be of least importance . . .'.[89] This callous attitude proceeded from a desire to make the Irish government reasonably self-sufficient. In 1579, when the queen ordered all pensioners discharged to save expenses, the council in Ireland objected that such ruthless actions would discourage men in the queen's service.[90] In general, this was a source of tension in conciliar relations with the queen, since the council traditionally recommended men who distinguished themselves in Irish service, and the queen increasingly cast the obligation back upon the government in Ireland.

c) military infrastructure—strongholds

The defensive network of strongholds maintained by the government was an essential cornerstone of the total military structure in Ireland (see Map 3). Immobile and semi-permanent, these fortifications were manned by constables and their men, ranging in number from eight to over fifty.[91] Some provided a local centre of control and administration in Gaelic Irish areas, while others offered protection to the inhabitants in settled regions near the Pale and supplemented the more anglicized and urban hubs of civilian authority. Fortresses which were used to quarter troops and store munitions were often traditional centres of military authority and they were rarely beleaguered or threatened. The wards in Carlow, Leighlinbridge, Monasterevan, Athlone and Dungarvan exemplified this kind of fortress. On the other hand, there were outposts on the frontier intended to harness the excesses of the potentially unruly Gaelic Irish and designed to serve as the vanguard for a new extension of conciliar control. These strongholds included newer forts such as Castlemaine in Co. Kerry and the Blackwater fort which defended the northern border of the

89. RIA, MS 24 F 17, f. 261–61v. In the same year the queen ordered the pensioners to be sent to Ulster or they would lose their stipends. PRO, SP 63/24/85v. Fourteen soldiers received 6*d.* per diem in 1579 in consideration that they had been 'decreeped and lamed in service, or growen by age or otherwise impotent and unable to serve . . .'. *Walsingham letter-bk*, p. 60.

90. *Walsingham letter-bk*, p. 242. In the reform of 1578 the queen ordered the pensioners limited to twenty-two men and not replaced on their deaths. BL, Cott. MS Titus B XII, f. 265v.

91. PRO, SP 63/35/2–16v. A full 'state of the garrison' report done to Burghley in 1572 by Lord Justice Fitzwilliam.

Pale, as well as established outposts such as Carrickfergus and Newry in Ulster.[92] While all these isolated garrisons were occasionally menaced by some recrudescence of Gaelic animosity, recent writers have stressed the level of cooperation achieved by experienced commanders such as William Piers at Carrickfergus and Nicholas Bagenall in his well-established community at Newry.[93]

During the period 1556 to 1578, the nature of these defensive bulwarks often changed. For example, the traditional garrison of Monasterevan, located within the Pale in Co. Kildare, was no longer manned after 1572. A precipitant of this relaxation of vigilance was the gradual development of the neighbouring shires of King's and Queen's Counties. Planted and re-named in 1556, and subsequently the object of frequent raids by the displaced O'Connors and O'Mores, nevertheless the fortress towns of Philipstown and Maryborough gradually employed fewer troops and in 1567 they became market towns. When the original concept of settlement was amended in 1563, forty-four of the eighty-eight individuals receiving estates were soldiers. There were only fifteen Palesmen and twenty-nine Gaelic grantees, but the total number rose to 262 by the end of the period. While the engrossment of lands by a few landholders such as Francis Cosbie and Henry Colley led to the dominance of key men, including the earl of Kildare, there were also a growing number of Gaelic tenants and a cultural adaptation which produced a mingling of customs in a new kind of social stability. Sussex had made ambitious plans for an 'integrated and self-sufficient community' based on a condominium of two legal systems with priority given to common law. The rebellion of Rory Oge O'More in 1573 and an undercurrent of low-level insurgency dashed these hopes, but the area witnessed a degree of assimilation and it ceased to be a source of general unrest after 1576.[94]

92. Traditionally, fortresses tended to look west, toward the unsettled regions of the Gaelic Irish. The wards in Athlone confronted Connacht, those in Monasterevan faced Leix and Offaly, while Dungarvan was a window on Desmond's lands in Munster. Carlow and Leighlin, however, were designed to face east and served as the military counter to the Cavanaghs, the O'Byrnes and the O'Tooles. Castlemaine and the Blackwater fort were both manned for the first time in 1575. PRO, SP 63/54/46v–47.

93. Brady, 'Sixteenth-century Ulster', p. 94; 'Government of Ireland', pp. 372–76. Brady claims they used accommodation and compromise with local lords wisely, yet prevented the realization of more comprehensive reforms. Canny argues that many of the English soldiers and their captains 'went native' and some eventually fought against the queen's forces, but it is more likely that they adopted certain Irish customs without losing their primary allegiance. See N. Canny, 'The permissive frontier: the problem of social control in English settlements in Ireland and Virginia, 1550–1650' in Andrews, et al., ed., *Westward enterprise*, p. 24.

94. Brady, 'Government of Ireland', pp. 145–48, 377–81. By 1571 the Cosbies amassed 4,200 acres and the Colleys had trebled their estates, frustrating the

The strategy of garrisoning troops to expand conciliar authority was a flexible one. Some changes took more time and were not completed before 1578. Roscommon was not garrisoned by an army unit until 1571 but it quickly became part of the defensive network of strongholds guarding the Pale, particularly because it was controlled by the lord president of Connacht.[95] Against these examples of the successful expansion of conciliar control, we must set the temporary fortresses, garrisoned for tactical or strategic advantage during a military campaign. There was in these cases no commitment to man the forts on a permanent basis, and they were used primarily during prolonged campaigns sparked by rebellion. Ballyadams and Stradbally, for example, were garrisoned as part of the plantation of Leix and Offaly during 1556. Similarly, Dunluce and other places were fortified during the Ulster projects of Essex and Smith from 1570 to 1572.[96]

The role of the Irish council in this protective system was to maintain the individual strongholds with able leaders, sufficient troops and adequate repairs. The queen was reasonably vigilant about her castles in 1558. Since she had urged Sussex to be '. . . continually travelling from place to place . . .', she ordered Roscommon, Athlone, Monasterevan, Carlow, Ferns, Enniscorthy and the forts in Leix and Offaly to be ready for him.[97] The erection and preservation of citadels of English influence was an important symbol of royal authority, so the queen demanded that the council supervise the regular upkeep of fortifications, towns and bridges. In 1565 Sydney was ordered to repair the 'decayed' towns and castles of Dublin, Kilmainham, Monasterevan, Leighlin, Carlow and Athlone.[98] In her instructions to the council in 1579, however, the queen ordered a moratorium on all new building without a special warrant from the privy council in England. Citing the growing burden of building costs, the queen ordered the Irish council to approve only buildings under £100 and then only if six councillors voted for it after a survey was made. But even with this new stringency, both Carrickfergus and Athlone were given new funds. Athlone in particular was to be repaired as the seat of the governors of Connacht.[99]

ambition of the government to create a settlement of smallholders. See also Ellis, *Tudor Ireland*, pp. 234, 242–43.

95. PRO, SP 63/31/154.
96. PRO, SP 62/1/51–52; 63/35/9–9v.
97. PRO, SP 63/2/52. In 1553 Mary had ordered a full survey of all the forts, the wards in them, the cost of them and which were deemed unnecessary. PRO, SP 62/1/4.
98. PRO, SP 63/13/110. In 1560 the queen had ordered a blockhouse built in Waterford for less than £250 with the help of the inhabitants. PRO, SP 63/2/42. For bridge-building see O'Keeffe and Simington, *Irish stone bridges*, pp. 30, 176, 190.
99. *Walsingham letter-bk*, p. 49.

The strategic deployment of troops in a defensive role required the maintenance of a delicate equilibrium. A proper balance was needed to keep up a minimum of mobile forces and adequate warders in the strongholds. Too few troops caused grave problems of inflexible response when the available men were inadequate to defend the garrisons. Fitzwilliam and the council complained in 1572 that they lacked enough forces since Elizabeth had just called for troop reductions. Citing the combined problems of the Smith plantation, the Fitzmaurice rebellion and the uprisings in the west, the council said the men in garrison were not enough to defend the Pale and to prosecute the rebels.[100] Occasionally, the queen's advisers would suggest where to deploy the troops in garrison, but that decision was generally left up to the council and the lord deputy. In 1580, for example, Gerrard wrote to Walsingham that the forces were split into 800 men to defend the Pale and guard the castles and 800 to fight the rebels. A new project was devised to expel the Irish from Wicklow and establish three new strongholds there to keep the region quiet.[101]

The council had the basic responsibility for the manning of new garrisons as well as old ones, and in 1578 it dissented vigorously from the suggestion that all the havens be fortified. Employing the example of Limerick, the council pointed out that a walled town could better defend itself than a small haven, and at less cost to the queen. The havens were but five miles apart all along the coast and it would cost a great deal to wall and defend each one. Further, when spending was inevitably cut back, the walls would soon decay unless sufficient townspeople were available to maintain them.[102] Failure to defend the havens meant that Fitzmaurice was able to sail unmolested into Smerwick, but the cost of such a stratagem would have been prohibitive in any case. Here again the council demonstrated the need for its competent advice at every stage of military planning.

The structure of the military establishment after 1556 incorporated three distinct forms of troop emplacements, distinguished by the mandates given to their officers. The primary type of military unit was the band of soldiers over which a captain had responsibility. These companies were typically 106 men in strength including their officers. They were positioned in strategic places during peace-time and when they were not engaged in expeditions they were accused of

100. PRO, SP 63/36/148–51v. In 1574 the council again complained that a great proportion of the 1,064 troops were needed to guard strategic places so only 314 could be spared to use against Desmond in the field. PRO, SP 63/45/182v.

101. PRO, SP 63/14/8v–9; 63/75/24. In 1566 the lord deputy was advised to do as he saw fit with regard to garrisons in Carrickfergus and Dundalk. PRO, SP 63/16/207v.

102. PRO, SP 63/61/3v–4.

disturbing the tranquillity of the realm since they were rarely paid on time. The captains and their bands constituted the major component of the standing army since they alone could be expanded by reinforcements. Secondly, there were the constables in the forts and wards. These men were occasionally also captains of large bands, but in their roles as constables they had both civil and military authority. In the memoranda of the garrison, they figure prominently from 1556 to 1578, and their numbers were increasing by the end of the period.[103] Henry Davells, for example, was named captain and constable in both Leighlin and Dungarvan in 1572. The ward of each castle was immobile and defensive, a fact which was confirmed in the instruction that 'these men never to be removed for any service'.[104] They may be distinguished from the third kind of military leader, the seneschal, in that the area over which they exercised command was more limited to the lands adjacent to their stronghold.

Similar to the constable yet endowed with broader powers of supervision was the seneschal. Originating with Bellingham's effort to extend administrative control over the rugged Wicklow mountains, the seneschals were backed by a band of soldiers who were stationed at a fortified stronghold near a region of Gaelic influence. Seneschals were given exceptional authority to collect rents and dues from the Gaelic septs under their control and to bring them as near as possible under the influence of the common law. While they were given commissions of martial law, these leaders were expected to govern the native Irish peaceably. Canny has explained that the use of seneschals was not designed to interrupt the landholding arrangements of the Gaelic chiefs or to threaten them with displacement, but simply to compel them to 'acknowledge the sovereignty of the queen'. However, it is misleading to suggest that Sussex had a kind of siege mentality when he 'sealed off' the Pale from Gaelic influences by positioning these fortresses along the borders.[105] The primary objective of government was not to isolate itself but to engage in the expansion of common law jurisdiction using the Pale as a secure foundation on which to build. Brady has suggested that the constables, captains and seneschals were alike empowered with instructions to rule according to local custom, blending common law with brehon law when practicable and pursuing assimilation rather than conquest or exclusion of the native Irish.[106]

103. PRO, SP 62/1/51–52; 63/1/8–9; 63/31/153–55v; 63/35/2–16v; 63/62/3–6v.
104. PRO, SP 63/35/8v.
105. Canny, *Elizabethan conquest*, pp. 34–36, 48–49. In the 1572 memorandum, ten captains and nine constables were named, but only one obscure seneschal of 'Sylanche'. PRO, SP 63/35/2–16v. And seneschals were also used for the more settled areas such as Co. Wexford.
106. Brady, 'Government of Ireland', pp. 114–15.

The constables, who were often also captains or governed with the assistance of another captain, combined civilian and military roles, since they were frequently responsible for the administration of justice and even the victualling of the town and garrison. Captain William Piers had the longest tenure of any constable, being commander of Carrickfergus from 1556 to 1578. Thomas Le Strange, on the other hand, was not a military man but a prominent gentleman of Co. West Meath. He was constable at Athlone from 1558 to 1566 and at Roscommon from 1571 to 1578. Captain Nicholas Heron, leader of a band of soldiers from 1556 to 1565, was perhaps the most active garrison leader. Heron was constable of Leighlin from 1558 until his death in 1568 and seneschal of Wexford. About 1558 he was named sheriff of Carlow and held that post until 1565. In 1563 he was made constable of Wexford castle, and throughout the period he was given the supervision of the MacMurroughs and Cavanaghs.[107] The consolidation of local power under the personal control of the constables was always a temptation, but the council recognized the importance of keeping strong men in these key roles. Sir Nicholas Malbie, for example, offered in 1576 to save the queen £500 per annum if he were given the fee farm of the towns of Athlone and Roscommon. He built up the town walls and his improvements in the castle at Roscommon may still be seen today.[108]

Various deputies, of course, used these offices to reward their followers and relatives. Sussex, for example, made his brother, Sir Henry Radcliffe, the commander of the two forts in Leix and Offaly from 1556 until his departure in 1564. Sir George Stanley, the marshal of the army, was made seneschal of Dalton's country, while Jacques Wingfield, master of the ordnance, commanded the O'Byrnes and O'Tooles. The politicization of the military posts was followed up by Sydney who placed his followers in key posts. However, this was far from a wholesale change and only half the constables were replaced. Canny's assertion that Sydney conducted a purge of all Sussex's men

107. Heron enjoyed a considerable salary for these duties, since the seneschalship of Wexford alone was worth £100 per annum. In 1563 he also earned £100 as captain of the Cavanaghs and £20 as constable of Leighlin. Others were not nearly so remunerative, though constables of Carrickfergus and Dungarvan each received £40 per annum. The constable of Monasterevan had to be content with only £10 per year. PRO, SP 63/8/127. Canny insists Heron was resented, even hated, for his widespread influence, but the effort to discredit him and other English office-holders generally was also a ploy of the Palesmen to attack the Sussex administration. Canny, *Elizabethan conquest*, p. 36.

108. *Cal. Carew MSS, 1575–88*, pp. 136–37. Although Malbie was granted his request, the queen particularly refused to grant the leadership of the forts in Leix and Offaly for life, being '. . . places of such strength and importance'. *Sidney S.P.*, pp. 80, 128. Avril Thomas, *The walled towns of Ireland*, 2 vols. (Dublin, 1992), ii, 13–17, 186–89; Leask, *Irish castles*, pp. 67–69.

is exaggerated.[109] The rotation of captains into Ireland about every five years offers another explanation of the periodic changes among constables when linked with the attribution of political advantage.

The most ambitious expansion of the military establishment was the new initiative to govern the provinces by establishing lords president and councils there. Conceived by Sussex and introduced under Sydney's administration, these governments in miniature were based on the successful councils in Wales and the North. Like their parent institutions, they were far more than military outposts, although some of the presidents and their officers were military men.[110] When Sydney built the bridge across the Shannon in 1565 he opened the way for military incursions into Connacht, and when the presidency was established in Athlone in 1569 it become a more important fortress town. Within three years the garrison at Roscommon was manned and by 1578 the government could claim it had extended its practical authority by its systematic programme of improving and garrisoning strategic sites. From the stronghold at Dungarvan, Co. Waterford through the Ormonde territories of Co. Tipperary to Roscommon and then east to Co. Longford along the borders of Co. Louth to Newry, a new perimeter of English influence was conceived (see Map 2).

Naturally, this was a slow and uneven process. At times, military setbacks neutralized hard-won territorial gains, but at the end of the period the number of garrisons permanently manned was measurably greater and the size of the Pale itself had grown as well. In military terms, English control was a moving frontier, depending on the activity of the chief governor. That is why the strongholds give a certain definition to the boundaries which the presidencies, despite their more formidable legal and financial apparatus, could not do. Some strongholds were manned outside the perimeter of this hegemony, and areas of English influence such as Cork, Limerick and Galway were beyond the emerging frontier. As the presidencies slowly expanded English power in Connacht and Munster, the network of fortifications complemented the efforts to expand English justice beyond the Pale and thus made it less vulnerable in 1578 than it was in 1556.[111]

109. Canny, *Elizabethan conquest*, p. 54. In fact, Sydney merely moved Cosbie from Monasterevan to Maryborough and old hands like Agarde and Colley could hardly be said to owe their positions to the lord deputy. See also Brady, 'Government of Ireland', pp. 174–75.

110. See Canny, *Elizabethan conquest*, pp. 47–50, 93–116; Brady, 'Government of Ireland', p. 114. See below for a fuller discussion of the lords president and regional councils and see chapter four for the legal business of the provincial councils.

111. It seems unexceptionable to include the traditional stronghold of Dungarvan within the ambit of conciliar control and to incorporate also the Ormonde towns of Cahir, Clonmel and Cashel. The inclusion of Roscommon and Longford is

d) reform and retrenchment

The average size of the army, based on all the components from horsemen to pensioners, was about 1,860 in any year between 1556 and 1578. Despite increasing pressures from the queen and privy council to reduce the size of the army in Ireland, there were provincial insurrections and a host of smaller disturbances which required substantial increases in the military establishment. Nevertheless, there was no steady rise over the two decades, and the restraints imposed on every chief governor by the queen's instructions suggest that the 'pattern' of conquest as a model for understanding the period is largely mistaken. In fact, the forces were augmented or reduced as the government balanced its needs against the desire for reform. At the beginning of Elizabeth's reign the forces were established at about 1,500 troops. Then in 1560 the army was increased to 1,920 to meet the threat of Shane O'Neill, reaching 2,250 troops in 1562. Retrenchment followed under the sniping Sir Nicholas Arnold and the levels were cut back to about 1,200 during 1564–65. When the clever, but impetuous, Shane O'Neill threatened a wholesale uprising in 1566, the cutbacks of the previous two years were quickly reversed, and in 1567 there were 2,990 troops in Ireland, the largest number before 1579. Sydney presided over further retrenchment during the ensuing years under the watchful eye of the queen, and the forces reached a low point of 1,483 in 1569. But the plantations of Smith and Essex in Ulster required more men, as did the new presidencies in Connacht and Munster, so from 1571 to 1574 the troop strength ballooned to well over 2,000 men. With the return of Sydney in 1575 Elizabeth exacted difficult terms for the strict curtailment of military spending. Sydney kept the forces between 1,500 and 1,800 men until in 1578 the Munster rebellion made further reductions impossible. From 1579 the troop strength rose to 3,400 and in the next year to 6,100 men. The carefully laid restraints of the government were thus abandoned, and this fundamentally changed the conditions on which Ireland was governed.[112]

arguable, but those points were bulwarks against the incursions of the O'Neills and were generally supportive of the English government. See Maps 2 and 3 and compare the political map of R.D. Edwards in *An atlas of Irish history* (London, 1973), p. 90.

112. Periodic musters were taken of the garrison in Ireland and these lengthy documents are largely to be found in the PRO. Changes in the size of the army paralleled rather inexactly the condition of war and peace in Ireland. In 1564 the council decided that, 'Forsomoche as generallie the wholle realme is in quiett, no rebellion beeng presentlie within the realme . . .', some 500 footmen and 200 horsemen could be discharged. RIA, MS 24 F 17, ff. 189v–90. But the figures might change radically in any given year. The troop strength in 1573–74 varied from 1,656 in April 1573 to 2,800 in March 1574, largely because of the needs of the Essex plantation. PRO, SP 63/45/37. For the figures 1558–78 see the

In 1556 the forces in Ireland were stabilized at an acceptable level and Queen Mary showed no immediate interest in obtaining a reduction. The council wrote to Mary on 1 March declaring that certain necessaries were lacking to withstand a possible French invasion. The message noted that the army '. . . exceadeth little one thousand men . . . ' and concluded that, 'We have neither money, munycion nor credit'.[113] These conditions were to plague the council for the next twenty years. At the beginning of her reign Elizabeth allowed Sussex considerable flexibility in the keeping of troops, saying,

. . . and thereupon no certayn limitacion can be well made to our sayd deputie in the keping of the nombers nowe appoynted, but that some time as he maye see good occasion to diminishe them so maye he se greater to augment them . . . .[114]

In crises such as the anticipated invasion in 1560 Elizabeth was ready with support and offered to send 300 more soldiers.[115]

From 1562, the queen began to declaim against the increasing military costs in Ireland and the council detected unmistakeable signs of flagging support. Instructions to the commissioners to be sent to Ireland in 1562 inquired suspiciously about the level of troop strength, the manner of payment and the victualling of the soldiers.[116] This created a natural tension beteween the council in Ireland, which perceived a growing need for more men and money, and the queen, who feared the consequences of increased military support to Ireland. The council, writing in October 1562, had decided to continue a band in service despite the order to discharge them. The perennial problem of defending the Pale and keeping an army in the field was stated thus:

. . . if Shane Onele, with his complices shulde at this tyme of the yere attempte to make warres upone her majesties Englishe subjects tharmy

following memoranda in PRO, SP 63: 1/8–9; 21/196;2/29; 3/100–14; 4/130; 7/ 193–94; 13/147–49; 22/84–94; 27/128–35; 31/153–55v; 54/45–48v; 56/44–50; 69/88–93; 77/38–48. See also BL, Cott. MS Titus B XIII, ff. 15, 175, 243–47. Compare these levels with the rate of 1542 which showed 549 men in military service and an annual charge of £7,942. *Cal. Carew MSS, 1515–74*, p. 200.

113. PRO, SP 62/2/32. On 20 March Sussex was instructed to keep the forces at current levels and 800 footmen would soon be sent over. ibid., f. 52.

114. PRO, SP 63/1/109.

115. PRO, SP 63/2/38. In 1574, fearing an uprising by Desmond, the queen sent 300 soldiers trained in the Low Countries with their captains. PRO, SP 63/44/25. It should also be noted that the council was reasonably cooperative in cost-cutting. On 27 September 1560 the council agreed to send back the 300 soldiers because of the 'universal quietness' then in Ireland. RIA, MS 24 F 17, f. 159v.

116. PRO, SP 63/6/163.

remayninge owte of the fortes after the dischardge of thes souldiers will not be sufficient to encounter with him and garde also the Englishe Pale to her majesties honor and the suretie of the realme.[117]

After the ordeal of Shane's rebellion, the queen insisted on holding the garrison to 1,555 men in 1568, forbidding the addition of any new troops.[118] Six years later Fitzwilliam pleaded that most of his soldiers were needed in defensive positions so he could not muster a mobile force to contend with Desmond.[119] The stringent economy measures of the queen deprived the lord deputy and council of their accustomed flexibility in managing the military establishment. Indeed, royal parsimony exposed the vulnerability of the Pale to attack without substantially reducing costs.

The most thorough attempt at retrenchment was made by Cecil in a 1572 memorandum based on the recent muster of 2,058 men. Cecil painstakingly annotated every item in the muster roll, suggesting the removal of some troops and the retention of others. Beginning with the treasurer at wars, Cecil saw no reason why he should be bound to keep a permanent retinue of horse and foot, and recommended that other bands be used to represent him. The marshal and the lord deputy were immune from cost-saving reductions, but the master of ordnance suffered a theoretical reduction of his entire band of 89 men at a saving of some £400. Cecil questioned the usefulness of small bands such as that of Edward Moore, and the retinue of the clerk of the check. He was particularly captious when he found a man with no office but two horsemen, saying ' I know of no office which this man hath nor reason whye he hath ether wages for himself or men in wages'.[120] On the other hand, he commended the work of Captains Piers and Cheston in Carrickfergus, and even recommended an increase of 250 men in Connacht.[121] Cecil was concerned here with making an intensive investigation of the rolls to discover if the military structure concealed needless waste. This close scrutiny was typical of

117. RIA, MS 24 F 17, f. 181. In 1569 the council made it lawful for Sydney to increase the garrison by hire or impressment, until the queen's pleasure were known, due to the rebellion of Fitzmaurice. ibid., ff. 315–16.

118. PRO, SP 63/25/109–11. The queen envisaged a mobile force of 882 and even determined where the balance should be garrisoned. PRO, SP 63/14/9. In 1569 Sydney defended his reputation against charges of prodigality, alleging that he had used 2,000 men less than his advisers counselled in the last rebellion. PRO, SP 63/30/98.

119. PRO, SP 63/45/182.

120. PRO, SP 63/35/6v.

121. ibid., ff. 2–16v. In August 1572 the queen called for a reduction of troop strength by 800 soldiers, noting that Sir Thomas Smith's band of 800 men was about to come over to Ireland. PRO, SP 63/37/56–56v.

Cecil's careful observation of Irish affairs. It was his meticulous and painstaking oversight of details that gave Irish policy what structure and substance it possessed.

In 1575 the queen decided on a dramatic reduction of the forces in Ireland, from the level in the preceding year of 2,800 to a maximum of 1,600 men. The order was accompanied by strict measures for the payment of discharged troops. This meant, of course, the end of the queen's support of the Essex plantation, however qualified it had been. Essex received the news with a good will, telling the council in Ireland where he thought the garrison in Ulster should best be quartered. But he hesitated to reduce the troops at once until the queen learned of the recent landing of the Scots and their pact with Turlogh Luineach O'Neill.[122] Essex failed to realize that the queen's decision was not based on military strategy but on cost accounting and that she had already bargained with Sydney to achieve the desired retrenchment. Instead of the 650 soldiers recommmended by Essex for Ulster alone, Sydney had contracted to employ 1,200 troops in all of Ireland, with about 300 of them in each province.[123] Brady has argued that this dramatic reduction was a dangerous truncation of the tenuous authority of the crown in distant provinces and it led to Sydney's removal from office after a political crisis which his policies did much to provoke.[124] An even more optimistic proposal was drawn up in 1578 designed to reduce military spending and cut the garrison to only 965 men. This 'new establishment' cut by half the retinues of the two leading officials and made similarly dramatic reductions in the bands, the wards and the hired kerne.[125] However, this last attempt at wholesale retrenchment had no chance of success. Within a few months, Fitzmaurice had landed on the coast of Munster, commencing the much-feared foreign invasion which required the deployment of more troops than any of Elizabeth's advisers had previously contemplated. Three efforts at substantial troop reductions from 1572 to 1578 mark the second decade of the reign as one of retrenchment in Ireland, but Elizabeth was engaged in a difficult paradox. By refusing to support sensible reforms with adequate means, she weakened the innovative structures and institutions designed to govern the provinces.

122. PRO, SP 63/50/162; 63/53/23–23v.

123. PRO, SP 63/53/164–64v.

124. Brady, 'Government of Ireland', pp. 208–09, 214–18, 221–22.

125. BL, Cott. MS Titus B XIII, ff. 243–47. A similar document of 1578 in Cecil's hand observed that the queen had made a series a stringent new regulations and that the reductions in men and expenses were not to be altered except in case of foreign invasions or rebellion. Within a few months both of these precipitants inaugurated a new spate of unprecedented military spending. BL, Cott. MS Titus B XII, ff. 265–68.

Her efforts to save money diminished the prospects for anglicization, permitting the insurrection to gather strength in its early stages, so that military expenses would eventually soar to record levels.

By 1579 the Munster rebellion was threatening to break out into other provinces. Nevertheless, the reductions in the garrison were still going forward according to official policy. Between March and September the queen and privy council experienced several reversals which contributed greatly to the ambiguities of the situation. It was clear by July 1579 that the instructions of the spring would have to be amended. Walsingham required a victualler to go to Bristol and to prepare for the transportation of 1,000 men, while the earl of Bedford was ordered to call up 600 men in the West Country. On 10 August news of the full-scale rebellion of Sir John of Desmond reached the privy council and £10,000 was immediately sent, along with Sir John Perrot and four ships carrying 500 soldiers. Then, on the death of Fitzmaurice, the privy council again reversed itself. Writing on 2 September the policy-makers in Westminster noted that some 3,300 men had been sent and now they would not all be needed. Yet, hesitating to dictate terms to the lord deputy and council, the queen's advisers said,

Notwithestanding we have thought it meet to leave to your owne judgement to retayne suche numbers ether more or less as to you and the rest of the Councell there shalbe thought meet, for that it wold be very herde for us to prescribe unto you peremptorily what were fitte to be don there.[126]

Twelve days later the lord justice complained that he lacked sufficient men simultaneously to defend the Pale and to prosecute the rebels. On 25 September Walsingham confessed that the privy council itself was at odds over the appropriate troop strength to be deployed, leaving no doubt that he favoured a reduction.[127] As the situation continued to change, so did the policy, but the council in Ireland maintained consistently that more men were needed. The normal tension between fiscal and military needs was strained badly by the rebellion, but the council in Ireland insisted on adequate troop strength and the queen and privy council deferred to the needs of the army.

The cost of the military establishment in Ireland was the greatest factor in Elizabeth's determined retrenchment, since it consumed two-thirds of the annual budget in the average year.[128] It is important to

126. *Walsingham letter-bk*, p. 155.
127. ibid., pp. 38–39, 110, 99, 121–23, 125–26, 153–55, 184, 187, 194, 239–40.
128. This figure was based on military proportions of the total budget for 1556–59, 1575 and 1578. See H.M.C., *De L'Isle and Dudley MSS*, i, 364–65; PRO, SP 63/53/164–64v. See below, chapter six, for a fuller discussion of the financial implications of military expenditures.

emphasize this fundamental weakness of the crown's military posture. The determination to reduce expenses in Ireland made it practically impossible to sustain a 'conquest' strategy of any kind and military policy was more often driven by the exigencies of fiscal reform rather than by the desire for land or colonization. While recent writers have acknowledged the queen's continual demands for retrenchment, they have refused to accept the implication that her military forces were prevented from pursuing an aggressive policy beyond the Pale except in cases of rebellion or foreign invasion.[129] With frequent increases of the troop strength in Ireland, expenditures rose uncertainly until 1575. From an average of about £17,500 per annum between 1558 and 1567, the military budget grew to about £25,000 per year during Sydney's last deputyship. Under Fitzwilliam the cost of the garrison had soared to £33,696 in 1571 alone.[130] Over the entire two decades the military budget averaged about £21,000 to £22,000 per annum, but the expenses fluctuated widely and it would be misleading to interpret periodic increases as evidence of a strategic commitment to expand government control by coercion.

Naturally, conditions of war and peace generally determined the size and cost of the garrison, but there were other variables which caused fiscal unpredictability. For example, different measurements were used to compute the total charges, since some estimates were made without counting the wards or the kerne or the pensioners. In addition, most statements omitted the extraordinary military charges, which were frequently considerable. These included the costs of victualling the forts and castles, the short-term hiring of more kerne or galloglasses, the transport of soldiers, munitions and money from England and the building or reparations of the queen's forts. The queen could command the size of the garrison by allowing or refusing increases in the bands, but she had little control over the hiring of kerne or galloglasses. This flexibility allowed the council in Ireland in February 1573, for example, to hire 600 kerne in the wake of the O'Connors' rebellion and cess them on the Pale and Counties Carlow and Wexford. By September, however, the council had to appeal for another 100 English footmen to aid their cause.[131]

Proportionate charges within the army tended to stabilize regardless of how much the overall troop strength was augmented. Hence, the average proportion of the bands of footmen and horsemen was

129. Canny, *Elizabethan conquest*, pp. 154–55; Ellis, *Tudor Ireland*, pp. 264–65.
130. PRO, SP 63/31/153–53v. Expenses were generally higher under Fitzwilliam as he maintained the army at an average rate of about 2,370 men, compared to the average of 1,550 under Sydney.
131. PRO, SP 63/3/77; BL, Cott. MS Titus B XIII, f. 246–46v; Bodl, Carte MS 57, f. 605–07.

about 40% of the total cost, and the wards in strongholds near the Pale represented about 20% of the burden. The retinues of leading officials were established in proportion to their dignity and seniority. The percentage of the total military establishment represented by these stable retinues varied with the size of the army, although they averaged about 25% of the total expenses. The only clearly declining figure was that of the kerne, who were used in far smaller numbers by 1578 and had been reduced from 10% to 2% of the total. Pensioners, gunners and others, had increased their share of the total cost, how-ever, and the potential for cutbacks there was ignored because of the need to find suitable perquisites for office-seekers and others. The council was thus saddled with certain fixed costs for the military based on the static figures for the retinues and the men in wards, totalling about 40% of the military budget. In practice, this meant a minimum force of about 400–500 men and a basic cost of at least £7,000 for the wards and the retinues alone. No amount of retrenchment cut significantly into these figures, and the privy council's reforms were thus aimed at the soldiers in bands.[132]

It was notorious among her advisers that the military was the 'chief cause of the consuming of her majestys treasure',[133] and yet she was unable to achieve meaningful reforms in the expenses of the gar-rison. The reasons for this are not far to seek. The real or imagined threats to her rule could not be treated lightly, and in a crisis the queen could be very supportive. In 1566, for example, she brought together 300 men from Berwick and another 700 from Bristol for service in Ireland under Colonel Edward Randolph.[134] However, in 1570 the queen estimated that the discharge of 500 soldiers would save about £4,000 Irish and she sent money for the purpose of giving them their release. On this occasion the initiative proceeded from the lord deputy and council who were '. . . desyrous to discharge us of certain nom-bres of souldiours remayning in wages unneedefull . . .'.[135]

The council was employed as a monitor of military expenses and as such it often had the responsibility for controlling the money spent on the army. In 1574 the queen ordered the council to restrict the spend-ing of £8,000 recently sent over to military causes only, rejecting the option of resolving old debts. Some £600 was to be advanced to the soldiers and £300 used for victuals, while the expenditure of the rest

132. These figures are very inexact because of the fluctuations in the total military budget. The retinues were not ordinarily augmented when the total size of the army increased, but occasionally, as in 1572, the entire force, wards and all, was increased to meet military projections. See PRO, SP 63/35/2–16v.
133. *Cal. Carew MSS, 1575–88*, p. 55.
134. *Sidney S.P.*, p. 30.
135. ibid., p. 121.

could only be warranted by the lord deputy and council.[136] For much of the period, military reform was a nettlesome point of contention between the queen and her officials in Ireland. Although Sydney succeeded in making substantial reductions, the ever-cautious Fitzwilliam paradoxically maintained troop levels at their highest peak.

The unreliability of figures taken from the musters makes it difficult to estimate the troop strength accurately. The function of the musters was to provide the basis for the issuance of rations, uniforms, arms and equipment. Further, the musters established the size of the garrison so that the treasurer at wars could make a full pay. It was for reasons of fiscal probity that the privy council intervened so frequently in the administration of the musters. The allegations of fraud and corruption, coupled with the growing financial burden of the military establishment, sharpened the vigilance of the queen and privy council. In 1575, for example, the privy council pointedly asked the council why the auditor had taken so long to compile a book of charges for the army, noting that no full pay could be made without such a summary.[137]

In general, the muster books were compiled annually under the direction of the clerk of the check, or the muster master. These muster books were laboriously copied out from the registers of each band, company and retinue, naming every member of each unit.[138] Cruickshank described the muster master as the supervisor of the actual registering of names, and the clerk of the check as the factotum who balanced the records of debit and credit.[139] But a memorandum of September 1563 indicates that the two offices were combined in Ireland. The first article considered which title would be of 'most estimation', that of clerk of the check or muster master. Having apparently decided that the clerk of the check had more dignity as a title, the next article queried whether the clerk should be able to take the musters without the express command of the lord deputy. The memorandum also discussed how often to take the musters, considering the great distances between garrisons, and whether the clerk should take the name of men in the retinues of the lord deputy, the vice trea-

136. PRO, SP 63/44/25v.

137. BL, Cott. MS Titus B XII, f. 156v. In 1566 the privy council anxiously awaited a statement from Arnold before making a full pay. PRO, SP 63/16/204.

138. The compilation of 1561 was titled 'Irlande. The booke of the laste musters of the Quene her majesties army, wardes and garrisons within her highnes said Realme'. The clerk of the check, in this case Matthew King, signed it at the end. PRO, SP 63/3/100–14. King occasionally made briefer abstracts of the army, summarizing the monthly wages of each band. SP 63/13/147–49. See also SP 63/22/84–94; 63/27/128–35; 63/54/45–48v; 63/77/38–48.

139. Cruickshank, *Elizabeth's army*, pp. 136–37, 145.

surer and others.[140] The musters were theoretically taken four times a year, but this regular pattern was not observed in practice, despite the repeated insistence of the council. In 1577 Sydney noted that the bands were badly understaffed because of the infrequent musters, and he issued a warrant dormant to Owen Moore, then clerk of the check. This document enabled the clerk to take the musters regularly, since he did not have to await a special warrant.[141] However, it is unlikely that this desideratum was fulfilled because of the great distances involved and the difficulty of travelling to points between Dungarvan and Carrickfergus. The dispersal of troops in the field and in garrison made the muster of forces in Ireland considerably more difficult than it would be for a unified army stationed in one area.

Musters were taken in large buildings or enclosures and at short notice to prevent fraudulent practices by the captains. Basic policies were implemented and interpreted there by the clerk of the check. Perhaps most fundamental was the practice of allowing a fixed number of dead pays in each company as a supplementary income to the captain or a means of providing the troops with extra money. In 1565 Sydney requested eight dead pays for every 100 troops in a unit as a condition of assuming the office of lord deputy. But the queen settled on six dead pays and this became the common proportion allowed to the captains, leaving a ratio of 94 able men in every band of 100 troops.[142] The abuse of dead pays by captains who commanded badly understaffed units allowed them to profit greatly from providing a full pay to a theoretically complete band of soldiers. Cruickshank explained the situation thus,

In the earlier part of the reign there was no machinery for replacing men who had died, deserted, or been invalided out of the army. Companies were therefore almost always below establishment, and could be brought up to strength only when new levies arrived from England . . . . This of course applied mainly to Ireland and the Netherlands where there were permanent garrisons . . . .[143]

A similar limitation was placed on the number of native Irish allowed in any band. Sydney's instructions of 1565 allowed only six

140. PRO, SP 63/9/51. The auditor was supposed to check the figures of the treasurer at wars and the clerk of the check, but he seldom appeared in Irish records.

141. PRO, SP 63/57/38. See also SP 63/14/10 for a renewal of the policy of quarterly musters. Sydney wanted to have musters taken more often than once each quarter.

142. PRO, SP 63/13/110; 63/14/10; BL, Cott. MS Titus B XII, f. 265v. In 1579 the queen ordered the council to take the pay of five horsemen allowed to Thomas Snagge, and to distribute it according to discretion. *Walsingham letter-bk*, p. 39. See also Cruickshank, *Elizabeth's army*, p. 154.

143. Cruickshank, *Elizabeth's army*, pp. 34–35; Falls, *Elizabeth's Irish wars*, p. 61.

Irish soldiers in every band of 100 and by 1578 the number was cut to five. This mandate was repeated in 1579, but an exception was made for guides and interpreters, and half of the horsemen of Ormonde and Kildare could be Englishmen born in Ireland. Since St Leger had been allowed ten Irishmen in every band of 100 in 1553, it appears that the reductions were part of a longer trend.[144] The difficulty of obtaining replacements and the willingness of mercenary Irish to serve for lower pay presented a great temptation to avoid these stiff regulations. On the whole, the council usually hired independent bands of kerne to supplement the English forces as needed, and it probably winked at evasions of the strict limitation on Irish troops within English bands. But it is unlikely that Irishmen formed the greater substance of any English units in this period, as some have claimed.[145]

The straightforward requirement of presenting the men in a company to be counted by poll (that is, by head count) was designed to facilitate the accurate accounting of the army. Soldiers were paid by their captains, who received weekly imprests, or advances, against the semi-annual full pay. Twice a year the accounts were theoretically brought up to date by payments to the captains from the treasurer at wars. A memorandum for the council of September 1563 ordered that captains must be made to pay their soldiers and their creditors based upon the number of pays and advances they had received since 1558.[146] Having the captain in charge of paying the troops was potentially a prescription for mutiny, since the basic pay of the soldiers was a subsistence rate. In 1571, for example, the council explained to the privy council that the mutinous soldiers of Malbie's band had been apprehended, but noted most urgently the need to pay them as they had gone so long without a full pay.[147]

If the captains held back any part of their pay, the soldiers came dangerously near destitution. Well before they reached that point, however, they would have resort to pillage, extortion or robbery from both the Irish districts and the Pale. In December 1562, for example, the account books of Fitzwilliam revealed that the last full pay had been made on 24 May 1560, and this was not untypical.[148] It is small wonder, then, that the grievances of the Pale against the soldiers at

144. PRO, SP 63/15/19; 62/1/5; BL, Cott. MS Titus B. XII, f. 265v; *Walsingham letter-bk*, p. 39.

145. Cruickshank, *Elizabeth's army*, p. 34.

146. PRO, SP 63/9/15.

147. PRO, SP 63/32/103–03v.

148. *The Fitzwilliam manuscripts: accounts from the Annesley collection*, ed. A.K. Longfield (Dublin, 1960), p. 54.

this time grew to unprecedented levels. To facilitate the payment of the troops after a muster, it was suggested that the warrants for payment to the captains be kept separately instead of engrossed, since that practice tended to delay unduly the payment authorized by the lord deputy.[149] But this technical adjustment did little to improve the payment of soldiers when musters and full pays were so infrequent.

Conditions in the military establishment were evidently corrupt and the muster system was notoriously inefficient. Since this led to a significant drain on the queen's revenue and to periodic outbursts of localized violence and more general resentment of the troops, the privy council sent into Ireland a host of new instructions in 1579. In a letter signed by the queen, the captains were accused of profiting from the understaffing of bands. She charged the clerk of the check to make quarterly general musters in conjunction with at least two commissioners from among the council. She advocated monthly payments made to the bands, but, noting the practical difficulties attending this policy, she accepted the reality of conventional payments to the troops by imprests, supplemented by semi-annual full pays. In order to assure the prompt payment of the troops, the queen ordered the treasurer to refuse to hold up a captain's pay over a debt.[150] In August of the same year, the queen was advised to have a surveyor attend both the musters and the payments and to have the soldiers paid by the poll in the presence of the clerk of the check.[151] This was designed to get around the corruption of the captains. In December the council assured the government in England that care was taken to pay only those men physically present at musters.[152]

While it is clear that abuses were common among the captains and other officials in Ireland, the government often failed to meet its minimal obligations to the army and the system encouraged certain kinds of abuses. One of the most egregious examples was noted by the council in a memorandum of 1574. In this case they reported that many captains did not reside at their garrisons but rather employed the troops at their own farms in and near the Pale.[153] Cruickshank has argued that the captains in some cases were going to Ireland without any troops, but there is no evidence for this assertion from the period under discussion. Indeed, the dispatches consistently decry

---

149. PRO, SP 63/9/51.
150. *Walsingham letter-bk*, pp. 40–41. If the captain were approached by a merchant on the day of a full pay, however, the government would reduce his pay and cancel the debt.
151. BL, Add. MS 32,323, f. 187v.
152. *Walsingham letter-bk*, p. 246.
153. PRO, SP 63/45/182v.

the inability to make full pays rather than the understaffing of bands except in the war year of 1579. A more balanced appraisal of the army in Ireland is needed which will examine carefully the assertions of 'invisible' companies and compare the management of accounts with the performance of military service.[154]

The council in Ireland normally maintained supervision of the army and its accounts, but the privy council in England retained final authority over the military establishment. This was forcefully brought home to the Dublin administration in the case of the commission of Sir Nicholas Arnold. Sussex's administration was coming under attack from the Palesmen who resented the incursions of the soldiers and the financial burden of provisioning them. A protest was mounted in Westminster against the arbitrary government of Sussex by Irish law students in 1561, and this was followed up by the visit of William Bermingham, the sergeant of Meath, who went to England in 1562 to reveal that the musters were taken fraudulently. He recommended a sudden muster to uncover the use of unauthorized dead pays, and his views were seized upon by the Dudley faction at court to undermine the authority of Sussex and his government in Ireland.[155]

In the wake of the charges of Bermingham and the Irish law students representing the interests of the Pale, a commission of inquiry was named to investigate the military establishment. Sir Nicholas Arnold led a preliminary study of the muster-master's accounts in 1562–63 and his report to the privy council led to a more formal and comprehensive mandate to try all the allegations of abuse under Sussex's leadership. The instructions of 1562 named leading men of the three largest shires in the Pale to aid Arnold, and advised '. . . if you shall see nedeful because of the Diversitie of the places to have any other to assiste you, we gyve you leve to make choise of any one or twoo of our Counsell there'.[156] Arnold, Thomas Wrothe and Gabriel Croft were named to go to Ireland and their commission was amplified beyond military concerns. It is doubtful that they were joined by councillors in Dublin since the incumbent officials were often the targets of the inquiry and they stood to lose much from careful scrutiny of their roles in the administration.[157]

154. Cruickshank, *Elizabeth's army*, pp. 136, 140.

155. PRO, SP 63/6/140. See Sussex's rejoinder in SP 63/7/22. Brady discusses the political factions which struggled over the Arnold commission and offers a convincing analysis of the downfall of Sussex and the ruin of his successor over the issues of military and financial administration. See 'Government of Ireland', pp. 158–70.

156. PRO, SP 63/6/140.

157. The commissioners were to investigate the discharge and addition of soldiers without the entering of their names in the book of musters. The accounts revealed

As a result of the revelations of the commission, a spate of reforms was discussed and recommended in September 1563. Cecil jotted down notes on the reform of the garrisons which went directly to the heart of the matter. He recommended sending special investigators from England periodically to oversee the taking of musters, and called for a general muster of all bands, from the retinues of principal officials to the Irish kerne. Each captain must deliver a book with the record of his men and every soldier was to be seen and called by his name. After the musters a general pay would be made only for those present at the roll calls, and the commissioners must try each cause of action over non-payment or the amount of pay. An unsigned memorandum presented the first of several additional queries on the right of captains to control the movement of their men. The captains' right to discharge or take in a private soldier, or to issue passports to return to England without a certificate from the clerk of the check was questioned. Another note recommended that captains should lead only one band since it was difficult to separate them for independent accounting at muster time. It also suggested that bands from English counties should be led by captains from those counties who would know the men and retain their loyalty.[158] These memoranda demonstrate once again the meticulous attention to detail which Cecil and his staff gave to Irish affairs, yet they also demonstrate the fatal flaw in his thinking. Any reforms which required the regular supervision of independent and non-resident English commissioners would quickly prove unworkable in practice and more costly than the pliantly corrupt methods of the incumbent officials.

The privy council continued to offer summaries of official policy on the musters in the annual instructions to the lord deputy and council. In 1565, for example, the lord deputy was reminded that he must issue a warrant for any new soldier succeeding to a place in an English band. The captains were allowed to employ Irish kerne only as temporary replacements to fill up their companies.[159] In the face of the Munster rebellion, the privy council attempted to tighten up military procedure, reducing the number of troops in the garrison but providing that bands be kept at full strength. No amount of cajoling and coaxing, however, could reform the fraudulent practices when

corruption in Fitzwilliam's band and thereafter he and other captains refused to cooperate with the commissioners, leaving them to poll the soldiers themselves. *Cal. Carew MSS, 1515–74*, pp. 354, 356, 363; PRO, SP 63/7/124–29.

158. PRO, SP 63/9/51, 53–54, 63. The writer noted the unhappy experience of a band of 'redcottes' who had lately come over from England. They had run away during an engagement with Shane O'Neill and the writer attributed this pusillanimous act to having a stranger for a captain.

159. PRO, SP 63/14/10.

the machinery for replacing the troops was so inadequate and the garrisons so far-flung. If the system was full of abuses, the conditions of Irish military service lent themselves to corrupt and fraudulent exploitation. And the council in Ireland was in no position to intervene since its leading members were themselves threatened by independent audits and sweeping reforms.

e) victualling

Another fundamental aspect of conciliar responsibility for the military was victualling. The requirement of victualling, or provisioning, the army gradually developed into an onerous burden after 1534 due to the slackening use of coyne and livery in the Pale. The Gaelic Irish system of free entertainment for the lord and his retainers, often called coyne and livery, was used at times by the English forces. The ordinances of 1534 limited the lord deputy's right to 'coyne' the king's subjects, requiring him to pay for victuals in ready money and to abide by a scale of charges fixed for his use in the Pale.[160] Prior to 1556, it seems, victualling was simply a flexible and ad hoc kind of purveyance similar to the more formal instrument of the cess. The difference, of course, since both had ponderous administrative mechanisms, was that the government could obtain victualling at any time from England or Ireland at the market price. The cess, by contrast, was sanctioned by a ceremonial meeting of the grand council and it had clearly articulated procedures based on an arbitrarily low price. In practice, the two systems commonly operated interdependently within Ireland. The daily allowance of the soldier in 1556 was already inadequate to provide for the basic amenities of life and inflation steadily eroded his earnings. The result was a marginal financial situation which worsened whenever large numbers of men were added to the army and thus thrust upon the reluctant English Pale.

Victualling had been supplementary to the cess for the army in 1556, but by 1579 it had become the primary instrument for provisioning the soldiers. The financial implications and political outcomes of these arrangements are discussed below (see chapter six). The basic impact of the changes was ultimately to free the Pale from the growing burden of cess and to fix the responsibility for victualling the army squarely on the government. Victuallers were ordinarily mentioned in connection with the accounts for cess before 1568, for they were the agents who delivered treasury money to the cessors in return for the prescribed provisions. In 1561 the council found it necessary to order three commissioners to supervise the payment of debts owed

160. PRO, SP 60/2/64. See also Ellis, *Tudor Ireland*, pp. 28, 134, 176–77.

to the cessors during the previous four years. It was alleged that the victuallers were holding the queen's money and a full pay was ordered to precede the forthcoming cess.[161] Thomas Might was undoubtedly one of these victuallers, as his name appears in connection with victualling the forts in Leix and Offaly in 1561.[162] In 1566 Might was named to receive the provisions of the cess, a role which adumbrated his appointment as general victualler two years later. Here the council demonstrated its attention to detail, controlling the amounts to be paid, the sites for victualling and the provisions themselves.[163] In 1568 he was appointed to the new post of surveyor general of the victuals and given complete responsibility for providing the garrisons with their necessary provisions. The organization of his staff is uncertain but he was in 1568 attended by numerous clerks, bakers, brewers, butchers, millers, porters, and wood cutters. In 1571–72 he was ordered by the council to place a man in Athlone and to take in and pay for the provisions levied on Counties Galway and Clare.[164] But for the most part Might obtained additional provisions from the English ports of Bristol and Chester.

While the council achieved a certain success in the establishment of new arrangements for victualling the troops, it frequently had difficulty paying for the provisions themselves. The varying size of the military establishment made planning difficult, and the periodic scarcities in Ireland meant that food must be brought from England at greater cost. In February 1558 the lord justice and council wrote that victuals were badly needed because of the dearth in Ireland and a full pay must be sent '. . . ffor by reason that both the marchaunt and countrey be so long unpaid of the old debt we be out of credit to borrowe . . .'.[165] A month later Sussex requested new powers for 'A commission generall to me and the counsell to take up victuell in Ingland [to] furnysshe the army in Ireland as we can agree with the partyes and the proporcions . . .'.[166] The council thus assumed the

161. PRO, SP 63/3/13.

162. In the Book of Accounts of 1561 Might is mentioned as victualler of the fort at 'Dingen' and he was paid at least £600 on some five occasions between 1558 and 1561. Victuallers named under 'old debts' or 'extraordinary payments' included such familiar military figures as Francis Cosbie, Henry Warren and Henry Colley, as well as lesser known officials such as James Brandon of Dundalk. Cosbie was described as victualler of the fort in Leix. PRO, SP 63/3/76–77.

163. RIA, MS 24 F 17, f. 229v.

164. *P.R.I. rep. D.K. 11*, p. 210, no. 1402; PRO, SP 63/23/17; 63/32/117; 63/36/149v–50. After 1568 the expenses of victualling amounted to roughly 10% of the annual expenditure in Ireland. BL, Cott. MS Titus B XIII, f. 186; PRO, SP 63/75/2–4.

165. PRO, SP 62/2/15.

166. ibid., f. 49.

burden of responsibility for victualling at a time when the troop strength was growing during the confrontation with Shane O'Neill.

The military build-up which has been attributed to Sussex must be viewed in the light of the logistical problems which he faced. The cumbersome and expensive process of victualling made troop increases particularly unwelcome, and the viceroy faced his gravest crisis in the deteriorating relationship with the Pale over this issue. Resentment at conciliar methods of provisioning had been brewing for a long time. The council in March 1557 had to require the townsmen of the Pale to victual the troops in a 'Proclamation for good ordre betwene the souldiours and the countrey . . .'. Allegations were made that townsmen in the Pale fled when they saw soldiers coming and that soldiers refused to pay for meat and drink. The council required the sergeant or constable of the town to see that the soldiers were fed and the people paid.[167] In 1559 a ringing indictment of conciliar military policy was delivered anonymously. The writer found the great number of soldiers quartered on the Pale nearly useless for defence and not necessary to preserve order there. He charged that they stayed in the Pale for greater comfort and then, when the Irish attacked the borders, the captains could not assemble the troops in less than four days. Furthermore, the critics alleged that the garrison at Carrickfergus was useless to defend the Pale and yet could not prevent the Irish from destroying the farms of English tenants.[168]

The need to impose large provisioning requirements on the Pale and the loyal areas was never greater than in 1562 when the grievances of the Anglo-Irish came to a head. The Book of Twenty-four Articles (see Appendix 3) condemned the cess as an intolerable burden on five small shires, especially when the payments were fixed at levels substantially below the market price. But the most virulent complaints were directed against the soldiers quartered on the Pale. It was claimed that they were not made criminally liable for crimes of murder and rape, that they extorted money and food from the farmers and that they never paid their bills, even after a full pay of the army. This vision of a prostrate Anglo-Irish countryside was challenged by Sussex and

---

167. RIA, MS 24 F 17, f. 44–44v. In 1556 the council had set the prices for victualling and required that no one seek more or less. But this inflexibility was of little use when prices were so unstable and soon the rate of 2s. per week per man was totally ignored. ibid., f. 7v.

168. PRO, SP 63/1/170–75. The critic further alleged that there were only 500–600 ploughlands at Carrickfergus before the garrison was enlarged, and that victualling for more troops had to come from the Pale. In the end, this cost more in transportation than the victuals were worth. It was finally necessary to abandon recently defended strongholds at Armagh, Belfast and elsewhere due to the great cost of victualling them.

the council in a series of retorts in the spring of 1562.[169] But the views of the Palesmen hardened while the government sought new avenues of approach. On 17 August 1562 the gentlemen of the Pale refused to consider a composition in lieu of the cess, because they were more interested in relief from the quartering of soldiers. The council, however, required them to consider only the cess and a stalemate was reached which forced the council to seek other alternatives for victualling at the end of the year.[170] The privy council in London requested a summary of conditions of the cess but did not intervene. Yet the notorious commission of inquiry which ultimately led to the replacement of Sussex as chief governor was already under consideration.

Early in 1563 Sussex found he had lost a good deal of support from the leading Palesmen. Lord Slane and others denied they had agreed to support Sussex in his expedition against Shane O'Neill and soon a confrontation developed over the victualling. Sussex ordered a meeting of the council on 18 February,

At which daye ther mette with me not on of the nobylyte and very fewe of the Counsell and Comyssioners of every Contye. Who in the behalf of them selfes, ther fellowes and the comons of every contye made dyrecte awenswer that they could not agre to the levying of that proporcyon and specyally of horsmeat for that it was not to be hadd and procedying further in partycularytes with them it was in fyne utterly denyed as a matter they wold not do . . . .[171]

The commissioners said they wanted to avoid a precedent for victualling soldiers who served away from the Pale since that represented a further burden on them. The arrival in late February of Chief Justice Plunket and Lord Howth with the queen's letters apparently stirred the Palesmen to make concessions. An agreement was soon reached which allowed the victualling and deferred the date of contribution, using two dates to spread the burden over a longer period.[172] However, the Palesmen were not completely assuaged. On 16 March the council reported that '. . . by the slackness of the people ther was little done . . .' and the orders were further deferred from 20 March to 3 April. The council explained to the queen that '. . . by the unseasonableness of the yeare, ther hath ben great skarcitie of grayne and great deathe of plow horses, so as the people be putt to a very great burden to performe the provisions . . .'.[173] There can be little doubt,

169. PRO, SP 63/5/133–36, 138–40, 145–77.
170. PRO, SP 63/6/183–84, 211–12; 63/7/74.
171. PRO, SP 63/8/24.
172. ibid., f. 29.
173. ibid., f. 39.

however, that a great part of their inability proceeded from a profound reluctance to contribute to another victualling.

As we have seen, the actions of the troops in the Pale and the corruption of the officials led to a thorough discrediting of the Sussex administration, both in the Pale and at Westminster. Resistance to subsequent requests for victualling and common payments for the troops continued under the brief administration of Sir Nicholas Arnold from 1564 to 1565. The situation deteriorated further when Fitzwilliam and the captains refused to surrender their accounts.[174] Consequently, it is difficult to support the notion that Sussex's government exercised a kind of military tyranny in Ireland.[175] There were inherent limitations on the size and extent of the garrisons and the bands; they were seldom fully paid; there were ongoing disputes between the troops and the landowners throughout the Pale; and the military policy of the lord lieutenant and council consisted of a series of linked responses to the depredations of Shane O'Neill and other rebellious lords and chiefs. Just as the government was not clearly conducting a rigorously conceived 'programmatic' military campaign, for reasons suggested above, the Gaelic chiefs and Anglo-Irish lords were not engaged in a politically motivated insurrection. In fact, the aims of government were quite conservative. Military policy under Sussex and his successors was connected to the objective of extending the rule of law and, as such, it was, of necessity, characterized by episodic, not systematic, reactions to outbreaks of violence and disorder.

In 1565 the queen instructed Sydney to take note of the grievances over victualling and to ensure that the soldiers were accountable at common law for felonies they had committed. This was the first time the queen had intervened in the issue. Sydney found conditions still depressed in the following year, and advocated an immediate full pay to the soldiers to prevent further extortions and robberies. The queen noted that the placing of the soldiers with poor inhabitants of the Pale aggravated their plight and in the following year Sydney saw that horsemen were quartered only on those who could support them with their boys and horses.[176] In May 1566 the council attempted a compromise by sending 250 soldiers to be positioned on the borders and assessing the Pale an increase of 4*d.* per diem for each of them to make up the difference in price and in the scarcity of victuals there.[177] This

174. Brady, 'Government of Ireland', pp. 158–71.
175. See Ellis, *Tudor Ireland*, pp. 246–50; Bradshaw, *Irish constitutional revolution*, pp. 260–63. Canny has moderated his view of Sussex in his more recent work, *Reformation to restoration*, pp. 65–73.
176. PRO, SP 63/14/11; 63/17/16–17.
177. RIA, MS 24 F 17, f. 219. Actually, Wexford was cessed in place of Louth because the marshal already drew heavily on the resources of the latter county for his garrison at Newry. This device was to last only from 1 May till 30 September.

measure was only a temporary one, and by 1568 the situation was approaching a crisis. The Irish council wrote in June 1568 that '. . . no mony can be had of this Cittie [Dublin]. . .' and that the garrisons in the north were dangerously short of victuals.[178] The decisive step was taken on 24 May at Greenwich when the queen agreed with Thomas Might for the regular provision of the forces in the north. At this point the council in Ireland lost its supervision of the victualling to the government in London, and henceforth the victualler bargained directly with Cecil for money and provisions. Just as this agreement subordinated the Irish council's authority over the government in Ireland, it also demonstrated the process by which that government was adapted to suit English principles and practices.

Might covenanted with the queen to provide 2,400 pecks of oats to the garrisons in the north and to pay 16*d*. Irish for every peck at distribution points to be named by the council. His appointment was registered on 28 June 1569 and his role was further clarified at that time. Might was to provide the garrisons with all their requirement of wheat, malt, beans, oats, beef, bacon, butter, cheese, wine, hogs, salt, herring, wood, coal, straw, hay and other necessaries. He became the most important link between the army and the government apart from the lord deputy and the treasurer at wars.[179] The council was not without some residual responsibilities, for it was directed to supply the victualler with essential transportation for both land and water carriage, and to enforce his privileges of taking oats, salt and other commodities from the Pale. Might was to inform the lord deputy of his remaining victuals every two months, and to surrender his books to the vice treasurer twice each year. The lord treasurer in England wrote to all customs officials in England and Wales to assist Might to export 25,000 lbs. of butter and 50,000 lbs. of cheese in a year. Might contracted to supply 800 men with their provisions, an obligation that required 230,400 lbs. of beef every year. The greatest burden, as it turned out, was the assumption of full responsibility from the queen, for,

The said Thomas covenants to discharge the Queen of all manner of wastes, losses, carriages, freights, charges, wages of clerks, and of bakers, brewers, coopers, labourers, and all charges and losses whatsoever incident to the said victualling saving such as may happen by the enemy or fire.[180]

178. Bodl, Carte MS 58, f. 587.
179. *Cal. S.P. Ire., 1509–73*, p. 378, no. 36; *P.R.I. rep. D.K. 11*, p. 210, no. 1402. The 2,400 pecks of oats were distributed by the council among eight counties. Meath provided 600 pecks; Dublin, West Meath, Kildare, Louth and Wexford gave 300 pecks each; and Carlow and Kilkenny brought in 200 pecks each. RIA, MS 24 F 17, f. 339v.
180. *Cal. Carew MSS, 1515–74*, pp. 379–81. Might was to have the storehouses of Carlingford, Newry, Armagh and Carrickfergus for his provisions. The enormity

The turning-point of 1568 wrested authority over the victualling from the council in Ireland and vested it in an experienced, wily veteran of Irish administration. Thomas Might entered into a bond, in the large amount of £4,000, for his proper performance in office, but he received far more from the queen in victualling money. In May 1568 alone he was given £3,000 for provisioning, but by November the auditor wrote to Cecil that there was no money left to pay Might according to his contract.[181] Within a year Might had assigned his office to Thomas Sackford, a cousin of Sydney, and the queen marvelled that '. . . he has been suffered to deal so negligently'. In truth, Might may have been unscrupulous, but Sackford fared little better and both men claimed to have suffered staggering losses. On 14 May 1570, some fourteen months after he assumed the post, Sackford gave up the office to Might, saying he had lost £1,000 in service to the queen. In 1572 the lord deputy accused him of so under-provisioning Newry that one band had to return to the Pale, but there was little doubt that Might had lost a great deal of money and he complained that he could get no credit. In 1574 the auditor, Jenyson, told Cecil that Might was £4,000 in debt.[182]

Sackford was again made victualler in 1574 and he executed the office until his death in 1582. The troops were removed from the Pale in 1571, but this did not resolve the problem of finding food for them. When the troops were quartered on the borders they were still victualled from the Pale and the council had to resolve the problems of distribution arising from periodic scarcities and other difficulties.[183] The dilemma of provisioning worsened after 1578 when the size of the army was doubled, and the intervention of the privy council then became more systematic and regular. In 1578 the council wrote to the privy council asking for enough provender for 4,000 men because of the scarcity in Ireland. The council also wrote to the mayors of Chester and Bristol to send over at once all the comestibles they had in store.[184] At that point most of the increase had to be taken up at

of his task is measured in the sheer size of the army's requirements: 1,200 quarters of wheat; 1,120 quarters of malt; 57,600 lbs. of cheese; and 28,000 lbs. of butter. If more than 800 men were to be victualled, the vice treasurer was to pay Might within twenty days after the delivery of the provisions.

181. Might was a veteran of 24 years' service in 1570 and he remained victualler until about 1582. *Cal. S.P. Ire., 1509–73*, p. 427, no. 26; p. 379, no. 1; p. 393, no. 17.

182. ibid., pp. 402, no. 30; 404; 459, no. 22; 461, no. 33, 3; 473, no. 41. *Cal. S.P. Ire., 1574–88*, p. 24, no. 24. See also *Sidney S.P.*, p. 109.

183. Bodl, Carte MS 57, f. 365.

184. PRO, SP 63/61/3–4v; *Walsingham letter-bk*, pp. 110–21. The council was responsible for distribution of the victualling as it came into Dublin and Might, who had received £7,000 in advances by 1580, was no longer trusted. The council

the ports of Bristol and Chester, and the monumental problems of catering for the troops thereafter consumed the time and energy of governments in Ireland and England alike.

Unlike the provisioning of the military in Ireland, responsibility for naval policy was more readily controlled from Westminster. During the turbulent episodes of warfare against Shane O'Neill and the Ulster Scots, the council sought and received the services of a warship which operated off the coast from 1565 until its withdrawal in 1568. The privy council in England placed in service as many as five ships during this period, and gave them their instructions without consulting the council in Ireland. Cecil resisted protestations from the council from 1571 to 1574 that a ship was needed, based on the rumours of a Spanish invasion. The small *Handmaid* was finally sent to Ireland in 1576 to be at the disposal of the lord deputy and remained there until 1587. Only in 1579 were the first large-scale naval operations conducted on the Irish coast and once again these were wholly controlled from England.[185]

THE GENERAL HOSTING

Only one aspect of military policy lay outside the basic structure outlined above, and this was the general hosting, or 'rising out' of the counties of the English Pale and its borderlands. While rarely mentioned in official correspondence with London, the general hosting was a basic part of the conciliar obligation to defend the Pale. It was, in fact, akin to the militia in England, although it was employed on a more regular and systematic basis to supplement or stand in for the garrisoned armed forces. The general hosting was ordinarily called out during the summer months between June and August and it remained in the field for about 40 days.[186] The origins of the hosting are obscure, but it seems that from the fourteenth century a military force of 1,000 men or more could be proclaimed by the governor and

feared '. . . the corruption to bee doubled in some when so many shalbe emploied'. PRO, SP 63/78/37.

185. Captain George Thornton and the *Handmaid* remained under the authority of the lord deputy and council, but the squadrons led by Sir John Perrot and Captain William Wynter were sent only to intercept the Spanish fleet. Five large warships were sent at first in 1579 and later a fleet of sixteen was dispatched. See Tom Glasgow, 'The Elizabethan navy in Ireland (1558–1603)', *Ir Sword*, vii (1966), 291–307, for a full treatment of the subject.

186. Of 26 general hostings in this period, some 20 of them, or 75%, were levied in June, July or August. The great majority were summoned for six weeks' service after 1556, but during 1543–55 the average length of service was only 30 days. See, for comparison, L. Boynton, *The Elizabethan militia, 1558–1638* (London, 1967).

council for the defence of the Pale. By the late fifteenth century the hostings were levied on all free tenants and magnates were required to attend with a customary quota of troops. This service was then made compulsory within the Pale and Co. Carlow and fines were levied for absence from the hosting.[187]

Prior to 1556, the general hostings were infrequent and they varied greatly in size and purpose. During the reign of Edward VI they became more common, and after 1556 they were called out annually until at least 1583, with few exceptions.[188] Although the stated objectives of the general hostings varied from year to year, the great majority of them were summoned to defend the northern borders of the Pale. In 1556 the hosting was called out to expel the Scots, and in 1557 more generally to suppress the rebels and repel a possible foreign invasion.[189] In many cases, however, the council simply mentioned 'sundry causes' as the reason for the general hosting. Imminent danger was therefore not necessary to justify calling out the forces of the Pale.

Meetings of the grand council were called to give assent to the general hosting. The consent of the nobility as representatives of the Pale was a perfunctory act, however, because few of them even attended these ceremonial meetings. Whereas about fourteen councillors were usually present for these occasions, only four of them were lay nobles. The formal recitation of the solemn reasons for the hosting was similarly routine. Noting the presence of the 'lords spiritual and temporal', the council explained the justification for the summons, and gave details of the duration, meeting place and proportions to be used.[190] In this respect, the general hosting required the same kind of assent as the cess, but there was no functional relationship between them. The cess was to victual the army for a year, while the hosting was a temporary force usually quartered on the Pale. Formal writs

187. Ellis, *Reform and revival*, p. 56.

188. In 1543 the general hosting was converted into money, and earlier 'risings out' referred to the appearance of several septs at the hostings. From 1547 to 1583 the general hosting was summoned annually with these exceptions: 1549, 1551, 1553, 1554, 1562, 1564, 1574. However, undated general hostings may be linked to the period 1553–55, and several special hostings took place in 1564. The absence of references in the council book to the year 1565 places in doubt the appearance of a hosting in Sydney's first year in office. RIA, MS 24 F 17, ff. 3, 17–21v, 47v, 75, 98, et seq.

189. RIA, MS 24 F 17, ff. 3, 47v, 156, 241–41v. The places chosen for the forces to rendezvous, such as Dundalk, Newry and the hill of Tara, also demonstrate the northern emphasis.

190. RIA, MS 24 F 17, f. 3 et seq. Ellis argues that it was an 'afforced' council meeting, following Quinn, which approved the general hosting. Prior to 1534 the procedures were evidently less systematic and the governor could call out a hosting of a week or less by writ of the privy seal and order up to 400 kerne to be quartered on the Pale. *Reform and revival*, pp. 56–57.

were sent to sheriffs, constables and justices of the peace to require all lords spiritual and temporal, knights, gentlemen and freeholders of the county to attend the lord deputy. Similar writs were sent to mayors, bailiffs and portreeves of the towns to require the forces of the county or barony to arm themselves and be ready to attend the hosting.[191]

In preparation for a general hosting, the local notables were often required to summon the men of the county for a general muster. They were instructed to divide themselves into circuits and to muster every barony on the same day, noting the name, the weapon and the ability of each man. In 1560 these musters were ordered only for the Pale, but in 1566 the council attempted to extend its military authority to the west by requiring musters from Counties Waterford, Tipperary, Limerick, Cork and Kerry. This experiment was not repeated, but by 1572 the council had extended the general musters to Carlow, Kilkenny, Wexford, Queen's and King's Counties.[192] This exemplified the geographical extension of conciliar effectiveness, although the hostings from those areas were normally under the direct control of a leading Anglo-Irish magnate such as Viscount Baltinglas. The council's injunction to the commissioners in 1574 was full and detailed.

The commissioners shall assemble and divide into companies, appointing a company of not less than 2 or 3 for each barony. They shall direct the barony constables to come before them on a certain day with lists of the persons in their baronies between the ages of 15 and 60, and to command the people to appear at the same time with all such horse, armour, bows, arrows, guns and other warlike apparel as they can put in readiness for the service of her majesty. Any able man not appearing shall forfeit 20s. On the day of muster they shall make lists of all men appearing, distinguishing archers, arquebusiers, billmen, horsemen, and kerns, also those who have a horsejack, spear, bow, sheaf or arrows, bill, gun, sword, or harbergeon of mail. This list, signed by the commissioners present, and also the lists of the constables, to be returned by the 20 August following.[193]

The number of men present at a general hosting varied considerably, despite the injunction to call out all the forces of each county. In general, the forces were well over 1,000 men, but on occasion the

191. *Cal. pat. rolls Ire., Hen VIII—Eliz*, pp. 495, 500.
192. *P.R.I. rep. D.K. 11*, pp. 57–58, 120; *12*, pp. 74–76, 111–12. For the earlier period, Ellis suggests that defence of the southern and western counties lay with the earls of Kildare, Ormonde and Desmond, availing of coyne and livery as needed to provide for their troops. *Reform and revival*, pp. 57–58.
193. *P.R.I. rep. D.K. 12*, p. 127. In 1579 the musters were taken in a state of emergency. Hence extra instructions were made to keep the beacons and watchers ready and to have post horses available at all times. The forces were to be ready to march on one hour's notice. PRO, SP 63/68/39–40.

council deferred the hosting on the small counties of West Meath and Louth.[194] Hence, Counties Dublin and Meath bore nearly the full burden alone because Co. Kildare was usually committed to serve with the lord deputy under the earl of Kildare. The city of Dublin and the town of Drogheda sent large contingents totalling about 100 men together, but the Irish chiefs contributed perhaps the greatest number to any hosting. These were the loyal chiefs of Irish septs located in the Pale or on the borders, and they filled up the ranks with Irish horsemen and kerne. O'Reilly, in particular, sent some 140 men to the average hosting. The O'Carrolls, Mageohegans, Magennises and Cavanaghs also contributed large numbers of Irish troops. Certain Anglo-Irish lords of the Pale such as Lord Slane and Lord Killeen also provided Irish kerne, while leading Anglo-Irish lords from beyond the Pale such as Ormonde and Upper Ossory were expected to bring their retinues, which generally included 40 kerne.[195] The presence of such a large and varied contingent under the leadership of native chiefs and lords is evidence of the level of cooperation which existed between the Dublin administration and its supporters. While the Palesmen and others could be vocal critics of increased charges for the garrisoned troops, they were reliable participants on many levels of local and national government, from the law courts to the militia.

The instrument of the hosting was employed by the council in different ways. Ordinarily, most of the men provided were described as 'archers on horseback', but a good number had muskets and pikes as well. Carts were requisitioned from each county to provide the carriage of necessary arms and victuals, and a certain number of carts was exchanged for garrons, or small pack horses native to Ireland, to haul them.[196] Special hostings of fewer men were sanctioned in the winter months and labourers were levied to cut passes through the woods. In 1557 a general muster of 400 labourers was ordered on the Pale to provide men for cutting passes and mending causeways in

194. There is precious little information on the size of the general hostings. Three musters were placed in the council book and they reveal figures of 1,431 (1556), 376 (1560) and 1,180 (1566). The smaller number may be partly explained by the absence of the Irish chiefs and the contributions of only Dublin and Kildare. On the other hand, the hosting required for 1579 was 1,800 to meet the anticipated foreign invasion. RIA, MS 24 F 17, ff. 17–21v, 128v–33, 221v–26v; PRO, SP 63/69/12; Bodl, Carte MS 56, ff. 50–51v; Carte MS 58, f. 7–7v.

195. Other contributing Irish chiefs were: O'Mulloy, O'Melaghlin, O'Madden, McMahon, McGuire, O'Hanlon and O'Magher. In addition, Francis Agarde and Nicholas Heron led the Irish forces of the O'Byrnes and Cavanaghs after 1560. RIA, MS 24 F 17, ff. 17–21v, 128v–33, 221v–26v.

196. Carts and garrons were often levied independently of the hosting for the use of the army, and this was done without the approval of a grand council. In May 1568, for example, 200 garrons were cessed on the Pale. RIA, MS 24 F 17, f. 308v.

Leix and Offaly. In an emergency, the council could levy a small contingent to assist the army as it did in 1566, sending 400 men from Co. Dublin to Kells for ten days to help the lord deputy against Shane O'Neill.[197] On the other hand, the hosting could be converted to money for military purposes. In November 1569 the council converted the announced general hosting into money, adding 10 days to the original 31 days' duration for the purpose of getting extra revenue. The council justified this expedient on the grounds that it was already late in the year and Irish kerne were needed for service against Fitzmaurice in Munster. In fact, the council occasionally ordered general hostings which were intended at the outset to be transformed into money. This practice could become an abuse if exploited arbitrarily by the council, and in 1568 the following proviso was extracted from the council by the nobility: 'Our meaning is, that if the warr in the north or the coming of the Skottes urge not this hosting, that then it shall not be converted into money to eny other uses.'[198]

Perhaps the most basic change in the general hosting was the increase in the number of days for which the men were called to serve. From an average of 30 days in the field, the number jumped to six weeks in 1556 and stayed there for at least two decades. In 1557 the Palesmen complained that '. . . they have of their owne benevolence been further charged then they heretofore have been accustomed to be'. The council assured them that '. . . this increase of charge growen and growing at these two laste hostinges and afore mencioned, shalbe no president [precedent] to burden the cuntreys hereafter . . .'.[199] The council did not then anticipate the growth of its military commitments during the following reign and this statement gives evidence of the cautious conservatism which typically marked its work. When more vigorous lords deputy expanded the territory which was subject to the hosting after 1563 to include the retinues of Desmond, Thomond and Clanricarde, the council explained that the distance was so great that they could not provide their own victuals. However, it was noted that each of those western earls had provided 50 horsemen when summoned in the previous year.[200] The average general hosting remained throughout the period at about 40 days and it was extended to new areas as well. We may conclude that this was in most respects an effort to enlarge the effective jurisdiction of the government rather than an aspect of military conquest, since the typical mandate of the traditional hosting was ordinarily quite limited.

197. RIA, MS 24 F 17, ff. 42, 241–41v.
198. H.M.C., *Haliday MSS*, pp. 275 (ff. 73v, 76); 279 (ff. 212v, 233v); 282 (f. 340).
199. RIA, MS 24 F 17, f. 48.
200. Bodl, Carte MS 58, f. 7v.

In 1566 the expedition of Sydney against Shane O'Neill provided a remarkable example of the link beteween the army and the hosting. A very large hosting was levied of 1,400 men and an extraordinary cess of victuals was also required. Desmond and his kinsmen came up from Cork and Kerry, together with Lords Dunboyne and Curraghmore, William Burke and others. The council was left to summon and organize the forces of the Pale, while Lords Delvin, Trimleston, Howth and Louth were stationed with their forces on the borders. Desmond and St Leger were left to command the rest with the aid of the council, while the lord deputy and the army went north against Shane. 'The wholle Rising out of thenglish pale within twoo dayes after were assembled . . . for the defense of the borders, to the number of thre thowsand beside the garrysons . . .', and these forces led by Delvin and Louth chased Shane when he ventured to attack the border towns.[201] Sydney had called for some 2,000 men, an unusually large force, yet Shane was able to burn some houses along the borders. The episode illustrates that an imposing mobilization of the forces of the Pale by an energetic lord deputy was still barely adequate in the face of a relentless and dangerous adversary.

By 1565 the lord deputy and council faced with some reluctance the necessity of expanding the size of the hosting. They acknowledged the resistance of the counties outside the Pale, in combination with leading Anglo-Irish magnates, which was difficult to overcome. For example, in July 1566 the council wrote to the leaders of Co. Waterford, exempting the county from the general hosting, '. . . considering the harvest season and other like busy tyme nowe at hand that it woold be no lytill hindrance to nude or barreyn that countie with horsemen or carriages or other like impositions . . .'.[202] Instead, the council levied a payment of 3*d.* per diem to hire 30 kerne for a quarter of a year on Co. Waterford. In 1574, the order of the council was almost apologetic in its tone, requiring a total of only 500 men to help Kildare defend the Pale against the threat of a Spanish invasion.[203] Resistance to the hostings rapidly eroded when the vulnerability of the Pale was exposed during the Munster rebellion. In 1579 the council noted the designs of O'Neill against the north and a very large defensive force of 2,600 men was levied on the Pale.[204] This exceptional troop strength represented the largest commitment from

---

201. PRO, SP 63/19/112–13.

202. RIA, MS 24 F 17, f. 233v. A similar accommodation was reached with Cos. Wexford, Kilkenny and Tipperary.

203. Bodl, Carte MS 56, ff. 50–51v, 59–60.

204. PRO, SP 63/69/11–12v. This number represented an increase of 1,800 men beyond the ordinary 'rising out' of 800 troops.

the Pale and its borders and it demonstrated the flexibility of the general hosting to meet emergency needs, despite the common resistance to it.

In summary, we may observe several important characteristics about the general hosting which illustrate the nature of government in Elizabethan Ireland. The hosting was a traditional instrument which could be used by the lord deputy and council in flexible ways, and it was expanded in this period to provide additional support for the increase of administrative effectiveness. However, the council observed caution and prudence in trying to reform the hosting and the Palesmen and the Anglo-Irish lords resisted efforts to link the annual 'rising out' of the militia to the work of the garrisons or to fiscal expediency. The conservative approach of the council was dictated by the need to maintain the willing cooperation of the loyal elements of the landowning élite. And this, in turn, demonstrates the practical modus vivendi which was at the heart of Tudor government in this period. Rather than an alien military conquest which ran roughshod over the legal rights and traditional independence of the native people of Ireland, the government produced a pragmatic mixture of modest reforms and cooperative expedients designed to offer stability and to speed the ultimate recourse to procedures of the common law.

THE LORDS PRESIDENT AND PROVINCIAL COUNCILS

Whereas the general hosting was a legacy from the later middle ages designed to protect and defend the English Pale, the development of the lords president and councils in both Munster and Connacht was an Elizabethan innovation. The concept of establishing regional councils to administer the outlying provinces was clearly based on the successful models of provincial administration in Wales and in the north of England. However, these extensions of conciliar supervision represented less an administrative revolution than a series of related expedients which were often undermined by the parsimonious queen and the balky local magnates they were intended to control. Adumbrated in the instructions to Sussex and in the advice of Thomas Cusake, the lords president and councils were established in two provinces only to become truncated and understaffed after a brief interval. It was clearly decided at the outset that the councils would become agents of English supervision and the rule of the common law. However, local insurgencies and political rivalries created so much unrest that the leadership of the council was entrusted to military men, for the most part, assisted by judges and law officers. What emerged from these experiments was the typical Tudor compromise, a hybrid institution that combined rule by martial law with the hearing of both civil lawsuits and criminal cases.[205]

Writing to Cecil on the state of Ireland in 1562, Cusake called for the establishment of presidents in Ulster, Munster and Connacht. His argument was the familiar one that the costs of such an enterprise would be borne by the country since the queen would soon be collecting revenue in all the provinces.[206] Sussex also championed the idea in several missives to Westminster and Sydney was promised in his instructions of 1565 that a council in Munster would be established with residences in Limerick, Cork and Waterford (see Map 3). The aim of such a council was explicitly to 'execute the laws' and the lord president was to be assisted by a judge and others 'learned in the law'.[207] It was anticipated that the queen would recover lost lands, revenues and lapsed rents, and Sydney's answer in July 1565 proposed his ally and neighbour in Kent, Sir Warham St Leger for the position of lord president. He called for a force of 100 troops to be associated with the lord president but also noted that the assent of the three earls in Munster would be crucial.[208] He sought a similar foundation in Connacht. St Leger was admitted to the council in Ireland in May 1565 in readiness for his service in the south. However, St Leger was unacceptable to the powerful earl of Ormonde and he was eventually cast in a much more modest role.[209]

a) Munster

Instructions were sent to the lord president and council of Munster on 1 February 1566 by the lord deputy and council. Despite the incomplete nature of these draft proposals and the reluctance of the queen to place St. Leger in office, we can learn much about the objec-

205. See Brady, 'Government of Ireland', pp. 209–13. His account stresses the initial commitment to common law principles of government, but exaggerates the subsequent embrace of military and despotic alternatives. See also L. Irwin, 'The suppression of the Irish presidency system', *IHS*, xxii (1980), 22–23.

206. PRO, SP 63/5/88.

207. PRO, SP 63/14/11v. See Canny, *Elizabethan conquest*, pp. 47–50. He views the Sussex proposals as inherently military, in contrast with Sydney's greater emphasis upon the use of judicial means, although both men relied on the same advisers and models.

208. PRO, SP 63/14/18–23v. Canny's argument that the presidency was calculated to undermine the authority of the great magnates ignores the essence of the Tudor compromise. Seeking to advance the causes of less influential local lords would not necessarily lead to political equilibrium and social stability, while any direct challenge to the traditional leadership of Ormonde and Desmond would lead to great unrest. In fact, the earls were not, in principle, unwilling to cooperate. See Canny, *Elizabethan conquest*, pp. 49–52, 99–100.

209. Canny, *Elizabethan conquest*, pp. 55–58, 99–100; Brady, 'Government of Ireland', pp. 184–85.

tives of the council in this era of relative tranquillity and about the relationship between the two governing bodies. The new council's jurisdiction was to include Counties Waterford, Tipperary, Limerick, Kerry and Cork, plus the countries of Thomond, Desmond and Ormonde. The councillors named to attend upon the new lord president included: the leading magnates (earls of Thomond, Ormonde, Desmond and Clancare); the archbishop of Cashel and the bishops of Cork, Waterford and Limerick; and three lay officials to be judges and clerk of the council. It is significant that in these early instructions there is no mention of a provost marshal and the overall tone of the document clearly suggests that a judicial role is intended. After reciting the 'daily disorders' that ruptured the peace in Munster, the council proposed a more speedy and efficient administration of justice there by sending a permanent council and president to hear cases.[210]

The guidelines of 1566 named civil administrators Nicholas White, Robert Cusack and Owen Moore to be resident members of the council and to serve with the lord president at all times. The ninth clause called for the council to hear and determine causes of action throughout Munster including the liberties or palatinates claimed by leading peers. Cases within the purview of the council included actions of real or personal property; inheritance; and criminal actions, especially if they threatened the peace. The councillors were particularly admonished to offer the queen's impartial justice to persons who pressed legal claims against such powerful adversaries as local lords, and to provide judicial remedies for cases in which the municipal courts, or other jurisdictions, acted in a partisan spirit. The council received warrants for oyer and terminer, for gaol delivery and for martial law, with the latter to be used only when other remedies failed. It should be noted here, of course, that commissions of martial law were exceedingly common and not intrinsically evidence of arbitrary rule.[211] The council was required to publish royal proclamations and to execute orders of the council in Dublin. Pursuant to its role as a provincial court, the council was also required to name three or four lawyers and clerks to serve at the judicial proceedings '. . . for making better answers and processes and to examine witnesses'.[212]

210. PRO, SP 63/16/40.
211. The standard commission of martial law did not apply to 40s. freeholders or those who possessed £10 in chattels, and it was clearly aimed at the idle men. James Dowdall's commission of 25 February 1575 for all of Munster contained this proviso: 'to be used only against such as cannot be reformed by the ordinary course of justice.' What is more, these commissions were issued both to Irish chiefs and to Anglo-Irish officials to be used for the security of the realm within their own territories. *P.R.I. rep. D.K. 12*, p. 143 (no. 2558); RIA, MS 24 F 17, ff. 192–93v.
212. PRO, SP 63/16/44–46.

While its role in the legal hierarchy was predominant, the new provincial institution also incorporated certain military features. Citing the disturbed condition of Munster, the lord president was allowed a retinue of 30 horsemen and 20 footmen with four officers. Using the model of the council in Wales, the lord president was ordered to retain a 'discreet person' as sergeant at arms to bear the mace of his office and to apprehend malefactors by arrest on warrant from the council. A porter who would have charge of the gaol was the only other official named to serve. However, since disorder was a common complaint, the lord president and his fellow commissioners were empowered to use the forces of the country in the queen's service. That is, they could call out nobles, sheriffs, mayors, bailiffs, justices, gentlemen and commoners to assist them against any rebels; they could use ordnance against any castle held against them; they might imprison a person in contempt of the court or sequester his goods; and they could use torture in cases of 'any great offence' and impose the death penalty on traitors and felons. However, no executions could be carried out until the lord deputy and council in Dublin were duly informed, within twenty days.[213]

Recent writers have emphasized the military activities and the stern ruthlessness of certain commanders such as Humphrey Gilbert, who served as colonel in Munster during the rebellions of 1569–71.[214] However, the records of the entire period, viewed across the spectrum of war and peace, rebellion and 'good order', indicate that provincial administration was intended primarily to provide access to the common law within a framework of security and stability. When necessary, the military garrisons at places like Dungarvan could be summoned, but widespread insurgency throughout the province could only be met by an exceptional force such as that commanded by Gilbert. Following the rebellion of Shane O'Neill in Ulster and his fortuitous demise at the hands of the Scots, Cecil drafted a memorandum calling for the establishment of a new provincial council at Armagh for the government of Ulster. His plan of December 1567 included the garrisoning of some thirteen places with wards and constables, and he required the lord deputy to reside at Armagh for 'some convenient time' in order to establish the new system.[215] Once again, the recent disorders of the province seemed to require a strong military presence there and the proposed council retained many features of a fortified

213. ibid.
214. Ellis, *Tudor Ireland*, p. 261; Brady, 'Government of Ireland', p. 212; Canny, *Elizabethan conquest*, pp. 101–02.
215. PRO, SP 63/22/139–42. Cecil even proposed trenching around the circumference of Armagh to secure it against attack. SP 63/24/85–87.

citadel. In the event, however, the council at Armagh was never established and the government relied on the trusted and experienced
veterans residing at Newry and Carrickfergus to provide a 'window
on the north' at far less cost to the queen. The colonies which were
subsequently established in Ulster under Smith and Essex were under-
manned, inadequately funded and strongly resisted by loyal stalwarts
such as Sir Brian MacPhelim O'Neill and Captain William Piers of
Carrickfergus. In any case, these provocative adventures were poor
substitutes for a systematic provincial administration and Lord
Deputy Fitzwilliam strenuously opposed them.[216]

Negotiations for the naming of a lord president in Munster had
proceeded very slowly. As St Leger had been rejected earlier, the
position was left dormant for several years prior to the outbreak of
rebellions, and the council named a series of commissions to travel to
the province and to hear causes of action. Sir Thomas Cusake was
sent on these judicial errands most frequently and he was joined by
other councillors such as the marshal, George Stanley, Sir William
Fitzwilliam and Francis Agarde.[217] A similar commission of 1567
was led by Chief Justice Plunket and the master of the rolls, Henry
Draycott. It contained 33 articles which required them to hear specific
causes of action and implement orders of the council throughout the
province.[218] This cumbersome and inefficient means of governing the
provinces led most observers to support the proposed councils and the
rebellions which began in 1569 made the changes more urgent.

In October 1568 new instructions for the council in Munster were
drafted by the lord deputy and council. While they relied on advice
and approval from London, it is interesting to note that it was the
Dublin administration that prescribed the mandate under which the
new government in Munster would operate.[219] Writing to Sydney in
November 1568, Cecil assured the chief governor that he had at last
obtained the queen's permission to establish two councils, in Munster
and in Connacht. Sir John Pollard was appointed as lord president in
Munster, although sickness eventually prevented him from accepting
the post, and Sir Edward Fyton was named lord president in Connacht.
Significantly, the queen continued to resist and Cecil called upon
Sydney to offer a new proposal which would make fewer demands on

216. Canny, *Elizabethan conquest*, pp. 73–90. Canny argues that Sydney was the
     mastermind of a grand scheme for the colonization of Ulster but it is far from
     clear that this was the foundation for Tudor policy in this period, as he implies,
     and both Cecil and the queen refused to commit resources to most of the overly
     optimistic colonization proposals. See also H. Morgan, 'The colonial venture of
     Sir Thomas Smith in Ulster, 1571–1575', *Hist Jn*, xxviii (1985), 261–67, 271–72.
217. PRO, SP 63/12/107; 63/2/66–72; 63/14/229.
218. Bodl, Carte MS 58, ff. 129–32.
219. PRO, SP 63/26/37–51.

the royal treasury.[220] Sydney responded that the need for a provincial governor was still very great but he suggested that the appointee should bring few English troops since those trained in Ireland were more experienced and would be of less charge to the queen.[221] By 1570, Sydney's appeals for a lord president were dramatically intensified against the background of rebellion. He did not view the role of Gilbert as anything better than an interim solution, and he claimed that the insurgency would have been prevented by a judicious provincial governor since '. . . the contrary ptes be the worse willing to serve when they be comaunded by their adversaries'.[222] Ormonde, likewise, reported earlier to Cecil that his service in Munster against the rebels was too expensive a burden for him and called for 'some grave and stowte presydent' such as Sir John Perrot.[223]

In the face of rebellion in 1570, Perrot made inflated requests for 200 horsemen and 200 footmen. Yet he also sought legal assistance from the council in Wales '. . . to take anie two Attornies and two clerks now attendinge on the counsell there to serve as Attornies and clerkes for the counsell at Mounster'.[224] A force of over 400 men certainly went far beyond the original conception of the provincial council as a judicial and administrative body. But subsequent instructions retained the original conciliar framework, and once the rebellion was ended in Munster the council in Dublin was exceedingly careful to defer to the 'discrete dealinge there' of the regional body.[225] Although Gilbert urged on the council a policy of ruthless coercion based on a return to the traditional pattern of arbitrary rule supported by purveyance, his successor practised a more moderate course. Canny's assertion that Perrot was '. . . primarily a military officer completing the task of Humphrey Gilbert' is not a wholly convincing account of the period of his administration, since he clearly had instructions to expand access to the common law.[226] His executions of rebels who were found guilty of treason from 1571 to 1573 is hardly surprising in the Tudor period, given the attitudes to disorder and social violence which accompanied any insurrection, and it is not at all clear that he thus undermined support for the idea of a presidency in Munster.[227]

220. PRO, SP 63/26/60–61.
221. PRO, SP 63/26/74–75.
222. PRO, SP 63/30/97–98.
223. PRO, SP 63/30/52–53.
224. PRO, SP 63/30/201–02.
225. PRO, SP 63/41/39.
226. Canny, *Elizabethan conquest*, pp. 102–03. See also Brady, 'Government of Ireland', pp. 210–12.
227. Ellis follows the customary argument that Perrot was a military despot, but cites no compelling evidence to support the alienation of the population of Munster.

Once Perrot obtained his desire to be dismissed in 1573, the queen refused to authorize a successor for several years. Nevertheless, the council in Ireland pursued its course by adopting several interim expedients. The veteran administrator, Francis Agarde, was named chief commissioner of the province until early in 1575, and the council thereafter called upon James Dowdall, second justice of queen's bench, to take up that role. Citing his experience as a judge, the council declared Dowdall '. . . is for all respectes except for marciall execucion only the moast mete and sufficyent man . . .', and called upon Henry Davells, then sheriff of Co. Waterford, to assist him in military matters.[228] The council's offer to make a judge the chief commissioner is persuasive of the intent to govern the province by the rule of law and the subsequent appointment of Sir William Drury as lord president of the council in Munster was followed by regular judicial hearings.[229]

It has often been argued that the government of Munster was typically entrusted to military men, yet this takes no account of the Tudor practice of requiring its administrators to be versatile in matters both civil and military. Sydney, for example, was acknowledged to be a competent commander as well as an impartial judge.[230] In their instructions to Sir William Drury as lord president in June 1576, the council in Ireland called for '. . . a Councell of a Convenyent number of psons, of ye three estates in the same partes to have an ordinarie contynuance for resorte of hir subiectes suites and Complaintes . . .'.[231] The lord president was to be assisted by James Dowdall, second justice of queen's bench; Nicholas Walshe and six other civil administrators; and Henry Davells as constable of the garrison at Waterford. Again, the model of the council in Wales was explicitly used and the clauses were based carefully on the original instructions composed

It is quite as likely that treason trials following a rebellion employed the rules of evidence just as they would have done in England and that cases heard under commissions of martial law were no more arbitrary in Ireland. See Ellis, *Tudor Ireland*, p. 261; Elton, *Policy and police*, pp. 297, 310, 325.

228. Bodl, Carte MS 57, ff. 602–03v.

229. See PRO, SP 63/70/211 for a summary of the government in Munster, emphasizing the continuity of officials there despite the hiatus in naming a lord president from 1573 to 1576. Ellis, following Canny, argues that the provincial administrations in Connacht and Munster were abandoned in 1572 and both writers ignore the surrogate roles of Agarde and Dowdall. See Ellis, *Tudor Ireland*, p. 266; Canny, *Elizabethan conquest*, pp. 103–04.

230. Ellis, *Tudor Ireland*, p. 261; Brady, 'Government of Ireland', pp. 209–12; Canny, *Elizabethan conquest*, pp. 47–49, 97, 101–03. Williams, *Council in Wales*, pp. 255–63. For Sydney as commander, see 'Henry Sidney's memoir of his government of Ireland', in *UJA*, iii (1855), 90–99.

231. BL, Add. MS 4,786, f. 49.

for St Leger in 1565, including the authority to hear causes of action throughout the province, even in franchises and liberties.[232] By the summer of 1578, the council in Ireland was instructed to complete the shiring of the provinces of Munster and Connacht, using the advice of the two regional councils, and to reduce the forces in garrisons there.[233] Despite the imminent commencement of the Munster rebellion, we must be careful not to exaggerate the impact on the early Elizabethan period of the violent, but parochial, disorders which periodically disturbed the peace. It is clear enough from the foregoing evidence that Drury was not primarily engaged in a military occupation and, indeed, he maintained a force of only 147 men as lord president in May 1577.[234]

b) Connacht

In the province of Connacht, similar instructions were laid down for a lord president and council. In 1568 the queen's patent allowed the governor of the province a retinue of 30 horsemen and 20 footmen along with one lieutenant. Ralph Rokeby was named as chief justice in Connacht to assist the new lord president, Sir Edward Fyton, and the council in Dublin was authorized to '. . . select a suitable man of this country, learned in the laws and with the knowledge of the Irish tongue, to be assistant to the said Justice'.[235] Robert Dillon was thus named as second justice in Connacht and John Crofton was appointed clerk of the council. Clearly, the queen intended the provincial government to proceed by common law and Rokeby wrote to Cecil in January 1569 proudly explaining the achievements of the new government. He said that the council had executed sundry malefactors, some of them by martial law; ordered idle men to be 'booked' or else proclaimed rebels; forced Irish subjects to cut off their long hair; and commanded the burning of idols and images in the churches of Galway itself.[236] After this galling introduction, the province reacted with predictable outrage. Rokeby's letter to Cecil in April 1570 was venomous in its denunciation of the Irish rebels. He casually explained that 'sundry' executions were ordered at the first session of 1570, after which the earl of Thomond blocked the plan to hold court sittings in Co. Clare and his forces chased the council ignominiously back to refuge in Galway.[237] Rokeby's oft-quoted comment that only

232. BL, Add. MS 4,786, ff. 43–51; Cott. MS Titus B XIII, ff. 215–22v.

233. BL, Cott. MS Titus B XII, ff. 265–68.

234. PRO, SP 63/58/84.

235. *Cal. pat. rolls Ire., Hen VIII—Eliz*, pp. 533–34.

236. PRO, SP 63/30/8–9.

237. PRO, SP 63/30/86–87v.

'fire and sword' could force the province to obedience must be weighed against several other factors. He was inexperienced in Ireland, a man of unswerving orthodoxy and implacable hostility, and he desperately sought to be recalled so he could return to England to be married.

The rebellion of the earl of Clanricarde's sons which began in 1569 troubled the lord president of Connacht greatly, although he had unwittingly done much to bring it about. Sir Edward Fyton was an assiduous correspondent who reported in February 1570 that Thomond had also gone into rebellion. His colourful description of affairs to the lord deputy deserves to be quoted at length:

Thus Your L. seeth wee have but Imperium precarium wee are favored to suffer everie man to doo what he liste, disobey processe, breake orders, comitt forces make unlawfull assemblies and wee, driven to speake faire, which our lacke of power muste needes be supplied otherwise wee shalbe but lyke Aesopes blocke whiche Jupiter threwe downe amonge the frogges in sted of a king'.[238]

Fyton called for 250 footmen to garrison Connacht and another 100 horsemen to bring the province to good order, and in March 1571 reported on a series of successful skirmishes with the rebels.[239] He continued to pursue the rebel leaders and he relentlessly used the gallows to execute their followers until his recall in 1572. Once again, the unsettled condition of the province during this period made recourse to the courts practically impossible and Fyton soon made matters worse by challenging the loyalty of the inept earl of Clanricarde.

Despite the episodes of conflict which punctuated his first three years in office as lord president, Fyton and the council evidently continued to govern by civil means. Writing to Cecil in January 1571 from Athlone, Fyton explained that he had held sessions that same month with the gentlemen of the shire at Roscommon and divided the new county into seven score ploughlands. He added, with some misgiving, that he had renewed the use of the Irish legal practice of 'kencogus', whereby each head of a family was made responsible for the acts of his followers. This custom required the Irish leader to bring into custody anyone charged with a felony or heinous crime, and it was employed to support the enforcement apparatus of English common law jurisdictions. Fyton enclosed a document in Latin written by a brehon of Connacht, James O'Scingin, to explain kencogus. But the lord president evidently scorned the practice, justifying his decision to use it in this way:

238. PRO, SP 63/30/30–31.
239. PRO, SP 63/30/30–31; 84–84v; 172.

We are dryven, partely by coldness of such as myght do good, but cheffely throwgh our owne wakenes [weakness], to make proffe what good wyll cum by allowyng agayne of that old Irysh law now long tyme forbidden called Kylcolgashe [kencogus]. And that your Lordship may the better understand how detestable it is, and what myschyf we be dryven to when we renue that as the best means we are able to use for mendyng of the cuntry, . . . I pray god there may be better meanes found and followed to brydle theym that such as be boath agaynst the law of god, nature and honesty.[240]

At this point an interesting transition occurred in the provincial government which may have reflected the frustration of policy-makers in Westminster with the scant accomplishments of the lords president. The queen's letters to the lord deputy in December 1572 named Fyton to be the new vice treasurer in Ireland, replacing Fitzwilliam who now occupied the role of chief governor. However, the queen also called on Fyton to retain his role in Connacht, with custody of the castle at Athlone and a small force of twenty men. His title was to be 'chief commissioner for the Government and province of Conaugh', but he was to retain the authority of a lord president.[241] In an apparent retreat from her original instruction, the queen explained that the remoter parts of Connacht were not yet ready to receive the continuous administration of justice or to have a president and council 'perpetually' in residence there. Nevertheless, she noted the revived loyalty of the leading magnates and commended the recent shiring of the province. So, in order to sustain the modest and tenuous achievements of her government, she created a commission under the great seal of Ireland to assist Fyton in a new tribunal designed to administer the province. The queen named the leading magnates and bishops, with lawyers to assist them, to hear cases in Connacht by oyer and terminer and to govern by common law. The queen called on Fyton to hold quarter sessions as in England, using one of the councillors in Ireland as a justice, and to reside 'a great part of the year' at Athlone and elsewhere in the province.[242] This decision was dictated, in part, by cost-cutting measures which the queen demanded, but it is also evidence of a willingness to experiment with moderation after the rigours of the initial introduction of the presidency and council in the western province. It is certainly difficult to see in this calculated withdrawal from military engagement a steadiness of purpose or a systematic belligerence.

240. *Facs. nat. MSS Ire.*, iv, sect. 1, pp. 29–30. Fyton added that he had shired Galway and Thomond and he was proceeding to make counties of Mayo and Sligo.
241. PRO, SP 63/38/132–35.
242. PRO, SP 63/38/132–35.

When the council in Ireland enlarged upon the queen's instructions in the following spring, it was clear that the new government in Connacht would replace military actions with legal remedies. The new commission was given '. . . full power and aucthoritie as Justices of oyer and terminer usuallie have . . .' to govern all the new shires by law '. . . or otherwies by their Discrecions as causes in equitie and conscience shoulde move them where the rules of the lawes shoulde be to [too] straight and harde . . .'.[243] This oblique reference to a kind of equity jurisdiction suggests the flexibility in approach that Brady has described as 'eclectic', or pragmatic, and it accords well with the observations of Cunningham that the government of Connacht after 1583 pursued the aim of moderate anglicization with the cooperation of local élites.[244] We can see here an implied criticism of the aggressive approach described by Rokeby in 1569 and a willingness to deal with the Irish more subtly and more tactfully in order to forestall future insurrections. The council reported to the queen in May 1573 that the government of Connacht would now proceed solely 'by commission of oyer and terminer', an interim solution which lasted until the appointment in July 1576 of Captain Nicholas Malbie, an experienced commander who had served for years at Carrickfergus with Captain Piers.[245]

The appointment of Malbie to serve as captain, and later as colonel, in Connacht may have been an effort to strengthen the military forces there, but the instructions emphasize other qualities in explaining how he was given the responsibility, without the title, of a lord president: 'For it is iudgemt and discrecon that bredeth good governement and not the title nor the Dignitie.'[246] Another rebellion broke out in June 1577 and the council reported that Malbie was unable to administer justice in the courts.[247] When Malbie was finally raised to the office of lord president of the council in Connacht in 1578, his instructions were nearly identical to those which were used to create the original government in Munster in 1565. Malbie was to be assisted by a chief justice, Thomas Dillon, and a clerk of the court, Edward White, who were to be continually present with him. The noble councillors who had been on the commission named in 1573 continued to serve in an advisory role and the council was given a mandate which combined both judicial and military responsibilities. They were to prosecute all

---

243. Bodl, Carte MS 57, f. 616.
244. Brady, 'Government of Ireland', p. 201; Cunningham, 'Composition of Connacht', 7–9, 13.
245. PRO, SP 63/40/124–25.
246. PRO, SP 63/56/33.
247. PRO, SP 63/59/13v.

rebels and conspirators and to raise troops as necessary, but only after obtaining permission from the council in Dublin.[248]

Most remarkable among these instructions of 1578, however, was the comprehensive treatment of common law procedures. Details of judicial administration took up 23 of the 34 clauses in the council's mandate. The council was authorized to collect rents and duties owed to the queen; to meet as a court in the regular terms for hearings of oyer and terminer; to encourage the Irish to abandon the brehon law and other Gaelic practices and to bring grievances before the provincial court; to sit for one month, at their discretion, during each term; to hire six clerks learned in the law and to use them as attorneys, naming one as queen's solicitor to examine accused criminals; and to expedite proceedings in the 'small causes of poor man's suits' by examining the case in the presence of both litigants and issuing an order there.[249] The councillors were further admonished not to impose levies on the local people for the quartering of judges when they sat as a court, explaining that,

The said L. Justice and Counsell doe thinke yt a thinge moste requisyte to draw the people to the love and lykinge of this establishmente by Justice, that theire Complainctes, cawses and greefes may wth smallest chardge come to speedie hearinge and order . . . .[250]

Naturally, the council in Ireland also provided for the enforcement of judicial decrees in Connacht and for an appropriate military response to outbreaks of violence or insurrection. Sheriffs were authorized to attach the person or property of a defendant who failed to appear in court; places of imprisonment, called the 'marshal's ward', were to be established in towns where sessions were to be held; and at all these sessions the Irish practices of coshery, bonaught, coyne and livery, and abuses such as black rent, maintenance of retainers and embraceries were prohibited.[251] Anyone who was suspected of a felony and who was thought to be concealing matters relevant to the case could be subjected to torture at the discretion of the council. Persons found guilty of perjury could be committed to the pillory, forced to wear papers or other insignia proclaiming their offence, or

248. BL, Add. MS 4,786, ff. 3–5.
249. ibid., ff. 5–6.
250. ibid., f. 5.
251. Coshery was the right to tallage exactions at will from substantial landholders for the use of Gaelic chiefs. Bonaught described the maintenance of Irish mercenary soldiers generally, while coyne and livery signified Gaelic exactions for the free quartering of the chief's dependants. Black rent was illegally extorted by Gaelic chiefs from Anglo-Irish landholders in return for their 'protection'. Embraceries is a term for the corruption of juries.

subjected to the 'nayling or cutting of ears'.[252] Native Irish chiefs and lords were required to bring to the clerk of the council all the names of men they claimed to lead ('booking'). And proper decorum was demanded of all persons appearing at sessions, including the wearing of English apparel and the banishment of weapons. In order to make these reforms effective, the lord president was authorized to follow malefactors beyond the borders of the province.[253] However, these manifestations of the severity of justice were not exceptional for Tudor courts, particularly in the aftermath of rebellion. The provincial governments were pragmatic innovations which were designed to provide flexible responses both to causes of action arising far from the courts in Dublin as well as to disturbances occurring beyond the perimeter of garrisons near the Pale.

c) comparisons

In order to demonstrate the flexibility and pragmatism of the provincial councils, we may compare the instructions to several of the principal administrators during the period. After Humphrey Gilbert was appointed as colonel in Munster to deal with the rebellion of 1569, he wrote to Cecil in October expressing his reluctance to accept the command.[254] However, he had already been named by letters patent to the post and Sydney had been expressly instructed to take all steps necessary to put down the insurrection. Gilbert was authorized to proceed by martial law; to conduct parleys with the rebels and offer protection at his discretion; to assemble all the queen's forces and to besiege any fortification of the rebels; to make proclamations as necessary and to cess the counties for his victuals; to add soldiers as needed without an accounting by the clerk of the check and to place troops in garrison where they were needed. Certain commissions were named from each county to assist him, but he had enormous discretionary authority in a time of crisis.[255] By contrast, instructions from the lord deputy and council to Perrot as lord president of Munster stressed his judicial authority. Writing in November 1572, the council called on Perrot to sequester the goods and apprehend the sailors of a ship docked at Youghal, using 'twelve honorable men' of the city as witnesses to appraise the number of the goods and furnishings of the ship, and to await the queen's further instructions.[256] Similarly,

---

252. BL, Add. MS 4,786, ff. 7–8.

253. ibid., ff. 8–9.

254. PRO, SP 63/29/133.

255. PROI, Lodge MSS, Extracts of patent rolls, pp. 129–31; *Cal. pat. rolls Ire., Hen VIII—Eliz*, pp. 535–37.

256. PRO, SP 63/40/51–52.

when Drury was lord president in Michaelmas term of 1576, the council held sessions at Cork and at Clonmel, hearing many cases alleging exploitation by the local aristocracy of a wide variety of victims. Presentments made at these sessions during two months of hearings included accusations of extortion, coyne and livery, forcible taking of victuals and general spoiling and wasting of the land.[257] In a comment remarkable for its blissful ignorance of an impending crisis, Sydney commended '. . . the universall quiet of Mounster, Connaught and Ulster . . .' in April 1578, giving due recognition to the achievements of Malbie and Drury in producing increased revenue for the queen. He told Elizabeth, with a singular lack of prescience, that the provincial governments would produce a reformed and stable Ireland, '. . . to the immortall fame of you and your posteritie forever'.[258]

In conclusion, then, we can observe several essential features of the new provincial governments. In the first place, it is certainly an exaggeration to describe the innovations as a presidential system since there were a number of false starts and, subsequently, long intervals when no presidents were named to the posts. However, the regional councils functioned continuously from 1569, using a variety of forms to achieve practical results in the face of changing circumstances in each province. The provincial councils were typical of the Tudor compromise, fashioned in a way which allowed expedient methods to be employed to meet new challenges. And the essentially judicial role of the councils was not allowed to lapse regardless of the mutations in the form of the provincial administration. Since these regional administrations were based in theory on the council in the marches of Wales, their ultimate objective was to employ judicial means rather than military ones. When necessary, they were organized for war and they confronted rebellious forces for several years at a time. But we should not dismiss too readily the effectiveness of the provincial councils sitting as courts of law in this period.

The assertion that the presidencies were 'diametrically opposed' in concept to the system of conciliar jurisprudence as practised in the council in Wales must be revised in light of the preponderance of the evidence. Canny has argued that the lords president were primarily

257. PRO, SP 63/56/114–18. Canny argues that Drury's term as lord president began well with major agreements struck between the government and the Munster lords and the holding of sessions at distant Tralee in Desmond's stronghold. Canny, *Elizabethan conquest*, pp. 106–07.

258. PRO, SP 63/30/93–94v. After the Munster rebellion the infrastructure of the regional governments returned to a modest size. The title of lord president was again diminished to the role of 'chief commissioner' in Connacht and the governor there was supported by only 100 footmen and 50 horsemen in 1584. BL, Cott. MS Titus B XIII, ff. 383–84v.

military leaders who were employed to discover crown lands which could be made available to unscrupulous English adventurers, and he has called the provincial councils 'stalking horses for colonization'.[259] However, the extensive instructions and the correspondence of the councils make no mention of the purpose of colonization. Canny points to only two examples. He has shown that Warham St Leger established a small colony at Kerrycurrihy, Co. Cork, after he was rejected as lord president. Yet he acknowledges that this fragile settlement was founded with the active support of his ally, the earl of Desmond. Moreover, Canny fails to explain the links between Richard Grenville's tenure as sheriff of Co. Cork and his subsequent enterprises as a colonizing adventurer. In addition, the argument of Fyton in 1572 that the queen's property could support 50 gentlemen in Connacht must be set against his many assertions of the impotence of crown government there.[260] Further, it is clear from all the commissions and instructions that each council was to include the leading local magnates as full members. They would hardly be likely to participate in efforts to diminish their own local power by making lands available to prospective English settlers. In fact, their presence on the council was expressly designed to promote more willing acceptance of the common law which offered them greater security of title.

The lords president and councils in the provinces were authorized by the privy council in Westminster and yet bound by the instructions sent by the council sitting in Dublin. It is clear that, by design, the autonomy of these regional governments in miniature was limited by intersecting layers of superior jurisdictions. This was done in part to restrain their use of military force and to curb excesses which might occur. We have been reminded often of the brutality and ruthlessness of Gilbert as colonel in Munster during the rebellion of 1569–72, but it is important to recall as well that no military tyranny succeeded him and that the council continued to function as a court under the leadership of a professional judge during the hiatus of 1572–75. Canny has asserted that the council in Connacht more nearly resembled the Welsh model in its handling of litigation and its efforts to complete the anglicization of local government. As we have seen, Fyton conducted sessions and named sheriffs to new counties. However, his tactless manner and bullying assertions of English jurisdiction soon alienated the local nobility, fomenting a series of rebellions against his aggressive methods. Local opposition, in fact, helped to drive him from his post in 1572, and we may question whether he had 'brought to conformity' large tracts of the province. Although he retained the

259. Canny, *Elizabethan conquest*, pp. 47–49, 92, 114–15.
260. ibid., pp. 77–79, 115.

office of lord president, he was largely an absentee from 1572 until 1574.[261] In the final analysis, the successes of the provincial councils rested mainly upon their tenacious and purposeful administration of common law procedures and the establishment of a framework for local government. Dramatic confrontations with leading magnates and their rebellious sons produced no lasting benefit for the crown.

The size of the military forces assigned to the provincial councils varied according to changing circumstances, as might be expected. The original instructions to the lord president of Munster authorized a small force of 30 footmen and 20 horsemen, but the size of this force grew enormously during the rebellion of 1569–72 and the costs helped to discredit the government of Sydney at that time. Nevertheless, by 1576 Sir William Drury led only 161 men in Munster while Malbie commanded a slightly larger force of 239 men in Connacht. The Munster rebellion caused a six-fold increase in the size of the military establishment and did much to change the conditions of Irish government, yet the provincial councils were supported by modest forces again by 1584. This suggests that the government had no intention of enforcing its will by a massive military conquest which it could ill afford. The factors which periodically inflated the number of troops are, of course, well known and negligent accounting methods make it difficult to estimate precisely the size of the garrisons located in Munster and Connacht. But it remains clear that the military role of the provincial councils was based on a flexible response to periodic outbreaks of disorder, while their judicial function was intended to provide systematic and continuous recourse to the common law.

Every commission sent to the provinces included judicial members, and all the instructions to lords president (including Perrot in 1571) provided them with legal assistance.[262] The argument that Perrot ruled arbitrarily by martial law and thereby alienated local lords exaggerates the impact of commissions of martial law. It is clear that administrators in England as well as in Ireland were frequently in the habit of challenging the impartiality of local juries and Canny offers no documentation for the assertion that Munstermen were wholly alienated by Perrot's tyrannical acts.[263] Recent writers have empha-

261. Canny implicitly recognizes the heavy burden carried by his archetype of 'conquest'. For example, he asserts that there were 'few insurrections' against Fyton's regime and that the common law jurisdictions were initially implemented without resistance in some key areas. Despite his initial characterization of the belligerence of the presidencies, Canny concludes that their aim was '. . . to facilitate the spread of English justice in the provinces . . .'. ibid., pp. 108–12, 116.

262. Canny declared Perrot retained no judicial administrators initially, but the instructions indicate that he was to be supported by a full legal staff, as were other lords president. Canny, *Elizabethan conquest*, p. 102; PRO, SP 63/30/ 201–02.

263. Canny, *Elizabethan conquest*, pp. 102–03; Ellis, *Tudor Ireland*, pp. 271–272.

sized that the aims of government in provincial administration were more restrained and moderate than has previously been supposed. Brady, for example, explained that the presidency in Munster aimed to expand the rule of the common law; enjoyed the cooperation of Desmond in 1566; and in any event had such a small military retinue that it could not impose arbitrary rule.[264]

Anglicization by the extension of the common law was the goal of new arrangements in Connacht and Munster after 1583. This moderate policy was less expensive than military confrontation and it ultimately proved more effective. Anthony Sheehan has recently argued for a new interpretation of the relations between native Irish groups and the provincial councils, citing areas of agreement and cooperation which have been hitherto neglected. He claims that the common law was often used in this period to protect the rights of native landowners, and Michael MacCarthy-Morrogh explains that this less ambitious policy was embraced largely because it was the cheapest way to govern Ireland.[265] Consequently, it may be necessary to revise the commonly accepted view that the 'Elizabethan conquest' of Ireland was the product of a grand design, launched by 'programmatic' governors, ambitious adventurers and fanatical reformers. The evidence seems to show that Tudor policy under Elizabeth was committed to certain modest goals, conservative in nature, which were adjusted to meet changing circumstances. The achievements of a government with limited means and pragmatic ends will usually be gradual, incremental and frustratingly incomplete. The effort to govern all of Ireland by establishing the lords president and councils constituted a genuine reform, but its successes were limited by its very moderation. Although the provincial councils combined both judicial and military objectives, some observers have obscured the complexity of their work by emphasizing the drama of episodic violence. Further research into the operations of the provincial administration may help to clarify these issues and perhaps lay to rest the essentially simplistic notion of an Elizabethan conquest based on illusory patterns of systematic abuse, exploitation and coercion.

CONCLUSION

Military policy in Elizabethan Ireland was intrinsically linked to the reforming purposes of the government. The expansion of effective jurisdiction under the council in Ireland was made possible by military

264. Brady, 'Origins of Desmond rebellion', 295–97. He sees Perrot as exceeding his authority in military rule, but finds Drury a moderate governor.

265. Sheehan, 'Native land claims in Munster', 297–98; MacCarthy-Morrogh, *Munster plantation*, pp. 21–22.

expedients which combined access to the common law with the enforcement of royal justice. The constables and seneschals made this possible in and near the Pale, while the new lords president and councils brought their small retinues to the provinces. The aim was, of course, to anglicize the population by degrees, offering them social stability along with protection from the brutal excesses of dynastic rivalries. It was expected that this would occasion the use of force, but the primary objective remained the extension of the common law by frequent court sessions held in the principal towns of all the provinces. Military policy was thus linked to judicial remedies and, in turn, the government anticipated the growth of revenue to pay for the queen's expenses in providing for her Irish subjects. The financial commitments and innovations of the Dublin administration form the next chapter of this study.

There have been many claims by historians that the government in this period was engaged in a full-scale military conquest. Canny, in particular, used the term to describe what he found to be two provocative innovations by Sydney after 1565: the introduction of provincial presidencies in Munster and Connacht and the establishment of two English settlements leading to the colonization of Ulster. While he acknowledged that the colonies failed badly, he exaggerated the extent to which they received meaningful support from the governments in London and in Dublin. Again, while Canny recognized the potential for the regional councils to furnish access to the common law in the provinces on a continuing basis, he argued that they themselves constituted an unwelcome intrusion into local politics. When rebellions flared up, the outrageous actions of certain English military leaders were cited by Canny as evidence of the hostile intent of the crown which lay concealed behind a veneer of respectability.[266] More recently, other leading historians have followed Canny's hypotheses, claiming that the government of Ireland constituted essentially a military occupation which received no support from the people. A corollary to this premise contends that the garrisons were evidence of an augmentation of military force which served as the prelude to colonization on behalf of a 'lobby of adventurers' who were supposed to have tremendous influence in the corridors of power.[267]

The historiography of the period has become something of an intellectual battleground. It is indeed hazardous to attempt to discover the balance between exaggerated claims of belligerence and overstated

266. Canny, *Elizabethan conquest*, esp. chs. 6 and 7 which purport to discover profound cultural alienation on the part of both English and Irish.
267. Ellis, 'Crown, community and government', 201–02; *Reform and revival*, pp. 214–15. Ellis correctly sees the inconsistencies in English policy but does not draw the conclusion that they made the government intrinsically weaker.

assessments of comity and social stability. On the one hand, we find Sydney's review of his campaigns in Ireland with its catalogue of virtually continuous struggle against his adversaries.[268] While, on the other hand, we encounter Thomas Cusake's assertion in 1562 that '. . . the quiete of this Realme universallie is suche as in no menes memorie the better hath bene sene'.[269] General observations that the Irish waged a defensive war against the government have been based principally on the evidence taken from the 1590s during the most widespread and violent conflict of the century.[270] But even such a sturdy veteran as Francis Agarde could, it seems, be seduced by the apparent calm during a period of intermittent peace. In 1576 he wrote to Walsingham that

. . . I can tell you that sithe I first knew it, the quietnes universallie and in all partes thereof was never greater . . . and the likeliehood of obedience (amongest the verie yrishe I meane) hathe not ben more. . . .[271]

In fact, it is useless to describe Irish warfare in this period without reference to the complex mingling of interests and rivalries on the side of the government by virtue of its alliance with Gaelic chiefs and Anglo-Irish lords. This complexity militates against the ingenuous doctrine of two hostile proto-nationalistic antagonists locked in combat, something which anticipates too much of later history.[272] It is often forgotten that Shane O'Neill and Desmond had acted with the government as well as against it, and that the council regularly taxed and mustered many septs of Gaelic Irish living near the Pale.

268. 'Sidney's memoir', *UJA*, iii, (1855), 91–99.

269. Cusake recognized, nevertheless, that the queen must always keep a force of 2,000 Englishmen in Ireland. PRO, SP 63/5/88. The council sent Cusake to England in 1563 with the report that Leix and Offaly were '. . . in good order and obedience', while the Gaelic septs in Wicklow were so well-behaved that '. . . ther is not at this presente one outlawe knowen in the hoole Contrey'. PRO, SP 63/9/34.

270. O'Domhnaill, 'Warfare in Ireland', 29–44. The council declared war on certain rebels such as Shane O'Neill and the O'Connors and O'Mores, but even these declarations were limited and hardly typical of conciliar government. RIA, MS 24 F 17, ff. 58v, 196, 234–35v. On the other hand, a desultory but chronic level of violence continued in this period among the Gaelic Irish in the form of cattle-raiding and plundering. See K. Simms, 'Warfare in the medieval Gaelic lordships', *Ir Sword*, xii (1975/76), 107–08.

271. PRO, SP 63/55/169. In March 1580 in the midst of the Munster rebellion, the council could write to the privy council that 'The whole pale in generall, god be thanked, is in verie good quiett, and the borders therof not muche molested . . .'. SP 63/72/20.

272. See, for example, Bradshaw's claim that the Gaelic Irish began to think in terms of ethnic nationalism and rebellion in protest against the 'Elizabethan conquest', citing Pearse on the origin of Irish patriotism. B. Bradshaw, 'Native reaction', pp. 73, 78–80.

If, indeed, there was no 'pattern' of military conquest in this period, is there an alternative model to explain government policy? We may question whether the government could afford an ambitious policy of conquest and colonization; we may doubt whether there was a clear and convincing consensus behind any systematic campaign of aggressive war in Ireland; and we may be sceptical of the use of small contingents in wards and garrisons for aggressive war when they were separated by miles of difficult terrain; but this leaves open the more general issue of the government's military purpose and direction. An alternative model exists, of course, which is not stupefyingly intricate. Military practice as pursued by the council consisted of a multi-layered structure of garrisons and wards, led by captains and constables who had civil authority as well as commissions of martial law; the new lords president and councils in Munster and Connacht, supported by a legal staff and a small military retinue; the traditional support of the general hosting which included numerous Irish chiefs and combined the forces of both English and Irish; and a network of support from the victuallers to the loyal towns and havens.

The policy which this structure was required to pursue was tentative and incomplete, based on a series of reforms and retrenchments which were increasingly dictated by the government in London. By 1578 the council in Ireland played the role of an informed intermediary in Irish military policy, helping to define conditions and to accommodate the structure to circumstances largely beyond their control. The Dublin administrators, both individually and as a group, wrote often to the queen and to Cecil on military matters. Their words were often punctuated by the hyperbole borne of genuine political crisis. But we must, in the last analysis, attempt to define the terms of Irish military policy without regard to exaggeration, either from the contemporary sources or from the spirited exchanges of modern historians. The intentions of the government were not fundamentally military. Access to the common law was guaranteed to citizens who accepted English government, and cooperation with the Anglo-Irish marked the course of English rule. The council itself was manned largely by Anglo-Irish civil officials and the lord deputy was an experienced administrator first, a commander second. While it is true that the use of martial law was fairly widespread, such use was limited primarily to the correction of idle men and vagabonds, those who had less than 40s. of property and were not formally retained by any lord or gentleman. The council was compelled to adopt a military strategy under certain conditions, but it did so only under pressure and the queen sanctioned very few ambitious military undertakings.

Elizabeth's military policy was directly linked to the ambitious goals set forth in the wake of her father's claim to the kingship of Ireland in

1541. In principle, the queen intended to govern her Irish subjects according to the terms of the common law. The establishment of new provincial councils and other reforms were designed to achieve the aim of a unitary sovereignty on terms which were entirely familiar to Elizabethan administrators. These inherently conservative statesmen used the models of conciliar government which had been successful in other Tudor borderlands. Indeed, Dr Ellis has recently called for a more inclusive study of Irish government in the overall context of Tudor dominions, and this proposal should now be applied to the Elizabethan era.[273] Since comparisons have also been offered which link the Elizabethan settlers in Ireland to Spanish conquistadores, it may not be amiss to suggest other useful contrasts relevant to conditions in the sixteenth century.[274] Ireland in this period, down to 1578, did not suffer civil war and invasion as did France during the age of religious wars. The Elizabethan government of Ireland was surely more measured and prudent than the Spanish government of Flanders in the same period, and the troops which mutinied in Antwerp hardly resembled the underpaid soldiers who occasionally plundered in the Pale. The level of disorder and rebellion in Ireland must be understood in relation to the conditions of the age. While the ideal of social stability in a well-governed commonwealth was clearly the government's objective, it is important to recognize how far they were from realizing it. Yet, just as we may acknowledge the extent and character of periodic social violence and insurrection, we must also avoid overstating their significance. Elizabethan Ireland was certainly not an 'age of equipoise', but equally it was not a tyranny based on conquest and colonization of an alien and defenceless population.

273. Ellis, 'Nationalist historiography', 1–18. Ellis is careful to observe the complexities in Gaelic society, but he persists in seeing the Elizabethan period as wholly distinct.

274. Canny, *Elizabethan conquest*, pp. 156–63; *Kingdom and colony*, ch. 1, 'Ireland as *Terra Florida*'; 'Identity formation in Ireland: the emergence of the Anglo-Irish' in N. Canny and A. Pagden, ed., *Colonial identity in the Atlantic world, 1500–1800* (Princeton, 1987), p. 175.

CHAPTER SIX

The council and fiscal experimentation: the exchequer, the coinage and the cess

INTRODUCTION

THE GOVERNMENT OF Elizabethan Ireland was chronically short of funds. Explanations for this fundamental weakness in the administration of the country have often been attributed to the accelerating expenses of conquest and colonization. However, fuller investigation of the evidence may reveal that multiple structural defects, compounded by inflation and external crises, contributed more to the general debilitation in the collection of revenue and management of expenses. Increased military spending doubtless exacerbated the combined effects of inefficiency, corruption, ponderous communications with the crown, inflation and economic regression.[1] What is more, the endemic pressures on the resources of government coincided with the new determination to expand the circumference of conciliar effectiveness beyond the Pale.

Bold initiatives such as the creation of lords president and councils, shiring of new counties and authorizing of colonial experiments represented potential drains on current revenue for the short term. But the frugal sovereign and her cautious policy-makers were quite reluctant to face the consequences of a fully-fledged campaign of reform. They countenanced limited increases in the revenue committed to Irish government, but they refused to sustain those commitments in the face of mounting debts, despite the knowledge that fundamental improvements would produce new revenue only gradually. The risks inherent in funding ambitious new programmes were evidently too great to be maintained by a conservative government which was beset by clamorous problems at home and abroad. While it would be incorrect to state that Cecil and others were simply disinterested in Irish matters, it is clear that Elizabethan administrators regarded Ireland as a drain on English resources which presented few realistic opportunities for amelioration in the near term. The expedients

---

1. Ellis, *Tudor Ireland*, pp. 49–50.

which were chosen to address the problems of Irish revenue administration were characteristic of the stop-gap approaches of a government preoccupied with other concerns.

This is not the place to attempt a full-scale study of financial administration in the first two decades of Elizabeth's reign. The objective of this chapter is to study the role of the privy council in Ireland in the financial aspects of governance and to examine two particular policies which aggravated both fiscal and political conditions, and which, as it happens, have significant constitutional implications: the debasement of the coinage and the attempt to impose composition for the cess. Most studies have agreed with the general proposition that the government was continually hampered by its inability to collect sufficient revenue to maintain itself without subventions from England.[2] As we have seen, the fundamental aim of Elizabethan policy in Ireland was the establishment of legal and political institutions designed to embrace all of her Irish subjects in a social compact which would, in turn, produce both obedience and good order. Yet, in all of her instructions to the lords deputy and council, Elizabeth and her councillors in Westminster also insisted on financial retrenchment. In 1568, for example, Sydney's instructions called upon him to assure the queen one year's rent from every new lease of land; to call in all debts and arrearages owed to the crown; to limit the daily allowance of councillors sent on commission; and to spend no more than £1,960 per month on the garrison.[3]

The principal defect in the government of Ireland in this period was thus the profound disjunction between the ambitions of the policy-makers and the means which they were prepared to use in support of them. As we shall see, no project was designed without a theoretically ample supply of money to provide for it. The reasons for the failure to develop adequate revenue in practice have little to do with a wilful mendacity or wholesale incompetence. Rather, they must be sought in the dynamic conditions of mid-Tudor Ireland which prevented the programmes of various chief governors from realizing their goals. Rebellion and disorder, of course, compounded other difficulties, while rising prices and changed trading relations were hidden but important factors. A reassessment of financial practice in the period will have to begin with a comprehensive analysis of the dynamic economic conditions which made planning so difficult.

Recent studies of the Irish economy under the Tudors have stressed the complexity of the situation while acknowledging the incompleteness

2. ibid., pp. 14–15; Brady, 'Government of Ireland', pp. 221–39; Canny, *Elizabethan conquest*, pp. 155–56.
3. PRO, SP 63/24/85–85v.

of the sources for a thorough investigation. No full-length study of the economy in the Elizabethan period exists, although several useful works have probed into the development of the towns, the customs and the economic conditions of Gaelic society.[4] This is due in part to a dearth of sources for economic performance, and this lack of evidence may also have plagued the queen's policy-makers, who consistently overestimated the profitability of crown revenues in Ireland. Nevertheless, traditional accounts of the primitive and under-developed circumstances of the Irish economy have exaggerated both the level of violence in the society and the lack of commercial contacts between its multiple elements. David Quinn and Kenneth Nicholls have discussed the great diversity inherent in Irish society, citing the many competing authorities and divided loyalties which nevertheless permitted a degree of genuine prosperity.[5] While it may be useful to describe the Irish economy by reference to its constituent parts, it is essential to remember that that economy was exceedingly intricate. Its many components were mingled and connected in ways which mitigate the stringent view of two hostile forces competing for the allegiance of a downtrodden people.

Dublin was the administrative capital of the country and a com-mercial centre as well. The population in this period has been estimated at between 5,500 and 8,000, making it the sixth largest urban centre in the British Isles. Despite the sand bar which still inhibits maritime commerce, Dublin was a trading port with mercantile contacts in England for the export of yarn, tallow and hides. In addition to the messengers and troops which arrived occasionally, the officials of the administration frequently brought in luxury goods, plus cloth and coal for the rest of the population.[6] Dublin was excep-tional in that it obtained the favour of a charter of incorporation as a county borough in 1548. This was testimony to its commercial and political importance and to the ambition of its powerful mercantile élite. This patrician class jealously guarded its new privileges and added to them. The local courts made every effort to preserve their judicial independence and the Trinity Guild of merchants obtained a charter offering them exclusive trading rights in the city in 1577.[7] In

4. Lennon, *Lords of Dublin*; A. Sheehan, 'Irish towns in a period of change, 1558–1625' in Brady & Gillespie, ed., *Natives and newcomers*, pp. 93 ff; M. O'Dowd, 'Gaelic economy and society', ibid., pp. 120 ff. See also the useful article by V. Treadwell, 'The Irish customs administration in the sixteenth century', *IHS*, xx (1976–77), 384–417.

5. Quinn and Nicholls, 'Ireland in 1534', in *N.H.I.*, *iii*, p. 20.

6. Canny, *Elizabethan conquest*, p. 4; Ellis, *Tudor Ireland*, p. 37; Sheehan, 'Irish towns', p. 95; Lennon, *Lords of Dublin*, pp. 31–34.

7. Lennon, *Lords of Dublin*, pp. 38–40, 93–99, 117–19.

an effort to expand their considerable privileges, the mayor and corporation of Dublin in 1582 sought to obtain exclusive rights to all trade within two miles of Dublin and the right to try all cases in their guild hall. But the council denied these requests with indignation as presumptuous and extravagant.[8]

Other important towns constituted a kind of 'urban hierarchy' throughout Ireland, and despite the real difficulties posed by a lack of roads and sufficient protection for overland transportation, there was substantial commercial contact between these centres and their hinterlands (see Map 1). The leading towns in this period were Waterford, Limerick, Cork, Galway and Drogheda, each of which contained between 2,400 and 4,000 inhabitants. These were all established ports which maintained significant commercial relations with continental trading centres in France and Spain as well as England and Scotland. During the Elizabethan period, these cities were granted renewed charters which provided them with certain freedoms from taxation and allowed them to retain the profits from forfeitures, fines and amercements. Sydney, in particular, attempted to stimulate local industry by encouraging the development of finished products for export, but the towns continued to export raw materials to their traditional markets and retained remarkable independence from the mercantile regulations of the Dublin administration. These provincial towns were largely self-governing regional capitals, dominated by a closed merchant oligarchy, yet with regular contact throughout a large hinterland dominated by both Gaelic and Anglo-Irish magnates.[9]

Country towns constituted a second level in the urban hierarchy, yet within this category there were substantial differences. The two largest were Kilkenny, the capital of the Ormonde sphere of influence in Munster, and Carrickfergus, the garrisoned 'window on the north' in Ulster. Although both were roughly equal in size at about 2,000 inhabitants, they represented markedly different urban social and political conditions. Kilkenny was the centre of a settled region which was dominated in practice by the powerful earls of Ormonde, and which enjoyed a traditional prosperity despite its lack of port facilities. Carrickfergus, on the other hand, was the site of a politically significant English garrison, led in this period by the veteran Captain William Piers, and the town maintained trading relations with both Scotland and with Gaelic Irish territories. It was more of an administrative capital, and later in the period both Limerick and Galway

8. BL, Cott. MS Titus B XIII, f. 348–48v.

9. Sheehan, 'Irish towns', pp. 97–103; Canny, *Elizabethan conquest*, pp. 4–6; Treadwell, 'Irish customs', 394–97, 405–08.

enjoyed similar status under the new lords president and councils for Munster and Connacht. The established market towns of the Pale possessed historic cultural and political links with the Dublin administration but they were distinct in character, both from the capital and from each other. Some were traditional garrisons as well as commercial centres; some were declining in relative prosperity while others were more fortunate; some were more independent of local magnates, especially those which were walled and fortified, while others sought protection (and accepted its consequences) from the lords and chiefs of their region. For example, the market town of Cavan, near Gaelic Ulster, benefited from the interest of the O'Reilly chiefs who supported its annual fair. The town itself harboured both natives of Co. Cavan and the Pale. Other towns of this type included Trim, Ardee, Navan, Athboy, Dundalk, Kells, Naas and Mullingar.[10]

Beyond the Pale itself, there were clusters of towns which enjoyed the support and protection of local peers such as Ormonde. The market towns of Clonmel, Cashel, Fethard and perhaps Carrick were in this category, while other Munster town such as Kinsale, Youghal, Dungarvan, Wexford and even New Ross were prosperous port towns which preserved more substantial autonomy. More distant from the Pale, but still identified as commercial centres, were the towns of Sligo, Baltimore, Bantry, Carlingford, and perhaps Rosscarbery, while Kilmallock, Armagh and others went into further decline in the period. The earl of Desmond presided over a fair at Tralee when he came to collect his rents from Co. Kerry, while the oft-disturbed region of the Wicklow Irish saw a considerable trade with Dublin and Carrickfergus in timber. Firewood was sold by the lords in Connacht to merchants in Galway, and there is evidence of sustained commercial activity throughout the country in the early Elizabethan period.[11] Furthermore, the strengthening of some garrisons may have augmented the size and importance of towns such as Carlow. In general, however, there is too little evidence to sustain the argument that increased military activity in the period after 1560 caused the uniform decline of Irish towns. While some became depopulated, others grew and recovered. Inflation was serious, but much local trade depended more on bartering than on currency. Higher taxes and rents, compounded by the increased use of purveyance, caused grievances in certain areas but the extent of these problems is uncertain.[12] The decline of trade and the disruption due to debasement of the coinage also demand further investigation if we are to develop a more accurate picture of the Irish economy in this period.

10. Sheehan, 'Irish towns', pp. 97–112; Canny, *Elizabethan conquest*, pp. 7–9.
11. Sheehan, 'Irish towns', pp. 97–112; Canny, *Elizabethan conquest*, pp. 8–10.
12. See Ellis, *Tudor Ireland*, pp. 39, 49–50.

The Gaelic areas of Ireland in the Tudor period have been traditionally regarded as backward and uncivilized, yet they too maintained urban settlements and conducted foreign trade, as we have seen. The links between Gaelic hinterlands and the predominantly Anglo-Irish towns were many, and they were made easier by the customary employment of 'gray merchants', traders who brought products from the countryside to be exchanged for durable goods in the towns and cities. Gray merchants were active in the annual fairs and they helped to sustain a kind of mercantile comity between the cultural antipodes of Irish society. The largely agricultural sectors in the Pale and the Gaelic areas were either planted in corn or used for grazing of cattle and sheep. Tenants in the Pale included both Anglo-Irish and Gaelic settlers, and there is too little evidence to be certain that the Pale was becoming either depopulated or heavily gaelicized in this period. Disruptions to the local economy were frequent, yet there was a certain resilience characteristic of the agrarian society which encouraged adaptation, rebuilding and mobility. Gaelic regions were often dominated by local lords who built the tower houses that commanded and protected a small settlement. Even the warlords like Shane O'Neill encouraged his tenants to plant wheat and till the soil, and despite the episodes of burning crops and cattle raids, the fragile economy of Gaelic Ulster could produce a stable and fruitful supply of cattle, sheep and horses for trade outside the province. When Sydney attempted to impose a standing army in Ulster based on the composition for cess, he sought merely to provide a stabilizing element which could be self-sustaining and provide adequate revenue for the crown.[13]

The economy of mid-Tudor Ireland was under-regulated when compared with mercantilist practices in England. What is more, statutory and other limitations on trade and business were difficult to enforce and therefore largely ignored in sectors distant from the Dublin administration. Several efforts by the council in Ireland to control the cross-channel trade with English ports were resisted by shrewd merchants who pleaded the privileges of their charter or earlier mercantilist legislation.[14] In the sketch of economic conditions noted above there is no attempt to provide even a rudimentary figure for the gross national product, or its Tudor equivalent. While modern planners would find this omission fatal to any effort to estimate potential revenue to the government, sixteenth-century fiscal administrators looked to the past for their guides and expected that conditions

13. Canny, *Elizabethan conquest*, pp. 5, 10–12; Ellis, *Tudor Ireland*, pp. 40–47; O'Dowd, 'Gaelic economy and society', pp. 123–29; Brady, 'Sixteenth century Ulster', pp. 80–83. For the sources of revenue among Gaelic lords, see Simms, *Kings to warlords*, pp. 129–46.

14. PRO, SP 63/33/17–17v; 63/40/27; 63/57/30; Bodl, Carte MS 55, f. 199.

would probably remain the same. As we know, of course, Elizabethan Ireland was a troubled and unsettled society, and this common insight may help in trying to establish how and why the government in Dublin so consistently failed to meet projected revenue expectations. In a changing economy, beset by social and political turbulence of an episodic nature, and altered in fundamental ways by the restructuring of central and local government, the collection of revenue and the estimation of productivity were exceedingly difficult. The conservative and traditional frame of reference in which most Tudor administrators were trained and expected to work prevented them from imagining the permutations which they would have to confront. Their response was discouragingly predictable: send more money!

The obsolete machinery of the unreformed Irish financial adminis-tration made it no easier for its poorly trained engrossers and remem-brancers to collect the revenue. Officials of the exchequer were the most numerous of any institution of government in Dublin. Foremost among the financial officers was the vice treasurer, not least because he combined three formerly distinct positions in one. In the commis-sion of 1556, Sydney was named vice treasurer and general receiver of the profits and casual revenues of the crown. He was named separately in the same commission as treasurer at wars in Ireland.[15] These three titles gave the incumbent direct personal supervision of nearly all the revenue and expenses in Ireland, and, because he was always an Englishman after 1534 (Andrew Wyse excepted), he became an instrument of the resumption of English control of the exchequer.[16] The auditor and the vice treasurer were named directly by the queen (rather than nominated by the lord deputy and council) and they stood outside the ordinary hierarchy of offices in the structure of the exchequer as the queen's representatives in the area of finance. Subordinate to the vice treasurer was the important chief baron, and below him were the second baron and chancellor of the exchequer, who used their offices as stepping-stones to more privileged and powerful positions. The sub-structure of financial administration generally followed the English model, from the chief remembrancer and chief engrosser to the transcriptors, clerks, marshals, ushers and other functionaries.[17]

15. PRO, SP 62/1/35–36. He had an annual fee of £66 13s. 4d. as vice treasurer and a separate fee of 6s. 8d. per diem as treasurer at wars. The treasurer had become a largely honorific office after 1495 with some residual duties in litigation in the upper exchequer. After 1534, when Brabazon was named vice treasurer, the treasurer surrendered practical control over Irish financial administration. Ellis, *Reform and revival*, pp. 99–102.

16. Ellis, *Tudor Ireland*, p. 174; *Reform and revival*, pp. 99–102.

17. See PRO, SP 63/64/6–6v and Ellis, *Reform and revival*, pp. 87–98, for a fuller review of the financial administration. Ellis is particular helpful on its pro-cedures and its relationship to English practice.

The vice treasurer was an important councillor in his own right and stood third in the hierarchy of civil administration behind the lord deputy and lord chancellor. The relationship between the vice treasurer and the council epitomized the nature of conciliar responsibility for finance. But the council as a whole was designed to serve as a check on the independence of the vice treasurer in order to prevent the fiscal abuses common under Sir William Brabazon and others. Whereas the vice treasurer had full control of daily affairs in the collection of revenue, he was restricted in the area of expenditure. The council authorized all extraordinary warrants and thus, in theory, curtailed unnecessary spending. Together with their supervision of accounts through periodic audits this should have given the council a great deal of practical control of Irish finance.[18] It is doubtful whether these checks were effective in practice, however, and the periodic difficulties of Fyton and Fitzwilliam as vice treasurers suggest that conflict and censure over matters of finance were not untypical.

In general, we may say that the financial administration from 1556 to 1578 was unable to keep up with the pace of change. As costs increased, the revenue to meet them was not augmented in Ireland. This required regular subventions from England and led to several expedients (debasement, composition) which tended to exacerbate conditions in Ireland rather than improve them. Agreements such as the programme inaugurated by Sydney's second administration were quickly unravelled by political resistance to new exactions and by the fundamental defects in revenue collection itself. It was not anticipated that the efforts to improve government based on extension of common law institutions throughout the realm would lead to greatly increased costs and in some cases to aggravated political conflict. In making the commitment to enhance the constitutional position of the government, the Elizabethan policy-makers unwittingly contributed to its decline. They did so, in part, because they lacked patience and foresight, but they also failed to understand the intricate dynamics of Irish society as it emerged in the later Tudor period. As we have seen, commercial contacts and substantial trade existed in and beyond Ireland and landowners possessed enough resources to contribute to expanded revenue. And the innovations in central and local government, from the court of castle chamber to the presidencies and county sheriffs, were created in part to relieve the burden of financial subsidies coming regularly from London. But the system was undermined by lapses of support and peremptory withdrawals of funding or official recognition. As a consequence, the progress made in these areas prior to the1580s

18. PRO, SP 62/1/35–36; *Walsingham letter-bk*, pp. 106–08. Instructions to the council regularly renewed its power to authorize extraordinary warrants and to take the account of the vice treasurer annually.

was slow and rather limited. Periodic retrenchment prevented even the most thoughtful and moderate reforms from coming to fruition. In the end, the council in Ireland surrendered most of its autonomy in fiscal matters to the privy council in Westminster but this transfer of authority did nothing to improve revenue collection. The purpose here was not intrinsically a repudiation of Anglo-Irish elements in the administration but merely to plug the holes in the leaky boat of Irish finances. Unfortunately, every effort to do so seemed to intensify the problem.

HISTORICAL BACKGROUND

The medieval lordship of Ireland experienced a gradual erosion of revenue during the fourteenth century, punctuated by efforts at reform which were not, however, sustained. During periods of more energetic leadership, such as the chief governorship of William of Windsor (1369–72), annual revenue nearly doubled. Yet the resulting disturbances led to disillusionment in Westminster and the retrenchment which followed seemed to adumbrate the Tudor experience of cyclical reform and consequent retraction. In the fifteenth century, revenues were diverted to continental wars and the amounts collected in Ireland to maintain the administration continued to decline. After 1399 the chief governor rarely controlled more than 4,000 marks and Irish revenue had fallen from an average of £2,000 per annum to under £900 per annum in 1446. This was inadequate to support the small retinue of 300–400 troops under his command, so the viceroy was compelled to resort to quasi-legal expedients to support the government. In order to pay creditors, the exchequer preferred to 'assign' revenue to be collected at certain points by issuing tallies which could then be redeemed at the source. This was reasonably efficient since the currency would not have to be carried to Dublin, but this system depended on the reliability of collectors and the relative prosperity of certain districts. The government also authorized troops to be paid through a levy of purveyance, and the soldiers resorted to Gaelic practices when necessary, such as coyne and livery.[19]

Dr Ellis has argued that the late fifteenth century witnessed an important period of reform which anticipated the changes engineered under Henry VIII by Cromwell, and, in part, made them possible. In financial matters, of course, the reforms were simply a series of more stringent efforts to collect revenue and to prune expenses. As a consequence, the annual English subvention to support the government of Ireland was reduced after 1470 and eliminated by 1485. After 1460

19. Ellis, *Tudor Ireland*, pp. 22–28.

the collection of customs was improved in the Pale ports and in 1494 Lord Deputy Poynings named a searcher and two controllers for Dublin and Drogheda. The revenue from customs was increased with the introduction of poundage in 1474, a tax of 12*d.* in the pound on goods entering and leaving Ireland, which was levied for the purpose of financing the defence of the Pale. It was made a permanent tax after 1499 and the customs revenue became lucrative enough by the mid-Tudor period that it was farmed out for a rent of £320 per annum. Yet the customs administration was inefficient, often left to deputies to carry out, and eventually alienated to the towns themselves by the terms of their charters and liberties after 1569.[20] The crown lands in the Pale included twenty manors prior to 1534 and urban properties which theoretically yielded annual rents and fee farms as well. However, the royal estates were also a significant source of patronage for each chief governor and an inducement to serve in an administration notorious for its late payment of salaries and stipends. Consequently, revenue from crown properties was limited due to the alienation of certain manors and the practice of returning fee farms to the cities to enable them to erect and repair their defensive walls (murage).[21] After Poynings' parliament of 1494, the subsidy became a regular and fundamental part of crown revenue, yielding about £600 per annum from 1499 to 1536, though the yield dropped after 1532 when it was levied annually. Finally, the income from fines, escheats, livery, reliefs and wardships were collected in the courts and these 'casualties' or casual revenues fluctuated along with the ordinary profits of justice and other irregular sources of income.[22]

The period between Poynings' tenure as lord deputy and the Kildare rebellion has been treated recently as a model of effective government under the leadership of the earls of Kildare. It has been argued by Ellis and others that the Geraldine 'ascendancy' in this period was a triumph of effective aristocratic governance since it was cheap and tractable, relying on the sinews of political patronage and making few demands on the English exchequer. When Henry VIII sent the earl of Surrey to Ireland as lord deputy with a mandate to expand the territory under direct control of the Dublin administration, expenses grew exponentially and the experiment lasted but two years, from

20. Treadwell, 'Irish customs', 391–97, 406–08; Ellis, *Tudor Ireland*, pp. 170–71; *Reform and revival*, pp. 72–74. Smaller rents were collected from Limerick, Cork, Youghal, Dundalk, Carlingford, and Carrickfergus.

21. Ellis, *Tudor Ireland*, p. 171; *Reform and revival*, pp. 74–77.

22. Ellis, *Tudor Ireland*, pp. 171–73; *Reform and revival*, pp. 70–71, 80–86. Crown expenses were modest under Kildare since officials' salaries were low and the costs of defence were borne largely by the deputy himself and limited to fortifying the Pale.

1520 to 1522. The argument in favour of Kildare's low-profile viceroyalty was strengthened, in the view of some writers, by comparison with the extravagant demands for English subventions made by the earl of Surrey. When Henry VIII realized it was costing him £10,000 per annum to maintain the army, he withdrew his support of Surrey and rejected the latter's requests for additional funds and an army of 6,000 men. Kildare was returned to office and Irish government was again inexpensive and unreformed.[23] Yet the primary goal of the Surrey experiment differed from that of Kildare. If Surrey's government were evidence of the inherently defective qualities of Elizabethan administrations to come, it was also perhaps an anticipation of the model which most late sixteenth-century monarchies would adopt. The effective centralization of fiscal and other branches of administration was simply the paradigm of the Tudor era and the option of turning back to a pattern of aristocratic governance that involved but a distant relationship to the crown was not tenable after 1558.

When Thomas Cromwell turned his formidable skills to the Irish problem of the sixteenth century, a series of important reforms was inaugurated. The provenance and the impact of these changes have been debated, but there is little doubt that major initiatives were launched in the aftermath of the Kildare rebellion. Brendan Bradshaw explains the programme of reform as representative of the thinking of Palesmen and humanists who considered Irish governance prior to 1534. He argues that the 'Ordinances for the government of Ireland' provided for profound improvements, including: (1) abolition of feudal and Gaelic exactions which competed with royal prerogatives to tax; and (2) reform of the central administration leading to more efficient collection of revenue due to the crown. Cromwell sent agents and commissioners to Ireland to seek out crown lands, make annual public audits and reform the exchequer. While the king and his advisers ruled out military conquest because it would be too costly, they pursued a policy of confiscation of the estates of defeated Geraldines and their supporters in the period 1534 to 1540. These new crown lands, however, were used to reward loyal Palesmen and bureaucrats in Dublin so they added disappointingly little in practice to the coffers.[24] Ellis, on the other hand, argues that the attainders were worth only £1,250 a year to the crown and the real costs of the rebellion and its aftermath exceeded that sum. While he agrees that the Cromwellian reforms extended royal power at the expense of aristocratic independence, Ellis claims that the legacy was to increase

---

23. Ellis, *Tudor Ireland*, pp. 80–110. Surrey was sent with a large military force to stay only six months and while he increased revenue by £350 per annum, his administration cost the crown an additional £8,000 each year.

24. Bradshaw, *Irish constitutional revolution*, pp. 100–06, 114–16, 123–24.

royal commitments without a commensurate improvement in Irish revenue to pay for them.[25]

The parliament of 1536–37 passed three financial measures: the subsidy was renewed for ten years; an act for first fruits required important ecclesiastical officials to pay the first year's income from their holdings to the crown; and the estates of certain absentee land-owners were resumed to the crown.[26] A bill to suppress the monasteries in Ireland, in conformity with similar legislation in England pursuant to the reformation, was opposed and delayed for over one year. When it was finally passed in 1537 in the expectation that crown revenue would be greatly increased, the council dallied and failed to imple-ment the legislation in areas beyond the Pale. Only eight monasteries were actually suppressed at that time and the lessees were mostly Cromwellian supporters who obtained favourable terms. Thus, the one singular opportunity for financial recovery presented to the Dublin administration in the early sixteenth century was almost immediately turned into political capital. Bradshaw has shown that even later suppressions were ultimately 'profitless' to the crown. Local landowners either obtained suspensions of the law or deferred payment of rents.[27] A commission in 1537, which included the moderate reformer Sir Anthony St Leger, attempted to save money by reducing the garrison from 700 to 340 men and leasing lands to loyal military men near the borders of the Pale. However, the smaller garrison was so weakened that it could not defend the newly won crown lands, and the receipts from monastic dissolutions were barely adequate to meet mounting expenses.[28]

When St Leger became lord deputy in Ireland in 1540 for the first time, he inaugurated a policy of moderation and consensus politics which Bradshaw has approvingly labelled 'the liberal revolution'.[29] The commission sent into Ireland in that year recommended reforms in the exchequer, higher salaries for royal officials and tighter controls on rev-enue administration, but the king rejected their advice. Consequently,

25. Ellis, 'Thomas Cromwell and Ireland', 516–18.

26. Ellis, *Tudor Ireland*, pp. 131–32. The act for resumption returned to royal ownership the Shrewsbury palatinate of Wexford and the Norfolk seigniory in Carlow. Co. Kildare was restored to the position of a normal shire after the earl had illegally made it a liberty prior to 1534.

27. B. Bradshaw, *The dissolution of the religious orders in Ireland under Henry VIII* (Cambridge, 1974), pp. 61–64, 70–77, 146–57, 160–61. Monasteries in Galway, Kinsale and Youghal, for example, were not suppressed at this time.

28. Ellis, *Tudor Ireland*, pp. 133–35. Landed revenue increased from IR£400 in 1533–34 to IR£3,100 by 1537, but total revenue never matched the expected windfall from dissolutions and in the period 1537–40 receipts averaged IR£4,500 annually as against expenses of about IR£4,400.

29. Bradshaw, *Irish constitutional revolution*, pp. 189 et seq.

the administrative revolution which was nearly complete in England was not replicated in Ireland despite the clear intent to expand the scope of the crown's effective authority.[30] St Leger proceeded to govern according to a pragmatic blend of expediency and leniency which produced goodwill in the Pale but forfeited credibility in his fiscal stewardship. The policy of surrender and re-grant, for example, has been described as a fiscal failure since it produced practically no new revenue from Gaelic chiefs, and crown lands beyond the Pale were not surveyed. St Leger's government was tainted by corruption from the outset. His vice treasurer, Sir William Brabazon, produced no credible audit of his accounts for twenty years and the indebtedness reported in the first seven years of the administration was £18,640. St Leger himself was a primary beneficiary of crown lands leased on favourable terms to leading members of the government. When St Leger was returned as lord deputy in 1553, there was considerable scepticism surrounding his leadership. A commission in that year reported the undervaluing of crown lands and the large debt in the exchequer which led to the removal of the vice treasurer, Andrew Wyse. The commission of Sir William Fitzwilliam sent in October 1554 initiated an extensive review and audit of accounts and his report demonstrated the fraud, peculation and corruption that so characterized the regime. St Leger was soon recalled and his clients in the administration were politically disgraced as a result.[31] The fall from power of such an experienced statesman demonstrated the vulnerability of chief governors in Ireland. It may also help to explain the attempts by the crown to harness the reform efforts of St Leger's successors, reining in their ambitious proposals at the first sign of excessive spending.

Despite the generally barren results of St Leger's government in terms of reform, certain administrative improvements were attempted. In 1544 a clerk of first fruits was named to expedite the payment of ecclesiastical revenues, but this initiative only highlighted the general absence of new structures such as the court of first fruits or the court of wards and liveries in England. An auditor was named for Ireland in 1547 to watch over the royal interests in Irish revenue. From the creation of the office, the auditor received duplicated receipts of all revenue, kept a note of all errors and developed a system of checking leases and grants. In 1552 the auditor was named to the first regular commission of accounts, composed of leading Irish councillors. These seven men were to clear all accounts annually and they superseded the upper exchequer in financial management. It was frequently

---

30. Ellis, *Tudor Ireland*, pp. 134–35.
31. Brady, 'Government of Ireland', pp. 76–96, 103–06.

through this body of commissioners that the Irish council exercised its responsibility for financial administration. However, this rationalization and institutionalization of the fiscal mechanism did not necessarily produce either efficiency or increased revenue. The first holder of the office soon allowed himself to be seduced by various schemes for underpayment of accounts, and subsequent auditors lacked the authority to impose needed reforms. A surveyor general was appointed in 1548 to improve the collection of rents due from crown lands, but no material advantage accrued to the government from this step.[32] Increasingly, the policy-makers in Westminster relied upon commissions of inquiry to look into the revenue administration since the annual deficits clearly demonstrated that optimistic forecasts of improvements were not realistic.[33]

The government of St Leger in Ireland has been credited with maintaining a peaceful and benign superintendence of affairs during a period of crises in England and elsewhere.[34] Yet his admirable restraint in the use of force and coercion must be weighed against his tolerance for, and encouragement of, rampant corruption at the highest levels of his administration. This undermined the credibility of the crown, weakened the financial basis of government, and caused his successors to seek new measures to balance the revenue and expenses in order to forestall the visits of sceptical commissioners. Their inability to do this is perhaps traceable to the discredit which befell the St Leger administration and tainted the efforts of succeeding chief governors.

THE COUNCIL AND ROYAL FISCAL POLICY

By 1566 the shortfall of Irish revenue below expenses was so great that the council constantly had to appeal to England for more money. This was made worse by the impact of rising prices and increasing expenses due to the expansion of military and provincial administration. One of the motivations behind the efforts to extend the perimeter of its authority was a determination by the government to

32. D.B. Quinn, 'Tudor rule in Ireland in the reigns of Henry VII and Henry VIII, with special reference to the Anglo-Irish financial administration' (unpublished Ph.D. thesis, University of London, 1934), pp. 23–24, 436, 538–48. Quinn first stated the argument that Tudor rule in Ireland rested on the resumption of direct control over the Irish exchequer.

33. Ellis, *Tudor Ireland*, p. 175. Ellis has shown that revenue forecasts averaged about £11,000 per annum from 1564 to 1585, yet the actual receipts remained under half of that figure (in 1540: £4,500; in 1558–59: £5,395; in 1561–62: £4,085; from 1555 to 1570 they averaged £4,150). The deficit soared from 1542 (when it was £4,700) to 1565 (when it averaged £21,400 per annum).

34. See the works of Bradshaw, *Irish constitutional revolution*; Brady, 'Government of Ireland'; Ellis, *Tudor Ireland*.

augment the revenue. This accelerated the vicious circle of Irish finance. The effort to enlarge the area of fiscal control by the crown meant, in turn, increased costs for the military, for provincial councils, for wardens and seneschals, for transportation and other incidental charges. Before the new sources of income could be identified and charges subsequently imposed on landowners and others, the policy-makers grew impatient with the lack of progress and called for cut-backs in the very administrative organs which were designed to help produce the money to pay for their work. Quinn has argued that the turning-point in Irish finance came as early as 1538 when it was determined that new revenue must be sought outside the Pale.[35] Yet the Elizabethan administrators and their predecessors failed to accept that enhanced income would only come in gradually, after new struc-tures based on English models were put into place. Sydney's hope that the provincial councils could ultimately be made to pay their own way through augmented revenues was never realized. But the alternatives of financial stagnation and a dangerous degree of autonomy for the greater part of the island were equally unacceptable, for both con-stitutional and financial reasons, so the basic commitment to extend the control of the government was continued.

The fundamental sources of Irish financial administration were fixed and were limited largely to the Pale. In 1580 the commission to authorize the receiver of the queen's casual revenues used the following categories to identify the extraordinary receipts of the crown: (1) parliamentary subsidies; (2) proffers of sheriffs and receipts of issues; (3) sales of wards, accounts of feodaries, fines for livery of land and marriages; (4) first fruits and twentieths and the accounts of ecclesiastical courts; (5) profits of the royal courts; (6) accounts of the hanaper; (7) forfeitures of recognizances, of merchandise, and of fugitives or felons; (8) fines for homage, pardons, etc.; and (9) the composition for bonaught of galloglasses.[36] From other sources we may add the arrearages from money owed to the Irish exchequer and the various loans contracted both in England and Ireland.

The revenue from Ireland was not growing to meet the increasing expenses of the government, although the sources of income were gradually changing. A note drawn up in 1575 by the auditor, Thomas

35. Quinn, 'Tudor rule', p. 441.
36. PRO, SP 63/73/49. The extraordinary receipts were those which varied in amount from year to year, often depending on the occurrence of casual events such as a wardship or marriage. These levies were often also called casualties, but extraordinary receipts encompassed more than these, for the payment of subsidy and sheriffs' proffers were annual, if not regular, events. Ordinary receipts were incomes from fixed rentals and the like. Ellis has estimated the annual income from wards and liveries at £105; from judicial profits at £150–350; and from absentees' lands at about £150. Ellis, *Tudor Ireland*, p. 172.

Jenyson, compared the revenue of Elizabeth with that of Henry VIII and demonstrated the static condition of the Irish receipts. His account showed that the income for one year under Henry VIII was £10,394 16s. 4d., while under Elizabeth in 1575 it was only £11,518 18s.[37] Jenyson also found that the traditional ordinary receipts, often called 'the old inheritance,' were slowly declining, although they still formed three-fourths of the entire annual income. An account of about 1559 described the ordinary receipts as the lands attainted and escheated to the crown, the land of suppressed monasteries, the land of the dissolved church of St Patrick's and the 'old inheritance'. The latter was, of course, the estates belonging traditionally to the sovereign. This revenue amounted to £12,145 out of a total of £14,566 for the year.[38]

The extraordinary revenue was growing and certain levies such as the impost of wines partially mitigated the effect of declining revenues from the ordinary receipts. While certain income from abbeys and spiritual estates grew larger, the revenue from attainted lands decreased as the estates were returned to the Geraldines and others. Profits from the lands of St Patrick's were returned to the church or granted away, so the net effect of these alterations in the sources of its income left the government with accelerating costs and the stubborn refusal of the exchequer to yield more money. Even worse, the accounts for 1575 to 1578 showed a decline, averaging but £4,866 during Sydney's second administration.[39]

The result of this arrested development in the gross receipts of Irish government was an increasing dependence on the English exchequer to make up the difference between receipts and expenses. From 1543 there was a generally upward trend in this dependency, although in any given year the trend might be temporarily reversed. Fluctuations might be explained by changes in the internal military or political situation, or by the determination of the queen to hold the line on Irish expenditure after authorizing an expensive new initiative. The average commitment of English revenue to the Irish

37. BL, Cott. MS Titus B XII, ff. 325–29. The date for Henry VIII is not given, but judging from the returns for suppressed abbeys and spiritualities (£4,937) it must be after 1539. See Bradshaw, *Dissolution of religious orders in Ireland*, pp. 98–130. The account for one year from Michaelmas 1562 showed £10,943 from Irish receipts. *Cal. Carew MSS, 1515–74*, pp. 364–65. Ellis, however, uses much lower figures, suggesting that estimates of £11,000 masked the actual receipts of crown revenue which averaged £4,250 in practice. Ellis, *Tudor Ireland*, p. 175.

38. BL, Add. MS 4,767, ff. 73–74.

39. PRO, SP 63/64/17v. The largest annual revenue in those years was £6,499 13s. 11d. The infusion of English revenue was nearly four times that from Ireland. Canny estimates the discrepancy thus: £31,847 from England, £4,305 from Ireland. Canny, *Elizabethan conquest*, p. 155.

government was over £20,000 in each year from 1556 to 1578. The account of Robert Holdiche, who was Vice Treasurer Sydney's deputy, showed that £40,000 was sent to the Irish exchequer from the mint in the Tower of London between 1556 and 1559. This was an average of about £11,428 per annum.[40] As the reign of Elizabeth progressed, this figure was at first doubled and finally quadrupled within twenty years. A memorandum of 29 September 1574 summarized the annual payments made out of English receipts to Ireland from Michaelmas 1558 to Michaelmas 1574. These payments averaged £22,798 per annum. During the last four years, however, from 1570/71 to 1573/74, the average commitment of English revenue jumped to £32,099.[41] After this increase, the government of Sydney apparently held the line with an average of £22,008 14s. per annum for just over three years (1575–1578).[42]

The Munster rebellion required such an enormous infusion of new monies into Ireland that the entire infrastructure of Irish government was exposed to intensified scrutiny and criticism. Support for Sydney's administration had already collapsed when the rebellion became truly dangerous and required revenue from England on a scale never before witnessed in Ireland. From 19 August 1579 to 8 August 1580 the English privy council authorized £76,765 to reinforce the Dublin government and protect the interests of the crown.[43] The interesting

40. H.M.C., *De L'Isle and Dudley MSS*, i, 373. The account of Sydney for 1556–58 (p. 364) contradicts the Holdiche account, but it seems to be out of harmony with all the other figures for the period. If the average English subvention for those years of £28,510 were correct, it would not have been reached again until 1571/72. This result would be at odds with all the other evidence from Quinn's researches as well as the work done here. Another account of Sydney from 1 May 1556 to 14 September 1559 tends to corroborate the first Sydney account, showing the total treasure received from England as £113,246 15s. 7d., an annual average of about £34,317 per annum. See PRO, SP 63/1/181. Therefore, even though the Holdiche account seems more credible, it would be best to withhold judgment on these years pending the results of further investigation. Canny uses an estimate of £18,975 during the 1560s. Canny, *Elizabethan conquest*, p. 155.

41. PRO, SP 63/47/170–71. Receipts from the exchequer were the principal source of payments for Ireland after 1544. See Quinn, 'Tudor rule', pp. 447–48. The generally upward direction of payments may also be shown from the fact that, after 1565–66, the amount was never below £15,000. In addition, the court of wards contributed £21,145 over the sixteen-year period. Other revenue may be unaccounted for, so this is only an estimate of annual revenue committed to Ireland.

42. BL, Add. MS 4,763, f. 266. The figures were: £19,150 (1575–76); £31,108 (1576–77); £15,255 (1577–78). Another summary of Sydney's receipts and expenses gives an average per annum of £19,605 for just under three years. PRO, SP 63/64/17–17v. Canny, however, extends the period to 1579 (the first year of rebellion) and his estimate of average English subventions is £31,847 annually. Canny, *Elizabethan conquest*, p. 155.

43. PRO, SP 63/75/47.

paradox which emerged was eloquent of the queen's intentions: she would never authorize enough money to reform and restructure her Irish dominion but she would spend both money and blood to preserve her sovereignty there. The near doubling of the previous highest sum (£43,304 in 1573/74) represented an increase so large that all hopes of making Ireland self-sufficient by using the models of aristocratic governance (Kildare's), benevolent paternalism (St Leger's) or moderate reform (Sussex and Sydney's) were dashed.[44] This was a decisive break from the past, both in terms of military requirements and fiscal pressures, yet the succeeding years offered no evidence that this was recognized in Westminster. The half-measures which were employed in Ireland after 1583 virtually guaranteed that a decade later new rebellion would sweep away the unfinished attempts at improvement. However, the dramatic increase in expenditure in 1579 gives the period 1556 to 1578 a unity within which we may see how the pragmatism of Tudor statesmen responded to opportunities for reform.

Although it is difficult to reconstruct the exact state of the Irish indebtedness, it is possible to survey the kinds of expenses the government regularly faced. Many of these were difficult to control, the kinds of casual expenses which accumulate unpredictably. But the bulk of the annual deficit resulted from the maintenance of the military establishment in Ireland. During most years, the combined diets and fees of the government officials plus the wages of the garrison amounted to 75% of the annual expenditure.[45] The garrison included the warders, Irish kerne, ministers of the ordnance and others, as well as the captains and their troops. The other expenses were quite miscellaneous, but they regularly included the following items: (1) pensioners, especially superannuated soldiers and the ex-religious; (2) annuities, particularly the large sums paid to Anglo-Irish magnates; (3) building and repairs, notably for town walls, bridges and castles; (4) payments to itinerant commissioners and to messengers; (5) old debts, carried over from former years; (6) transportation for grain, for troops and for the posts; (7) victualling for the garrison; (8) and other extraordinary payments such as hiring of boats.[46]

The fluctuations in the yearly expenses of the Irish government make it somewhat misleading to refer to the state of finance as the

44. PRO, SP 63/47/170v.

45. See, for example, H.M.C., *De L'Isle and Dudley MSS*, i, 379 for Sydney's account of 1556–59. For the years 1575–79 see PRO, SP 63/64/17. Here the ordinary wages for three years were £57,523 while the extraordinary charges were £21,401, a ratio of nearly 3:1.

46. The book of accounts for 29 March 1561 has a virtually complete summary of the expenses of the government for a year. See PRO, SP 63/3/76–77. See also the detailed Fitzwilliam account books in PRO, SP 65, especially vol. vii.

annual deficit. A shortfall in receipts vis-à-vis expenses was expected each year and the requests for revenue from England were made regularly. However, the infusions of English money, when they came, usually were not enough to offset the expenses which had grown up in the meantime, so the government was, in effect, always in debt. It is often impossible to estimate annual averages from the surviving evidence, because the arrears were carried over from year to year. Accounts were usually made on the basis of several years' indebtedness, and complicated by imprests and loans contracted in the interim to stem the tide of approaching insolvency. Besides, the surviving accounts from the State Papers are often contradictory, in that the expenses itemized vary considerably in comparable records. The cost of governing Ireland from 1556 to 1578 may be roughly estimated at between £23,000 and £26,000 a year, and it may have been much higher. The summaries of several years' indebtedness indicate a backlog of over £30,000 which, in any one year, would have a greater impact than the annual expenses would suggest. One reason for such a state of arrearage was the common financial expedient of the full pay, a complete payment on all wage accounts to bring the arrears up to date. A full pay was usually made on the arrival of a new lord deputy, but otherwise it was lamentably infrequent. On 31 July 1565 the account of Sir William Fitzwilliam was taken which revealed a debt of some £32,553 since the last full pay made on 24 March 1560.[47]

A summary of the deficits in this period will help to demonstrate the nature of the fiscal crisis. Both Sussex and Sydney began their respective administrations with programmes of reform which were based upon interlocking policies of garrisoning troops, expanding common law administration and financial stringency. Fitzwilliam, on the other hand, was seen as an interim governor and he offered no plans or principles to guide government spending. In all three administrations, however, the costs of government outstripped the expectations and the income of the incumbents. Sussex (as Lord Fitzwalter in 1556) commenced his government with ambitious proposals to widen the effective territory under the queen's control, and he reckoned upon an initial deficit in order to pay for garrisoning and colonization. Indeed, he proclaimed that the council would pay all the debts of the former deputy, and the council ordered St Leger to put up a recognizance of £5,000 as surety for his repayment in England of the outstanding sum of £3,214.[48] He envisaged that increased revenue would be available to pay for the larger military establishment within two years, but the size of the army was increased from

47. *Fitzwilliam accounts*, ed. Longfield, pp. 111–13.
48. RIA, MS 24 F 17, ff. 5v–6.

500 troops to 1,500 troops by the middle of 1557 and one year later the number stood at about 2,500 men.[49] Fluctuations in the size of the establishment continued, but the protracted struggle against Shane O'Neill exhausted the treasury and the patience of the queen. Sussex relied on irregular payments from England to maintain his government, and the average indebtedness was rising steadily from 1556 to 1564 when he left Ireland. The average expenses were well over £23,000 per annum and in some years they reached £34,000. From 1560 to 1565 the annual debt averaged about £6,000–7,000. Estimates of crown revenue in 1560 anticipated income of £12,000, yet in the entire period the average revenue actually realized was only £4,500 per annum.[50] The required infusions of English treasure set a precedent for the period that no lord deputy could reverse, despite the repeated attempts of Sussex's successors.

The first administration of Sydney in 1565 came on the heels of a hostile commission of inquiry led by Sir Nicholas Arnold. The partial success of this sceptical inquisition raised doubts about relying too heavily on English subventions to support grandiose military expeditions by the chief governor. Sydney was thus unable to secure the generous terms on which Sussex commenced his government. He promised to be more economical and to use a smaller garrison which would cost only £1,288 per month. He committed himself to make no increase in the military establishment without approval from Westminster and he forecast that the cost of his administration would be only £15,500 per annum.[51] When he was returned to Ireland as lord deputy in 1568 his government was then in arrears, but new political crises required a senior military leader to confront the threat of rebellion. The garrison was nevertheless capped at 1,500 men and Sydney was to make no new grants or leases without a new survey. By 1571 the rebellions had destroyed all his sanguine projections for fiscal stringency. The army had been increased to over 2,000 men and campaigns had brought the annual charges of government to nearly £40,000 per annum. The debt owed by the government was £61,135 in 1571 and this increased in the next year to £73,154. Furthermore,

49. Brady, 'Government of Ireland', p. 131.

50. *Fitzwilliam accounts*, ed. Longfield, pp. 59, 111–113; BL, Add. MS 4,767, ff. 73–75; H.M.C., *De L'Isle and Dudley MSS*, i, 372. The average expense for the years 1559–1566 was £23,282 according to Fitzwilliam's account in PRO, SP 63/1/181. The book of accounts for 1561, an enrolled document of considerable detail, showed an indebtedness of £34,194, but the varying terms of each entry, ranging from six months to over two years, render it difficult to use for a yearly deficit. PRO, SP 63/3/76–77. See also Brady, 'Government of Ireland', pp. 131–32, who estimates the annual cost of government from 1556 to 1565 at £35,777.

51. Brady, 'Government of Ireland', p. 180.

the long-delayed auditors' report on Fitzwilliam's ten-year account was produced in 1570 and it showed a prodigal expenditure of £348,000 throughout the period.[52] Sydney's removal was a foregone conclusion.

During the interim administration of the hapless Sir William Fitzwilliam, the garrison was reduced to 1,300 men. The new lords president attempted to govern the provinces while the inept colonists in Ulster merely aggravated political friction there and added almost £130,000 to the queen's indebtedness.[53] Fitzwilliam was certainly the most desperate of chief governors and he pleaded for four years alternately to be released from office or else to have a substantial sum to correct the deficit. By 1574 he claimed that the government had lost its credit in Dublin through heavy borrowing and pleaded for more English revenue.[54] In May 1575 he was plainly beside himself, complaining that he had used up all the money available just to victual the soldiers for April and that now he expected a mutiny. He was unable to obtain money from either the Pale or the city of Dublin, so he resorted to an unusual expedient. He said, 'But when bothe fayled me, I was driven to make a loan emongst all the Counsell; and so every man made owte a share, where by this danger is avoyded, and the victualling furnished for one month more'.[55] Fitzwilliam clearly saw this as a last resort and the practice could not have been common, but it is instructive that when in dire straits the government could be relied on, in effect, to save itself. Nine days after this letter, on 12 May, Fitzwilliam concluded another missive with this appeal: 'We are here ronne so fare into Debte as wee are ronne cleane out of creditt, so as we muste truste no more to our olde shiftes, but onely and flattly to that which comith thence.'[56]

When Sydney was returned for his last administration in 1575, he engaged in a covenant with the queen to provide economical reform

---

52. PRO, SP 63/34/56; BL, Cott. MS Titus B XIII, f. 186; Brady, 'Government of Ireland', pp. 197–207.

53. Ellis, *Tudor Ireland*, p. 268.

54. PRO, SP 63/44/103. The council wrote in 1574 that they had borrowed heavily to pay for defence of the Pale and the victualling of troops, both '. . . emongest some of our selfes . . .' and from the mayor and city of Dublin. Other debts were contracted from nobles and gentlemen outside Ireland, and the council requested permission to use money on hand to pay off these debts and thus restore the credit of the government. PRO, SP 63/44/67.

55. PRO, SP 63/51/3. Fitzwilliam further explained that the last sum sent from England, £6,000, was used up in paying discharged soldiers and for other causes.

56. Bodl, Carte MS 55, f. 7. What is needed is a study of the full indebtedness of the government at this period and the extent of their reliance on the Dublin merchants for short-term loans. However, a study such as Robert Ashton's *The crown and the money market 1603–1640* (Oxford, 1960) is clearly beyond the scope of this work and almost certainly too ambitious for the surviving evidence.

based on a compact with the Palesmen. He promised to eliminate all traditional forms of taxation in kind in return for an agreement to provide regular taxation, a 'composition for the cess' (see below for the political implications of this policy). Sydney was forced to trim his original proposal to a garrison of 1,100 men and an annual charge to the queen of only £20,000 to be paid in regular instalments. Despite the optimistic remark of Francis Agarde to Walsingham in 1576 that the rents and revenues had increased dramatically, the promise of systematic reform was once again undermined by events.[57] Sydney was unable to get the hard-headed Vice Treasurer Fyton, for example, to go along with his positive projections of revenue. Unlike the other councillors, Fyton balked at signing one of several articles intended for Cecil on the state of the realm. The third article held that the revenue had increased and Fyton set out to demonstrate that this was not the case. He noted that the receipts from Munster and Connacht had actually declined in the past two years and he had no reason to expect new sources of revenue there. Further, he challenged the notion that the composition in lieu of cess represented a net gain in revenue, and averred he would not acknowledge any increase in revenue '. . . tyll I see yt come in'.[58]

By the end of 1577, Sydney's administration was almost £9,000 in debt, politically disgraced at court and betrayed by its own supporters.[59] Just as Drury was about to take the helm as lord justice in 1578, the queen made a feeble attempt to rescue the situation, promising to pay only some of the old debts. Rather than the blanket payment promised in 1556, the council was ordered to determine which creditors were most pressing and '. . . metest speedely to be paid . . .' so they would not make their claims directly to the queen or the lord treasurer in England.[60] The persistent failures to develop new sources of revenue or to control expenses have been explained as the inevitable consequences of an extravagant military policy and a feckless political dialogue with the leading men of the Pale. But it is

57. PRO, SP 63/55/169.

58. PRO, SP 63/60/69v. Only with reluctance did he sign another article affirming that he expected the revenue from Munster and Connacht to pay for the cost of the garrisons there, although he noted the respective deficits were then at £1,200 and £2,500 per annum. PRO, SP 63/60/70. In defence of his projections Sydney had made a summary of lands and revenue recovered by him for the crown during his two administrations. He claimed that these totalled £10,672. PRO, SP 63/64/1–3.

59. PRO, SP 63/64/17v. Fluctuations in the debt showed again some inconsistency. The debt for 1576–77 was £6,051 in comparison to a debt of £1,556 in 1575/76 and £1,343 in 1577/78. Brady, 'Government of Ireland', pp. 208, 221, 239.

60. BL, Cott. MS Titus B XII, ff. 379v–80.

important to examine other reasons for the chain of political losses resulting from the inability of chief governors to rule Ireland economically. Despite the lack of a comprehensive study of financial administration and the paucity of systematic data for fiscal management, we must analyze why so many proposed solutions for ending the deficit came to naught.

Chronic deficiencies in funds for Ireland were aggravated by the necessary lag in time between a demonstrated need for more revenue and the mobilization of English resources to transport the money to Ireland. In addition, the smaller Irish receipts were always very slow in arriving at the exchequer. In between full pays for the garrison and officials, and in lieu of imprests from money on hand, the council could borrow money from Dublin merchants to meet immediate needs of the government. This expedient was certainly used by every lord deputy and council but there is too little evidence to indicate much about the nature of the loans, their duration, their terms, and the record of the government in repaying them. In a letter of 24 March 1567 the queen remonstrated with Sydney against the practice of '. . . dyvers emprests made there by your ordre by certein merchants who come hither at tymes unlooked for with your letters requyring very speedy payment . . .'.[61]

The largest structural defect in the financial administration was the unreformed Irish exchequer. Its officials were regularly accused of corruption and ineptitude, and the problem was acute even at the beginning of the period. Fitzwalter was ordered to correct the abuses and disorders in the exchequer in 1556 and his instructions set the tone of official exasperation. It was there implied that the cause of the losses of revenue from wardship, liveries, sales of wood, customs, subsidies, and other accustomed profits was negligence rather than extortion or peculation. Article 5 summed up the situation thus:

In our Exchequer also are some disorders, and by negligence of that our Court, the arrearages of our rents and revenues are notably great, and have so encreased that much thereof is become desperate and illeviable, where, if our officers there had been diligent to call upon the accomptants and farmers, no such arrearages should now remain.[62]

Elizabeth required the council to resolve the problem of declining receipts from the courts, from unprofitable leases and from certain

---

61. *Sidney S.P.*, p. 53. At the least, the queen was concerned about the unpredictability of sudden visits to Westminster from anxious Dublin creditors. On a similar occasion, the council lacked money to pay the expenses of Irish magnates travelling to London. They decided to take 200 marks from certain merchants of Dublin to be repaid to those merchants in London. PRO, SP 63/13/67.

62. *Cal. Carew MSS, 1515–74*, p. 254.

casual revenue. She delivered the following tirade to the council in 1559: '. . . there is not one of that counsaill, but must confesse, that the revenue of that land hath thes many yeres daily decayed, and the charge of gouvernaunce daily encreased, which be twoo thinges muche contrary to good gouvernaunce.'[63] Even with regular annual surveys, the growth of Irish receipts had to depend on poorly trained clerks working in the exchequer, so the privy council in England tried to amend this with detailed instructions to the lord deputy and council. The first instruction to Sussex in 1559 was to acquaint every officer of the exchequer with his precise duties and obligations and the manner in which he had failed to meet them. The queen sent along with Sussex the book of the exchequer procedure in England, thinking that it would instruct them in the arcane mysteries of the treasury.[64] By comparison, the English exchequer was reformed in 1554 after the amalgamation of revenue courts there, yet the crown generally appointed only 29 of the 94 official places. Mid-level clerks efficiently ran the day-to-day operations of the exchequer, but the process was still cumbersome, prone to the encroachment of the patronage system and dominated by an oligarchy of well-entrenched families and their kinfolk. Consequently, it would be misleading to suggest that Irish practice deviated entirely from the English paradigm of intensely personal government which was improved only gradually by piecemeal reforms.[65]

In 1560 the queen sent Gilbert Gerrard, the attorney general in England, on a mission to Ireland to devise orders and rules for the better administration of Irish finance. After conferring with the lord deputy and council, Gerrard made up and signed a book of instructions for the proper management of the exchequer.[66] However, even the personal intervention of an experienced English official had little effect. When Sir William Gerrard was sent to Ireland as lord chancellor in 1575 he was handed the responsibilities formerly assigned to

63. PRO, SP 63/1/125. See also *Cal. Carew MSS, 1515-74*, pp. 254-55; PRO, SP 63/24/85; 63/14/7.

64. PRO, SP 63/1/126, 130. The book was signed by principal officers of the English exchequer and contained the form of each office. Brady argues that senior officials were either disinterested (Sussex) or distracted (Fitzwilliam) by the burden of other responsibilities, leaving the clerks unsupervised. Brady, 'Government of Ireland', pp. 47-50; 'Court, castle and country', pp. 33-35.

65. J.D. Alsop, 'Government, finance and the community of the exchequer', in C. Haigh, ed., *The reign of Elizabeth I* (Athens, Georgia, 1985), pp. 101-04, 109-17, 122-23.

66. BL, Add. MS 4,767, ff. 128-30. Basically the instructions required semi-annual accounts to be made up by each official so that arrears would not build up. In 1562 new instructions called for an investigation of exchequer accounts and an attempt was made to assess the effects of Gerrard's visit. PRO, SP 63/6/142.

special commissioners. He described his extra duties thus: '. . . her Majestie chardged me I should have eye to the state of that lande and to her revenue there, sayinge she would looke to me to have answers as well defectes of governement and waste of her threasure as she would from her deputie . . . .'[67] Ultimately, a recommendation was made to discharge certain officials of the exchequer whose fees could not be justified by the amount of work they performed. In 1579 it was proposed to allow the offices of chief and second engrosser and chief and second chamberlain to lapse upon the death or removal of their holders. A parting shot was levelled at the surveyor general whose continuance in office was also questioned.[68] Negligence, as opposed to corruption, was therefore the typical charge. As in England, however, patronage and its consequent partner, political faction, suffused the exchequer. The private clerks and deputies who carried on much of the work were clients of powerful officials and allied in a network of mingled public and private interests.[69]

The instructions sent to the council in Ireland included not only the full articulation of the rules and procedures of the exchequer officials, but some reforms aimed at other financial agents as well. Tax farmers, tenants, customers and others persistently evaded the performance of their obligations and the orders sent to the council required a better accounting from them. The instructions of 1556 particularly addressed the abuses of customers, saying, 'We will also that our said Barons and officers of our Exchequer shall especially see that all customers and searchers do make their accompts duly, and put into the said court good sureties for the true administration of their offices in their own persons . . .'.[70] In 1569 the council was ordered to resume lands, liberties, franchises, abbeys and other estates in law which had been divested from the queen, presumably due to the corruption or complicity of local officials.[71] Finally, in the systematic inquiry which was made into the running of the exchequer in 1579, several commissions were named to deal with defaults and arrearages of the tax farmers. Those within the Pale were to be called in to Dublin and to yield up a bond for the payment of their rent.

67. 'Gerrard's report', ed. McNeill, 94.

68. *Walsingham letter-bk*, pp. 76–77.

69. Brady, 'Government of Ireland', pp. 49–54; Alsop, 'Government and finance', pp. 103, 112–13, 117.

70. *Cal. Carew MSS, 1515–74*, pp. 255–57. Treadwell has shown that the appointment of officials of the customs (customers, searchers, controllers) was gradually alienated from the Dublin administration and that port towns in the Elizabethan period often kept customs revenue for themselves. 'Irish customs', 391–93, 406–08.

71. PRO, SP 63/27/22.

Outside the Pale enforcement of the lease agreements was even more troublesome, so an itinerant commission was named to investigate and to collect outstanding debts from farmers beyond the five counties.[72] This system was more clear-sighted and more systematic than any before it, but it had even less chance of success since the Munster rebellion was gathering strength just at this time.

A major aspect of official corruption was the granting of extraordinary payments for rewards, gifts, buildings, repairs and other services which were not warranted by the queen or her designated officials. This manner of peculation and illegal patronage was the subject of several orders designed to place effective curbs on unusual charges. Perhaps mindful of the onerous legacy of the previous administration, Sussex in 1558 asked for an augmentation of conciliar power so that these payments could be stopped. His request stated, 'I and the Counsell to graunt warrants Joyntly for all extraordinary charge to be thoughte mete'.[73] In 1578 the queen gave instructions to the lord justice and council to regulate all further extraordinary warrants over the sum of £10. The chief governor was in those cases to call together

. . . all those of our Counsell beeinge within viij milles of the place where you or eyther of you shalbe, soe as you ever have the number of fower besydes yourself to conferre and consyder of the demaunde before you graunte anie allowances, and then callynge before you the partie demaundinge the allowance, throughtlie [sic] dulye and consyderatelie, to examine the cause, wherin yf you shall doubt of the trueth of anie thinge necessarie to be consydered of towchinge the grauntinge or denieing of the allowance demaunded you may for your further satysfaction, examine the partie or anie other upon their corporall oathes . . . And we will that our treasorer shall have noe allowance upon his accompte for anie paymente contrarie to this order.[74]

It may be doubted whether this cumbersome procedure was frequently employed as a check on the corruption of officials, although the substance of the order was renewed about 1585. The council was here seen as the last resort of official rectitude and was strongly admonished to take this obligation seriously.[75]

The councillors were not always scrupulous in their financial dealings, however, and occasionally the instructions of the queen concentrated on their own activities. Few were ever caught out in blatant malversation, although Nicholas White was accused by the attorney

72. *Walsingham letter-bk*, pp. 71–73.
73. PRO, SP 62/2/49.
74. BL, Cott. MS Titus B XII, f. 382.
75. BL, Add. MS 4,786, ff. 39–40.

general in 1577 of failure to produce his accounts as master of the rolls
for three full years. The most common indictment of the councillors
was that they enriched themselves through the perquisites of office
which they controlled. The venerable former lord chancellor, Thomas
Cusake, had acquired sixty-one receiverships from the dissolution of
the monasteries by 1540, for example.[76] An ingenious tax levied on
wine brought to Ireland in alien ships also resulted in an exemption
for '. . . everie of the privie Counsell three tonnes yerelie free and
dischardged of the said ympost or custome'.[77] When the councillors
obtained an estate by virtue of the influence they wielded, they scarcely
improved the general financial conditions by withholding the rental
for years at a time. The preamble to an instruction of 1585 suggested
that this practice had become common, declaring that,

. . . a great parte of the Revenues have bene hitherto by Deputies and
Commissions devised to suche as have beene in former tyme Councillors
ther, so as they and their heires and executors have bene bolde to retayne
theire rentes longe behind hand and for lack of demaundes and distresses
or entries for forfeytures greate arrearages accrued . . .[78]

The councillors found other ways to enrich themselves. They made
demands for a large 'entertainment', or provisioning, whenever they
went on commission, a practice for which they were chastised in an
order of 1586.[79] An amount of peculation was to be expected in this
age, of course, and the exchequer provided the largest number of
official places for the operation of political faction. Brady has argued
that Anglo-Irish officials saw the Dublin administration as an extension
of their own local government and matters of self-interest therefore
always preceded the carrying out of crown policy.[80]

For the most part, there were no clever new initiatives designed to
raise the quality of administrative performance and prevent misfeasance
in office. Rather, the council was called upon to offer a more systematic
and rigorous oversight of the financial apparatus through a series of
commissions of inquiry. The most active of these was the commission
of accounts. It had been established as a permanent board as early as
1546 to oversee Irish finance, and its membership was invariably
drawn from the council.[81] The personnel varied from the 1559 body

76. Quinn, 'Tudor rule', p. 427.
77. PRO, SP 63/27/23.
78. BL, Add. MS 4,786, f. 39.
79. ibid., f. 22.
80. Brady, 'Court, castle and country', pp. 29, 35–36, 41.
81. Quinn, 'Tudor rule', p. 546. Commissions of 1537 and 1540 set the pattern for
    the resumption of English control over Irish finance and led to the board of
    commissioners. See ibid., pp. 433, 456–459.

of nine men to the forum of 1568, which included only the lord chancellor, the chief baron, the master of the rolls and the auditor.[82] The commissioners were instructed to call before them the vice treasurer and his books, rolls and other documents; to hear and determine his accounts; and to record the results in two books, one to be delivered to the exchequer and the other to be used to discharge the debts.[83] The accounts of the master of the ordnance and the victualler had to be taken first. To illustrate how cumbersome and ineffective this procedure was, the commissioners were required in 1585 to take the account of the vice treasurer for the past six years, and thereafter to take the accounts annually.[84] It is almost certain that annual accounts were never achieved in this period.

Another major reason for declining revenue was the persistent failure to lease crown estates at their full market value. The office of surveyor general was created in 1548 to take regular surveys of the crown lands and to keep his records in the exchequer, and the council was periodically instructed to support the work of the surveyor with a commission. In 1559, for example, a commission was authorized to make new leases based on the most recent survey and to recover lands previously leased at below the market value as occasion permitted.[85] In some cases, they were ordered to seek out means to have the lease set aside and then to renegotiate it on better terms, a device which might be called 'sanctioned' corruption today.[86] In May 1568 another commission was required to lease land within the Pale '. . . or any part of our contreys where our lawe hath had usuall execution', with a reservation of at least one year's rent to the queen.[87] Similar commissions in 1576, always headed by six or more councillors, were directed to seek out concealed lands of monasteries and to recover

82. PRO, SP 63/1/77–78; 63/25/78; 65/7/1–2v. See also BL, Cott. MS Titus B XIII, f. 394–94v. The 1559 commission may have been seen as too unwieldy since later bodies were limited to about five members. The 1559 board included second level administrators such as the second baron, the chief remembrancer and the chancellor of the exchequer. This pattern, too, was not followed. Only the chief baron and the auditor were named to every commission.

83. PRO, SP 63/25/78.

84. BL, Cott. MS Titus B XIII, f. 394.

85. PRO, SP 63/1/110, 126. Decayed revenues were blamed largely on the liberal grants made in England at values below the survey. To remedy this, the privy council recommended the making of new leases at a higher rent with the inducement of a longer lease. Also cited in the decay of revenue was the devaluation of property through rebellion or devastation by roving bands and the continuation of a devalued rent after the property was restored to full productive capacity. *Walsingham letter-bk*, pp. 69–70.

86. PRO, SP 63/2/39.

87. PRO, SP 63/24/85.

debts due to the queen.[88] The council was thus directly involved in the surveying and leasing of crown estates and the queen made it responsible for improving the profitability of the crown lands. This was another example of conciliar management of finance in which the council's independent authority to act on the queen's behalf suffered under the constant pressure to augment the revenue.

One notable attempt to secure reliable figures from an independent account resulted in a spectacular failure and scuttled the administration of Sussex. According to Dr Brady, the Dudley faction at court insisted on a full audit of the army's accounts after Sussex had maintained a military establishment of over 2,000 men for several years. Sir Nicholas Arnold was named to head a commission in 1562 which produced convincing evidence of corruption and negligence in the army and discredited the Sussex regime.[89] In October 1563 Arnold returned to Ireland with Thomas Wrothe and William Dixe to conduct a comprehensive account of the administration, including the musters, the arrearages and the profits owed to the crown. Dixe was charged with auditing the account of the vice treasurer in particular. He estimated the crown's debt at between £30,000 and £40,000 after a year of inquiries punctuated by the resistance, corruption and negligence of many officials in both the army and the exchequer.[90] The Arnold commission subverted the Sussex government, as it was intended to do, and Arnold became lord justice when Sussex was recalled in April 1564. But the interim character of his government and the general reluctance to cooperate with his policies of retrenchment undermined all his efforts to obtain support. After spending a year as a uniquely disagreeable and truculent lord justice, Arnold was recalled without producing the projected audits. In a way, this presaged the difficulty of succeeding administrations in obtaining comprehensive accounts. In August 1578, for example, the privy council wrote to the council in Ireland to command Thomas Jenyson to finish the audit begun four years before, '. . . so as thereby we may understand what hir Majestie oweth there . . .'.[91]

When Sydney was appointed as chief governor in 1565 he quickly recognized that the political atmosphere was exceedingly tense. There was incipient rebellion in the provinces and general resistance to the commission of inquiry in the Pale, while in Westminster the queen would not tolerate continued deficits. Sydney accepted these conditions and reckoned that he could govern prudently with a smaller

88. *P.R.I. rep. D.K. 12*, pp. 183, 191.
89. Brady, 'Government of Ireland', pp. 159–71.
90. *Cal. Carew MSS, 1515–74*, pp. 355, 363; Bagwell, *Ireland under the Tudors*, ii, 69–70.
91. *Walsingham letter-bk*, p. 25. See also *Sidney S.P.*, p. 66, no. 16.

military force while restoring order and confidence in the government. Recent writers have argued that he intentionally exaggerated his claims to govern efficiently, though his prior experience as vice treasurer should have prepared him for the hazards of Irish financial administration.[92] But Sydney was initially popular and many expected him to establish agreements which would allow him to reduce the size of the garrison.

Despite the excessive charges which he subsequently incurred, he was returned in 1568 with new instructions to cut costs and raise revenue. Sydney was instructed to call a parliament to increase the resources of government and he introduced legislation to renew the subsidy, to regulate certain trade and to control exports. A new import duty on wines was expected to yield £6,000 each year, while the forfeiture of the O'Neill estates in Ulster would allow the crown to dispose of a vast amount of territory at favourable rents. Finally, Sydney extended the shiring of the country to new lands in the expectation that sheriffs would collect additional revenue. Together with the innovation of the lords president and councils designed to expand the use of the common law, these measures were expected to provide an annual yield of up to £14,500 or more.[93] In the event, these optimistic projections were never realized. The mercantilist legislation had the effect of reducing the volume of Irish trade, the naming of 16 official ports of entry was, in practice, a dead letter, and the new impost of wines yielded little steady income.[94] Nevertheless, it is certainly unreasonable to charge Sydney with a cynical intent to overwhelm a debilitated government with bootless proposals which had no chance of becoming effective.

Perhaps the most significant step toward financial reform was taken in 1575 when Sydney began his second term as lord deputy. This proposed improvement was unique because it was a general reform, aimed at spending limits rather than specific abuses. It was comprehensive in that it encompassed all financial departments. Sydney himself proposed the retrenchment in a memorandum calling for a fixed sum of £20,000 per annum from the English treasury for three years. With this amount and an estimated £6,000 from Irish revenue, he intended to end the deficits of the Fitzwilliam administration. Sydney's hopes were fixed upon the prospects for augmenting Irish revenue through the presidency system. He wanted to hold the cost of the military establishment to about £21,000.

92. Ellis, *Tudor Ireland*, pp. 245–46, 250–51; Brady 'Government of Ireland', pp. 197, 206.

93. Brady, 'Government of Ireland', pp. 198–200; V. Treadwell, 'The Irish parliament of 1569–71', *RIA Proc*, lxv (1966), sect. c, 55; Ellis, *Tudor Ireland*, pp. 258–59.

94. Treadwell, 'Irish customs', 389, 394–97, 405–417.

The proposal was a milestone in Irish financial administration because it was the first time the queen had agreed to commit English revenue to Ireland in advance of expenditure. For this reason Cecil and the queen were sceptical, and they devised a policy of fiscal restraint designed to keep Sydney to his bargain. The lord deputy's instructions, penned by Cecil, required great circumspection in financial matters. Together with the council, Sydney was ordered to assess the queen's debts comprehensively, to whom these were owed, when they fell due, how they were contracted and how they were paid. They were further instructed to devise means whereby some debts could be postponed or reduced by sums owed to the queen, and to note whether defaults proceeded from delay or outright evasion. Sydney was to receive the £20,000 in quarterly payments, and Cecil insisted that no further expenses be incurred. He ordered the discharge of unnecessary soldiers serving in Ulster and other areas.[95] Cecil was determined to give effect to this policy of retrenchment, using Sydney as his instrument. But the project came to naught since it coincided with the constitutional conflict over the cess and it quickly proved too inelastic in the straitened circumstances of Irish finances.

The supervisory role of the lord deputy and council over Irish finance was manifest in the continuous stream of instructions received from the queen and her privy council in Westminster. Crown policy was created in England from a congeries of experienced advice, cautionary tales and ambitious projects. While the primary aim of Tudor administrators was to provide order and stability through recourse to an expanded role for the common law, a significant addendum to this formula was the requirement to limit costs and augment income. The relentless pressure on the council in Ireland to achieve both an extension of its practical authority and an increase of revenue to support it had the effect of encroaching on its independence, and in most respects the council lost power due to the resumption of direct control over the Irish exchequer from England. Paradoxically then, the supervisory role of the council and its management of the financial administration were expanded just at the time that its voice in policy-making was subordinated to the authority of Westminster. The annual deficit was the defining problem of every administration and the council had usually to answer for it.

95. BL, Cott. MS Titus B XII, ff. 155–58; PRO, SP 63/53/164–65v. See Brady, 'Government of Ireland', pp. 208 ff., for the view that Sydney's proposals were dangerously over-ambitious because of his competition for office with the equally bold earl of Essex.

THE ELIZABETHAN RECOINAGE: A MODEL OF CONCILIAR MANAGEMENT

The effort to reform the currency at the beginning of Elizabeth's reign offers an opportunity to examine how the council in Ireland operated at the initial junction of administrative policy and performance. The role of the council during several stages of the recoinage was prominent, since it appeared that this was an issue which could easily be managed from Dublin. In fact, however, the proclamations of the council did not succeed in making the new coins generally acceptable throughout the realm and there was periodic and covert resistance to them. Nevertheless, the concentrated attention to the recoinage helps to illustrate certain key features of conciliar management in Ireland. First, we see the practical dependence of the Irish council on the privy council in Westminster for the establishment of policy. The councillors in Dublin were arbitrarily given a comprehensive plan which was likely to be opposed and then told to implement it. Secondly, it is clear that the actual articulation of the new policy was made the full responsibility of the council in Ireland. To this task they turned with bureaucratic zeal, issuing a large number of detailed proclamations and using the local network of sheriffs, captains, courts and commissions to circulate the queen's order. Thirdly, we are in a position to assess the character of their enforcement of the provisions. In this respect, the council was limited by political pragmatism and a clear sense of the unmanageability of their task beyond the Pale. While they recognized the damage that the reform of the coinage might do to the economy, they were powerless to change it and they largely ignored the consequences. It is exceedingly difficult to find prosecutions for disobeying conciliar proclamations relative to the recoinage. This, in turn, is eloquent of the delicate political and constitutional equilibrium which had been achieved in Elizabethan Ireland. The council was simply expected to manage affairs for two distinct interests which were becoming difficult to reconcile: that of the queen and that of her loyal subjects in Ireland.

The aim of this study is to analyze the general quality of conciliar governance, so it is necessary to touch upon matters of economics and finance. However, since very little has been written on either subject in this period, the focus of this section is largely on administrative mechanisms designed to reform the coinage. It is also important to view monetary policy in terms of the larger thrust toward the rule of law throughout Ireland. The council used its ample authority to issue proclamations and orders for the management of the recoinage, but it did so in accordance with established legal conventions. Penalties for misuse of the coinage, or avoidance of the council's orders, were draconian but they were given little effect. There is no suggestion that the council used extra-legal means to compel acceptance of the queen's orders, and the tenor of their statements permits the inference to be drawn that they may have disagreed with the policy. The council was often called upon to serve in the role of honest broker for Elizabethan political initiatives and in this matter of the recoinage we can see that the council gave shape to royal policy in a way that preserved the dignity of the crown without compromising the independence of the merchants and others who relied on a steady economy. Throughout the entire process, there is no hint of military conquest or arbitrary ruthlessness and the diplomatic handling of the affair suggests that the council was capable of managing the business of the realm with quiet efficiency, if not dramatic improvement.

Medieval coinage in Ireland generally copied the English coins in form and substance. In the early fourteenth century a shortage of both Irish and English coins occurred due to the closing of the Dublin mint, yet by 1450 Ireland was overrun by inferior coins of both Irish and English origin which had been worn, clipped, sheared and disfigured over time. This situation led to a period of experimentation beginning in 1460 with the restoration of the Dublin mint. New Irish coins of varying weights and fineness were minted throughout the late fifteenth century, reflecting in part the political disturbances in England affecting the monarchy. The proliferation of mints after 1467 included authorized ones at Dublin, Waterford, Limerick, Galway, Trim, Drogheda and Carlingford, plus unofficial ones at Cork, Wexford, Kinsale and Youghal. This led to general confusion in the coinage which the first Tudor king set about to correct. Henry VII managed to gain control of the Dublin mint through the making of key appointments to it. The inferior Irish coin produced thereafter amounted to a de facto debasement of the currency. Against the advice of the council in Ireland, the king maintained a separate, lower standard of Irish coin. The mint was closed in 1506 because the king, who had changed his stance and would no longer accept coinage using a dual standard, was sufficiently powerful to be able to enforce his will on the ambivalent Anglo-Irish.[96]

By 1534, a 'farrago' of obsolete and obsolescent coins circulated in Ireland, the result of three centuries of periodic exploitation and general neglect.[97] After 1534, the government of Henry VIII minted

96. R.H.M. Dolley, 'The coinage to 1534' in *N.H.I., ii: Medieval Ireland 1169– 1534*, ed. A. Cosgrove (Oxford, 1987), pp. 822–26; S.G. Ellis, 'The struggle for control of the Irish mint, 1460–*c*.1506', *RIA Proc*, lxxviii (1978), sect. c, no. 2, 30–34. See the recent revisionist account of the fifteenth century reforms by J. Moore McDowell, 'The devaluation of 1460 and the origins of the Irish pound', *IHS*, xxv (1986), 19–28.

97. Dolley, 'Coinage to 1534', pp. 825–26; 'Anglo-Irish monetary policies, 1172– 1637', *Historical Studies: VII*, ed. J.C. Beckett (London, 1969), p. 57.

new coins for Ireland, including the notable Irish 'harp' of sixpence. However, the fineness of the coin was less than sterling and by 1547 an effective debasement had occurred resulting in an Irish coin of only 3 oz. fine. Further confusion was caused by the resurrection of the Dublin mint in 1548 which produced another adulterated Irish sixpence coin of only 4 oz. fine. The Dublin mint was dismantled by Mary and the London mint was used to strike new Irish coins of 7 oz. fine in 1553, but within two years the government was dumping light and thin coins of only 3 oz. in Ireland once again.[98] Both St Leger and Sussex, alarmed at the increasing costs of government, submitted to the issue of large quantities of the debased 3 oz. coins. Despite the reform of the English coinage by revaluation, Irish currency continued to be a source of fiscal and economic weakness and confusion.[99]

Under the reign of Elizabeth a serious effort at reform of the coinage was undertaken at the behest of Sussex himself. After 1558 the policy was to allow English sterling to be accepted in Ireland at a premium of one third greater than Irish currency (the English shilling of 12*d.* sterling would be accepted as 16*d.* Irish).[100] A comprehensive reform of this sort required the concentrated vigilance of the council in Ireland, and for a period of three years the council guided the reform of the coinage. During Mary's reign only an isolated case of 1557 was taken up by the council involving two counterfeiters from Liverpool who were incarcerated for a few days. In 1559, however, the campaign of monetary reform began when Fitzwilliam was sent back to Ireland in July with a 'masse' of money and the lord deputy was instructed to establish the rates for it by proclamation. An English sixpence was to be worth eight pence of Irish money. Further, certain base money of Ireland was to be devalued by the deputy acting in conjunction with two or three of the council. But '. . . before any decays be made . . .' the lord deputy and council were to pay off all the queen's debts and pay the soldiers as well.[101] This expedient was typical of the manipulation of the currency that attended every attempt to reconstruct it.

Many proposals were heard by the privy council in England during this period but few were designed to benefit Ireland. Most writers

98. R.H.M. Dolley, 'The Irish coinage 1534–1691' in *N.H.I., iii: Early modern Ireland, 1534–1691*, ed. T.W. Moody, F.X. Martin and F.J. Byrne, pp. 408–12. See also J.D. Gould, *The great debasement: currency and the economy in mid-Tudor England* (Oxford, 1970).

99. ibid.; Brady, 'Government of Ireland', pp. 134–35. About £13,000 of the debased coins were issued under St Leger, and £85,000 shipped to Ireland under Sussex from 1556 to 1558.

100. Dolley, 'Irish coinage 1534–1691', p. 412; Brady, 'Government of Ireland', p. 135.

101. RIA, MS 24 F 17, f. 35; PRO, SP 63/1/153–54.

tended to agree with the unknown observer who in 1559 suggested that the base Irish money should be rated at its lowest intrinsic worth. He argued that when Irish money was substantially debased, Irish merchants were forced to trade with the English on favourable terms. But if the Irish currency were of equal value with the English, their merchants would compete in international trade and English bullion would be carried away to other countries.[102] This mercantilist argument apparently carried great weight with the queen and her advisers; instead of a wholesale recoinage they re-established a subordinate relationship for Irish currency. In May 1560 Sussex complained to the queen that the base money used in Ireland caused great harm to the soldiers and officials in the queen's pay. Elizabeth promised a quick solution, since plans had been under way for several months.[103]

The recoinage in England was proclaimed there on 27 September 1560 as a measure to reform the standard and weight of the English currency. A month later, on 29 October, the council in Ireland issued a proclamation to explain the implications of recoinage. The reform was announced as a revaluation of the English testoon from 6d. to 8d. Irish and a proportionate revaluation for the other English base money in Ireland. A stern warning was also delivered not to receive those base coins for any other price but the one proclaimed by the government. Finally, the council ordered all local officials to see that reasonable prices were asked in the market place, '. . . for the advoyding of the gredynes of sondry persons that wolde take occasion hereby to rayse and enhanse the prices of all thinges . . .'.[104] This proclamation was soon found to be insufficient because it failed to give complete figures on the effective devaluation of Irish money and it contained inadequate provisions to implement the decree. The council, as usual, had to rely heavily on the local officials for enforcement. But their first task was to offer clear and comprehensive guidelines to the new multiform structure of the circulating currency in Ireland.

In a letter to the council of 21 December 1560, the queen laid out her plans in considerable detail. She set the value of three kinds of testoons of varying quality as 4½d. (7d. Irish), 2¼d. (3½d. Irish) and the Irish harp testoon at 7d. Irish (it was forbidden to use it in England).[105]

102. BL, Add. MS 40,061, f. 18.

103. PRO, SP 63/2/41.

104. RIA, MS 24 F 17, f. 162–62v.

105. PRO, SP 63/2/120. The testoon was a silver coin with a portrait, first used by Henry VII. In 1543 it was worth 12d., but it was debased rather quickly and was recalled in 1548. Thereafter, the testoons varied widely in valuation. See A. Feavearyear, *The pound sterling: a history of English money*, 2nd. ed., rev. by E. V. Morgan (Oxford, 1963), p. 74.

The object of the reform was theoretically to restore Irish coinage to its true value as it was before Henry VIII ascended the throne. The queen intended to coin all future money in fine silver for Ireland as well as England but she first consulted her councillors for their opinions. She asked,

> . . . yet if any part of this our resolution shall seeme to you uppon consultation and advise unmeet either for itself or in respect of present tyme . . . we meane not so to prescribe directly to you thexecution, . . . but that you may . . . advertising us . . . know our further pleasur. . . .[106]

She called on the council further to do what they thought best regarding the base testoon, which was about to go out of circulation, and reminded them that it was illegal to transport base money out of Ireland.[107] This amplification of the policy of recoinage was duly passed on by the council, although not in the form of a proclamation. Despite these early opportunities to advance their own projects for currency reform, the councillors were unusually reticent on the issue until the implications became clear. On the whole, the council made no significant contribution to the planning of reform.

The enforcement of the recoinage, however, was left entirely to the council. It began with an unusually vigorous spate of activity in which five proclamations were made in four days, from 23 to 26 January 1561. The council was motivated by the anticipation of widespread evasions of the new valuation and it recognized the need for speed. Two proclamations were aimed at internal economic abuses. The first decree made it illegal to reject the English coins at their proclaimed rates in the Irish market place. The local officials were admonished to require all men to '. . . accepte, take and pay all coignes of Englande at suche rates and vallewes as they were proclaymed to be current within this realme . . .'.[108] Offenders were to be apprehended and punished according to the statute law. The second such decree proscribed the practice of certain merchants who bargained for the coin they would take in payment for goods or victuals. Noting the great disorder this had caused in Irish commerce, and castigating the offenders for their greed, the council reserved to itself the right to penalize each offender according to his misdeeds. The penalties were made retroactive to 20 October 1560.[109] The government was apparently convinced that business could be thus manipulated to ensure the acceptability of the new valuations. Although

106. PRO, SP 63/2/120.
107. ibid., f. 121.
108. RIA, MS 24 F 17, f. 165–65v.
109. ibid., ff. 167v–68.

mercantilist policies were never fully effective in the Irish economy, as we have seen, this strategy was central to the council's objective of managing commercial relations.

Three other proclamations were issued which dealt with international trade. Here the council's authority was more limited in its implementation of the recoinage, but it proved remarkably resourceful. On 24 January the council decreed that anyone transporting English base coin from England to Ireland could be incarcerated. Local officials were ordered to search diligently for such miscreants and an ingenious means of detecting them was found. To differentiate them from other testoons of similar appearance, the base testoons had been marked with a portcullis in England since they were devalued. Anyone found trying to make payment with such a testoon was to be arrested for transporting English base coin illegally.[110] A similar proclamation was made to require all searchers in Irish ports to seek out base coin in ships leaving Ireland and to confiscate the money.[111] The final proclamation on 26 January was directed against foreign merchants who received payment in Irish money and thus transported it out of the realm. To remedy this, the council required merchant aliens to put up a surety that they would spend all Irish money taken in payment before leaving the country.[112] In an economy notoriously short of usable currency, this solution may have been intended to solve two problems at once.

A new valuation of the Irish coinage was anticipated by the queen early in her reign and once the recoinage in England had been set in motion her advisers gave their attention to Ireland. A flurry of memoranda and communications in mid-February 1561 dealt with the conversion of Irish currency, the proportions of Irish to English money, and the coin to be used to make a full pay.[113] On 8 March 1561 the queen wrote to the lord justice and council announcing her decision to call down the Irish coinage. She ordered the council to proclaim that all English testoons valued at 4*d.* sterling should be valued at 6*d.* Irish until the last day of April, when they were to be collected and brought back to England for re-minting. The base testoon was devalued as well, but English pennies in circulation there were to remain at the current value of 2*d.* Irish. The Irish harp testoon was devalued from 7*d.* to 6*d.* and the harp groat valued at 2*d.* These measures were to be proclaimed by 25 March and the council was further to consider the best place for a new Irish mint.[114]

110. ibid., ff. 166–167.
111. PRO, SP 63/3/11; RIA, MS 24 F 17, ff. 169v–70.
112. RIA, MS 24 F 17, ff. 168v–69.
113. PRO, SP 63/3/45–66.
114. PRO, SP 63/3/74–75.

The council issued a proclamation on 24 March 1561 which made explicit the authorization for recoinage by paraphrasing the instructions from the queen plus an exculpatory preamble. Citing the evils that resulted from the uncertain values in the currency, the council carefully laid out the reasons for the recoinage, saying the object was '. . . to reduce the said moneys coigned and nowe currant within this realme, as well Englishe as Irishe, as neighe to their values as may be in lyke manner as her majestie hathe already attempted within her realme of Englande . . .'.[115] The proclamation delivered other palliatives designed to show why the recoinage was necessary and how it would influence the economy. It was, of course, a regular function of the council to demonstrate the need for such a fundamental change and it applied particularly to such a sensitive subject as the alteration of the currency. The council's order recited the new valuations as contained in the queen's letter and made arrangements for the coins to be brought in to the treasury in Dublin. The council then continued in its justification of the expedient, summarizing the harmful effects of the confused currency by saying,

. . . the dyverstyie of standerdes of her highnes moneys currant within this realme as well Englishe as Irishe, with the unequall valuacions thereof, dothe gretely annoye her majesties commen weale here as a matier whereby, besides sondry other myschieffes, all maner of pryses of thinges bothe growing in this realme and brought and conveighed into the same from forren partes, growe dayly excessyve, to the manifest hurte of her crowne, grevous detryment of her nobylyte and lamentable opression and ympoverishement of her subjectes of this her realme, specially suche as lyve upon her highnes pay ether in cyvill or marshall offices or services.[116]

An ambitious project was put before the council in 1561 by Lord Lieutenant Sussex designed to achieve an unprecedented response beyond the Pale and an unusual degree of cooperation from the merchant community. He required the printer to produce forty proclamations to be sent throughout the five counties of the Pale, to Co. Carlow and to the port towns in those counties. For Counties Wexford, Kilkenny, Waterford, Tipperary, Cork and Limerick, the council was ordered to send the proclamations in letters to the sheriffs, mayors and other local officials. In addition, a means was devised to organize the collection of base money, enlisting the support of local merchants. The lord lieutenant proposed that '. . . certen marchauntes of the principall cyties and townes of this Realme shulde be commoned

115. RIA, MS 24 F 17, f. 173.
116. ibid.

[communicated] with to take upon them to amasse together apon there credicte all the base quoynes with in this Realme . . .'.[117] The council was to call before it the merchants of the towns of Dublin, Drogheda and Waterford and to bargain with them to have all the base money in their possession transferred to the Tower of London. They would have adequate compensation for their troubles when the money reached the Tower.[118]

The attempt to extend the effective jurisdiction of the council in this case to twelve counties and the enlistment of merchants' support demonstrates the willingness, if not the ability, of the council to expand the authority of the Dublin administration. Similar efforts had been made to enforce the terms of the customs laws, without much effect, and it is evident that this scheme, too, was premature. The difficulties inherent in the project and the independence of the merchants conspired to defeat it. Yet we may observe the intent of the Sussex government to follow common law procedures, relying on the instruments of local government to implement crown policy. The measures employed were conventional and conservative, based on the precedents established by the concurrent recoinage in England. The objective of the government was, ultimately, to produce a more fully integrated economy which was capable of responding to the emerging command structure of Tudor mercantilism. In all of the devolution of power from the queen and council on this issue there was no mention of the use of military means.

When the lord deputy and council drew up the original proclamations, they plainly anticipated disobedience. As a result, they went to some pains, not only to justify the recoinage in the clearest terms, but to charge all local officials to see that reasonable prices were offered in markets and fairs under their jurisdiction. A subsequent, undated proclamation restated the long-standing prohibition against transportation of '. . . plate, vessell, masse, bullyon, nor juelles of golde or sylver . . .'[119] out of the realm. The order required searchers to pursue diligently any suspected wrongdoer and offered as an inducement one-fourth of the total of forfeited coins or plate. On 25 March the council wrote to the queen, declaring their fears of merchants hoarding currency and of aliens removing money from Ireland.[120] Uncertainty about the value of various coins contributed to the non-compliance of merchants, and the council found it necessary on

117. PRO, SP 63/4/35.

118. ibid.

119. RIA, MS 24 F 17, ff. 174–75. The proclamation was clearly made in the month following the recoinage because it followed the original proclamation of 24 March and preceded an entry of 23 April 1561.

120. PRO, SP 63/3/87–88.

23 April to declare the official value of the red harp and the rose half-penny without first consulting the queen.[121] Evasions and sharp practices continued despite the activity of the council because the local officials disdained to prosecute offenders. The council records reveal no trials of or penalties imposed on those who violated the proclamation, so we may assume that enforcement was left in the hands of reluctant municipal administrators.

It took the councillors nearly a year to take up with the queen the devaluation of their own salaries, although this particular outcome of the recoinage was understood much earlier. On 9 February 1562 several councillors wrote to the queen, complaining that the value of their salaries was reduced by one third because of the recoinage. They requested new warrants to raise their fees to the old levels, but this plea apparently fell on deaf ears.[122] The further complication of a third variant in the coinage was then raised by the council on 24 August. They argued that, since they had been paid in a bastard currency, known as Irish sterling, which had a value intermediate between the English sterling and the current Irish money, the statement of their fees in sterling had become quite confusing. The recoinage had eliminated the Irish sterling as a currency, so the council requested new patents of office stating their fees more clearly in current Irish money.[123] Responding to this suggestion in a letter of 11 October the queen said, 'I therefore authorise you our deputie and counsaill there . . . to cause all the said patentes and writinges to be newly made in form as you have mencioned . . .'.[124] The council had earlier complained of the baneful effects of increasing prices on their fixed salaries and this appeal to stabilize official compensation effectively symbolized the concerns of the entire country.

The currency reform which was designed to address insecurity in the financial and economic sectors of Elizabethan Ireland produced mixed results. More research is required at the local and provincial

---

121. RIA, MS 24 F 17, f. 175v. Proposals for a mint, discussed at some length in a council letter of 5 May 1561, were mysteriously dropped. PRO, SP 63/3/173. And as late as 14 July the council was correcting errors in the official correspondence and questioning the values of still more old coins of earlier recoinages.

122. PRO, SP 63/5/67.

123. PRO, SP 63/6/190. The problem of a third currency may be explained by the great variety of coins found then in Ireland, and the relatively higher value of those Irish coins in use before the 'Great Debasement'.

124. PRO, SP 63/7/82; PROI, Lodge MSS, Extracts of the patent rolls, f. 97. This decree may have solved the problem temporarily, but as late as 1586 it came up again. The queen demanded to know why some officials were being paid in sterling, contrary to her orders. She requested the names of these men, noting that they were profiting from this offence at the rate of twenty-five per cent. BL, Add. MS 4,786, f. 22v.

level to determine how the new currency operated and to what extent the proclamations of the council in Ireland were enforced in practice. Michael Dolley has suggested that the new currency was issued in such small numbers that it made little impact, but the decision to permit English sterling to circulate in Ireland at a premium of one third led to a more uniform standard throughout the country. This 'ascendancy of sterling' was the product of a benign neglect on the part of the council, but it facilitated trade and it seems to have had the effect of gradually driving out of circulation the worn, sheared and clipped variants of earlier currencies. It was not until 1601 that another attempt was made to issue a distinctive Irish coinage.[125] Recent research has suggested that the towns in the first two decades of Elizabeth's reign experienced some improvement in their commercial activity, a fact which may have been partly due to the newly stabilized currency. But the mercantilist policies of the government which were designed to facilitate trade were largely ignored, and the prosperity enjoyed by some of the leading towns was more likely the product of their own enterprise and ingenuity.[126]

In summary, the policy of currency reform and its attendant outcomes affords the observer an opportunity to analyze the work of the council in Ireland from several perspectives. It is clear, for example, that the council intended its proclamations on economic matters to be effective throughout the country and it is strong early evidence of the determination to expand conciliar jurisdiction. Furthermore, the constitutional position of the council in the administrative hierarchy of Irish governance is clarified after an analysis of its multiple roles. Whereas the queen had full control of the policies and the monetary technicalities of the recoinage, the council was entirely responsible for the implementation of the reform. Its powers of enforcement were thus enhanced for this occasion, and the mandate for change was unimpeded by entrenched factions such as it was in the ordinary revenue administration. The council demonstrated that it could act with celerity and decisiveness when occasion demanded, outlawing anticipated abuses, developing penalties for defaulters and attempting to neutralize resistance to the reform. It acted as a conduit for the policy made in England, but that was only the beginning of its work. It clarified and amended that policy, enforced and defended it against the recalcitrant and employed local officials to execute its instructions. Finally, the episode allows us to observe a model of Elizabethan government which is more complex and more convincing than the conventional view of conquest and colonization. The council in Ireland

125. Dolley, 'Irish coinage 1534–1691', p. 413.
126. Sheehan, 'Irish towns 1558–1625', pp. 105–11.

provided a political and administrative medium through which royal mandates and Irish concerns could be filtered. In order to balance the competing interests in Irish governance the council had to exercise discretion and to remain alert to the dynamic and intricate cross-currents in Irish politics and society. This was acutely evident as well in the constitutional crisis over the cess.

THE CONTROVERSY OVER CESS

The political and constitutional controversy which developed over the rights of the chief governor and council to levy impositions on the Pale illustrated once again the convergence of the three fundamental responsibilities of the council: military policy, legal jurisdiction and financial administration. The cess was normally a tax in kind, analogous to purveyance in England for the crown, and the increasing pressures on the council to produce more revenue in Ireland led to an increase in the number and the uses of the cess after 1556. Since it was required for the maintenance of the military establishment, the council regularly set the rates of the levy and the area on which it was to be assessed. The council heard repeated appeals from the leading men of the Pale against the cess in quasi-judicial proceedings and ultimately heard cases brought before it when sitting as the court of castle chamber. However, the council as a tribunal was in this case seen as an interested party, even an adversary, since it was responsible for both financial and judicial policies. The gradual but inexorably increasing cascade of protest against the cess drew the Palesmen into a constitutional battle with the council which involved the queen and her government in Westminster. This in turn led to an estrangement of the parties which were normally relied upon to form the core of loyal subjects in Ireland. Driven to find alternative sources of revenue, and committed to fashion a more systematic legal framework throughout Ireland for the administration of justice, it is difficult to see how the council could have avoided the conflict. At the end of the period, the council's role as honest broker in the conciliation of competing interests in Ireland was seriously compromised, despite its genuine attempts to achieve a new agreement.

a) historical definition

The historical background to the controversy must take into account both English and Irish forms of taxation in kind. In the first place, there was an undoubted right of the crown in England to demand payment in kind for royal entertainment. As early as the mid-thirteenth century this right had been expanded to include the supply of royal forces during wartime and even the repair of bridges and buildings on behalf of the crown. During the wars of Edward I the royal demand for money became so great that baronial resistance led to the granting of a series of charters by which the king agreed to place limits on the rights of purveyance. Royal officers were forced to seek proper authorization for taking up money or goods for the king's table or other sanctioned public purposes, but the right to purvey was not questioned and in practice the goods or services were obtained at well below market prices (if they were paid for at all). Ultimate responsibility for this exercise of the royal prerogative generally fell upon the sheriff and he could require money, supplies, labour, transportation or a combination of them. In fact, this became a recognized source of additional revenue for the crown and it led to many complaints throughout the later middle ages in England.[127]

By the reign of Elizabeth, this right had become institutionalized, yet resistance to purveyance continued unabated. The purveyors themselves had become notorious for their corruption since they had the right to obtain supplies at below market price and then apply to crown officials for reimbursement. It was expected that they would profit from the exchange by adding a commission to the charges at both ends of the transaction, but their arbitrariness caused such a stir that Cecil developed a composition for payment during the 1570s. A new arrangement was struck with the counties directly so that their levy was taken up by justices of the peace at the market price and sold to the crown at the fixed rate, with the difference made up by a tax (or composition) for the entire county. The system was still open to abuses and criticism mounted during the war years of the 1590s, but the crown had become accustomed to this form of non-parliamentary taxation and it was estimated to be worth about £35,000 per annum by 1603.[128]

In Ireland, a cognate concept of billeting and supply had existed for centuries as a right of the lords and kings. The anglicized term 'coyne and livery' has been used to describe the system by which Gaelic chiefs required support from their subjects in the form of taxes in kind. The acknowledged profits to the king from 'hosting, tribute and maintenance' were enforceable by distraint of property, and there were many conditions under which a legitimate exercise of these rights might be occasioned. Both Anglo-Irish and Gaelic chiefs used coyne and livery in the later middle ages and in 1297 a complaint was made to a parliament at Dublin about the excessive charges of

127. B. Lyon, A *constitutional and legal history of medieval England* (London, 1960), pp. 368, 379, 394–95, 524.

128. Williams, *Tudor regime*, pp. 75–76.

billeting. By the sixteenth century a blending of customs throughout Ireland led to the hybridization of taxes, fines, surcharges and other exactions based upon feudal, Irish and royal concepts. For example, the practice of 'cutting', or imposing a general tax on the inhabitants of the country was used to describe a tax without consent. Irish chiefs, furthermore, could legitimately impose a tax or surcharge on their own tenants and so pass on to them a fine or other levy required by the queen's government. There is such variety in the terms and conditions in use by the mid-sixteenth century that a direct tribute to the chief from land under his control might be legitimized in any number of ways. The *cios*, for example, could be levied as a fixed quantity of livestock, or foodstuffs, or sums of money, or a tax on land or cattle, and the same term was used in the fifteenth century to describe a tax on every ploughland levied by the chief governors for the defence of the Pale.[129]

While the system of coyne and livery clearly developed as a peculiarly Irish exaction in the form of beef, oats, butter, malt and beer, the custom was adopted by Anglo-Irish lords and then by the government itself. In practice, it had become a fairly onerous form of arbitrary taxation based on custom of long standing, but in the later sixteenth century some tenants began to have recourse to the common law in protest against its excessive use. The chief governors depended on the subventions of the English exchequer for their salaries, but the money was often late in arriving, so the deputies and justiciars since the fifteenth century had begun to rely on local sources for provisioning. Their military retinues were not large and they followed the practice of coyne and livery for their troops in the Pale, even though it was much resented.[130] The fusion of these two systems, purveyance with coyne and livery, was substantially complete by the end of the fifteenth century, at least in practice. The billeting of troops, a device closely related to the cess, often led to conflict and both Poynings and Surrey made efforts to improve the system. Poynings simply increased the daily rates charged for boarding troops and their horses, while Surrey increased the soldiers' wages.[131] Though it may be true that the precise meaning and the origin of cess was not clear by the mid-sixteenth century, the practice of taxing the country in kind for the maintenance of the chief governor and his troops was well established. In

129. Simms, *Kings to warlords*, pp. 129–44.

130. Nicholls, *Gaelic and gaelicised Ireland*, pp. 31–38; A. Cosgrove, 'The emergence of the Pale, 1399–1447', in *N.H.I., ii: Medieval Ireland, 1169–1534*, ed. A. Cosgrove (Oxford, 1987), pp. 539–42.

131. Brady, 'Government of Ireland', pp. 320–21. Poynings set the rates in 1495 and obtained parliamentary sanction for them. They were largely unchanged until the mid-1550s.

the same way, the habit of protest against arbitrary exactions was customary, if not particularly successful.

As Dr Ellis has shown, the conduct of government during the 'Kildare ascendancy' from 1496 to 1520 allowed the Anglo-Irish and Gaelic lordships to practise a kind of self-help within conditions of limited autonomy. The earls of Kildare as lords deputy balanced an intricate network of local chiefs and lords, using a combination of English law and Irish custom, and managed affairs in Ireland without the need of a large military force or liberal subventions from the English exchequer. Since there were no exceptional pressures on the resources of the government, and the earl managed to govern inexpensively while maintaining the crown's interests in Ireland, the period witnessed no increase of arbitrary charges on the Pale, and hence no protests.[132] However, the earl of Surrey's administration established a new model of intervention, and the chief governors after 1534 increased the size of the military and exhausted traditional sources of revenue. The Ordinances for the government of Ireland, promulgated as a reform measure in 1534, called upon the lord deputy to keep to a fixed rate when allowed to use coyne and livery. Further, the chief governor was the only one to be allowed the use of coyne and livery, and he was instructed to limit the number of men in his retinue when he went on progress in the Pale, an implied reference to the levy for the lord deputy's household.[133] Although the ordinances employed the concept of coyne and livery in the same sense as purveyance, the Irish exaction was subsequently stigmatized as a particularly arbitrary native custom to be eradicated, while the cess was regarded as a perfectly legitimate English practice. The tax gradually evolved into a customary financial expedient. This was due largely to the failure to realize fully the potential income from dissolved monastic lands which, coupled with rising prices and corruption in the unreformed exchequer, put new pressure on the government to produce more revenue. Just at this time, efforts to impose new religious doctrines in Ireland were accelerating and the government was slowly attempting to extend the geographical reach of its effective authority. Not surprisingly, the lords deputy looked to the prosperous regions of the Pale to augment the English treasure which slowly and fitfully made its way to Ireland.

The first lord deputy to increase the exactions on the Pale was Sir Anthony St Leger. He began in 1541 to levy provisions for his household at fixed prices and he converted the obligation to attend

132. Ellis, *Tudor Ireland*, pp. 85–89, 93–97.

133. PRO, SP 60/2/65v. In article 31, Cos. Kildare and Louth were required to bear the same 'cess' as Co. Dublin (f. 70).

the general hosting into cash, an expedient which called into question the right to consent to new forms of taxation. However, this had certainly been done before and it was common among the Gaelic chiefs, so it raised no outcry at the time. The precedent of establishing a customary tax on the Pale which could be altered to suit the needs of the government was rather ominous. Yet it is also important to recall the long tradition of exceptional forms of taxation which had been so widely adopted by the late fifteenth century. When Lord Deputy Bellingham later converted the general hosting into money and used the carriages supplied by the Pale to help in building the forts in Leix and Offaly, the mayors of Dublin and Drogheda protested. Yet again, the government used an argument which rested on the traditional rights of the crown to protect the realm and to use the cash payment in lieu of provisions.[134] The untested allegations of the Palesmen and the arbitrary extension of royal power were not yet on a collision course. Bellingham in particular made regular and judicious payment and accepted that the country had a right to be consulted in the levying of the cess. Grumbling about the imposition ceased after 1551 when it was repeated, but only once, under Lord Deputy Croft.[135]

b) the council's responsibility for the cess

From 1556 to 1578 the cess was of fundamental importance in the business of the council in Ireland. The levy was akin to the older imposition of coyne and livery still in use as an arbitrary form of tax; in theory, the cess replaced these capricious and uncontrolled exactions of the feudal aristocracy with a regulated governmental tax assuring adequate compensation for the victuals provided. A contemporary writer defined it in the following manner:

Cesse is prerogative royall her majestie hath within that Realme to take certaine proporcions of Beefes, corne, porke, muttons and grains at meane prizes towardes the victualling of the Garrison and provision of the deputies howseholde, for the easing of her highnes charges there, which said proporcions ar charged oppon the inhabitauntes of the Englishe pale onely and indifferently cessed uppon everie Baronie.[136]

In 1577 Sydney explained the cess to the queen in terms that stressed the military nature of it more strongly. He said, '. . . it is a quantitie

134. *Cal. Carew MSS, 1575–88*, p. 88. The imposition fell on seven counties, including the Pale, and it served as the prototype for all future cesses.
135. Brady, 'Government of Ireland', pp. 319–23. Brady's treatment of the controversy over cess is exhaustive and convincing. Although he may exaggerate the nature of the change in its use after 1540, he is certainly right in claiming that the reaction was of great political and constitutional significance.
136. BL, Cott. MS Titus B XII, f. 337.

of victuall, and a prisage sett uppon the same, necessarye for soch soldiers as here your Majestie is contented to be at chardge with for their defence . . .'.[137]

The council was directly and solely responsible for the timing, the proportions and other details of the tax. The word 'cess' was used loosely to cover all types of military exactions, such as the levy to support troops on a general hosting, or for carriage of supplies, or the conversion of the cess into money. However, two other kinds of cess were used more often: the general cess for victualling the army and the cess of provisions for the lord deputy's household. They may be distinguished in several respects. In the first place, the general cess was levied more widely, falling on most counties and on Irish countries beyond the Pale, while the lord deputy's cess was generally exacted from the Pale alone. Secondly, the proportions of the lord deputy's cess were smaller than the general cess. Thirdly, the kinds of victuals levied for the governor's household were much more varied. In every general cess there were five staples: wheat, oat malt, beer malt, beef and pork. In addition to these, the lords deputy's household required such provisions as mutton, geese, veal, chicken, eggs, butter and lamb.[138]

When the two kinds of cess were imposed on the Pale simultaneously it strained the resources of every barony and, coupled with the aggravation of receiving an arbitrarily low price, this led to a series of grievances culminating in the crisis of 1575–79. Brady has demonstrated that increasingly active campaigning after 1556 necessitated annual cesses on the Pale and surrounding countries, while the practice of billeting troops on the ordinary citizens caused unusual distress. Payments for lodging and food were set at low prices and were grossly inadequate, though it is possible that the established quantities of food were set very high in theory because the government recognized the inherent limits of the country's productivity and laid claim to a higher proportion of it than was really practicable. Furthermore, we may view with some scepticism whether Sydney was able to collect for his own household over 3,000 animals in 1567 and over 10,000 in only seven months of the following year.[139]

The procedure employed by the council in granting a cess involved the ceremonial meeting of a grand council, that is, the lords and nobles of the realm together with the council in Ireland. The perfunctory nature of the meeting and the nobles' consent was ultimately challenged in the confrontation of 1575–79, when the advocates of the Pale asserted that such a use of the prerogative right

137. PRO, SP 63/58/90.
138. PRO, SP 63/59/61–62; 63/57/71–72.
139. Brady, 'Government of Ireland', pp. 324–31.

to purveyance must first obtain the full consent of all the taxpayers' representatives in a parliament. Until 1575, however, these grand council meetings were pro forma and not genuine consultative assemblies. The procedure outlined above was invariably followed whenever a general cess was levied, but the privy council was empowered to act alone when a smaller or a supplementary cess was needed. It was, of course, this very expedient which was later attacked by agents of the Pale who found it to be an egregious exploitation of conciliar management of the cess. The constitutionality of this exercise of the prerogative was taken up before the queen in Westminster and the council in Dublin, but no conclusive ruling was ever obtained. The formal pronouncement was first recorded on 9 November 1556 at a meeting of '. . . the lorde deputie, the lordes and nobles of this realme, with the rest of the king and quenes majesties counsaill . . .'.[140] Their agreement on a 'universell cesse' of corn and beef set the precedent for all subsequent levies of what became known as the general cess for one year. Most of the exactions for the lord deputy's household were also announced in this way.

One of the central issues of the emerging dispute was the inflexible pricing which had become crystallized for the entire period in 1557. Lord Chancellor Gerrard later explained that the soldiers had always been given daily allowances which were adequate for their needs until inflation exposed their vulnerability to steadily increasing prices:

. . . in tymes paste, they could victuall theim selves, and with the reste provide theim clothes and other necessaryes, . . . yet by reason that corne and catell, and all other achates [purchases] of late years arose to greater prises then before, therfore, the lord deputie and counsell, callinge to theim the nobilitie, used yearly to consider . . . what proporcion of victualls should be needfull to be levied of the countrye . . . .[141]

The prices for the general cess were set arbitrarily low as a measure to help the soldiers, but at first they were allowed to go up. The compensation paid for a peck of wheat in 1549 was 3s., in 1556 it was 3s. 4d. and by 1577 it had reached 4s.[142] But there it stopped. The price for beef remained the same throughout the period at 12s., and the prices of all commodities were unchanged after 1557. The market value for these items was substantially higher. For example, beef cost from 20s. to 40s. depending on the season. In defence of the cess of 1575, Sydney argued that all the officials and soldiers had received their pay only in Irish money since 1562, the year of the

140. RIA, MS 24 F 17, f. 27v.
141. 'Gerrard's report', ed. McNeill, p. 104.
142. RIA, MS 24 F 17, ff. 27v, 59v.; *Cal. Carew MSS, 1575–88*, p. 88.

recoinage, which effectively devalued their salaries during a time of accelerating costs. He explained that '. . . the prises of all things be farre deerer now than they were then . . .', and claimed he would be willing to end the cess if he could have his pay in sterling.[143]

The role of the council in the administration of cess was concentrated largely in the planning and scheduling of the tax, and attention was paid to the smallest details. The council levied the exact proportion of cess on each county and called for 'indifferent', or equitable, assessments on the baronies and ploughlands. In general, the council imposed a cess during the autumn so that the times of collection would coincide with the period of greatest need for the garrison.[144] The council carefully set down the places where the collection of victuals and payment of compensation would be made. These places tended to remain the same throughout the period and they represented not merely convenient collection points but centres of government power and authority. They were: Navan (for Louth), Trim (Meath), Mullingar (West Meath), Naas (Dublin), Athy (Kildare and Carlow), Wexford (Wexford) and Leighlin (Kilkenny). Other areas, including Irish countries, used one of those places to bring in their victuals, unless urgency required them to be brought at once to a fort or garrison, such as Fort Protector (Ballyadams in Co. Leix). In some cases the council also established the names of the victuallers who would be at each meeting-place, and the standard of measure to be used (there were four local standards at this time).[145]

While the council in Ireland controlled all aspects of the cess up to a point, the direct enforcement of it, as of so much else, depended on the sympathies and abilities of local officials. In 1559 the council explained in some detail the duties of the local officials, beginning with the apportionment of the county levy to each barony by a conference of the lords and gentlemen of the county. The burden of collecting the cess fell on the cessors of each barony. These were local men named to their offices annually, who were responsible for the gathering of the purveyance in each barony, with an equal proportion taxed upon every ploughland.[146] Besides the collection of victuals, the cessors were required to levy carts to carry them and to oversee the transportation of the barony's cess to a collecting point. The cessors were instructed to make up two 'perfect books' containing the names of all men in the barony who ought to bring in grain and

143. BL, Add. MS 4,763, f. 413.
144. See, for example, RIA, MS 24 F 17, f. 229v. The dates for the cess varied between Christmas and Trinity.
145. ibid., ff. 68–68v, 93.
146. ibid., ff. 105, 206.

the portions imposed upon them. One of these records was kept at the fort in Offaly by the victualler, and when the cessor guided his wagons and carts to the fort and there placed on record in the book the portion each man had contributed, he was paid according to the rate ordered by the council.[147]

Abuses were manifold and defaults common, so the council ordered the cessors to warn defaulters and then to 'distress' them for the delinquent proportion of victuals. At the same time, the officials were to complain against them to the justices of the peace, who in turn committed the offenders to ward until they paid their debt.[148] The council's reliance on this extensive, but fragile network of local administrations goes far to explain its lack of success in taxing counties as far distant as Limerick and Cork, and even Waterford. The problem of enforcement of its decrees, of course, led the council to embrace proposals for the shiring of new counties and for the creation of the lords president and councils in Munster and Connacht. A kind of low-level passive resistance to the cess may have been tolerated by local officials and we lack sufficient evidence at this time to demonstrate how well the judiciary implemented conciliar policy on this sensitive matter. Brady has emphasized the abuses of the administration, which were indeed outrageous in some cases, but it is also clear that the levies on the country were not actually collected in the amounts assessed.[149]

The general impact of the cess must be measured in different ways. The size of the taxable area, the quantity of victuals levied, and the frequency of the exactions should be considered in order to estimate the overall effect. The taxable area was in theory much wider than the Pale, and in the best of times the council could impose the levy on all or part of some sixteen (modern) Irish counties (see Map 2). There are few extant documents which reveal the practical effectiveness of the cess in each county or Irish sept. In general, however, we know that there were twenty-four cesses for victuals levied in the twenty-two year period under consideration, and eleven of those were general cesses, imposed on a wide area for the better part of a year.[150] Comparing the size of different exactions is difficult

147. ibid., f. 105–05v.

148. ibid.

149. Brady, 'Conservative subversives', pp. 18–20.

150. The evidence for the period to 1572 rests mainly on the council book, which registered every cess. For the period 1572–79 we have the table to the council book and, more important, the extracts culled from the original council book by Gerrard up to 1577. Since Gerrard was seeking to prove the historic precedents for cess and the general acceptability of it, we may assume he took pains to note down every example of cess in the council book, for it is certainly

because of the varying proportions of wheat, beef, pigs, malt, etc. However, the largest cesses actually levied, in terms of the total number of items, were the proportions administered in 1558 and in the succeeding two years. The tax authorized by the council under Sydney in 1575 was the largest ever proposed, but it was substantially reduced before it was collected.[151]

It is customary to think of the Pale as bearing a tax burden equally shared among the five counties, but this is demonstrably inaccurate for the period from 1556 to 1578. Some counties of the Pale provided supplies consistently for the government, while others were considerably less reliable. The herculean labours of Co. Meath obscured the contributions of other counties because it was most frequently taxed and nearly always provided a double proportion in even the largest cesses. Dublin and Kildare were consistently cessed as well, but they were taxed at only half the rate of Co. Meath. They were particularly reliable because they were effectively the 'home counties' of the Dublin government. The council was unable to cess West Meath at the same rate as the other counties, though it contributed its proportion in nearly every cess. And Co. Louth was the weakest link in the Pale, contributing only one-third of the cumulative proportion of Co. Meath in but two-thirds of the number of cesses. The council was occasionally forced to excuse Co. Louth from a cess already imposed.[152] The Pale was usually the only area contributing both to the cess for the lord deputy's household and to the cesses of troops and money for the army. In addition, two Irish septs, the MacGeoghegans and the McLoughlins, were regularly assessed independently of the Pale though they inhabited parts of Meath and West Meath. Clearly, then, the Pale counties shouldered by far the heaviest burden of cess, though they did not share it equally.

Outside the Pale, there was considerable differentiation in the taxable areas and a surprising customary reliance by the council on certain Irish countries for contributions to cess. Wexford stood by itself in the number of cesses and the quantity of victuals it provided and yet cumulatively it produced only a little over half that of Co. Louth. Wexford may be considered more similar to the Pale than to the other counties, but its peripheral location and traditional independence gave it a separate status. Kilkenny was the next most

fuller than the extant table. However, Brady argues that large cesses imposed by Fitzwilliam and Sydney are not recorded, and that formally authorized cesses understate the actual obligations of the country. See *Cal. Carew MSS, 1575–88*, pp. 87–101; Brady, 'Government of Ireland', pp. 324–25.

151. See Brady, 'Government of Ireland', p. 325 for a table of comparative exactions.
152. For examples of the proportional breakdown of the cess, see RIA, MS 24 F 17, ff. 92–93v, 102–02v, 177–78, 229–29v.

important contributor to the cess, which was unremarkable considering it was the stronghold of the normally reliable Butler dominions. More surprising were the consistent and substantial levies imposed on the O'Reillys' country (modern Co. Cavan) by the council. This Irish region, so close to the predatory Shane O'Neill during the wars of Sussex's chief governorship, contributed at a greater rate than more settled counties, such as Carlow and Tipperary (see Map 4).[153]

Other areas outside the Pale were taxed frequently, although only about half as often as Co. Meath. The council relied upon them consistently for the purveyance of both grain and cattle. Included here were the counties of Carlow and Tipperary and the Irish countries of the Annaly (modern Co. Longford), the Byrnes (south Co. Wicklow) and the McMahons (Co. Monaghan, including the baronies of Ferney and Dartry which were separately cessed). These areas were ordinarily taxed in both the general cess and, in the cases of Carlow and Tipperary, in special supplementary exactions as well. The counties contributed less than Kilkenny because there was less cultivable land there, and the Irish countries were required to provide about half the amount of O'Reilly's contribution to cess. At the lowest level of assessment we find Co. Waterford, Upper Ossory, O'Kelly's country (Co. Roscommon) and O'Carroll's country (north Co. Tipperary). Waterford was cessed less frequently than other Anglo-Irish counties and at a substantially lower rate. Upper Ossory was unusual in that it was cessed like a county (i.e., in grain) and also like an Irish country (i.e., in cattle). All these areas outside the Pale were taxed often and at substantial rates, another indication that the council aimed to extend the perimeter of its control using its taxing authority and widening the tax base. The cumulative totals of cesses levied between 1556 and 1578 indicate that the council believed it could obtain victuals from these areas consistently. Indeed, if the augmentation of the area under its control could have been achieved by planning and by demonstrated intention, the council would have made great progress.[154]

The efforts of the council to expand its authority were not limited to the areas of traditional loyalty to the crown. In Leix and Offaly, for example, the plantations were begun during the early period and the council levied cesses on the Pale and other counties to pay for the garrisons there. But in 1562 the first cess was levied on the recently

153. If we compare the relative value of the cesses, O'Reilly was far more valuable to the council. The Gaelic Irish, like O'Reilly, contributed beef at 12s. each while Kilkenny contributed grain at 4s. the peck. The cumulative value of O'Reilly's cess was nearly three times that of Kilkenny (£1,272 v. £450).

154. See the map of the cess (Map 4), and Appendix 2, showing the taxed areas and the proportions of victuals cessed on them.

planted counties and by 1566 the council was emboldened to require 1,000 pecks of grain from each of them, as King's and Queen's Counties.[155] On the other hand, Counties Limerick and Cork, together with certain Irish countries, were only cessed once, and that in very doubtful terms.[156] These abortive attempts demonstrate, nevertheless, the desire of the council to augment its effective jurisdiction through extension of its taxing authority. Certainly it took more than a conciliar decree to develop new taxable areas, and the council suffered the indignity of having its influence ignored instead of rejected. But, in general, the operation of cess was extended to many more areas by 1574, and the policy was implicitly connected to expanding both judicial and military oversight in Munster and Connacht.

The real productiveness of the cess was generally lower than the council had hoped, but we must recall that the political and economic conditions of the Pale and the other areas were frequently unstable so that the gathering of provisions could be very difficult. Perhaps this is another reason that the cess was imposed during the colder season of the year, when sporadic fighting and marauding, especially outside the Pale, routinely ceased. In the cess of 22 October 1562, the council recognized the doubtful nature of the imposition outside the Pale. The last article of the order for cess said,

. . . that if the proporcions cessed upon the counties of Kilkenny, Lymerycke and Corke be brought in, that then the counties of Dublin, Kyldare, Westmethe, Methe and Lowthe shalbe dischardged after equall porcions of so moche cessed upon them as shalbe upon the forsaid counties leavyed.[157]

In the general cess of 1566 the council said '. . . it is alleagid to be doubtfull whether the said graine can be levied in eche of these counties according the proporcion . . .', so they allowed the counties to pay the cess in money in lieu of victuals.[158]

The cess for the lord deputy's household was generally more comprehensive than the general cess because it demanded a greater variety of provisions. When it was levied for one year from Michaelmas 1561, a carefully detailed account was later provided for the council. This unusually complete document gives the fullest direct and substantial evidence for the real productiveness of the cess, broken down by baronies and by the kind of victual levied. Eight counties were cessed but victuals came in from only four of them. Among

155. RIA, MS 24 F 17, f. 229.
156. ibid., ff. 229, 180.
157. ibid., f. 180.
158. ibid., f. 229–29v.

these (Dublin, Meath, Kildare and West Meath) the total victuals returned was about 53% of the amount imposed. Dublin was the most productive county, providing 80% of the taxed victuals actually collected. Meath and Kildare contributed about one-half and West Meath about 40%. But the complete non-performance of Louth, Wexford, Kilkenny and Tipperary must have been far more disturbing than the relatively tepid response of some counties of the Pale.[159] In an attempt to calculate the total impact of this cess on the Pale, Dr Brady has estimated the total charge to be £20,957 for the year.[160] However, the returns from this cess were certainly far less than the original exaction and the crippling effects which he describes were probably exceptional.

In general, the issue of non-compliance with council orders for the cess may be attributed to poor economic conditions and ineffective local enforcement as well as to political resistance. The council met these evasions by using different tactics to compel performance. In 1572, for example, when Co. Louth was again unable to provide its share of victuals, the council proposed a surcharge on the price paid for the victuals in order to buy cattle in another county.[161] The arrears of Co. West Meath were handled more roughly. The council was plainly angered when, in 1575, it had to provide for the garrison out of the queen's revenue at the highest market prices. As a penalty, the government demanded a new cess to cover the past three years of defaults. To put teeth in its proclamation, the council ordered the sheriff to distrain and sell the goods of anyone in arrears for this 'delinquent' cess.[162] On this occasion, the council devised an appropriate punishment for non-performance, but in most cases it was unwilling to compel a county or even a barony to provide victuals, relying instead on the influence of local enforcement. This was hardly the tyranny which recent writers have described as the stain of Elizabethan conquest.

Nevertheless, the country must have struggled painfully at times under the combined effects of frequent cesses and corruption in victualling, compounded by unsettled political conditions, inflation and economic downturns. Brady has estimated that the country was forced to subsidize every soldier at the rate of about twenty-nine shillings per month, although the difficulties of collecting this amount were substantial, as we have seen. What made matters worse, of course, was the behaviour of unpaid soldiers who committed crimes

159. BL, Add. MS 4,767, ff. 144–49.
160. Brady, 'Government of Ireland', pp. 333–36.
161. Bodl, Carte MS 57, f. 365.
162. Bodl, Carte MS 56, ff. 77–78.

against the very people who were required to support them. Reports of murder and theft were acknowledged by the government, albeit reluctantly, and incidents of outright extortion by soldiers against ordinary husbandmen are recorded too. While the soldiers were forbidden to demand money from the people, they would pressure local tenants and farmers into accepting a kind of composition to avoid damage to their possessions or violence to their families. It is not known how many accepted these conditions, but it is certain that some simply left the land and went to live beyond the Pale, reduced to begging and sympathetic to rebellion. Of course, billeting lent itself to extortions of this kind, and to make matters worse, soldiers on the move went foraging (or pillaging) through the countryside, leaving their captains to arrange for payment in some arbitrary fashion once they had gone.[163]

The captains themselves apparently cheated the most. They defrauded both the government and the country by maintaining their troops below strength and charging for the full complement of men. They bargained for lower prices based on immediate payment, and they profited from the hides of cattle and other 'wastage', turning the entire enterprise of cessing into a private business.[164] What is more, the chief governors toured the Pale regularly, using their official residences as a means whereby to obtain victualling by the traditional form of purveyance, and in some cases selling the surplus to increase their own total compensation.[165] While the total impact on the Pale is difficult to quantify because the evidence is so patchy, we can imagine that the presence of the military garrisons was a chronic irritant, and at times a devastating burden on the settled areas of the Pale.

Malfeasance in office at the local level was a symptom of the problem as well. The council was largely unable to control the performance of unpaid local officials, and the cessors in particular were accused of making illegal exemptions in return for payment of a bribe; of taxing poor men who could not afford to pay the levy; and of over-burdening certain baronies and selling the surplus grain in the market at a profit to themselves.[166] Sir Peter Carew charged in 1572 that the cessors sometimes doubled or trebled the charge on a barony and kept the difference in price, and that they occasionally used coercion and

163. Brady, 'Government of Ireland', pp. 328–30.

164. ibid., pp. 332–33.

165. Brady, 'Government of Ireland', pp. 330–31. Special purveyors for the chief governor's household, known as 'cators', were notorious for their extortionate demands and made their own profits by paying low prices for excessive levies.

166. See the Book of 24 Articles (of grievances): PRO, SP 63/5/133v. This is printed in extenso as Appendix 3. Also see BL, Cott. MS Titus B XII, f. 340.

violence in taking provisions.[167] The sheer incompetence of victuallers
was a chronic problem from the beginning of the period, for they
often neglected to compensate the cessors for victuals. On 25 January
1561 the council hastily arranged for an immediate payment of two
years' obligation for the cess, supervised by three commissioners at
each of five places within the Pale.[168] Naturally, the council could not
provide supervisors for every assessment, and the non-payment and
underpayment for victuals continued.[169]

Self-interested abuses of the system, coupled with the genuine
scarcity of goods in the country, caused active resistance to the cess.
When the cess was levied at the queen's price the merchants sought
better compensation for their goods, and the grain was thus transported
out of the Pale. Consequently, the council attempted to manipulate
market forces by prohibiting the transportation of grain and forbidding
alien merchants from coming on market days to buy it.[170] A more
subtle form of resistance was the frequently heard allegation of exemption or freedom from cess. Many tax farmers challenged the right of
the council to impose the charges on certain estates. In August 1566,
for example, Nicholas Herbert petitioned the council for redress
against the cessors of the barony who were illegally imposing levies
on his estates of Cotlandstown. Herbert claimed exemption from the
impost based on lawful inheritance 'time out of mind' and the council
appointed a commission to investigate the matter.[171] In the province
of Connacht a right of exemption from cess was granted to two Galway
merchants after a hearing before the lord president and council on 6
March 1571. The provincial court heard the claim of John Blake fitz
Richard and John Blake fitz Nicholas that their lands in five towns of
Co. Galway were free from all charges for victualling by virtue of their
original titles. After hearing testimony at general sessions from the
'chief gentlemen' of the county, the council sitting as a court ordered
the cessors to cease demanding any levy on the Blakes' estates.[172]
Finally, on 21 May 1571 the council in Dublin issued a definitive order
that all freedoms granted by concordatum, private letters or other
special circumstances should end by the last day of that month. The
proclamation noted that certain baronies paid nothing for cess while

167. PRO, SP 63/25/56–57.
168. RIA, MS 24 F 17, f. ff. 144v–46. The victuallers for Irish countries were to pay
the captains or chiefs of those countries by the same date.
169. PRO, SP 63/35/56–57.
170. RIA, MS 24 F 17, f. 60–60v.
171. ibid., f. 87v; H.M.C., *Haliday MSS*, pp. 193, 146–48; *Cal. pat. rolls Ire., Hen
VIII—Eliz*, p. 547.
172. *Blake family records*, ed. Blake, pp. 115–17. This is interesting evidence of the
resort to legal remedies in the nascent protest against cess.

others bore the entire burden. The practice of cessors charging too much on some baronies was also proscribed, and landowners were prohibited from concealing land for the purpose of avoiding their assessments.[173] This decree halted the importunities of most landowners for the grant of new freedoms, although many continued to claim those they already held.[174] These forms of resistance indicate that the Pale was far from helpless in the face of continuous demands for victualling. We should be cautious in treating the very large demands for cess as the sole evidence of its real impact. Not everyone in the Pale laboured under a promethean burden from the exactions. It is probable, for instance, that the council concealed evasions on the part of its own membership.

c) innovation and resistance

In general, the mechanism of cess was flawed, difficult to administer and prey to the vicissitudes of political confrontation and economic crisis. It was challenged repeatedly by those who bore the brunt of it. In response, the council gradually became more sympathetic to the grievances of farmers in the Pale. The proportion of victuals cessed grew smaller because the taxable area was broadened and many soldiers were garrisoned outside the Pale. Despite these concessions, murmurings against the levy persisted, finally erupting into a critical confrontation over the cess of 1575. Signs of protest and disaffection were evident when the first annual cess was levied in 1556, a relatively large one due to the military expeditions of Sussex. The levy in 1557 was quite small but one lawyer was arrested in the parliament of that year for challenging the lord deputy's use of the prerogative, and the attorney general, Barnaby Scurlocke, was dismissed for supporting the emergent opposition. The more far-reaching protests of two leading councillors, Archbishop Dowdall of Armagh and the earl of Desmond, were aimed at depredations of the army rather than the apparatus of the general cess, yet they added fuel to the grievances within the Pale itself.[175]

173. PRO, SP 63/32/199–200.

174. PRO, SP 63/35/56–57. Carew sued for an exemption in the next year based on ancient rights in the barony of Idrone.

175. Brady, 'Government of Ireland', pp. 136–41. Brady sees Sussex's 'programmatic' government committed to a kind of fiscal opportunism through which he would exploit the traditional cess and use it to substitute for additional revenue. Using the advice of John Alen, Sussex proclaimed continuous cesses, commandeered enormous supplies and billeted the military on the Pale. The implication that this was an unconstitutional extension of prerogative power may be drawn, but the evidence does not indicate a systematic use of the cess as a kind of financial tyranny throughout the period, though it caused substantial distress.

In 1558 the council virtually revolutionized the levy by extending it to eleven Irish countries which, with Carlow, Tipperary, Waterford, and Upper Ossory, assumed the full burden of 18,000 cattle.[176] This was the largest cess of the entire period and the proportions were required for three years until further reductions were made in 1561 and 1562. However, in 1561 the benefit of a reduced general cess was neutralized by the imposition of a second annual purveyance, the cess for the lord deputy's household imposed on the Pale and three other counties for one year.[177] In 1562 the cess was extended to its farthest limits, including 14 counties and 12 Irish countries.[178] Brady has argued that these large exactions were the product of the grandiose ambitions of Sussex and others, made worse by the evident fact that the government in Westminster was unable or unwilling to offer adequate support for the military campaigns against Shane O'Neill which proved to be so expensive.

According to Dr Brady, these early years witnessed the growth of a self-conscious opposition within the Pale, organized by able and experienced lawyers who presented the case of the country against the government through petitions, appeals and finally by arguments made in Westminster. Three of the leading 'commonwealth men', as they were called, came from Co. Meath and represented the well-educated landed gentry of an anglicized culture. Sir Christopher Chyvers, Barnaby Scurlocke and William Bermingham were joined by others in this period to put up a united front against the cess while protesting their loyalty to the crown.[179] While it is tempting to describe this opposition as an embryonic political party, the 'organizational core' is difficult to detect and the movement did not clearly sustain itself beyond episodes of concerted petitioning. Nevertheless, it is significant that the leaders chose to articulate their grievances against the government in a fashion which made use of common law procedures. If the aim of the council were to produce the habit of recourse to the law as a means of expressing popular discontent, this confrontation must have been a bittersweet irony.

As a consequence of the 'commonwealth' movement, the council found itself busily rebutting alleged injustices and grievances in 1562

176. RIA, MS 24 F 17, f. 92v.
177. BL, Add. MS 4,767, ff. 144–49. Even worse, when the lord deputy left for England Lord Justice Fitzwilliam was granted yet another cess on a month-to-month basis during his tenure. Bodl, Carte MS 58, f. 13.
178. RIA, MS 24 F 17, ff. 179–80.
179. See Brady, 'Conservative subversives', pp. 11–12, 17–23; Brady, 'Government of Ireland', pp. 344–48. The anonymous indictment of military policy delivered in 1559 may have been authored by these men since it anticipated some of the grievances which soon emerged more directly from the Pale. See PRO, SP 63/1/170–75.

and trying at the same time to find alternatives to the general cess. In that year the simmering resentment of the Pale exploded into plain view with a book of twenty-four articles written and signed by some twenty-six Anglo-Irish law students at the inns of court. Chief among their grievances were allegations that: (1) the five counties of the Pale bore the full burden of cess; (2) the lord deputy could cess at his pleasure in small amounts; (3) the soldiers quartered on the Pale paid cheap rates and abused their rights; and (4) the farmers were driven off the land by penalties of forfeiture for non-payment.[180] A swift rejoinder drafted by the council countered that seven counties contributed to the cess, not five, and that the cess had been reduced in quantity since Bellingham first introduced it. The council rightly pointed out that the Irish countries had removed the burden of the cess of beef from the Pale. It was further noted that the council obtained the agreement of the representatives of the Pale to every cess through the meeting of the grand council.[181]

The queen and privy council quickly joined in the dispute. Elizabeth and her advisers were sympathetic to the legitimate grievances of the Pale, summoning the law students to three separate interviews while admonishing them as well for their presumption. Brady has argued that political factions at court now entered the picture. He believes that Lord Dudley employed William Bermingham, one of the leading Pale lawyers, to present the case against Sussex's administration and that his testimony led to the disgrace of Dudley's political rival, Sussex.[182] While the intervention of Elizabethan courtiers was only an occasional matter, the autonomous development of an opposition within the Pale is not in doubt, and the accusations of Bermingham and others led to a commission of inquiry. On 7 July 1562 the privy council called for the council in Ireland to aid the queen's commissioners, led by Dudley's client, Sir Nicholas Arnold. He was sent to Ireland to inquire '. . . how the Cesses myght be either spared in the whole or in part, or how the same might be diminished to the lesse charge of our subiettes and people there and yet not lesse to our surety and service'.[183]

At this point the queen began to undermine the position of the council, reducing its independence by requiring the reconsideration of the cess. The council had untrammelled financial responsibility

180. PRO, SP 63/5/135–36. See Appendix 3 for transcription of the 'Book of 24 Articles'. Kenny has recently argued that sharing a common residence in London contributed to the solidarity of Irish law students, perhaps leading to the subsequent use of King's Inns as a centre of political opposition after 1567. Kenny, *King's Inns*, pp. 49–50, 60, 66.

181. PRO, SP 63/5/138–40; 150–55v; 177–79.

182. Brady, 'Government of Ireland', pp. 157–60.

183. PRO, SP 63/6/143.

for the cess until 1562 and the queen did nothing to usurp its position in that year. But, gradually, more constraints were imposed on the management of the cess and, as the grievances of the Pale were made known, the position of the council as the initiator of the cess became more tenuous. On the other hand, the council was composed principally of Anglo-Irishmen with estates in the Pale and they were accustomed to the role of brokering the interests of the queen and the country. On 17 August 1562 the lord deputy and council met with agents of the Pale to establish an agreed contribution for cess, but their efforts were rebuffed by the gentry, who sought first of all the elimination of the troops. A project to recall to the queen's possession one-fourth of the crown's former spiritual holdings was allowed to lapse, and subsequent levies of the cess were reduced in size.[184] In the spring of 1563 resistance to the cess reached a critical stage when some of the councillors themselves refused to attend the council meeting and petitions addressed to the lord deputy and council claimed that the dearth in the country prevented any contribution to the victualling.[185] Most of the councillors were placed in an untenable position by this apparent conflict of interest. They were bound by oath to serve the queen's purposes and they were rewarded with many privileges, including possession of some of the ancient freedoms from cess itself. Yet the Palesmen were their neighbours and kinsfolk and their sympathies must have been divided, at best. The views of individual councillors were not generally recorded, but we may assume that, as their fortunes were joined to the Elizabethan ship of state, their attitudes reflected the quintessential pragmatism of their ruler.

The Arnold commission of 1563–64 and the attendant disgrace of Sussex offered a moratorium from the cess, although when Arnold became lord justice on an interim basis he was compelled to rely on the unwieldy instrument of the general hosting to supply provisions for the troops.[186] His government was crippled by the legacy of political intransigence from the Pale; by opposition within the council itself; and by slender resources due to inadequate funding from England. When Sydney was offered the role in 1565, he was ordered to try to ease the burden on the Pale and to seek out other means of victualling the army. He placed the foot soldiers in garrisons and border towns

184. PRO, SP 63/6/183–84; 213–14. A proposal to hold a parliament to authorize new forms of taxation came to naught. SP 63/6/183v.

185. PRO, SP /63/8/24, 29, 39. Brady's suggestion that this amounted to a 'general strike' seems rather inflated, though he demonstrates that meetings and petitions were orchestrated by leading opponents of the cess. William Bermingham was chosen to present the case of the Pale at court, using a subsidy collected for his maintenance by covert agreement within the Pale itself. Brady, 'Government of Ireland', pp. 346–50.

186. *Cal. S.P. Ire., 1509–73*, pp. 213–14.

beyond the Pale where they could not practise extortion or abuse the local farmers. He planned further to remove horsemen on to the greater estates in the Pale in order to reduce the burden on ordinary husbandsmen, though this plan eventually fell through.[187] He revived the apparently moribund general cess for victuals on 4 November 1566, greatly increasing the burden of cess on the Pale, but reducing that on Irish countries. Sydney explained that the tacit agreement with the Palesmen to forbear the customary cess had cost the crown £2,000 per annum.[188] Yet in the same year he proposed that supplies could be bought in England at market prices and brought to Ireland for little more than the difference in valuation (33%) between English sterling and Irish money. The expedient proved to be unmanageably complex and cumbersome, causing delays and debts which served to undermine his regime by 1567.[189]

When Sydney was returned to office in 1568, he was ordered to manage the accounts in Ireland more carefully. One of his most ambitious experiments was to undertake a new contract with the seasoned veteran of purveyance, Thomas Might, who agreed to provide victualling for the troops in return for regular payments from England (see chapter five for details). Might had been involved in the administration of the cess as a victualler, one who paid the cessors from the treasury, and he presumably saw an opportunity to profit from the unwieldy system which had grown to be such a political liability. The contract for victualling called for Might to engage in a bond for the full performance of the equivalent of the cess which he attempted to provide from the English ports of Bristol and Chester. But strict terms of payment and provisions, coupled with unanticipated price increases, quickly undermined the position of the ambitious Might, who soon complained that he could get no credit in the country. He assigned his office to Thomas Sackford who also suffered enormous losses and by 1574 it was reported that Might and Sackford had accumulated debts of over £5,000 in service to the queen.[190] In consequence, this effort to relieve the council of the responsibility for cess had the paradoxical effect of worsening the credit position of the country. It caused the succeeding administration of Fitzwilliam to thrash about for new measures.

187. PRO, SP 63/14/11; 63/17/16–17; RIA, MS 24 F 17, f. 219.

188. *Sidney S.P.*, p. 17. In 1562 the general cess for the Pale brought in a total of 7,790 pecks of grain; in 1566 it was up to 15,000 pecks. RIA, MS 24 F 17, ff. 229–30.

189. Brady, 'Government of Ireland', pp. 159–67, 338–39.

190. *Cal. S.P. Ire., 1509–73*, pp. 378, no. 36; 379, no. 1; 427, no. 26; 459, no. 22; 461, no. 33. 3; 473, no. 41; *P.R.I. rep. DK. 11*, p. 210, no. 1402; *Cal. Carew MSS, 1515–74*, pp. 379–81; *Sidney S.P.*, p. 109; RIA, MS 24 F 17, ff. 324, 339v.

Before he left his post, Sydney entered a covenant with the representatives from the Pale to alleviate the abuses from billeting of troops. The council established in 1571 an agreement '. . . with condicion that the soldiors of tharmy should be removed from the Cesse of thinglyshe pale and placyd to Lye in garrysons upon the ffruntiers'.[191] Writing to the privy council in March 1571, the council in Ireland took a balanced view, blaming low pay for the soldiers' disorders and agreeing that the burden of billeting the troops on the Pale was creating poverty and dearth.[192] This accord was based in part on the promise of a successful victualling agreement, and the Palesmen further allowed a yearly provision of oats to victual the garrisons at prices levied below market value. The agreed price was to be 12*d.* for a peck of oats, a substantial reduction from the 16*d.* paid in 1562. On 14 February 1572 all the soldiers were to be garrisoned outside the Pale.[193] Sydney's handling of the dispute over the cess to this point serves to illustrate his command of Irish politics. He proved to be flexible and creative, relieving the Pale of the billeting of troops and turning over the victualling contract to a seasoned purveyor. His responsiveness to the barrage of criticism levelled at his government was statesmanlike, rather than tyrannical.

Nevertheless, the debts to the country mounted and the victualling agreement produced only delays and other difficulties. In May 1572 the council threatened to add a surcharge on Co. Louth if they defaulted on the agreement for 127 'beefes', forcing them to increase the cess on Co. Dublin.[194] And in 1577 Captain Malbie complained that he was owed 3,837 pecks of grain because of the defaults of the Pale in victualling his troops for the previous five years.[195] So, in 1573 the new lord deputy, Sir William Fitzwilliam, entered into a contract to provide victualling under an agreement with the crown. In return for a waiver of the accumulated debts in the Pale, Fitzwilliam guaranteed regular compensation for victualling the troops based on subventions from the treasury in England for three years. But the disbursements from England were delayed, prices rose and resistance grew again.[196] In October 1574 five leading men of the Pale petitioned

191. PRO, SP 63/59/54.

192. PRO, SP 63/31/130.

193. ibid. See also the recommendations by Edmund Tremayne in 1571. PRO, SP 63/32/181. A subsequent meeting with the Palesmen on 18 February 1572 agreed on funding for troops in garrison at below the market price and attempted to settle all outstanding accounts. *Cal. Carew MSS, 1515–74,* p. 419.

194. Bodl, Carte MS 57, f. 365; Carte MS 56, f. 23–23v.

195. PRO, SP 63/59/54–55v.

196. Brady, 'Government of Ireland', pp. 340–41. Fitzwilliam originally demanded £5,000 per annum, but by early 1574 he was already £6,000 in debt and he

the council in Ireland against the cess. One of the petitioners was Richard Nettervill, who became the leading spokesman for the Pale during the heat of the crisis from 1575 to 1579. Reciting the familiar litany of complaints against low prices, disorderly troops marching through the Pale and broken promises to reduce the burden of cess, they asked permission to plead their case before the privy council in England.[197] Fitzwilliam and the council in Ireland sent word to England that the petitioners would appeal to the higher authority of the privy council, while defending their own actions on the basis of custom and precedent. The lord deputy argued that he had reduced the cess for his household and complained that the Palesmen represented only the interests of self-serving landlords who wished to increase their exactions on their own tenants.[198]

When Sydney left Ireland at the end of his second term as chief governor, he was disillusioned and frustrated. Feeling that he had been abandoned by the queen and her ministers, he was only too anxious to return to England in 1572. Yet his reputation for competence had been tarnished. He was a proud and ambitious Tudor administrator who felt marginalized as a courtier and he sought opportunities to be restored to the dignity of office in service to the queen. Sydney was known for surrounding himself with experienced and able men on whom he could rely for advice, and he had employed the sage clerk of the privy council, Edmund Tremayne, as his private secretary in Ireland from 1569 to 1571. Tremayne found other office on his return to England, but he also used his time to ponder the state of Ireland, as so many politicians had before him. The result of his reflections was a cogent argument for the reform of Irish government, based on adherence to the common law and a gradual anglicization of the country using military garrisons to assure political and social stability. Significantly, he rejected the policies of coercion and colonization as too expensive, too confrontational and too prone to the cultural reversal which seemed to follow all previous efforts.[199] Sydney found the strategy attractive and in 1573 he began to seek another appointment as lord deputy in Ireland where he might restore his name and fortune.[200] A central component of the Tremayne programme of reform was the composition for the cess.

eventually faced both the fraudulence of his own victualler and the non-compliance of the country.

197. PRO, SP 63/48/113v–14.

198. PRO, SP 63/48/111–11v, 114v; BL, Cott. MS Titus B XIII, f. 206–06v.

199. Huntington Lib, Ellesmere MS 1,701. This document was prepared in manuscript form in 1573 for the use of Sir Walter Mildmay, but an earlier version of it was apparently in circulation by 1572.

200. Brady explains that Sydney campaigned to undermine the administration of Fitzwilliam and to discredit the proposals of the earl of Essex, who were his presumed rivals for the office. Brady, 'Government of Ireland', pp. 218–22.

Tremayne's discourse took the form of a rhetorical essay which rehearsed the familiar bifurcation of Irish government and society into English and Gaelic models. He claimed that Irish lords and chiefs ruled by tyranny, using alien concepts of law and treating their tenants in an arbitrary manner. The consequences were that the people lacked access to impartial justice; the queen's rule was not respected; and the revenue due to the crown was nearly always in default. Tremayne argued that Ireland could be made to contribute to its own reform, based upon a comprehensive synthesis of earlier proposals. First, law and order must be restored and that would require the maintenance of a military force to assure obedience. Tremayne called for the establishment of sufficient garrisons in the provinces to assure the security of the realm which, in turn, would be administered by the new lords president and councils. Secondly, in order to pay for this expansion of the Dublin administration, he explained that the lords and chiefs in each region would be required to contribute to the maintenance of the military, along with their tenants. Thirdly, the social arrangements which encouraged local independence would be radically transformed. The lords would be required to give up their rights to coyne and livery in exchange for established annual rents and other exactions upon their tenants.[201] This would serve two important public purposes. At first, the disorder and violence associated with challenges to arbitrary taxation among local aristocrats would be curbed. In consequence, the stability of the countryside would promote greater agricultural productivity and trade, permitting the government to substitute a composition payment for the more arbitrary levy of coyne and livery. Finally, Tremayne linked his proposal for Irish social reform with higher expectations of the government:

Herewith also must be ordered that all men paie for that they take as well the quenes garrison as others, for otherwise pretending to remove a tyranny you shall use an exaccon as grevous to the pore people as that which you wold seme to reforme. And yet with the good consents of the lordes & comons there mought be a reasonable rate granted as well for ye diettes of the Soldiors.[202]

The plan of Treymayne was rather complex and perhaps overly sanguine, since it relied upon the cooperation of powerful local magnates and its ostensible purpose was to rule by intimidating the unruly elements in Irish society rather than by coercing them. In a

---

201. Huntington Lib, Ellesmere MS 1,701, ff. 1–7. See Brady, 'Government of Ireland', pp. 213–18 for an excellent discussion of the Tremayne proposal and its political implications.

202. Huntington Lib, Ellesmere MS 1,701, f. 6.

conservative and traditional culture, beset by powerful forces for change, a comprehensive reform programme was unlikely to be well-received. Yet the objectives of the policy were wholly consistent with the overall design of Elizabethan government. Tremayne put it thus: 'But as her majestie is the naturall lieg soveryne of bothe the Realmes, so shold there be made no difference of Subjectes so farre forthe as both shall showe like obedience to her majesties lawes'.[203] In form, this was a policy of conciliation, yet Sydney set about establishing the composition for cess in a highly arbitrary manner. The basic conditions which had so agitated the Palesmen were still present and these lingering difficulties were manifested in the smouldering rancour against the instrument of purveyance itself, the cess. Nevertheless, on 24 September 1575, within two weeks of his arrival, Sydney met with the leading nobles of the Pale and the majority of the council to levy the annual cess for his household.[204] The following day he met again with this grand council and a general cess was agreed upon for victualling the soldiers, on the understanding that they would no longer be quartered on the Pale. This was the largest cess ever imposed by the council and nobility, nearly doubling the highest previous one.[205] Sydney aggravated these ominous beginnings by ordering, on the next day, another contribution of £175 from the Pale for carriage of the victuals. The effect of his three days' meeting with the nobles and council was to accelerate suddenly the problem of the cess, to upset the delicate equilibrium fostered by Fitzwilliam, and to aggravate relations with the Pale. Although nearly every major interest in the Pale had clamoured for his return as lord deputy, he almost immediately poisoned the goodwill they were ready to offer him and they, in turn, made his tenure an unusually difficult one.[206]

d) a constitutional crisis

Why would Sydney resort to a policy of intimidation when he badly needed the support of the Pale? What prompted this sudden reversal of form, abandoning the tone of conciliation for one of confrontation? Brady has suggested that this was a 'finely calculated bluff' which was designed to agitate the Pale and prepare their minds for the more moderate terms of composition for cess. Sydney was to offer a fixed cash payment of £2 13s. 4d. per ploughland instead of the prevailing

203. ibid., f. 5.
204. *Cal. Carew MSS, 1575–88*, p. 100
205. H.M.C., *Haliday MSS*, p. 284: *Cal. Carew MSS, 1575–88*, p. 99. The total cess of grain was more than doubled on the Pale and the price offered for wheat and beer malt was 8d. less than what had been given as the 'queen's price' since 1557.
206. 'Gerrard's report', ed. McNeill, 106.

rate for cess which was nearly £9 on every ploughland. What is more, he tried to drive a wedge between the members of the landed élite, arguing that the new composition would be levied equally on all landholders, thus eliminating the elaborate terms for freedoms and exemptions from cess enjoyed by a privileged few.[207] But his primary motivation was surely the agreement which he had previously struck with the queen to govern strictly according to fixed terms and to increase the revenue from the queen's loyal subjects. In return for a guaranteed £20,000 per annum from the English exchequer, he had covenanted to govern Ireland without any extra charges to the crown. Handicapped by this compact, he needed to maximize the Irish revenue at once, and could ill afford to continue the queen's payment for victualling. The previous arrangements which had so straitened the administration of Fitzwilliam were now replaced by the terms of his reform programme.[208] This bargain, to which the members of the council in Ireland were not privy, explains his rash action and his tenacious defence of the cess in the ensuing years. Yet, if Sydney were desperate to compel acceptance of this new offer, the Palesmen were equally determined to resist it, and the council's role as mediator between competing interests was now strained to breaking-point. Ultimately, Sydney would lose support even from his most loyal advisers, the councillors themselves.[209]

The uproar that followed the levy of the general cess led to a significant reduction in the quantities imposed on the Pale to about the level of the last substantial cess in 1566. In fact, the country largely refused to provide the cess and many of the leading noblemen had remained away from the meeting of the grand council. In view of their resistance, and the generally poor harvests of the past two years, the council met on 17 November 1575 to agree upon a lower quantity of grain. But the prices remained below the usual rate, which was considerably beneath the market price anyway. Since the troops were now garrisoned outside the Pale, the council noted bitterly that, '. . .

207. Brady, 'Government of Ireland', pp. 223–25.
208. PRO, SP 63/53/164–64v; BL, Cott. MS Titus B XII, ff. 155–58.
209. Brady argues that Sydney was the consummate pragmatist, interested primarily in achieving short-term goals which would bring him personal glory. However, the thrust of Tremayne's argument was, in part, that all previous programmes of reform had failed because they were too short-sighted and unsystematic. Surely the veteran Sydney could foresee the confrontations his composition would invite. We can suppose, perhaps, that he was relying on the legacy of good-will from his previous government and his undoubted political skills to obtain grudging acceptance of a reform which he genuinely believed would unite the country and help it to prosper. Only this long-range objective would truly bring him public acclaim and he was willing to risk the certainty of immediate resistance to bring this about. See Brady, 'Government of Ireland', pp. 224, 228.

when so many soldiers [formerly] lay at cesse within five of those shires, with their boys and horses, and with such extortion and disorder as the counties did complain of, they consumed a greater proportion than the said former cesse amounted'.[210] In addition, the proportion of cess for the lord deputy's household was lowered to conform with the quantity Fitzwilliam had received in 1574. These measures, however reluctantly they may have been adopted, represented undoubtedly a tactical retreat on the part of the council in the face of the outburst of the Pale. Cautious restraint might have rescued the predicament, but the queen unwittingly exacerbated the situation when she ordered the council in January 1576 to increase support for the Essex expedition in Ulster. Two thousand pecks of grain were to be cessed on the Pale at below market prices beginning on 1 May 1576 and carried to the victualler for the use of Essex.[211]

During the spring of 1576, the privy council in England and the council in Ireland worked out alternatives to the tax and suggested their introduction to the spokesmen of the Pale, without, however, any success. On 24 January the privy council wrote to the lord deputy advocating an annual contribution of £2,000 from the Pale in lieu of cess.[212] The Pale turned down a proposal by Sydney to charge five marks on every ploughland in the place of cess, although this represented a substantial reduction from the £8 or £10 then charged on every ploughland. Consequently, when a last attempt at negotiations failed, the council reimposed the cess on 22 August 1576 on the same terms as the previous year. The frustration of the council was evident in the strident tone of the proclamation, which began by citing the great benefit to the Pale of the withdrawal of the soldiers since 1572. These bitter words announced a virtual ultimatum to the Pale:

. . . her Majestty, having for the most part the space of four years before the last year sustained the whole charge and losses in providing for all their victualling, except oats, contributed for their horses out of th'English Pale, which losses of victualling her Majesty will no longer be at.[213]

The imposition of this second general cess, in addition to the usual cess for the household of the governor, seemed to crystallize the opposition.

---

210. *Cal. Carew MSS, 1575–88*, pp. 100–01. Most quantities were reduced, although the levy of plain oats was nearly doubled to 13,000 pecks, and the price for wheat and beer malt remained lower than before.

211. Bodl, Carte MS 56, f. 457–57v.

212. *Cal. Carew MSS, 1575–88*, p. 37.

213. ibid., p. 101. On 17 August the council attempted to appease the Palesmen by ordering the mayor of Dublin to compel all captains and soldiers resident in the city to contribute to the cess. PROI, MS 2,546.

Based on its earlier antipathy to the purveyance, a well-organized, disciplined and calculated reaction developed.

Although they did not yet fully recognize the gravity of the challenge, the lord deputy and council were determined to tackle the real cause of the grievances. Sydney was convinced that the freedoms exempting many leading Palesmen from the cess cast an inequitable burden on the rest of the taxpayers. He found that nearly half the ploughlands had been granted such freedoms and in November 1576 a proclamation abruptly ended these exemptions. Sydney defended his cancellation of the new freedoms by showing that they were not lawful in the first place.[214] The legal and constitutional basis of the controversy over the cess was now taking shape. An indication of the mood of the Pale was the bill of indictment preferred against the lord deputy and council in Co. Meath for misconstruing the law. Included in the bill was an insolent reference to the execution of Sir Robert Tresilian, chief justice of king's bench under Richard II who was hanged for malfeasance in office.[215] A petition of the Pale against the cess was delivered to the council less than two months after the proclamation ending freedoms and exemptions.[216] It was clear that the stance of the Pale would be based on common law precedents and an understanding of the legitimate constitutional basis for the exercise of the royal prerogative.

Whereas the year 1576 was dominated by sporadic attempts to negotiate a new agreement, the following year witnessed an open confrontation. But deference preceded defiance. The initial act in the campaign was the petition to the lord deputy and council of January 1577, a submissive document couched in respectful language and intended to disarm the council. Although it was not immediately provocative, this represented nonetheless a direct challenge to the queen's right of purveyance. The charges and grievances were familiar ones, but the substance of the petition was this:

Of which abuses and oppressions we ar nowe (after long tollerance) of necessitie driven to complayne unto your Honnors beinge noe longer able to endure the same, and beinge nowe reduced and brought to utter decaye and poverte there by, . . . we ar constrayned most humbly to beseche your Honnors to have suche gracious and charitable consideration of this our myserie as thereby hence foorthe her Majesties subiects be noe furder exacted nor oppressed other then her Highenes lawes and statutes of the realme dothe warrant and allowe of . . .[217]

---

214. *Cal. Carew MSS, 1575–88*, pp. 66, 70–71, 478. Five years earlier, an attempt by Fitzwilliam to eliminate exemptions from cess had apparently failed (above, pp. 389–90). PRO, SP 63/32/199–200.

215. See *DNB*, s.v. 'Tresilian, Sir Robert'.

216. 'Gerrard's report', ed. McNeill, 107.

217. ibid., p. 137.

The novelty of this language lay not in the charge of abuses and exploitation, but in the explicit challenge to the council on the basis of misinterpretation of the law. Here is revealed the continuity with prior demonstrations of protest, particularly that of the law students in 1562. When this new manifestation of outrage took place, some of the leading protagonists were indeed the same, now lawyers themselves, who had brought their case before the queen fourteen years earlier. The constitutional principles being debated in 1576 and 1577 highlighted the apparent contradictions of a government seeking to rule in accordance with the common law while using military stratagems and dubious financial practices.

The initial reaction of the council was low key, for the petition was treated as if it were a theoretical inquiry rather than a serious threat to the stability of the Pale. They admitted the inherent abuses of the system but said the manner of imposing the cess was warranted by law. As Gerrard described it later, '. . . the lords deputie and counsell had neither aucthoritie nor colde consent to dispossesse her Majestie of that she and her predecessors had so longe enioyed'.[218] When the petitioners declared their intent to appeal beyond the authority of the council in Ireland, they were refused licence to go to England, but allowed to depart on their own recognizances. The signers of the petition included five of the leading peers of the Pale and fifteen eminent knights and gentlemen acting for the disaffected majority, so the council could ill afford to restrain them by coercion. On 10 January 1577 the importunate critics wrote to the queen, explaining the events of the past weeks, and recommending the three agents they would be sending to present their case in England. Two of these, Richard Nettervill and Henry Burnell, had signed the twenty-four articles of 1562 when they were law students. The senior among them was Barnaby Scurlocke, attorney general under Mary and Elizabeth from 1554 to 1559, who had been dismissed in a previous controversy with the council.[219]

At this point in the dispute the argument ceased to focus on fiscal abuses and started to concentrate rather on the legal principles and precedents behind the cess. Sydney reported to the privy council on 27 January that, 'The only gall of the Pale for this present is the wilful repining at the cesse, which is stirred up by certain busyheaded lawyers and malcontented gentlemen . . .'.[220] Certain of these malcontents whose new freedoms had been cancelled had refused to provide the cess in 1576, the matter then being taken up at the court

218. ibid., p. 131.
219. PRO, SP 63/57/1–1v. The peers included Viscount Gormanston and the Lords Delvin, Howth, Trimleston and Killeen.
220. *Cal. Carew MSS, 1575–88*, p. 66.

of castle chamber in Hilary term. Here the link between the lawyers and disaffected gentlemen was made clear, for two of the three lawyers representing the Palesmen in castle chamber, Burnell and Scurlocke, were also chosen to argue the case before the queen. The defence advanced three premises which they claimed were also binding on Ireland. They contended that: (1) nothing could be taken from a free subject without 'present payment'; (2) no imposition could be laid upon the subject without the consent of a parliament or grand council; and (3) grants of freedom were to be continued according to an act of 1536. The lord chancellor, in response, provided the justification for the employment of the cess firmly on the prerogative powers of the crown, citing the customary payments made by the Pale since the reign of Henry IV. Of course, Gerrard was correct to assert the sovereign's right of purveyance which, by custom, was levied for defence of the country without the sanction of a parliament or grand council. However, the Irish form of provisioning was imposed during times of peace to maintain an extensive military establishment and there was no exact English precedent for this. The agents for the Pale contended that the cess amounted to a form of regular taxation for which the consent of the community was needed and they denied that the crown's prerogative could, in effect, alter the occasional charge for protection of the realm into a continuous levy.[221]

The language of the dispute had risen to the level of comparative constitutional relations between England and Ireland. The lawyers for the Pale were intent on challenging the viceroy's rightful power to increase the tax burden on the loyal counties, but they showed no interest in challenging Elizabeth's sovereignty in Ireland. Quite the contrary, this controversy took the form of lawful resistance, not incipient rebellion. Nevertheless, questioning the legal basis for the crown's taxing authority touched the prerogative too nearly for the queen to allow the council in Ireland a free hand. Gerrard had tried to get the lawyers to cancel their suit in Westminster, offering to negotiate a new agreement if they agreed to the cess for 1577. But they were persuaded by Nettervill that the lord chancellor only sought to delay their journey until it was too late to appeal to the queen. As a result they departed about the end of February 1577. Meanwhile the case before the council sitting in castle chamber was continued to Easter and then to Trinity term, as other Palesmen had joined in the suit and the court was anxious to hand down a definitive ruling. When the defence of the prerogative was finally taken up in England, the initiative of the council in Ireland was dramatically reduced. This political act enfeebled the council at a critical juncture in its evolution,

221. PRO, SP 63/58/45–48.

but the intervention of the crown was ultimately no more than another spasmodic gesture. A potentially important transition in Irish governance was once again left moribund.[222]

The trouble brewing in Ireland had not gone unnoticed at Westminster, but the English reaction to the mission of the three lawyers immediately transformed the issue. Once the queen had intervened directly, the very nature of the dispute was intensified and complicated. Walsingham had reported the arrival of the agents for the Pale in April, assuring Sydney that his reputation would be saved from libel.[223] But the queen, noting that the charges '. . . tendeth manifestie to th' overthrowe of our prerogative . . .', was indignant at the failure of the council to incarcerate the spokesmen for the Pale. When she wrote to the council on 14 May 1577 she had already committed the three agents to prison. She charged the council with neglecting its duty:

> We cannot but be greatlie offended with this presumptuous and undutyfull manner of proceding and therfore must let you knowe, that we do fynd that you and the rest of our Counsell there did varry myche fayle in your dutyes in suffering our royall prerogatyve so to be impugned by them in open speches and argumentes tending to so notorious a contempt of us and our authoritie, and not to be principall actores and dealeres therein which if you had don (as for our honor had ben convenyent) this matter might have ben remedied at ye beginning.[224]

The privy council in England charged that the agents wanted not the mere reduction of cess but the outright abolition of it. Nevertheless, while recognizing the political and constitutional implications of their grievances, the privy council called on the lord deputy to abate the quantity of cess levied on the Pale as a measure of economic relief.[225] The queen wrote to Sydney, in particular, noting that a sinister complaint had arisen against him for rapacity since it was rumoured that he had entered into a private bargain with the queen for his own aggrandizement.[226]

The reaction of the council in Ireland to the agents' mission to the queen was at first hesitant and cautious. Gerrard moved slowly toward a conclusion of the case pending in the court of castle chamber. He

222. 'Gerrard's report', ed. McNeill, 131–33; PRO, SP 63/58/45–48; *Cal. Carew MSS, 1575–88*, pp. 78–79.

223. H.M.C., *De L'Isle and Dudley MSS*, ii, 53.

224. PRO, SP 63/58/67; *Cal. Carew MSS, 1575–88*, pp. 78–79.

225. *Cal. Carew MSS, 1575–88*, pp. 79–80.

226. Brady, 'Government of Ireland', pp. 224–25, 229–31. Popular suspicion of Sydney's designs had been raised by officials like Nicholas White, by freeholders of Galway, and by the earls of Desmond and Clanricarde.

assembled all those who had been party to the original case, questioned them individually on the prerogative, and then committed them to ward in Dublin castle.[227] Once the council had received the queen's scathing rebuke, it proceeded with a great deal more determination and speed. On 20 June the lord deputy and council wrote to the queen, excusing their conduct by pointing to the many admonitions they had addressed to the Pale to negotiate a new agreement. They had employed restraint and discretion, they said, because '. . . we conceived, that had wee then punished them, they would have bruted into the eares of the common sorte, that we went aboute rather by authoritie, and with severitie to suppresse them in a rightfull cawse . . .'.[228] This circumspect handling of the initial confrontation was due in part to the need to rescue flagging support from the Palesmen for the entire programme of composition. It is also further evidence of the commitment of the lord deputy and council to govern according to the principles of the common law. It is hardly the attitude one would expect from rapacious conquistadors.

The entire summer of 1577 was consumed with fruitless efforts to develop a substitute for the cess. The basic problem, of course, was that once the gentlemen of the Pale decided to challenge the levy, they would settle for nothing less than its complete abolition. In their view, the cess lacked constitutional foundation; once approved, it could be expanded arbitrarily and indefinitely. The queen was sympathetic to their specific grievances against the cess, but she could not allow her subjects to eliminate wholly a traditional right of her prerogative. Meanwhile, Sydney had sent his able secretary, Edward Waterhouse, to plead his case at court along with his famous son, Sir Philip. Sydney's central argument was that the composition for cess in the Pale was a cornerstone of the new policy of the government.[229] To remove it now would cause the entire edifice to collapse. Hence, the stalemate of the summer, punctuated by the pleas of the imprisoned petitioners whom the council refused to release without a satisfactory submission on their part. The intractable Palesmen continued to assert that,

. . . they do nowe as allwaies they have bene willinge acknowledge, that hir majestie maie take up accordinge hir prerogative, necessarie victuall for hir armye and garrison at reasonable prices, and that also hir L. Deputie for Lick [*sic*] Causes, maie take victualls with Consent of the nobilitie, and Counsell of this Realme in cases of urgent necessitie as farr forthe anny waie as her highnes prerogative extendeth unto.[230]

227. 'Gerrard's report', ed. McNeill, 107–08.
228. PRO, SP 63/58/139.
229. Brady, 'Government of Ireland', pp. 231–32.
230. PRO, SP 63/58/149v. They included the five peers among the original petitioners. Some of the gentlemen quickly gave in, however, such as Nicholas

The most probable reason for the stubbornness of the Pale was that they had the ear of the queen. The tenacity of the imprisoned gentlemen in Dublin was explained by Sydney as the result of the encouragement given them in connection with their suit in Westminster. On 17 June Elizabeth wrote to Sydney that she disapproved of the heavy burden on the Pale, particularly during peace time.[231] Walsingham reproved Sydney in August for taxing the lands of the powerful Ormonde with cess, an indication that other influences were at work in London in support of the Pale's representatives.[232] In September the lord deputy proposed a new cess which the leading spokesmen consented to bear, in view of the demonstrable need of victualling the troops, although they refused to subscribe to it. At this point the council, fearing the recriminations of the queen at a new levy being imposed without final resolution of the dispute, instructed Lord Chancellor Gerrard to go to England. He was required to explain the proceedings of the harried council and, implicitly, to wrest the initiative away from the agents pleading the case of the Palesmen before the queen.[233] At last the council understood that a successful defence of their position would have to be presented in person by an able spokesmen in Westminster.

The role of Gerrard was to defend the actions of the lord deputy and council, but in order to do this he had to locate a modus vivendi with the Pale. As lord chancellor, he was experienced in the practical uses of equity jurisdiction to discover opportunities for compromise in exceptionally difficult cases. Charged with the implementation of the government's policy of law reform, he saw this occasion as the chance to create a model for negotiated settlements between the queen's interests and those of her Irish subjects. Consequently, he chose the via media. He called on the Pale to accept the cess at this time in return for a promise from the lord deputy not to impose any

Nugent and Christopher Fleming. They explained that they were duped by the leaders and never meant to challenge the queen's prerogative. *Cal. Carew MSS, 1575–88*, pp. 103–04.

231. *Cal. Carew MSS, 1575–88*, p. 105. The agents had shifted their ground, moving from the provocative argument of illegal exactions to the more congenial gambit of financial hardship. They protested about the cost of cess, the extortions of soldiers and the danger to the Pale of an expensive new subsidy under colour of the composition. Then they offered a compromise contract which would supplement the soldiers' pay and allow them to undertake victualling. See Brady, 'Government of Ireland', pp. 233–34.

232. H.M.C., *De L'Isle and Dudley MSS*, ii, 60.

233. BL, Add. MS 4,763, ff. 411–13; PRO, SP 63/59/45–47; 'Gerrard's report', ed McNeill, 136–37. The general cess and the cess for the household were duly ordered and the victualling agreement of the queen again put into effect, at least temporarily. PRO, SP 63/59/61–62, 116–17.

future cess without the approval of a parliament or grand council. He sought the development of alternative proposals for victualling and made clear in his report that the current system was indeed rife with abuses, corruption and inefficiency. Gerrard's principal argument was that comprehensive legal and administrative reform would move the Pale to accept the justice of crown policy and improve revenue at the same time. So, when the Palesmen finally shifted the grounds of their challenge to cess from controversial legal attestations to more practical economic issues, Gerrard pursued the opportunity for a rapprochement. Brady has argued that, in doing so, he consciously undermined the position of the lord deputy. But the main thrust of Gerrard's report is clearly to offer a comprehensive policy for judicial and administrative reform, not to destroy the reputation for statesmanship of his erstwhile patron. And his argument was consistent with the primary aims articulated by Tremayne and embraced by Sydney.[234]

Gerrard had examined all the council books and older records, and he gave a magisterial summary of purveyance in Ireland. His defence of the conciliar actions and his justification of the cess persuaded the queen nearly as much as his insistence on her prerogative rights. At the conclusion of his arguments, the queen wrote an encouraging letter to Sydney on 1 November 1577. She declared that, 'Sufficient matter was produced by the Chancellor for justification of you and that Council, and all your doings in the continuance of the cess; and we found that our subjects have not been oppressed or in any way abused'.[235] The queen further ordered the council to call the petitioners to the council board again and to compel them to submit to the cess. Accordingly, the gentlemen were commanded to appear at the court of castle chamber on 31 January 1578. The querulous critics at length admitted that the agents in England had encouraged them to hold out at all costs, and each man separately refused to submit. After five days of this the council fined them and committed them all to prison.[236] This failure to obtain submissions was ominous for the lord deputy and council since they had just regained the queen's support. Frustrated by their inability to obtain a satisfactory concession, they were once again compelled to rely upon intimidation and lame threats which did little to influence the resolute Palesmen.

234. See 'Gerrard's report', ed. McNeill, 93 ff; Brady, 'Government of Ireland, pp. 226, 235–38. It is difficult to accept Brady's assertions that Gerrard sought the chief governorship for himself, or that his judicial reforms made the more comprehensive programme of Sydney 'obsolete'.

235. *Cal. Carew MSS, 1575–88*, p. 117. The lord chancellor's report to the council is fully transcribed in 'Gerrard's report', ed. McNeill.

236. BL, Add. MS 47,172, f. 43–43v; PRO, SP 63/60/21–23. Lord Delvin appeared as spokesman for the Pale and his stature at court may explain why the petitioners were not to be intimidated by star chamber procedure.

By the spring of 1578 the recall of Sydney was widely rumoured and on 20 March the queen ordered him back to England to confer with her on the matter of the cess. Three days later Walsingham wrote that he would be summarily recalled as governor and that he must end the dispute over the cess at once. The uncertainty and divisiveness of the entire affair aggravated tenuous financial conditions so that by Michaelmas 1577 the government was nearly £9,000 in debt.[237] There was great disillusionment in both England and Ireland with Sydney's rule. He had forfeited most of his hard-won support, but the privy council had approved one final attempt at an accommodation with his adversaries. The three agents were released at last from the Tower and told to take their proposals to the council in Ireland. Sydney and the council were ordered to consider the new plan and then to call before them all the lords and gentlemen of the Pale. This was an effort to go beyond the obdurate nucleus of petitioners to retrieve some additional support in the Pale at large. If the council obtained an agreement, the names of the lords and gentlemen were to be entered and subscribed in the council book to prevent future misunderstandings. The English privy council recognized the damage done by the controversy to the credibility and reputation of the lord deputy. They called for harsh and public penalties against offenders in the court of castle chamber. But they also recommended clemency and subtler handling in case an accord was reached.[238] The queen's advisers gave every indication of weariness at this juncture, but the complainants showed no signs of giving up. On 1 June the privy council wrote to Sydney to use the council meeting instead of parliament to try to obtain agreement on the cess. In an expression of lingering confidence in their mission, they said, '. . . for that it is thought many of the thinges required to passe by Parliament may be as sufficiently perfected by order of the Lord Deputie and Councell, as by statute lawe; and that if the composition of the cesse [be accepted], the lawe for the subsidye shall not need to be revived'.[239]

It was not until 24 July, after the return of the lord chancellor, that 'The Conference betweene ye Lord deputie and Counsell and the nobilities Knights and Gentry of the English pale [was] assembled at Dublin . . .'.[240] The meeting was significant because it involved representatives from eleven counties and both sides indicated a willingness to compromise. The spokesmen for the Pale proposed an

237. *Cal. Carew MSS, 1575–88*, p. 128; H.M.C., *De L'Isle and Dudley MSS*, ii, 79; Brady, 'Government of Ireland', p. 239.
238. PRO, SP 63/60/51–52.
239. *Walsingham letter-bk*, p. 2.
240. BL, Add. MS 4,763, f. 263.

alternative to the cess, thereby dropping their demand for its complete abolition. And the council was ready to compromise on the need to save the queen from greater charges for victualling. The basic points were quickly agreed upon. The Pale would provide 9,000 pecks of oats for 300 horses and fully discharge the queen of victualling for 1,000 soldiers. In return, the council would pay, in advance, the sum of £4,881 sterling every half year, and compensate the farmers with 16d. for each peck of oats. But these amicable beginnings were frustrated by the difficult problems that recurred in every discussion of details of the cess. The Pale wanted the Irish countries to contribute and the council disagreed. And, on the chronic problem of the cess for the lord deputy's household, no agreement was reached. The problem with this proposal was that it contained all the elements of earlier controversies arising over the carriage of victuals, arrearages, defaults and especially the household cess. Nevertheless, the participants at the conference signed the document, however provisional and incomplete the settlement was, and sent it along to the queen and privy council.[241]

The council was cautiously optimistic about reaching a final resolution of the problem and set about arranging the financing of the new cess. On 4 September the consent of the privy council was received and the council in Ireland contacted the agents for the Pale with a view to securing their adherence to the new pact. But Nettervill and Burnell dashed their hopes. They agreed to seek the affirmation of the Palesmen, but declared they would accept this only as an interim solution and they would again petition the queen for redress.[242] It was now clear that this was not what the Pale had sought from the beginning of the dispute, and they had come too far to retreat in the face of a reduced version of the original tax. The cess had been increased arbitrarily in the past and this could be done again. In the face of sparse and withering support for the composition, the council was forced to seek a temporary agreement as the time for levying the cess was already past. The council met along with representatives of the Pale in October and agreed upon a cess for 15 weeks to begin on the first of November.[243]

Sydney had left Ireland in September. His justification for the cess was based squarely on the royal prerogative and the practical needs of the troops which were maintained to protect the crown's loyal

241. ibid., ff. 263–66.
242. PRO, SP 63/62/29. To make matters worse, Captains Francis Cosbie and Robert Harpoole, acting as agents for 'Queen's County', appeared before the council at the end of September to protest against their liability to cess since they were also required to support billeting of troops. PRO, SP 63/62/200–01v.
243. PRO, SP 63/65/104–04v.

subjects. In principle, his argument was neither unconstitutional nor immoderate. What is more, the queen was indeed jealous of her prerogative rights and eager to defend them. However, Elizabeth was also a pragmatist and her support of Sydney waned in the face of political realities. In the first place, the representatives of the Pale demonstrated their loyalty to the crown yet they also demonstrated exceptional tenacity. Further, Sydney himself proved incapable of expedient compromise and he became increasingly the bête noire of the opposition, preventing a resolution by his manner as well as his policies. And finally, the queen recognized in their legal and constitutional challenge to the cess both the affirmation of common law principles and the danger of seeming to skirt legality.[244] Once again, the careful handling of the matter is inconsistent with claims that this was a tyrannical government bent on military conquest.

Meanwhile, rumours of an impending invasion from Spain had been gathering force, and Lord Justice Drury needed to court the goodwill of the Pale. He announced that he was determined to lay no charge on the country and to pay in hard currency for all that he bought.[245] The emergence of the final solution had a great deal to do with the more tractable lord justice and the imminent danger of a Spanish expedition to Ireland. By the spring of 1579 the long dispute had entered its final stages. When the temporary cess was ended in February, the familiar problems lingered over the defaults of certain baronies and the reasonable amounts for the lord deputy's household.[246] Another interim cess of three months was mooted and in March the privy council sought a final accord based on the composition proposed the previous July. Instead of victualling the soldiers, the Pale was required to pay 1*d.* per diem toward the cost of their sustenance, and to provide 9,000 pecks of oats.[247] At last the council met with the nobles and gentlemen on 29 May. The agents suggested that they continue the payment, which had ended in February, of 1*d.* per diem for the soldiers. The council debated this and agreed upon a sum of £2,000 sterling for one year from 1 June 1579 to 31 May 1580.[248] This was based on £375 for the purchase of 9,000 pecks of oats and about £1,520 for the soldiers at 1*d.* per diem. Six of the principal gentlemen agreed to enter into bonds of recognizance for the payment of this sum (i.e. £2,000). The spokesmen for the Pale thus won their struggle against the cess, for the substitution of a money payment immediately solved many of the disputed aspects

244. Brady, 'Government of Ireland', pp. 350–57.

245. *Walsingham letter-bk*, p. 31.

246. PRO, SP 63/65/128–29v.

247. *Cal. Carew MSS, 1575–88*, p. 153; *Walsingham letter-bk*, pp. 79–80.

248. PRO, SP 63/66/197–98.

of the imposition. Cessors could not overcharge a barony as the price was fixed at 3s. 4d. for each ploughland. And the queen was forced to assume the burden of victualling the troops, a substantial and growing liability.

The Pale had little chance to savour its victory, for in July 1579 James Fitzmaurice landed at Dingle and within a year the south of Ireland was engulfed in conflict. On 12 May 1580 the council was called upon to renew the composition for the cess for another year, and to prosecute those who failed to contribute.[249] Later in 1580 the new lord deputy, Lord Grey, experienced resistance to the cess for his household and referred the case to the English privy council. That body gave its consent to the cess at reasonable prices and the council in Ireland accordingly ordered the levy on eight counties, hoping thereby to reduce the charge on the Pale.[250] Acknowledging the abuses, bribery and extortions of some purveyors of the cess, the council in Ireland made the following decree:

It ys ordered to prevent those disorders hereafter, that the steward in howshold to the governor for the tyme beinge, before he delyver to any suche Purveyors his Comyssion, to deliver to him the false [faults] and Disorders aforesaid articulated in wrytinge and by othe to Inhibite him from offendinge therein, to thend that upon Conviccion of any of them so offendinge he maye not onely receave the punyshement for falcite [falsity], but also for perjurie to lose his eares.[251]

After the ravages of the Desmond rebellion, the new accord proved to be the prototype for later compacts. In 1586 the composition in lieu of cess was renewed because the leading peers approved it. The queen instructed the lord deputy to '. . . Cause to be Assembled the Nobilitie and Graund Counsell according to former usadg in like Cases and to move them to renewe and accepte the said composicion . . .'.[252]

After thirty years the Pale had finally won the struggle against the cess. They had achieved the ouster of the troops in 1572 and the end of victualling the army in 1579. The arguments on both sides were compelling, so it is not surprising they reached an early stalemate. The burden on the Pale was undoubtedly great, if rather uneven. The abuses of the cessors, the disorders of the soldiers, and the arbitrary increases of the cess made it a dangerous instrument in the hands of

249. BL, Stowe MS 160, f. 132–32v.

250. PRO, SP 63/77/10–10v.

251. ibid., f. 10v.

252. BL, Add. MS 4,786, f. 24. Besides the five counties of the Pale, Kilkenny, Tipperary, Wexford, Carlow, Leix and Offaly were contributors to the composition.

an unscrupulous lord deputy. On the other hand, the army had to be maintained, prices were indeed high, and the frequent increases of the troops exacerbated the problem of victualling. The constitutional confrontation did not reach an elevated threshold of reasoned debate nor did it probe deeply into subtle interpretations of the law. Gerrard tried to overwhelm the spokesmen for the Pale with historical precedents and Sydney tried to terrify them with long gaol sentences. Yet even when the challenge moved from legitimate complaints against fiscal abuses to the dangerous ground of the queen's prerogative, the ranks of the Palesmen were remarkably solid. They had gone over the head of the lord deputy and council and appealed directly to the queen, thus undermining the government's position in Ireland. In doing so, the Palesmen became alienated from their own government, although they won grudging admiration as formidable adversaries.

Debate over taxation without adequate representation or consent of the governed was eventually raised to a matter of high principle, although the government preferred to treat it as a matter of expediency. The Palesmen discovered that the most effective political strategem was also the most profound. In their challenge to the legal and constitutional bases for the cess, they were consciously straining the underlying precepts of English sovereignty in Ireland. Yet, by the nature of their appeal to the queen and their calculated use of common law procedures and axioms, the country's heterodox position remained a moderate one. If, then, the confrontation witnessed the development of a loyal opposition in Ireland, this was certainly consistent with the emergence of a similar trend in the English parliamentary tradition. Recent claims that the Palesmen were creating an incipient Irish nationalism are highly exaggerated.[253] But it is clear that the confrontation over the cess led to the establishment of a core group of articulate spokesmen for the Anglo-Irish interests in the Pale by 1578. When the rebellions in Munster and Leinster introduced a new era of confrontation in Elizabethan Ireland, this determined resistance became further entrenched, isolated and estranged.[254]

In summary, the lord deputy and council lost the victualling agreement for the army, although they obtained a contribution in lieu of cess that accomplished their ends satisfactorily. To some extent the council hurt its own cause by its initial tergiversation over the petition

253. Bradshaw, *Irish constitutional revolution*, pp. 276–82, 287. See also Ellis, 'Nationalist historiography', 4–5, 16–17; 'Crown, community and government', 201–02.

254. Brady, 'Conservative subversives', pp. 20–25. See also H.C. Walshe, 'The rebellion of William Nugent, 1581', in R.V. Comerford et al., ed., *Religion, conflict and coexistence in Ireland: essays presented to Mgr Patrick J. Corish* (Dublin, 1990), pp. 28–29.

of 1577. Their greatest defeat was a loss of prestige. For the queen was forced to abandon her measured aloofness because of their inability to get a new agreement, and the gentlemen of the Pale successfully resisted their heavy-handed attempts at intimidation. The intervention of the queen and privy council was increasing throughout the conflict, and they reluctantly took the initiative in its later stages. As a result, the council in Ireland lost its practical independence in the management of cess. The triumph of the Pale was a hollow one, of course, since the rebellions of the ensuing decades effectively ruined the economy. And the constitutional position of the government was strengthened, para-doxically, by the very success of the country's appeal to law and precedent. It is difficult to find in the behaviour of the crown or the council in Ireland the arbitrary and unrelenting despotism of a govern-ment bent solely on military conquest.

CONCLUSION

To many contemporary observers, cost was the overriding consid-eration in the government of Ireland. The inability to generate more revenue or to manage expenses undermined the efforts by each chief governor in the period to achieve political success, and nearly every administration ended in disaster because of financial malpractice or incompetence. But this is to give priority to the means of royal policy over its stated ends. In the final analysis, the Elizabethan objective for the government of Ireland was to rule according to the common law throughout the realm. In order to give practical effect to the concept of 'unitary sovereignty', the government conceived a systematic anglicization of the administrative structure, from the central courts to the shiring of new counties to the establishment of lords president and councils beyond the Pale. As we have seen, the interlocking features of this policy were judicial, military and financial. The rule of law must be established by providing access to common law jurisdic-tions, but the country must first be pacified and stabilized. Military garrisons were thus placed at strategic points throughout Ireland, and increased as necessary to meet local resistance to English rule. This apparently rational programme failed to take account of many factors, not least of which was the accelerating cost of maintaining troops on a permanent basis. It was not military campaigns as such, but the broadened scope and steadfast durability of the military establishment which placed so much pressure on the resources of both English and Irish exchequers. The early Elizabethan period, as we have seen, witnessed a flurry of contrivances and experiments which were designed to meet the costs of governing Ireland. And the ultimate failure of all these efforts to establish the financial basis for expanded governance placed the entire edifice of crown policy in jeopardy.

At the beginning of the period, a series of reforms were introduced to strengthen the infrastructure of revenue collection. The auditor and the surveyor general had been created to provide discipline and accountability. Instructions from the English exchequer were formally introduced in Ireland, though they were not systematically implemented. The Elizabethan recoinage was the most systematic attempt to construct an anglicized model of governance and it manifested the character of the regime. Through its enforcement of the terms of recoinage, the council demonstrated that it was the conduit for royal policy, empowered with the authority to do the queen's will. The council acted also as a mediator between English and Irish interests, balancing the exigencies of financial requirements and economic resources. But the goal of fair and impartial justice in financial administration was frustrated by political rivalry, economic weakness and entrenched corruption. At the outset, commissions were sent from England to examine the accounts of Sussex's government and every chief governor in the period was accused by independent observers of a lack of fiscal probity. In consequence, the privy council in England imposed on each successive administration binding conditions and imperatives which increased the pressure on the council in Ireland to identify new resources and to cut costs. The contract for victualling the troops and the decision to quarter them beyond the Pale; the new impost for wines; and the composition for cess were characteristic of the diverse financial mechanisms employed in response to the frequent directives to control expenses and produce more revenue. In the end, when all these policies failed to stem the tide of red ink from chronic deficits, the council forfeited its position of intermediary as well. In the crisis over the cess, the canny agents of the Pale conspired successfully to present their case directly to the queen in Westminster.

While anglicization was not a total failure in Ireland prior to 1578, neither did it succeed in producing the integrated economy which was one of the principal aims of the government. The impact of innovations on fiscal policy produced mixed results. Efforts to extend the perimeter of government control by expanding its taxing authority were too ambitious and led to the constitutional crisis over the cess. The recoinage was accepted on a piecemeal basis which was largely influenced by local conditions. And the exchequer's institutional reforms were undermined by the corruption, faction, and other abuses which were inherent in the administration more generally. The most fundamental problem was the government's unrealistic planning. The queen and privy council insisted on financial stringency while at the same time encouraging bold reforms which would put increasing pressure on the rickety apparatus of revenue collection. Royal policy ignored the dissonant features of its own stated goals. A government which was known and appreciated for its pragmatism, produced a policy which was reactive, short-sighted, stop-gap and unenlightened. By the end of the period, the leading members of the Anglo-Irish community had become alienated from their own government and the crown had finally drifted into a political and constitutional crisis largely of its own making.

But the government succeeded in its most fundamental aim. Despite the obstinacy of the agents of the Pale and the convoluted processes through which the negotiations over cess were conducted over five years, the matter was handled strictly according to principles of the common law. Of course, the leaders were imprisoned for a time both in England and Ireland, and threats of coercion were uttered. But the controversy was a model of recourse to common law procedures, and the insistence of the Palesmen on their rights as loyal subjects was a portent of profound constitutional questions which would come before the crown in the next century. The case was heard in the court of castle chamber and discussions were continued thereafter using the council board as the venue for practical compromise. If the argument from necessity was unable to win against the principle of legitimacy, that was indeed a victory for the rule of law in Ireland. And comparable debates were being heard at just the same time in England concerning the abuses of the royal prerogative, with similar results. The determination to govern according to tenets of the common law was a commitment which made a return to the rule of the feudal aristocracy impossible, despite its small budget and low profile. For similar reasons, a retreat to the gradualist inertia of St Leger's government was politically unattractive to the queen and privy council. The tragedy of Tudor rule, if such it was, concerned the disjunction of means and ends, the lack of convergence between the needed reforms of early modern governance and the ability to pay for them.

CHAPTER SEVEN

The role of the council assessed

A POLICY OF REFORM

THE PRIVY COUNCIL IN IRELAND played an unusual role in the Elizabethan state. It was the broker and intermediary of competing factions. It was a composite body which took its instructions from England and sought to rule on behalf of the queen without adequate resources. It was hampered by local resistance and social unrest; yet it struggled to implement the design and structure of common law institutions in areas which were culturally distant from the locus of royal power. While the potent aim of the government was evidently anglicization through 'institutional development and reform', as Dr Brady has noted, the outcome was often frustrated by the erratic character of crown policy which moved from periodic bursts of reforming energy to feeble withdrawals of support.[1] Within the parameters of this oscillating boundary, the privy council in Ireland governed with caution and restraint. Knowing that the queen might refuse to countenance a bold initiative which met with stiff resistance, the chief governor and council were placed in a precarious position. They were charged with the practical work of enforcing 'unitary sovereignty' throughout Ireland, but the policy of anglicizing which thus evolved was based on a set of unrealistic assumptions.[2] It did not necessarily follow that the creation of an administrative model based on the structure of government in Westminster would lead to the emplacement of English institutions on the regional and local levels. When the shiring of new counties and the creation of lords president and councils were introduced, there was an impatience for results that would quickly produce revenue to pay for the expanded perimeter of the queen's government. And when military garrisons were strengthened to provide stability and security in the countryside, which would in turn facilitate the work of judges on assize and justices of the peace, the queen balked at the expense. As a consequence, the piecemeal reforms which were achieved by the council in Ireland in this period appear to be rather

1. Brady, 'Court, castle and country', p. 38.
2. ibid., pp. 25–28, where Brady points to the constitutional significance of the act of 1541 which served to justify the encroachment of crown authority on formerly independent Irish lords and chiefs.

lame and fragmented. The hoary cliché of a debilitated central government which had to rely on the use of excessive force to control an
alienated population has done nothing to increase the reputation of
conciliar management of affairs. Yet there is evidence to show that
the council in this period achieved some success in its aims.

Since the primary intent of the government was to expand the
jurisdiction of the common law, the final evolution of the council
itself into the court of castle chamber was an important achievement.
In this role the council manifestly enhanced its supervision of the
entire apparatus of judicial administration and it increased its caseload,
in part, by hearing more causes of riot. Most of the litigants were
members of the gentry or the peerage, but it does not appear that the
council automatically favoured their interests. A related effort to give
wider access to the common law was the creation of lords president
and councils in both Munster and Connacht, but the work of these
new institutions was delayed by partisan resistance and the disinterest
of the queen. These were provincial courts which were made up of
judges and other legal officers and attended by the local aristocracy.
They were supported by small contingents of troops and they were
designed to promote order and civility through a combination of judicial and military means. They were not inherently martial institutions.
The work of the judges on assize, the justices of the peace and the ad
hoc commissions of the council itself was interdependent with that of
the provincial councils, and the concept of expanding access to the
common law was intrinsic to each of these initiatives. The placement
of troops in garrison to defend the interests of the crown was a
critical interlocking part of the effort to govern through constitutional
means, not a substitute for the rule of law. The incremental additions
to local government were designed to enforce the proclamations for
the recoinage, the victualling agreement and the efforts at composition
for the cess. The ultimate aim of Tudor policy was simply to complete
the circle of acknowledged sovereignty throughout crown dominions
and to enable the administration to collect taxes everywhere which
would pay its costs. But the actualization of that policy would have to
await the measured steps taken to expand the effectiveness of common
law rule in Ireland.

LAYERS OF RESISTANCE

When the council attempted to move beyond the founding of key
English institutions of government to the implementation of Elizabethan policy, it was faced with layers of resistance. In the first place,
the creaking, antiquated machinery of the Dublin administration was
unreformed and unreconstructed. The exchequer and the courts, in

particular, suffered from a kind of ossification which was compounded by the effects of patronage and nepotism. In the second place, some of the new office-holders such as John Chaloner, secretary of state, were unimaginative book-ends who offered neither independent judgment nor creative energy to the process of reform. In the third place, the central administration was understaffed and overworked so that new conventions of crown authority might be created without either personnel or purse to give substance to them. In the fourth place, political bickering both in Ireland and in England could forestall the most well-intentioned advancement of constitutional norms of government by substituting personal advantage for royal purpose. In the fifth place, the queen withdrew her support for new policies suddenly and fitfully. She was short-sighted and reactive in her Irish policy, and she responded to crises by sending money and troops with the understanding that they would be immediately withdrawn when troubles were resolved. The dissonance of royal policy did much to undermine the effectiveness of royal government in this period. And finally, the defiance of reform at the local level crippled the work of the council. Resistance took the form of indifference and inertia more than outright rebellion, but the long delays and sudden departures associated with local administration made truculence pay off for the reactionary elements of the provincial aristocracy. The composition for the cess was meant to be the apotheosis of reform, but it eventually became the rallying-cry for opposition. The final paradox of Elizabethan governance in this period was to turn the victory of legal principle into political defeat for the very English reformers who sought to rule by constitutional forms and judicial solutions. The resort to lawyerly debate on the legal grounds for the cess itself was an indication that the leaders of the Pale élite still accepted the terms of anglicization. It does not necessarily follow that this incipient loyal opposition became a proto-nationalist Irish party in the process.

Recent assessments of Elizabeth's reign have accused the queen of a crystalline obstinacy when it came to needed reforms and delicate matters of diplomacy. Dr Elton has said that the 'chief purpose of her reign was to make time stand still'.[3] The queen's essential ambivalence may be illustrated by her instructions to Sydney as viceroy. In regard to persistent Irish suitors, she deferred to the judgement of the deputy and council, saying,

. . . we have thought good to referre the further consyderacion of them unto you and our consayle there for that by the dyversytye of government

3. G.R. Elton, *English law in the sixteenth century: reform in an age of change* (London, 1979), pp. 12–13.

of that realme from this, summe Matier unknowen unto us touchinge our servyce and state of the countrey may appere unto you, and induce therby reason to accorde or forbere the graunte of sute.[4]

On the other hand, the queen rebuked her viceroy for his urgent nomination of Sir Warham St Leger as lord president of the new council in Munster. Having first given her consent to the appointment, she subsequently withdrew it. When the lord deputy complained that Ormonde had sabotaged the candidacy of his nominee, Elizabeth replied,

For first we did not mislyke generally of planting a counsell there but we did mislyke in deed to see you so addicted to the favour of thearle of Desmond . . . as to place St Leger the President of the Counsell . . . so as we assure you, neither needid we the information of the Earle of Ormond to disallow St Leger to be President, nether (to say the truthe) did we upon his information first mislyke the choice of him . . . .[5]

It is apparent that the queen's involvement in Irish affairs had more to do with the political matrix of the English court than with the current needs of Irish administration. But her chief policy-makers were more consistent, and increasingly more well-informed, on matters of Irish government.

The essential conservatism of the crown's Irish policy was based on its simplicity. The aim was to recreate in Ireland a microcosm of English government which would allow the maintenance of quiet and good order using limited resources.[6] This, in fact, was the consistent purpose of cautious Elizabethan administrators and it was not less applicable to Ireland than it was to England itself. Dr MacCaffrey has stated that the ends of government were to 'improve existing practice' so that a 'unified regime' could enjoy the benefits of 'relative political stability'.[7] Elton disagrees with MacCaffrey's appreciation of Cecil's statesmanship and opportunism, arguing that the 'last echo' of genuine reform was crafted rather weakly by Cecil in the 1560s.[8] In regard to Irish policy, however, Cecil hewed to a consistent line with the queen, nagging her into approval of new Irish institutions which her viceroys had sought for over a decade. Unlike Cromwell, who took the citadel of royal indifference by storm and paid the price for his temerity,

---

4. 'Additional Sidney state papers', ed. D.B. Quinn, *Anal Hib*, no. 26 (1970), 96.

5. *Sidney S.P.*, p. 67.

6. For the limited aims of the privy council in England, see Pulman, *Elizabethan privy council*, pp. 249–50.

7. MacCaffrey, *Shaping Elizabethan regime*, p. 21; *Making of policy*, pp. 13, 503.

8. Elton, *English law*, pp. 12–13. See MacCaffrey, *Making of policy*, p. 19, for his view of Cecil.

Cecil was a reformer for a different age. But piecemeal reforms which endure may be the more effective by virtue of their tranquil and hesitant origins. Indeed, a study of Cecil's Irish policy would vastly improve our understanding of the practice of government by executive forums such as the council in Ireland.[9] Despite his great respect for tradition, Cecil was aware that the Irish council ruled in the absence of frequent parliaments and that its decrees lacked the corporate authority of statute law. His careful management of Irish affairs was based on his preference for conventional norms of Tudor government and his recognition that Ireland was constitutionally exceptional.[10]

BALANCED PRAGMATISM: A NEW PARADIGM

It is in this connection that we must revise the currently accepted paradigm of the Tudor conquest of Ireland. Prior to the 1580s, the government pursued grand constitutional ends with severely limited means. The chief governor was constantly exposed to hostile criticism from both England and Ireland and his initiative was limited by royal parsimony and partisan attacks. Fitful changes in policy direction, the withdrawal of financial support, and the replacement of viceroys after less than five years in office did little to ensure continuity and stability in Irish politics. As a consequence, we must seek a different model of governance. There was no constitutional revolution in the period, although important structural innovations were put into place. The council in Ireland pursued instead a policy of compromise. Its administrative innovations were incomplete and they were achieved through evolution rather than 'programmatic' infusions of executive authority. The council was part of the constitutional anomaly of Irish government, a broker of interests and a filter through which the competing agendas of reform could be screened. Dr Brady has argued that all Tudor governments in Ireland followed the nostrum of law reform as the basis of improved management and supervision, yet few of them sustained a commitment to it in practice.[11] Thus, the

9. In Conyers Read's classic biography, the author dismissed Cecil's role in Ireland with these words, 'I have found nothing in the record of Burghley's relations to Ireland to throw fresh light either upon the history of the island or of the man'. C. Read, *Lord Burghley and Queen Elizabeth* (London, 1960), p. 10. One suspects that his search of the Irish record was very limited.

10. Canny has argued, in contrast, that Cecil was 'the most enthusiastic advocate of an aggressive policy in Ireland' and a strong supporter of colonization. This effort to superimpose clarity, structure and pattern on the untidy reality of Elizabethan Ireland serves to support Canny's belief that there was a comprehensive plan to subjugate Ireland to military rule. *Elizabethan conquest*, pp. 62–63, 73–76.

11. Brady, 'Court, castle and country', p. 47; 'Introduction' to *Natives and newcomers*, pp. 14–17.

Elizabethan government of Ireland to 1578 was the product of balance, practical adjustment and conditional settlements. In England itself, there was a similar disjuncture between majesty and pretension. Professor Hurstfield has reflected on the 'illusion of power' in late Tudor governance. He found that every English monarch was perilously short of funds and limited by an administrative structure which was inadequate to pursue its political objectives. Despite the superficial trappings of royal pomp, he said, 'The Elizabethan state had all the emblems of a great power with miserably inadequate means to support it'.[12]

In its reliance on local government and traditional methods of enforcement, the queen's government masked its systemic frailty by its insistence on constitutional forms. In practice, of course, these inchoate agents of the policy of anglicization enjoyed only limited support from both the centre and the periphery. The acute contradictions which often developed from the interplay of theory and practice were nowhere more marked than in the expansion of conciliar jurisdiction through the shiring of Irish counties. No new counties had been shired since the thirteenth century until Henry VIII created Co. West Meath in 1543. The new shires of Queen's and King's Counties were created by act of parliament in 1556. But the settlement of these counties was continually frustrated by the rebellious O'Connors and O'Mores.[13] In the parliament of 1569–71 Sydney attempted to realize the claims of the government to rule all of Ireland by shiring Ulster and Connacht. It is possible to date the shiring of Counties Monaghan, Longford, Leitrim, Sligo and Fermanagh from this act, but in practice there was little administrative effort to control these areas. Survey commissions were named in 1570 and 1571, however, and in the case of Co. Longford an interesting, though very tentative, order was made. The lord deputy decreed in October 1570 that,

. . . considering that the country is now shire ground, and no longer under Irish law, [he] has resolved that the office of captain should be extinguished, and that her Majesty's laws and the currency of her writs shall take place as is convenient, but believes the services of some such officer necessary, till the authority of a sheriff be better known.[14]

12. J. Hurstfield, *The illusion of power in Tudor politics*, Creighton lecture (London, 1979), p. 25.

13. See R. Dunlop, 'The plantation of Leix and Offaly', *EHR*, vi (1891), 61–96. Dunlop chronicled the resistance to settlement far more ably than he described the plantation itself, and there is room for a new study.

14. *P.R.I. rep. D.K. 11*, p. 241 (no. 1605). On 4 February a commission was named '. . . to limit and nominate them [the Annaly and the McGrannells' country] a shire or county . . .', citing the act 11 Eliz., sess. 3, c.9. ibid., p. 223 (no. 1486).

Whereas in 1559 commissions were sent both to create sheriffs in the loyal shires and to name captains among the native Irish, ten years later the government was committed '. . . to change the name of captain to seneschal, a degree or name more usual in places of civil governance . . .'.[15] Furthermore, commissions of the peace commonly associated the provincial aristocracy with itinerant councillors or members of the new regional boards.[16] This was not a tyrannical regime, therefore, because it possessed only a skeletal local administration and it lacked the resources to support a 'conquest'.[17]

The contrast between the public posture of Irish government and its concealed susceptibilities should not lead us to the conclusion that the resistance to reform was inspired by nationalist opposition. The simplistic view that the government pursued aggressive military conquest which was violently opposed by well-defined ethnic and political unity is untenable.[18] Rather, the response to assertions of central authority in the provinces was variable and often muted. The bardic poets who described Ireland in general political terms were merely using conventional images and they, too, thought and wrote primarily about dynastic and provincial themes.[19] Further, there was great complexity within the native Irish population well into the late sixteenth century. Dr Cosgrove has recently described the Anglo-Irish as neither English nor Gaelic in the later medieval period, and he noted the persistence of their unique identity well into the Tudor century.[20] Dr Brady has explained that the role of the earl of Desmond in the Munster rebellion was politically

Other commissions were named to survey the county lines or to delimit native Irish countries in Waterford, West Meath, Tipperary, Antrim, Down and other areas of Ulster, Connacht and Munster. See *P.R.I. rep. D.K. 11*, pp. 224, 230–34, et seq.

15. *P.R.I. rep. D.K. 12*, p. 40 (no. 1760), where Ross Mageohegan was named the seneschal of his ancestral lands in Co. West Meath, now the barony of Moycashell, in 1571. For sheriffs and captains, see *P.R.I. rep. D.K. 11*, pp. 33–34. Despite the transformation of the title, the seneschal continued to receive the fees and dues granted to Irish captains.

16. *P.R.I. rep. D.K. 9*, pp. 82–83; *11*, p. 93.

17. See also Williams, *Tudor regime*, pp. 458, 463, for the structural limitations of Tudor government in its reliance on local militia and ad hoc policies. For a careful study on the shiring of the native Irish territories see the essay by C.L. Falkiner, 'The counties of Ireland: an historical study of their origin, constitution and gradual delimitation', *RIA Proc*, xxiv (1903), sect. c, pt. 4, 169–94. Falkiner is indefinite on some of this, but he usefully pointed out that Sussex was '. . . the first to conceive any large plan for an efficient administrative settlement of Ireland . . .' based on the shiring of the country (at 182).

18. Bradshaw, 'Native reaction to the westward enterprise', pp. 78–79. Bradshaw uses only a few poems to prove his case of 'purely rebel songs'.

19. B. Cunningham, 'Native culture and political culture, 1580–1640' in Brady & Gillespie, ed., *Natives and newcomers*, p. 150.

20. A. Cosgrove, 'The writing of Irish medieval history', *IHS*, xxvii (1990), 110–11.

fortuitous and had little to do with his inveterate opposition to English rule.[21] And other writers have shown that Gaelic attitudes to the English were governed by the limited vision of local élites engaged in contests for power in counties and countries far from Dublin. Cunningham and Gillespie have written,

There appears to have been no sharp division on political lines between natives and newcomers. Each had succeeded in understanding the other in its own terms. Even in the early seventeenth century Annals of the Four Masters, there is no real sense of racial antagonism between the crown and the Irish in the late sixteenth century. There is even an acceptance of the new order and the structures it brought with it.[22]

Brady's argument for an emergent opposition party within the Pale is limited to the constitutional crisis over the cess and he blames the excessive violence and ruthlessness of Lord Grey in the aftermath of the Munster rebellion for the crystallization of political resistance to the government.[23]

In order to clarify the work of the council and the response of the country to its superintendence of affairs, we must consider the entire spectrum of conciliar activity. The aim of this work has been to restore a balanced perspective to discussion of Irish government in the Elizabethan period by broadening the scope of analysis. To a large extent, the nature of the documents has compelled us to consider the practice of government rather than its theoretical foundations. In the process of interpreting the wide range of council actions, we must come to recognize the complexity of its work, the diversity of its views and the ambiguity of its results. We must be aware of the gap which often separates intention from action, just as we should be sensible of the inherent limitations of sixteenth-century governments generally. The purpose here is neither to diminish the significance of single events nor to legitimize the occasional use of violence for the ends of government. Rather, it is to suggest that intensive analyses of the council's work can help us to avoid the distorting mirror of isolated occurrences and excessive schematizing.[24] The massacre of O'Mores

21. Brady, 'Desmond rebellion', 300–04, 309–11.
22. Cunningham and Gillespie, 'Englishmen in Irish annals', 5, 12–15, 18, 20. For a different view which stresses the durability of Gaelic opposition to reform, see Morgan, 'End of Gaelic Ulster', 8–31.
23. Brady, 'Conservative subversives', pp. 26–30.
24. See, for example, the sensationalist treatment by J.P. Myers, 'Murdering heart, murdering hand: captain Thomas Lee of Ireland, Elizabethan assassin', *Sixteenth Century Journal*, xxii (1991), 47–60 which argues that cruelty and selective assassination were at the core of official Irish policy. For a critical overview of research designs which are too narrowly drawn, see Elton, *Reform and renewal*, p. 4.

and O'Connors at Mullaghmast and the slaughter of the Scots by the earl of Essex in Ulster were important aspects of the generally roguish behaviour of the English soldiery, but this does not justify an inordinate emphasis on the stories of outrageous and provocative breakdowns in relations with the native Irish. The council itself demonstrated a clear preference for praxis over theory in its work and we may do well to follow this example in our analysis of Irish government. An appreciation of the continuities of government, the efforts to balance the competing interests of Irish culture and English crown, and the tangled intricacy of the task which the council faced will take us further toward a comprehensive understanding of Elizabethan Ireland than the narrowly defined and mono-causal treatments which have proliferated throughout Irish historiography.

In general, studies of Tudor Ireland have focused on military conflict, on models of conquest and colonization, and on competing ideologies. The research agenda should be expanded to include reviews of the effectiveness of government at the local and provincial levels; statistical analyses of inflation and landholding patterns and the relative health of the economy over time; and studies of litigation which may reveal more about the relationship between law and society. It would be useful to conceive of the perimeter of conciliar jurisdiction in relation to multiple factors such as the imposition of cess, the placement of garrisons, the effective boundaries of the provincial councils and judges of assize, and the level of recourse to common law remedies. As Brady and Gillespie have observed, the discussion of theoretical alternatives is premature since we lack sufficient information on the administrative context for the English government of Ireland.[25] Another useful approach to Irish historiography would be to incorporate ancillary disciplines into the discussion of the success or failure of English rule. New studies in anthropology and cross-cultural communication may be used to understand the limits of the possible in Tudor Ireland and to revise our expectations for ambitious projects such as law reform. On the other hand, sociological perspectives may assist us in an appreciation of the *modus vivendi* which was established in certain areas of Ireland where conflict and confrontation were muted or largely avoided. The existence of distinct cultural and linguistic blocs which have been submerged within larger national boundaries would suggest that symbiotic relationships may be an useful model for understanding semi-independent regions such as Brittany, Catalonia, Asturias and Flanders. In much the same way, symbiosis characterizes the pattern of contacts between late Tudor Ireland and the Elizabethan state. There has been so much concentration on the

25. 'Introduction' in Brady & Gillespie, ed., *Natives and newcomers*, pp. 14–17, 21.

colonial models in the study of Elizabethan Ireland that it has often been forgotten that Ireland is an integral part of Europe.

Comparative studies of Tudor Ireland have recently been initiated by Dr Ellis and others. He has examined the government of the North of England and compared Tudor borderlands in Scotland and Wales with the situation in Ireland. Ellis has found that local and dynastic politics dominated the concerns of every provincial regime and that the central government pursued anglicization in Wales and other dominions by the extension of the common law.[26] For the council in the marches of Wales, Dr Williams has established that Tudor rule was effectively broadened by increased litigation. He has argued that the council in Wales faced problems of a refractory native populace which was wedded to low-level disorder, resentful of increased taxation, and suspicious of outside influence. Nevertheless, he views the levels of dissent and disruption as common by sixteenth-century standards and finds that the increased caseload of the council was the result of a more systematic effort to apprehend and punish offenders. Lord Chancellor Gerrard compared cattle-raiding in Leinster with similar disturbances in the Welsh marches and he bemoaned the corruption of fellow councillors in Wales and Ireland alike.[27] In England itself there were atavistic tendencies at the local level in contrast to the proclaimed ideal of the ordered commonwealth. Disorders which resulted in litigation might range from cases of robbery and assault and abduction to misdemeanours linked to football, bowling, cards and alehouses. Cases of riot brought before the justices in Essex, for example, covered '. . . everything from a rebellion to a trio of sour-minded rustics trampling down another's grass'.[28] This is not to suggest that Ireland was little different in its social organization or its level of political sophistication from England or other early modern states. It is simply an assertion of the need for a more ample framework within which to make judgements about the work of the Tudor council in Ireland.

AFTER 1578

Whatever the position one takes about the preceding decades, it is clear that the successive rebellions which began in 1579 changed the

26. Ellis, *The Pale and the far North: government and society in two early Tudor border-lands* (Galway, 1988), pp. 5–32; 'Nationalist historiography', 1–18; 'England in the Tudor state', *Hist Jn*, xxvi (1983), 211–12.

27. Williams, *Council in Wales*, pp. 313–14, 320–23.

28. F.G. Emmison, *Elizabethan life: disorder* (Chelmsford, 1970), p. 100. Evidence of substantial, and rising, violence and disorder in the period has been confirmed in the work of Samaha and Cockburn. See Samaha, *Law and order*, pp. 16–17; J.S. Cockburn, 'The nature and incidence of crime in England, 1559–1625', in Cockburn, ed., *Crime in England, 1550–1800* (Princeton, 1977), pp. 53–60.

landscape of Irish politics. Dr Canny has argued that an era of compromise and tact between the Old English and the Dublin administration ended after 1579 in an estrangement of the Pale élite from the Elizabethan regime.[29] Dr Brady has stressed the combination of events—the political crisis in the Pale over cess, the fiscal debilitation of the government and the shock of rebellion—which culminated in the alienation of the Anglo-Irish.[30] The fragile equilibrium of limited military commitments and tightly managed fiscal restraint was made irrelevant by the sudden appearance of an Irish rebel with papal backing in a 'crusade' against the government. We might add that the recall of Sydney in 1578 led to a series of weakened chief governors. Both Drury and Pelham lacked substantial authority as interim lords justice, while Lord Grey possessed meagre experience and demonstrated a talent for exacerbating dangerous situations. The remarkable continuity of conciliar membership quickly evaporated after 1578 with the long-anticipated demise of both chief justices, the departure and death of the lord chancellor, and the deaths of the secretary of state and the vice treasurer. One third of the membership of the council in 1578 had been eliminated within three years and another third of that forum had died by 1585.[31] As influence passed to veteran English leaders such as Adam Loftus, the solitary representatives of cooperation and compromise, Sir Lucas Dillon and Sir Nicholas White, passed their remaining days on the council with little effect until both died in 1593.

In the decade following the recall of Sydney, Ireland seemed to lurch from one crisis to another. The rebellion in Munster consumed arms and treasure for nearly five years until the death of the earl of Desmond in 1583. The rapacious brutality of Lord Deputy Grey against both Gaelic and Anglo-Irish rebels led to his dismissal and served as a catalyst to the forces of opposition in the Pale. When Sir John Perrot launched a new initiative to extend English authority by the composition for cess in 1585, he coupled this renewed threat of fiscal tyranny with an insistence on religious conformity throughout the realm. Not surprisingly, his parliament witnessed full-scale opposition and the council in Ireland was the scene of bitter feuding between Loftus and the lord deputy.[32] When Perrot was recalled in 1588 the

29. Canny, 'Identity formation', p. 164.
30. Brady, 'Desmond rebellion', 312; 'Conservative subversives', pp. 26–30.
31. Men of experience such as Malbie, Cowley and the moderate Bishop Brady died in 1584, while the death of Kildare in 1585 was lamented as a loss for Anglo-Irish interests in the Pale. Archbishop Lancaster, a stalwart supporter of Loftus, died in 1583.
32. Ellis, *Tudor Ireland*, pp. 284–96; Brady, 'Conservative subversives', p. 28; Treadwell, 'Irish parliament of 1585–6', 261–77, 285–306.

new chief governor was the aged Sir William Fitzwilliam. The choice of a secondary figure who had failed to provide effective leadership in an earlier lieutenancy in Ireland is at first glance an odd one. But Fitzwilliam also brought unique advantages to this role. He offended no one. He had years of experience in Ireland and knew the country well. He had no particular agenda for reform and little energy with which to pursue one. Consequently, he emerged as the ideal compromise candidate for a healing interim. His second viceroyalty was, of course, equally disastrous, but the selection of Fitzwilliam is perhaps an effective characterization of Elizabethan Irish policy. As it moved from one end of the spectrum to the other, embracing first reform and then retrenchment, Elizabeth's government of Ireland manifested all its flaws. Yet there is another aspect to the story.

Recent writers have determined that the Tudor government of Ireland was largely a failure, but the structure of an English administration is clearly discernible by 1578 and the emergence of a fully-fledged Tudor state was largely achieved by gradual anglicization in 1603.[33] Those who have concentrated their attention exclusively on politics and confrontation may have missed the slow development of constitutional forms in Irish government which conservative statesmen regarded as essential to Tudor rule. The estrangement of the native population is still a hotly contested issue, but we can point to a recent study of the Munster plantation which demonstrated the use of common law procedures and the mixed results which were obtained there. The commission of 1588, which was headed by the English chief justice of common pleas, refused to accept evidence of Irish land titles. But the subsequent commission of 1592, led by officials of the Dublin and Munster administrations, showed greater knowledge of the situation and more equitable treatment of the litigants.[34] The complexity of the Munster arrangements is not uncharacteristic. As Dr Ellis has observed, political authority was extended throughout nearly all of Ireland save Ulster by 1590, despite the resistance of local forces. And when English troops were demobilized after 1603 Irish government returned to the earlier model of a reduced military force and inexpensive government based on the gradual anglicization of Irish institutions.[35] The incompleteness of this process and the complexity of the problems faced by each regime in Dublin make it difficult to assess the achievement of Elizabethan rule in Ireland. The assertion that it was a conquest seems exaggerated in view of the limited

33. Ellis, *Tudor Ireland*, pp. 315–18. Ellis finds Elizabethan rule 'committed' to energetic reform, but 'irresolute' in its application (p. 318).

34. Sheehan, 'Plantation of Munster', 297–98, 303–13.

35. Ellis, *Tudor Ireland*, pp. 297, 314. See also Simms, *Kings to warlords*, p. 148 for the view that Gaelic lords accepted the Tudor kingdom of Ireland by 1603.

resources committed to Irish governance. But equally, the claim that it was a failure appears to focus primarily on the political estrangement of key elements of the Irish polity. Perhaps the most convincing case can be made for a Tudor compromise, one in which competing interests, rival strategies, conflicting personalities and structural defects hampered the government and prevented all but the most heroic measures from having immediate success. In the end, the intermittent process of anglicization throughout the period achieved the profoundly undramatic result of binding Irish subjects to the rule of English common law.[36]

In conclusion, the aims of the lord deputy and council were exceedingly conventional. Once peace and stability were achieved, the gradual extension of the common law would guarantee the preservation of order. The response to sporadic unrest had to be a military one, for the judicial apparatus and the habit of recourse to litigation were not sufficiently developed in Ireland. Efforts were made to combine judicial and military programmes in order to win over the native Irish outside the Pale. But these attempts were shackled by the fiscal restraints imposed by the queen. Some disturbances occasionally congealed into large-scale insurrections in one province, but the coercive measures used to put them down were designed to overawe the native Irish, not to exterminate them. When a large-scale revolt broke out, the expenses of governing Ireland rose dramatically and the result was always to jeopardize previous gains in a withdrawal of the queen's support after the end of the conflict. The tension between these three cornerstones of conciliar policy was always present. Judicial reforms required a preliminary military presence which in turn meant spending more money. Fiscal restraint compelled force reductions which threatened the fragile tranquillity of the country. Only a firm commitment to move ahead simultaneously on all three fronts would allow the desired extension of the common law. Elizabeth's failure to do this meant that the gains of one administration were often wiped out in the orgy of retrenchment and recrimination which followed. Steady progress toward the expansion of Tudor authority in Ireland came largely in spite of the last Tudor sovereign.

What was the role of the privy council in Ireland in the process of anglicization? An intermediate answer must begin with the impetus for reform. As we have seen, the act of 1541 ended the basis for constitutional dualism and English officials thereafter embraced the theoretical model of unitary sovereignty throughout royal dominions. To this campaign for an expanded jurisidiction of conciliar government,

36. For the transformation of Irish law and the Irish legal profession, see C. Kenny, 'Exclusion of Catholics', 337–46; Pawlisch, *Sir John Davies and the conquest of Ireland*.

a number of individual Irish councillors made important intellectual contributions. The proposals of Sussex and Sydney were based in part on these models, and the privy councillors at Westminster developed their own independent sources of information. When this varied field of inquiries was mixed with the inveterate caution of the queen, it is hardly surprising that it produced mixed results. Nevertheless, the council in Ireland presided over the building of new structures in Irish government, leading to the creation of a microcosm of English administration. If the process was still incomplete by 1578—the exchequer was still unreformed, for instance—it is clear that the concept of juridical unity had been adopted and that the English model of governance was being slowly extended beyond the Pale. If the new institutions were initially rather weak, and the practical diffusion of authority resisted centralization, the essential thrust of conciliar government was plain. The council issued proclamations to reform the coinage, to authorize the shiring of new counties, to call litigants and juries to account for their actions at court, and to require the victualling of troops. Members of the council served on judicial commissions of inquiry; commissions to be sheriffs of Irish counties; and commissions to take musters, to recover debts, and to execute ecclesiastical laws.[37] In matters of high policy, the council arrogated to itself the exercise of direct law-making powers by means of the 'act of state', an expedient which was increasingly used in the absence of frequent Irish parliaments. It was, in sum, a working executive committee, an active force in the management of the realm, and an engine of constitutional change.

37. *P.R.I. rep. D.K. 11*, pp. 34, 71, 78; *12*, p. 183; *13*, p. 48.

Map 1 Principal cities and towns subject to royal authority, 1556–78[1]

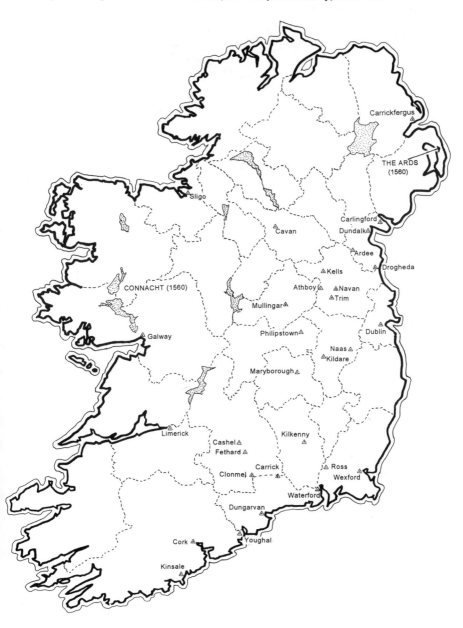

1. Based on 'Parliamentary constituencies, 1560–86' by T.W. Moody in Moody et al., *N.H.I.: ix*, map no. 49 (revised and amended).

Map 2 The shiring of Tudor Ireland, including areas subject to the cess by county and by lordship[1]

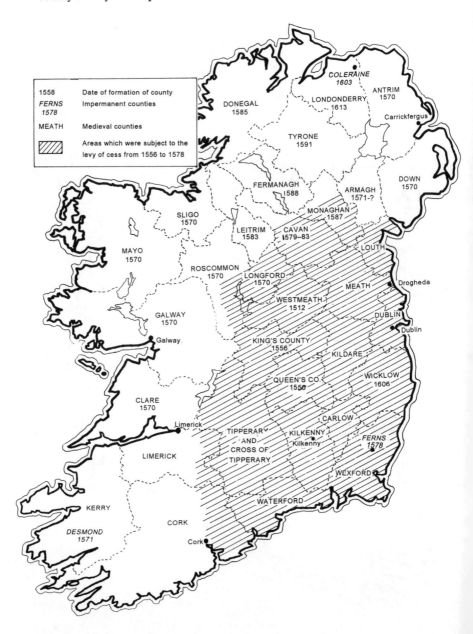

1. Based on 'Counties, 1542–1613' by K.W. Nicholls in Moody et al., ed., *N.H.I.: ix*, map no. 45 (revised and amended).

Map 3 The provincial government: garrison towns and centres for the new provincial councils after 1570[1]

1. Based on 'Anglo-Irish and Gaelic lordships in the late 15th century' by K.W. Nicholls in Moody et al., ed., *N.H.I.: ix*, map no. 47 (revised and amended).

Map 4 The administration of the cess and the mustering of troops: Irish lord-ships subject to the levy of cess and primary collecting points in the Pale[1]

1. Based on 'Anglo-Irish and Gaelic lordships in the late 15th century' by K.W. Nicholls in Moody et al., ed., *N.H.I.: ix*, map no. 47 (revised and amended).

The signet of Ireland

The signet was in the possession of the secretary of state from 1560 and it was used to seal council documents as well as documents signed by the lord deputy alone. Examples of the seal survive in a number of conciliar letters and decrees. It was about one inch in diameter and the border contained the full title of the queen: 'Eliz[abeth] D[ei] G[ratia] Ang[liae] Hib[erniae] Reg[ina]'. PRO, SP 63/6/194. One of the earliest intact examples of the seal was made on a council document of 24 October 1563 which clearly described the seal as the 'Queens Majesties signett'. In the centre was the symbolic Irish harp, bordered on the top by the queen's initials, E.R., and on the bottom by a rose and portcullis. At the very top of the border was a crown. BL, Carte MS 58, f. 22. A nearly perfect example is in Carte MS 58, f. 24v. A photo-reproduction is shown below.

8 Photograph of the seal produced by the signet of Ireland. The signet was used to authenticate documents produced by the council in Ireland and it was held in the custody of the secretary of state for Ireland from 1560.

The burden of cess

Furnished below are the details of the cess for 1561, the imposition that provoked the Book of 24 Articles and the bringing forward of other grievances.

Units (of grain or beef)	Counties or Irish countries
2,400 pecks of wheat and malt	Meath
1,040 pecks of wheat and malt	West Meath
1,040 pecks of wheat and malt	Dublin
1,040 pecks of wheat and malt	Kildare
400 pecks of wheat and malt	Wexford
200 beef cattle; 100 swine	O'Reilly
100 beef cattle; 25 swine	The Annaly
30 beef cattle; 15 swine	MacCoghlan
60 beef cattle; 30 swine	O'Kelly
100 beef cattle; 50 swine	O'Byrnes
20 beef cattle; 50 swine	O'Tooles
140 beef cattle; 20 swine	Carlow (including Kavanaghs country)
100 beef cattle; 40 swine	Upper Ossory
100 beef cattle; 50 swine	O'Carroll
100 beef cattle; 50 swine	Tipperary
100 beef cattle; 50 swine	Waterford
50 beef cattle; 25 swine	Ferney
30 beef cattle; 50 swine	Dartry
60 beef cattle; 30 swine	O'Kellys (beyond the Suck River)
100 beef cattle; 50 swine	McMahons

The Anglo-Irish counties of the Pale contributed to the cess in prescribed units of grain (wheat, malt and beer malt). The Gaelic Irish countries, such as O'Reilly's country, were required to levy a prescribed number of beef cattle and pigs for the cess. In the loyal southern counties under the domination of Ormonde, levies of grain or

of cattle might be imposed, but the Desmond counties of Limerick
and Cork were infrequently charged with smaller amounts of cattle.
Kilkenny, Louth, Leix and Offaly were normally cessed for purveyance
although not in 1561, as we have seen above. Other Irish countries
which customarily contributed to the cess were O'Ferralls, MacMahons
(but see Ferney and Dartry above) and MacGeoghegans. Smaller and
less frequent levies were imposed on the MacLoughlins, O'Maddens
and O'Mulloys. See RIA, MS 24 F 17, ff. 177–78 and chapter 6, above,
pp. 376–81.

APPENDIX THREE

The Book of 24 Articles

Printed below is the text of the Book of 24 Articles, a book of grievances presented to the government in England by Irish law students who were studying at the inns of court in London during the political contest over the cess in 1561 and 1562. When a second annual purveyance, the cess for the lord deputy's household, was added to the burden on the Pale in 1561, there was an outcry from leading gentry. These men were lawyers and landholders who formed an inchoate opposition which was dubbed the 'commonwealth men'. In 1562 the lord deputy and council imposed the largest cess of the period, extending it to 14 counties and 12 Irish lordships. The Book of 24 Articles was composed by law students to offer a definitive account of the machinations of the council in the matter of cess; to show how the new exactions were an unconstitutional departure from previous forms of taxation; and to insist on the right of the Palesmen to protest against arbitrary increases in purveyance. The articles concluded with an appeal for redress from the queen. The lord deputy and council promptly defended their actions, but the queen launched an investigation into the matter and the entire affair became highly politicized. The Book of 24 Articles indicates that the council in Ireland functioned within a highly developed political culture and that arbitrary methods of government were met with lawful resistance.

It is worth adding that this first salvo in the battle over cess was answered by a detailed list of responses, including the 'Annsweare made to the boke of articles on the state of the English Pale 1560 to 1561 delivered to the lordes of the privy council by certen Irish students' (PRO, SP 63/5/138–40v;150–55v). Another reply to the students was apparently penned for Sussex (ff. 160–65) and an answer to his rebuttal was then made by the students along with certain gentlemen of Ireland (ff. 145–49;168–69v). A digest of the book and the answers was then made for reference, using two columns to compare the allegations and responses (ff. 173–75; 177–79v). On 27 May 1562 a group of 29 Irish gentlemen of the English Pale signed a letter to the queen asserting both their loyalty to the crown and their inability to pay the cess (PRO, SP 63/6/22), indicating that overt dissension had spread widely in the Pale. The lord lieutenant and council reported to the queen that they had sent a commission to confer with the gentlemen of every county, but their offer to redeem certain leases made in each county as an alternative to charging cess was rejected. The council met with representatives of the Pale for several days, suggesting a parliament which would authorize a tax upon anyone who held any of the queen's spiritual possessions in fee farm. The gentlemen were then dismissed with the injunction that they were ultimately responsible for the administration of the law as justices of the peace in their shires, including the execution of all orders sent to them by the council. A stalemate had been reached and neither side wished to aggravate the matter in question with further accusations, despite the lack of resolution (PRO, SP 63/6/183–83v).

For purposes of the printed transcription, I have followed the original text except where I have extended contractions and silently added punctuation to clarify the sense of the original. Brackets are used to indicate editing emendations and clarifications where the meaning is obscure, and to note words which could not be identified with any certainty. The original document is PRO, SP 63/5/133–36v.

A boke comprehendinge Dyvers articles favoring [?] the miserable estate of the Englishe pale of Ireland
Annis 1560 & 1561

Firste the circuite or precinckte of that parte of the Englishe pale which in effecte beareth onely almanner of ymposicions and cesses for the governors house the fortes and soldiors is but fyve small shires viz The Counties of Dublyn, Meath, Weastemeath, Lowth and Kildare. And the same fyve shires are by estimacion scarse as bigg as some one shire here in England. And parcell of the said shires are alredy so ympoverished through the extreame charges of warre and cesses that there be but thre shires which in effecte beareth the hole charge. viz The Counties of Dublyn, Meath and Kyldare:

Item the said shires are devided into Carewes [a measure of land] or plowelandes every plough lande conteyninge six score Acres whereof every one payeth yerely xiij s. iiij d. subsidie unto the Quenes Majestie

Item the said fyve shires as often as is thought good by the governor are charged with asmuch wheate and malte by the name of cesse as he thinckes mete for the furniture of his house, victuling of the fortes and soldiors. Which charge of cesses began in the tyme of Sir James Croftes and was then but viij peckes A plough Lande but hath since growen by litle and Lytle to that rate that every Carewe or plough Lande is charged at this daie with xviij peckes whereof more then the half is wheate, the residue malte. The peck wheate conteyning xvj gallons, the peck malte xviij; for the wheate is paid but iiij s. the peck and for the malte but ij s viij d. The same at the market solde the wheate at xxvj s. viij d: The malte at xiij s. iiij d. And yet the nomber of souldiors litle increased in respecte of thincrease of charge upon the Cuntrey. [f.133]

Item every plough Lande in the shires aforesaid was charged ech [each] of those yeres for provision of the governors hous and fortes with one choise befe, thre muttons, the thirde parte of a porke, one gallon of Butter; The befe taken up at viij s. sterlinge being comonly solde in the cuntrey for xxxiij s. iiij d. sterl. The mutton take up for xij d. sterlinge being comonly solde for iiij s. str. The gallon of butter taken up for xij d. str. being sold for iiij s. str. The porke taken up for v s. being comonly solde for xv s . str.

Item note that before this certainty began in ceasses of beafes, muttons, porkes etc., The governors Cators mighte and Did take up As much As them listed At the price abovesaid, which abuse was since redused to the certenty before mencioned by the governour and counselles order, meanynge thereby to redres the extorcion used by the cators under color of their comyssion, which although the same doth seme by order reformed yet the pore people stande intollerablie burdened as appereth.

Item those cesses before notwithstandinge. The governors Cator doth still take up poulterie and other small cates at pleasure as beckon [?] from the roffe [ruff, or perch] veale pig lambe etc. and also other private men hath their cators. To the subiectes greate charge and empoverishment.

Item a certaintie of provision beinge rated and thought sufficient to serve the Lorde levetenantes house for a hole yere and the same levied holly before maie [May] the same yere, yet in the Absence of him the lorde justice for the tyme had his cators that toke up of newe at his pleasure: As manie beves muttons and other Cates etc. paying at the price before mencioned comonly called the quenes price. [f. 133v]

Item the pore men of the fyve shires are alwaies charged with carynge of their corne ceassed to the fortes on their owen horses, being alowed but viij d. for the horse, the places distante from the fortes forty miles, some more, some les in somuch as they have Dyvers tymes offred their corne grates [gratis] to be Discharged of the caryage, and some by favour are so Discharged, so remayneth the pore subiecte without any penny for his Corne.

Item whereas this cesse or greate charge of the Cuntry of Corne, beves etc. is duely levied and taken up, it sholde seme the same to be hable to victuall a farre greated [sic] Crue [crew] of soldiors then are in the fortes. And whereas a meane was Devised and moved to Disburden the Cuntrey of this intollerable charges to the Quenes maiesties greate benefite yf the same were then put in execucion, yet that Devise and mocion toke no effecte. By reason whereof the pore cuntrey remayneth charged as aforesaid.

Item more the said fyve shires are inforced to aunswere caryage to every iorney with cartes, carres and carters, Also cartes, carres and labourers to repaire and builde private mens houses, walles and Ditches. And moreover the governors, marshall and other mens stuff and caryage at all tymes when they please or commaunde, having for the same but small alowaunce or none.

Item all those charges not withstandinge there lyeth contynually (except in iorneys made ones or twice a yere which contynueth never above xl^{ti} Daies) on the plough Lande in many places of the Englishe pale two horsemen soldiors which are to be accounted foure men and foure horses by reason every soldior hath his boy and two horses whose infinite charge and unruelie Doinges are not possible to be written.

Item in the said Englishe pale where they lie there is no syrvice[?] to be don for the same, save for them, is as is met [meet] and as aunswerable to the Lawes As is any parte of England. [f. 134]

Item every soldior hath for his two horses every xxiiij owres [hours] xij sheaves of oates Duble banded, and for lack of otes viij sheaves of wheate and paieth but ij d. for every xij sheves of otes or viij sheaves of wheate, whereof every xlviij sheaves maketh a peck worth in the cuntrie beinge otes x s. str for which they paie xiij d. and no more, and when he taketh wheate he payeth but after the same rate. And for wante of corne in sheafe the soldior will have iiij gallons and a half [of] clene [without chaff?] corne every daie and nighte and no les, which charge is so grevous to the husbandman As some hath compounded with the captaines to forgive there allowaunce for iiij^{or} yeres to be Discharged of horses [for] the vth yere wheerunto the captaine hath agreed.

Item the Soldior hath besides this of the farmer haie lytter and glaie, that is, the sheafe strucken with the thresher once or twise. And so taketh the same to his horse with out paying any thinge therefore, which is a great Distruccion of corne and no lyttle undoing to the farmer.

Item every soldiors two horses consumeth after the rate aforesaid besides haie and glaie in iij quarters of a yere, During which tyme they are at harde [?] meate, lxvi peckes, every peck conteyning xviij gallons. The reste of the yere they runn in the medowes paying nothinge, so as the charges of fyndinge iiij horses on every plough landes where they lie in corne onely During these iij quarters commeth to the some of lx^{li}[£] sterlinge at the leaste, over and besides the subsidie to the Quenes maiestie, The cesses to the governors hous and the fortes, and the souldioures owne table with his woman and boy as a nomber hath.

Item the sowldiar is not aunswerable at the comon lawe for any debt, trespasse or Demaunde neithe[r] araignehable for murder, rape nor any other kinde of felonie or Disordre but is triable as they say by their Marshiall lawe. So that it hath bene sene that soldiars being at their Araynement at the barr hath bene by the Marshalles owne handes attempted to have bene taken thense to the derogacion of the Quenes highnes lawes. And the soldiers that is tried by that lawe is seldome or never ponished for their factes [deeds] aforesaide wherof they commytt A nombre. [f. 134v]

Item every soldior for him self payeth but ii d. a weake and for his boie i d. and will not contente him self with such there as the husbandman hath for his owen provision but mislikinge the same will kill such victuelles as he beste fancieth. As moste comonly is his ostice [host's?] pigges, capons, hens or chickins yf any be in the house and for wante of these his oste [host] must agre with him to give him clerely xv d. sterlinge a daie to be clerely rid and Discharged of him els will the soldior take his ostice [host's] pledge and Dyne thereon at the next Alehouse. And notwithstandinge an order of late taken for reformacon of the unruelines or misorder in this article specified, yet is it still usal [usual]. Also some captaines notwithstanding this small allowaunce hath after a paie made to them by the Quenes Maiestie lefte the husbandman unpaid for the souldiors borde, who besides that he hath but this ij d. a meale for the weke daies muste be faine to geve him his meales on the sondaie grates [gratis].

Item the extremetie of the said Ceasses, bearing of horses & burdeninge of the souldiors and their boies, with the charges of al manner [of] Cariages before mencioned doth cause the pore men to give up their houses, and they with their wives and children do runne a begging, leving their tenures and farmes utterly waste without manuringe or occupying the same for grasinge or any other commoditie, in so much that in some one Barrony which is not above the tenth parte of one of the said shires there are xx^{ti} farmes waste and utterly void at this present. An in other Barronies, some more, some les. And of soundry other farmes the half ar lefte unsowen for lack of sede, the corne being consumed with horsses.

Item a commission was this yeres graunted by the governor there that though pore men wanted [i.e. lacked] corne and were not hable to paie the cesses by reason of those intollerable charges, that notwithstandinge, the shreves and collectors sholde take their Chattelles and goodes and sell the same. And of the monie thereof levyed to bye at the markettes accordinge as corne was solde there so did the pore men paie at the market xxvi s. viij d. sterlinge the peck, upon his goodes and was allowed therefore but iiij s. sterlinge, to his utter undoinge. [f. 135]

Item whereas a mas of treasure currant mony of England was these yeres sente by her Maiestie into Ireland for the payment of the armie and other her dettes, the same was retained in the handes of the governors undisbursed for a longe season untill such tyme as the base coine had a fall by proclamacion here in England, some testors to iiij d. ob and some to ij d. str. [?]. After which tyme the same was proclaimed to viij d. sterling the teastor there. And of the iiij d. ob none was sene to come a brode [abroad]. Then was the ij d. str. [?] disbursed after that rate unto the cuntrie for certaine such dettes as was Due for ceasses As well ymmediately before levied As for other ceasses then presently graunted but not levied nor leviable for longe tyme after, whereas other olde dettes of her maiestie was then lefte and yet do remaine unpaid. Then after the Cuntrie was paid they were proclaymed to the same rate that they were here in England, save a farthinge in a pece, by reason whereof the subiettes had greate los. Whereas yf the said monie had byn paid in convenient tyme the great losses unto the pore subiectes had not byn so grevous.

Item Whereas the cuntry hath remayning upon them there accustomed charge of horsses, men and boies, A newe crewe of Souldiors being late come thether, and to be placed, considering the farmer not hable to bere there the exaccions and them together, they were faine to be ceassed upon the borrowe [borough] townes. And bicause there Lyvinge is by trafike and merchaundice so as they have no provision but what they bie for their penie, there allowaunce is made the greater, for where the husbandman hath but ij d. thei are allowed iiij d. a meale whereof the farmer muste paie the one half to be Discharged of this newe burden.

Item notwithstandinge these enormities of the soldiors charges, there is an olde oppression called Coyne & lyverie on all borders by the Captaines of the severall borders and the same usid by the nobilitie and Dyvers gentilmen there in many places within the Englishe pale, which is an extorcion such as is not to be suffred amonge Englishe subiectes. [f. 135v]

Thus it evidently appereth that this litle plott being no more in quantitie by estimacon then some one shire of England as is aforesaid, besides the intollerable Disorder of the unruelie soldior[s] over and above the charges that the Quenes Majestie is at, is charged yerely with thirtie thowsand poundes sterlinge at the leaste; besides that the Lordes, gentilmen, Cities and borough Townes goeth to every iorney (which is the onely tyme of servise) At their owen proper costes and charges without any allowance. By reason whereof the pore & miserablie [sic] cuntrie runneth Dailly into waste and utter decaie to the greate grief of the Landelordes who thereby are undon and also to the famishing of the selie [poor, helpless] and myserable tenantes who in those yeres doth Die in the streates and highwaies for faulte of sustenance. And those of the pore labouring men which are in beste case contented onely for their meate & drincke to serve without any other wages or salary. And Dyvers other[s] contrary to their nature and bringing up are glad to flete out of the Englishe pale and to Dwell under the savage and rude sorte of Irish men chosing rather to inhabite under them then to abide the excessive burden wherewith they are Laden in the place where thei and their forefathers have Dwelte welthelie since Henry the secondes Daies. At which tyme our auncestors went from hens and placed them selves there.

Item that in this present boke nothing is Comprehended nor showed save such thinges as have ben don in those selfe yeres, though greate abuses hath byn in other yeres heretofore, nor nothing therein written other then are moste true and provable; Wherefore if any Dowte do arise in any parte hereof, Or yet any parcell thereof be denied for troth, yf it shall please the Quenes Maiesty to sende the copie hereof with her highnes lettres to the [f. 136] Sheriffes lordes and gentilmen of the same fyve shires and to the maiestrates, officers of Cities, borough Townes and franchises in the same, Willinge and commaundinge them upon their allegaunce to call their comminalties and to enquire of the troth thereof and to certifie what they knowe and that they fele them selves greved with all, As well in the premisses as in other thinges. And of the same to certifie her Maiestie under their handes and seales, Then her highnes shall thereby fynde the mere troth in any Matter or clause so Denied. Wherefore it maie please her Maiestie to have respecte & consideracon of the premisses. And for the love of god and charities sake to provide some Due and present redres therein.

Drawen & Executed by thos whose names ensuethe.

John Talbote	J Moy [?] Barnewall	Rychard Mellnyth [?]
Willm Bathe		Frauncis Delahide
Henry Burnell	Robert Dillon	Johne Bathe
John Rochefort	Michaell More	Georg [?] Cusake
Walter Golding		
Edward Barnewall	Thomas Dyllon	Gerald Weste
Richard Bassnett	Robert Bathe	Richard Sedgrave
Patrick Flemynge	Patrick Bathe	Bartholome Dardyth [?]
Christophor Hemyng [?]	John Mellnyth [?]	Robert Felde
John Waylshe	Thomas Dillon fitzRobert	

Chronological patterns of conciliar membership, 1556–1578

The lists of councillors given below are designed to illustrate the patterns and continuities of conciliar membership. The position at eight different dates is indicated: 1556, 1562, 1565, 1569, 1573, 1575 and 1578.

In 1556 the administration of Sussex began with an infusion of new members and a nucleus of holdovers from previous administrations. In 1559 the impact of Elizabeth's reign was felt on the council and in 1562 a number of new men were brought on the council. In 1565 Sydney began his first tenure as lord deputy, and in 1569 he was briefly returned to office. Fitzwilliam was named lord deputy to replace Sydney in 1573, although he did not have a distinct following in the council. In 1575 Sydney returned for a second term as lord deputy and in 1578 he was removed.

1556—Agarde, Alen, Aylmer, Bathe, Ormonde, Curwen, Dowdall, Baltinglas, Kildare, Fitzwilliam, Harbert, Hay, Lokwood, Parker, Plunket, Radcliffe, H., Radcliffe, T., Stanley, Sydney, Travers, Walsh.

1559—Agarde, Alen, Aylmer, Bathe, Ormonde, Curwen, Cusake, Dillon, R., Baltinglas, Kildare, Fitzwilliam, Harbert, Lokwood, Parker, Plunket, Radcliffe, H., Sussex, Stanley, Sydney, Travers, Warren, Walsh, Wingfield.

1562—Agarde, Bathe, Ormonde, Chaloner, Curwen, Cusake, Dillon, R., Baltinglas, Kildare, Fitzwilliam, Harbert, Loftus, Lokwood, Parker, Plunket, Radcliffe, H., Sussex, Stanley, Travers, Wingfield.

1565—Agarde, Arnold, Bagenall, Bathe, Brady, Ormonde, Chaloner, Curwen, Cusake, Dillon, R., Baltinglas, Kildare, Fitzwilliam, Harbert, Loftus, Lokwood, Plunket, Radcliffe, H., St Leger, Sydney.

1569—Agarde, Bagenall, Bathe, Brady, Ormonde, Carew, Chaloner, Cusake, Dillon, R., Draycott, Fyton, Kildare, Fitzwilliam, Lancaster, Loftus, Plunket, St Leger, Sydney, Weston.

1573—Agarde, Bagenall, Brady, Ormonde, Carew, Chaloner, Dillon, L., Dillon, R., Fyton, Kildare, Fitzwilliam, Garvey, Lancaster, Loftus, Perrot, Plunket, Weston, White.

1575—Agarde, Bagenall, Brady, Ormonde, Carew, Chaloner, Cowley, Dillon, L., Dillon, R., Fyton, Kildare, Fitzwilliam, Garvey, Gerrard, Lancaster, Loftus, Malbie, Plunket, Sydney, White.

1578—Bagenall, Brady, Ormonde, Chaloner, Cowley, Dillon, L., Dillon, R., Drury, Fyton, Kildare, Garvey, Gerrard, Lancaster, Loftus, Malbie, Plunket, Sydney, White.

Biographical studies

The biographical statements that follow assemble information on the membership of the council in Ireland which is particularly relevant to its structure, character and personality. They are not biographies as such, but rather individual studies conducted *en passant*. The national origins, family connections, education, office-holding and activity on the council of each member are indicated. Other information shows the political outlook of the men who sat on the council.

AGARDE, FRANCIS (d. 1577)

Son of English-born Thomas Agarde, who was vice treasurer of the mint in Ireland, Cromwell's servant and confidant, later agent of St Leger and Vice Treasurer Brabazon.[1] No university education. Appears in 1548 as leader of a troop of cavalry in Scotland under Admiral Lord Seymour de Sudeley.[2] Constable of Ferns castle 1553, of Wexford castle 1554.[3] Councillor in 1553, remained on council board for twenty-four years.[4] Captained a band of horsemen in the standing army until 1566, then became seneschal of the O'Byrnes and O'Tooles on the borders of Co. Dublin.[5] Commanded a small band of twenty-four Irish kerne in subsequent general hostings.[6] Served on many important commissions and military expeditions.[7] Chief commissioner in Munster during 1574–75.[8] Estates in Co. Dublin, especially at Grange Gorman.[9] Daughter Cecilie m. Captain Henry Harrington who erected mural monument to Agarde in 1584.[10] Agarde was the

1. Quinn, 'Tudor rule', p. 634; Brady, 'Government of Ireland', p. 53.
2. Agarde monument, Christ Church cathedral, Dublin.
3. Hughes, *Patentee officers*, p. 1.
4. PRO, SP 62/1/3–7.
5. Agarde monument, Christ Church cathedral; *Cal. Carew MSS, 1575–88*, pp. 44–45.
6. RIA, MS 24 F 17, f. 226.
7. *Cal. S.P. Ire., 1509–73*, p. 254; *Cal. Carew MSS, 1515–74*, pp. 265–67, 349.
8. *Cal. S.P. Ire., 1574–85*, pp. 14, 38–40, 51.
9. PROI, Lodge MSS, Records of the rolls, i, 140.
10. Agarde monument, Christ Church cathedral.

most assiduous councillor of entire period, the leading military adviser on the council, an informant of the queen's principal secretaries.

ALEN, SIR JOHN (d. 1561)

Son of Warin Alen of Cotteshall, Norfolk, who was an uncle of the senior John Alen, archbishop of Dublin and lord chancellor in 1528. Entered Gray's Inn in 1522. Went to Ireland as secretary to his cousin, the archbishop, in 1528. Clerk of the council before 1532.[11] Master of the rolls in 1533. Chancellor of the exchequer in 1535, Cromwell's leading adviser on Irish affairs, enjoyed favour of Cecil after 1559.[12] Became lord keeper and then lord chancellor, 1538, and the next year headed the commission for the suppression of religious houses.[13] Made accusations against Lord Deputy St Leger in 1546; recalled to England same year on charges of corruption; deprived and committed to the Fleet, but restored as lord chancellor and made a knt in 1548. Superseded as chancellor in 1550 by his rival, Cusake, but continued active on the council. MP for Kinsale, 1559. Married a Cheshire woman but left no issue.[14] Enriched through corrupt management of dissolution of religious houses, particularly by the grant of St Wolstan's, Co. Kildare.[15] On council nearly thirty years, excluding absences in England. Not a leading councillor after 1556, attended infrequently, but valued for his experience.

ARNOLD, SIR NICHOLAS (?1507–80)

Second son of John Arnold (d. 1546) of Churcham, Gloucestershire, who was a clerk of the crown in Wales. Nicholas became a gentleman pensioner in 1526, entered Cromwell's service after 1530 and became a member of the king's bodyguard in 1538.[16] MP for Gloucestershire, 1545. Commanded garrisons in Queensborough (1545) and Boulogne (1546–49). Noted for heroic defence of Boulogne in 1549 against 3,000 French. Knt in 1550.[17] Aligned with Northumberland, fell from favour under Mary, suspected of plotting against her. After 1558, joined Dudley faction, served with Sydney on Welsh council. Sheriff of Gloucestershire, 1559.[18] Sent to Ireland in 1562–63 as head

11. Ball, *Judges*, i, 198.
12. Hughes, *Patentee officers*, p. 2; Brady, 'Government of Ireland', pp. 57, 100.
13. Ball, *Judges*, i, 199; Hughes, *Patentee officers*, p. 2; Bradshaw, *Dissolution of religious orders in Ireland*, pp. 111–21.
14. Ball, *Judges*, i, 199.
15. Bradshaw, *Dissolution of religious orders in Ireland*, pp. 46, 56, 67–68, 252–55.
16. *DNB, supplement*, s.v. 'Arnold, Sir Nicholas'.
17. ibid.
18. ibid.; Brady, 'Government of Ireland', p. 159.

of commission to investigate the corrupt exchequer and made allegations of fiscal abuse against Sussex's administration.[19] Returned as lord justice in 1564 and 1565 in absence of Sussex. Confronted by refusal of Vice Treasurer Fitzwilliam and military captains to yield their accounts. Irascible temperament led to many conflicts on the council, notably with Stanley, Radcliffe, and Ormonde.[20] Replaced by Sydney early in 1566. Escaped retribution of Sussex, and thereafter retired to local administration in Gloucestershire.[21] Spent less than four years in Ireland.

AYLMER, GERALD (d. 1559)

Younger son of Bartholomew Aylmer of Lyons, Co. Kildare.[22] No record of legal education, though named second justice of common pleas in 1528.[23] Chief baron of the exchequer in 1534. Active against Geraldine rebels, though earlier a partisan of Kildare. Became a client of Cromwell and was promoted to chief justice of king's bench in 1535.[24] Served on the council for some twenty-five years. Named to various commissions, particularly for the court of wards, and served as lord justice in 1552.[25] An able military figure, he was employed in the field against the Geraldines and the O'Neills. Knt in 1539.[26] Estates in Meath augmented due to his leadership with Alen of the commission to dissolve religious houses.[27] Like Alen, he came infrequently to council although he held chief justiceship until his death in 1559. Continuous membership less certain. Named to council in 1553 and 1559 but omitted from 1556 instructions.[28]

BAGENALL, SIR NICHOLAS (?1510–90)

Second son of John Bagenall of Newcastle-under-Lyme, erstwhile mayor of the town. Elder brother Sir Ralph a committed Protestant. Nicholas became a gentleman pensioner of Henry VIII, and in 1539 was sent to Ireland, served in military role, perhaps as a captain.

19. *Cal. Carew MSS, 1515–74*, pp. 354–62; Brady, 'Government of Ireland', p. 160.
20. *Cal. S.P. Ire., 1509–73*, pp. 292–94, 299–300; Brady, 'Government of Ireland', pp. 165–70.
21. *DNB*; *Cal. S.P. Ire., 1509–73*, pp. 303–12.
22. Hughes, *Patentee officers*, p. 5.
23. *Ball, Judges*, i, 196–97.
24. Ball, *Judges*, i, 197; Hughes, *Patentee officers*, p. 5.
25. Hughes, *Patentee officers*, p. 5.
26. Ball, *Judges*, i, 197.
27. Bradshaw, *Dissolution of religious orders in Ireland*, pp. 82–83, 239.
28. PRO, SP 62/1/3–7; 63/1/90; *Cal. Carew MSS, 1515–74*, pp. 252, 279.

Returned to England by 1544, fought at Boulogne, 1545.[29] Named marshal of the army in Ireland, 1547.[30] Knt in 1551. Estates in Newry, 1549, and Carlingford, 1552, which became chief bulwarks of northern frontier, fortified colonies with Irish and English tenants.[31] On Mary's accession, replaced by Sir George Stanley as marshal, possibly due to suspicion of machinations of Protestant brother, Ralph. MP in England, 1559, for Stoke-on-Trent.[32] Sought renewal of office, returned to Ireland in 1560 as captain, restored to marshalship in 1566 by Sydney.[33] Held the office for twenty-five more years, resigning in favour of son, Henry, 1590.[34] Daughter m. Hugh, earl of Tyrone. Employed almost exclusively in the northern frontier, became patron of Magennis and other Irish chiefs, resisted new colonization enterprises.[35] Hence not in regular attendance at the council board.

BATHE, JAMES (d. 1570)

Belonged to one of the great Anglo-Irish families. Entered Middle Temple 1522, master of the revels 1524.[36] Chief baron of the exchequer, 1535 until his death in 1570.[37] Served as agent of Cromwell in reporting dissensions within the government. Enriched by the grants of five monastic estates at the dissolution.[38] Resided in 1546 at Drimnagh castle, Co. Dublin, which he obtained through his wife, a widow of Robert Barnewall.[39] Obtained grant of lands at Drumcondra in 1553, augmented by Elizabeth in 1565.[40] Succeeded by Sir Lucas Dillon, who had m. his daughter. Son, John, became chancellor of the exchequer.[41] Served on the council for thirty-five years, named frequently to commissions of the court of wards, of ecclesiastical causes and judicial inquiries.[42] One of the most diligent councillors, yet not involved in exchange of ideas with leading statesmen.

29. *DNB, supplement,* s.v. 'Bagenall, Sir Nicholas'.
30. Hughes, *Patentee officers,* p. 6.
31. *DNB*; Canny, *Elizabethan conquest,* pp. 76, 85; Brady, 'Government of Ireland', pp. 372–74.
32. *DNB.*
33. ibid.; Brady, 'Government of Ireland', p. 175.
34. Hughes, *Patentee officers,* p. 6.
35. Brady, 'Sixteenth-century Ulster', pp. 94–95.
36. Ball, *Judges,* i, 203.
37. Hughes, *Patentee officers,* p. 8.
38. Bradshaw, *Dissolution of religious orders in Ireland,* pp. 92, 202, 239.
39. Ball, *Judges,* i, 204.
40. PROI, Lodge MSS, Records of the rolls, i, 157–58.
41. Ball, *Judges,* i, 204; Hughes, *Patentee officers,* pp. 8, 41.
42. Ball, *Judges,* i, 204; PRO, SP 63/25/115–16; *P.R.I. rep. D.K. 9,* p. 81 (no. 214).

BRADY, HUGH (*c.* 1527–84)

Born at Dunboyne, Co. Meath, of Anglo-Irish stock.[43] Attended
Oxford, and perhaps Cambridge, where he may first have met Cecil.[44]
Named bishop of Meath by patent of 21 October 1563, made a
councillor in December 1563.[45] Praised for his preaching in Irish,
solemnity, hospitality.[46] Attended the lord deputy on many progresses
and expeditions. On ecclesiastical commission from 1564, a voice for
moderate church reform, dispute with Loftus in 1566 over nomination
to archbishopric of Dublin.[47] Allied with Weston and Sydney from
1567, lost influence due to conflicts after 1578.[48] The most diligent
ecclesiastical councillor without a temporal office, he was named to
many commissions of the peace and was used often on conciliar
embassies both in and out of the Pale.[49] His diocese of Meath produced
little income and strong resistance to the reformation.[50]

BUTLER, THOMAS, 10th earl of Ormonde (1532–1614)

Probably the greatest Irish peer of the Elizabethan period. Eldest son
of James Butler, the 9th earl. Educated with Prince Edward at court
from 1544. Knt at his coronation, 1547.[51] Succeeded to the earldom
in 1546.[52] Returned to Ireland in 1554, made a councillor in 1556.
Named lord treasurer of Ireland in 1559. Lifelong feud with Desmond
Geraldines over property rights in Munster. Called to England after
a pitched battle with earl of Desmond in 1565. Spent much time in
England, but a great political force whenever he returned to Ireland.
In 1570 returned to induce his rebellious brothers to submit to lord
deputy.[53] Prevented insurrection in Clare and probably terrified
Thomond into fleeing to France.[54] Led the government forces against
Desmond in 1574 after latter had escaped from Dublin, and again in
the first stages of Desmond rebellion, 1579–81. Governor of Munster

43. *DNB, supplement,* s.v. 'Brady, Hugh'; Walshe, 'Elizabethan settlement', 354.
44. *Cal. Carew MSS, 1515–74,* p. 298; Walshe, 'Elizabethan settlement', 356.
45. *DNB.*
46. *Cal. S.P. Ire., 1509–73,* p. 298.
47. *DNB*; Walshe, 'Elizabethan settlement', 364–69.
48. Walshe, 'Elizabethan settlement', 369–73.
49. *P.R.I. rep. D.K. 12,* pp. 129, 184; *13,* pp. 34, 124–25; PRO, SP 63/25/115–16.
50. Walshe, 'Elizabethan settlement', 359–63.
51. G.E.C., *Peerage,* s.v. 'Ormonde, Sir Thomas Butler, 10th earl'.
52. *Cal. Carew MSS, 1515–74,* pp. 252–57; Brady, 'Government of Ireland', p. 107.
53. *DNB,* s.v. 'Butler, Sir Thomas, 10th earl of Ormonde'; Brady, 'Thomas Butler, earl of Ormond', pp. 52–55.
54. RIA, MS 24 F 17, ff. 266–83.

in 1583 and again in 1594–96. Supported the government in Tyrone's rebellion.[55] A favourite of Elizabeth, he obtained her support for his coveted rights to the prise wines and he helped poison the reputation of Sydney at court.[56] Held vast estates in the south-east, possessed considerable personal patronage in his own territories and was linked by a large network of family alliances to all the important peers in Munster, even including Desmond.[57] Though active in Irish politics, he was never an assiduous councillor. The expansion of conciliar jurisdiction was most effective in territories under the influence of Ormonde. Political fortunes declined sharply after 1600 due to Tyrone rebellion, failure to establish heir to earldom.[58]

CAREW, SIR PETER (1514–75)

Second son of Sir William Carew of Mohun's Ottery, Devon.[59] Educated in Exeter and at St Paul's School, London, travelled to France and Italy in 1530.[60] Served as a gentleman of the privy chamber to Henry VIII from 1530, employed on frequent embassies, campaigned in France, 1544–45. MP for Tavistock and Devon in 1545 and 1553, respectively, sheriff of Devon in 1547.[61] Under Mary, fled to continent after opposing royal marriage, was apprehended, placed in Tower until 1556.[62] Restored to favour under Elizabeth, he successfully pressed claims to certain estates in Ireland. With support of Leicester and Sydney, went to Ireland in 1568, won his cases heard before the council in Dublin. Took barony of Idrone as residence, challenged the neighbouring Butlers, who revolted along with Fitzmaurice in 1569.[63] Was named captain of Leighlin castle, petitioned council to be free of the cess.[64] Made a councillor on winning estates 1569, seldom attended meetings, alienated Ormonde and the Butlers. Spent most of his time in Carlow or in England. One of the rare examples on the council of the English adventurer, his participation in the government was only peripheral.[65] His first cousin, Sir George Carew, became president of Munster in 1600.

55. *DNB*. See also Cyril Falls, 'Black Tom of Ormonde', *Ir Sword*, v (1961), 10–22.

56. RIA, MS 24 F 17, ff. 77v–78, 325–26v.

57. G.E.C., *Peerage*.

58. Brady, 'Butler and reform', pp. 58–59.

59. *DNB*, s.v. 'Carew, Sir Peter'.

60. J. Hooker, 'Life of Sir Peter Carew' in *Cal. Carew MSS, 1515–74*, pp. lxvii–lxxi.

61. *DNB*.

62. Hooker, 'Life', pp. lxxxix–xciv.

63. ibid.

64. Hughes, *Patentee officers*, p. 24; *Cal. S.P. Ire., 1509–73*, p. 456.

65. But see Canny, *Elizabethan conquest*, chs. 4, 6, 7, who sees Carew as a model of English 'freebooter'.

CHALONER, JOHN (d. 1581)

An English official of gentry stock, limited education. Had been an auditor in Calais until it was lost to France.[66] Recommended by Sussex to be the new secretary of state in Ireland, 1560.[67] Reluctant to accept it, Chaloner spent the next twenty years trying to be gracefully removed from the office.[68] A councillor from his assumption of office, he was at first quite regular in attendance. In precedence, he was the last to sign council orders. Used frequently on conciliar commissions.[69] Unlike his successor, Geoffrey Fenton, he was never a significant political force on the council. After 1571 he came infrequently to council meetings. Tried to resign his office in favour of his son, Thomas, who became register of the council in 1576.[70] Alleged by son to have spent thirty-four years in service of the queen.[71] Estates in the Pale, especially Lambay island, prominent in municipal government, alderman of Dublin.[72]

COWLEY, SIR HENRY (d. 1584)

Probably a son of Robert Cowley, English-born master of the rolls, who d. in England in 1546. His brother would thus be Walter Cowley, principal solicitor in Ireland.[73] Henry obtained important estate of Castle Carbery, Co. Kildare, some time before 1551.[74] Captain of a band of troops, in 1556 took charge of fort at Daingean, later called Philipstown, from Kildare.[75] In course of the plantation of Leix and Offaly, Cowley supervised collection of provisions and implements, paid cessors, and guarded convoys to Philipstown.[76] Named to many commissions by council, especially for disputes in King's Co. Mediated contention between O'Mulloys in 1566.[77] Created seneschal of King's Co. in same year.[78] Pleaded continually for more men, for regular pay.[79] Reported the steady losses to rebels in 1573 and 1574 during

66. PRO, SP 63/8/109.
67. PRO, SP 63/2/38.
68. PRO, SP 63/8/109; 63/36/10v.
69. RIA, MS 24 F 17, ff. 192–92v, 323; *P.R.I. rep. D.K. 13*, pp. 34, 124–25.
70. Hughes, *Patentee officers*, p. 25.
71. *Cal. S.P. Ire., 1574–85*, p. 373.
72. ibid., p. 311; Lennon, *Lords of Dublin*, pp. 237–38.
73. Ball, *Judges*, i, 203.
74. *Cal. S.P. Ire., 1509–73*, p. 114.
75. RIA, MS 24 F 17, ff. 4, 22.
76. ibid., ff. 105–05v, 171.
77. ibid., ff. 210v–11. See also *Cal. S.P. Ire., 1509–73*, pp. 241–42, 244.
78. Hughes, *Patentee officers*, p. 33; *Cal. S.P. Ire., 1509–73*, pp. 293–96.
79. *Cal. S.P. Ire., 1509–73*, pp. 471, 493, 515, 524.

Rory Oge O'More's rebellion.[80] Commended frequently for his wise government, governed according to common law.[81] A regular informant of Cecil, replaced as seneschal in 1574 and nominated as councillor. Example of a veteran military leader elevated for his experience.[82] Knt in 1576.[83] Not a diligent councillor, but useful for his knowledge of military affairs. A persistent suitor, held estates in Co. Kildare, augmented by grants of Edenderry and many other lands.[84] M. secondly, daughter of Sir Thomas Cusake, and both his sons m. daughters of Archbishop Adam Loftus. Ancestor of dukes of Wellington.[85]

CURWEN, HUGH (1507–68)

Born near Penrith, Westmoreland, took B.C.L. at Brasenose College, Oxford in 1528, D.C.L. in 1532. Became chaplain to Henry VIII in same year.[86] From 1533 to 1553 steadily supported the reformation.[87] Despite his Protestant background, Queen Mary named him archbishop of Dublin in 1555, and, after his consecration, appointed him the lord chancellor in Ireland in succession to the disgraced reformer, Cusake.[88] Was named as councillor in Sussex's instructions of 1556.[89] Served as lord justice in the following year.[90] Accepted oath of supremacy 1560. Named to many commissions by the council.[91] Among the most active councillors until 1566, rarely left Dublin, so attended nearly every meeting during his tenure. Accused of corruption, laxity in both temporal and spiritual offices. From at least 1563 suffered from sickness, sought his removal to an English bishopric, supported in this by Sussex and Sydney.[92] Nominated to see of Oxford in 1566, replaced as chancellor in August 1567 by Sir Robert Weston.[93] Loftus, who had charged him with corruption and

80. *Cal. S.P. Ire., 1574–85*, pp. 3, 8.

81. Bagwell, *Ireland under Tudors*, ii, 227–28; *Cal. S.P. Ire., 1509–73*, p. 495.

82. PRO, SP 63/45/184.

83. J. Burke, *Burke's genealogical and heraldic history of the peerage, baronetage and knightage*, ed. P. Townsend, 104th ed. (London, 1967), p. 2616.

84. *Cal. S.P. Ire., 1509–73*, pp. 212, 348, 374, 474, 491.

85. Burke, *Peerage*, p. 2616.

86. Ball, *Judges*, i, 207.

87. *DNB*, s.v. 'Curwen, Hugh'. Ball is far more credible on the early career.

88. ibid.; Hughes, *Patentee officers*, p. 36; Ball, *Judges*, i, 207.

89. *Cal. Carew MSS, 1515–74*, p. 252.

90. *DNB*.

91. *P.R.I. rep. D.K. 9*, p. 81; *11*, p. 72.

92. PRO, SP 63/18/110v, 113v–34; *Cal. S.P. Ire., 1509–73*, pp. 162, 234.

93. *Cal. S.P. Ire., 1509–73*, pp. 162, 345.

licence, replaced him as archbishop.[94] Lacked a clear policy as chancellor, did nothing to improve judicial practice, probably retarded efforts to reform judiciary.

CUSAKE, SIR THOMAS (1490–1571)

Son of John Cusake of Cussington, Co. Meath, member of a great Pale family. Entered Inner Temple in 1522, master of the revels in 1524.[95] Successfully sought chancellorship of the exchequer in 1532, second justiceship of common pleas in 1534.[96] Active agent of Cromwell for suppression of religious houses, served on several commissions, obtained lucrative nunnery at Lismullen in which he established his residence.[97] Speaker of Irish house of commons in 1541. Wrote treatise on Irish government, leading Anglo-Irish reformer aligned with moderate lord deputy, St Leger, authored policy of surrender and re-grant.[98] Named master of the rolls, 1542. Appointed keeper of the seal in 1546, became lord chancellor in 1550, each time at the expense of the beleaguered Sir John Alen.[99] Served as lord justice in 1552, wrote an important treatise for Northumberland on state of Ireland, calling for provincial presidencies led by Anglo-Irish peers.[100] Removed from office by Mary in 1555, probably on account of his support of the reformation, also tainted by financial scandals of St Leger's last viceroyalty in 1553.[101] Restored to council by Elizabeth in 1559.[102] Among the most active councillors of the period, industrious, constant in attendance, employed on nearly every important commission.[103] Embassies to Shane O'Neill, Desmond, other truculent adversaries of administration. Corresponded often with Cecil, offered his advice on state of Ireland, undermined Sussex administration with charges of profligacy and coercion in 1562.[104] Recommended by

94. ibid., pp. 298, 328; *DNB*; Ball, *Judges*, i, 208.

95. Ball, *Judges*, i, 200.

96. ibid.; Hughes, *Patentee officers*, p. 37.

97. Ball, *Judges*, i, 201; Bradshaw, *Dissolution of religious orders in Ireland*, pp. 58, 89, 113, 189, 201.

98. *DNB*, s.v. 'Cusack, Sir Thomas'. See Bradshaw, *Irish constitutional revolution*, pp. 112, 190–94, 260 on Cusake as architect of 'commonwealth liberalism' in Ireland.

99. Ball, *Judges*, i, 201; Hughes, *Patentee officers*, p. 37.

100. Canny, *Elizabethan conquest*, pp. 39, 96.

101. Ball, *Judges*, i, 201; *Cal. S.P. Ire., 1509–73*, pp. 80, 126–27; PRO, SP 62/1/3–7; Brady, 'Government of Ireland', p. 93.

102. *Cal. Carew MSS, 1515–74*, pp. 252, 279. See also PRO, SP 63/8/132.

103. RIA, MS 24 F 17, ff. 80, 81v, 140v–41, 145–45v, 283v, 336v–37.

104. PRO, SP 63/5/33, 88; 63/10/14; Ball, *Judges*, i, 201. Brady sees him as part of Leicester faction after 1559. 'Government of Ireland', pp. 57, 162.

Sydney in 1566 to succeed Curwen as lord chancellor.[105] The most trusted Anglo-Irish supporter of crown till his death in 1571, also active in municipal government of Dublin.[106]

DILLON, SIR LUCAS (d. 1593)

Eldest son and heir of Sir Robert Dillon, chief justice of common pleas. Entered Middle Temple in 1551.[107] Became queen's solicitor general in 1565 and attorney general in 1566.[108] M. Jane, daughter of James Bathe, chief baron of the exchequer; and secondly m. Marion Sharl, widow of Sir Christopher Barnewall, in 1578. Frequently employed on conciliar commissions.[109] Became a councillor himself in 1570 when he succeeded father-in-law as chief baron.[110] A reliable informant of Cecil, he was the most active supporter of moderate reform on the council, and the ablest of the Anglo-Irish judges.[111] Knt in 1575.[112] Frequently accompanied the lord deputy on expeditions, hearing cases in town and camp.[113] Considered for chancellorship in 1581 and for chief justiceship of queen's bench in 1583, but Loftus and others charged him with covert Catholicism. One of few supporters of Lord Deputy Perrot in 1580s, suffered from charges against his cousin, Sir Robert Dillon the younger. Estates in Co. Meath, especially Newtown Trim, inherited from his father.[114] Acknowledged the most diligent and most loyal of the Anglo-Irish councillors.

DILLON, SIR ROBERT (the elder) (1500–80)

Third son of James Dillon of Riverston, Co. Meath. Eldest brother was Sir Bartholomew, a chief justice of king's bench.[115] Son was Lucas, noted above. Uncertain legal education, probably attended an inn of court. Named attorney general in 1535, obtained large monastic

105. PRO, SP 63/18/133–34.
106. PRO, SP 63/32/11v; Lennon, *Lords of Dublin*, pp. 240–41.
107. Ball, *Judges*, i, 201.
108. Hughes, *Patentee officers*, p. 41.
109. ibid.; Ball, *Judges*, i, 212; RIA, MS 24 F 17, ff. 216v, 333, 334v; J. Jocelyn, 'The renaissance tombs at Lusk and Newtown Trim', *RSAI Jn*, ciii (1973), 153–66.
110. *Sidney S.P.*, pp. 124–25; PRO, SP 63/30/115v.
111. PRO, SP 63/53/53; LPL, Carew MS 628, f. 312.
112. *DNB, supplement*, s.v. 'Dillon, Sir Lucas'.
113. *Cal. Carew MSS, 1575–88*, p. 126; Ball, *Judges*, i, 212.
114. Ball, *Judges*, i, 212; Walshe, 'Elizabethan settlement', 374.
115. Ball, *Judges*, i, 206.

estates, leading member of the social and political oligarchy in the Pale.[116] Estates at Newtown Trim, Co. Meath. Acted as civil governor of Athlone in 1548, became second justice of common pleas in 1555, elevated to chief justiceship in 1559. Knt in 1567.[117] Served on several commissions in the Pale, but not a particularly active councillor, rarely attended meetings after 1571.[118] Sydney and Fitzwilliam sought his removal but Elizabeth vacillated. His office usually executed by the second justice during last decade of his life.[119] A target of Gerrard's judicial reforms from 1576.[120]

DOWDALL, GEORGE (1487–1558)

Born in Drogheda, Co. Louth, to an important merchant family. Of uncertain education, but reputedly a learned man. Prior of Ardee monastery, in 1543 became archbishop of Armagh.[121] A devoted Catholic, led opposition to George Browne, Protestant archbishop of Dublin under Edward VI. Deprived of rank of primate by Lord Deputy Croft in 1550, fled to France. Restored to full authority as primate of all Ireland under Mary, led reaction against Protestant divines. Obtained Ardee monastery as a grant with life interest from Mary in 1554.[122] Named to the council in 1553 and throughout Mary's reign.[123] Rarely attended council board, apparently resided both at Armagh and Dublin.[124] Sought establishment of a college for religious training in 1558.[125] By 1557 led opposition to Sussex's campaigns in Ulster, travelled to court to challenge viceregal government in 1558, but died within the year.[126]

DRAYCOTT, HENRY (d. 1572)

A native of Denby in Derbyshire, uncertain education, may have been a protégé of Sir Anthony St Leger. Obtained a lease of crown lands

116. Hughes, *Patentee officers*, p. 41; Bradshaw, *Dissolution of religious orders in Ireland*, pp. 53–56, 75, 117, 240.

117. Hughes, *Patentee officers*, p. 41; Ball, *Judges*, i, 206; *DNB, supplement* s.v. 'Dillon, Sir Robert'.

118. *P.R.I. rep. D.K. 9*, p. 81; *11*, p. 72; PRO, SP 63/25/115.

119. PRO, SP 63/50/4; 63/72/147.

120. LPL, Carew MS 628, f. 312.

121. *DNB*, s.v. 'Dowdall, George'.

122. ibid.

123. PRO, SP 62/1/51; *Cal. Carew MSS, 1515–74*, p. 252.

124. Hughes, *Patentee officers*, p. 44.

125. Walshe, 'Elizabethan settlement', 358.

126. *DNB*; Ellis, *Tudor Ireland*, pp. 235–37.

in Co. Wexford and Co. Louth at the dissolution of religious houses.[127] Named comptroller of the pipe in the exchequer in 1541, became chief remembrancer in 1544 and chancellor of the exchequer in 1561. Appointed treasurer of the lordship of Wexford in 1544.[128] Estates at Mornington, Co. Meath from about 1551. MP for Naas in 1559.[129] Became third baron of the exchequer in 1563 and continued to hold that office after appointment three years later as master of the rolls.[130] Appointed to the council in 1566, a very active member, employed on several commissions for ecclesiastical causes.[131] Named to hear disputes between Ormonde and Desmond in 1566.[132] Had a good reputation for integrity as a judge, yet not known as a reformer, had no proposals for the government of Ireland.

DRURY, SIR WILLIAM (1527–79)

Son of Sir Robert Drury of Buckinghamshire, educated at Gonville Hall, Cambridge, became a follower of Lord Russell under Henry VIII. Campaigned in France in 1544, assisted Russell in putting down Western rebellion of 1549.[133] Out of favour under Mary, but in 1559 sent to Scotland on embassy, named marshal and governor general of Berwick in 1564. Knt in 1570 during Northern rebellion, intervened often in Scotland, attacked Edinburgh in 1573.[134] His appointment as lord president in Munster rumoured during 1574, delayed until he was placed at Cork in August 1576.[135] Cessed the province, executed masterless men, arranged settlements among Munster lords. Not an active councillor in Dublin because of his duties in Munster, though he led all relevant commissions in that province.[136] Succeeded Sydney as chief governor in August 1578, viewed as an interim replacement, valued for his military experience in face of Munster rebellion.[137]

127. Ball, *Judges*, i, 209; Bradshaw, *Dissolution of religious orders in Ireland*, pp. 194, 238.
128. Hughes, *Patentee officers*, p. 44.
129. Ball, *Judges*, i, 210. See also RIA, MS 24 F 17, f. 123v; PROI, Lodge MSS, Extracts of patent rolls, pp. 84–85.
130. Hughes, *Patentee officers*, p. 44.
131. RIA, MS 24 F 17, ff. 192–93v, 330; PRO, SP 63/25/115–16; Hughes, *Patentee officers*, p. 44.
132. *Sidney S.P.*, p. 43.
133. *DNB*, s.v. 'Drury, Sir William'.
134. ibid.
135. *Cal. S.P. Ire., 1574–85*, pp. 28–29, 80, 83, 99; Ellis, *Tudor Ireland*, pp. 270–71.
136. *P.R.I. rep. D.K. 12*, p. 184.
137. PRO, SP 63/61/3–4v; U. North Carolina, Southern Historical Collection, Preston Davie Papers (1560–1903), item no. 4.

Drury's instructions hampered the military campaign because the queen insisted on financial retrenchment and troop reductions.[138] His administration of one year was made more difficult by the need to be away in Munster and he was berated for not writing to the privy council.[139] He devoted himself entirely to military matters, controlled Connacht through Malbie's actions and obtained pledges from the Irish septs on the borders of the Pale. Taken ill in summer 1579, d. at Waterford in October.[140]

FITZEUSTACE, ROLAND, 2nd Viscount Baltinglas (1505–78)

Son and heir of first Viscount Baltinglas, Sir Thomas Eustace, who was created in 1541. Namesake of grand-uncle Roland Fitzeustace, Baron Portlester, who was lord treasurer from 1454 to 1492. Took livery of his father's estates in Cos. Kildare and Wicklow in 1549.[141] Dependable supporter of the English government, although occasionally found in the opposition, particularly on the issue of cess.[142] Useful on commissions of peace and on embassies to Shane O'Neill, Desmond and other Irish chiefs.[143] Attended more council meetings than any peer except Kildare, yet never specifically mentioned as a councillor. Regularly attended grand councils, appeared at a number of working council meetings from 1556 to 1565. Increasingly took the side of the Anglo-Irish Pale and fell out of favour. Sydney tried to send him to the Tower along with other Anglo-Irish peers, but the queen wanted to hear the charges first and there is no record of his incarceration.[144] After 1566 did not again appear at council meetings. His son became a partisan of the gentlemen of the Pale in the controversy over cess and in 1579 joined the rebels against the government.[145]

FITZGERALD, GERALD, 11th earl of Kildare (1525–85)

First son of the ninth earl of Kildare by his second wife, half-brother of Silken Thomas. Removed from the Pale during Geraldine rebellion of 1534, escaped to continent in 1540 after Geraldine confederation failed.[146] Educated in Verona, Mantua and Florence, served with

138. BL, Cott. MS Titus B XII, ff. 265–68, 378–85, 610–25.
139. *Walsingham letter-bk*, pp. 186–87.
140. ibid., pp. 164–65, 185–86; PRO, SP 63/65/64–65; Ellis, *Tudor Ireland*, pp. 280, 330.
141. G.E.C., *Peerage*, s.v. 'Baltinglas, Roland Fitzeustace, 2nd viscount'.
142. *Cal. S.P. Ire., 1509–73*, pp. 174, 195, 416.
143. ibid., pp. 185, 408; *Cal. pat. rolls Ire., Eliz*, p. 11.
144. G.E.C., *Peerage*; *Sidney S.P.*, p. 62.
145. *DNB*, s.v. 'Eustace, James'.
146. G.E.C., *Peerage*, s.v. 'Kildare, Gerald Fitzgerald, 11th earl'.

Cosimo di Medici. Returned to England in 1547, m. daughter of Sir Anthony Browne, knt in 1552. Served Mary in Wyatt's rebellion, restored to earldom and returned to Ireland in 1554.[147] A councillor from 1556, used on commissions to guard the Pale, sent on embassies to Shane O'Neill and other Irish chiefs, led his own forces in general hostings and military expeditions.[148] Represented Geraldine interests in the Pale, defended Pale against rebels, served as mediator with Gaelic chiefs. Worked against Sussex in England in 1562, later suspected of treasonable relations with rebels Rory Oge O'More and the earl of Desmond. Imprisoned in 1575, again in 1580.[149] The greatest magnate in the Pale, employed by the council on all important commissions, endowed with power to govern Pale in absence of deputy in 1574, yet never completely trusted despite his military and political standing.

FITZWILLIAM, SIR WILLIAM (1526–99)

Eldest son of Sir William Fitzwilliam of Milton, Northamptonshire. Uncertain education, presented at court of Edward VI by Sir John Russell, became marshal of king's bench and a gentleman of the king's chamber.[150] Sent to Ireland in 1554 to conduct commission of inquiry into financial malpractice. Named to the council in 1554. Accused St Leger of corruption, became a supporter of new viceroy, Sussex, in 1556.[151] Vice treasurer in succession to Sydney in 1559.[152] Served as lord justice in 1560, 1561, 1567 and 1571 before becoming lord deputy himself in 1572.[153] The next most active councillor of the period, served on nearly every important commission, went on expeditions with the chief governors, but failed to reform the exchequer and amassed a debt to the crown of £7,000 by 1569.[154] Ineffective as lord deputy, he was victimized by dissension on the council and the diverting of resources to the plantation in Ulster.[155] Viewed as a supporter of coercive measures in bringing about Elizabethan settlement, but did little to enforce them.[156] His disputes with Fyton and Essex

147. *DNB*, s.v. 'Fitzgerald, Gerald, 11th earl of Kildare'; Ellis, *Tudor Ireland*, p. 233.
148. *Cal. Carew MSS, 1515–74*, p. 252; *P.R.I. rep. D.K. 9*, p. 81; *Cal. S.P. Ire., 1509–73*, pp. 169, 179, 183.
149. PRO, SP 63/2/15; *Cal. S.P. Ire., 1574–85*, pp. 53–54, 64, 69, 265, 276, 297.
150. *DNB*, s.v. 'Fitzwilliam, Sir William'.
151. Brady, 'Government of Ireland', p. 105.
152. *Cal. Carew MSS, 1515–74*, p. 252; Hughes, *Patentee officers*, p. 51.
153. Hughes, *Patentee officers*, p. 51.
154. PRO, SP 63/25/15–16; *Cal. pat. rolls Ire., Hen VIII—Eliz*, p. 511; Brady, 'Government of Ireland', p. 207.
155. PRO, SP 63/41/52–52v, 54–54v, 66–66v, 152; Bodl, Carte MS 56, f. 44–44v.
156. Walshe, 'Elizabethan settlement', 367.

left him out of favour with the queen and he was recalled in 1575.[157] Spent next twelve years attending to local affairs at estate of Milton. Recalled as lord deputy in 1588, presided over the despatch of the Armada's survivors, made long expedition in 1588 to Ulster. Engaged in several confrontations with Ulster chiefs, especially the rebellion of McGuire in 1593. Finally replaced in 1594, sick and going blind.[158]

FYTON, SIR EDWARD (1527–79)

Eldest son of Sir Edward Fyton of Gawsworth, Cheshire. Little known on education or early career. Had licence to enter his father's lands in 1557.[159] Knt in 1566.[160] Named first lord president of Connacht in 1569, held Athlone castle from about 1570 and refused to give it up.[161] Began his tenure by erecting Cos. Clare, Galway and Roscommon, holding sessions, proscribing Gaelic customs. Alienated earl of Thomond after holding assizes in Ennis. Earl of Clanricarde fled from Connacht briefly and his sons rebelled in 1571.[162] Held the earl responsible for his sons' rebellion, charged him with treason before the council but refused to press charges.[163] When the earl was released, Fyton hanged many of his kinsmen and they in turn burned much of Athlone, leading to Fyton's recall as president in 1572. Returned to Cheshire in October, but was named vice treasurer in 1573 in succession to Fitzwilliam. Retained his standing in Connacht as chief commissioner for the province, a somewhat empty title.[164] Quarrelled often with the chief governor, especially over his withholding a pardon issued by the council.[165] Barely reconciled with Fitzwilliam, he refused in 1574 to go on commission to Munster despite his ample military experience. In 1578 refused to sign a document certifying the growth of Irish revenue under Sydney.[166] Failed to obtain the reversion of his office for his son, Sir Edward the younger. Attended council meetings fairly often as lord president. One of the most diligent councillors as vice treasurer after 1573. Irascible, temperamental, self-righteous, he was not an ideal councillor except for his vigorous defence of what he deemed to be the queen's interest.

157. PRO, SP 63/45/112; 63/50/164.
158. *DNB.*
159. *Cal. pat. rolls, Philip and Mary,* iii, 374.
160. *DNB,* s.v. 'Fitton, Sir Edward'.
161. Hughes, *Patentee officers,* p. 49.
162. *DNB*; PRO, SP 63/29/58; 63/30/30–31; 84–84v, 172; Ellis, *Tudor Ireland,* pp. 262–65.
163. PRO, SP 63/32/116–17, 124–25; Bodl, Carte MS 56, f. 59.
164. *DNB*; PRO, SP 63/40/95–95v, 130–33.
165. PRO, SP 63/41/52–52v; Bodl, Carte MS 56, f. 44–44v.
166. PRO, SP 63/42/184–86; 63/60/69–70.

GARVEY, JOHN (1527–95)

Eldest son of John O'Garvey of Morisk, Co. Mayo, born in Kilkenny. Educated at Oxford, temp. Edward VI, received D.D. Named dean of Ferns in 1558, then archdeacon of Meath and rector of Kells in 1559. In 1560 became a prebendary of St Patrick's, Dublin.[167] Employed on many ecclesiastical commissions, became a leading clerical official of the Pale.[168] Succeeded Thomas Lokwood as dean of Christ Church in 1565, but was not immediately placed on the council. In 1572 the council nominated him to be bishop of Ardagh and recommended that he be created a councillor.[169] Though a council member by at least 1573, the deanship probably did not confer ex officio council membership.[170] Allowed to keep his archdeacon's position along with the deanship, he enjoyed favour of the queen. Became bishop of Kilmore in 1585 and continued to hold his earlier preferments. Appointed archbishop of Armagh in 1589 and allowed to dispense with first fruits.[171] Known as one of the most faithful Anglo-Irish supporters of the crown.

GERRARD, SIR WILLIAM (d. 1581)

Son of Gilbert Gerrard of Lancashire, cousin was another Gilbert, master of the rolls in England. Admitted to Gray's Inn in 1543, called to bar in 1546. Became an ancient of Gray's in 1555, reader in 1560.[172] MP for Preston, 1553; Chester from 1555 to 1572. Became recorder of Chester in 1556, justice of Brecknock circuit in 1559. Named to council in marches of Wales, 1560; vice-justice of Chester in 1561; vice-president of Wales in 1562.[173] A thoughtful and diligent councillor in Wales, responsible for several important proposals for reform of government.[174] Named as lord chancellor in Ireland in April 1576, probably at behest of Sydney, lord president of council in Wales.[175] Had the confidence of Cecil, Walsingham and the English privy council, was sent to England to explain the council's dealings regarding

167. DNB, s.v. 'Garvey, John'.
168. PRO, SP 63/14/18–23; 63/16/109–10.
169. PRO, SP 63/38/1, 3–3v.
170. Garvey first signed a council document on 8 February 1573 (PRO, SP 63/44/80). The first official recognition of his membership was in 1576. See P.R.I. rep. D.K. 12, p. 184.
171. DNB.
172. DNB, s.v. 'Gerrard, Sir William'.
173. Ball, Judges, i, 217.
174. Williams, Council in Wales, pp. 62–64, 83–84, 169–70, 260–64.
175. Hughes, Patentee officers, p. 56; DNB; Williams, Council in Wales, p. 267.

cess in 1577.[176] Led a vigorous movement for judicial reform, wrote often on the state of Ireland, proposed regular assizes and the replacement of aged Anglo-Irish judges.[177] Though an active administrator and judge, he did not attend council frequently, spent many months in England, generally had greatest impact outside the council.

HARBERT, SIR FRANCIS (d. 1566)

Of uncertain origin, but probably an English soldier who arrived in Ireland in 1534 in the company of Lord Deputy Grey.[178] Commended by Sir William Brereton for his courage in the war against the Geraldines.[179] A trusted informant of Cromwell, gave frequent opinions on the state of Ireland, looked for preferment and reward in the distribution of dissolved monastic lands.[180] Sought and lost Holmpatrick, but received forfeited lands of Kildare, particularly manor of Portlester, Co. Kildare.[181] In 1537 he was nominated by Cromwell to command a garrison in Ireland and to have some of the king's lands. Knt before 1547. As early as 1546 he was recommended to be on the council in Ireland and he was apparently a councillor in 1547.[182] Although not formally named to the Marian council, signed the council book as early as 3 June 1556, was officially included on Elizabethan councils.[183] Valued for his long experience in Irish government. Though not a diligent councillor, served on the body twenty years, useful on commissions, especially near his estates in Cos. Kildare and Meath.[184] Died early in 1566. Early champion of plantation, urged English settlers as a solution to unrest on borders of Pale.[185]

HAY, DAVID (?d. after 1564)

A native of Slade, Co. Wexford, of uncertain education and background, member of the leading family of that community.[186] An

176. PRO, SP 63/57/97–98; 63/59/17–17v; 63/75/24–24v; LPL, Carew MS 628, ff. 141v–43; BL, Add. MS 4,763, ff. 411–13.

177. PRO, SP 63/55/189–89v; 63/56/105–05v; 63/66/1–1v; LPL, Carew MS 628, ff. 311v–14; 'Gerrard's report', ed. McNeill, pp. 119–20, 124, 136, 183–87.

178. Bradshaw, *Dissolution of religious orders in Ireland*, pp. 52, 56–57.

179. *Cal. Carew MSS, 1515–74*, pp. 57–58.

180. ibid., p. 90; *Cal. S.P. Ire., 1509–73*, pp. 19, 36, 38; Bradshaw, *Dissolution of religious orders in Ireland*, pp. 56–57, 75.

181. *Cal. S.P. Ire., 1509–73*, pp. 36, 38, 61.

182. ibid., pp. 29, 75, 77.

183. RIA, MS 24 F 17, f. 3; PRO, SP 63/14/18; *Cal. Carew MSS, 1515–74*, p. 279.

184. RIA, MS 24 F 17, ff. 19, 129v, 132.

185. ibid., f. 210v; PRO, SP 63/16/110; *Cal. Carew MSS, 1515–74*, p. 90; *Cal. S.P. Ire., 1509–73*, p. 36.

186. Lewis, *Topographical dictionary*, ii, 518.

active member of the council from June 1556 to November 1557, but not mentioned in the instructions, nor employed on conciliar commissions.[187] Hay was arrested and held on charges of treason, along with his son, in 1564. Imprisoned for twenty-five weeks, released when no evidence was found. No mention at the time of his being a former councillor.[188] The most questionable in list of councillors, included because he signed at least eleven orders and decrees in council book.

LANCASTER, THOMAS (d. 1583)

English-born native of Cumberland, educated at Oxford. Consecrated bishop of Kildare by Archbishop George Browne in 1549; regarded as a moderate Protestant. Held deanery of Ossory in commendam, assisted in consecration of John Bale as bishop of Ossory in 1553.[189] Deprived in 1553 under Mary for being married, retired during Marian reaction. Restored to favour under Elizabeth, became treasurer of Salisbury cathedral in 1559 and a royal chaplain.[190] Went to Ireland with Sydney in 1565, attended him on expeditions. During this time a reliable informant of Cecil on military affairs, especially Shane O'Neill's rebellion. Continued to write to Cecil thereafter on the state of Ireland.[191] Nominated in 1567 to succeed Loftus as archbishop of Armagh, consecrated in Dublin in 1568. Allowed to keep pluralities due to poverty of see, resided largely in Dublin.[192] An active councillor from 1568, useful on ecclesiastical commissions, known as strong supporter of persuasion, advocate of moderate Protestant policy based upon preaching, education and vernacularization.[193] After 1580 he devoted much of his attention to the erection of a free school at Drogheda.[194]

LOFTUS, ADAM (1533–1605)

Second son of Edward Loftus of Yorkshire, entered Trinity College, Cambridge in 1556. Preferred by Mary to rectory in Norfolk, 1556; vicarage in Lincolnshire, 1557.[195] Became chaplain to Lord Lieutenant

---

187. RIA, MS 24 F 17, ff. 5, 60v.

188. ibid., f. 194–94v.

189. *DNB*, s.v. 'Lancaster, Thomas'.

190. ibid.

191. *Cal. S.P. Ire., 1509–73*, pp. 312, 319, 334.

192. ibid., pp. 379, 425, 441, 447; *DNB*.

193. PRO, SP 63/25/116; Bradshaw, 'Sword, word and strategy', pp. 484–85.

194. *Cal. S.P. Ire., 1574–85*, pp. 260, 302, 308.

195. *DNB*, s.v. 'Loftus, Adam'.

Sussex in 1560, presented to rectory in Co. Meath in 1561. Nominated to archbishopric of Armagh in 1561, vacant since death of Dowdall. Ordinary election impossible due to Shane O'Neill's control of Armagh, so Loftus went to England in 1562, obtained temporalities, was consecrated in 1563 at Dublin. Lived in Dublin, allowed to augment living with deanery of St Patrick's in 1565.[196] A learned, eloquent preacher, active Protestant reformer, became chief of commission for ecclesiastical causes in 1565.[197] Returned to England in 1566, took D.D. at Cambridge, nominated to archbishopric of Dublin in 1567, held the post until his death nearly forty years later.[198] Coveted the chancellorship, named lord keeper on death of Weston in 1573; again in absence of Gerrard in 1577 and 1579. Replaced Gerrard as lord chancellor after interim as lord keeper in 1581. Served as lord justice in 1582, 1597, and 1599.[199] Reconciled Lord Deputy Fitzwilliam with Essex in 1575 prior to their recall.[200] Engaged in 1577 in a protracted controversy over the newly created commission of faculties, designed to grant licences, dispensations and faculties. Loftus was outraged at the usurpation of episcopal privileges, demonstrated a contentious nature later displayed in arguments with Lord Deputy Perrot.[201] Loftus belatedly led establishment of Trinity College, Dublin, served as its first provost. Left a prodigious record as lord chancellor, but openly enriched himself in the bargain, obtained great estates near Dublin, erected impressive castle at Rathfarnham in 1590. Had twenty children, many of whom became important public figures.[202] As archbishop, led the struggle to establish reformation in Ireland, an advanced Protestant, friendly with Cartwright, even sought archbishopric for him.[203] Favoured aggressive strategy for reformation based on external conformity, penal legislation, enforced by court of high commission.[204] Among the most diligent councillors, represented clerical interest, active on ecclesiastical and other commissions.[205] Quarrelled openly after 1565 with moderates Brady, Weston, Lancaster

196. ibid.; Ball, *Judges*, i, 215.
197. *Cal. S.P. Ire., 1509–73*, p. 261; PRO, SP 63/25/115–16; Ford, *Protestant reformation in Ireland*, pp. 19–21.
198. *DNB*; Walshe, 'Elizabethan settlement', 364–68.
199. Hughes, *Patentee officers*, p. 81.
200. PRO, SP 63/50/164.
201. *DNB*; BL, Harl. MS 35, ff. 253–58; BL, Cott. Titus B XIII, ff. 263–70v; *P.R.I. rep. D.K. 13*, p. 25; *Cal. pat. rolls Ire., Eliz*, pp. 24–25; PRO, SP 63/65/150–50v.
202. *DNB*; Walshe, 'Elizabethan settlement', 364–65.
203. *Cal. S.P. Ire., 1509–73*, p. 351.
204. Bradshaw, 'Sword, word and strategy', pp. 480–81, 485–86.
205. *P.R.I. rep. D.K. 12*, pp. 129, 183, 191; *13*, pp. 34, 48, 124–25.

over pace of religious change. Led the conciliar opposition to Perrot's personal handling of public affairs, obtained recall and disgrace of the lord deputy.[206]

LOKWOOD, THOMAS (d. 1565)

Of uncertain origin and education, but probably Anglo-Irish. Participated in the campaign against images in 1539, was then dean of Christ Church.[207] Named to the council at least as early as July 1550, when St Leger received his instructions, remained on the council until his death.[208] Used on various commissions in Co. Dublin, particularly for ecclesiastical purposes.[209] Apparently a trimmer, since in 1557 he participated in commission to recover chalices and ornaments of churches which had been confiscated and sold by him in commission of 1539.[210] A steady, reliable councillor, not particularly active on commissions outside the Pale, d. 1565.[211]

MALBIE, SIR NICHOLAS (1530–84)

Native of Yorkshire, uncertain background or education, though reportedly learned.[212] Mentioned in 1556 as participant in Leix and Offaly plantation.[213] Found guilty of coining in 1562, pardoned on condition of service in France with Ambrose Dudley, earl of Warwick. Became Warwick's secretary, 1563, sent to Spain, 1565, adherent of Dudley faction in England. On return, went to Ireland with, or shortly after, Sydney, became sergeant major of the army there.[214] Stationed at Carrickfergus with Captain Piers to check Scots from 1566. Commended by Sydney for negotiations with Sorley Boy MacDonnell, employed against Butlers in 1569, rewarded with grant of customs at three eastern ports in 1571.[215] A frequent and diligent informant of Cecil, commented perceptively on affairs in the north. Advocated a military policy, warned against troop reductions in 1572.[216] In 1571

206. *DNB*; Walshe, 'Elizabethan settlement', 364–68.

207. Bradshaw, *Dissolution of religious orders in Ireland*, p. 104.

208. *Cal. Carew MSS, 1515–74*, pp. 226, 231, 279; PRO, SP 62/1/3; 62/2/70.

209. RIA, MS 24 F 17, ff. 119–20, 123; *P.R.I. rep. D.K. 9*, p. 81; *11*, p. 72; *Cal. pat. rolls Ire., Hen VIII—Eliz*, pp. 354–55.

210. *P.R.I. rep. D.K. 9*, p. 78.

211. *Cal. S.P. Ire., 1509–73*, p. 271.

212. *DNB*, s.v. 'Malby, Sir Nicholas'.

213. *Cal. S.P. Ire., 1509–73*, p. 134.

214. *DNB*.

215. ibid.; Hughes, *Patentee officers*, p. 86; *Cal. S.P. Ire., 1509–73*, pp. 348–50, 353.

216. *Cal. S.P. Ire., 1509–73*, pp. 422, 428, 436, 480, 500.

obtained grant of barony in Co. Down on condition he plant and settle it within eight years. The settlement a failure due to pressures from north, excesses of Smith and Essex plantations.[217] Admitted a member of council in Ireland 1575, knt and named colonel of Connacht province in 1576, ending tenure of Fyton and the interim commission.[218] Active governor of Connacht, harried the Burkes into quiescence, strict but impartial judge, commended by natives for his fairness.[219] Appointed president of Connacht in 1579, acted as commander in Munster during sickness of Drury in same year. Defeated rebels handily in every confrontation, kept Connacht quiet while Ormonde, then Grey subdued Munster rebellion, 1580–83.[220] Overcame charges in London that he governed with cruelty and corruption. Obtained large estates in Athlone and Roscommon, but apparently died in debt.[221] Not an active councillor because employed in his province, but useful on important commissions, and a reliable informant on the state of Ireland.[222] Perhaps the ablest provincial governor of the period, an early advocate of coercion and plantation, anticipated composition of Connacht in 1577 by agreement with provincial landholders.[223]

PARKER, JOHN (d. 1564)

A native of Tenterden, Kent, went to Calais in retinue of Lord Lisle, then to Ireland in 1540 as secretary to Lord Deputy St Leger.[224] Obtained rich monastery of Selsker, Co. Wexford in 1542 and Holmpatrick, Co. Dublin in 1545 by fraudulent underpayment, linked to financial scandal of Brabazon.[225] Became an usher in the exchequer in 1540, and constable of Dublin castle in 1544. Appointed master of the rolls in 1552, succeeding Sir Patrick Barnewall.[226] Named to Mary's council in 1553, remained a councillor till his death, though

217. ibid., p. 532; *DNB*; Canny, *Elizabethan conquest*, pp. 76, 85.

218. *DNB*.

219. ibid.; *Annals of Loch Cé*, p. 459; Cunningham & Gillespie, 'Englishmen in Irish annals', 12–13.

220. *DNB*; *P.R.I. rep. D.K. 13*, p. 125; Hughes, *Patentee officers*, p. 86.

221. *Cal. S.P. Ire., 1574–85*, pp. 360–75; PROI, Lodge MSS, Records of the rolls, i, 140.

222. PRO, SP 63/59/59–59v; *P.R.I. rep. D.K. 12*, pp. 184, 191; *13*, p. 34.

223. Canny, *Elizabethan conquest*, p. 114; Cunningham, 'Composition of Connacht', 1–2, 8–9.

224. Ball, *Judges*, i, 205.

225. Bradshaw, *Dissolution of religious orders in Ireland*, pp. 194, 238; Brady, 'Government of Ireland', pp. 93–94.

226. Hughes, *Patentee officers*, pp. 101–02.

not very diligent.[227] Unusually active outside the council, owned a
ship called the *Peter* in 1545, organized the defence of Carrickfergus
in 1551. Obtained rule of border lands in Co. Meath in 1553, MP
for Trim in 1559, established a millinery in 1559.[228] Employed on
various commissions by the council, including one in 1560 to settle
disputes between Ormonde and Desmond.[229] Took the side of gentlemen of the Pale in the dispute over cess in 1562, became enemy of
Sussex, was nearly stripped of his lands and offices. Held vast estates
in Pale but apparently died in debt.[230]

PERROT, SIR JOHN (1527–92)

Reputed a bastard son of Henry VIII, took name of Thomas Perrot
of Pembrokeshire. Educated at St David's and in the household of
the marquis of Winchester. Preferred by Edward VI, knt in 1547, in
retinue of Northampton to France in 1551. Briefly imprisoned for
Protestant views under Mary, later sued successfully to obtain Carew
castle in Pembrokeshire. MP Sandwich 1555, Pembrokeshire 1563.
One of leading patriarchs in Wales, allied with Leicester faction.
Appointed by Elizabeth the vice admiral of Welsh seas in 1558, split
time between Wales and court.[231] In 1570 reluctantly assumed post
of president of council in Munster.[232] Arrived early in 1571 to subdue
Fitzmaurice rebellion, engaged rebels successfully but without
achieving peace, accepted submission of Fitzmarice in 1572 after
long exhausting campaigns. Introduced common law trials, claiming
that Munster accepted the rule of English law, though he had executed
some 800 men.[233] Named to council in 1570 but rarely sat, spent
nearly all his time in Munster, especially at Cork, known to espouse a
military policy in Ireland. Sought his revocation immediately, finally
departed for England in July 1573 without licence, returned to
Wales, sat on council there.[234] In 1579 led a squadron of ships to Ireland
to patrol waters of south-west, await Spanish invaders.[235] Returned in
1584 as lord deputy to supervise plantation of Munster. Engaged in

227. PRO, SP 62/1/3; *Cal. Carew MSS, 1515–74*, p. 279.
228. Ball, *Judges*, i, 205–06; *P.R.I. rep. D.K. 11*, p. 40.
229. RIA, MS 24 F 17, ff. 140–41v; *P.R.I. rep. D.K. 9*, p. 81; *11*, p. 72; *Cal. pat. rolls Ire., Hen VIII—Eliz*, p. 343.
230. PRO, SP 63/59/59–59v; *P.R.I. rep. D.K. 12*, pp. 184, 191; *13*, p. 34.
231. *DNB*, s.v. 'Perrot, Sir John'; Williams, *Council in Wales*, pp. 231–32, 239–40.
232. *Sidney S.P.*, p. 137; *Cal. S.P. Ire., 1509–73*, pp. 427, 436–37.
233. *Cal. S.P. Ire., 1509–73*, pp. 457–58, 461, 482–83, 487, 497; Canny, *Elizabethan conquest*, pp. 101–04.
234. *DNB*; Ellis, *Tudor Ireland*, pp. 261, 264–65.
235. *Cal. S.P. Ire., 1574–85*, pp. 182–83, 187–89, 192.

numerous expeditions to Ulster and the west, without much result. Disputed Loftus over erection of a school at St Patrick's, failed to get his bills through contentious parliament of 1585–86, opposed by Anglo-Irish resistance to cess, attainders.[236] Implemented moderate composition of Connacht, allied with Anglo-Irish reformers on council, but recalled in 1588 and placed in Tower. Found guilty of speaking contemptuously of queen, d. before sentencing.[237]

PLUNKET, SIR JOHN (d. 1582)

Son of Christopher Plunket of Dunsoghly, grandson of a previous chief justice, member of distinguished family that included three peerages (Barons Dunsany, Killeen, Louth).[238] Obtained valuable estates at dissolution near Trim, Co. Meath in 1546.[239] Educated at Inner Temple, acted as master of revels in 1518. Attendant to Robert Fitzsymons, vicar general of see of Dublin; and to chief justice of common pleas, Richard Delahide (before 1535), who was married to a near kinswoman of Plunket.[240] Under Edward VI he served as controller of the household to Bellingham and other lords deputy.[241] Named to the council in 1556 though he held no major office, became chief justice of queen's bench in 1559.[242] The most active Anglo-Irish councillor of the period, attended nearly all the meetings, employed on many important commissions.[243] Attended council infrequently after 1577. Known for his judicious temperament, fairness, yet espoused no policy independently, was relatively inactive in correspondence with London.[244] Estates in Co. Dublin continually augmented by suits of acquisitive Plunket.[245]

236. Ellis, *Tudor Ireland*, pp. 285–93.

237. *DNB*; B. Cunningham, 'The composition of Connacht in the lordships of Clanricarde and Thomond, 1577–1641', *IHS*, xxiv (1984), 8–9.

238. Ball, *Judges*, i, 208.

239. Bradshaw, *Dissolution of religious orders in Ireland*, p. 240.

240. Ball, *Judges*, i, 208.

241. ibid.; *Cal. S.P. Ire., 1509–73*, pp. 84, 90–91, 102.

242. Hughes, *Patentee officers*, p. 106; *Cal. Carew MSS, 1515–74*, pp. 252, 279; PRO, SP 62/2/51; 63/1/122; 63/14/18.

243. *Cal. S.P. Ire., 1509–73*, pp. 354, 364, 373, 453; RIA, MS 24 F 17, ff. 119, 144, 146; PRO, SP 63/25/115–16; *Cal. pat. rolls Ire., Hen VIII—Eliz*, pp. 343, 354–55; *P.R.I. rep. D.K. 9*, p. 78; *12*, p. 129.

244. LPL, Carew MS 628, f. 311v.

245. PRO, SP 63/24/33; PROI, Lodge MSS, Extracts of patent rolls, pp. 84–85, 114–119; *P.R.I. rep. D.K. 11*, p. 43.

RADCLIFFE, SIR HENRY, 4th earl of Sussex (1532–93)

Brother of Thomas Radcliffe, earl of Sussex, b. about 1532. MP for Maldon in 1555, for Hampshire in 1571, for Portsmouth from 1572 to 1583.[246] Went to Ireland with his brother in 1556, made a councillor the following year and became lieutenant of the forts in Leix and Offaly. As military governor of the new plantation he organized defences and received supplies levied on the Pale. Had the right to take pledges and to exercise martial law.[247] An active councillor, employed on many commissions, also commanded a band of soldiers.[248] Reported occasionally to Cecil on military affairs.[249] Sought his release in 1564 on return of Sussex to England, but in 1565 was detained by Lord Justice Arnold for debts of £8,000 discovered during extensive investigation of musters. Radcliffe protested vigorously to Cecil, obtained his release and defended himself before the privy council in England.[250] Appointed warden of Portsmouth in 1571, succeeded to earldom in 1583. Complained that he inherited a bankrupt estate, continued in local offices in Hampshire, active in defences against the Armada, elected K.G. in 1589.[251]

RADCLIFFE, SIR THOMAS, 3rd earl of Sussex (1525–83)

Eldest son and heir of 2nd earl of Sussex, known as Lord Fitzwalter from 1542 to 1556. Educated at Cambridge, knt in 1544, commanded a band of troops at Pinkie in 1547.[252] Embassies to France and Brussels in 1551, 1553, 1554. MP for Norfolk in 1553, named warden and captain of Portsmouth in 1549, appointed captain of gentlemen pensioners for life in 1553.[253] Replaced St Leger as lord deputy of Ireland in 1556. Succeeded to earldom in 1557. Presided over establishment of feeble plantation in Leix and Offaly, named brother Sir Henry Radcliffe as lieutenant of the two forts.[254] Challenged Shane O'Neill over control of Ulster, attacked MacDonnell Scots who inhabited Antrim.[255] Challenged authority of leading aristocratic

246. *DNB*, s.v. 'Radcliffe, Sir Thomas'. See note at end of article.

247. RIA, MS 24 F 17, ff. 42–43, 56–58.

248. *Cal. S.P. Ire., 1509–73*, pp. 136–37, 208; *P.R.I. rep. D.K. 9*, p. 81; *11*, p. 72.

249. *Cal. S.P. Ire., 1509–73*, pp. 170, 174, 185.

250. RIA, MS 24 F 17, f. 202; *Cal. S.P. Ire., 1509–73*, pp. 250–54.

251. G.E.C., *Peerage*, s.v. 'Sussex, Henry Radcliffe, 4th earl of'.

252. G.E.C., *Peerage*, s.v. 'Sussex, Thomas Radcliffe, 3rd earl of'.

253. *DNB*, s.v. 'Radcliffe, Sir Thomas, 3rd earl of Sussex'.

254. *Cal. Carew MSS, 1515–74*, pp. 252–57; RIA, MS 24 F 17, ff. 27v–28, 44–44v, 56–58; Brady, 'Government of Ireland', pp. 147–48.

255. PRO, SP 62/2/51–55; 63/1/105; 63/2/36–37; RIA, MS 24 F 17, ff. 58v–59.

dynasties, Butlers and Geraldines, in 1560. Proposed councils for each province and espoused creation of the court of castle chamber.[256] From 1561, continually harrassed by critics of his administration including Councillors Parker, Kildare and Dowdall; challenged in England by St Leger and the Irish students at the inns of court. Parliaments in 1557 and 1560 established the plantations and Elizabeth's ecclesiastical settlement, but failed to resolve Sussex's financial problems.[257] Failed to contain Shane O'Neill, unable to prevent his audience with the queen in 1562. Charged with corruption by Bermingham, suffered the indignity of Arnold's commission to investigate allegations of maladministration from 1562 to 1564.[258] As chief governor espoused an active military policy combined with judicial process, planned extension of English institutions. A very diligent councillor, held many meetings in the field, apparently made more use of council than his successors. Recalled in 1564, he remained in England and became the rival of Leicester for power at court. Sent to Austria to negotiate queen's marriage with Archduke Charles in 1567–68. In 1568 created lord president of council in the North, led royal forces against the insurgents in Northern rebellion. Recalled to court in 1572, named lord chamberlain of household, continued to favour marriage alliance with one of continental powers. After 1575 a leading privy councillor, regarded as voice for moderation and pragmatism.[259]

ST LEGER, SIR WARHAM (1525–97)

Second son of Lord Deputy Sir Anthony St Leger, of Leeds, Kent; fought in Scotland with Protector Somerset in 1547, remained prisoner there for some three years. Released in 1550, supported Mary against Wyatt's rebellion in 1554, may have served briefly in Ireland under his father. Sheriff of Kent in 1560.[260] Obtained favour of Sydney, his Kentish neighbour, named to the council in Ireland in 1565, knt in the same year, nominated as first president of council in Munster.[261] Not an active councillor, spent most of his time on commission in Munster, resided at Cork, employed on occasional military expeditions.[262] Suspected by queen of partiality to Desmond and opposed

256. Brady, 'Government of Ireland', p. 114; *Cal. Carew MSS, 1515–74*, pp. 330–36, 342–43.
257. Ellis, *Tudor Ireland*, pp. 236–40.
258. *Cal. Carew MSS, 1515–74*, pp. 354–62.
259. *DNB*; MacCaffrey, *Elizabethan regime*, p. 256; Pulman, *Elizabethan privy council*, pp. 48–50.
260. *DNB*, s.v. 'St Leger, Sir Warham'.
261. ibid.; PRO, SP 63/14/18; 63/16/22, 109–10.
262. RIA, MS 24 F 17, ff. 215–15v, 246.

by Ormonde, rebuked for handling of cases between the two earls in 1566, ordered to suspend all their pending cases. Rejected as president of Munster in 1566, a year after his nomination.[263] Continued to serve as chief commissioner in Munster on interim basis, obtained manor of Kerricurrihy near Cork from Desmond by 1569, also leased friary in Limerick.[264] Replaced in 1569, went to England to pursue hopes of settlement in south-west Munster, organized a corporation to sponsor full-scale plantation of English colony there, but lost crown support.[265] Had custody of Desmond from 1570 to 1572 at Leeds castle, Kent.[266] In 1579 returned to Munster as provost marshal of province, was briefly commander-in-chief in Munster during Desmond rebellion in 1581. Pursued his plans for colonization in the subsequent plantation of Munster. Died at Cork in 1597, having spent most of his career in the province.[267]

STANLEY, SIR GEORGE (d. before 1573)

Probably from Lancashire where he had his estates in 1557. May have been related to the earl of Derby, perhaps a younger brother.[268] Appointed marshal of the army in Ireland in succession to Bagenall in 1553.[269] Named to the council in instructions of 1558, but probably sat from 1553.[270] An active councillor, attended many meetings. Employed on a number of commissions, including one in 1560 to decide the dispute between Ormonde and Desmond.[271] Went on many expeditions with Sussex, named general of Ulster in 1556 with broad powers to hear causes and to use martial law.[272] This plan was abandoned in 1557, thereafter Stanley employed mainly on borders of Co. Meath to keep order, bring in the cessed corn.[273] Arnold commission found him heavily in debt to the queen and to his soldiers; he was charged with gross negligence, leading to his recall as marshal.[274]

263. *Sidney S.P.*, pp. 23–24, 50, 67.
264. *Cal. Carew MSS, 1515–74*, pp. 392, 417.
265. Canny, *Elizabethan conquest*, pp. 77–84.
266. *Cal. S.P. Ire., 1509–73*, pp. 411, 413, 449–50, 452.
267. *DNB*; MacCarthy-Morrogh, *Munster plantation*, ch. 1.
268. *Cal. S.P. Ire., 1509–73*, p. 144; *Cal. Carew MSS, 1515–74*, p. 276; *DNB*, s.v. 'Stanley, Sir Edward, 3rd earl of Derby'.
269. Hughes, *Patentee officers*, p. 122.
270. PRO, SP 62/2/51–55; RIA, MS 24 F 17, f. 42.
271. *Cal. S.P. Ire., 1509–73*, p. 161; RIA, MS 24 F 17, ff. 140–41v; *P.R.I. rep. D.K. 9*, p. 81; *11*, p. 51; Hughes, *Patentee officers*, p. 122.
272. RIA, MS 24 F 17, f. 8; *Cal. Carew MSS, 1515–74*, pp. 260, 262, 275–76.
273. RIA, MS 24 F 17, f. 185; *Cal. S.P. Ire., 1509–73*, pp. 229, 243.
274. RIA, MS 24 F 17, f. 188; *Cal. S.P. Ire., 1509–73*, pp. 205, 210, 249, 266–67, 277, 292–93, 325.

Though his debts were serious, he had support of Sussex and the queen, who nominated him to be president in Munster in 1567 as recompense for his removal from office.[275] He apparently never recovered from his indebtedness, d. between 1570 and 1572.[276]

SYDNEY, SIR HENRY (1529–86)

Eldest son and heir of Sir William Sydney, the chamberlain and steward of Prince Edward's household before 1547. Raised from childhood with the prince, named one of the four gentlemen of the privy chamber in 1547, knt in 1550.[277] Embassy to France in 1550, m. Mary, daughter of John Dudley, duke of Northumberland, in 1551. Briefly lost favour in 1553, but obtained goodwill of Philip II in 1554.[278] Appointed vice treasurer of Ireland in 1556 and named to the council.[279] Served as lord justice three times from 1557 to 1558, and acted on numerous commissions.[280] Among the most active councillors of Sussex's lord deputyship, frustrated by inability to obtain chief governorship, returned to England in 1559. Named lord president of council in the marches of Wales in 1560. Initiated practical reforms in judicial procedures of that council.[281] Appointed to succeed Sussex as lord deputy after interim tenure of Arnold. Owed political success to influence of his patron, Leicester.[282] Negotiated successfully with queen for terms of office, fiscal restraint and new councillors.[283] Largely responsible for the creation and establishment of the provincial councils and the court of castle chamber, presided over the final defeat of Shane O'Neill. Sought a nucleus of experienced officials on Irish affairs within the privy council to whom he could write. Peripheral encouragement to private colonizers and adventurers such as Carew and St Leger.[284] Nearly recalled from office in 1568, was

275. *Cal. S.P. Ire., 1509–73*, pp. 306, 336, 339, 344. Sussex had nominated him to be lord justice in 1558. ibid., p. 150.
276. Sussex noted he was very sick in 1570, badly needed a reward of £400 for his past services. ibid., pp. 428, 528.
277. *DNB*, s.v. 'Sydney, Sir Henry'.
278. *Letters and memorials*, ed. Collins, i, 82–85.
279. Hughes, *Patentee officers*, p. 119; *Cal. Carew MSS, 1515–74*, p. 252; PRO, SP 62/2/51.
280. Hughes, *Patentee officers*, p. 119; *P.R.I. rep. D.K. 9*, p. 81; *Cal. pat. rolls Ire., Hen VIII—Eliz*, pp. 354–55, 363.
281. Williams, *Council in Wales*, pp. 252–55.
282. Brady, 'Government of Ireland', pp. 172–81.
283. Hughes, *Patentee officers*, p. 119; PRO, SP 63/13/109–11; 63/14/2–15, 18–23, 32–43; 63/16/109–10; *Cal. pat. rolls Ire., Hen VIII—Eliz*, p. 493.
284. PRO, SP 63/26/60, 71; 63/28/131; 63/30/97; 63/32/162–66v; 63/13/111; *DNB*; Canny, *Elizabethan conquest*, pp. 46–75, 114–15.

sent back to Ireland in middle of new crises. Parliament of 1569–71 a turbulent and captious assembly, passed mercantilist legislation and attainders against rebels, rejected fiscal reforms. Rebellions in Munster of 1569–71 quelled by Sydney with help of Ormonde, who criticized Sydney's arbitrary handling of dissidents.[285] Recalled at his own urging in 1571, spent the next four years in Wales and at the court. Failed to implement his earlier proposals, saw council in Wales split by factions, corruption.[286] At his nomination to a second lord deputy-ship in 1575, bargained for terms of a regular continuous payment from England of £20,000 per annum, promised to limit spending, reform administration.[287] Three years later he returned in disgrace, the victim of uncontrollable military spending and an extended dispute over the cess.[288] Among the ablest of Tudor lords deputy, initially won the confidence of nearly all sectors of opinion in Ireland. The most active chief governor in the field, a determined judicial reformer, forfeited goodwill of the Pale in constitutional crisis over the cess. Recovered political influence at court after 1578, but faced opposition of Whitgift and others in his presidency of Wales to 1583.[289]

TRAVERS, SIR JOHN (d. 1562)

Of Anglo-Irish birth, military training, named first master of the ordnance in 1540.[290] Named to the council probably in 1541, at least by 1543, and continuously thereafter until his death.[291] Knt before 1550. Acquired substantial estates from dissolution, established his house at Monkstown, Co. Dublin.[292] An active councillor for many years, given regional commands in Co. Wicklow and Ulster at various times. Employed on many commissions of the council.[293] Diligent in his attendance at meetings from 1556 to 1561. In 1558 joined in his

285. Ellis, *Tudor Ireland*, pp. 257–64; Brady, 'Government of Ireland', pp. 194–201, 206.
286. Williams, *Council in Wales*, pp. 257–66.
287. *Cal. Carew MSS, 1575–88*, p. 19.
288. H.M.C., *De L'Isle and Dudley MSS*, ii, 59, 61–62, 66, 69, 75–76, 78–79. See Brady, 'Government of Ireland', pp. 319 ff.
289. MacCaffrey, *Making of policy*, p. 436; Williams, *Council in Wales*, pp. 257–75.
290. *Cal. S.P. Ire., 1509–73*, p. 52; *Cal. Carew MSS, 1515–74*, pp. 162–63; Hughes, *Patentee officers*, p. 130.
291. *Cal. Carew MSS, 1515–74*, pp. 182, 207, 226, 252, 279; *Cal. S.P. Ire., 1509–73*, p. 67; PRO, SP 62/2/51; 62/1/3.
292. *Cal. Carew MSS, 1515–74*, pp. 173, 224; Bradshaw, *Dissolution of religious orders in Ireland*, pp. 176–177, 194, 241.
293. Bradshaw, *Dissolution of religious orders in Ireland*, p. 194; *P.R.I. rep. D.K. 9*, p. 81; *11*, p. 72; *Cal. pat. rolls Ire., Hen VIII—Eliz*, pp. 354–55, 368; RIA, MS 24 F 17, ff. 18, 119–23, 338v; Hughes, *Patentee officers*, p. 130.

office of master of the ordnance by Jacques Wingfield, probably on account of his advanced age. Died in May 1562.[294]

WALSH, WILLIAM (1512–77)

Son of William Walsh, perhaps of Co. Meath. Became a Cistercian, educated at Oxford, obtained D.D. degree. Returned to Ireland, lived at Bective abbey until its dissolution.[295] Commissioner to deprive married clergy in 1553, including Edward Staples, bishop of Meath. Appointed successor to Staples by Cardinal Pole, obtained temporalities of office in 1554, but not consecrated until 1564 by the pope. Sat on council from 1556 to 1559 although not officially named in the instructions.[296] Not a very active councillor, appointed to occasional commissions, limited himself to ecclesiastical duties.[297] Refused the oath of supremacy in February 1560 and preached against the Book of Common Prayer at Trim. Deprived in July 1560, continued preaching in Meath during Bishop Brady's tenure, imprisoned on several occasions until 1565. Remained in custody for seven years until he escaped in 1572, made his way to Toledo, d. in 1577 at Alcala.[298]

WARREN, HUMPHREY (d. 1561)

Probably of English birth, military training, first appears in Ireland in 1551 as one of six captains sent to serve in the king's army. Named to commission governing Cork, Limerick and Kerry with three other captains and the earl of Desmond.[299] In 1556 appeared on commission under newly appointed general of Ulster, Sir George Stanley. Went on many expeditions with Lord Deputy Sussex.[300] Named to the council in 1559, but continued to serve in military capacity, appointed to commission to negotiate with Shane O'Neill in 1561. Died suddenly in November 1561.[301] May have had lands in Co. Meath.[302] Not a diligent councillor, his tenure too brief to have had much impact, his membership probably an effort by Sussex to gain support for his military policies on the council.

294. *Cal. S.P. Ire., 1509–73*, pp. 147, 195.
295. *DNB*, s.v. 'Walsh, William'.
296. ibid.; RIA, MS 24 F 17, f. 8.
297. *Cal. pat. rolls Ire., Hen VIII—Eliz*, p. 368.
298. *DNB*; Walshe, 'Elizabethan settlement', 363.
299. *APC*, iii, 136, 145, 263; *Cal. S.P. Ire., 1509–73*, pp. 115, 118.
300. RIA, MS 24 F 17, f. 8; *Cal. Carew MSS, 1515–74*, pp. 260, 266–67, 275–76.
301. PRO, SP 63/1/122; *Cal. Carew MSS, 1515–74*, p. 279; *Cal. S.P. Ire., 1509–73*, pp. 160, 165, 177, 182.
302. RIA, MS 24 F 17, ff. 129, 145.

WESTON, SIR ROBERT (1515–73)

Son of John Weston of Staffordshire. Fellow of All Souls College, Oxford in 1536, graduated B.C.L. in 1538. Principal of Broadgates Hall from 1546 to 1549, vicar general of Exeter under Miles Coverdale, 1551–53. MP for Lichfield, in 1559.[303] Nominated to succeed Curwen as lord chancellor in 1566, arrived in Ireland in 1567, acted as lord justice briefly in 1568. Salary augmented with deaneries of St Patrick's Dublin (1567) and Wells (1570).[304] Assiduous as a councillor, but not as active as Gerrard on assizes and circuits. Plagued by ill-health while in Ireland, but served on many commissions in the Pale. A moderate Protestant allied with Brady and Lancaster in favour of policy of persuasion. Reported on condition of the Irish judiciary, advocated building schools, reforming clergy.[305] A reliable informant of Cecil, particularly during his tenure as lord justice. Letters grew less frequent as ailments overtook him after 1571, he petitioned continuously for recall.[306]

WHITE, SIR NICHOLAS (d. 1593)

Son of James White, steward of James, earl of Ormonde, member of notable Kilkenny family of White's Hall. Entered Lincoln's Inn in 1552, called to the bar in 1558, attorney for earl of Ormonde. MP for Kilkenny in 1559, JP for Kilkenny in 1563, recorder of Waterford in 1564.[307] On several commissions of the council, including commission for government of Munster, before being named a councillor himself in 1569.[308] Named constable of Wexford castle the same year, replacing Thomas Stukeley, and granted lands in Counties Wexford, Kildare, and Dublin.[309] Named master of the rolls in 1572 while on a trip to England, disputed with Loftus the right to custody of the great seal in 1573.[310] Advocate of moderate policy in church reform along with Brady, Cusake and Weston.[311] One of the most active councillors, a reliable informant of Cecil, from whom he received substantial preferment. An independent bureaucrat, took

303. *DNB*, s.v. 'Weston, Sir Robert'; Ball, *Judges*, i, 211.

304. Hughes, *Patentee officers*, p. 138; *Sidney S.P.*, pp. 59–60; *DNB*.

305. Walshe, 'Elizabethan settlement', 369; *DNB*.

306. *Cal. S.P. Ire., 1509–73*, pp. 358, 360–65, 370–74, 400–02, 404, 439, 495.

307. Ball, *Judges*, i, 213–14; *DNB*, s.v. 'White, Sir Nicholas'.

308. RIA, MS 24 F 17, f. 99–99v; PRO, SP 63/16/22, 109–10; *Sidney S.P.*, pp. 23, 102.

309. Hughes, *Patentee officers*, p. 138; *Sidney S.P.*, pp. 100–01, 129.

310. *DNB*; Hughes, *Patentee officers*, p. 138.

Fyton's side in 1573 dispute and aligned with Pale gentry in cess controversy in 1577, but in 1584 became a partisan of incumbent Lord Deputy Perrot. In each case suffered antagonism of his colleagues and in 1578 nearly lost his office.[312] Unusually adept at both military and judicial affairs, yet described by Gerrard in 1577 as a 'depe dissembler' and a corrupt judge.[313] Active in military campaigns of Munster rebellion, knt in 1584, commissioner for composition of Connacht in 1585. Nearly lost office in 1588 for supporting Perrot, arrested by Fitzwilliam in 1590, examined in castle chamber and released. Retained office, but was dismissed from council.[314]

WINGFIELD, JACQUES (d. 1587)

English-born, perhaps a scion of the prominent Wingfield family of soldier-statesmen who served Henry VIII.[315] With prior military experience, came to Ireland with Sussex in 1556 as a captain of troops. Had command of the marches of Dublin next to the O'Byrnes and O'Tooles.[316] In 1558 named to hold mastership of the ordnance jointly with Travers, became sole master in 1562 on Travers' death.[317] Named to the council in 1559 and sat regularly for several years.[318] In 1562 allowed Shane O'Neill to surprise the rearguard of Sussex's army, suffered heavy losses, nearly lost his office as a result.[319] He was named to many commissions thereafter by the council, continued to receive estates, was named constable of Dublin castle in 1566. But after 1564 he never again signed the council book.[320] Though he may have been re-admitted to membership after 1579, it appears his exclusion was a penalty for his defeat in 1562. In 1573 had a protracted dispute over patronage with Lord Deputy Fitzwilliam.[321] Joined St Leger's project for a colony in south-west Munster in 1569. Continued active in military affairs, especially in Munster rebellion, d. in office in 1587.[322]

311. Walshe, 'Elizabethan settlement', 367.
312. Ball, *Judges*, i, 214; *DNB*; Brady, 'Government of Ireland', pp. 58, 353.
313. LPL, Carew MS 628, f. 311v.
314. *DNB*; Ball, *Judges*, i, 214.
315. *DNB*, s.v. 'Wingfield, Sir Richard'.
316. *Cal. Carew MSS, 1515–74*, pp. 257, 346; *APC*, vi, 288, 301.
317. *Cal. S.P. Ire., 1509–73*, p. 147; Hughes, *Patentee officers*, p. 140.
318. *Cal. Carew MSS, 1515–74*, p. 279; RIA, MS 24 F 17, f. 102–02v.
319. Bagwell, *Ireland under Tudors*, ii, 24–25, 29; *Cal. S.P. Ire., 1509–73*, p. 198.
320. RIA, MS 24 F 17, ff. 192–93v, 196v; *Cal. S.P. Ire., 1509–73*, p. 293; *Cal. Carew MSS, 1515–74*, p. 299; Hughes, *Patentee officers*, p. 140.
321. *Cal. S.P. Ire., 1509–73*, pp. 507, 513, 517–18.
322. Canny, *Elizabethan conquest*, pp. 69, 78–79.

Bibliography

MANUSCRIPT SOURCES

Bodleian Library, Oxford University

Carte manuscripts	55–59, 131	Fitzwilliam papers, 1556–94
Rawlinson manuscripts	D657	Gerrard report on the state of Ireland, 1577
	A237	Revenue accounts, 1559–60
	C98	Instructions to lord justice and council

British Library, London

Additional manuscripts	4763	Letters and papers of the council; tables of the council books
	4767	Instructions to lord deputy and council; revenue accounts of Mary
	4783	Extracts from Sydney papers
	4785	Letters of Queen Elizabeth to lords deputy
	4786	Letters from council; instructions for provincial councils
	4792	Tables of council books, 1543–1605
	4801	Letters of various sovereigns to council, 1547–1603
	4813	Chronicle of Ireland, 1559–90
	4819	Instructions to lord deputy and council, 1556–1663
	32,323	Letters from privy council, 1571–81
	40,061	Papers on currency reform; depositions taken before the council
	47,172	Records of the court of castle chamber
Cottonian manuscripts	Augustus I	Maps of sixteenth-century Ireland
	Titus B XII, XIII	Instructions to council; letters and papers of council

Cottonian manuscripts (contd.)

	Vespasian F XII	Letters of queen, and of Dundalk corporation, to council
Harleian manuscripts	35	Letters and papers of council, 1560–86
	497	Documents on state of garrison, 1571–79
	697	Council book for Munster province
Royal manuscripts	18 D III	Burghley atlas, including maps of Ireland
Sloane manuscripts	2442	Instructions from council to Tremayne
Stowe manuscripts	160	Letters of privy council to council in Ireland, 1578–81
Lambeth Palace Library		
Carew manuscripts	597	Pelham letter book, 1578–79
	600	Instructions from council to Tremayne
	602	Letters from council to Queen Mary
	605	Hooker's Life of Sir Peter Carew
	609	Report of Sussex on state of Ireland
	611	Proceedings of council; revenue accounts
	614	Report on state of Ireland 1561
	619	Letters on cess controversy
	628	Tables of council books, 1543–1605; Gerrard's report on law officers; instructions to council

Public Record Office, London	
State Papers 31, vol. 1	Transcripts of Carte papers
State Papers 60, vols. 1–12	State papers of Ireland, Henry VIII
State Papers 61, vols. 1–4	State papers of Ireland, Edward VI
State Papers 62, vols. 1–2	State papers of Ireland, Mary
State Papers 63, vols. 1–86	State papers of Ireland, Elizabeth I, 1558–81
State Papers 64, vols. 1–3	Maps of Ireland, 1558–1625
State Papers 65, vols. 6–9	Accounts of the vice treasurer of Ireland, 1559–75

Public Record Office, Dublin	
Ferguson manuscripts, vols. 6–7	Copies of Elizabethan letters and patents

Public Record Office, Dublin (contd.)
Lodge manuscripts
Extracts of patent rolls	Patent rolls of Ireland, 1509–1603
Patentee officers and offices in Ireland	Lists of office-holders
Records of chancery rolls, vol. 1	Chancery records, 1509–1603
Manuscript 2440	Letters from King's and Queen's Counties to council
Manuscript 2531	Abstracts of grants and charters, Henry VIII
Manuscript 2532	Extracts from council books, 1548–95
Manuscript 2543	Inquisitions post mortem, 1509–1603
Manuscript 2546	Dublin charters, 1509–1603

Royal Irish Academy, Dublin
Manuscript 24 F 17	Council book of 1556–71

Trinity College Library, Dublin
Caulfield papers	Sarsfield family letters
Manuscript 581	Letters regarding cess, 1577
Manuscript 745	Sidney state papers, 1565–70
Manuscripts 842, 843, 845	Table of Red Council Book; letters and papers of council
Manuscript 852	Cases tried in court of castle chamber

Huntington Library, San Marino, California
Ellesmere manuscript 1701	Edmund Tremayne's essay on Ireland

Louis Round Wilson Library, University of North Carolina, Chapel Hill
Southern Historical Collection
Preston Davie papers	Letter of Elizabeth I to Sydney

PRINTED SOURCES

'Additional Sidney state papers, 1566–1570', ed. D.B. Quinn, *Anal Hib*, no. 26 (1970), 91–102.
Annals of Connacht. ed. A.M. Freeman. Dublin, 1944.
'The annals of Dudley Loftus', ed. N. White, *Anal Hib*, no. 10 (1941), 225–38.
Annals of the Four Masters. ed. J. O'Donovan. 7 vols. Dublin, 1849.
The Annals of Loch Cé. A chronicle of Irish affairs from AD 1014 to AD 1590. ed. W. Hennesy. 2 vols. Dublin, 1939.
A bibliography of royal proclamations of the Tudor and Stuart sovereigns, 1485–1714. ed. R. Steele. vols. 5–6 of *Bibliotheca Lindesiana*. Oxford, 1910.
Blake family records, 1300–1600. ed. M.J. Blake. London, 1902.
Burke's genealogical and heraldic history of the peerage, baronetage and knightage. ed. P. Townend. 104th ed. London, 1967.
'Calendar of the Harris manuscripts (now in the National Library of Ireland)', ed. C. McNeill, *Anal Hib*, no. 6 (1934), 248–449.
'Calendar of the Irish council book for 1581–86', ed. D.B. Quinn, *Anal Hib*, no. 24 (1967), 93–180.
Calendar of the patent and close rolls of chancery in Ireland, of the reigns of Henry VIII, Edward VI, Mary and Elizabeth. 2 vols. ed. J. Morrin. Dublin, 1861–62.

A collection of state papers relating to affairs of the reigns of Henry VIII, Edward VI, Mary and Elizabeth, 1542–1570 . . . left by William Cecil, Lord Burghley, and now at Hatfield House. ed. S. Haynes. 2 vols. London, 1759.

The complete peerage of England, Scotland, Ireland, Great Britain and the United Kingdom. ed. G.E. Cokayne, rev. V. Gibbs. London, 1910.

Desiderata curiosa Hibernica: or a select collection of state papers during the reigns of Elizabeth, James I and Charles I. 2 vols. ed. J. Lodge. Dublin, 1772.

The dictionary of national biography. ed. L. Stephen and S. Lee. 21 vols. Oxford, 1917.

'Financial records available for Irish history, 1461–1558', ed. D.B. Quinn, *Anal Hib*, no. 10 (1941), 3–69.

'The Fitzwilliam manuscripts at Milton', ed. C. McNeill, *Anal Hib*, no. 4 (1932), 287– 326.

A full view of the public transactions of Queen Elizabeth. ed. P. Forbes. 2 vols. London, 1740–41.

Gilbert, J.T., ed. *Facsimiles of national manuscripts of Ireland.* Vol. iv, sect. 1. London, 1882.

Great Britain. Historical Manuscripts Commission. *Calendar of the manuscripts of the marquis of Salisbury preserved at Hatfield House.*

—— *The manuscripts of Charles Haliday, esq., of Dublin. Acts of the privy council in Ireland, 1556–1571.*

—— *The manuscripts of the marquess of Ormonde, formerly at Kilkenny Castle.* 3 vols.

—— *Report on the manuscripts of the earl of Egmont.* vol. 1.

—— *Report on the manuscripts of Lord De L'Isle and Dudley preserved at Penshurst Place.* vols. 1–2.

Great Britain. Privy Council. *Acts of the privy council of England.* new ser. vols. 1–11.

Great Britain. Public Record Office. *Calendar of the Carew manuscripts preserved in the archiepiscopal library at Lambeth, 1515–1574.*

—— *Calendar of the Carew manuscripts preserved in the archiepiscopal library at Lambeth, 1575–1588.*

—— *Calendar of the patent rolls preserved in the Public Record Office.* Philip and Mary. vols. 1–4.

—— *Calendar of the patent rolls preserved in the Public Record Office.* Elizabeth I. vols. 1–2, 4–5.

—— *Calendar of state papers, domestic series, of the reigns of Edward VI, Mary and Elizabeth, 1547–1580.*

—— *Calendar of state papers, Ireland, 1509–1573.*

—— *Calendar of state papers, Ireland, 1574–1585.*

—— *Letters and papers, foreign and domestic, in the reign of Henry VIII.*

Great Britain. Record Commission. *Liber Munerum Publicorum Hiberniae ab anno 1152 usque ad 1827: or the Establishment of Ireland.* ed. R. Lascelles. 2 vols.

Hibernia Anglicana: or the history of Ireland from the conquest thereof by the English to this present time. ed. R. Cox. London, 1689.

Hibernica: or some antient pieces relating to Ireland. ed. W. Harris. Dublin, 1747.

Holinshed's chronicles of England, Scotland and Ireland. ed. R. Holinshed. vol. 6. London, 1808.

Ireland (Eire). Irish Manuscripts Commission. *Dignitas decani.* ed. N.B. White.

—— *The Dowdall deeds*. ed. C. McNeill and A.J. Otway-Ruthven.

—— *Extents of Irish monastic possessions, 1540–1541*. ed. N. White.

—— *The Fitzwilliam manuscripts: accounts from the Annesley collection*. ed. A.K. Longfield.

—— *Sidney state papers, 1565–1570*. ed. T. O'Laidhin.

—— *The Walsingham letter book, 1578–79*. ed. J. Hogan and N. O'Farrell.

Ireland. Public Record Office. Reports of the Deputy Keeper of the Public Records of Ireland. 9th through 13th reps.

—— *Calendars to fiants in the reigns of Edward VI, Mary and Elizabeth*.

Ireland under Elizabeth and James I. ed. H. Morley. London, 1890.

Irish Free State. Irish Manuscripts Commission. *Calendar of Ormonde deeds, 1172–1603*. vol. 5. ed. E. Curtis.

—— *Chronicle of Ireland, 1584–1608 (Sir James Perrott)*. ed. H. Wood.

—— *Liber Primus Kilkenniensis*. ed. C. McNeill.

—— *The Tanner letters*. ed. C. McNeill.

Irish historical documents, 1172–1922. ed. E. Curtis and R.B. McDowell. London, 1943.

Irish history from contemporary sources, 1509–1610. ed. C. Maxwell. London, 1923.

Letters and memorials of state . . . written and collected by Sir Henry Sydney, Sir Philip Sydney, et. al. ed. A. Collins. London, 1746.

The Oxford English dictionary. ed. J.A.H. Murray, H. Bradley, W.A. Craigie, C.T. Onions. 12 vols. Oxford, 1933.

'Report on the state of Ireland, 1577–78, by lord chancellor Gerrard', ed. C. McNeill, *Anal Hib*, no. 2 (1930), 93–291.

'Sir Henry Sidney's memoir of his government of Ireland.' *UJA*, iii (1855), 90.

Spenser, Edmund. *A view of the present state of Ireland*. ed. W.L. Renwick. Oxford, 1970.

Stafford, Thomas. *Pacata Hibernia: Ireland appeased and reduced, or a history of the wars of Ireland under Elizabeth*. ed. S. O'Grady. 2 vols. Dublin, 1810.

State papers concerning the Irish church in the time of queen Elizabeth. ed. W.M. Brady. London, 1868.

Tudor royal proclamations. ed. P.L. Hughes and J.F. Larkin. 3 vols. New Haven, 1964–69.

Ware, Sir James. *The antiquities of Ireland*. ed. W. Harris. Dublin, 1762.

SECONDARY SOURCES: BOOKS

Adair, E.R. *The sources for the history of the council in the sixteenth and seventeenth centuries*. London, 1924.

Andrews, J. *Ireland in maps, an introduction*. Dublin, 1961.

Andrews, K.R., Canny, N.P. and Hair, P.E.H., ed. *The westward enterprise: English activities in Ireland, the Atlantic and America, 1480–1650*. Liverpool, 1978.

Asplin, P.W.A. *Medieval Ireland, c. 1170–1495: a bibliography of secondary works*. Dublin, 1971.

Aylmer, G.E. *The king's servants: the civil service of Charles I, 1625–1642*. London, 1961.

Bagwell, R. *Ireland under the Tudors*. 3 vols. London, 1890–95.

Baker, J.H. *The legal profession and the common law: historical essays*. London, 1985.

Ball, F.E. *The judges in Ireland, 1121–1921*. 2 vols. London, 1926.

Baldwin, J.F. *The king's council in England during the middle ages*. Oxford, 1913.

Bayne, C.G. and Dunham, W.H., Jr., ed. *Select cases in the council of Henry VII*. Selden Soc, vol. lxxv. London, 1968.

Beckett, J.C. *The making of modern Ireland, 1603–1922*. London, 1966.

—— *The Anglo-Irish tradition*. Ithaca, NY, 1976.

Bellamy, J. *Crime and public order in England in the late middle ages*. London, 1973.

Bindoff, S.T., Hurstfield, J., and Williams, C.H., ed. *Elizabethan government and society: essays presented to Sir John Neale*. London, 1961.

Black, J.B. *The reign of Elizabeth*. 2nd ed. Oxford, 1960.

Blatcher, M. *The court of king's bench, 1450–1550*. London, 1978.

Boynton, L. *The Elizabethan militia, 1558–1633*. London, 1967.

Brooks, C.W. *Pettyfoggers and vipers of the commonwealth: the 'lower branch' of the legal profession in early modern England*. Cambridge, 1986.

Brooks, F.W. *The council of the North*. London, 1953.

Bradshaw, B. *The dissolution of the religious orders in Ireland under Henry VIII*. Cambridge, 1974.

—— *The Irish constitutional revolution of the sixteenth century*. Cambridge, 1979.

Brady, C., ed. *Worsted in the game: losers in Irish history*. Dublin, 1989.

Brady, C. and Gillespie, R., ed. *Natives and newcomers: essays on the making of Irish colonial society, 1534–1641*. Dublin, 1986.

Brady, C., O'Dowd, M. and Walker, B., ed. *Ulster: an illustrated history*. London, 1989.

Bryan, D. *Gerald Fitzgerald, the great earl of Kildare, 1456–1513*. Dublin, 1933.

Bryson, W.H. *The equity side of the exchequer: its jurisdiction, administration, procedures and records*. Cambridge, 1975.

Burke, O.J. *The history of the lord chancellors of Ireland, 1186–1874*. Dublin, 1879.

Butler, W.F.T. *Confiscation in Irish history*. Dublin, 1917.

Canny, N.P. *The Elizabethan conquest of Ireland: a pattern established, 1565–1576*. Hassocks, 1976.

—— *The formation of the Old English élite in Ireland*. Dublin, 1975.

—— *From reformation to restoration: Ireland, 1534–1660*. Dublin, 1987.

—— *Kingdom and colony: Ireland in the Atlantic world, 1560–1800*. Baltimore, 1988.

—— *The upstart earl: a study of the social and mental world of Richard Boyle, first earl of Cork, 1566–1643*. Cambridge, 1982.

—— and Pagden, A., ed. *Colonial identity in the Atlantic world, 1500–1800*. Princeton, 1987.

Challis, C.E. *The Tudor coinage*. Manchester, 1978.

Chart, D.A. *An economic history of Ireland*. Dublin, 1920.

—— *The story of Dublin*. London, 1907.

Clarke, A. *The Old English in Ireland, 1625–42*. Ithaca, NY, 1966.

Cockburn, J.S., ed. *Crime in England, 1550–1800*. London, 1977.

—— *A history of English assizes, 1558–1714*. Cambridge, 1972.

Coleman, C. and Starkey, D.R., ed. *Revolution reassessed: revisions in the history of Tudor government and administration*. Oxford, 1986.

Collinson, P. *The religion of Protestants: the church in English society, 1559–1625*. Oxford, 1982.

Conway, A. *Henry VII's relations with Scotland and Ireland, 1485–1498*. Cambridge, 1932.

Cosgrove, A. *Late medieval Ireland, 1370–1541*. Dublin, 1981.

—— ed. *A new history of Ireland- ii: Medieval Ireland, 1169–1534*. Oxford, 1987.

—— ed. *Studies in Irish history presented to R.D. Edwards*. Dublin, 1979.

Cotton, H. *Fasti ecclesiae Hibernicae: the succession of the prelates and members of the cathedral bodies of Ireland*. Dublin, 1845–60.

Crone, J.S. *A concise dictionary of Irish biography*. London, 1928.

Cross, C., Loades, D. and Scarisbrick, J.J., ed. *Law and government under the Tudors: essays presented to Sir Geoffrey Elton on his retirement*. Cambridge, 1988.

Cruickshank, C.G. *Elizabeth's army*. 2nd ed. Oxford, 1966.

—— *Army royal: Henry VIII's invasion of France, 1513*. Oxford, 1969.

Cullen, L.M. *The emergence of modern Ireland, 1600–1900*. New York, 1981.

Curtis, E. *A history of Ireland*. London, 1936.

—— *A history of medieval Ireland from 1110–1513*. London, 1923.

Dicey, A.V. *The privy council*. London, 1887.

Dietz, F.C. *English public finance, 1485–1641*. 2 vols. 2nd ed. Urbana, Ill., 1964.

Donaldson, A.G. *Some comparative aspects of Irish law*. Cambridge, 1957.

Dunlop, R. *Ireland from the earliest times to the present day*. London, 1922.

Eager, A.R. *A guide to Irish bibliographical material: a bibliography of Irish bibliographies*. London, 1964.

Edwards, R.D. *Church and state in Tudor Ireland: a history of penal laws against Irish Catholics, 1534–1603*. Dublin, 1930.

—— *Ireland in the age of the Tudors: the destruction of Hiberno- Norman civilization*. London, 1977.

Ellis, S.G. *The Pale and the far North: government and society in two early Tudor borderlands*. Galway, 1988.

—— *Reform and revival: English government in Ireland, 1470–1534*. London, 1985.

—— *Tudor Ireland: crown, community and the conflict of cultures, 1470–1603*. London, 1985.

Elton, G.R. *England under the Tudors*. 2nd ed. London, 1969.

—— *English law in the sixteenth century: reform in an age of change*. London, 1979.

—— *The parliament of England, 1559–1581*. Cambridge, 1986.

—— *Policy and police: the enforcement of the reformation in the age of Thomas Cromwell*. Cambridge, 1972.

—— *Reform and renewal: Thomas Cromwell and the common weal*. Cambridge, 1973.

—— *Reform and reformation: England 1509–1558*. London, 1977.

—— *Star chamber stories*. London, 1958.

—— *The Tudor constitution: documents and commentary*. 2nd ed. Cambridge, 1982.

—— *The Tudor revolution in government: administrative changes in the reign of Henry VIII*. Cambridge, 1953.

Emmison, F.G. *Elizabethan life: Disorder*. Chelmsford, Essex, 1970.

Evans, F.M.G. *The principal secretary of state*. Manchester, 1923.

Falkiner, C.L. *Essays relating to Ireland, biographical, historical, topographical*. London, 1909.

—— *Illustrations of Irish history and topography*. London, 1904.

Falls, C.B. *Elizabeth's Irish wars*. London, 1904.

—— *Mountjoy: Elizabethan general*. London, 1955.

Fitzgerald, Brian. *The Geraldines: an experiment in Irish government, 1169–1601*. London, 1951.

Fletcher, A. *Tudor rebellions*. London, 1983.

480   *Anglicizing the government of Ireland*

Fletcher, A. and Stevenson, J., ed. *Order and disorder in early modern England.* Cambridge, 1985.

Ford, A. *The Protestant reformation in Ireland.* Frankfurt-am-Main, 1985.

Fortescue, J.W. *A history of the British army.* vol. 1. London, 1899.

Frame, R.F. *English lordship in Ireland 1318–1361.* Oxford, 1982.

Freeman, T.W. *Ireland: its physical, historical, social and economic geography.* London, 1950.

Gilbert, J.T. *A history of Dublin.* 3 vols. Dublin, 1861.

—— *A history of the viceroys of Ireland.* Dublin, 1865.

Gillespie, R. *Colonial Ulster: the settlement of East Ulster, 1600–1641.* Cork, 1985.

Gladish, D.M. *The Tudor privy council.* Retford, 1915.

Gould, J.D. *The great debasement: currency and the economy in mid-Tudor England.* Oxford, 1970.

Green, A.S. *The making of Ireland and its undoing, 1200–1600.* London, 1908.

Guth, D.J. and McKenna, J.W., ed. *Tudor rule and revolution: essays for G.R. Elton from his American friends.* Cambridge, 1982.

Guy, J. *The cardinal's court: the impact of Thomas Wolsey in star chamber.* Hassocks, 1977.

—— *The court of star chamber and its records to the reign of Elizabeth I.* London, 1985.

—— *Tudor England.* Oxford, 1988.

Gwynn, A. *The medieval province of Armagh, 1417–1545.* Dundalk, 1946.

Gwynn, A. and Hadcock, R.N. *Medieval religious houses: Ireland.* London, 1970.

Hamilton, E.W., Lord. *Elizabethan Ulster.* London, 1919.

Haigh, C. *Elizabeth I.* London, 1988.

—— ed. *The reign of Elizabeth I.* London, 1985.

Hand, G.J. *English law in Ireland, 1290–1324.* Cambridge, 1967.

Hardiman, J. *The history of the town and county of Galway.* Dublin, 1820.

Hayes, R., ed. *Manuscript sources for the history of Irish civilization.* Boston, 1965.

Hayes-McCoy, G.A. *Irish battles.* London, 1969.

—— *Scots mercenary forces in Ireland (1565–1603).* London, 1937.

—— *Ulster and other Irish maps, ca. 1600.* Dublin, 1964.

Hechter, M. *Internal colonialism: the Celtic fringe in British national development, 1536–1966.* London, 1975.

Heinze, R. *The proclamations of the Tudor kings.* Cambridge, 1976.

Helmholz, R.H., ed. *Canon law in Protestant lands* (Comparative studies in continental and anglo-american legal history, bd. 11). Berlin, 1992.

Hinton, E.M., ed. *Ireland through Tudor eyes.* Philadelphia, 1935.

Hoak, D.E. *The king's council in the reign of Edward VI.* Cambridge, 1976.

Hogan, D. and Osborough, W.N., ed. *Brehons, serjeants and attorneys: studies in the history of the Irish legal profession.* Dublin, 1990.

Hogan, E. *Distinguished Irishmen of the sixteenth century.* London, 1894.

Hogan, J. *Ireland in the European system.* vol. 1. London, 1920.

Hughes, J.L.J., ed. *Patentee officers in Ireland, 1173–1826.* Dublin, 1960.

Hurstfield, J. *Elizabeth I and the unity of England.* London, 1960.

—— *Freedom, corruption and government in Elizabethan England.* London, 1973.

—— *The illusion of power in Tudor politics.* London, 1979.

—— *The queen's wards: wardship and marriage under Elizabeth I.* London, 1958.

Ireland (Eire). Irish Manuscripts Commission. Sir William Herbert, *Croftus sive Hibernia liber.* ed. and transl. A. Keaveney and J.A. Madden.

Ives, E.W. *The common lawyers of pre-reformation England.* Cambridge, 1983.
James, M.E. *Society, politics and culture: studies in early modern England.* Cambridge, 1986.
Jackson, D. *Intermarriage in Ireland, 1550–1650.* Montreal, 1970.
Jennings, R. *Glimpses of an ancient parish: Newcastle, Co. Wicklow 1189–1989.* n.d. [1989].
Johnston, E.M. *Irish history: a select bibliography.* London, 1969.
Jones, F.M. *Mountjoy, 1563–1606: the last Elizabethan deputy.* Dublin, 1958.
Jones, W.J. *The Elizabethan court of chancery.* Oxford, 1967.
Jones, W.R.D. *The mid-Tudor crisis, 1539–1563.* London, 1973.
Kearney, H.F. *Strafford in Ireland, 1633–1641: a study in absolutism.* Manchester, 1959.
Keir, D.L. *A constitutional history of modern Britain, 1485–1937.* 3rd ed. London, 1947.
Kenny, C. *The King's Inns and the kingdom of Ireland: the Irish 'inn of court', 1541–1800.* Dublin, 1992.
Kiernan, T.J. *The financial administration of Ireland to 1817.* London, 1930.
Leask, H.G. *Irish castles and castellated houses.* Dundalk, 1946.
—— *Irish churches and monastic buildings.* 3 vols. Dundalk, 1955.
Lee, J., ed. *Irish historiography, 1970–79.* Cork, 1981.
Lehmberg, S.E. *Sir Walter Mildmay and Tudor government.* Austin, Tex., 1964.
Lennon, C. *Richard Stanihurst, the Dubliner, 1547–1618.* Dublin, 1981.
—— *The lords of Dublin in the age of the reformation.* Dublin, 1989.
Lewis, S. *A topographical dictionary of Ireland.* 2nd ed. 2 vols. London, 1849.
Loach, J. and Tittler, R., ed. *The mid-Tudor polity, c. 1540–1560.* London, 1980.
Loades, D.M. *The reign of Mary Tudor: politics, government and religion in England, 1553–1558.* London, 1979.
—— *The Tudor court.* London, 1987.
Longfield, A.K. *Anglo-Irish trade in the sixteenth century.* London, 1929.
Loomie, A.J. *The Spanish Elizabethans.* New York, 1963.
Lydon, J.F. *The lordship of Ireland in the middle ages.* Toronto, 1972.
—— ed. *England and Ireland in the later middle ages.* Dublin, 1981.
—— ed. *The English in medieval Ireland.* Dublin, 1984.
Lyon, B. *A constitutional and legal history of medieval England.* London, 1960.
MacCaffrey, W.T. *The shaping of the Elizabethan regime.* Princeton, 1968.
—— *Queen Elizabeth and the making of policy, 1572–1588.* Princeton, 1982.
MacCarthy-Morrogh, M. *The Munster plantation: English migration to southern Ireland, 1583–1641.* Oxford, 1986.
MacCurtain, Margaret. *Tudor and Stuart Ireland.* Dublin, 1972.
McEldowney, J.F. and O'Higgins, P., ed. *The common law tradition: essays in Irish legal history.* Dublin, 1990.
MacLysaght, E. *Irish life in the seventeenth century.* 2nd ed. Cork, 1950.
—— *Irish families, their names, arms and origins.* Dublin, 1957.
Mant, R. *History of the church of Ireland from the reformation to the revolution.* London, 1840.
Maxwell, C. *A short bibliography of Irish history.* London, 1921.
Moody, T.W., ed. *Irish historiography, 1936–1970.* Dublin, 1971.
—— Martin, F.X. and Byrne, F.J., ed. *A new history of Ireland- iii: Early modern Ireland, 1534–1691.* Oxford, 1976.
—— ed. *A new history of Ireland- ix: Maps, genealogies, lists.* Oxford, 1984.

Morton, G. *Elizabethan Ireland*. London, 1971.

Nicholls, K. *Gaelic and gaelicized Ireland in the middle ages*. Dublin, 1972.

—— *Land, law and society in sixteenth-century Ireland*. Dublin, 1976.

O'Connor, G.B. *Elizabethan Ireland, native and English*. Dublin, 1906.

O'Faolain, S. *The great O'Neill: a biography of Hugh O'Neill, earl of Tyrone, 1550–1616*. London, 1942.

O'Flanagan, J.R. *The lives of the lord chancellors and keepers of the great seal of Ireland*. 2 vols. London, 1870.

O'Keefe, P. and Simington, T. *Irish stone bridges: history and heritage*. Dublin, 1991.

Otway-Ruthven, A.J. *The history of medieval Ireland*. London, 1968.

Pawlisch, H.S. *Sir John Davies and the conquest of Ireland: a study in legal imperialism*. Cambridge, 1985.

Philpin, C.H.E., ed. *Nationalism and popular protest in Ireland*. Cambridge, 1987.

Ponko, V., Jr. *The privy council and the spirit of Elizabethan economic management, 1558–1603*. Trans Am Philos Soc, n.s., vol. lviii. Philadelphia, 1968.

Prest, W.R. *The inns of court under Elizabeth I and the early Stuarts, 1590–1640*. London, 1972.

—— *The rise of the barristers: a social history of the English bar, 1590–1640*. Oxford, 1986.

Pulman, M.B. *The Elizabethan privy council in the fifteen-seventies*. Berkeley, 1971.

Quinn, D.B. *The Elizabethans and the Irish*. Ithaca, NY, 1966.

Rae, T.I. *The administration of the Scottish frontier, 1513–1603*. Edinburgh, 1966.

Read, C., ed. *Bibliography of British history: the Tudor period, 1485–1603*. 2nd ed. Oxford, 1959.

—— *Mr. Secretary Cecil and Queen Elizabeth*. London, 1955.

—— *Lord Burghley and Queen Elizabeth*. London, 1960.

—— *Mr. Secretary Walsingham and the policy of Queen Elizabeth*. 3 vols. Oxford, 1925.

Reid, R.R. *The king's council of the North*. London, 1921.

Richardson, H.G. and Sayles, G.O. *The administration of Ireland, 1172–1377*. Dublin, 1963.

—— *The Irish parliament in the middle ages*. Philadelphia, 1952.

Richardson, W.C. *The history of the court of augmentations, 1536–1554*. Baton Rouge, La., 1961.

—— *Tudor chamber administration, 1485–1547*. Baton Rouge, La., 1952.

Richey, A.G. *Lectures on the history of Ireland, 1534–1609*. London, 1870.

Ronan, M.V. *The reformation in Dublin, 1536–1558*. London, 1926.

—— *The reformation in Ireland under Elizabeth, 1558–1580*. London, 1930.

Samaha, J. *Law and order in historical perspective: the case of Elizabethan Essex*. New York, 1974.

Scofield, C.L. *A study of the court of star chamber*. Chicago, 1900.

Sharpe, J.A. *Crime in early modern England, 1550–1750*. London, 1984.

Silke, J.J. *Kinsale: the Spanish intervention in Ireland at the end of the Elizabethan wars*. Liverpool, 1970.

—— *Ireland and Europe, 1559–1607*. Dublin, 1966.

Simms, K. *From kings to warlords: the changing political structure of Gaelic Ireland in the later middle ages*. Dublin, 1987.

Slack, P., ed. *Rebellion, popular protest and the social order in early modern England*. Cambridge, 1984.

Slavin, A.J., ed. *Tudor men and institutions*. Baton Rouge, La., 1972.

Smith, A.G.R. *The government of Elizabethan England.* London, 1967.
— *The emergence of a nation state: the commonwealth of England 1529–1660.* London, 1984.
Stephens, N. and Glasscock, R.E., ed. *Irish geographical studies in honour of Emyr Estyn Evans.* Belfast, 1970.
Thomas, Avril. *The walled towns of Ireland.* 2 vols. Dublin, 1992.
Thomson, G.S. *Lords lieutenants in the sixteenth century.* London, 1923.
Tillyard, E.M.W. *The Elizabethan world picture.* London, 1963.
Webb, J.J. *Municipal government in Ireland: medieval and modern.* Dublin, 1918.
Williams, P. *The council in the marches of Wales under Elizabeth I.* Cardiff, 1958.
— *The Tudor regime.* Oxford, 1979.
Wilson, P. *The beginnings of modern Ireland.* Dublin, 1912.
Wood, H. *A guide to the records in the Public Record Office of Ireland.* Dublin, 1919.
Woodward, D.M. *The trade of Elizabethan Chester.* Hull, 1970.
Wrightson, K. *English society, 1580–1680.* London, 1982.
Youngs, F.A. *The proclamations of the Tudor queens.* Cambridge, 1976.

SECONDARY SOURCES: ARTICLES

Abbott, L. 'Public office and private profit: the legal establishment in the reign of Mary Tudor', in *The mid-Tudor polity, c. 1540–1560.* ed. J. Loach and R. Tittler. London, 1980.
Adair, E.R. 'The privy council registers.' *EHR*, xxx (1915), 698.
Adams, S. 'Eliza enthroned? The court and its politics', in *The reign of Elizabeth I.* ed. C. Haigh. London, 1985.
Alsop, J.D. 'Government, finance and the community of the exchequer', in *The reign of Elizabeth I.* ed. C. Haigh. London, 1985.
— 'The structure of early Tudor finance, c. 1509–1558', in *Revolution reassessed: revisions in the history of Tudor government and administration.* ed. C. Coleman and D.R. Starkey. Oxford, 1986.
Andrews, J.H. 'Geography and government in Elizabethan Ireland', in *Irish geographical studies in honour of Emyr Estyn Evans.* ed. N. Stephens and R.E. Glasscock. Belfast, 1970.
Appleby, J. and O'Dowd, M. 'The Irish admiralty: its organisation and development, c. 1570–1640.' *IHS*, xxiv (1985), 229.
Baker, J.H. 'Criminal courts and procedure at common law, 1550–1800', in *Crime in England, 1550–1800.* ed. J.S. Cockburn. Princeton, 1977.
Barnes, T.G. 'Due process and slow process in the late Elizabethan and early Stuart star chamber.' *Am Jn Legal Hist*, vi (1962), 221; 315.
— 'Mr. Hudson's star chamber', in *Tudor rule and revolution: essays for G.R. Elton from his American friends.* ed. D.J. Guth and J.W. McKenna. Cambridge, 1982.
— 'Star chamber mythology.' *Am Jn Legal Hist*, v (1961), 1.
Barry, J. 'Guide to records of the genealogical office, Dublin, with a commentary on heraldry in Ireland and a history of the office.' *Anal Hib*, no. 26 (1970), 3.
Beier, A.L. 'Vagrants and the social order in Elizabethan England.' *Past & Present*, no. 64 (1974), 3.
Berry, H.F. 'The sheriffs of the county of Cork: Henry III to 1660.' *RSAI Jn*, xxxv (1905), 39.

Bottigheimer, K. 'The failure of the reformation in Ireland: une question bien posée.' *Jn Eccles Hist*, xxxvi (1985), 196.

—— 'Kingdom and colony: Ireland in the westward enterprise, 1536–1660', in *The westward enterprise: English activities in Ireland, the Atlantic and America, 1480–1650*. ed. K.R. Andrews, N.P. Canny, P.E.H. Hair. Liverpool, 1978.

Boyce, D.G. 'Brahmins and carnivores: the Irish historian in Great Britain.' *IHS*, xxv (1987), 225.

Boynton, L. 'The Tudor provost-marshals.' *EHR*, lxxvii (1962), 437.

Bradshaw, B. 'Cromwellian reform and the origins of the Kildare rebellion, 1533–34.' *R Hist Soc Trans*, 5th ser, xxvii (1977), 69.

—— 'The Edwardian reformation in Ireland, 1547–53.' *Archiv Hib*, xxxiv (1977), 83.

—— 'The Elizabethans and the Irish.' *Studies*, lxvi (1977), 38.

—— 'George Browne, first reformation archbishop of Dublin, 1536–1554.' *Jn Eccles Hist*, xxi (1970), 33.

—— 'Nationalism and historical scholarship in modern Ireland'. *IHS*, xxvi (1989), 329.

—— 'Native reaction to the westward enterprise: a case-study in Gaelic ideology', in *The westward enterprise: English activities in Ireland, the Atlantic and America, 1480–1650*, ed. K.R. Andrews, N.P. Canny, P.Hair. Liverpool, 1978.

—— 'The opposition to the ecclesiastical legislation in the Irish reformation parliament.' *IHS*, xvi (1969), 285.

—— 'Robe and sword in the conquest of Ireland', in *Law and government under the Tudors: essays presented to Sir Geoffrey Elton on his retirement*. ed. C. Cross, D. Loades, J.J. Scarisbrick. Cambridge, 1988.

—— 'Sword, word and strategy in the reformation in Ireland.' *Hist Jn*, xxi (1978), 475.

—— '"A treatise for the reformation of Ireland, 1554–5"', by E. Walshe. *Ir Jur*, xvi (1981), 299.

Brady, C. 'Conservative subversives: the community of the Pale and the Dublin administration, 1556–1586', in *Radicals, rebels and establishments* (Historical Studies: XV). ed. P.J. Corish. Belfast, 1985.

—— 'Court, castle and country: the framework of government in Tudor Ireland', in *Natives and newcomers: essays on the making of Irish colonial society, 1534–1641*. ed. C. Brady and R. Gillespie. Dublin, 1986.

—— 'Faction and the origins of the Desmond rebellion of 1579.' *IHS*, xxii (1981), 289.

—— 'The killing of Shane O'Neill: some new evidence.' *Ir Sword*, xv (1982), 115.

—— 'The O'Reillys of East Breifne and the problem of "surrender and regrant".' *Breifne*, vi (1985), 233.

—— 'Sixteenth-century Ulster and the failure of Tudor reform', in *Ulster: an illustrated history*. ed. C. Brady, M. O'Dowd, B. Walker. London, 1989.

—— 'Spenser's Irish crisis: humanism and experience in the 1590s.' *Past & Present*, no. 111 (1986), 17.

—— 'Thomas Butler, earl of Ormonde (1534–1614) and reform in Tudor Ireland', in *Worsted in the game: Losers in Irish history*. ed. C. Brady. Dublin, 1989.

Brand, P. 'The early history of the legal profession of the lordship of Ireland, 1250–1350', in *Brehons, serjeants and attorneys*. ed. D. Hogan and W.N. Osborough. Dublin, 1990.

Butler, T.B. 'King Henry VIII's Irish army list.' *Irish Genealogist*, i (1937), 3; 36.

Butler, W.F.T. 'Irish land tenures, Celtic and foreign.' *Studies*, xiii (1924), 291; 524.

—— 'The lordship of MacCarthy Mor.' *RSAI Jn*, xxxvi (1906), 349; xxxvii (1907), 1.

—— 'The policy of surrender and re-grant.' *RSAI Jn*, xliii (1913), 47; 99.

Canny, N.P. 'Dominant minorities: English settlers in Ireland and Virginia, 1550–1650', in *Minorities in history* (Historical Studies: XII). ed. A.C. Hepburn. London, 1979.

—— 'Edmund Spenser and the development of an Anglo-Irish identity.' *Yearbook of English Studies*, xiii (1983), 1.

—— 'The formation of the Irish mind: religion, politics and Gaelic Irish literature, 1580–1750,' in *Nationalism and popular protest in Ireland*. ed. C.H.E. Philpin. Cambridge, 1987.

—— 'Hugh O'Neill, earl of Tyrone, and the changing face of Gaelic Ulster.' *Stud Hib*, x (1970), 7.

—— 'Identity formation in Ireland: the emergence of the Anglo-Irish', in *Colonial identity in the Atlantic world, 1500–1800*. ed. N. Canny and A. Pagden. Princeton, 1987.

—— 'The ideology of English colonization: from Ireland to America.' *William and Mary Quarterly*, 3rd ser., xxx (1973), 575.

—— 'The permissive frontier: social control in English settlements in Ireland and Virginia, 1550–1650', in *The westward enterprise: English activities in Ireland, the Atlantic and America, 1480–1650*. ed. K.R. Andrews, N. Canny, P. Hair. Liverpool, 1978.

—— 'Protestants, planters and apartheid in early modern Ireland.' *IHS*, xxv (1986), 105.

—— 'Rowland White's "Discors touching Ireland", c. 1569.' *IHS*, xx (1976), 439.

—— 'Rowland White's "The dysorders of the Irisshery" 1571.' *Stud Hib*, xix (1979), 147.

—— 'Why the reformation failed in Ireland: une question mal posée.' *Jn Eccles Hist*, xxx (1979), 423.

Chart, D.A. 'The break-up of the estate of Con O'Neill.' *RIA Proc*, xlviii (1942), sect. c, no 3, 119.

—— 'The Public Record Office of Northern Ireland, 1924–1936.' *IHS*, i (1938), 11.

Clarke, A. 'The history of Poynings' law, 1615–1641.' *IHS*, xviii (1972), 207.

Cockburn, J.S. 'The nature and incidence of crime in England, 1559–1625: a preliminary survey', in *Crime in England, 1550–1800*. ed. J.S. Cockburn. Princeton, 1977.

Coleman, C. 'Artifice or accident? The reorganization of the exchequer of receipt, c. 1554–1572', in *Revolution reassessed*. ed. C. Coleman and D.R. Starkey. Oxford, 1986.

Cosgrove, A. 'The Gaelic resurgence and the Geraldine supremacy, c. 1400–1534', in *The course of Irish history*. ed. T.W. Moody and F.X. Martin. New York, 1967.

—— 'The writing of Irish medieval history.' *IHS*, xxvii (1990), 97.

Crawford, J.G. 'The origins of the court of castle chamber: a star chamber jurisdiction in Ireland.' *Am Jn Legal Hist*, xxiv (1980), 22.

Cregan, D.F. 'Irish Catholic admissions to the English inns of court, 1558–1625.' *Ir Jur*, n.s., v (1970), 95.

—— 'Irish recusant lawyers in politics in the reign of James I.' *Ir Jur*, n.s., v (1970), 306.

Cunningham, B. 'The composition of Connacht in the lordships of Clanricard and Thomond, 1577–1641.' *IHS*, xxiv (1984), 1.

—— 'Native culture and political change in Ireland, 1580–1640', in *Natives and newcomers*. ed. C. Brady and R. Gillespie. Dublin, 1986.

—— and R. Gillespie. 'Englishmen in sixteenth-century Irish annals.' *Ir Econ Soc Hist*, xvii (1990), 5.

Curtis, E. 'A survey of Offaly by Robert Cowley, 1550.' *Hermathena*, xlv (1930), 312.

—— 'The clan system among the English settlers in Ireland.' *EHR*, xxv (1910), 116.

Davies, C.S.L. 'The Pilgrimage of Grace reconsidered.' *Past & Present*, no. 41 (1968), 54.

—— 'Popular religion and the Pilgrimage of Grace', in *Order and disorder in early modern England*. ed. A. Fletcher and J. Stevenson. Cambridge, 1985.

Delany, V.T.H. 'The history of legal education in Ireland.' *Jn of Legal Education*, xii (1960), 396.

—— 'The palatinate court of the liberty of Tipperary.' *Am Jn Legal Hist*, v (1961), 95.

Dolley, R.H.M. 'Anglo-Irish monetary policies, 1172–1637.' *Historical Studies: VII* (1969), 45.

—— 'The pattern of Elizabethan coin-hoards from Ireland.' *UJA*, xxxiii (1970), 77.

Duggan, C.G. 'Troop movements in the Irish seas.' *Ir Sword*, ix (1970), 174.

Dunlop, R. 'The plantation of Leix and Offaly.' *EHR*, vi (1891), 61.

—— 'The plantation of Munster, 1584–89.' *EHR*, iii (1888), 250.

—— 'Sixteenth century schemes for the plantation of Ulster.' *Scottish Hist Rev*, xxii (1924), 51; 115; 199.

—— 'Some aspects of Henry VIII's Irish policy', in *Owens College historical essays*. ed. T.F. Tout and J. Tait. London, 1902.

Edwards, R.D. 'History of the penal laws against Catholics in Ireland, 1534–1691.' *IHR Bull*, xi (1933–34), 185.

—— 'Ireland, Elizabeth I and the counter-reformation', in *Elizabethan government and society: essays presented to Sir John Neale*. ed. S.T. Bindoff, J. Hurstfield, C.H. Wiliams. London, 1961.

—— 'The Irish bishops and the Anglican schism, 1534–1547.' *Ir Eccles Record*, 5th ser, xlv (1935), 39; 196.

—— 'The Irish reformation parliament of Henry VIII, 1536–37.' *Historical Studies: VI* (1968), 59.

—— 'Tudor religious policy in Ireland, 1534–58.' *Ir Eccles Record*, 5th ser, xliii (1933), 54.

—— and T.W. Moody. 'The history of Poynings' Law, 1495–1615.' *IHS*, ii (1941), 415.

—— and D.B. Quinn. 'Sixteenth century Ireland, 1485–1603: the last thirty years.' *IHS*, xiv (1968), 15.

Ellis, S.G. 'Crown, community and government in the English territories, 1450–1575.' *Hist*, lxxi (1987), 187.

—— 'England in the Tudor state.' *Hist Jn*, xxvi (1983), 201.

—— 'Henry VII and Ireland, 1491–1496', in *England and Ireland in the later middle ages*. ed. J.F. Lydon. Dublin, 1981.

—— 'Henry VIII, rebellion and the rule of law.' *Hist Jn*, xxiv (1981), 513.

—— 'Historiographical debate: representations of the past in Ireland: whose past and whose present?' *IHS*, xxvii (1991), 289.

—— 'The Irish customs administration under the early Tudors.' *IHS*, xxii (1980), 1.

—— 'The Kildare rebellion and the early Henrician reformation.' *Hist Jn*, xix (1976), 807.

—— 'Nationalist historiography and the English and Gaelic worlds in the late middle ages.' *IHS*, xxv (1986), 1.

—— 'Parliament and community in Yorkist and Tudor Ireland', in *Parliament and community* (Historical Studies: XIV). ed. A. Cosgrove and J.I. McGuire. Belfast, 1983.

—— 'Parliaments and great councils, 1483–99: addenda et corrigenda.' *Anal Hib*, no. 29 (1980), 96.

—— 'Privy seals of chief governors in Ireland, 1392–1560.' *IHR Bull*, li (1978), 187.

—— 'The struggle for control of the Irish mint, 1460-c. 1506.' *RIA Proc*, lxxviii, (1978) sect. c, 17.

—— 'Thomas Cromwell and Ireland, 1532–40.' *Hist Jn*, xxiii (1980), 497.

—— 'Taxation and defence in late medieval Ireland: the survival of scutage.' *RSAI Jn*, cvii (1977), 5.

—— 'Tudor policy and the Kildare ascendancy in the lordship of Ireland, 1496–1534.' *IHS*, xx (1977), 235.

Elton, G.R. 'Crime and the historian', in *Crime in England, 1550–1800*. ed. J.S. Cockburn. Princeton, 1977.

—— 'The Elizabethan exchequer: war in the receipt', in *Elizabethan government and society*. ed. S.T. Bindoff, J. Hurstfield, C.H. Williams. London, 1961.

—— 'Informing for profit: a sidelight on Tudor methods of law-enforcement.' *Hist Jn*, xi (1954), 149.

—— 'King or minister? The man behind the Henrician reformation.' *Hist*, xxxix, (1954), 216.

—— 'The law of treason in the early reformation.' *Hist Jn*, xi (1968), 211.

—— 'Parliament', in *The reign of Elizabeth I*. ed. C.A. Haigh. London, 1985.

—— 'The problems and significance of administrative history in the Tudor period.' *Jn British Studies*, iv (1965), 18.

—— 'The rule of law in the sixteenth century', in *Tudor men and institutions*. ed. A.J. Slavin. Baton Rouge, La., 1972.

—— 'Tudor government' (review article). *Hist Jn*, xxxi (1988), 425.

—— 'Tudor politics: the points of contact. II. The council.' *R Hist Soc Trans*, 5th ser, xxv (1975), 195.

—— 'Why the history of the early Tudor council remains unwritten.' *Annali della Fondazione per la Storia Amministrativa*, i (1964), 268.

Falkiner, C.L. 'The counties of Ireland: an historical sketch of their origin, constitution and gradual delimitation.' *RIA Proc*, xxiv (1903), sect. c, 169.

—— 'The parliament of Ireland under the Tudors.' *RIA Proc*, xxv (1905), sect. c, 508; 553.

Falls, C. 'Black Tom of Ormonde.' *Ir Sword*, v (1961), 10.

—— 'The Elizabethan soldier in Ireland.' *History Today*, i (1951), 40.

—— 'The growth of Irish military strength in the second half of the sixteenth century.' *Ir Sword*, ii (1955), 103.

Ferguson, J.F. 'The court of exchequer in Ireland.' *Gentleman's Magazine*, n.s., xliii (1855), 37.

Ford, A. 'The Protestant reformation in Ireland', in *Natives and newcomers*. ed. C. Brady and R. Gillespie. Dublin, 1986.

Fletcher, A. 'Honour, reputation and local officeholding in Elizabethan and Stuart England', in *Order and disorder in early modern England*. ed. A. Fletcher and J. Stevenson. Cambridge, 1985.

Frame, R.F. 'The immediate effect and interpretation of the 1331 ordinance *una et eadem lex*: some new evidence.' *Ir Jur*, n.s., vii (1972), 109.

—— 'The judicial powers of the medieval Irish keepers of the peace.' *Ir Jur*, n.s., ii (1967), 308.

—— 'Power and society in the lordship of Ireland, 1272–1377.' *Past & Present*, no. 76 (1977), 97.

Freeman, T.W. 'Historical geography and the Irish historian.' *IHS*, v (1946–47), 139.

Glasgow, T. 'The Elizabethan navy in Ireland (1558–1603).' *Ir Sword*, vii (1966), 291.

Graham, J.M. 'Rural society in Connacht, 1600–40,' in *Irish geographical studies in honour of Emyr Estyn Evans*. ed. N. Stephens and R.E. Glasscock. Belfast, 1970.

Green, A.S. 'Irish land in the sixteenth century.' *Eriu*, iii (1907), 1.

Griffith, M.C. 'The Irish record commission, 1810–1830.' *IHS*, vii (1950–51), 17.

Guy, J. 'Law, faction and parliament in the sixteenth century.' *Hist Jn*, xxviii (1985), 441.

—— 'Law, lawyers and the English reformation.' *History Today*, xxxv (1985), 16.

—— 'The privy council: revolution or evolution?,' in *Revolution reassessed*. ed. C.Coleman and D.R. Starkey. Oxford, 1986.

Hart, A.R. 'The king's serjeant at law in Tudor Ireland, 1485–1603', in *Brehons, serjeants and attorneys*. ed. D. Hogan and W.N. Osborough. Dublin, 1990.

Haigh, C. 'The church of England, the catholics and the people', in *The reign of Elizabeth I*. ed. C. Haigh. London, 1985.

Hammerstein, H. 'Aspects of the continental education of Irish students in the reign of Elizabeth I.' *Historical Studies: VIII* (1971), 137.

Hayes-McCoy, G.A. 'The army of Ulster, 1593–1601.' *Ir Sword*, i (1960), 105.

—— 'The early history of guns in Ireland.' *Galway Arch Soc Jn*, xviii (1938), 43.

—— 'Gaelic society in Ireland in the late sixteenth century.' *Historical Studies: IV* (1963), 45.

—— 'The making of an O'Neill: a view of the ceremony at Tullaghoge, Co. Tyrone.' *UJA*, xxxiii (1970), 89.

—— 'The renaissance and the Irish wars.' *Iris Hibernia*, iii (1957), no. 5, 43.

—— 'Strategy and tactics in Irish warfare, 1593–1601.' *IHS*, ii (1941), 255.

Herrup, C. 'Law and morality in seventeenth century England.' *Past & Present*, no. 106 (1985), 102.

Hoak, D. 'Rehabilitating the duke of Northumberland: politics and political control, 1549–53', in *The mid-Tudor polity, c. 1540–1560*. ed. J. Loach and R. Tittler. London, 1980.

—— 'The king's privy chamber, 1547–1553', in *Tudor rule and revolution*. ed. D.J. Guth and J.W. McKenna. Cambridge, 1982.

—— 'Two revolutions in Tudor government: the formation and organization of Mary I's privy council', in *Revolution reassessed*. ed. C. Coleman and D.R. Starkey. Oxford, 1986.

Hogan, J. 'The Irish law of kingship.' *RIA Proc*, xl (1932), sect. c, 186.
Hurstfield, J. 'Political corruption in early modern England.' *Hist*, lii (1967), 16.
Irwin, L. 'The Irish presidency courts, 1569–1672.' *Ir Jur*, xii (1977), 106.
—— 'The suppression of the Irish presidency system.' *IHS*, xxii (1980), 21.
Ives, E.W. 'Law, history and society: an eternal triangle', in *Litigants and the legal profession*. ed E.W. Ives. London, 1983.
—— 'Promotion in the legal profession of Yorkist and early Tudor England.' *LQR*, lxxv (1959), 348.
—— 'The reputation of the common lawyers in English society, 1450–1550.' *U of Birmingham Hist Jn*, vii (1960), 130.
Jackson, D. 'The Irish language and Tudor government.' *Eire-Ireland*, viii (1973), 21.
James, M.E. 'The concept of order and the Northern rising.' *Past & Present*, no. 60 (1973), 49.
Jefferies, H.A. 'The Irish parliament of 1560: the anglican reforms authorised.' *IHS*, xxvi (1988), 128.
Jocelyn, J. 'The renaissance tombs at Lusk and Newtown Trim.' *RSAI Jn*, ciii (1973), 153.
Jones, N.L. 'Elizabeth's first year: the conception and birth of the Elizabethan political world', in *The reign of Elizabeth I*. ed. C. Haigh. London, 1985.
Jones, W.J. 'Conflict or collaboration? Chancery attitudes in the reign of Elizabeth I.' *Am Jn Legal Hist*, v (1961), 12.
—— 'Due process and slow process in the Elizabethan chancery.' *Am Jn Legal Hist*, vi (1962), 123.
Kenny, C. 'The exclusion of catholics from the legal profession in Ireland, 1537–1829.' *IHS*, xxv (1987), 337.
—— 'The four courts in Dublin before 1796.' *Ir Jur*, xxi (1980), 107.
Knafla, L.A. 'Sin of all sorts swarmeth': criminal litigation in an English county in the early seventeenth century', in *Law, litigants and the legal profession*. ed. E.W. Ives. London, 1983.
Lambert, G.W. 'Sir Nicholas Malby and his associates.' *Galway Arch Soc Jn*, xxiii (1948), 1.
Lehmberg, S.E. 'Star chamber: 1485–1509.' *Huntington Lib Qtrly*, xxiv (1961), 189.
Lennon, C. 'The counter-reformation in Ireland, 1542–1641', in *Natives and newcomers*. ed. C. Brady and R. Gillespie. Dublin 1986.
—— 'Richard Stanihurst (1547–1618) and Old English identity.' *IHS*, xxi (1978), 121.
Longfield, A.K. 'Anglo-Irish trade in the sixteenth century as illustrated by English customs accounts and port books.' *RIA Proc*, xxxvi (1924), sect. c, 317.
Lough, S.M. 'Trade and industry in Ireland in the sixteenth century.' *Jn of Political Economy*, xxiv (1916), 713.
MacCaffrey, W.T. 'Place and patronage in Elizabethan politics,' in *Elizabethan government and society*. ed. S.T. Bindoff, J. Hurstfield, C.H. Williams. London, 1961.
—— 'Elizabethan politics: the first decade, 1558–1568.' *Past & Present*, no. 24 (1963), 25.
McCavitt, J. '"Good planets in their several spheares"—the establishment of the assize circuits in early seventeenth century Ireland.' *Ir Jur*, xxiv (1989), 248.

McCracken, E. 'The woodlands of Ireland, circa 1600.' *IHS*, xi (1958–59), 271.

MacCulloch, D. 'Kett's rebellion in context.' *Past & Present*, no. 84 (1979) 36.

McDowell, J. Moore, 'The devaluation of 1460 and the origins of the Irish pound.' *IHS*, xxv (1986), 19.

McKerral, A. 'West Highland mercenaries in Ireland.' *Scottish Hist Rev*, xxx (1951), 1.

MacNeill, Eoin. 'Military service in medieval Ireland.' *Cork Hist Soc Jn*, lxvi (1941), 6.

Manning, R.B. 'Violence and social conflict in mid-Tudor rebellions.' *Jn British Studies*, xvi (1977), 21.

Moody, T.W. 'The Irish parliament under Elizabeth and James I: a general survey.' *RIA Proc*, xlv (1939), sect. c, 41.

Mooney, C. 'The Irish church in the sixteenth century.' *Ir Eccles Record*, 5th ser, xcix (1963), 102.

Morgan, H. 'The end of Gaelic Ulster: a thematic interpretation of events between 1534 and 1610.' *IHS*, xxvi (1988), 8.

—— 'The colonial venture of Sir Thomas Smith in Ulster, 1571–1575.' *Hist Jn*, xxviii (1985), 261.

Murphy, B. 'The status of the native Irish after 1331.' *Ir Jur*, ii (1967), 116.

Myers, J.P. 'Early colonial experiences in Ireland: captain Thomas Lee and Sir John Davies.' *Eire-Ireland*, xxiii (1988), 8.

—— 'Murdering heart . . . murdering hand: captain Thomas Lee of Ireland, Elizabethan assassin.' *Sixteenth Century Jn*, xxii (1991), 47.

Neale, J.E. 'The Elizabethan political scene.' *Brit Acad Proc*, xxxiv (1948), 97.

Nicholls, K.W. 'Some documents on Irish law and customs in the sixteenth century.' *Anal Hib*, no. 26 (1970), 103.

—— 'A calendar of salved chancery proceedings concerning Co. Louth.' *Louth Arch Soc Jn*, xviii (1972), 112.

O'Baille, M. 'The Buannadha: Irish professional soldiery of the sixteenth century.' *Galway Arch Soc Jn*, xxii (1946–47), 47.

O'Domhnaill, S. 'Warfare in sixteenth century Ireland.' *IHS*, v (1946), 29.

O'Dowd, M. 'Gaelic economy and society,' in *Natives and newcomers*. ed. C. Brady and R. Gillespie. Dublin, 1986.

Osborough, W.N. 'Ecclesiastical law and the reformation in Ireland', in *Canon law in Protestant lands*. ed. R.H. Helmholz. Berlin, 1992.

—— 'Executive failure to enforce judicial decrees: a neglected chapter in nineteenth century constitutional history', in *The common law tradition*. ed. J.F. McEldowney and P. O'Higgins. Dublin, 1990.

O'Sullivan, M.D. 'The fortification of Galway in the sixteenth and early seventeenth centuries.' *Galway Arch Soc Jn*, xvi (1934), 1.

—— 'Irish lawyers in Tudor England.' *Dublin Review*, clxxix (1926), 1.

Otway-Ruthven, A.J. 'The chief governors of medieval Ireland.' *RSAI Jn*, xcv (1965), 227.

—— 'Knight service in Ireland.' *RSAI Jn*, lxxxix (1959), 1.

—— 'The native Irish and English law in medieval Ireland.' *IHS*, vii (1950), 1.

—— 'Royal service in Ireland.' *RSAI Jn*, xcviii (1968), 37.

Patterson, N. 'Gaelic law and the Tudor conquest of Ireland: the social background of the sixteenth-century recensions of the pseudo-historical Prologue to the *Senchas már*.' *IHS*, xxvii (1991), 193.

Piveronus, P.J. 'Sir Warham St Leger and the first Munster plantation, 1568–69.' *Eire- Ireland*, xiv (1979), 15.

Pollard, A.F. 'Council, star chamber and privy council under the Tudors.' *EHR*, xxxvii (1922), 337, 516; and xxxviii (1923), 42.

Povey, K. 'The sources for a bibliography of Irish history, 1500–1700.' *IHS*, i (1939), 393.

Quinn, D.B. 'Anglo-Irish local government, 1485–1534.' *IHS*, i (1939), 354.

—— 'The bills and statutes of the Irish parliaments of Henry VII and Henry VIII.' *Anal Hib*, no. 10 (1941), 71.

—— 'A discourse of Ireland (circa 1599): a sidelight on English colonial policy.' *RIA Proc*, xlvii (1942), sect. c, 151.

—— 'The early interpretation of Poynings' law, 1494–1534.' *IHS*, ii (1941), 241.

—— 'Edward Walsh's conjectures regarding the state of Ireland [1552].' *IHS*, vii (1946–47), 303.

—— 'Government printing and the publication of Irish statutes in the sixteenth century.' *RIA Proc*, xlix (1943), sect. c, 45.

—— 'Guide to English financial records for Irish history, 1461–1558, with illustrative extracts, 1461–1509.' *Anal Hib*, no. 10 (1941), 1.

—— 'Henry Fitzroy, Duke of Richmond, and his connexion with Ireland, 1529–1530.' *IHR Bull*, xii (1935), 175.

—— 'Henry VIII and Ireland, 1509–34.' *IHS*, xii (1961), 318.

—— 'Ireland and sixteenth-century European expansion.' *Historical Studies: I* (1958), 20.

—— 'Ireland in 1534', in *A new history of Ireland- iii: Early modern Ireland, 1534–1691*. ed. T.W. Moody, F.X. Martin, F.J. Byrne. Oxford, 1976.

—— 'The Irish parliamentary subsidy in the fifteenth and sixteenth centuries.' *RIA Proc*, xlii (1935), sect c, 219.

—— 'The Munster plantation: problems and opportunities.' *Cork Hist Soc Jn*, lxxi (1966), 19.

—— 'Parliaments and great councils in Ireland, 1461–1586.' *IHS*, iii (1942), 60.

—— 'Renaissance influences in English colonization.' *R Hist Soc Trans*, 5th ser, xxvi (1976), 73.

—— 'Sir Thomas Smith (1513–1577) and the beginnings of English colonial policy.' *Am Phil Soc Proc*, lxxxix (1945), 543.

Ranger, T. 'Richard Boyle and the making of an Irish fortune.' *IHS*, x (1957), 257.

Richardson, H.G. 'English institutions in medieval Ireland.' *IHS*, i (1939), 82.

—— 'The Irish parliament rolls of the fifteenth century.' *EHR*, lviii (1943), 448.

Rutledge, V.L. 'Court-castle faction and the Irish viceroyalty: the appointment of Oliver St John as lord deputy of Ireland in 1616.' *IHS*, xxvi (1989), 233.

Samaha, J. 'The recognizance in Elizabethan law enforcement.' *Am Jn Legal Hist*, xxv (1981), 189.

Sayles, G.O. 'The vindication of the earl of Kildare from treason, 1496.' *IHS*, vii (1950– 51), 39.

Schofield, R. 'Taxation and the political limits of the Tudor state', in *Law and government under the Tudors*. ed. C. Cross, D. Loades, J.J. Scarisbrick. Cambridge, 1988.

Schwind, M. 'Nurse to all rebellions: Grace O'Malley and sixteenth century Connacht.' *Eire-Ireland*, xiii (1978), 40.

Sheehan, A.J. 'Irish towns in a period of change, 1558–1625', in *Natives and newcomers*. ed. C. Brady and R. Gillespie. Dublin, 1986.

—— 'Official reaction to native land claims in the plantation of Munster.' *IHS*, xxiii (1982–83), 297.

—— 'The population of the plantation of Munster: Quinn reconsidered.' *Cork Hist Soc Jn*, lxxxvii (1982), 107.

Silke, J.J. 'The Irish appeal to Spain of 1593: some light on the genesis of the "Nine Years War".' *Ir Eccles Rec*, xcii (1959), 279.

—— 'Spain and the invasion of Ireland, 1601–2.' *IHS*, xiv (1966–67), 295.

Simms, K. 'The brehons of later medieval Ireland', in *Brehons, serjeants and attorneys*. ed. D. Hogan and W.N. Osborough. Dublin, 1990.

—— '"The king's friend": O'Neill, the crown and the earldom of Ulster', in *England and Ireland in the later middle ages*. ed. J.F. Lydon. Dublin, 1981.

—— 'Warfare in the medieval Gaelic lordships.' *Ir Sword*, xii (1975–76), 98.

Starkey, D.R. 'Court and government', in *Revolution reassessed*. ed. C. Coleman and D.R. Starkey. Oxford, 1986.

—— 'Which age of reform?' in *Revolution reassessed*. ed. C. Coleman and D.R. Starkey. Oxford, 1986.

Strickland, W.G. 'Irish soldiers in the service of Henry VIII.' *RSAI Jn*, 6th ser, xiii (1923), 94.

Treadwell, V. 'The Irish court of wards under James I.' *IHS*, xii (1960–61), 1.

—— 'The Irish customs administration in the sixteenth century.' *IHS*, xx (1976–77), 384.

—— 'The Irish parliament of 1569–71.' *RIA Proc*, lxv (1966), sect. c, 55.

—— 'Sir John Perrott and the Irish parliament of 1585–6.' *RIA Proc*, lxxxv (1985), sect. c, 259.

Valkenburg, A. 'Gerald, eleventh earl of Kildare (1525–1585): a study in diplomacy.' *Kildare Arch Soc Jn*, xiv (1966), 293.

Walshe, H.C. 'Enforcing the Elizabethan settlement: the vicissitudes of Hugh Brady, bishop of Meath, 1563–84.' *IHS*, xxvi (1989), 352.

—— 'The rebellion of William Nugent, 1581', in *Religion, conflict and coexistence in Ireland: essays presented to Mgr Patrick J. Corish*. ed. R.V. Comerford, et al. Dublin, 1990.

Weikel, A. 'The Marian council revisited', in *The mid-Tudor polity, c. 1540–1560*. ed. J. Loach and R. Tittler. London, 1980.

Welply, W.H. 'Edmund Spenser's brother-in-law, John Travers.' *Notes and Queries*, clxxix (1940), 74; 92; 112.

White, D.G. 'Henry VIII's Irish kerne in France and Scotland, 1544–1545.' *Ir Sword*, iii (1958), 213.

—— 'The reign of Edward VI in Ireland: some political, social and economic aspects.' *IHS*, xiv (1964–65), 197.

Williams, P. 'The crown and the counties', in *The reign of Elizabeth I*. ed. C. Haigh. London, 1985.

—— 'The star chamber and the council in the marches of Wales, 1558–1603.' *Board of Celtic Studies Bull*, xvi (1956), 287.

Wood, H. 'Commercial intercourse with Ireland in the middle ages.' *Studies*, iv (1915), 250.

—— 'The court of castle chamber or star chamber of Ireland.' *RIA Proc*, xxxii (1914), sect. c, 152.

—— 'The office of chief governor of Ireland, 1172–1509.' *RIA Proc*, xxxvi (1923), sect. c, 206.

—— 'The offices of secretary of state and keeper of the signet or privy seal.' *RIA Proc*, xxxviii (1928), sect. c, 51.

—— 'The titles of the chief governor of Ireland.' *IHR Bull*, xiii (1935), 1.

Youings, J.A. 'The council of the West.' *R Hist Soc Trans,* 5th ser., x (1960), 41.
Youngs, F. 'Towards petty sessions: Tudor JPs and the division of counties', in *Tudor rule and revolution: essays for G.R. Elton.* ed. D.J. Guth and J.W. McKenna. Cambridge, 1982.

UNPUBLISHED MATERIALS

Brady, C. 'The government of Ireland, c. 1540–1583.' Unpublished Ph.D. thesis, Trinity College, Dublin, 1980.
Canny, N.P. 'Glory and gain: Sir Henry Sidney and the government of Ireland, 1558–1578.' Unpublished Ph.D. thesis, University of Pennsylvania, 1971.
Quinn, D.B. 'Tudor rule in Ireland in the reigns of Henry VII and Henry VIII, with special reference to the Anglo-Irish financial administration.' Unpublished Ph.D. thesis, University of London, 1934.

Index

Carlow (contd.)
county, 37, 179–80, 203, 215, 279, 286, 299, 302–03, 365, 376, 385, 405, 430
Carrickfergus, 58, 107, 249, 256, 264, 269, 275–77, 279, 283, 289, 296, 299, 311, 317, 331–32, 338, 460, 462
Carrick-on-Suir, 91, 332
Cartwright, Thomas, 156, 459
Cashel,
archbishop of, 309
town, 280, 332
castle chamber, court of, 175–76, 180, 189, 192–93, 208, 216, 242, 335, 402, 409, 411, 465, 467
entry book of, 219, 227, 231
litigants in, 228, 369, 397–98, 401, 471
Cavan, county, 229, 332
Cavanaghs, or Kavanaghs, clan, 64, 72, 167, 197–98, 275, 279, 304, 379
Brian McCahir, 199, 239
Cecil, William, Lord Burghley, 10–11, 30, 36, 42, 44, 70–72, 74–76, 79, 88, 91, 97, 100, 112–13, 117–18, 124, 126, 128, 135–36, 140–42, 144–45, 150–51, 160, 163, 168, 170, 189–90, 210, 213–14, 219–20, 241, 263, 265–66, 269, 274, 284–85, 293, 299–301, 308, 310–12, 314–15, 319, 326, 328, 349, 358, 370, 413–14, 442, 445, 448–50, 456, 458, 460, 464, 470
cess (*see also* purveyance), 9, 37, 53, 61, 64, 66–67, 71, 87, 105, 120, 122, 132, 143–44, 149, 163, 169, 172, 234–35, 294, 297, 302, 369–407, 418, 420, 430, 432–33, 457, 462–63, 468
cessors, 382–84, 434
conciliar responsibility for, 373–84
constitutional crisis, 392–407, 417, 453
historical definition, 369–73
innovation and resistance, 384–92
Chaloner, John, secretary of state, 47, 50–51, 63, 75, 77, 103, 106, 113, 203, 412, 439–40, 447
Chaloner, Thomas, clerk, 447

chancellor, lord (of Ireland), 32–33, 42, 45, 60, 157–59, 185, 223, 355, 402
Chyvers, Christopher [or Cheevers], 197–98, 385
Chester, 216, 269, 295, 300–01, 388, 455–56
chief baron of the exchequer (Ireland), 42, 45, 223, 334
chief governors (*see also* lords deputy, lords lieutenant), 4, 10, 17, 23, 24, 34, 73, 79, 83, 117, 119, 129, 170, 223, 371, 414
Christ Church cathedral, Dublin, 32, 57, 164
Clancare, earl of (*see* MacCarthy More)
Clanricarde, earl of (*see* Burke)
Clare, county (*see also* Thomond), 215, 295, 314, 445, 455
clerk of the check, 266, 288, 291, 293
Clonmel, 203, 280, 320, 332
Coccrell, Ralph, clerk of council, 71, 74
coinage, debasement of (*see* recoinage)
Colclough, Anthony, 115, 226
colonization, colonial policy in Ireland, 1, 2, 6–7, 19, 37, 82, 93, 102, 129, 135, 139, 141, 149, 158, 172, 242, 244, 321, 326–28, 390, 418, 461, 466
commissions, 213
ecclesiastical, 140, 143, 156–58, 188, 445, 458–59
of faculties, 157, 459
of inquisition, 245, 423
of the council, 70, 79, 189–90, 204–05, 209, 243, 411
of martial law, 206
of oyer and terminer, 139, 205, 317
common law, 2, 7, 10–13, 26, 31, 83, 144, 162, 175, 178, 278, 404, 409–10, 418, 422
composition (for cess), 94, 391–92, 403, 405, 408, 411–12, 420
Connacht,
composition of, 461, 463, 471
council of, 3, 9, 20, 43, 133, 140–43, 192, 208, 229, 243, 248–49, 265, 314, 326, 461
province of, 107, 121, 126, 214, 229, 275, 280, 380, 383, 415, 453

The Irish Legal History Society

Established in 1988 to encourage the study and advance the knowledge of the history of Irish law, especially by the publication of original documents and of works relating to the history of Irish law, including its institutions, doctrines and personalities, and the reprinting or editing of works of sufficient rarity or importance.

PATRONS

The Hon. Mr Justice T.A. Finlay,
Chief Justice of Ireland

Rt Hon. Sir Brian Hutton,
Lord Chief Justice of
Northern Ireland

LIFE MEMBER

Rt Hon. Lord Lowry,
Lord of Appeal in Ordinary

COUNCIL, 1991

PRESIDENT

The Hon. Mr Justice Costello,
Judge of the High Court

VICE-PRESIDENTS

Professor G.J. Hand,
University of Birmingham

His Honour Judge Hart, Q.C.

SECRETARY

Professor W.N. Osborough,
Trinity College, Dublin

TREASURER

Daire Hogan, esq.,
Solicitor

ORDINARY MEMBERS

His Honour Judge Carroll,
Judge of the Circuit Court

Professor D.S. Greer,
Queen's University, Belfast

Dr Art Cosgrove,
University College, Dublin

Professor John Larkin,
Trinity College, Dublin

Dr D.V. Craig,
Director, National Archives